Enforcing Obligations *Erga Omnes* in International Law

The concept of obligations *erga omnes* – obligations owed to the international community as a whole – has fascinated international lawyers for decades, yet its precise implications remain unclear. This book assesses how this concept affects the enforcement of international law. It shows that all States are entitled to invoke obligations *erga omnes* in proceedings before the International Court of Justice, and to take countermeasures in response to serious *erga omnes* breaches. In addition, it suggests ways of identifying obligations that qualify as *erga omnes*. In order to sustain these results, the book conducts a thorough examination of international practice and jurisprudence as well as the recent work of the UN International Law Commission in the field of State responsibility. By so doing, it demonstrates that the *erga omnes* concept is now solidly grounded in modern international law, and clarifies one of the central aspects of the international regime of law enforcement.

Christian J. Tams is a Lecturer at the Walther Schücking Institute for International Law at the University of Kiel, Germany.

Established in 1946, this series produces high quality scholarship in the fields of public and private international law and comparative law. Although these are distinct legal subdisciplines, developments since 1946 confirm their interrelation.

Comparative law is increasingly used as a tool in the making of law at national, regional, and international levels. Private international law is now often affected by international conventions, and the issues faced by classical conflicts rules are frequently dealt with by substantive harmonisation of law under international auspices. Mixed international arbitrations, especially those involving state economic activity, raise mixed questions of public and private international law, while in many fields (such as the protection of human rights and democratic standards, investment guarantees and international criminal law) international and national systems interact. National constitutional arrangements relating to 'foreign affairs', and to the implementation of international norms, are a focus of attention.

The Board welcomes works of a theoretical or interdisciplinary character, and those focusing on the new approaches to international or comparative law or conflicts of law. Studies of particular institutions or problems are equally welcome, as are translations of the best work published in other languages.

A list of books in the series can be found at the end of this volume.

Enforcing Obligations *Erga Omnes* in International Law

Christian J. Tams
Walther Schücking Institute
University of Kiel (Germany)

CAMBRIDGE
UNIVERSITY PRESS

CAMBRIDGE UNIVERSITY PRESS
Cambridge, New York, Melbourne, Madrid, Cape Town, Singapore,
São Paulo, Delhi, Dubai, Tokyo

Cambridge University Press
The Edinburgh Building, Cambridge CB2 8RU, UK

Published in the United States of America by Cambridge University Press, New York

www.cambridge.org
Information on this title: www.cambridge.org/9780521128896

First published 2005
Reprinted 2007

A catalogue record for this publication is available from the British Library

ISBN 978-0-521-85667-6 Hardback
ISBN 978-0-521-12889-6 Paperback

Transferred to digital printing (with new Epilogue) 2010

Contents

Foreword

The subject of obligations *erga omnes* - obligations to the international community as a whole - their character and possible consequences has been with us ever since the stray dictum of the International Court in the *Barcelona Traction* case in 1970. The shares in that Canadian company may have become worthless, but huge resources have been put into explaining and accounting for this particular product of the company's failure. And as so much has been said, so opinions have differed. The phrase was used incidentally only to mark out the terrain of diplomatic protection as an inherently bilateral sphere of interstate relations. It was a pretext for an apology for the Court's earlier decision in *Second South West Africa* - a disaster from a public relations point of view for the Court and a turning point in its relations with the Third World - in short it was law as politics. It showed the Court confronting a new structure of international law, where what matters are not bilateral but multilateral relations and multilateral norms - self-determination, non-discrimination, the prohibition of aggression, fundamental human rights. It showed the Court evading the challenge presented by the concept of peremptory norms of general international law, adopted over the dissent of France at the Vienna Conference in 1969. Where the States (or most of them) would boldly go with a fundamental assertion of core substantive values - or at least of the *possibility* of such values - the Court would timorously follow, reducing those values to a procedural concept of standing to sue. And so on.

The conceptual split which the two Latin phrases - *jus cogens* and *erga omnes* - caused in the academy has still not been fully traced. Could they not be different aspects of the same underlying concept - fundamental values of juridical interest to all and therefore not waivable without general assent? The International Law Commission in its Articles on

Responsibility of States for Internationally Wrongful Acts used both terms (in Articles 40 and 48) without implying that there is any radical distinction between them. It also used the notion of a group of States (Article 48(1)(a)), immediately contrasted with the international community as a whole - not, be it noted, the international community of States. Historically we have had a world in which there were hundreds of States and State-like entities - countless hundreds in 1648 - and a world in which there were around 60, at the numerical low point of 1945. Currently in the oscillation of numbers of States we seem to be stuck just short of 200 - but such numbers are evidently arbitrary. Perhaps all the States there are now are simply a 'group of States', the group of entities that happen to be States at this time, a contingency not a category.

There is much here that needs careful, painstaking and dispassionate analysis, avoiding dogma and the a priori. Christian Tams provides all this. Of course his is not the only work in the field but it may be judged by some distance the best, and not merely because it has the temporary advantage of being the most recent. It is well researched, historically informed, well-written and balanced in its judgements. It does not oversell the subject but deals with it lucidly and thoroughly, convincing the reader where more strident works on the subject might not. It is a significant contribution, which I believe will help mark out Christian Tams as one of the very best international lawyers of the coming generation.

James Crawford
Lauterpacht Research Centre for International Law
16 July 2004

Preface

The concept of obligations *erga omnes* has fascinated international lawyers for some time. It has raised high hopes about the protection of fundamental interests shared by the international community as a whole, yet its precise implications remain, at best, uncertain. My own interest in the concept goes back to a seminar, held at the Christian-Albrechts University of Kiel (Germany) in early 1998, which clearly exposed both aspects – high hopes and lack of certainty. Internships at the United Nations International Law Commission, during the final stages of its work on State responsibility (1999–2001), made me realise that obligations *erga omnes* not only present an intellectual challenge, but are eminently relevant to States.

This book assesses to what extent the fascinating, yet elusive, concept of obligations *erga omnes* has had an impact on the rules of modern international law. It is based on research undertaken at the Universities of Cambridge and Kiel. It was submitted as a PhD thesis to the University of Cambridge in late 2003, and was subsequently awarded the Yorke Prize 2005. My research in Cambridge was supervised by Professor James Crawford, to whom I am much indebted. As the International Law Commission's Special Rapporteur on the topic of State responsibility, he was in a unique position to provide expert guidance. His comments and advice proved most helpful. At the same time, I have greatly appreciated his tolerance of criticism of the Commission's work.

In addition, a great number of people have helped me develop my thoughts on the topic. They include Judge Bruno Simma (The Hague); Professors Jost Delbrück (Kiel), Rainer Hofmann (Frankfurt), and Colin Wabrick (Durham); Chester Brown and Ben Olbourne (both at London); Martin Mennecke (Copenhague); Dr. Andreas Paulus (Munich); as well as Dr. Guigelmo Verdirame, Dr. Matthew Conaglen, and Dr. Roger O'Keefe (all at Cambridge). Between 2000 and 2003, while I was a member of Gonville & Caius College, Cambridge, my research was generously supported by the College's W. M. Tapp Fund. I am grateful to the Trustees of the Fund, in particular to Dr. Pippa Rogerson, as well as to the following bodies: the Whewell Fund; the Cambridge European Trust; Studienstiftung des deutschen Volkes; Evangelisches Studienwerk Villigst; Deutscher Akademischer Austauschdienst. Thanks are also due to Cambridge University Press, in particular to Finola O'Sullivan, Annie Lovett, and Jan Miles-Kingston, for all their help in turning this manuscript into book form.

Finally, my deepest thanks are owed to my parents, Christa and Dr Gerhard Tams, and to Ina Wiesner, for all their support and encouragement. This work is dedicated to them.

Notes on citation

Citations in the book follow a modified social sciences (Harvard) style, with abbreviated references in the footnotes and full references in the bibliography.

A full bibliographical reference such as

Delbrück, Jost, 'Laws in the Public Interest - Some Observations on the Foundations and Identification of erga omnes Norms in International Law', in: *Liber Amicorum Günther Jaenicke - Zum 85. Geburtstag* (Götz *et al.* eds., 1998), 17

therefore is given in the footnotes as

Delbrück (1998), 17

Where necessary, different entries published in the same year are distinguished by 'a' or 'b', i.e. Delbrück (1999a), Delbrück (1999b).

Documents issued by the International Law Commission are not included in the general bibliography, but listed separately.

Cases cited in the footnotes are listed in the Table of cases, which also gives shorthand titles used in the text.

Websites were checked on 20 December 2004.

Table of cases

1. International Court of Justice

2. Permanent Court of International Justice

3. Arbitral Awards

4. Judgments of the ICTY and ICTR

The relevant decisions are available at: http://www.un.org/icty/cases/indictindex-e.htm and http://wwww.ictr.org respectively

5. European Court/ Commission of Human Rights

European Commission of Human Rights

European Court of Human Rights

6. GATT/ WTO Reports

7. Other International Decisions/ Proceedings

8. National decisions

a. Germany

b. United Kingdom

c. United States

d. Decisions of other national courts

Abbreviations

A.C.	Appeal Cases (England and Wales)
ACHR	(Inter-)American Convention on Human Rights
AFDI	Annuaire français de droit international
AJIL	American Journal of International Law
AJPIL	Austrian Journal of Public International Law
All ER	All England Law Reports
AnnIDI	Annuaire de l'Institut de Droit International
ASR	Articles on State Responsibility (International Law Commission)
AVR	Archiv des Völkerrechts
Bd(e).	Band/Bände
BDGVR	Berichte der deutschen Gesellschaft für Völkerrecht
BGBl.	Bundesgesetzblatt
BISD	Basic Instruments and Selected Documents (GATT)
BYIL	British Yearbook of International Law
CAT	Convention Against Torture
CCPR	(International) Covenant on Civil and Political Rights
CEDAW	Convention on the Elimination of All Forms of Discrimination Against Women
CERD	(International) Convention on the Elimination of Racial Discrimination
CSECR	(International) Covenant on Social, Economic and Cultural Right
CTS	Consolidated Treaty Series (Parry ed.)
Diss.Op	Dissenting Opinion
Doc.	Document

DRC	Democratic Republic of Congo
EC	European Community
EC Bull.	Bulletin of the European Communities
ECHR	European Convention of Human Rights and Fundamental Freedoms
ECJ	European Court of Justice
ECOSOC	(United Nations) Economic and Social Council
ECR	European Court Reports (ECJ)
ed(s).	edition/editor(s)
EJIL	European Journal of International Law
ELR	European Law Review
EPIL	Encyclopaedia of Public International Law
et al.	*et aliter*
ETS	European Treaty Series
EURATOM	European Atomic Energy Community
Eur. Comm'n HR	European Commission on Human Rights
Eur. Ct. HR	European Court of Human Rights
EWCA (Civ.)	England and Wales Court of Appeal (Civil Division)
FCN	Friendship, Commerce and Navigation (treaties)
FRY	Federal Republic of Yugoslavia
GA	(United Nations) General Assembly
GATT	General Agreement on Tariffs and Trade
GYIL	German Yearbook of International Law
HJIL	Harvard Journal of International Law
HRLJ	Human Rights Law Journal
HRQ	Human Rights Quarterly
ibid.	*ibidem*
ICAO	International Civil Aviation Organization
ICJ	International Court of Justice
ICLQ	International and Comparative Law Quarterly
ICTR	International Criminal Tribunal for Rwanda
ICTY	International Criminal Tribunal for the Former Yugoslavia
id.	*idem*
IDI	Institut de droit interational
i.e.	*id est*
ILA	International Law Association
ILC	International Law Commission
ILM	International Legal Materials

ILO	International Labour Organisation
ILR	International Law Reports
Indian JIL	Indian Journal of International Law
JIR	Jahrbuch für Internationales Recht
LJIL	Leiden Journal of International Law
LNTS	League of Nations Treaty Series
LOSC	Law of the Sea Convention
MichJIL	Michigan Journal of International Law
MN	Marginal note
NILR	Netherlands International Law Review
NQHR	Netherlands Quarterly for Human Rights
Nordic JIL	Nordic Journal of International Law
NRG	Nouveau Receuil Général (Martens)
NYIL	Netherlands Yearbook of International Law
OAS	Organization of American States
OJ	Official Journal of the European Communities
ÖZÖR	Österreichische Zeitschrift für Öffentliches Recht
para(s).	paragraph(s)
PCIJ	Permanent Court of International Justice
Proc. ASIL	Proceedings, American Society of International Law
RBDI	Revue belge de droit international
RdC	Recueil des Cours
Res.	Resolution
RGDIP	Revue générale de droit international public
RIAA	Reports of International Arbitral Awards
RIW	Recht der Internationalen Wirtschaft
SADC	Southern African Development Community
SAYIL	South African Yearbook of International Law
SC	(United Nations) Security Council
SchwJIR	Schweizerisches Jahrbuch für Internationales Recht
Sep.Op.	Separate Opinion
Ser.	Series
Strasbourg Court	European Court of Human Rights
TEC	Treaty Establishing the European Community
TEU	Treaty Establishing the European Union
UKTS	United Kingdom Treaty Series
UN	United Nations
UNC	United Nations Charter
UNTS	United Nations Treaty Series

UNYB	United Nations Yearbook
US	United States
VCLT	Vienna Convention on the Law of Treaties
Virginia JIL	Virginia Journal of International Law
Vol.	Volume
VwGO	Verwaltungsgerichtsordnung (Germany)
WTO	World Trade Organization
Yb.	Yearbook
YbILC	Yearbook of the International Law Commission
YbECHR	Yearbook of the European Convention of Human Rights
ZaöRV	Zeitschrift für ausländisches öffentliches Recht und Völkerrecht
ZÖR	Zeitschrift für Öffentliches Recht

Introduction

1.

On 5 February 1970, after international legal proceedings spanning twelve years, and more than two decades after the dispute had arisen, the President of the International Court of Justice, Judge Bustamante y Rivero, read out the Court's judgment in the *Case Concerning the Barcelona Traction, Light and Power Co., Ltd.*[1] In that judgment, the Court held that, under international law, the nationality of corporations depended on national incorporation rules and that the violation of shareholders' rights did not normally constitute a separate breach of international law. The Barcelona Traction, Light and Power Co., having been incorporated under Canadian law, therefore was to be treated as Canadian, although 88 per cent of its shares were held by Belgian shareholders, and Belgium could not espouse claims of diplomatic protection. Highly controversial at its time, this holding remains the crucial judicial pronouncement on the nationality of corporations to date.[2]

[1] ICJ Reports 1970, 3.
The company was declared bankrupt in 1948 by a Catalan district judge, and eventually was taken over by a Spanish finance magnate. After diplomatic representations by various countries, Belgium, in 1958, instituted proceedings against Spain before the ICJ. These were discontinued in 1961 to allow for direct negotiations between the company and its new Spanish owners, but re-entered on the Court's list in 1962 after the negotiations had failed (ICJ Reports 1961, 9). At the beginning of the second phase of the proceedings, Spain raised four preliminary objections against the admissibility of Belgium's claims, of which the Court dismissed two and joined the other two to the merits (ICJ Reports 1964, 6). When it actually declared the case inadmissible, in 1970, the written pleadings exceeded 60,000 pages in length, see Sette-Camara (1994), 1071; Ragazzi (1997), 10 (his note 44).

[2] See Judge Oda's separate opinion in the *ELSI case*, ICJ Reports 1989, 83–87; and further Brownlie (2003), 466–471; Akehurst/Malanczuk (1997), 266–267; Verdross/Simma (1984), 880–881.

A quick glance at the textbooks, however, reveals that *Barcelona Traction* is more than a controversial decision on the question of diplomatic protection of corporations. Two paragraphs of the judgment have taken on a life of their own and have inspired much discussion among States, courts, commissions, and commentators. Although they did not affect the rules of nationality, nor indeed any other central aspect of the case before the Court, these two paragraphs are among the most famous judicial pronouncements in the ICJ's history. Since they provide the starting-point of the present study, they merit to be quoted in full.

> 33. When a State admits into its territory foreign investments or foreign nationals, whether national or juristic persons, it is bound to extend to them the protection of the law and assumes obligations concerning the treatment afforded to them. These obligations, however, are neither absolute nor unqualified. In particular, an essential distinction should be drawn between the obligations of a State towards the international community as a whole, and those arising vis-à-vis another State in the field of diplomatic protection. By their very nature, the former are the concern of all States. In view of the importance of the rights involved, all States can be held to have a legal interest in their protection; they are obligations *erga omnes*.
>
> 34. Such obligations derive, for example, in contemporary international law, from the outlawing of acts of aggression, and of genocide, as also from the principles and rules concerning the basic rights of the human person, including protection from slavery and racial discrimination. Some of the corresponding rights of protection have entered into the body of general international law (*Reservations to the Convention on the Prevention and Punishment of the Crime of Genocide, Advisory Opinion, I.C.J. Reports 1951, p. 23*); others are conferred by international instruments of a universal or quasi-universal character.[3]

In the three-and-a-half decades that have passed since 5 February 1970, this passage (which will be referred to as the *Barcelona Traction* dictum) has puzzled courts and commentators, including, at times, the ICJ itself. On its basis, international lawyers have begun to discuss the concept of obligations *erga omnes*, or obligations owed to the international community as a whole.[4] The importance of this category of obligations, at least from a conceptual point of view, is widely acknowledged today. It is brought out with particular clarity in the International

For early and continuing discussions of the Court's approach see Seidl-Hohenveldern (1971), 255; Higgins (1971), 327; Mann (1973a), 259; van Dijk (1980), 414–416; Wallace (1992), 356; Henkin (1995), 89; Seidl-Hohenveldern (1996), 115.

[3] ICJ Reports 1970, 32 (paras. 33–34).

[4] Although not identical in meaning, both expressions are generally treated as synonyms. The present study employs the former expression, as it is the more common. For a different approach see e.g. article 48 (1)(b) ASR and para. 9 of the ILC's commentary.

Law Commission's Articles on State Responsibility, adopted in 2001, which recognise its impact on the rules governing the invocation of responsibility,[5] and expressly cite para. 33 of the *Barcelona Traction* judgment as evidence of a modern approach, pursuant to which State responsibility can no longer be reduced to bilateral relations between pairs of States.[6] Many commentators are prepared to go beyond that. To them, the emergence of obligations *erga omnes* marks no less than a paradigm shift in international law. Delbrück sees it as part of 'the ongoing process of the constitutionalization of international law';[7] to many others, obligations *erga omnes* (together with the related concept of peremptory norms) reflect 'a common core of norms essential for the protection of communal values and interests', which transcend the bilateralism and parochial State concerns dominating traditional international law.[8] The Latin phrase '*erga omnes*' thus has become one of the rallying cries of those sharing a belief in the emergence of a value-based international public order based on law. Indeed, such is the degree of fascination that even sceptical commentators like Prosper Weil (whose earlier work is widely regarded as a highly influential *critique*) acknowledge that the concept is one of the 'pièces maîtresses de l'arsenal conceptuel du droit international d'aujord'hui.'[9]

As often, the reality is neither so clear nor so bright. One problem is readily admitted by commentators: whatever the relevance of obligations *erga omnes* as a legal concept, its full potential remains to be realised in practice. The international community's failure effectively to react against humanitarian catastrophes, for example in Pol Pot's Cambodia or during the 1994 Rwandan genocide, makes solemn proclamations of a core of fundamental values ring hollow.[10] Bruno

[5] See article 48 (1)(b) ASR and paras. 2, 8–10 of the ILC's commentary to that provision. See further para. 2 of the introductory commentary to Part Three, Chapter I, and para. 2-3 and 7 of the introductory commentary to Part Two, Chapter III.

[6] See commentary to article 1 ASR, para. 4. [7] Delbrück (1999a), 35.

[8] See ILA Study Group (2000), para. 105. For similar statements or approaches see e.g. Ragazzi (1997) (stressing the moral foundations of the *erga omnes* concept and its relevance for the quest 'for peace and justice among States through the promotion of their common good' (218)); Tomuschat (1995), 15; Fassbender (1998), 75–85 and 126–128; Fassbender (2003), 5–7; Karl (2002), 277.

[9] Weil (1992), 286 and 287 respectively. Weil's criticism seems to have become mollified over time: contrast Weil (1983), 430–433, and Weil (1992), 284–291.

[10] See e.g. Kooijmans (1990), 92–93, and further Hannum (1989), 82, for a critical comment on the reluctance of States to institute ICJ proceedings against Cambodia, which had, *inter alia*, accepted the Court's compulsory jurisdiction under article 36, para. 2 of the ICJ Statute.

Simma's much-quoted observation encapsulates this feeling of disappointment: 'Viewed realistically, the world of obligations *erga omnes* is still the world of the "ought" rather than of the "is"'.[11]

This comment, however, only identifies part of the problem. It is difficult to disagree with the factual assessment - as will be shown in subsequent chapters, obligations *erga omnes* often have yet to enter 'the world of the "is"'. On the other hand, the observation seems to suggest that, as a matter of law, the *erga omnes* concept was fully developed, and that all that remained to be done was to implement it in practice. If this assessment were correct, further legal analysis would be unnecessary, and should be substituted by political pledges and action. Of course, however, it is not correct.[12] Difficulties with the *erga omnes* concept cannot be reduced to problems of implementation, or differences between *is* and *ought*, *Sein* and *Sollen*. Despite the wealth of analysis and the host of solemnly-worded statements, commentators continue to disagree about even the most fundamental issues. Having reviewed the ICJ's jurisprudence, Thirlway doubts whether the *Barcelona Traction* dictum is 'little more than an empty gesture'.[13] On the basis of a rather summary reference to international practice, Rubin arrives at the same result.[14] More specifically, there is no agreement about the scope of the *erga omnes* concept, and the legal consequences flowing from that status remain unclear. A brief glance at the jurisprudence of the ICJ and the many academic works addressing obligations *erga omnes* shows that the concept has become a sort of legal *panacea*; it is said to affect the legal regime of law enforcement, but also the *pacta tertiis* principle, the question of persistent objection, the territorial and temporal application of obligations, etc.[15] Thirty-five years after the *Barcelona Traction* judgment (and quite apart from problems of implementation), there is thus very often no agreed *ought* and basic aspects of the legal regime of obligations *erga omnes* remain 'very mysterious indeed'.[16] Given these controversies, it may be no coincidence that its implemetation has proven tortuous.

[11] Simma (1993a), 125. See also Zemanek (2000a), 10 ('The Tortuous Implementation of the Idea in Practice').

[12] Simma's own work, which discusses many aspects of the legal regime of obligations *erga omnes* and is frequently referred to in subsequent chapters, testifies to this.

[13] Thirlway (1989), 100. [14] Rubin (1993), 172. [15] For references see below, Chapter 3.

[16] Brownlie (1988a), 71.

2.

The present study attempts to demystify aspects of the 'very mysterious'[17] concept and thereby to facilitate its implementation. Apart from suggesting ways of identifying obligations *erga omnes*, it assesses whether all States, acting individually, are entitled to respond to breaches of such obligations by (i) instituting contentious proceedings before the International Court of Justice and (ii) resorting to countermeasures against the State responsible for the breach. The subsequent chapters will show that these questions are highly controversial, and involve a host of intricate issues, such as the interrelation between different sources of international law and the role of individual States in the process of safeguarding general interests of the international community. Nevertheless, they represent only some of the issues raised by the *erga omnes* concept. The decision to focus on identification, ICJ proceedings and countermeasures (and to ignore other questions) is to some extent due to space constraints. But it is also based on a number of assumptions about the function of the *erga omnes* concept, its influence on the rules governing responses against wrongful acts, and the role of States in the process of securing compliance with international law. Before proceeding with the actual analysis, these assumptions and caveats may be briefly explored, as they help situate countermeasures and ICJ claims within the broader framework, and delimit the scope of the present study. Four points seem particularly relevant.

The first relates to the function of the *erga omnes* concept. The present study focuses on the *enforcement* of international law, i.e. on attempts to induce a State to cease its wrongful conduct and to remedy its consequences.[18] The underlying assumption is that obligations *erga omnes*

[17] Brownlie (1988a), 71.

[18] For similar definitions see Schachter (1991), 227; Shihata (1996–1997), 37; Dahm/Delbrück/Wolfrum (1989), 90–91; Weschke (2001), 2; Ferencz (1983), xv. It must be admitted that there is no agreement about how to interpret the notion of 'enforcement' in international law. Literature in well-developed fields of international law (such as international environmental law, international humanitarian law, or disarmament law) often includes positive, incentive-based measures, preventive measures, or, more generally, all other means aimed at safeguarding compliance with legal systems; see e.g. Bothe (2000), 23; Bothe (1996), 13; Beyerlin (2000), 231–240; Kessler (2001), 48–50; Ladenburger (1996).

Others have adopted a narrower approach than the one pursued here, e.g. by restricting enforcement to measures requiring justification (see Morrison (1995), 43), or by solely focusing on judicial means of enforcement (such as, for example, Jennings (1987), 3). Article 53 UNC, addressing the role of regional arrangements in the

first and foremost affect this area of the law.[19] This assumption is widely shared, and finds support in the above-quoted *Barcelona Traction* dictum, especially the Court's recognition of the 'legal interest' of all States in seeing obligations *erga omnes* observed. However, it has already been mentioned that the *erga omnes* concept is said to influence a wide variety of other legal issues, often entirely unrelated to questions of law enforcement. These other *erga omnes* effects are not usually acknowledged in the legal literature, which is one of the factors mystifying the concept. The present study discusses, and puts forward a distinction between, different types of *erga omnes* effects to avoid these complications.[20] Beyond that, however, it remains focused on *erga omnes* effects in the field of law enforcement.

Secondly, by analysing countermeasures and ICJ proceedings, the present study focuses on what will be called measures of *decentralised enforcement by States*. In contrast, it does not address other forms of law enforcement, notably (i) means of direct recourse, by individuals, groups of individuals, or legal persons against infringements of their rights, or (ii) the institutional enforcement of obligations within the framework of international organisations. While the former distinction is relatively unproblematic, the line between institutional and decentralised enforcement may not always be easy to draw, as it requires an analysis of the often complex interplay between international organisations and their member States. For the purposes of the present study, institutional enforcement will be defined as a measure authorised by the agreement establishing an international organisation. In contrast, decentralised enforcement comprises measures that cannot be evaluated in the light of the institutional rules alone.[21] Following this approach, decentralised enforcement thus covers measures taken by groups of States and may even include measures agreed within the framework of an international organisation, as long as these are directed against non-member States.[22]

The decision to focus on decentralised enforcement by States is based on a simple assumption. It is assumed that State enforcement remains

enforcement of UN sanctions, is equally based on a narrower (treaty-specific) understanding; see Ress/Bröhmer in: Simma (2002a), Article 53, MN 3–7. On 'enforcement' by the Security Council see below, footnote 23.

19 Contrast notably Ragazzi (1997), who sees enforcement rights as mere 'corollaries' (p. xii) of the *erga omnes* concept.

20 See below, Chapter 3.

21 See the similar distinction drawn by Alland (1994), 26.

22 Following this use of terminology, there may thus well be collective decentralised measures.

an essential aspect of protecting general interests under international law. This does not mean that enforcement by non-State actors was irrelevant. Quite to the contrary, direct recourse and institutional enforcement are increasingly relevant – few today would question the importance of systems of judicial protection of individuals in fields such as human rights or investment protection, or of institutional responses under Chapter VII of the United Nations Charter.[23] What is more, the different forms of enforcement are interrelated: as will be shown below, by conferring enforcement competence upon individuals or international organisations, States may have restricted their own enforcement rights.[24] Decentralised enforcement by States therefore is only one (and not necessarily the most appropriate)[25] way of securing compliance with general interests of the international community. The subsequent analysis, however, is based on the assumption that, at the present stage of international law, it remains indispensable, as it is the only form of enforcement that is independent of treaty-based mechanisms.

Thirdly, the present study focuses on two specific measures of decentralised law enforcement, namely countermeasures and ICJ proceedings. Again, this is not to suggest that these are the only forms of conduct by which States could enforce international law. The above definition of enforcement (comprising all attempts to induce another State to cease its wrongful conduct and to remedy its consequences) is sufficiently broad to cover a variety of responses, ranging from verbal protests to the use of military force.[26] The decision to focus on countermeasures and ICJ proceedings is based on a third assumption: these two forms of response are most likely to be affected by the *erga omnes* concept. There are two aspects to this assumption:

[23] On the relevance of direct recourse see e.g. Brown Weiss (2002), 798. As regards Chapter VII UNC, it must be conceded that Security Council action under articles 41 and 42 UNC are based on a wider understanding of the term '*enforcement*'. Unlike in the present study, Security Council *enforcement* action does not presuppose a breach of the law, but is based on political considerations about whether a specific situation amounts to a threat to the peace, breach of the peace or an act of aggression. While the Council will usually only respond if international law has been violated, it is conceivable that situations brought about by lawful conduct should qualify as threats to, or breaches of, the peace. For a comprehensive discussion of the functions of Security Council enforcement action see Frowein/Krisch in Simma (2002a), introductory commentary to Chapter VII, especially MN 17–24. See further Wolfrum in Simma (2002a), Article 1(1), MN 17–19; Dinstein (2001), 250–251; Schachter (1991), 390.

[24] See below, Chapter 7. [25] See Tomuschat (1995), 15.

[26] Contrast the narrower understanding noted above, footnote 18.

The first aspect relates to the function of the *erga omnes* concept. As stated above, the present study discusses how the concept affects the regime of law enforcement. Without prejudicing the subsequent analysis, it is understood that, if anything, it *enhances* the prospects of enforcement, and that States can respond against *erga omnes* breaches in a way not otherwise open to them. As a consequence, it would be rather beside the point to discuss enforcement measures that are *always* available to all States, irrespective of whether the breach, against which they are directed, affects an obligation *erga omnes*. This notably applies to measures that are intrinsically lawful and do not require any justification. Protests and verbal condemnations are one example; under modern international law; they are part of the regular informal diplomatic relations and can no longer be considered a (*prima facie* unlawful) interference in the domestic affairs of another State.[27] Unfriendly, but lawful, responses against breaches (retorsions) are the second type of response in point.[28] As will be shown below, the distinction between countermeasures and retorsions is often difficult to draw in practice. Both can be qualified as sanctions by which States seek to exercise pressure on other States.[29] Whether a specific response is *prima facie* unlawful and requires justification, or still unfriendly but lawful, can only be decided on a case-by-case basis, having regard to the applicable legal rules and taking account of the development of the law.[30] These practical difficulties notwithstanding, the distinction is crucial as a matter of law. By definition, responses can only qualify as retorsions if they remain intrinsically lawful. If it passes that test, it does not require

[27] See Crawford, Fourth Report, para. 35; ILC, commentary to article 42 ASR, para. 2.

[28] On retorsions see Partsch (2000b), 232; Tomuschat (1973), 184–185; Alland (1994), 25; Elagab (1987), 4 and 29–30.

There is some disagreement over the precise definition of the notion of 'retorsion'. In the view of some authors, it denotes unfriendly (but lawful) responses against prior wrongful acts, while others extend it to cover unfriendly responses against prior unfriendly (but lawful) acts as well. Of these, the former, narrower, understanding seems preferable, as it maintains a minimum of coherence in what is already a very vague notion. For a discussion of the terminological issue see Dzida (1997), 49–50.

[29] For a different understanding of the term 'sanction' (comprising only centralised enforcement) see Abi-Saab (2001), 32; White/Abass (2003), 522. For a broader approach (as used here) see draft article 30 of the ILC's first reading text; Dupuy (1983), 505; and cf. Crawford (2001a), 57 for a discussion.

[30] For example, calls for compliance with human rights standards may have, at one time, been considered an unlawful intervention in another State's internal affairs, whereas today they would be considered permissible. See further below, Introduction to Chapter 6.

to be justified, but can be taken by all States. Whether protests or retorsions are lawful, therefore, does not depend on the specific (*erga omnes*) character of the prior breach against which they are directed.

The second aspect concerns the areas of law in which the *erga omnes* concept is being invoked. Even when leaving aside measures always available to all States, enforcement can take various forms. Apart from countermeasures and judicial proceedings, States can notably seek to enforce general interests by forcible means or by exercising national jurisdiction over a particular form of conduct or a particular group of persons. Unlike retorsions and protests, these two forms of responses are not always available, and States wishing to react against breaches are required to justify their respective conduct under the rules of jurisdiction and those governing the use of force. There have indeed been suggestions in the literature that the *erga omnes* concept should provide such justification. As regards jurisdiction, writers have drawn a parallel between the *erga omnes* concept and the rules governing extra-territorial jurisdiction.[31] Van Alebeek has even suggested a direct link between the two, arguing that 'the ... principle [of universal jurisdiction] should now be seen as having its theoretical basis in the concept of *erga omnes* obligations'.[32]

As regards forcible measures, there have equally been claims that obligations *erga omnes* should be enforceable by way of humanitarian intervention. In the view of Michael Reisman, 'military intervention ... [even qualified as] a primary means of enforcing some *erga omnes* norms concerned with human rights.'[33]

However, both statements are speculative and do not reflect the present state of international law. As regards the former, it cannot of course be excluded that the *erga omnes* concept should come to regulate questions of jurisdiction. Cases such as the *Fur Seals Arbitration* or the more recent *Tuna II* and *Shrimps/Turtle* disputes suggest that States indeed may seek to safeguard general interests by claiming a right to exercise extra-territorial jurisdiction.[34] At present, however, there is little indication that an alignment of the two concepts has taken or will take place. Historically, the law of jurisdiction has evolved as a distinct branch of international law and continues to be treated

[31] Jørgensen (2000), 222–223; Boed (2000), 299–302; Sands (2003), 184–191; Bianchi (1999), 271–274.

[32] van Alebeek (2000), 34. [33] Reisman (1993), 171.

[34] See Moore (1898), Vol. I, 755; 33 ILM (1994), 839; WT/DS58/AB/R respectively; and cf. Sands (2003), 184–191.

separately from the rules governing claims made on the international plane. In line with this development, the International Court, when recognising the legal interest of all States in seeing obligations *erga omnes* observed, discussed international claims, but did not make any statement, even inferentially, about the exercise of national jurisdiction.[35] As regards State practice, States asserting a right to exercise extra-territorial jurisdiction have not relied on the *erga omnes* concept, nor have national courts applying principles of universal jurisdiction.[36] The link between jurisdiction and obligations *erga omnes* thus seems more tenuous than van Alebeek's statement suggests.[37]

The same applies to measures involving the use of force. As will be shown below,[38] traditional instances of humanitarian intervention do form part of the historical context in which obligations *erga omnes* have to be seen. However, under modern international law, the legality of measures involving the use of force is first and foremost governed by the UN Charter.[39] Whether humanitarian intervention is permissible under present-day international law therefore is almost exclusively discussed with respect to article 2, para. 4 UNC, which – following the two most prominent arguments advanced by supporters – either does not prohibit the use of force for humanitarian purposes,[40] or recognises a non-written exception based on customary international law.[41] In contrast, debates following the recent military operations in Kosovo, Afghanistan and Iraq suggest that the *erga omnes* concept is of limited (or no) relevance to the dispute. States

[35] Higgins (1994), 57.

[36] If anything, national courts seem to have taken the view that all States could exercise universal jurisdiction over breaches of obligations arising from peremptory norms (*jus cogens*). See below, section 4.2.2.b for a discussion.

[37] Cf., however, below, section 4.1, for brief comment on article 218 LOSC, which recognises a right of port States to exercise jurisdiction over certain discharge offences in any part of the sea. Interestingly, this provision (unless other broad jurisdiction-conferring clauses) is frequently cited in support of the *erga omnes* concept.

[38] See below, section 2.2.2.d.

[39] For comprehensive discussions of the concept of humanitarian intervention see e.g. Gray (2000a), 26–42; Gray (2000b), 240; Chesterman (2001); Beyerlin (1995), 926; Lillich (1967), 325; Lillich (1974), 229; Teson (1997); Brownlie (1974), 217; Brownlie (1963), 338–342; Akehurst (1984), 95; Verwey (1986), 57.

[40] See e.g. Goodrich/Hambro (1946), 68–69; D'Amato (1987), 57–73; Teson (1997), 150–157; similarly the United Kingdom's argument in the *Corfu Channel case*, ICJ Pleadings, Vol. III, 296.

[41] See Lillich (1967), 325; Oppenheim/Lauterpacht, Vol. I (1955), 312–313 and 319–320; Fonteyne (1973), 203; and, more recently, Teson (1997), 177–179.

have hardly ever invoked it and commentators usually treat it *en passant.*[42]

In the light of these considerations, it would seem premature to assert that the *erga omnes* concept should have a decisive influence on the rules of jurisdiction or the legal regime governing the use of force. In contrast, the connection with ICJ proceedings is apparent (the *Barcelona Traction* dictum having been given in that context), while effects on the rules of countermeasures (a generally available concept, counted, together with inter-State proceedings, among the classical means of inter-State dispute settlement) seem at least plausible and have been discussed for a long time.

Fourthly, the present study focuses on whether States are *entitled* to respond to *erga omnes* breaches by way of ICJ proceedings and countermeasures. It does not discuss whether there could be circumstances under which their entitlement (if any) could turn into a *duty* to react.[43] Nor does it seek to assess whether States could join other States' enforcement action, e.g. by intervening in judicial proceedings under articles 62 and 63 of the ICJ Statute.[44] Two other caveats are probably more important. While focusing on the entitlement to take countermeasures or institute ICJ proceedings, the present study does not discuss whether these enforcement measures may be used to secure specific forms of reparation, such as restitution or compensation. This question involves a range of complex issues, such as the relation between different States, or claimant States and actual victims (individuals or groups of

[42] For example, there is no reference to obligations *erga omnes* in the detailed discussions by Gray (2000a), 26–42; Chesterman (2001); or Teson (1997). Franck (2002), 135, and Zygojannis (2003), 60, refer to obligations *erga omnes* in passing, while Empell suggests that in future, *erga omnes* considerations *should* inform debates about humanitarian intervention (378–383).

[43] Cf. Sicilianos (1990), 174; Klein (1998a), 63; Wengler (1964), 920–928; and further Thierry (2001), 219; Corten/Klein (1996).

The matter is often discussed with respect to States' duties under common article 1 of the Geneva Conventions, see e.g Kessler (2001), 102–120; Schindler (1995), 204–205; Condorelli/Boisson de Chazournes (1984), 67. See also ICJ's advisory opinion in the *Israeli Wall case*, available at www.icj-cij.org, paras. 157–159, in which the Court carefully distinguished between a *duty* to respond based on common article 1 of the Geneva Conventions and *rights* of response based on the *erga omnes* concept.

See further Judge *ad hoc* Lauterpacht's separate opinion in the *Genocide case*, ICJ Reports 1993, 444–445 (para. 115) (assessing whether States have a duty to intervene in order to prevent genocide); and 43 ICLQ (1994), 714 (editor's note providing information about Bosnia's intention, soon abandoned, to institute ICJ proceedings against the United Kingdom alleging a breach of that duty.)

[44] See e.g. Palchetti (2002), 139.

individuals) of *erga omnes* breaches, which international lawyers have only begun to address, and on which there is very little concrete practice.[45] Insofar as the present study discusses the existence of a right to take countermeasures, or to institute ICJ proceedings, this right therefore is understood as a right to react with a view to stopping on-going breaches or to secure a declaration of their unlawfulness.[46] Finally, this also means that there can be no detailed discussion of the relation between different claimants asserting a right to respond against *erga omnes* breaches[47] – a question that heavily depends on rules governing reparation and the eventual distribution of the proceeds secured by way of restitution or compensation.[48]

3.

Of course, the *erga omnes* concept has been the subject of a number of earlier studies, many of which focus on the decentralised enforcement of obligations *erga omnes*. In view of the continuing interest in it, and the remaining controversies, a reassessment nevertheless seems justified; this in particular because more recent developments have helped clarify some of the underlying issues. The ICJ and its members have pronounced on specific features of obligations *erga omnes* in the *East Timor, Genocide, Gabčíkovo cases*, as well as, most recently, the *Israeli Wall case*.[49] Perhaps more importantly, as has been stated already, the ILC's Articles on State Responsibility, completed in 2001, recognise the pivotal role of the *erga omnes* concept. Part Three of the ILC's text constitutes

[45] On the question see the various contributions in Tomuschat/Randelzhofer (1999); and cf. further paras. 12–14 of the ILC's commentary to article 48 ASR.

[46] See Brownlie (1998), 124–126; Gray (1987), 96–108, on the manifold functions that declaratory relief may serve.

[47] See, however, below, section 7.2.3.a, for brief comment on article 51 UNC.

[48] On the issue see article 48, para. 2b ASR, requiring that claims 'must be made in the interest of the direct victims of the wrongful act', while acknowledging that 'this aspect of article 48 (2) involves a measure or progressive development' (commentary to article 48 ASR, para. 12).

As regards the relation between States seeking to vindicate obligations *erga omnes* and direct beneficiaries of such obligations see also Portugal's arguments in the *East Timor case*, ICJ Pleadings, *Réplique*, para. 9.49 and Memorial, paras. 9.12–9.13 (arguing that compensation should be paid into a fund used to support the direct beneficiaries). For scholarly discussion see von Schorlemmer (2003), 265–271, 283–287.

[49] See ICJ Reports 1995, 90 (*East Timor*); 1996, 595 (*Genocide*); 1997, 7 (*Gabčíkovo*), and 43 ILM (2004), 1009 (*Israeli Wall*) respectively. The text of the *Israeli Wall* opinion is also available at www.icj-cij.org.

the most comprehensive attempt to date to spell out the legal consequences flowing from *erga omnes* breaches and to define the position of States affected by such breaches. The present study will take into account these more recent developments, which so far have hardly been discussed in detail.[50]

It should nevertheless be noted at the outset that, important though it is, the ILC's text has not settled matters. There is little doubt that the Commission's work has shaped, and continues to shape, the modern law of State responsibility. It has brought about an objective understanding, pursuant to which a State incurs responsibility whenever it fails to comply with its international obligations, irrespective of factors such as damage or fault, thus freeing the law of responsibility from fruitless doctrinal controversies about the definition of damage and fault, and the restrictive focus on the reparation of material wrongs.[51] The present study proceeds on the basis of this modern understanding of responsibility, brought about, to a large extent, by the ILC. However, the Commission's work will not be treated as 'the law'.[52] The Commission is not (and does not claim to be) infallible. Unless States should decide to conclude a Convention on State Responsibility,[53] its text is not an independent source of the law, but is influential if, and to the extent that, it reflects international practice and jurisprudence. Whether it does needs to be assessed, and commentators seeking to do so are more than glossators explaining the meaning of legal rules. In the light of these considerations, the

[50] Cf., however, the study by Empell (2003), published after the completion of the Articles on State Responsibility. For general assessments of the ILC's work see Crawford (2002a); Dupuy (2003), 305; Dupuy (2002b), 354–398; Tams (2002a), 759; as well as the various contributions to symposia organised by the American Society of International Law and the European University Institute, published in 96 AJIL (2002), 773–889; 13 EJIL (2002), 1053–1255, respectively.

[51] See article 2 ASR. On the implications of this reorientation see Pellet (1996), 10–13; Pellet (2001), 289–291; Simma (1986a), 366–370; Tams (2002a), 765–766. For attempts to retain notions of damage, while at the same time coming to terms with responsibility relationships transcending bilateral contexts see Cottereau (1991), 21–39; Stern (2001), 3.

[52] It sometimes seems to be treated as such: see e.g. Shaw (2003), 696–721.

[53] Although this question is still under consideration, it seems unlikely that States should convene a conference on State responsibility with a view to concluding a treaty. In its Report to the General Assembly, the ILC had proposed that the Assembly should 'take note' of the ILC's text. This it has done in GA Res. 56/83 and again in GA Res. 59/35. For a brief summary of the debate cf. Crawford (2002a), 58–60; id., Fourth Report, paras. 21–26; and further Caron (2002), 857.

present study intends to be more than a guide to the ILC's work. Where relevant – for example in the sections addressing countermeasures[54] – the Commission's work will be duly taken into account. However, its evaluation cannot replace the assessment of international jurisprudence and practice relating to obligations *erga omnes*.

Finally, two further preliminary remarks may be made regarding the way in which this material is assessed in the following. The first point to make is that the present study seeks to approach the *erga omnes* concept in a neutral and uncommitted way. This may be an evident point to make, as all academic research should aim to be objective. In view of the strong views provoked by the *erga omnes* concept, it is nevertheless worth stressing. In fact, it seems fair to say that commentators addressing obligations *erga omnes* have at times been influenced less by legal argument than by the high expectations or severe concerns raised by the concept. This is brought out with particular clarity in discussions about the existence (or otherwise) of a right to take countermeasures in response to *erga omnes* breaches. Commentators placing great faith in the *erga omnes* concept often simply assume that such a right exists. Without worrying about State practice or international jurisprudence, they confidently treat it as an automatic consequence of the above-quoted *Barcelona Traction* dictum.[55] On the other end of the spectrum are writers who reject outright the idea that States could take countermeasures in the general interest. Equally unconcerned with practice or jurisprudence, some of them have asserted that recognising such a right would lead to 'mob violence' or 'vigilantism'.[56] As will be shown in more detail below,[57] both approaches fail to appreciate the complexity of the issues involved. Whether States can take countermeasures in response to *erga omnes* breaches is one of the most controversial issues in the law of State responsibility. The existence (or otherwise) of such a right is neither excluded nor does it follow as a matter of course from a certain hypothesis. It depends on a thorough evaluation of international practice and jurisprudence, which cannot be substituted by

[54] See below, Chapter 6. While elaborating a regime of countermeasures, the Commission did not have a mandate to define the conditions governing the making of claims before international judicial bodies, such as the ICJ. These depend on the constitutional documents of the relevant institution, as interpreted in the institution's subsequent jurisprudence, see Bryde (1994), 180.

[55] For references see below, Chapter 6.

[56] See Marek (1978–1979), 481; McCaffrey (1989), 244, and cf. further below, Chapter 6.

[57] See below, Chapter 6.

generalised assertions, or by firmly held views about the allegedly 'true nature' of the *erga omnes* concept. Hoping to avoid a biased approach, the present study will not reiterate the high hopes or grave concerns raised by that concept. Instead, it seeks to assess whether, and to what extent, obligations *erga omnes* have already affected the rules of present-day international law.

Secondly, the present study seeks to analyse the concept of obligations *erga omnes* in its historical context. Again, it may seem an obvious point to make that legal concepts should not be addressed in isolation. But again, the point is worth making, as this is precisely what often happens to the *erga omnes* concept. While first mentioned, as a law enforcement concept, in 1970, obligations *erga omnes* have a longer history. Most commentators accept that the two paragraphs first expressing it were included into the *Barcelona Traction* judgment in an attempt to mitigate the effects of the 1966 (second) *South West Africa* judgment – a decision that had come to epitomise a narrow approach to questions of law enforcement and had provoked concern about the Court's allegedly conservative approach.[58] In order fully to appreciate the relevance of the *erga omnes* concept, it is, however, not sufficient to juxtapose *South West Africa* (1966) and *Barcelona Traction* (1970): restrictive approaches to law enforcement cannot be reduced to the former any more than modern, broader approaches start with the latter. Before dealing with obligations *erga omnes* proper, it will therefore be necessary to clarify a number of relevant concepts and to analyse the traditional rules governing the enforcement of international obligations. Only by presenting these in some detail, it is believed, can the *erga omnes* concept be fully evaluated, and its novel features grasped.

[58] On *South West Africa* see below, section 2.1.2.

For comment on the relation between *South West Africa* and *Barcelona Traction* see e.g. Kamminga (1992), 153; Thirlway (1989), 94 and 98; Crawford (1996), 588–589; Joergensen (2000), 219; Dugard (1996), 549 and 554; Simma (1994a), 295; Byers (1999), 196 (his footnote 144). In view of Judge Schwebel *Barcelona Traction* 'decisively displaced' *South West Africa* (*Nicaragua case* (provisional measures), ICJ Reports 1984, 190). Judge Lachs, whom many see as the person responsible for the inclusion of paras. 33 and 34, later observed that the statement on obligations *erga omnes* 'was not necessary in the judgment, but it was a good opportunity to nail down certain provisions of the law and indicate where states are obliged to act vis-à-vis the international community as a whole', Lachs (1988), 464. Lachs' role in the drafting of the *Barcelona Traction* judgment is, for example, discussed by McWhinney (1995), 25, 36–38; Higgins (1995), 19; cf. also McWhinney (1991), xix. It should be noted that others have claimed the crucial role for Judge Jessup, see e.g. Schachter (1986), 892. For Lachs' own account see Lachs (1986), 897–898.

4.

In the light of these considerations, Part I (Chapters 1 and 2) of the present study assesses the background against which the *erga omnes* concept has to be seen. Part II (Chapters 3 to 7) addresses the legal regime governing obligations *erga omnes*. More specifically, Chapter 3 introduces the distinction (hinted at above) between different types of *erga omnes* effects. Chapter 4 suggests ways and means of identifying obligations *erga omnes*. Chapters 5 and 6 focus on the two rights of protection relevant to the present study: they analyse whether States are entitled to respond to *erga omnes* breaches by instituting ICJ proceedings or by taking countermeasures. Finally, Chapter 7 deals with the relation between rights of protection based on the *erga omnes* concept and other enforcement rights available to States.

PART I • BACKGROUND TO THE *ERGA OMNES* CONCEPT

The specific features of obligations *erga omnes* cannot be fully appreciated if the concept is interpreted in isolation. Part I of the present study intends to avoid this problem by addressing a number of basic issues. It proceeds in two steps. Chapter 1 addresses fundamental legal concepts; its aim is to clarify the basic parameters, within which the subsequent analysis evolves. Chapter 2 presents the historical background by providing an overview over the traditional, pre-*Barcelona Traction* rules of law enforcement. Taken together, both chapters are intended to set the stage for the subsequent discussion of specific problems raised by the *erga omnes* concept.

1 Clarifications

The concept of obligations *erga omnes* and the rules governing the enforcement of international law do not exist in a legal vacuum. Their analysis, in the following chapters, depends on a number of basic concepts and notions. The purpose of this chapter is to introduce and clarify these concepts and notions. Three aspects in particular are to be considered: Section 1.1 briefly summarises legal rules governing countermeasures and ICJ proceedings as the two means of law enforcement relevant to the present study. Section 1.2 introduces the concept of standing to react against internationally wrongful acts, whose interpretation occupies much of the subsequent analysis. Finally, section 1.3 addresses the distinction between individual and general legal interests, which is at the heart of modern discussions about standing.

1.1 Countermeasures and ICJ proceedings

As a first step, it is necessary to introduce the two forms of responses addressed in the following: countermeasures and ICJ proceedings. At the outset, it is worth reiterating that although focusing on the two forms of responses, this study is not about the law of countermeasures or ICJ claims as such. It is assumed that if indeed, all States should be entitled to respond against *erga omnes* breaches, their responses would have to conform with the normal requirements governing ICJ claims and countermeasures. Subsequent chapters will therefore not address these other requirements, but take them for granted. The relevant legal rules can be summarised as follows:

The concept of countermeasures (traditionally referred to as 'reprisals')[1] constitutes a form of permitted self-help recognised under general

[1] The traditional term 'reprisals' was at times said to imply an idea of vengeance. As a consequence, international tribunals and the ILC have, in recent decades, preferred to

international law. More specifically, a countermeasure can be defined as the act of non-compliance, by a State, with its obligations owed to another State, decided upon in response to a prior breach of international law by that other State and aimed at inducing it to respect its obligations.[2] The concept is characterised by a considerable degree of flexibility. In principle, the reacting State is free to choose which obligations it intends to disregard. Moreover, there is no requirement of a prior third-party assessment of whether the target State has actually committed a wrongful act.[3] Given this flexibility, it is not surprising that the reacting State's entitlement to resort to countermeasures is subject to a number of restrictions, both procedural and substantive.

As to the former, it is agreed that the target State must have been confronted with a demand for compliance, and attempts to negotiate, prior to the actual taking of countermeasures.[4] As to substance, limits relate to the duration, intensity and direction of the measure adopted. Since countermeasures aim at inducing compliance with the law, they must stop when the violation in response to which they were taken stops, and ought to be reversible.[5] With regard to their intensity, reactions must be necessary and commensurate, i.e. their effects must be proportionate with the effects of the initial wrongful act.[6] In addition, a countermeasure must not involve violations of rules of *jus cogens* (notably the prohibition against the use of force), or affect obligations to

speak of 'countermeasures', see *Air Services*, 54 ILR 337 (para. 80); *Gabčíkovo case*, ICJ Reports 1997, 55 (para. 82); article 49 ASR; and cf. Alland (1994), 24–25; and para. 3 of the ILC's introductory commentary to Part Three, Chapter II ASR for a discussion. The present study uses the modern term, as it has now become accepted.

2 See articles 22, 49 ASR; *Institut de droit international* (1934), 708 (article prémier); Elagab (1987), 3; Partsch (2000a), 201; Zemanek (2000b), 227; Dzida (1997), 19. For judicial and arbitral support see e.g. *Gabčíkovo case*, ICJ Reports 1997, 55–57 (paras. 83–87); *Air Services*, 54 ILR 337–341 (paras. 80–98); *Naulilaa*, RIAA, Vol. II, 1025–1026; *Cysne*, *ibid.*, 1052.

3 In contrast, in order for responsibility to be precluded, there must have actually been a previous wrongful act. Jurisprudence, including the award in *Air Services* (which is at times interpreted to the contrary), rejects the view that conduct by the respondent State would be justified if the respondent unjustifiedly believed in the existence of a prior breach. See also commentary to article 49 ASR, para. 3; and, for a discussion, Elagab (1987), 49–50; Zoller (1984), 95–97.

4 *Gabčíkovo case*, ICJ Reports 1997, 56 (para. 84); *Air Services*, 54 ILR 338–339 (paras. 84–87); see also article 52, para. 1 ASR.

5 *Gabčíkovo case*, ICJ Reports 1997, 56–57 (para. 87); article 49, para. 3 ASR.

6 *Naulilaa*, RIAA, Vol. II, 1028; *Air Services*, 54 ILR 338 (para. 83), *Gabčíkovo case*, ICJ Reports 1997, 56 (paras. 85–87). As the latter two decisions clarify, the assessment of whether a certain response is commensurate not only depends on a quantitative assessment of the losses, but may also take into account the gravity of the wrongful act. This is expressly confirmed in article 51 ASR.

settle disputes by pacific means.[7] Finally, reactions can only be justified if they are directed against the State responsible for the initial breach of international law. Countermeasures therefore cannot justify violations of rights of other ('third') States.[8]

Being customary in character, the concept of countermeasures can be relied on by all States irrespective of their participation in a particular treaty. Conversely, it may be modified or excluded by special rules, notably treaty rules prescribing specific forms of third-party dispute settlement, which, expressly or by implication, restrict the availability of measures of self-help.[9]

Given the breadth and flexibility of the concept, it is at times difficult to distinguish countermeasures from other justifications. Since this problem will be addressed more fully below, it may be sufficient briefly to note the two main areas of conflict. First, where a State responds against a prior wrongful act that constitutes an armed attack, it can take forcible and non-forcible measures of self-defence.[10] While forcible action cannot be justified as a countermeasure, non-forcible responses can come within the scope of both concepts. Secondly, similar problems arise where States suspend or terminate treaties in response to prior breaches of the same treaty. Quite apart from the concept of countermeasures, such conduct often can be justified under the maxim *exceptio inadimpleti contractus*, as codified in article 60 VCLT, or other concepts of general treaty law.[11] Of course, there remain crucial conceptual differences between the different justifications.[12] Self-defence and article 60 VCLT (unlike countermeasures) on the one hand presuppose qualified

[7] See generally article 50 ASR and, as regards the question of dispute settlement clauses, the ICJ's judgments in the *ICAO* and *Hostages cases*, ICJ Reports 1972, 53, and ICJ Reports 1980, 28 (para. 53). On *jus cogens* rules see further below, section 4.2.2.

[8] See especially *Cysne case*, RIAA, Vol. II, 1056–1057 (where the tribunal held that '[o]nly reprisals taken against the provoking State are permissible'), and further commentary to article 22 ASR, para. 5.

[9] See article 52, paras. 3 and 4 ASR for the ILC's attempt to codify the existing law. Whether or not an existing treaty excludes resort to countermeasures is a matter of treaty interpretation. For a discussion see below, Chapter 7.

[10] Dahm (1962), 56–59; Bowett (1972a), 3; Dzida (1997), 50–52; and cf. Malanczuk (1987), 197; Alland (1987), 143.

[11] Dzida (1997), 52–54; Malanczuk (1985), 311–314; and cf. Sicilianos (1993), 341.

[12] See Simma (1970), 20–24; Dahm (1962), 59–60; Dzida (1997), 50–54; Schlochauer (1974–1975), 269; Malanczuk (1985), 311–314; and para. 4 of the ILC's introductory commentary to Part Three, Chapter II ASR. Contrast e.g. Kelsen (1932), 481 (self-defence a subcategory of reprisals/countermeasures); and Akehurst (1970), 6 (*exceptio* a subcategory of reprisals/countermeasures).

breaches of the law (an armed attack; a material breach of a treaty), but on the other hand permit farther-reaching responses (the use of force in the first case; the suspension or even termination of obligations in the second). Moreover, at least in theory, self-defence and treaty-based responses are meant to be protective reactions, by which the responding State seeks to re-establish a certain contractual or military balance rather than to *enforce* international law against recalcitrant States. In practice, however, the line between the different justifications will often be difficult to draw. Where a State responds against an armed attack or a material treaty breach, it will not always be readily apparent whether it does so in order to restore a certain equilibrium (by way of self-defence or *exceptio*) or in order to enforce international law by way of countermeasure. What is more, express statements clarifying on which concept a State relies are only rarely available. Conceptual distinctions notwithstanding, the broad and flexible concept of countermeasures thus often overlaps with other justifications.

No such problems arise with respect to ICJ proceedings. Still, the legal rules governing proceedings are more difficult to summarise since ICJ judgments can be sought in a variety of situations and are not limited to responses against violations of international law. When focusing on that scenario, the following aspects can be outlined:

Unlike in the case of countermeasures, a State seeking an ICJ judgment entrusts the resolution of a dispute to an international body established by treaty. It follows that contentious ICJ proceedings can only be instituted by States participating in the regime-creating treaty, the ICJ Statute, and subject to the conditions set out in it or developed in the Court's jurisprudence.[13] Apart from the basic conditions *ratione personae* set out in articles 34 and 35 of the ICJ Statute, these can be divided into jurisdictional and admissibility requirements. Pursuant to article 36 of its Statute, the Court's jurisdiction rests on the principle of consent of the parties. Consent may be given after the dispute has arisen[14] or in advance. In the latter case, it is possible to distinguish between declarations under the optional clause and treaty-based compromissory clauses.[15] Optional clause declarations, by which States accept the general jurisdiction of the Court, have at present been

[13] Schwarzenberger (1986), 459, speaks of 'constitutional limitations'.

[14] In the case of a *compromis* or *forum prorogatum* (see article 40, para. 1 of the ICJ Statute and article 38, para. 5 of the Court's Rules).

[15] See article 36, paras. 1 and 2 of the ICJ Statute, and cf. article 36, para. 5 and article 37 for the transfer of jurisdiction from the PCIJ to the ICJ.

made by sixty-five States, but are often subject to reservations.[16] Leaving aside general dispute settlement conventions,[17] compromissary clauses usually recognise the Court's jurisdiction over specific treaty-based disputes. The principle of consensual jurisdiction therefore severely restricts the effectivity of judicial law enforcement, both with respect to the availability of judicial recourse and with respect to the legal rules that may be the subject of litigation.

As for admissibility, it is implicit in article 38 that the Court's competence in contentious proceedings is restricted to the solution of 'disputes'. In the Court's practice, this requirement has been interpreted to mean that there has to be, between the parties, a 'disagreement on a point of law or fact, a conflict of legal views or interests',[18] which is not merely hypothetical and still exists at the time of the decision.[19] The admissibility of claims is further restricted by doctrines of general procedural law, such as *res judicata*,[20] *désistement*,[21] litispendence,[22] the concept of the indispensable third party,[23] or rules against delay in bringing the claim.[24] Further conditions depend on the specific

[16] Cf. the list of declarations available at http://www.icj-cij.org/icjwww/ibasicdocuments/ibasictexts/ibasicdeclarations.htm.

[17] For examples of such broadly formulated jurisdictional clauses see e.g article 1 of the 1957 European Convention for the Peaceful Settlement of Disputes (320 UNTS 243); or article 17 of the 1928 General Act for the Pacific Settlement of Disputes (as revised, 71 UNTS 101).

[18] *Mavrommatis Palestine Concessions*, PCIJ, Ser. A, No. 2 (1924), 11.

[19] On hypothetical disputes see *Northern Cameroons case*, ICJ Reports 1963, 33–34 and further Sep.Op. Fitzmaurice, *ibid.*, 117; on moot questions (i.e. disputes that have become hypothetical after the institution of proceedings) *Nuclear Tests cases*, ICJ Reports 1974, 253 and 457.

[20] As derived from the combined effect of articles 59, 60 of the ICJ Statute; see *Barcelona Traction case* (preliminary objections), ICJ Reports 1964, 20; *Chorzow Factory case*, Diss.Op. Anzilotti, PCIJ, Ser. A, No. 13 (1928), 23.

[21] Articles 68, 69 of the Rules of the Court.

[22] As discussed e.g. in *German Interests in Polish Upper Silesia*, PCIJ, Ser. A, No. 6 (1925), 19–20, *Chorzow Factory*, PCIJ Reports Ser. A, No. 9 (1927), 31–32, or the *South West Africa case*, ICJ Reports 1962, 345. Cf. de Visscher (1966), 174–176; and Shany (2003), 239–245 with many further references.

[23] As applied in the *Monetary Gold* and *East Timor cases*, ICJ Reports 1954, 32, and 1995, 100–105 (paras. 23–35) respectively. See further the discussion of the concept in the *Nauru* and *Nicaragua* (provisional measures) *cases*, ICJ Reports 1992, 259–262 (para. 55); ICJ Reports 1984, 185 (para. 35); and more recently the interim order in *Armed Activities (Congo/Uganda)*, available at www.icj-cij.org, para. 38.

[24] See e.g. the Court's orders on provisional measures in the *Kosovo* proceedings brought against Belgium and the Netherlands, where the Court held that applicants were not entitled to present additional bases of jurisdiction during the course of the oral pleadings, see ICJ Reports 1999, 124 and 542 (paras. 42–44 respectively).

jurisdiction-conferring title or the specific claim that is being brought. Duties to exhaust prior means of dispute settlement (negotiations or conciliation),[25] to settle the dispute by other means (e.g. arbitration),[26] or the nationality of claims and exhaustion of local remedies rules governing cases of diplomatic protection[27] are prominent examples of such special admissibility requirements.[28]

Where these conditions are satisfied, the Court will pronounce on the merits of the applicant's claims. Its decision is final and entails binding legal obligations between the parties.[29] However, neither the Statute nor the Court's Rules address the execution of judgments.[30] In the absence of voluntary compliance, execution therefore is a matter for the UN Security Council or for self-help, including, for example, by way of countermeasure.[31]

As this brief survey reveals, countermeasures and ICJ proceedings do not simply coexist side by side, but are interrelated. The continuing importance of countermeasures under international law is largely a consequence of the relative lack of compulsory jurisdiction. Where recourse to binding judicial dispute settlement (including before the ICJ) is available, countermeasures may well be excluded. Where ICJ

[25] See e.g. article 7 of the 1922 Mandate Agreement, which formed the subject of the *South West Africa cases*, or the negotiations clause contained in the *compromis* submitting to the Court the *Lybian-Chad Territorial Dispute* (ICJ Reports 1994, 6). In contrast, the Court has held that in the absence of such specific clauses, there is no general condition pursuant to which contentious proceedings have to be preceded by negotiations; see e.g. *Land and Maritime Boundary (Cameroon Nigeria)* (preliminary objections), ICJ Reports 1998, 303 (para. 56).

[26] As discussed in the *Ambatielos case*, ICJ Reports 1952, 28 (Preliminary Objections) and 1953, 10. Article 95 UNC specifically safeguards the rights of UN members to opt for other forms of inter-State adjudication.

[27] As for the nationality of claims see *Mavrommatis Concessions case*, PCIJ, Ser. A, No. 2 (1924), 12; *Nottebohm case*, ICJ Reports 1955, 24; as for the local remedies rule see *Interhandel case*, ICJ Reports 1959, 27. On the procedural character of the local remedies rule see e.g. article 44 ASR, and further Doehring (1995), 240.

[28] In addition to adding new types of conditions, special rules may of course modify the existing general rules. Treaty clauses specifically governing the question of legal interest provide a typical example in point; many of these clauses are discussed below, section 2.2.1.a.

[29] Articles 59, 60 of the ICJ Statute; article 94, para. 1 UNC.

[30] The parties can of course empower the Court to supervise compliance, as in the *Gabčíkovo case*, see article 5, para. 3 of the *compromis*, referred to in the Court's judgment, ICJ Reports 1997, 12.

[31] See article 94, para. 2 UNC. On enforcement by way of self-help see Collier and Lowe (1999), 178; Magid (1997), 334–335; on the possible role of third parties, see below, section 2.2.2.c.

judgments are not complied with, countermeasures may come into play again as a means of enforcement. Furthermore, the survey also shows that law enforcement through countermeasures and ICJ proceedings is very different in a number of respects. Differences between the two types of responses notably relate to

- their availability (general availability versus availability subject to acceptance of the Court's jurisdiction),
- their objectivity (private assessment of whether there has been a breach versus institutionalised third-party evaluation), and
- their functioning (coercion versus creation of legal obligations).

These differences notwithstanding, countermeasures and ICJ proceedings are both means of putting pressure on a State that has violated international law, each subject to its own conditions and restrictions. The question remains whether States respecting these various conditions and restrictions can always respond against all types of breaches of international law. The short answer to this question has already been given in the Introduction. As has been stated there, unlike other forms of enforcement action, countermeasures and ICJ claims are not always available to all States. Instead, States are required to show that the previous breach was of such a character to entitle them to respond. This specific entitlement is of crucial relevance to the present study. It will be analysed in the subsequent section.

1.2 The notion of standing

Much of the analysis in subsequent chapters is but an interpretation of this specific entitlement. The analysis takes place on the basis of a specific legal concept: the notion of '*standing*'. The present section does not intend to anticipate its interpretation, but merely to clarify the parameters within which that interpretation evolves. To that extent, it makes a number of basic points about the notion of 'standing'.

A preliminary point relates to terminology. The notion of 'standing' is used in many different ways. Legal dictionaries define it as 'the right to make a claim', or the right to 'enforc[e] a duty'.[32] Of course, this is a rather general definition. Whether States have the 'right to enforce a duty' by way of countermeasure or ICJ proceedings depends on a variety of conditions, most of which have been summarised already. The

[32] See e.g. *Black's Law Dictionary* (7th ed.), 1413.

relevant entry in the *Encyclopedia of Public International Law*, having noted that '[t]here is no uniform concept of standing in international law', indeed discusses issues such as access to court, jurisdiction of courts, or procedural capacity.[33] Since none of these is addressed in the following, the above-quoted definition needs to be refined. This can be done by qualifying the way in which the requirement of standing (as understood here) affects the right to make a claim. Different conditions do so in different ways, for example by restricting the availability of a specific forum or by identifying the classes of legal actors qualified to appear before it. Unlike these requirements, 'standing', as used here, is a condition qualifying the relation between the State seeking to respond against a violation of the law and the legal rule against whose violation the response is directed.[34] It can be defined as the requirement that a State seeking to enforce the law establishes *a sufficient link* between itself and the legal rule that forms the subject matter of the enforcement action.[35] This is usually formulated either by qualifying the position of the State with regard to the observance of the obligation (which must have been *interested*, *concerned*, *protected*, etc.) or by describing the effects that the prior breach has had on it (hence qualifications such as *affected*, *aggrieved*, *injured*, etc.).[36]

Although the term 'standing' is most often used in judicial proceedings, this requirement applies to both countermeasures and ICJ proceedings. This does not mean that States having established standing to

[33] Matscher (2000), 594.

[34] This has been described very differently, for example as a question of 'proximity [. . .] to a breach' (German comments on State responsibility, UN Doc. A/CN.4/496, 19 (para. 123)); or as an issue of 'involve[ment] in the injury' (Riphagen, Third Report, YbILC 1982, Vol. II/1, 37 (para. 95)). See further Günther (1999), 24–28; Hafner (1988), 212–222.

[35] Just as 'standing' has many meanings, the specific meaning chosen here has been described very differently. What is labelled here as an issue of standing is addressed also under any of the following rubrics: *locus standi* or *jus standi*, legal interest, interest to sue or *intérêt pour agir*, capacity or special capacity, *qualité (pour agir)*, interest in bringing an action, right or cause of action, all of which are used to describe partly identical or overlapping conditions restricting the exercise of enforcement measures. For a survey of terminology see Matscher (2000), 594; Günther (1999), 20–28.

[36] As the Court clarified in *South West Africa*, the problem of standing is not part of the question whether there is a legal dispute, but must be addressed separately (see ICJ Reports 1962, 343; and further M'Baye (1988), 288; van Dijk (1980), 25). By drawing this distinction, the Court rejected the defendant's argument that for there to be a legal dispute, applicants would have to establish a right to react in defence of the relevant legal rules. For a discussion contrast the opinions of Judges Mbafeno and Spender/ Fitzmaurice, ICJ Reports 1962, 447 and 559 respectively; and see further Cassese (1975), 173; Günther (1999), 13–19.

institute ICJ proceedings are, by necessity, also entitled to respond to breaches by way of countermeasure. It is not excluded that the two rules could be different in scope - whether this is so is a question of interpretation, which will be addressed in subsequent chapters. The basic test - the requirement of a sufficient link between the State seeking to respond and the legal rule in question - however is the same. Hence texts spelling out the legal regime of countermeasures, while not always using the term 'standing', restrict the right to respond against breaches to 'aggrieved States',[37] States suffering 'prejudice',[38] or, most commonly, 'injured States'.[39] Despite the lack of an agreed terminology, 'standing' in the sense used here therefore is a requirement common to both countermeasures and ICJ proceedings; its main features can be studied without distinguishing the two forms of enforcement.

At least traditionally, the requirement of standing has received scant attention. In recent years, the situation has begun to change, partly as a result of the ILC's protracted discussions in the context of State responsibility. Nonetheless, a considerable number of works, including specialised works on the law of responsibility, ignore it altogether.[40] Others address it in a simplistic way, e.g. by briefly distinguishing instances of so-called 'direct claims' by States from those of diplomatic protection of nationals.[41] This may have been the result of a pragmatic approach used to thinking in terms of causes of action rather than to discussing questions of standing in the abstract. It may also reflect the fact that the bulk of diplomatic, judicial, or arbitral practice traditionally involved claims brought by way of diplomatic protection, in which problems of standing mainly arose as an aspect of the nationality of claims rule. The traditionally narrow understanding of the law of State responsibility, which viewed responsibility as a reciprocal relationship between pairs of States, or reduced it to a mechanism for obtaining reparation, also facilitated narrow approaches to questions of standing. Finally, these

[37] Elagab (1987), 55.

[38] *Institut de droit international* (1934), 708 (article prémier).

[39] *Gabčíkovo case*, ICJ Reports 1997, 56 (para. 84); article 49 ASR; and already article 40 of the ILC's first reading draft articles.

[40] See e.g. O'Connell (1970), Vol. II; O'Brien (2001); von Münch (1963); Accioly (1959), 349; Jiménez de Aréchaga and Tanzi (1991) (but cf. the brief reference, at 357–358, to international crimes of States).

[41] For example, Greig (1976), 522–525; Fawcett (1968), 110; Berber (1964), 18–19; Rousseau (1983).

may also have been informed by the belief that categories of standing were self-explanatory.

Whatever the reasons, this lack of debate is highly problematic. Although it may in many cases be evident whether a States has standing, the relevant legal rules are considerably more complex than the works referred to in the previous paragraph suggest. In order to underline this point, the present section introduces what are believed to be the three basic features of the rules of standing: their normativity, flexibility, and diversity. Given the relevance of the issue, and the relative absence of literary discussion, these features will be explored in some detail.

1.2.1 Standing as a normative concept

The most fundamental question to be addressed is how to distinguish States having standing to respond against violations from States lacking it. Making standing dependent on the establishment of an 'interest', of 'injury', 'concern', or of 'affectedness' is of little help; it begs the question which State can be said to have an interest in the observance of a legal rule or under which circumstances it can claim to be affected or injured by a breach of international law. The problem is corroborated by the fact that the terms used are defined by reference to one another – 'interest', for example, can be defined as 'the relation of being *concerned* or *affected* in respect of advantage or detriment'.[42] Furthermore, the different categories are inherently vague and can be defined in a variety of ways. To focus again on the notion of interest, Judge Morelli once hinted at a subjective approach when observing that '[e]ach State is the judge of its own interest'.[43] Clearly, if this was the relevant test (which Judge Morelli did not suggest), the notion of standing would be trivial or meaningless, as States intending to respond would always be interested.

Objective approaches, however, need not necessarily be more practicable. If 'interested' simply meant 'being concerned' (as in the above definition), all States would always be somehow interested in every legal rule. State A's decision to impose import duties on goods from State B might be a cause of concern to State C (which supplies much of

[42] *Shorter Oxford Dictionary* (1973), Vol. I, 1093 ('interest', section I. 1.) (emphasis added). Interest of course has many other meanings. In the words of Devlin, J, 'anybody who was asked what it [interest] meant would at once want to know the context in which it was used before he could venture an opinion' (*Bearmans Ltd v. Metropolitan Police District Receiver* [1961] 1 All ER 391).

[43] Diss.Op. Morelli, *South West Africa case* (preliminary objections), ICJ Reports 1962, 570.

the goods to State A) and State D (whose industry depends on cheap exports from State B). State E, an ardent supporter of free trade, might want to see the import duties removed as a matter of principle. Finally, F could claim to be affected because it depended on the (hitherto good) relations between States A and B. The example shows that each legal rule involves, to quote Judge *ad hoc* Skubiszewski, 'a myriad of interests',[44] often classified as economic, political, humanitarian, or similar.[45] One might even accept the proposition that since the international legal system safeguards the interests of all States, every single wrongful act inevitably affects the general interest of all States in seeing international law observed.[46] Were standing to be made dependent on these broad notions of interest, rules on standing would be as meaningless as under a subjective test.

In order to avoid the problems of subjectivity and over-breadth, it is therefore necessary to define *which* types of interests, and *which* forms of concern, are sufficient to establish standing. Of course, this is largely a question of interpretation and as such will be addressed in subsequent chapters. At a very general level, however, the required distinction is based on a clear and simple criterion. When it comes to deciding whether a State has standing or not, the international legal system (just as other legal orders[47]) draws a distinction between interests that are *legally protected*, and those that are not. A State seeking to establish standing therefore has to show that the breach against which it intends to react has affected its legally protected positions, usually referred to as 'rights' or 'legal interests' as opposed to mere interests.[48] This differentiation does not answer the question whether a specific interest is protected by the law. However, it clarifies the point of reference and

[44] Diss.Op. Skubiszewski, *East Timor case*, ICJ Reports 1995, 256 (para. 103).

[45] See e.g. Diss.Op. Koretsky, *South West Africa case*, ICJ Reports 1966, 242.

[46] Riphagen, Fourth Report, YbILC 1983, Vol. II/1, 21; Sinclair, YbILC 1983, Vol. I, 130 (para. 27); McCaffrey (1989), 243. See also Judge *ad hoc* Skubiszewski's dissent in *East Timor*, ICJ Reports 1995, 256 (para. 103), and Brigitte Boellecker-Stern's similar observations relating to the notion of moral damage (Boellecker-Stern (1973), 25).

[47] Expressing the point in terms of a distinction between (legally protected) rights and (not protected) interests, while conceding that terminology was not uniform, counsel for Spain in the *Barcelona Traction case* observed: 'La distinction du droit et de l'intérêt est une donnée probablement inéluctable de tout système juridique', ICJ Pleadings, Vol. IX, 520. See further de Hoogh (1996), 12.

[48] At the present stage, it is not necessary to differentiate between rights and legal interests. Whether a meaningful distinction can be drawn between the two is discussed below, section 1.2.3.

introduces a yardstick against which the permissibility of responses against international wrongs is to be assessed.

Given the considerable controversy surrounding questions of interpretation, it may be pointed out that this basic premise is undisputed. The ILC's long-standing efforts to determine which States are entitled to invoke the responsibility of other States, and to do so by way of countermeasure, are but attempts to differentiate legally protected positions from other, non-legal, interests. Explaining the need for this distinction, Willem Riphagen observed:

> Whether a particular State has an interest in the performance of its international obligations by another State is a matter of fact. In the long run every State has an interest in the observance of any rule of international law [. . .]. But this by no means authorizes . . . every State to demand the performance by every other State of its international obligations, let alone take countermeasures in case of non-performance of those obligations.[49]

The same distinction is brought out with particular clarity in the jurisprudence of the ICJ, more particularly the judgments in the *South West Africa* and *Barcelona Traction cases*. In fact, the measure of agreement can be gauged from the fact that while the decisions adopt widely diverging interpretations of what constitutes a legally protected position, they affirm the underlying issue of principle in nearly identical terms. In *South West Africa*, the Court had to address the defendant's contention that the applicants had no 'legal right or interest', and that the case should therefore be dismissed. At the preliminary objections stage, a narrow majority of the Court rejected this argument because it did not share the defendant's interpretation of the relevant legal rule, article 7(2) of the 1922 Mandate Agreement.[50] As for the matter of principle, however, it fully accepted that applicants, in order to have standing, needed to establish a 'legal right or interest' in the subject-matter of the dispute.[51] Four years later, at the second stage of the *South West Africa case*, the Court accepted the defendant's interpretation of article 7(2) and effectively reversed its earlier decision. As regards the question of principle, it reiterated the point in a passage that bears to be quoted at some length:

> Throughout this case, it has been suggested, directly or indirectly, that humanitarian considerations are sufficient in themselves to generate legal rights and

[49] Riphagen, Fourth Report, YbILC 1983, Vol. II/1, 21.
[50] ICJ Reports 1962, 342–344. On *South West Africa* see further below, section 2.1.2.
[51] ICJ Reports 1962, 343. The French translation of the phrase ('*un droit ou un intérêt juridique*') suggests that the attribute 'legal' is meant to qualify both rights and interests.

obligations, and that the Court can and should proceed accordingly. The Court does not think so. It is a court of law, and can take account of moral principles only in so far as they are given a sufficient expression in legal form. [. . .]

Humanitarian considerations may constitute the inspirational basis for rules of law, just as, for instance, the preambular parts of the United Nations Charter constitute the moral and political basis for the specific legal provisions thereafter set out. Such interests do not in themselves amount to rules of law. All States are interested - have an interest - in such matters. But the existence of an 'interest' does not of itself entail that this interest is specifically juridical in character. [. . .] In order to generate legal rights and obligations, it must be given juridical expression and be clothed in legal form.[52]

Finally, a further four years later, in *Barcelona Traction*, the Court addressed Belgium's claim that the State of nationality of the shareholders should be entitled to bring claims of diplomatic protection where shareholders had suffered financial losses. In terms remarkably similar to those used in the previous judgments, the Court dismissed this argument, which it considered to be

merely a different way of presenting the distinction between injury in respect of a right and injury to a simple interest . . . [A]s the Court has indicated, evidence that damage was suffered [by the shareholders] does not *ipso facto* justify a diplomatic claim. Persons suffer damage or harm in most varied circumstances. [. . .] Not a mere interest affected, but solely a right infringed involves responsibility.[53]

These as well as a variety of other[54] pronouncements show that the fault line between States having standing, and those failing to establish it, is drawn in legal terms. In order to be entitled to institute ICJ proceedings or to resort to countermeasures, it is not sufficient for a State to point to specific factual consequences of a breach, or to political or humanitarian concerns to which a breach has given rise. While of course legal rules can accommodate such political, humanitarian or economic concerns, States wishing to establish standing need to show that these concerns have been 'clothed in legal form'.[55] Standing therefore is first and foremost a normative concept.

[52] ICJ Reports 1966, 34 (paras. 49–51). See the similar observation in the 1962 dissent of Judges Spender and Fitzmaurice, ICJ Reports 1962, 466.

[53] ICJ Reports 1970, 36 (para. 46). Cf. also *ibid.*, 38 (para. 54) and 46 (paras. 86–87).

[54] See e.g. Judge *ad hoc* Skubiszewski's dissent in *East Timor*, ICJ Reports 1995, 255 (para. 101) (drawing a distinction between States concerned in the outcome of proceedings, and States having standing to institute them); *Nuclear Tests cases*, Joint Diss.Op., ICJ Reports 1974, 369–370; *Barcelona Traction case*, Sep.Op. Ammoun, ICJ Reports 1970, 325–326; *Lac Lanoux case*, RIAA, Vol. XII, 314–317.

[55] ICJ Reports 1966, 34 (para. 51).

1.2.2 *Standing as a flexible concept*

So far, there has been deliberately no attempt to analyse the types of legally protected positions whose infringement is considered to give rise to standing. As the above-quoted pronouncements show, two different categories are usually held to be relevant: rights and legal interests. The question is whether these terms have a fixed meaning, which would predetermine in which situations States have standing to take countermeasures or institute ICJ proceedings. It is submitted that neither of them has. Of course, specific types of interests will be most likely to qualify as a right or legal interest. However, in principle, virtually every interest *can* be legally protected. The scope of potential rights and legal interests is unlimited; which interests qualify, and which not, depends on an interpretation of the law. The normative criterion of standing therefore is flexible and depends on the evolution of the law.

As regards the notion of legal interests, this proposition seems to be generally accepted. It is indeed rather straightforward. The distinction between legal and other, non-legal, interests requires an analysis of the legal rules applicable at the relevant time. All that distinguishes the two categories of interests is that one is 'clothed in legal form',[56] whereas the other is not. Nothing suggests that only specific types of interests could be elevated to the higher level of legal interests. Which have, and which not, cannot be decided *a priori*, but requires an analysis of the law. The circle of potential legal interests thus is not predetermined.

The situation is more controversial as regards the notion of rights, especially if these are further qualified and referred to as 'subjective rights'.[57] Many commentators seem to think that making standing dependent on the infringement of a (subjective) right implies a restrictive approach to standing pursuant to which States can only respond to breaches that affect their individual legal positions. The ILC's debates during the second reading of the draft articles on State responsibility provide a telling example. When discussing provisions governing the invocation of responsibility, the Commission had to revise draft article 40 of the first text adopted in 1996, which defined injury as an 'infringement of a right'.[58] During the second reading, the reference to rights

[56] *Ibid.*

[57] See e.g. *South West Africa*, Diss.Op. Winiarski, ICJ Reports 1962, 449, at 455–456; Ago, Second Report, YbILC 1970, Vol. II, 192 (para. 46); *id.*, Sixth Report, YbILC 1977, Vol. II/1, 22 (para. 52), *id.*, Eighth Report, YbILC 1980, Vol. II/1, 18 (para. 9).

[58] See draft article 40, para 1 [1996].

was heavily criticised. According to James Crawford, it implied 'that all responsibility relations could be assimilated to classical bilateral right-duty relations (an assumption contradicted by the International Court in the *Barcelona Traction* case)'.[59]

Roberto Ago's famous comment about the 'correlation between a legal obligation ... and a subjective right'[60] fared little better. In view of Bruno Simma, the statement embodied 'a rigidly traditionalist view - according to which the law exhausts itself in correlative rights and obligations of its subjects'.[61]

Both criticisms however are unjustified. Before exploring the issue, it is necessary to make a preliminary point about the frequent references to subjective rights. Some of the discussion about the notions seems to be based on the assumption that the circle of subjective rights were narrower than that of other rights. This assumption is unfounded and the qualification of specific rights as 'subjective' is of little help. In fact, whether subjective rights can be meaningfully distinguished from other types of rights, may be open to doubt.[62] In English language works addressing questions of standing, 'subjective right' appears to be used as a direct translation from other languages, in which the notion of '*droit subjectif*' or '*subjektives Recht*' is indeed very common. These languages use the same expression (*droit*, *Recht*, etc.) in order to describe (i) the sum-total of legal rules (i.e. 'law'), and (ii) a claim that enjoys legal protection ('right'). The qualifications 'subjective' and 'objective' thus are necessary in order to distinguish two different meanings of the same expression.[63] In contrast, where (as in the English language) the two different meanings mentioned above are expressed by entirely different words, such as 'law' and 'right', the attributes seem superfluous.[64] The

[59] See Crawford (2002a), 24 and 25. See further *id.*, Third Report, paras. 83–85.

[60] Ago, Second Report, YbILC 1970, Vol. II, 192 (para. 46). During the first reading, the Commission had agreed; cf. commentary to draft article 3, YbILC 1973, Vol. II, 182 (para. 9).

[61] Simma (1994a), 232 and 231.

[62] For a different criticism, based on the vagueness of the term 'subjective', see Crawford (2000), 34–35.

[63] See e.g. (for Germany) Maurer (2002), § 8, MN 3–4; *Creifelds Rechtswörterbuch* (2002) (entry 'Recht', section I.); for France: *Dictionnaire économique et juridique Navarre* (1992) ('droit', alinea 1° and 2°); for Spain: *Diccionario de términos jurídicos* (2000) ('derecho', alinea (a) and (b)).

[64] Of course, it remains entirely possible that the distinction between objective and subjective rights could acquire other meanings in the English language. Within international legal discourse, Judge Ranjeva's separate opinion in *East Timor* (which will be discussed below, section 5.2.5.) provides another example. All that is claimed here is

present study will therefore not use the misleading expression 'subjective rights'.[65]

As regards the distinction between rights and legal interests, very little suggests that the scope of the former term is as limited as Crawford and Simma assert. Both suggest that legal positions labelled 'rights' were, by necessity, allocated to one subject, and enabled it to enforce a duty against one other subject - exchanges of benefits under bilateral treaties (e.g. State A's duty to pay for goods from State B) might be thought of as archetypal examples. This, however, is a rather narrow approach to the notion of 'right'. To be sure, legal systems will usually accept that legal positions allocated to one subject in its individual capacity qualify as rights.[66] However, this by no means implies that other legal positions could not qualify. In fact, the very definition of rights as 'legally protected interests'[67] - which has dominated much of the continental legal debate about rights - casts doubt on whether rights and legal interests can be neatly distinguished. A brief glance at national legal systems, which have adopted very different approaches, confirms this view. While a detailed comparative assessment is beyond the scope of the present study, the point may be illustrated by contrasting English and German law. English law has indeed traditionally favoured a narrow concept of rights, usually restricted to bilateral disputes involving one person's claim and another person's duty.[68] This did not prevent English courts from progressively recognising claims by individuals acting outside such bilateral contexts. However, these claims were admitted on the basis of a more flexible test, codified in the English 1981 Supreme Court Act, under which standing required the showing of a 'sufficient [legal] interest'.[69] Accordingly, the narrow understanding of the notion of 'right' could remain unchanged. German courts, when faced with claims outside 'classical bilateral right-duty relations' (to use Crawford's terminology),[70] had to

that the attribute is superfluous (in the English language) when distinguishing *droit subjectif* from *droit objectif*.

[65] See further de Hoogh (1996), 19–20; Ago, Eighth Report, YbILC 1980, Vol. II/1, 18 (para. 9).

[66] See below, section 1.3, for a brief assessment from the perspective of international law.

[67] Jhering (1877), 328. Cf. *Barcelona Traction case*, Sep.Op. Ammoun, ICJ Reports 1970, at 325 (para. 33), and, for an analysis of the various 'interest theories', Bauer (1986).

[68] See e.g. Crawford (2000), 23–24. For a thorough review of common law approaches to questions of standing see Bradley (1969), 327; König (1979).

[69] Section 31(3) of the 1981 Supreme Court Act provides in the relevant part: '[T]he Court shall not grant leave to make ... an application unless it considers that the applicant has a *sufficient interest* in the matter to which the application relates' (emphasis added).

[70] See above, footnote 59.

follow a different approach, since the relevant provisions of German constitutional and administrative law make standing dependent on the potential violation of a right ('*subjektiv-öffentliches Recht*').[71] When German courts began to admit claims by individuals outside bilateral contexts (such as claims aimed at the quashing of administrative acts granting construction permits for nuclear power plants[72] or claims by companies against State subsidies hindering economic freedoms[73]), they therefore had to expand the initially narrow concept of 'right'. While German public law still aims at protecting individual legal positions, it has long recognised that great numbers of individuals can hold parallel or identical rights to see a particular obligation observed.[74] For present purposes, this is important insofar as it shows the flexibility of the notion of 'right', which at least under German public law has come to comprise legally protected interests outside bilateral contexts.

Coming back to the international level, the very language of article 40 shows that the ILC, during the first reading of its work, also leaned towards this second, broader approach - hence the express confirmation that in a variety of non-bilateral disputes, one State's duty corresponded to rights of more than one State.[75] While one might hold differing views on whether this choice of terminology is particularly well suited or preferable to the language of legal interests, it is surely one possible way of addressing the matter.

The above considerations suggest that the scope of potential rights is not as limited as critics suggest. The term can be, and has been, used in different ways. Just as in the case of legal interests, what qualifies as a right cannot be determined *a priori*. Courts or commentators making standing dependent on the infringement of a right (or even a subjective

[71] Cf. paragraph 42(2) of the *Verwaltungsgerichtsordnung* (Code of Administrative Courts) and article 19, para. 4 of the German Basic Law, both requiring claimants seeking the quashing of administrative or executive acts to establish that the act in question affects a right ('*subjektiv-öffentliches Recht*'). On the rationale of judicial review of administrative action under German law see Wahl in Schoch/Schmidt-Aßmann/Pietzner (2003), introductory commentary to paragraph 42(2) VwGO, MN 11-16; Günther (1999), 30-32; and cf. Skouris (1979), and Bleckmann (1971), 19, for a comparative assessment.

[72] See e.g. BVerwGE 61, 256. [73] BVerwGE 30, 191; BVerwGE 65, 167.

[74] Cf. Kopp/Schenke (2003), para. 42 VwGO, MN 78; Wahl in Schoch/Schmidt-Aßmann/Pietzner (2003), introductory commentary to para. 42(2) VwGO, MN 95-96; Bauer (1986), 138-139. Needless to say that the notion of a *subjektiv-öffentliches Recht* has occupied German public lawyers for decades; for influential attempts to assess it see Bühler (1914); Henke (1968); Bauer (1986).

[75] Commentary to draft article 40, YbILC 1985, Vol. II/2, 26-27 (paras. 17-26); and already YbILC 1976, Vol. II/2, 76.

right) thus should not be held to adopt a narrow approach to the question. Whether a specific legal position qualifies as a right is a matter of interpretation, and of interpretation only.

1.2.3 *The diversity of rules governing standing*

Finally, it needs to be assessed which types of legal rules have a bearing on the question of standing. It has already been stated at the outset that many works hardly address this question, or simply distinguish direct State claims from claims espoused by way of diplomatic protection.[76] By so doing, they seem to suggest that the question was governed by a handful of immutable rules. This, however, would be quite misleading: the legal rules addressing questions of standing are of a considerable diversity. Two factors are chiefly responsible for this.

First, rules of standing can be of different levels of generality. There is of course a set of residual rules; from these, States can derogate by entering into special agreements. Crucially, the two sets of (special and residual) rules do not exist in isolation, but are interrelated. The residual regime forms part of the legal context in which treaties – unless they deliberately deviate – have to be interpreted.[77] Conversely, certain types of treaty regulation may mature into general rules and become part of the residual regime.[78] Furthermore, as the ILC's attempts to spell out the existing law demonstrate, the residual rules themselves are rather diverse. In the first reading draft articles, the relevant provision on standing, draft article 40 [1996], comprised a total of 376 words.[79] While the relevant second reading provisions, articles 42 and 48 ASR, are shorter, they equally take up a variety of distinctions between different categories of norms and provide special rules for special circumstances. There is thus not one single residual rule. Conversely, special rules may be rather general in character. As will be shown below, there are suggestions that certain classes of treaties or certain categories of obligations (whether conventional or customary) should

[76] See above, references in footnotes 40–41.

[77] See article 31, para. 3c VCLT and most recently Judge Simma's separate opinion in the *Oil Platforms case* (para. 9).

[78] See e.g. *North Sea Continental Shelf case*, ICJ Reports 1969, 41 (para. 71), for the proposition that treaties can provide evidence of customary international law.

[79] This was severely criticised during the second reading, see e.g. Crawford, Third Report, para. 96.

be subject to special rules of standing.[80] The respective rules would accordingly apply in a wide variety of cases; whether they could still properly be called 'special' or would already be part of the diversified residual regime, may be a question of perspective.

Secondly, legal rules can address questions of standing directly or indirectly. 'Direct rules' shall denote provisions that specifically address the right of States to invoke responsibility in a specific way, namely by way of either countermeasure or ICJ proceedings. Such rules will usually be conventional in character. Treaties directly authorising resort to countermeasures are rare, but article 35 of the Universal Postal Convention, which recognises the right of *all* parties to ignore their treaty obligations in respect of a State that breaches its obligation to respect the freedom of transit, provides an example in point.[81] As regards judicial claims, the much more common direct rules are often part of a jurisdictional clause establishing the competence of a particular court. Article 7 of 1922 Mandate Agreement, which was at issue in the *South West Africa cases*, is an example in point; it established the Court's jurisdiction over 'any dispute whatever [that] should arise between the Mandatory and another Member of the League of Nations relating to the interpretation or the application of the provisions of the Mandate'.

In the presence of such a direct regulation, it is clear that judicial claims or countermeasures are a permissible means of responding against a prior breach. All that is left to decide is whether the State wishing to respond actually fulfilled the criteria laid down in the applicable legal rule.[82]

Very often, however, no provision directly addresses means of law enforcement. In this case, standing to take countermeasures or to institute ICJ proceedings may be a consequence of the rules governing the invocation of responsibility more generally. As has been stated above, countermeasures and legal claims are specific means of invoking the responsibility of other States. It follows that rules governing the

[80] See especially section 2.2, for examples. The category of obligations *erga omnes* would be another example, should it be subject to a special regime of standing.

[81] 364 UNTS 3. For further examples see below, section 2.2.1.a. Whether article 35 codifies a specific form of countermeasure may be questioned; it might as well be interpreted as a special rule allowing for the suspension of treaties in the sense of article 60 VCLT. The qualification depends on whether one is prepared to accept that by withholding treaty benefits under the Postal Convention, States seek to enforce the law.

[82] This of course may involve detailed discussion, as will be exemplified below (section 2.1.2) with respect to the *South West Africa cases*.

invocation of responsibility (but failing to specify the permissible means of enforcement) may imply a right to do so by way of countermeasure or ICJ claim. These 'indirect rules' in turn may be customary or conventional. In its work on State responsibility, more particularly article 42 and 48 ASR, the ILC has attempted to spell out the former. In contrast, common article 1 of the 1949 Geneva Conventions or article 94 LOSC are examples of treaty-based indirect rules. Under article 94 LOSC, a specific State (the flag State) is authorised to exercise jurisdiction over ships, which is widely interpreted as a recognition of that State's right to react against infringements of rights enjoyed by ships.[83] Under common article 1 of the 1949 Geneva Conventions, all States shall 'ensure respect' with the Geneva rules, which is generally held to establish a right of all treaty members, irrespective of their involvement in a particular armed conflict, to observe other States' compliance with the Convention rules.[84] Both provisions therefore indicate which States have standing to respond to breaches of the law. Neither of them, however, specifies what forms this response may take.[85] Whether States are entitled to resort to countermeasures or institute ICJ proceedings depends on the relation between the different rules of standing. This again is largely a matter of interpretation; however, two preliminary points can be made.

For once, in theory, direct and indirect rules need to be distinguished. It cannot simply be taken for granted that States entitled to invoke another State's responsibility should always be entitled to do so by way of ICJ claim or countermeasure. In fact, it has already been stated in the Introduction that at least for the case of military measures, it is widely accepted that law enforcement by means of force is subject to more stringent conditions than the general right to invoke another

[83] Geck (1992), 1055; Churchill and Lowe (1999), 257; and the judgment of the ITLOS in the *M.V. Saiga (No. 2) case*, 38 ILM (1999), 1323. Whether or not this means that other States are completely precluded from exercising diplomatic protection (e.g. in response to violations of rights of their nationals sailing on board the ship) is a matter of controversy; see - apart from the *Saiga* judgment - Geck (1992), 1055; von Münch (1979), 231; Watts (1957), 52; and cf. further below, section 2.2.1.b, for an analysis of the PCIJ's approach in the *Wimbledon case*.

[84] See e.g. para. 9 of the 1968 Teheran Resolution on Human Rights in Armed Conflict, UN Doc. A/CONF.32/41, 18; Pictet (1952), Article 1, 27; Gasser (1993), 25; Condorelli/Boisson de Chazournes (1984), 24. For a thorough discussion see Kessler (2001), 68–72.

[85] Especially with respect to common article 1, the matter is much discussed: see Condorelli/Boisson de Chazournes (1984), 17; Gasser (1993), 15; Schindler (1995), 199; Kessler (2001).

State's responsibility. The Articles on State Responsibility equally accept that while a rather large number of States may be entitled to invoke the responsibility of other States, not all of them are entitled to do so by way of countermeasure – hence the distinction between a narrowly defined circle of 'injured States' (as defined in article 42 ASR) and a broader circle of 'other States entitled to invoke responsibility' (in the sense of article 48 ASR).[86] Whether this differentiation is justified will be analysed subsequently.[87] For present purposes, it is sufficient to note that indirect rules on standing, following the ILC, do not necessarily imply a right to take countermeasures.

A similar question arises with respect to ICJ claims. Nothing would stop the ICJ from making standing dependent on more stringent conditions than the general right to invoke responsibility: the availability of judicial relief first and foremost depends on the statutory provisions addressing questions of standing or the jurisprudence of the respective judicial body.[88] Even the preliminary discussion undertaken so far, however, suggests that, while formally distinct, standing to invoke responsibility and standing to institute ICJ proceedings are closely linked. As the above-quoted passages show, the Court seemed to accept that standing to institute proceedings would follow the general rules of responsibility. Hence damage suffered by shareholders in *Barcelona Traction* did not justify a '*diplomatic* claim' nor involved 'responsibility'.[89] Equally, in *South West Africa*, the Court's interpretation of the applicable jurisdictional clause (notably its statement that the applicants had an interest, but no 'legal right', and its decision to deny standing for lack of a 'legal interest') was phrased in general terms rather than specifically addressing standing in judicial proceedings.[90] Its eventual decision to dismiss the applicants' judicial claim therefore effectively amounted to saying that they had no right to invoke the defendant's responsibility. Conversely, the relevant ICJ decisions on questions of standing to institute proceedings have been widely recognised as having shaped the general rules of standing to invoke responsibility.[91] While theoretically

[86] Contrast articles 49 and 54 ASR for the implications of this distinction; and see para. 8 of the introductory commentary to Part Three, Chapter II ASR.

[87] See below, Chapter 6. [88] See already above, Introduction (footnote 54).

[89] ICJ Reports 1970, 36 (para. 46) (emphasis added).

[90] See ICJ Reports 1966, 34 (para. 51).

[91] See the frequent references to the *South West Africa* and *Barcelona Traction* judgments in the ILC's work on State responsibility: introductory commentary to Part Three, Chapter I, para. 2; commentary to article 48, paras. 2, 7–9, 11.

distinct, the two rules therefore have evolved along parallel lines. This in turn would seem to suggest that a State that can establish a general right to invoke another State's responsibility should be presumed to have standing to do so by way of ICJ proceedings.[92]

1.2.4 Interim conclusions

To sum up, the legal rules governing standing are considerably more complex than is often assumed. In principle, standing applies to both enforcement measures relevant to the present study; States seeking to respond to breaches of the law by way of countermeasure and ICJ proceedings must establish a sufficient link between themselves and the legal rule whose infringement they allege. They will succeed in doing so where they have a right or legal interest in the observance of the relevant rule. Whether this is so cannot be determined *a priori*, but depends on an interpretation of the law. This interpretation involves rules of different generality as well as direct and indirect rules. It is, moreover, complicated by the fact that standing to take countermeasures may well be subject to different, more stringent, conditions than standing to institute ICJ proceedings. In the light of these considerations, it is now possible to assess how rules of standing have been applied in practice.

1.3 Standing to enforce individual legal positions

It has been stated in the Introduction that the concept of obligations *erga omnes* protects general interests of the international community. Accordingly, subsequent chapters analyse whether (or under which circumstances) States have standing to defend general interests under international law. The present section addresses a preliminary issue. It first introduces the basic distinction between individual and general interests, on which the subsequent discussion hinges. In a second step, it briefly shows that where States seek to protect their individual interests, the question of standing presents few problems and can be dealt with summarily. Having addressed it at this preliminary stage, subsequent chapters will concentrate on the more controversial issues raised by the *erga omnes* concept.

[92] See also para. 2 of the ILC's commentary to article 42 ASR, noting that the invocation of responsibility (addressed by the ILC) would include 'an application before a competent international tribunal'.

1.3.1 *The basis of the distinction*

It has been said already that the rules of standing distinguish interests protected by the law from other ('mere') interests.[93] Whether a specific interest is legally protected largely depends on whether it is individual or general in character. Unlike the distinction between legally protected, and other, interests, this distinction first and foremost depends on a factual assessment of the situation. Although not always easy to apply, it is based on a very simple criterion. In line with the ordinary meaning of the term, interests qualify as 'individual interests' if they concern one actor in its personal capacity. In contrast, interests will be referred to as 'general interests' if they are shared by a majority of actors. Applied to the present context of law enforcement by States, the crucial distinction therefore needs to be drawn between breaches of international law that affect one State in its individual capacity and those that affect it as a member of a group.

While individual interests are necessarily allocated to one State, general interests may be shared by groups of different sizes. A small number of riparian States may have a general interest in the use of a particular watercourse. All State parties to a multilateral treaty may be interested in seeing the treaty rules complied with. Finally, all States (as members of the international community of States) may have a general interest in seeing some, or even all, rules of customary international law performed. Whether the respective general interests are legally protected and can be vindicated by way of countermeasure or judicial proceedings must be decided in each individual case; as will be shown below, it may depend on factors as diverse as the structure or source of the obligation breached, the gravity of the infringement, or the number of State parties sharing a general interest.

By comparison, the identification of individual legal interests presents fewer problems. Of course, the mere fact that a State has been individually affected by a specific breach of international law does not mean that it necessarily has standing to respond against it. Just as general interests, individual interests need to be *legally protected* in order to give rise to standing. In the *Barcelona Traction case*, to take but one example, Belgium was certainly individually affected by Spain's treatment of the Barcelona Traction company – after all, it was the State of nationality of the majority of shareholders who had to bear the brunt of the financial losses. In the

[93] See above, section 1.2.1

view of the Court, this particular individual interest, however, was not legally protected; in the absence of any treaty rule to the contrary, there was no room for diplomatic claims on behalf of shareholders.[94] Difficulties need nevertheless not be overstated. In fact, in most cases, the identification of individually injured States presents very few problems. To illustrate the point, the subsequent subsection will give a short overview of the main categories of individual legal interests recognised in international law.

1.3.2 *Categories of individual legal positions*

Although the need to distinguish between legal and other interests arises with respect to both individual and general interests, it does not usually present major problems in the former case. Two main categories of individual legal interests can be distinguished. First, States have standing to respond against breaches of bilateral rules that have been established in their favour. And secondly, even if the rule in question applies between more than two States, States are entitled to respond if the obligation breached was owed to them. Both categories present few problems, as can be seen be seen, *inter alia*, from the ILC's work on State responsibility, during which the relevant provisions, articles 42 (a) and 42 (b)(i) ASR (unlike the other rules on standing), proved uncontroversial.

1.3.2.a Bilateral legal rules and similar situations

If a wrongful act affects bilateral rules that apply between two States only, the situation is straightforward. In this case, the question of standing can be answered even without assessing the effects of the breach. If one State violates a bilateral obligation, the other State has standing to respond against the breach, simply because it is the exclusive beneficiary. Five types of such bilateral legal rules can be distinguished.

The obvious example in point is that of legal relations arising under bilateral treaties. Where one State party disregards its obligations, it is undisputed that the other has standing to respond to breaches.[95] Two other, less common, situations are analogous. One is the case of bilateral custom.[96] A State establishing the existence

[94] See above, Introduction.

[95] See commentary to article 42, para. 7. Breaches of bilateral treaties are one of the most common grounds prompting the other treaty party to resort to countermeasures or ICJ proceedings. These disputes have not given rise to problems of standing.

[96] Cf. *Rights of Passage case*, ICJ Reports 1960, 39; Degan (1997), 243–246; Akehurst (1974–1975), 28–31. As Soerensen (1960), 43, has observed, the distinction between bilateral custom and a (tacit) bilateral agreement is often artificial.

of a rule of bilateral custom, applying only in relation to itself and another State, is entitled to respond to a breach of that rule.[97] Unilateral undertakings (promises), assumed by one State in relation to another State, provide the second analogy.[98] If one accepts that one State, by virtue of a unilateral act, can assume binding obligations, it can do so not only in relation to all States (as France was said to have done in the *Nuclear Tests cases*),[99] but also *vis-à-vis* a specifically defined other State (such as Denmark in the case of the *Ihlen declaration*).[100] In this situation, the other State as the exclusive beneficiary of the legal rule is entitled to respond to breaches of the promise.[101]

Outside the case of bilateral treaties and analogies, two further situations can be envisaged. The first is that of a binding inter-State judgment or award in favour of one State.[102] Under normal circumstances, this judgment will only be binding *inter partes*, i.e. between the two parties to the arbitration or adjudication.[103] Unless the specific dispute settlement mechanism provides for an institutional form of execution,[104] it has been accepted that the State favoured by the judgment

[97] Hence, India, in the *Rights of Passage case*, despite raising a variety of objections, did not dispute Portugal's right to invoke responsibility allegedly entailed by India's violation of a customary right of passage between Daman and the Portuguese enclaves; see ICJ Reports 1960, 39–43.

[98] Commentary to article 42 ASR, para. 6; de Hoogh (1996), 37. On unilateral undertakings see Brownlie (2003), 612–615; Degan (1997), 287–306.

[99] Cf. ICJ Reports 1974, 270 (para. 51), and 474 (para. 53), where the Court found that 'the French government [had] conveyed *to the world at large*, including the Applicant, its intention to effectively terminate these [atmospheric] tests' (emphasis added). The pronouncement is further discussed below, section 3.3.3.

[100] *Eastern Greenland case*, PCIJ, Ser. A/B, No. 53, (1933), 69–73.

[101] No issue of standing therefore arose when Denmark as the exclusive beneficiary of the obligation, invoked the *Ihlen declaration* before the Court.

[102] Commentary to article 42 ASR, para. 7. Whether international decisions really are a case of exclusive injury is however a matter of debate; cf. below section 2.2.2.c.

[103] In the case of *ad hoc* arbitration, this will follow from the bilateral character of the *compromis*. In the case of institutionalised arbitration or adjudication, it is usually regulated in the treaty establishing the judicial or arbitral body, see article 59 of the ICJ Statute or article 296, para. 2 LOSC.

[104] Such provisions are not infrequent. Article 94 UNC, which recognises the Security Council's special role, is the most prominent example. For further examples see article 33 of the ILO Constitution, articles 84–88 of the ICAO Convention, article 39 of the European Convention for the Pacific Settlement of Disputes, or article 50 of the Pact of Bogota, (whose application led to the ICJ proceedings in the *Arbitral Award case* between Nicaragua and Honduras, see ICJ Reports 1960, 192). In the presence of such special clauses, it must be determined whether institutional enforcement is meant to be exclusive. At least in respect of article 94, this question must be answered in the

can take coercive action in order to secure compliance, as has happened, for example, in the *Socobel case* or in the aftermath of the *Corfu Channel case.*[105] The final case is that of a *stipulation pour autrui.*[106] While transcending the formally bilateral context, it is widely accepted that such treaties are subject to similar rules. In particular, the third State in whose favour the right has been created will be treated as an exclusive beneficiary, and consequently has standing to respond against breaches.[107]

1.3.2.b Special injury

In most cases, internationally wrongful acts affect rules that apply between more than two States, and that do not benefit one State only. Multilateral treaties are the most evident example; by definition, they apply between more than two States. To these, obligations of customary international law have to be added; with the exception of bilateral custom, they are equally binding on more than two States.[108] In these cases, there is no exclusive beneficiary of the rule; all States bound by it have some general interest in seeing it observed (which, of course, is not necessarily legally protected). The distinction between States having standing and States not having standing therefore cannot be drawn by simply analysing who is a party benefiting from the rule. Identifying

negative; individual enforcement action thus remains possible (Oellers-Frahm (1976), 667–669; Guillaume (1997), 444–445).

105 In *Socobel*, the Belgian government instituted proceedings before the PCIJ against Greece, which had allegedly violated its international obligation to comply with an arbitral award rendered in favour of the Société commerciale de Belgique, see PCIJ, Ser. A/B, No. 78 (1939), 160; and for the subsequent proceedings before the civil tribunal of Brussels see *Socobel v. Greek State*, 18 ILR 3.

In the aftermath of the *Corfu Channel case*, the United Kingdom took a variety of steps to satisfy the ICJ's award of damages; these eventually led to the arbitral and judicial proceedings in the *Monetary Gold* dispute: see RIAA, Vol. XII, 13 (for the arbitral award), ICJ Reports 1954, 19 (for the ICJ proceedings), and further below, section 2.2.2.c. In addition to these cases, States have often exercised diplomatic or economic pressure to enforce judgments or awards; the United Kingdom's decision to make the conclusion of a bilateral commercial agreement dependent on the prior execution of the *Lena Goldfield award* (36 Cornell Law Quarterly (1950–1951), 42) is a prominent example in point; see Guillaume (1997), 444; Oellers-Frahm (1976), 657.

106 Cf. article 36 VCLT and the PCIJ's judgment on *Free Zones of Upper Savoy and the District of Gex*, PCIJ, Ser. A/B, No. 46 (1932), 147–148. Treaties creating proper rights of third parties have to be distinguished from those creating obligations, which, by way of a reflex, might benefit third States without however granting them actual rights; see Verdross/Simma (1984), 483.

107 See para. 7 of the ILC's commentary to article 42 ASR; and further draft article 40, para. 2(d) of the 1996 text.

108 Crawford (Hague Lectures), 4.

individually injured States nevertheless remains unproblematic if the breach has specially affected one State in a legal position. Of course, whether special effects are legally relevant again depends on an analysis of the law. In two situations, however, this is universally accepted.

Multilateral obligations that are required to be performed in relation to one particular State are the first, and most important, case in point.[109] Although the *legal rules* apply between a plurality of States, the *obligations* arising under them are owed to one State in particular. In the case of a breach, that State therefore is specially affected and entitled to respond. A brief reference to obligations in the field of diplomatic or consular relations may illustrate the point. Despite their multilateral (customary or conventional) character, these obligations have to be performed between pairs of receiving and sending States.[110] A receiving State's duty to respect diplomatic immunities under article 39 of the Vienna Convention on Diplomatic Relations, although deriving from a multilateral rule, therefore, always arises in relation to one specific (sending) State. As a consequence, in the case of a breach, that (sending) State is specially affected and entitled to respond.

Obligations in the field of diplomatic or consular law are not the only multilateral obligations that are required to be performed in a bilateral context. Obligations arising under rules regulating the use of economic or military pressure (including those outlawing the use of force), obligations concerning questions of extradition or rights of transit or passage are further examples in point.[111] Since all of these rules are required to be performed between pairs of States, they are frequently referred to as 'bilateralisable' obligations, or 'bundles of bilateral relationships'.[112]

[109] On the following see Simma (1972), 152–155; Feist (2001), 49–52 and 123–124; Sicilianos (1990), 107–110; and further below, section 1.2.1.a.

[110] See the respective articles 2 of the Vienna Diplomatic and Consular Conventions. The relevant provisions setting out, for example, the diplomatic provisions therefore usually make express reference to sending and receiving States. In international jurisprudence, cases involving alleged breaches of diplomatic and/or consular law have not given rise to problems of standing (see e.g. the proceedings in the *Hostages*, and *Breard cases*; ICJ Reports 1980, 3 and 1998, 244 respectively).

[111] See Sachariew (1986), 63–67 with further references. The proceedings in the *Barcelona Traction case* suggest that identifying the State to whom performance is due may involve complex questions of interpretation, especially in cases of diplomatic protection. As that case shows with particular clarity, in order to have standing, a State has to be specially affected *in a legally protected position.*

[112] See e.g. Sicilianos (1990), 107; Simma (1994a), 364; Sachariew (1988), 277; Annacker (1994a), 30; ILC, commentary to article 42, para. 8.

In addition, a State may also be specially affected if the breach of a multilateral obligation at the same time affects its personal or territorial sovereignty. As will be discussed more fully below,[113] not all multilateral obligations apply between pairs of States only. Even where this is not the case, breaches can, however, have special effects on particular States. As the brief reference to Belgium's position in the *Barcelona Traction case* has shown, not all special effects are legally relevant. However, where the breach affects sovereign rights of one particular State, it is generally accepted that they are, and that the specially affected State has standing to respond against the breach. The point may be illustrated with reference to the *Nuclear Tests cases*, in which the two applicants sought from the Court a declaration that France was prohibited from conducting atmospheric nuclear tests.[114] In view of the applicants, a customary rule to this effect had come into existence. France's obligation under this alleged rule was not owed to one State in particular; it had to be performed *vis-à-vis* all States. To establish standing, both applicants, *inter alia*, argued that their territory would be contaminated by radioactive fallout, and that they would therefore be specially affected by France's conduct.[115] While the Court did not address the issue, having declared the dispute moot, the separate and dissenting opinions confirm that New Zealand and Australia, as specially affected States, would have had standing to bring the case.[116] More generally, the case illustrates that where breaches of multilateral obligations affect sovereign rights of particular States, those State are entitled to respond.[117]

1.4 Concluding observations

The present chapter has sought to clarify a number of basic issues underlying the specific questions to be addressed in the course of the subsequent analysis. Apart from outlining the legal regime governing

[113] See below, section 2.1.1. [114] ICJ Reports 1974, 253 and 457 respectively.

[115] See especially ICJ Pleadings, *Nuclear Tests*, Vol. I; Vol. II, 82. In addition, the applicants also relied on the *erga omnes* concept; cf. on this point below, section 5.2.5.a.

[116] See e.g. joint Diss.Op. Onyeama, Dillard, Jimenez de Arechaga, Waldock, ICJ Reports 1974, 369 (para. 117); Sep.Op. Petrén, *ibid.*, 303–304; Diss.Op. Barwick, *ibid.*, 427–428. The same is implicit in Judge de Castro's dissent, see *ibid.*, 38–90. For the Court's findings on mootness see ICJ Reports 1974, 269–270 (paras. 50–52) and 474–475 (paras. 52–55) respectively.

[117] See further Sachariew (1986), 109–116; Picone (1983), 78; and para. 12 of the ILC's commentary on article 42 ASR.

countermeasures and ICJ proceedings, it has shown that both enforcement measures can only be taken by States that have established an entitlement to do so. The notion of standing, used to describe this requirement, is normative and flexible and the subject of very diverse legal rules. Standing presents few problems where States seek to respond against internationally wrongful acts affecting their individual legal positions. In contrast, it is highly controversial whether States have standing to defend general interests, i.e. interests shared by groups of States. This question is addressed in the next chapters, first in historical perspective, later with specific regard to the *erga omnes* concept.

2 Traditional approaches to standing

In order to evaluate how the *erga omnes* concept has affected the international rules of standing, it is necessary to assess the *status quo ante*. The present chapter analyses whether international law prior to the Court's *Barcelona Traction* judgment recognised the right of States to respond to wrongful acts that did not affect them in their individual legal positions. Quite frequently, this is flatly denied. Following a popular analysis, traditional international law consisted of bilateral or bilateralisable legal rules, which gave rise to reciprocal rights and duties between pairs of States. Riphagen for example described traditional international law as 'bilateral-minded', while Verdross (in more guarded terms) spoke of the 'essentially relative character of international obligations'.[1] These characterisations were based on two propositions. First, States individually injured by breaches of international law have standing to respond. Secondly, their right to respond is exclusive. The first of these propositions has been addressed already; it is uncontroversial and remains true today. In contrast, it is highly contentious whether, prior to the emergence of the *erga omnes* concept, standing was limited to the defence of individual legal positions. This will be discussed in the present chapter.

A brief look into the classic treatises of international law shows that debates about standing in the general interest have a long history.[2] Grotius' claim that kings 'have the right to demand punishment not only on account of injuries committed against themselves or their subjects, but also on account of injuries which do not directly affect

[1] See Verdross (1964), 126; Riphagen, Third Report, YbILC 1982, Vol. II/1, 38 (para. 97).
[2] See Meron (1998), 122–130; Frowein (1994), 406–408; Alland (1994), 359–360; Nolte (2002), 1084–1086.

them but excessively violate the law of nature or of nations in regard to any persons whatsoever'[3] is only the best known but by no means the only early pronouncement on the issue. In eighteenth-century literature, Bynkershoek and Vattel disagreed on whether England had been entitled, in 1662, to take reprisals against the Netherlands in order to vindicate rights of the Sovereign Order of Malta – one stressing the need to sanction wrongful conduct, the other cautioning against anarchy.[4] One century later, Bluntschli and Heffter produced lists of breaches of international law against which each and every State should have standing to react,[5] while Phillimore and von Bulmerincq warned against intervention in the name of a greater good.[6]

The present section does not attempt to recapitulate these debates. Instead, it focuses on issues of standing that had received support in practice or jurisprudence and that were discussed at the time of the Court's *Barcelona Traction* judgment. This restrictive focus seems necessary because, contrary to a popular perception, standing to protect general interests was much discussed in the years preceding the emergence of the *erga omnes* concept. The growing recognition, in the course of the twentieth century, of multilateral obligations transcending the bilateral relations between pairs of States put pressure on the allegedly 'bilateral-minded' system – a problem touched upon already in relation to the *Nuclear Tests cases*.[7] Given the special consequences of France's alleged breaches of international law, Australia and New Zealand in that case could claim to be specially affected in their individual legal positions. However, what if the radioactive fallout had not reached one particular State's territory, but polluted the high seas, i.e. an area of the world not allocated to one State in particular? The least that can be said is that a regime premised on individual injury would have had difficulties in determining standing.[8]

The problem of course is not specific to the issue of nuclear tests, but arises wherever a State violates multilateral obligations that cannot be

[3] Grotius (1646/1925), book II, chapter 20, § 40.

[4] Contrast de Vattel (1758/1916), book II, § 348 and van Bynkershoek (1744/1946), chapter 22, § 5. On the incident see also Phillimore (1879), vol. III, 30–31.

[5] Bluntschli (1868), 263–265 (§§ 471–473); Heffter/Geffcken (1882), 222 (para. 104).

[6] Phillimore (1879), Vol. I, 442; Vol. III, 30–31; van Bulmerinq (1889), 84–85; similarly Martens (1864), tome 2, 198 (para. 261).

[7] See above, section 1.3.2.b For the quotation see Riphagen, Third Report, YbILC 1982, Vol. II/1, 38 (para. 97).

[8] See Birnie/Boyle (2002), 196, for a similar observation.

performed in relation to one other State, and which therefore are not – in the above terminology – 'bilateralisable'.[9] It was brought to the fore by the gradual emergence of obligations of States to respect human rights of their nationals. As the ICJ declared in its 1951 *Genocide opinion*:

> In [the 1948 Genocide] convention, the contracting States do not have any interests of their own; they merely have, one and all, a common interest, namely the accomplishment of those high purposes which are the *raison d'être* of the convention. Consequently, in a convention of this type, one cannot speak of individual advantages and disadvantages to States, or of the maintenance of a perfect contractual balance between rights and duties.[10]

Less than a decade later, the European Commission for Human Rights similarly confirmed the specific character of human rights obligations in the *Pfunders case*, where it stated that

> the purpose of the High Contracting Parties in concluding the [European] Convention was not to concede to each other reciprocal rights and obligations in pursuance of their individual national interests . . . but to establish a common public order of the free democracies of Europe with the object of safeguarding their common heritage of political traditions, ideals, freedom and the rule of law.[11]

Although neither of these pronouncements had a direct bearing on the question of standing,[12] both exposed the limits of the concept of individual injury very clearly. By disregarding its obligations under

[9] See above, section 1.3.2.b.

[10] ICJ Reports 1951, 23. During the pleadings, the point had been forcefully made by the British government, which had argued that the parties' obligations under the Genocide Convention 'are not obligations to be executed towards or for the benefit of other States' (ICJ Pleadings, 64).

[11] 4 YbECHR (1961), 138; and see further *ibid.*, 140.

[12] In the *Genocide opinion*, the Court stressed the specific character of the convention when discussing the permissibility of reservations; it was part of the reasoning leading the Court to endorse the object and purpose test, which eventually informed article 19(c) VCLT. On the case see Klein (1995b), 544; Ruda (1975), 133–156.

In the *Pfunders case*, the Commission found that because of the specific character of the European Convention, Austria could file an inter-State complaint in relation to breaches that had taken place prior to its own accession to the European Convention. Although rejecting the contrary Italian position, the Commission held that the complaint was partly inadmissible on other grounds and otherwise manifestly unfounded; hence there had been no violation of the Convention (see 6 YbECHR (1963), 740). As regards standing, the case presented no major difficulties since (then) article 24 expressly recognised the right of '[a]ny High Contracting Party' to bring inter-State complaints. On the provision see below, section 2.2.2.a.; on the *Pfunders case* see Jacobs/White/Ovey (2002), 20–21; Simma (1972), 179–182; Golsong (1963), 92–95.

either of the two conventions, a State might well act in contravention of a 'common' or 'general interest' or even of a 'common public order'. However, neither of these violations would usually affect any State in its individual legal positions.[13]

The international legal system did not respond to these challenges in a uniform way. Partly, States tried to deal with the problem at an institutional level, i.e. by establishing international organisations capable of addressing issues of common concern. In the special field of human rights, individuals themselves were increasingly given procedural capacity to vindicate their rights. As regards the subject of the present inquiry, assertions, by States, of a right to respond against wrongful acts affecting general interests met with very different reactions. Two statements, made by ICJ judges in the context of the preliminary objections judgment in the *South West Africa cases* show the degree of uncertainty and disagreement. Invoking 'the old tag ... *pas d'intérêt pas d'action*', President Winiarski restated what might be characterised as the restrictive approach in its purest form. He was adamant that 'an interest [had to be] personal and direct;' it was a general principle of law that legal actors could only respond to breaches of individual legal positions.[14]

Judge Jessup put forward a very different view, arguing that '[i]nternational law has long recognised that States may have legal interests in matters which do not affect their financial, economic, or other "material", or, say, "physical" or "tangible" interests'. In specific situations 'States [therefore have] a legal interest in the general observance of the rules of international law.'[15]

The contrast between the two statements, as indeed the procedural history of the case in whose context they were made, shows that the traditional regime of standing was not static but in a state of tension. In order to convey this impression, the following analysis does not proceed chronologically, but distinguishes restrictive tendencies from early attempts to recognise a right of standing in the absence of

[13] Based on the arguments referred to in the context of the *Nuclear Tests cases*, States obligations *vis-à-vis* their own nationals would have to be distinguished from human rights obligations owed to foreigners. Breaches of the latter would of course specially affect the foreigner's State of nationality, as would breaches committed on the territory of a foreign State.

[14] ICJ Reports 1962, 455 and 456.

[15] ICJ Reports 1962, 425; and further *ibid.*, 428–430. For similar observations see already Jessup (1948), especially at 2 and 154.

individual injury. For the sake of convenience, it does not distinguish between countermeasures and ICJ proceedings, but treats both forms of law enforcement together.[16]

2.1 Restrictive tendencies

Under a restrictive approach, States are only entitled to institute ICJ proceedings or resort to countermeasures in response to wrongful acts that affect their individual legal positions. Just as in President Winiarski's above-quoted pronouncement, statements in favour of this approach often took the form of claims that States did not have standing to vindicate general interests.[17] A statement by Eagleton (who was critical of the narrow approach allegedly dominating international practice) is particularly clear. In his view, 'Responsibility [under traditional international law] was acknowledged only in relation to another state; it was based on 'tort' or 'delict' [...]. The two states concerned fought it out as between themselves, and no one else had the right to interfere.'[18]

For the purposes of the present discussion, statements like these are of little help – they may or may not have been correct at the time they were made, but they do not advance the analysis. In contrast, two other restrictive tendencies are of considerable relevance and will be analysed. The dominance of what may be termed a 'structural analysis' of multilateral obligations is the first aspect. As will be shown, there emerged, in the decade before the Court's *Barcelona Traction* judgment, a particular way of classifying and interpreting multilateral obligations.

[16] In addition to countermeasures and ICJ claims, see below, section 2.2.2.d for a brief discussion of forcible enforcement action.

For the reasons stated in the Introduction (above, text accompanying footnotes 31–37), the present chapter does not address instances of enforcing general interests by asserting national jurisdiction over foreign conduct deemed to contravene common values. As a consequence, no attempt is made here to discuss nineteenth-century tendencies to suppress the slave trade. The well-known British and US American decisions on the matter reflect the tension between effective enforcement and respect for other States' rights on the other: see e.g. *United States v. 'La Jeune Eugénie'*, 26 Federal Cases 832 (1822) on the one hand, and *The 'Antelope'*, 23 US (10 Wheaton) 64 (1825), or *The 'Le Louis'*, 2 Dodson 210 (1817) on the other. For a detailed examination cf. Rubin (1997), 82–137.

[17] Cf. e.g. Tsuruoka's Working Paper on State Responsibility, YbILC 1963, Vol. II, 250 (para. 14); Anzilotti (1902), 84; Strupp (1920), 13–16; Münch (1963) 137–138; similarly the many writers maintaining the need for a narrowly conceived notion of damage as a precondition of responsibility. It must be conceded that many of these commentators *de lege ferenda* argued for a broader approach.

[18] Eagleton (1951), 423.

Codified in article 60 VCLT, this structural analysis has exercised considerable influence on the law of State responsibility, in particular the rules of standing. The second aspect to be addressed is the ICJ's treatment of the *South West Africa case*, which – as stated above[19] – epitomises a restrictive approach disavowed by the *Barcelona Traction* dictum.

At the outset, it should be said that neither the *South West Africa* judgment nor article 60 VCLT (or indeed the structural analysis upon which it is based) constitute absolute, pure, applications of the restrictive approach as encapsulated in President Winiarski's statement quoted above. Both engage with the problem of multilateralism, and acknowledge the possibility that individual States might be entitled to vindicate general interests. At the same time, they reduce this possibility to a minimum by subjecting it to strict conditions. It therefore seems justified to address them together as applications of a restrictive approach to questions of standing.

2.1.1 A structural analysis of multilateral obligations

The structural analysis of multilateral obligations is the first factor restricting the right of States to defend general interests. The expression 'structural analysis' is used here to denote a specific approach to the classification of multilateral obligations, which places great emphasis on the structure of performance of the respective obligations. This approach has never been formulated in the abstract. Instead, it is implicit in Sir Gerald Fitzmaurice's ILC Reports on the law treaties, which constitute an attempt to come to terms with the problem of different categories of multilateral obligations – a problem that had been exposed in, for example, the ICJ's advisory proceedings in the *1951 Genocide* case or the European Commission's report in *Pfunders*.[20] This structural analysis eventually provided the basis for article 60 VCLT, addressing the right of States to suspend or terminate treaties in respond to breaches. Given the close relation between countermeasures and treaty-based responses under article 60, this alone would be sufficient to warrant some further analysis. The impact of the structural analysis on the rules of standing, however, goes beyond article 60 VCLT. The ILC's deliberations on what was to become article 60 VCLT constituted the

[19] See above, Introduction (footnote 58).

[20] See above, footnotes 10 and 11. It is interesting to note that Fitzmaurice – acting in his (then) capacity as agent of the British government – first presented his typology of obligations during the pleadings in the *Genocide case*: see ICJ Pleadings, especially at 64 and 387–388.

first general debate about issues of standing and had a profound influence on, for example, its work on State responsibility.[21] Although originally developed within the framework of the law of treaties, Fitzmaurice's classification of multilateral obligations has been applied to all types of legal relations, irrespective of their source,[22] and is generally accepted as workable and analytically sound.[23] Although not always acknowledged, the structural analysis of multilateral obligations thus is of considerable relevance for the present study. In order fully to understand its influence on the rules of standing, it is necessary to first introduce the three categories upon which it based.

2.1.1.a Three categories of obligations

Fitzmaurice was not the first to suggest a distinction between different types of multilateral obligations. His analysis heavily drew on the earlier work by Triepel and Bergbohm, who had drawn a basic distinction between law-making treaties or agreements on the one hand (*Vereinbarungen*, or *traités-lois*), and contractual treaties (*Rechtsgeschäften*, or *traités-contrats*) on the other.[24] Their so-called *Vereinbarungstheorie* was based on recognition that under some treaties, parties assume identical obligations, whereas others provide for corresponding rights and duties that are to be performed reciprocally, between pairs of States.[25] For all its flaws,[26] this approach clarified the crucial relevance of the notion of

[21] See the express references to article 60 VCLT in paras. 4, 5, 12, 13 of the Commission's commentary to article 42 ASR; and cf. further Crawford (2002a), 39.

[22] Sachariew (1986), 33; Crawford, Third Report, para. 91; Crawford (2000), 30; de Hoogh (1996), 79 (his footnote 143); and cf. also article 42 ASR.

[23] See e.g. Dupuy (2002b), 380–383; Reuter (1995), 174–175 (para. 302); Simma (1972), *passim*; (Verdross/Simma 1984), 341 and 517–518; Schwelb (1967a), 309; Sicilianos (1993), 341; Elias (1974), 114–115; Feist (2001), 47–57, 122–131; Sachariew (1988), 273; Bleckmann (1974); Hafner (1988), 187; as well as article 42 ASR.

It is important to note that this general support for the categories distinguished by Fitzmaurice does not necessarily extend to the *prescriptive* parts of the structural analysis; see below, footnote 75.

[24] Triepel (1899), who in turn relied on Bergbohm's earlier study published in 1887. The influence of Triepel's theory is, for example, discussed by Partsch (1962), 389; and Gihl (1937), 47–53.

The influence of earlier approaches on Fitzmaurice's classification of treaties is particularly obvious in draft article 8 of his First Report, YbILC 1956, Vol. II, 108.

[25] Triepel (1899), 46; Bergbohm (1887), 81.

[26] For a critical analysis of the *Vereinbarungstheorie* see Lauterpacht (1927), 156–159; McNair (1930), 105–118; Feist (2001), 28–32; Reuter (1995), 23–24 (paras. 56–59); Rousseau (1973), 68–69. The debates triggered by Triepel's theory need not be recapitulated here. Suffice it to say that in many respects, the *Vereinbarungstheorie*

reciprocity.[27] In line with it, Fitzmaurice first drew a distinction between reciprocal and other multilateral obligations. In a second step, which went beyond the existing analysis and constitutes the main innovation of Fitzmaurice's structural analysis, the latter category of other, non-reciprocal obligations was further divided into absolute obligations (also referred to as 'internal',[28] 'self-existent'[29] or 'objective'[30] obligations) and interdependent (or 'integral'[31]) obligations.

The first distinction was not only based on the *Vereinbarungstheorie*, but also equates with what has been said above about multilateral obligations – in fields such as diplomatic or consular law – that require to be performed in relation to one particular State, and, although multilateral, give rise to reciprocal rights and duties.[32] Fitzmaurice himself defined reciprocal obligations as 'consist[ing] of a mutual and reciprocal exchange of benefits or concessions as between the parties', which comprised obligations in such fields as diplomatic or consular law, extradition treaties, or under the rules regulating the use of economic or military pressure.[33] In contrast, the performance of absolute and

proved simplistic, and that one of Triepel's main claims – that only law-making treaties were a source of law – was flatly rejected by international practice; contrast Triepel (1899), 62 on the one hand, and article 38, para. 1(a) of the ICJ Statute.

27 This explanatory value is recognised by most critics of the distinction, see e.g. Lauterpacht (1927), 157; Oppenheim/Lauterpacht, Vol. I (1955), 878–90.

28 Provost (2002), 133–134.

29 Fitzmaurice, Second Report, draft article 19 (1)(iv), YbILC 1957, Vol. II, 31.

30 See e.g. the Eur.Comm'n HR, *Pfunders case*, 4 YbECHR (1961), 140; Eur.Ct. HR, *Ireland v. United Kingdom case*, Ser. A, No. 25 (1978), para. 239; Simma (1994a), 364–369.

31 In fact, this third type of obligations is usually described as 'integral', see Crawford, Third Report, para. 91 (but contrast the statement in para. 106(b), footnote 195); Crawford (2000), 29–31; Gomaa (1996), 34–35; Simma (1970), 76; Sicilianos (1993), 348. This choice of terms, however, is problematic, and has given rise to many misunderstandings. For example, both interdependent and absolute (self-existent, objective) obligations are often said to require an 'integral performance', cf. Fitzmaurice, Second Report, draft article 19 (1)(iv), YbILC 1957, Vol. II, 31; *id.*, Fourth Report, draft article 18 (3)(e), YbILC 1959, Vol. II, 46; Sachariew (1988), 276–277. To make matters worse, absolute (objective, self-existent) obligations have also been qualified as 'integral', see Sachariew (1986), 21–22.

In order to avoid these problems, the third category will be referred to as 'interdependent obligations', which conforms with Fitzmaurice's description of its main feature.

32 See above, section 1.3.2.b.

33 See e.g. Second Report, draft article 18(1)(a), YbILC 1957, Vol. II, 30. Similar descriptions can be found in his Second Report, draft articles 19 (1)(ii)(a) and 29(1)(ii) and commentaries thereto, YbILC 1957, Vol. II, 31, 36, 54 (para. 124) and 68 (para. 209) respectively; Third Report, draft article 18(2) and commentary, YbILC 1958, Vol. II, 27 and 41 (para. 78); see also Fourth Report, draft articles 18 and 20 and commentaries, YbILC 1959, Vol. II, 45, 46, 66 (para. 82) and 70 (para. 102) respectively. On the category see also

interdependent obligations cannot be reduced to reciprocal exchanges between pairs of States. In both cases, the obligation in question is not to be performed in relation to one State in particular. Instead, all States bound by it have the same interest in seeing the obligation observed – hence the observation that they required an 'integral performance'.[34] This does not mean however that the two categories are identical. Quite to the contrary, the structural analysis offers a key to distinguishing between both categories by pointing to the interrelation between the obligations assumed by States.

Pursuant to Fitzmaurice, 'absolute obligations' require States to adopt a parallel conduct within their own sphere of jurisdiction.[35] The performance, by each State, of these obligations is in no way dependent on the corresponding performance by other States, and compliance does not result in *any* exchange of benefits.[36] Expectations of reciprocity of course might have played a role during the creation of the obligation in question – as is particularly evident in the process of treaty-making during which different States often express very different views on whether parallel obligations are acceptable. However, the actual application of the multilateral obligation is characterised by a complete absence of reciprocity.

It is in this regard that interdependent obligations markedly differ. Pursuant to the structural approach, an obligation qualifies as interdependent if the performance, by all States, is inextricably linked.[37] Just as with absolute obligations, interdependent obligations cannot be split up into pairs of legal relations. However, unlike absolute obligations,

Simma (1972), 152–155; Sachariew (1988), 277–278; Riphagen, Sixth Report, YbILC 1985, Vol. II/1, 7 (para. 14).

[34] Fitzmaurice, Second Report, draft article 19 (1)(iv), YbILC 1957, Vol. II, 31; *id.*, Fourth Report, draft article 18 (3)(e), YbILC 1959, Vol. II, 46; Sachariew (1988), 276–277; and similarly Simma (1994a), 338, 351–352. Cf. also *Shorter Oxford Dictionary* (1973), 1088, which defines integral as 'something entire and undivided' (section B.1).

[35] See Fitzmaurice, Second Report, draft article 19 (1)(iv) and commentary, YbILC 1957, Vol. II, 31 and 54 (paras. 125–126); Third Report, draft articles 18 (2), 19 (b) and commentary, YbILC 1958, Vol. II, 27–28, 41 (para. 78), 44 (paras. 91–93); Fourth Report, draft articles 18 (3)(e), 20 (1) and commentary, YbILC 1959, Vol. II, 45–46, 66 (para. 82) and 70 (para. 102) respectively.

[36] In the words of Fitzmaurice, 'neither juridically, nor from the practical point of view, [...] the obligation of any party [is] dependent on a corresponding performance by the others', YbILC 1957, Vol. II, 54 (para. 126).

[37] See Fitzmaurice, Second Report, draft articles 19 (1)(ii)(b) and (iii) and commentary, YbILC 1957, Vol. II, 31 and 54 (para. 126); Third Report, draft article 18(2), 19 (a) and commentary, YbILC 1958, Vol. II, 27–28, 41 (para. 78) and 44 (paras. 91–93); Fourth Report, draft articles 18 (3)(e) and 20 (1), YbILC 1959, Vol. II, 45, 46, 66 (para. 82) and 70 (para. 102).

they have to be performed between the parties, not independently by each of them. They are premised on an implied understanding that the purpose of the obligation can only be attained if *each* party complies with it.[38] Interdependent obligations thus incorporate reciprocity between all States (aptly described as 'global reciprocity' by Sicilianos),[39] and one State's non-compliance puts into question the purpose for which they have been entered into. When this is the case depends on an interpretation of the relevant obligation, and, at least in theory, the line between absolute and interdependent obligations may not be as clear as the structural approach suggests. In practice, however, a very narrow understanding of the category has helped avoid problems. In his Reports, Fitzmaurice had stated that prohibitions on the use of specific weapons, or obligations of disarmament, were interdependent in character.[40] Beyond these, rules prohibiting the exercise of sovereign rights in internationalised areas (most notably in Antarctica or in Outer Space) are the only further, generally agreed, examples.[41]

Absolute obligations have given rise to more problems. There is broad agreement about the absolute character of human rights obligations, or obligations providing for common standards of safety, e.g. at sea.[42] To these examples, which were already referred to by Fitzmaurice, one might add other standard-setting obligations, notably in the environmental field.[43] However, it is crucial to note that the category of absolute obligations cannot be limited to these examples.[44] Precisely because it is based on a structural analysis, the category comprises *all* obligations that are to be performed independently, irrespective of

[38] Cf. only Crawford, Third Report, para. 91; Crawford (2000), 29–31; Feist (2001), 49–52; Gomaa (1996) 34–35; Simma (1970), 76; Sicilianos (1993), 348.

[39] Sicilianos (2002), 1135. [40] YbILC 1957, Vol. II, 54 (para. 126 with footnote 73).

[41] See e.g. article I of the 1959 Antarctic Treaty (402 UNTS 71), or article II of the 1967 Outer Space Treaty (610 UNTS 205). The narrow character of the definition is for example stressed in the ILC's commentary to Article 42 ASR, para. 15.

[42] See e.g. Second Report, YbILC 1957, Vol. II, 54 (para. 125). In his Fourth Report, he spoke more generally of conventions of a social or humanitarian character, draft article 18 (3)(e), YbILC 1959, Vol. II, 46 (footnote 12).

[43] Environmental treaties often express this standard-setting character by describing the object of protection as a 'common heritage' or a 'good of mankind', or by stressing the 'intrinsic value' of preserving, for example, wild flora and fauna. See Beyerlin (1996), 605–611 with references. On the general interest character of obligations in the environmental field see Charney (1991), 162; Nettesheim (1996), 195–199; Günther (1999), 128–130; Brunée (1989), 791.

[44] Among the few writers discussing absolute obligations outside the said categories are Sachariew (1986), 90–92, and Simma (1994a), 337.

their content. This is notably the case for all obligations requiring States to adopt a uniform conduct. This includes, for example, the duty to harmonise national laws, e.g. by outlawing specific forms of behaviour (such as torture, hijacking of airplanes, or forgery),[45] or by adopting common rules of private law (e.g. under the Hague Conventions or CISG).[46] As regards executive, administrative, or judicial action, absolute obligations, for example, require States to prosecute perpetrators of certain wrongful acts, or to maintain specific archives, registers, or records.[47] To give but one example, article 7(e) of the 1971 Convention on Psychotropic Substances[48] obliges States parties to ensure 'that persons performing medical or scientific functions keep records concerning the acquisition of the substances [referred to in Schedule 1] and the details of their use.'

Contrary to the narrow focus of much of the academic debate, the category of absolute obligations therefore is not limited to obligations in the humanitarian, ecological, or social field.

2.1.1.b The legal regime

Following Fitzmaurice, the structural analysis provides the key to a differentiated legal regime governing multilateral obligations. In his Reports, he spelled out his approach in respect to three different areas of the law: suspension and termination of treaties in response to prior breaches,[49] modification of treaties through subsequent agreements,[50] and non-performance of treaty obligation by way of countermeasures (reprisal)[51] – a topic eventually not addressed in the Vienna Convention. In its subsequent work, the Commission did not always adhere to Fitzmaurice's structural analysis of multilateral obligations. Under Fitzmaurice's successor, Sir Humphrey Waldock, it opted for a pragmatic approach, often expressly disagreeing with what was considered to be an over-refined structural differentiation.[52] Interestingly, the situation is

[45] See e.g. article 4 of the 1984 Torture Convention (1465 UNTS 85); article 3 of the 1971 Montreal Convention (974 UNTS 178) and article 3 of the 1929 Geneva Convention on Counterfeiting Currency (112 LNTS 371).

[46] See, for example, article 7 of the 1955 Hague Convention on the Law Applicable to the International Sale of Goods (510 UNTS 147); and cf. Simma (1994a), 337.

[47] Sachariew (1986), 91–92. [48] 1019 UNTS 175.

[49] Second Report, draft articles 18–19, 29, YbILC 1957, Vol. II, 30–31, 35–36.

[50] Third Report, draft articles 18 and 19, YbILC 1958, Vol. II, 27–28.

[51] Fourth Report, draft articles 18 and 20, YbILC 1959, Vol. II, 45–46.

[52] See e.g. Waldock, Second Report, YbILC 1963, Vol. II, 76–77 (para. 15).

different with regard to responses against breaches. The one provision addressing questions of standing, article 60 VCLT, indeed is clearly informed by Fitzmaurice's analysis. Of course, treaty suspension and termination under that provision is subject to a number of conditions not applicable to other responses against breaches; notably responses can only be directed against material breaches of treaties.[53] Notwithstanding this difference, debates preceding the adoption of article 60 VCLT had to address the same question that is of relevance here: Under which circumstances should States be held to have standing to respond against treaty breaches? On the basis of the *travaux préparatoires* and Fitzmaurice's Reports, it is possible to extrapolate a 'structural' regime of standing.

This legal regime neatly follows the pattern of performance of the different categories of multilateral obligations. With respect to multilateral obligations of a reciprocal character, the specially affected State's right to respond therefore is exclusive. In the framework of the Vienna Convention rules, this is expressly provided for by article 60, para. 2(b), which reserves the right to suspend treaties to specially affected States and thus echoes draft provisions contained in Fitzmaurice's Second Report.[54] The eventual adoption of that provision was preceded by extensive debates that clearly exposed the different understandings of multilateral obligations. Waldock had initially recognised the right of 'any other party' to react against breaches of multilateral treaties by way of suspension or termination.[55] This 'solidarity view'[56] was criticised within the ILC, but nevertheless found its way into draft article 42, para. 2(a), adopted in 1963.[57] Its supporters argued that allowing each party to respond could deter States from violating treaties.[58] On a less practical note, they stressed the general legal interest of all parties in seeing treaties complied. The point was made with particular clarity by Rosenne, who '[a]s a matter of principle, ... felt strongly

[53] See above, section 1.1.

[54] Fitzmaurice, Second Report, draft articles 18(1)(a) and 19(1)(iv), YbILC 1957, Vol. II, 30–31.

[55] See his proposed draft article 20, para. 4a, YbILC 1963, Vol. II, 73.

[56] Simma (1970), 68.

[57] YbILC 1963, Vol. II, 204. In contrast to Waldock's draft article 20, para. 4a, article 42, para. 2a only recognised the right of all parties to suspend (but not to terminate) the treaty in relation to the defaulting State.

[58] See e.g. Waldock's Second Report, YbILC 1963, Vol. II, 77 (paras. 15–17).

that all parties to a multilateral treaty had the same interest with regard to the observance of a treaty, so long as it was in force.'[59]

Critics of draft article 42, para. 2(a) responded that by allowing all States to suspend or even terminate multilateral treaties, the Commission would endanger the stability of treaty relations.[60] They also observed that there were different types of multilateral obligations, and that different States had different interests in seeing them observed. Various Commission members as well as a number of governments in particular stressed the need for a distinction between 'the general interest of all the parties and the specific and direct interest' of parties individually affected.[61]

It was this latter, more restrictive position, which eventually prevailed, and found its way into article 60, para. 2(b).[62] As is clarified by the commentary to that provision, only individually injured States are entitled to respond to breaches of multilateral treaties.[63] For present purposes, it is important to note that although the Commission did not always acknowledge it, article 60, para. 2(b) implements Fitzmaurice's proposals to the letter. Based on a structural analysis, it equates violations of reciprocal obligations with breaches of bilateral treaty obligations.[64] In contrast, the general legal interest in seeing multilateral obligations observed is not sufficient to warrant a right to respond.

[59] YbILC 1966, Vol. I/1, 60 (para. 26). The point was reiterated by Castren and Briggs, *ibid.*, 61 (paras. 40 and 47 respectively). Waldock's observation that all treaties contained 'a contractual element' points in the same direction, see Second Report, YbILC 1963, Vol. II, 77 (para. 15). It should be noted that Rosenne subsequently reversed his position, see YbILC 1966, Vol. I/1, 128 (para. 7).

[60] See Verdross, YbILC 1963, Vol. I, 294 (para. 62). Cf. also Schwelb (1967a), 321–326; Rolin (1967), 359–361.

[61] Cadieux, YbILC 1966, Vol. I/1, 62 (para. 60). Similar remarks were made by Yasseen, *ibid.*, 62 (para. 55), de Luna, *ibid.*, 63 (para. 70), Rosenne, *ibid.*, 128 (para. 7); as well as the Dutch and United States governments, YbILC 1966, Vol. II, Annex, section 17 (318).

[62] The eventual wording of the narrower formulation gave rise to further controversy. In particular, there were different views on whether all parties to a multilateral treaty had a 'right' or a '(legal) interest' in its observation. By referring to special effects, article 60, para. 2(b) avoids this question rather salomonically. For details of the drafting process see Simma (1970), 69–70.

[63] YbILC 1966, Vol. II, 255 (para. 8). See further Simma (1970), 67–75; Feist (2001), 152–154; Hafner (1988), 190; Hutchinson (1988), 188–189.

[64] Consequently, suspension under article 60, para. 2(b) only takes effect between the State specially affected and the responsible State, but leaves the other legal relations intact.

Given their special structure of performance, such bilateralisation is impossible with regard to the other two categories of multilateral obligations. In line with what has been said about the interrelation between the obligations assumed by States, the structural approach clearly distinguishes between absolute and interdependent obligations. As to interdependent obligations, article 60 VCLT opts for a completely multilateralised regime.[65] Pursuant to para. 2(c), all States can respond if the breach of an obligation 'radically changes the position of every party with respect to the further performance of its obligations'. Despite the unclear wording, the ILC's commentary leaves no doubt that this formulation is intended to cover the special case of interdependent obligations whose objective can only be achieved if all States perform their respective obligations.[66] This again mirrors the draft articles submitted by Fitzmaurice in 1957, which had recognised the right of 'the other parties ... [to] ceas[e] to perform any obligations of the treaty ... which are of such a kind that ... their performance by any party is necessarily dependent on an equal or corresponding performance by all the other parties.'[67] Based on a structural analysis of the underlying patterns of performance, the legal regime governing interdependent obligations thus gives broad room to decentralised responses to breaches.[68]

The situation is different with regard to the remaining category of absolute obligations. As has been stated, these obligations are not to be performed between States, but independently by each of them. Pursuant to a structural approach, it follows that the breach, by one State, leaves the obligations of other States unaffected and conversely does not entitle them to respond individually. In draft article 19, para. 1(iv) of his Second Report, Fitzmaurice expressly stated that the breach of an absolute obligation:

[65] In addition to article 60, para. 2(c) VCLT, see also commentary to article 42 ASR, para. 13; as well as draft article 40, para. 2(e)(ii) of the ILC's first reading text; YbILC 1985, Vol. II/1, 26–27 (para. 19).

[66] YbILC 1966, Vol. II, 255, para. 8. See further Simma (1970), 75–77; but contrast Sicilianos (1990), 115–116. In the case of treaty suspension, article 60, para. 2(c) furthermore stipulates that the suspension has legal effects *vis-à-vis all* other parties (*inter omnes*); see Simma (1970), 76–77.

[67] Draft article 19, para. 1(ii)(b), YbILC 1957, Vol. II, 31.

[68] This point is made very clearly in the ILC's commentary to article 42 ASR, para. 14, where the Commission observes: 'The other States parties ... must all be considered as individually entitled to react to a breach. This is so whether or not any one of them is particularly affected ...'

(a) Can never constitute a ground of termination or withdrawal by any of the parties;
(b) Cannot even (to the extent to which that otherwise be relevant or practicable) justify non-performance of the obligations of the treaty in respect of the defaulting party or its nationals, vessels, etc.[69]

Two years later, this position was confirmed with respect to the law of countermeasures: 'Action by way of reprisals may only be resorted to . . . . [p]rovided that the treaty concerned is not a multilateral treaty . . . where the force of the obligation is self-existent, absolute and inherent for each party, irrespective and independently of performance by the others'.[70] By implication, article 60 VCLT produces the same result. Individual States can only suspend multilateral obligations if they are either specially affected (para. 2(b)) or if the obligation in question is interdependent (para. 2(c)). Since interdependent obligations are distinguished from absolute obligations, para. 2(c) is clearly inapplicable. As regards para. 2(b), unless they exceptionally affect individual legal positions of one particular State (e.g. its nationals, its territory, etc.[71]), breaches of absolute obligations simply do not 'specially affect' any of the other States; hence no State is entitled to respond individually.[72] Redressing breaches of absolute obligations therefore becomes a matter of collective or institutionalised action pursuant to article 60, para. 2(a).[73]

The - seemingly neutral - structural analysis of obligations therefore has important implications on the question if standing. By focusing on patterns of performance, it makes the law dependent on sociological characteristics of different categories of multilateral obligations.[74] As a

[69] Draft article 19, para. 1 (iv), YbILC 1957, Vol. II, 31.

[70] Draft article 18, para. 3(e), YbILC 1959, Vol. II, 46. The same provision misleadingly refers to 'integral' obligations. However, this is due to Fitzmaurice's inconsistent use of that term, and casts further doubt on the usefulness of the term 'integral'. The passage quoted, as well as the cross-references given by Fitzmaurice, clearly show that the provision is intended to cover interdependent obligations.

[71] See above, section 1.3.2.b.

[72] As a further safeguard, article 60, para. 5 VCLT provides that humanitarian treaties may never be suspended or terminated for grounds of breach by another State. The importance of this clause, however, is often overestimated. Even without article 60, para. 5, States could not usually suspend humanitarian treaties, since breaches do not specially affect them.

[73] Under that provision, suspension or termination of treaties remains possible if all State parties (but for the wrongdoing State) so decide.

[74] In the words of Simma (1994a), 365, 'sociological characteristics have spilled over into legal analysis.'

consequence, decentralised responses to breaches are only permissible where there is an exchange of benefits between States. This means that, in the absence of individually sustained injury, decentralised reactions are only permitted in response to breaches of interdependent obligations. In contrast, outside that narrowly defined category, the general interest of each and every State in the observance of reciprocal or absolute obligations is not sufficient to trigger an individual right of response.[75]

The structural approach thus indirectly favours institutional or collective responses to breaches. While in the case of treaty regimes, such collective enforcement or supervision can be institutionalised through the creation of supervisory bodies, no equivalent possibility exists with respect to norms of general international law. Despite the narrow exception of interdependent obligations, the structural analysis thus facilitates a restrictive approach to standing.

2.1.2 *A restrictive interpretation of treaty provisions: the* South West Africa case

Unlike the often-neglected structural analysis, the *South West Africa case* is widely recognised as a landmark case on the rules of standing.[76] Indeed, more than any other event, the Court's judgment of 18 July 1966 stands for a restrictive approach. It is not always acknowledged that the case did not concern the general rules of standing, but the interpretation of a special treaty-based jurisdictional clause, article 7(2)

[75] Especially with regard to absolute obligations, this approach has not gone undisputed. Many commentators have claimed that the structural approach developed by Fitzmaurice would render absolute obligations practically unenforceable; see e.g. Simma (1994a), 364–375; Weschke (2001), 64–71; Arangio-Ruiz (1977), 246–251; Simma (1972), 176–219. Possibly in response to this criticism, the European Court of Human Rights, in the *Ireland v. United Kingdom case*, stated that 'the Convention comprises *more than* reciprocal engagements between the contracting States. It creates, *over and above a network of mutual, bilateral undertakings*, objective obligations', ECHR, Ser. A, No. 25 (1978), 90 (emphasis added).

Subsequent chapters will analyse whether Fitzmaurice's analysis of absolute obligations remains persuasive today. For the time being, it is important to note that the interpretation of absolute obligations described in the text neatly follows from the sociological analysis upon which the structural approach is based.

[76] Literature on the case is immense; see the extensive coverage by Dugard (1973) (with many further references); and further *id.*, (1966), 429; Higgins (1966), 573; Friedmann (1967), 1; Bernhardt (1973), 24–30; Degan (1966), 9; Kappeler (1966), 335; Ginther (1971), 99–114; Boellecker-Stern (1973), 68–82; Fleming (1967), 241; de Visscher (1966), 17–28; Reisman (1966–1967), 31–90; Johnson (1967), 157. For a very clear summary see Klein (2000a), 494–497.

of the South West African mandate agreement.[77] That the case should have acquired such notoriety therefore may seem curious. In fact, the immediate effects of the decision were rather trivial – all the Court held was that the jurisdictional clause of a 1920 treaty (which was soon-to-be terminated)[78] did not confer standing on two applicant States. However, the interpretation of the specific treaty clause was informed by a restrictive understanding of the general rules of standing. In line with what has been said above, about the blurred line between special and residual rules of standing,[79] the implications of the *South West Africa* judgment therefore extend well beyond article 7(2) of the 1920 mandate agreement. This factor, more than anything else, justifies the importance attached to the decision.

In the circumstances of the case, the two applicant States, Liberia and Ethiopia, alleged that South Africa's administration of South West Africa/ Namibia[80] violated the terms of the 1920 mandate agreement. In the agreement, the League had entrusted the administration over the former German colony to South Africa, which in turn had accepted different types of obligations. Under the so-called 'special interest provisions', South Africa recognised certain rights of nationals of other League members, such as the right of foreign missionaries to 'prosecute their calling'.[81] Under the so-called 'conduct provisions' (which were at stake before the Court) South Africa had agreed to adopt a certain conduct *vis-à-vis* the mandate population, e.g. to 'promote to the utmost the material and moral well-being and social progress' of the inhabitants.[82] Formally a bilateral treaty concluded between South Africa and the League of Nations, the mandate agreement was multilateralised through the inclusion of a broadly formulated jurisdictional clause. Article 7(2), on whose interpretation the proceedings hinged, read as follows:

> The Mandatory agrees that, if any dispute whatever should arise between the Mandatory and another Member of the League of Nations relating to the interpretation or the application of the provisions of the Mandate, such dispute, if it cannot be settled by negotiation, shall be submitted to the Permanent Court of International Justice provided for by Article 14 of the Covenant of the League of Nations.

[77] LNOJ 1921, 89. South West Africa was classified as a C-mandate in the sense of article 22 of the Covenant. Whereas article 22 set out the general principles of the mandate system, the actual Mandate Agreement spelled out the rights and duties of the mandatory.

[78] See GA Res. 2145 (XXI). [79] See above, section 1.2.3.

[80] The mandate territory was renamed by the General Assembly in 1968, see GA Res. 2372 (XXII).

[81] Mandate agreement, article 5. [82] Mandate agreement, article 2(2).

As is well known, the Court's interpretation of this provision changed considerably in the period between the 1962 judgment on preliminary objections, in which the applicants' standing was accepted, and its eventual reversal[83] on 18 July 1966.[84] This evolution (or regression) raises questions about the relation between interim and merits proceedings, as well as issues of institutional ICJ law – notably the question of whether the Court, in 1966, was bound by the earlier decision.[85] Neither of these problems will be addressed in the following, nor will the obvious question of whether the Court's ultimate decision was convincing. Instead, the subsequent analysis will focus on how the Court approached the interpretation of the treaty-based clause from a methodological point of view, and on whether its approach sheds light on the general rules of standing.

In this regard, it is important to note that judges did not only read article 7(2) very differently, but were equally divided on how to approach the question of interpretation. In terms of method, judges representing the 1962 majority largely relied on narrow, textual grounds. In their view, article 7(2) was formulated in clear enough terms. It used very broad language ('any dispute whatever', 'another Member of the League', 'interpretation or application of the provisions') and expressly referred to individual League members. Furthermore, it did not provide much support for the distinction between conduct or special interest provisions.[86]

[83] The Court in 1966 maintained not to have reversed the 1962 judgment. Instead, it argued that there was a distinction between the *locus standi* of applicants – on which it had decided in 1962 – and the legal interest entitling them to a judgment on the merits, see ICJ Reports 1966, 36–38 (paras. 59–61). This distinction has been generally rejected, not the least because the parties to the dispute had assumed that questions of legal interest were no longer at stake; see Dugard (1973), 332–346; Higgins (1966), 577–582; Klein (2000a), 497. In his dissent, Judge Jessup laconically stated that '*something* must have been finally decided by the 1962 Judgment', ICJ Reports 1966, 333 (emphasis in the original).

[84] The two judgments discussed in the following were decided by the closest of margins (8:7 in the first case, 7:7 – with the President's casting vote deciding – in the second). Both prompted a flow of dissenting opinions, some of which reveal deep division between the judges. This is particularly apparent in the introductory phrase of Judge Jessup's dissent, in which he took the view that 'the Judgment which the Court has just rendered [was] completely unfounded in law', ICJ Reports 1966, 325.

See further Dugard (1973), 374–375 and Anand (1968), 144–145 for a summary of reactions from outside the Court. The changes in the composition of the Court that enabled the 1962 minority to reappear as a majority in 1966 are recalled in Dugard (1973), 291–292.

[85] For a discussion of these issues see the references in footnote 83.

[86] '[Article 7] refers to any dispute whatever relating not to any one particular provision or provisions, but to "the provisions" of the mandate, obviously meaning all or any provisions, whether they relate to substantive obligations of the Mandatory toward the

To the 1962 majority, there was thus not much reason to look beyond the wording of the applicable jurisdictional clause, or to engage in a general discussion about notions such as 'dispute' or 'legal interest':

> The language used is broad, clear and precise. [. . .] [T]he manifest scope and purport of the provisions of this Article [i.e. article 7(2)] indicate that the Members of the League were understood to have a legal right or interest in the observance by the Mandatory of its obligations both toward the inhabitants of the Mandated Territory, and toward the League of Nations and its Members.[87]

Whatever the position under general international law, article 7(2) thus was considered to be a special rule settling the issue.

In contrast, the 1966 majority held that article 7(2) presupposed the distinction between special interest and conduct provisions. To a limited extent, their reasoning was based on specific features of article 7(2) or the mandate agreement as a whole. Historically, the role of individual League members within the mandate system had been limited, which seemed to warrant a narrow interpretation.[88] Furthermore, the requirement of prior negotiations was said to imply a restrictive reading of article 7(2).[89] However, the crucial argument allegedly supporting the distinction derived not from the applicable treaty, but from considerations of a general nature in whose light the mandate agreement had to be interpreted. President Winiarski's dissent from the 1962 judgment contains the clearest exposition of this contextual approach. In his view, it was

> a principle of international law that every conventional provision must be interpreted on the basis of general international law. The relevant words of Article 7 cannot be interpreted in such a way as to conflict with the general rule of procedure according to which the Applicant State must have the capacity to institute proceedings.[90]

Analysing the general rules of standing thus became a necessary aspect of treaty interpretation. There was, however, no agreement as

inhabitants of the Territory or toward the other Members of the League . . . ', ICJ Reports 1962, 343. This is conceded by Judges Spender and Fitzmaurice in their dissenting opinion, see ICJ Reports 1962, 550.

87 ICJ Reports 1962, 343. See already the separate opinions of Judges McNair and Read in the advisory opinion on the *International Status of South West Africa*, ICJ Reports 1950, 158 and 165; as well as Judge Nyholm's analysis of the history of the League mandates in the *Mavrommatis Jerusalem Concessions (Jurisdiction) case*, PCIJ, Ser. A, No. 10 (1927), 26.

88 Cf. ICJ Reports 1966, 39–40 (paras. 66–68). See also the analysis of the *travaux préparatoires* by Judges Spender and Fitzmaurice, ICJ Reports 1962, 554–559.

89 Diss.Op. Spender/Fitzmaurice, ICJ Reports 1962, 550–552; Diss.Op. Winiarski, *ibid.* 457–458.

90 ICJ Reports 1962, 455. For a similar statement see ICJ Reports 1966, 41 (para. 72).

to the content of the general rule of procedure. President Winiarski's own restrictive view on the matter – pursuant to which only individual interests could be vindicated before the Court – has been referred to already, as has Judge Jessup's more progressive approach.[91] The 1966 majority adopted a less categorical approach than Winiarski, conceding that legal interests 'need not necessarily relate to anything material or "tangible"'.[92] It also recognised that States remained free to agree on treaty provisions that allowed for standing irrespective of individual injury.[93] Clauses conferring such broad enforcement rights however would have to be formulated in unequivocal terms. In the words of the 1966 judgment 'rights or interests [in the enforcement of general interests], in order to exist, must be clearly vested in those who claim them, by some text or instrument, or rule of law . . . '[94]

In the view of the majority, article 7(2) did not reach the required threshold; despite its broad formulation, it was not held to 'clearly vest' into the applicants a right to institute ICJ proceedings in response to alleged breaches of the mandate's conduct provisions.[95] When inquiring why the Court, in 1966, established such a high threshold, the relevance of the general rules of standing becomes particularly evident. In view of the majority, article 7(2), if interpreted in the broad manner advocated by the applicants and confirmed in 1962, would have been an entirely unusual provision. Throughout the whole judgment, the Court was at pains to stress that article 7(2) was not exceptional enough to justify what would have been – so the majority – a radical break with the general rules of international law. Hence, the Court could see 'nothing in [article 7(2)] that would take the clause outside the normal rule'; and it was 'not capable of carrying the load the Applicants seek to place on it'.[96]

[91] See above, footnotes 14 and 15. Not surprisingly, many judges dissenting from the 1966 judgment agreed with Judge Jessup's 1962 separate opinion. In their view, article 7(2) deviated from the general rules on standing, but was not an altogether exceptional provision and thus could be taken at face value; see the dissenting opinions of Judges Wellington Koo, ICJ Reports 1966, 226–229; Koretsky, *ibid.*, 246–248; Forster, *ibid.*, 478–480; M'Bafeno, *ibid.*, 501–505.

[92] ICJ Reports 1966, 32 (para. 44). This refers back to Judge Jessup's earlier remark, ICJ Reports 1962, 425.

[93] ICJ Reports 1966, 40 (para. 67), where the Court cited the 1919 Polish Minorities Treaty as an example. On this treaty see below, section 2.2.1.a.

[94] ICJ Reports 1966, 32 (para. 44); and see also *ibid.*, 40 (para. 67). For a similar observation see Voeffray (2004), 91–92.

[95] See especially ICJ Reports 1966, 41–42 (para. 72). Elsewhere, article 7(2) was referred to as a 'common-form jurisdictional clause' (at 39, para. 65).

[96] ICJ Reports 1966, 39 and 42 (paras. 65 and 72 respectively).

In fact, one might even say that the result of the analysis was predictable when the Court introduced the relevant section of the judgment by observing that 'it would be remarkable if ... so important a right [such as that alleged by the applicants] had been created ... by an ordinary jurisdictional clause'.[97]

Article 7(2) was thus interpreted in the light of what was perceived to be a restrictive general rule of standing. This was corroborated by the fact that the two applicants were not themselves party to the treaty against whose alleged breach their response was directed.[98] Finally, the Court also rejected the applicants' argument that article 7(2) ought to be interpreted broadly because inter-State legal proceedings were the only feasible means of enforcing the conduct provisions effectively. This was said to ignore the realities of the mandate system and amounted, as the Court observed in a much-quoted dictum,

> to a plea that the Court should allow the equivalent of an '*actio popularis*' or right resident in any member of a community to take legal action in vindication of a public interest. But although a right of this kind may be known to certain municipal systems of law, it is not known to international law as it stands at present: nor is the Court able to regard it as imported by the 'general principles of law' referred to in article 38, paragraph 1(c), of its Statute.[99]

In the literature, the *South West Africa* judgment is often reduced to this last quotation. The preceding discussion shows that this is an unjustified simplification. In fact, neither the applicants nor the 1962 majority had relied on the concept of *actio popularis* - they simply interpreted article 7(2) differently. The Court's remark therefore seems at best unnecessary.[100] Instead, what did divide the two camps was their perception of the general rules of standing. Only on the basis of a

[97] ICJ Reports 1966, 38, (para. 63).

[98] See e.g. ICJ Reports 1966, 39 (paras. 65–66). It is sometimes maintained that the Court would have decided otherwise had the applicants been parties to the mandate agreement, see Simma (1981), 646; and cf. also Gray (1987), 212. But this is speculative since the 1966 majority based its decision on a number of general considerations, of which the applicants' formal third-party status was only one. See further Sep.Op. Bustamante, ICJ Reports 1962, 380; Diss.Op. Forster, ICJ Reports 1966, 479; Diss. Op. Jessup, *ibid.*, 378 (mentioning the right of third States to institute proceedings for violations of the minorities treaties).

[99] ICJ Reports 1966, 47 (para. 88). See already Diss.Op. Winiarski, ICJ Reports 1962, 452.

[100] See the remarks by Judge Jessup, ICJ Reports 1966, 387. As Judge Kooijmans (1997), 76, correctly observed, the case 'was not so much a question of an *actio popularis* in 1966, as of an interpretation of a normal treaty'; similarly Simma (1981), 646; Voeffray (2004), 94–95; Brownlie (2003), 452.

restrictive analysis of these general rules was the 1966 majority able to contextualise – viz. to restrict – article 7(2). As far as treaty clauses are concerned, the Court's eventual decision thus created a presumption against the existence of treaty-based enforcement rights irrespective of individual injury.[101] That the restrictive approach was upheld in the presence of a broadly formulated jurisdictional clause shows the strength of this presumption.

As far as the general rules are concerned, the Court's approach was not only based on, but also confirmed, the restrictive approach to standing. In fact, one cannot fail to note that *South West Africa* squares very well with the results of the structural approach to multilateral obligations.[102] Following a structural analysis, the conduct provisions of the mandate gave rise to absolute obligations, as they were to be performed independently by the mandatory, and their performance did not depend on conduct of the League or its members. Insofar as the Court was hostile to recognising any individual right of enforcement, its judgment was therefore perfectly in line with the structural approach to multilateral obligations more generally. As for its implications, the eventual decision in *South West Africa* – just as the structural approach – reduced the perspectives of inter-State litigation about matters of general concern, but instead reinforced the need for institutional solutions to these problems. Not surprisingly, subsequent stages of the Namibia dispute were handled on an institutional level, i.e. by the political organs of the United Nations.[103]

2.2 Expansive tendencies

Traditional approaches to standing cannot, however, be reduced to the structural analysis of obligations, or restrictive judgments like that in the *South West Africa case*. In order to give a balanced account of the state

[101] Brownlie (2003), 452; Crawford (2002a), 24–25.

[102] Judge Fitzmaurice's participation in the 1966 judgment – which, according to Merrills (1998), 15, 'plainly owed much to Fitzmaurice's drafting' – further supports that the *South West Africa* case has to be seen against the background of a structural approach to multilateral obligations.

[103] See Crawford (1996), 587–590, and, more generally, Dugard (1973), 376–542, for an account of the developments following the Court's 1966 judgment.

It is telling that in their joint dissent, Judges Spender and Fitzmaurice had explicitly suggested that the dispute should be dealt with by a political or technical commission such as the former Permanent Mandates Commission, the UN Trusteeship Council or the General Assembly; see ICJ Reports 1962, 467.

of the law prior to the *Barcelona Traction* judgment, it is necessary also to discuss early expansive approaches to standing. As will be shown in the following, assertions, by individual States, of a right to vindicate general interests were by no means uncommon. These assertions were not always universally welcomed; in fact, as will be shown below, claims of self-proclaimed guardians of general interests at times met with rather sceptical responses. However, even so, it is important to note that such claims were made and that they often enjoyed considerable support. Many of these debates about early attempts to enforce general interests are not duly reflected in literature, and the relation between the *erga omnes* concept and its antecedents is not always acknowledged.[104] By addressing accepted and controversial examples in point, the following discussion seeks to present a more nuanced account of the context in which the *erga omnes* concept has to be seen. Taking up the differentiation introduced above,[105] it distinguishes treaty-based and general rules of standing. Although the former remain, in principle, treaty-specific, they cannot be entirely separated from the general regime, and by ignoring them, one would fail to acknowledge the interrelation between treaty and custom, which the proceedings in the *South West Africa case* so clearly bring out.

2.2.1 *Treaty-based rules of standing*

Whatever the state of the general rules, States of course remain free to regulate the question of standing by agreeing on treaty-based *leges speciales*. Just as the general regime can influence the interpretation of treaty provisions, such special clauses can shape the general rules, and thus cannot be ignored. For the sake of convenience, the subsequent

[104] See, however, Meron (1989), 188–190 who qualifies common article 1 of the 1949 Geneva Conventions as a 'precursor of the concept of obligations *erga omnes*' (190) and draws a parallel between that concept and some of the earlier instances of standing in the absence of individual injury. Similarly, Oxman (1997), 27, has observed that 'an obligation whose breach gives rise to a legal right to complain by any state is an obligation *erga omnes*. This is *not a new idea*' (emphasis added). Delbrück (1999a), 17, and Ragazzi (1997) have also analysed prefigurations to the *erga omnes* concept in more detail. They have done so, however, on the basis of a broader understanding of the concept that does not focus on the enforcement of obligations. As a consequence, both try to establish that even prior to the Court's *Barcelona Traction* judgment, international law recognised the possibility of objective law established in the general interest. However, this is at best a first step in explaining the historical context in which the *erga omnes* concept has to be seen, and neither Delbrück nor Ragazzi elaborate on prefigurations in the field of standing.

[105] See above, section 1.2.3.

analysis will distinguish between unequivocal and ambiguous treaty provisions. As the *South West Africa case* suggests, this distinction is not categorical.[106] However, for practical reasons, it seems helpful, as the interpretation of ambiguously formulated provisions is more likely to be influenced by considerations of a general nature, and, conversely, less likely to be treaty-specific.

2.2.1.a Unequivocal treaty clauses

Even restrictive decisions like the 1966 *South West Africa* judgment did not question the right of States to deviate from the general regime by agreeing on special treaty clauses (provided that their intent to deviate was expressed in clear enough terms).[107] The most obvious way to do so is for States to provide, in unequivocal terms, that all States can respond against treaty breaches irrespective of individual injury. On the basis of the differentiation, introduced in Chapter 1, between direct and indirect rules of standing,[108] it is possible further to distinguish between (i) clauses explicitly recognising a right of all treaty parties to bring judicial proceedings, (ii) clauses explicitly recognising a right of all treaty parties to take countermeasures, and (iii) clauses implicitly recognising such a right by clarifying which parties are entitled to invoke the wrongdoing State's responsibility.

In the presence of clauses of the third type it needs to be asked whether States, in the absence of individual injury, would be entitled to invoke responsibility by way of countermeasure and/or before a court; they would therefore hardly be unequivocal. Similarly, it has been stated already that clauses explicitly authorising a right to resort to countermeasures are relatively rare.[109] Both, therefore, will be left to a side here. The situation is different as regards judicial proceedings. Even prior to the Court's *Barcelona Traction* judgment, a host of widely ratified conventions recognised, in clear and unequivocal terms, a right of all treaty parties to bring

[106] See section 2.2.1.b. As that case confirms, whether the express terms of a treaty provision are clear and unequivocal is itself is a matter of interpretation. See also Oppenheim/Jennings/Watts (1992), 1267, who observe: 'The finding whether [the wording of] a treaty is clear or not is not the starting point but the result of the process of interpretation.'

[107] Cf. ICJ Reports 1966, 32 (para. 44).

[108] See above, section 1.2.3.

[109] See above, section 1.2.3. For examples cf. article 8 of the Statute of the International Regime of Maritime Ports, 58 LNTS 301; or article 4, para. 4 of the Multilateral Agreement of Non-Scheduled Air Services in Europe, 310 UNTS 229. Similar provisions can be found in a number of Postal Conventions, such as article 35 of the 1957 Convention (364 UNTS 3), article 33 of the 1952 Convention (169 UNTS 43), or article 78 of the 1924 Convention (40 LNTS 19).

proceedings in defence of a general interest. As regards regional treaties, the Treaties establishing the European Communities and the European Convention on Human Rights provide well-known examples.[110] Outside the regional context, three classes of treaties can be distinguished.

The elaborate system of international labour law provides the first example. Although not providing for dispute settlement before a permanent international court, the ILO experience may be briefly mentioned, as it has had a lasting influence on the subsequent development of proceedings in the general interest.[111] Under article 26 of the ILO Constitution, adopted in 1919, '[a]ny of the [ILO] Members has the right to file a complaint with the International Labour Office if it is not satisfied that any other Member is securing the effective observance of any Convention which both have ratified . . . '

A member State thus can bring complaints in response to breaches of any ILO Convention in force between itself and the State against which the response is directed.[112] Complaints are dealt with by a quasi-judicial Commission of Inquiry, whose Report is subject to appeal before the ICJ.[113] Practice under article 26 is scarce, but clearly confirms that ILO members can institute proceedings in the general interest and irrespective of any individual injury.[114] ILO members facing inter-State proceedings have not contested the standing of States filing the complaints, the

[110] See then article 170 TEC (now article 227); article 142 EURATOM; article 24 ECHR (now article 33). Prior to the *Barcelona Traction judgment*, article 24 had been invoked three times, (by Greece against the United Kingdom; in *Pfunders* by Austria against Italy; and by various European countries against Greece). On the Greek case see further below, section 2.2.4.; for a survey of inter-State applications see Voeffray (2004), 142–152; Prebensen (1999), 446; Tomuschat (2003), 200–202. Practice under article 170/227 TEC is analysed by Dashwood and White (1989), 388.

[111] Ehrmann (2000), 64–69; Meron (1989), 189–190 (his note 172). Voeffray (2004), 108, aptly speaks of '*un mécanisme précurseur*'. Three of the dissenters in the 1966 *South West Africa case* expressly referred to the ILO Constitution as an early example of proceedings in defence of general interests; see ICJ Reports 1966, 226 (Wellington Koo), 252 (Tanaka), 377 (Jessup).

[112] There are currently 185 ILO Conventions (December 2004). At the time of the 1966 *South West Africa* judgment, 126 Conventions had been concluded.

[113] See articles 26–34 of the ILO Constitution; and further Golsong (1963), 40–48; Schwelb (1972), 48–49; Valticos (1987), 847; Leckie (1988), 277–289. In addition to ILO member States, the ILO Governing Body, and ILO Delegates can also file complaints. For a survey of the ILO supervisory mechanism see also Nielsen (1995), 129; Swepston (1999), 85.

[114] So far, six inter-State complaints have been registered under article 26 (some of which were settled at an early stage). In addition to the two examples mentioned in the text, these are three separate complaints by France against Panama in the 1970s and the *Tunisia/Libya complaint*. For a survey see Leckie (1988), 278–281.

first of which (by Ghana against Portugal and Portugal against Liberia) were registered in 1961.[115] In its Report in the *Portugal/Liberia complaint*, the Commission specifically stressed Portugal's 'constitutional right ... as a Member of the International Labour Organization' to bring proceedings in cases concerning 'the observance, in the territories of another State, of general welfare treaty provisions', observing that the language of article 26 was 'broad, clear and precise'.[116]

Article 26 of the ILO Constitution was by no means the only treaty clause recognising the general legal interest of all State parties in seeing the treaty observed. In the 1966 *South West Africa* judgment, the Court itself had given the example of the 1919 Polish Minorities Treaty, whose article 12 recognised the right of all Principal Allied and Associated Powers (i.e. the United States, the United Kingdom, France, Italy, and Japan) and all members of the League Council to refer to the PCIJ disputes about Poland's treatment of minorities.[117] This treaty, however, was only the first of a series of multilateral agreements comprising the comprehensive attempt at settling the minorities issue after the end of World War I.[118] Clauses modelled on its article 12 were notably contained in the Peace Treaties with Austria, Bulgaria, and Hungary;[119] the Minorities Treaties concluded with Czechoslovakia, Yugoslavia, Romania, and Greece;[120] and unilateral declarations submitted to the League Council

[115] For the Commissions' Reports see 45 ILO Bull. (1962), No. 2, Supplement II; 46 ILO Bull. (1963), No. 2, Supplement II.

[116] *Portugal/Liberia complaint*, 46 ILO Bull. (1963), No. 2, Supplement II, 155 (para. 384) (expressly quoting Judge Jessup's separate opinion in the 1962 *South West Africa case*, ICJ Reports 1962, 428).

[117] 225 CTS 412. Cf. ICJ Reports 1966, 40 (para. 67); and already above, footnote 93. While the circle of States entitled to institute proceedings was therefore restricted to treaty parties or Council members, its number remained considerable. Pursuant to article 4 of the Covenant, originally four seats on the League Council were reserved to States other than the principal allied and associated powers. In view of the growing membership of the League, this number was increased to six (in 1923), nine (in 1926), and eleven (in 1939), while Germany and Russia, when joining the League (1926 and 1934 respectively), were granted permanent seats on the Council. It follows that, for example, in 1930, fourteen States would have been entitled to institute PCIJ proceedings in response to a breach of any of the minorities treaties. On the organisation of the League Council see Weber (1995), 850.

[118] For a comprehensive survey of the system see Green (1970), 180; Musgrave (1997), 32–61; Rosting (1923), 641; Thornberry (1991), 38–52. For a comparison between minority treaties and obligations *erga omnes* see Gazzini (2000), 21–24.

[119] See 226 CTS 8 (article 69); 226 CTS 332 (article 57) and 6 LNTS 187 (article 60) respectively.

[120] See 226 CTS 170 (article 14); 226 CTS 182 (article 11); 5 LNTS 335 (article 12); 28 LNTS 244 (article 16) respectively.

by Albania, Lithuania, and Iraq.[121] Finally, Lithuania also agreed to a very similar clause in the 1924 Memel Agreement,[122] as did Poland in the 1922 Geneva Convention on Upper Silesia.[123]

All State parties to these agreements accepted two propositions. First, disputes about the treatment of minorities within their territory should be treated as international disputes, which meant that the plea of domestic jurisdiction was precluded. Secondly, States referred to in the jurisdictional clauses were entitled to bring disputes before the PCIJ.[124] In terms of a structural approach, States accepting the minorities treaties had assumed absolute obligations whose performance in no way depended on the conduct of other treaty parties. In contrast to the general rules discussed above,[125] the drafters of the minorities treaty system sought to guarantee treaty compliance by allowing for decentralised legal proceedings in the general interest.

Finally, a considerable number of treaties protecting other humanitarian issues followed the same approach. By way of example, many of the dissenters in the 1966 *South West Africa case* referred to the 1948 Genocide Convention,[126] whose article IX provides:

> Disputes between the Contracting parties relating to the interpretation, application or fulfilment of the present Convention, including those relating to the responsibility of a State for genocide or any of the other acts enumerated in article III, shall be submitted to the International Court of Justice at the request of any of the parties to the dispute.

The Genocide Convention is by no means the only universal human rights treaty convention providing for a general right of all parties to institute ICJ proceedings in response to breaches.[127] At the time of the

[121] See LNOJ 1921, 1162 (article 7); LNOJ 1922, 586 (article 9); LNOJ 1933, 1347 (article 10). In negotiations with the League, Estonia and Latvia successfully objected to an internationalisation of the minorities question, as did Turkey during the negotiations following the conclusion of the Treaty of Sèvres; see Robinson *et al.* (1943), 163–167.

[122] 29 LNTS 85 (article 17). In contrast to the above-mentioned clauses, article 17 conferred a right to institute PCIJ proceedings only on the principal allied powers.

[123] Martens, NRG, 3 Ser., Vol. 16, 645 (article 72).

[124] Schwelb (1972), 49. On the special character of the relevant jurisdictional clauses and the role of the PCIJ see further Mandelstam (1923), 400–405 and 449–453; Feinberg (1937), 600–601; Robinson *et al.* (1943), 135–150.

[125] See above, section 2.1.1.

[126] 78 UNTS 278. For references to the case see e.g. Diss.Op. Wellington Koo, ICJ Reports 1966, 228; Diss.Op. Forster, *ibid.*, 478; Diss.Op. M'Bafeno, *ibid.*, 503–504; Diss.Op. Jessup. *ibid.*, 379.

[127] It has traditionally been discussed whether article IX would allow State parties to the Genocide Convention to invoke the responsibility of other States; see e.g. the declarations by Judges Oda, Vereshchetin, and Shi in the 1996 *Genocide case*, ICJ Reports 1996, 625

1966 *South West Africa* judgment, this right was explicitly recognised (sometimes subject to prior attempts at negotiation) in any of the following conventions:

- 1926 Slavery Convention (article 8)
- 1949 Convention for the Suppression of the Traffic in Persons and of the Exploitation of the Prostitution of Others (article 22)
- 1951 Refugee Convention (article 38)
- 1952 Convention on Political Rights of Women (article 9)
- 1952 Convention on the Right of Correction (article 5)
- 1954 Convention on the Status of Stateless Persons (article 34)
- 1956 Supplementary Slavery Convention (article 10)
- 1957 Convention on the Nationality of Married Women (article 10)
- 1961 Convention on the Reduction of Statelessness (article 14).

In addition, other treaties – such as the 1965 Convention on the Elimination of all Forms of Racial Discrimination[128] or the 1960 UNESCO Convention Against Discrimination in Education[129] (article 8) – recognised a right of all parties to institute ICJ proceedings once non-judicial means of dispute settlement, specifically provided for in the respective treaties, had failed to produce results.

Unlike the ECHR or the ILO Constitution,[130] few of these conventions had, as of 1966, been the basis of formal inter-State proceedings. The much-neglected *Memel Statute case*,[131] however, shows that international courts had little difficulty in applying such clearly formulated dispute settlement clauses. When in 1932, the Lithuanian government dismissed the President of the Memel Directorate, Germany referred the matter to the attention of the League Council. Negotiations having led to no avail, the four allied powers represented on the Council invoked article 17 of the 1924 Memel Treaty[132] and asked the Court to determine

and 631 respectively. The Court's 1996 judgment answers the question in the affirmative, see *ibid.*, 616 (para. 32); Gray (1997), 692–693; and further Jørgensen (1999), 273. For comment on Judge Oda's approach, see further below, section 5.2.5.c.

128 See article 22 (requiring the prior exhaustion of treaty complaint procedures).

129 See article 8. It seems that this provision, which allows for recourse to the ICJ 'failing other means of settling the dispute', would have to be read in accordance with the 1962 Protocol to the Convention, whose article 12 establishes an inter-State complaints procedure. Cf. further Leckie (1988), 269–271.

130 On which above, footnotes 110 and 114–116.

131 For the Court's judgment on preliminary objections see PCIJ, Ser. A/B, No. 47 (1932), 243; for the merits *ibid.*, No. 49, 294. Lamers (1995), 1431, provides a brief summary of the case (without, however, addressing the problem of standing). For a discussion of that aspect see Diss.Op. Jessup, ICJ Reports 1966, 375–377; Voeffray (2004), 49–52.

132 See footnote 122.

whether the Lithuanian conduct had been in line with the provisions of the Memel Statute. Neither of the applicants was in any sense specially affected by the events in Memel, as the British Agent conceded when stating: '[T]he Applicant Powers are not here [before the Court] to defend their particular interests, nor to maintain any rights of their own which they allege to have been infringed. Their only interest is to see that the Convention to which they are Parties is carried out by Lithuania . . .'[133] In view of the clear and unambiguous formulation of article 17, neither the Court nor the defendant considered this to be problematic. The *Memel Statute case* thus constitutes an early example of proceedings brought in defence of a general interest. By implication, it is unlikely that the other - similarly unequivocal - jurisdictional clauses referred to in the previous section should have given rise to problems.[134]

The preceding survey shows that such jurisdictional clauses were by no means uncommon. Again, it needs to be stressed that their adoption is a matter of treaty law and does not necessarily affect the general rules of standing. Also, one can hardly fail to notice that practice was far from regular. Nevertheless, the sheer number of treaties allowing for decentralised responses in defence of a general interest, as well as the existing instances of practice described in the previous section, cast doubt on President Winiarski's above-quoted dictum according to which a legal interest *necessarily* had to be personal and direct.[135] On the basis of the preceding discussion, the least that can be said is that prior to the *Barcelona Traction* judgment, a great number of treaties had adopted a very different approach.

2.2.1.b Equivocal clauses broadly interpreted: the *Wimbledon case*

Even in the presence of ambiguous jurisdictional clauses, the position was not as clear as the 1966 *South West Africa* judgment might suggest. When faced with treaty clauses that were formulated in equivocal terms, international courts did not always accept a presumption against standing in the general interest. The 1962 *South West Africa* judgment, which has been addressed above, is an obvious example for a broader approach, but of course has to be seen in the light of its subsequent

133 PCIJ, Ser. C, No. 59, 173. Similar observations were made by the Italian agent (*ibid.*, at 190).

134 In his dissent in the case of the *Minority Schools in Upper Silesia*, Judge Huber similarly had little difficulty to accept the broad formulation of article 72 of the Geneva Convention on Upper Silesia, see PCIJ, Ser. A, No. 15 (1928), 50.

135 Cf. ICJ Reports 1962, 456.

reversal. *South West Africa* (1962) however was in line with the decision in the *Wimbledon case*, in which the PCIJ interpreted a vaguely formulated jurisdictional clause in the broadest possible terms.[136]

In the circumstances of the case, the SS *Wimbledon*, a British steamship chartered by a French company and shipping war material to the Polish port of Danzig, was denied access to the Kiel Canal by German authorities.[137] Germany argued that because Poland was at war with Russia, for Germany to allow passage would be in violation of the rules of neutrality. The United Kingdom, France, Italy, and Japan took the case to the PCIJ, arguing that under articles 380–386 of the Treaty of Versailles, Germany had to permit access to vessels of all nations. Article 380 of that treaty, to which Russia was not a party, provided that 'The Kiel Canal and its approaches shall be maintained free and open to the vessels of commerce and war of all nations at peace with Germany on terms of entire equality.'

On substance, the Court controversially held that the law of neutrality did not justify a violation of article 380 of the Treaty of Versailles; Germany thus had been wrong to deny access to the Kiel Canal.[138] Notwithstanding the problems of this interpretation,[139] the Court's elaboration on rules of standing is of greater relevance here. In order to establish standing, the four applicants had relied on article 386 of the Treaty of Versailles, which provided that: 'In the event of violation of any of the conditions of Articles 380 to 386, or of disputes as to the

[136] PCIJ, Ser. A, No. 1 (1923), 15. On the case see von Münch (2000), 1482; Ragazzi (1997), 24–27; Klein (1980) 6–9; Wolgast (1926); Wehberg (1923), 1255, 1277, 1301.

[137] See the summary of facts contained in the judgment, PCIJ Reports, Ser. A, No. 1 (1923), 18–20.

A similar incident had occurred in September 1920, when the Danish vessel *Dorrit* (also chartered by a French company and shipping military material to Poland) was denied access to the Kiel Canal by German authorities; cf. the diplomatic correspondence attached to the Wimbledon judgement, PCIJ, Ser. C, No. 3, vol. suppl., 20.

[138] In view of the majority, the Kiel Canal had been 'permanently dedicated to the whole world', which meant that passage by war ships or vessels shipping war material was not incompatible with the neutrality of the riparian sovereign; see PCIJ Reports, Ser. A, No. 1 (1923), 28. Contrast, however, the dissenting opinions of Judges Anzilotti and Huber and Judge *ad hoc* Schücking, *ibid.*, 35 and 43 and further von Münch (2000), 1483–1484; Wehberg (1923), 1301–1302.

The concept of permanent dedication has often been interpreted as an early example of objective treaties or status regimes: see McNair (1957), 28–30; Klein (1980), 6–9; Ragazzi, 24–27; Delbrück (1999a), 20–21. On this aspect see below, section 2.2.2.b.

[139] For example, the majority assumed that article 380 of the Treaty Versailles forced Germany to disregard the rules of neutrality *vis-à-vis* the Soviet Union, i.e. the belligerent State affected by the shipping of war material to Poland. This broad interpretation is astonishing given the non-participation of the Soviet Union in the Treaty of Versailles.

interpretation of these Articles, *any interested Power* can appeal to the jurisdiction instituted for the purpose by the League of Nations.'[140]

The original meaning of this passage has never been fully clarified. It is tempting to argue that article 386 intended to allow inter-State proceedings under more lenient conditions than the regime of general international law, requiring only the showing of an interest (as opposed to a legal interest).[141] On the other hand, given the vagueness of the term 'interest', this choice of terminology would have invited misunderstandings. Some commentators have suggested that by referring to 'interests', the drafters had merely wanted to affirm the general regime of standing, the distinction between legal and other interests not having been fully explored at the time of Versailles.[142]

In any event, the ease with which the Court admitted all four claims is surprising. Of course, the United Kingdom, as the State of registry of the SS *Wimbledon*, was entitled to espouse claims for diplomatic protection.[143] Equally, France could claim to be specially affected by Germany's conduct, as the charter firm bearing the financial loss was incorporated under French law.[144] Italy and Japan however had no interest in the subject matter other than the general interest of all State parties in the observance of the treaty regime. Not surprisingly therefore, Germany raised the question of standing.[145] In response, neither Japan nor Italy thought it

140 Emphasis added. Article 37 of the Court's Statute makes clear that the reference to 'jurisdictions instituted by the League of Nations' was meant to establish the jurisdiction of the PCIJ.

141 Günther (1999), 46–47; Hutchinson (1988), 179–184; Ragazzi (1997), 25; see also the ILC's introductory commentary to Part Three Chapter I ASR, para. 5 (mistakenly referring to article 396). This reading is supported by the fact that the Court did adopt a stricter test when deciding about Poland's request for intervention under article 62 of the ICJ Statute (requiring the showing of 'an interest of a legal nature'); see PCIJ, Ser. A, No. 1 (1923), 11; and cf. Salvioli (1926), 12–13.

142 Bos (1957), 217–218. Graefrath (1984), 74–75 and Gray (1987), 211–212, also seem to accept that the PCIJ's interpretation of article 386 is of general relevance.

143 On the nationality of ships, and the right of flag States to exercise diplomatic protection for ships see articles 91, 94 LOSC; and further von Münch (1979), 231.

144 In terms of the modern law, this would have been problematic, as the flag State's right of diplomatic protection is often held to be exclusive; see e.g. Geck (1992), 1055; ITLOS, Saiga case, 38 ILM (1998) 1323; but contrast von Münch (1979), 246–247. As appears from the German pleadings as well as from contemporary literature, France was held to be the State mainly affected by wrongful act; see e.g. German counter-memorial, PCIJ, Ser. C, No. 3, Vol. III, 42; Salvioli (1926) 11–12; Hutchinson (1988), 179–180 (his note 94).

145 German counter-memorial, PCIJ, Ser. C, No. 3, Vol. III, p. 42: 'Le Gouvernement allemand croit devoir laisser à l'appréciation de la Cour la question de savoir si les gouvernements des Puissances alliés qui, conjointement avec le Gouvernement

necessary to establish in which respect they were interested in the outcome of the proceedings. The Court seemed to share their view, as it confined itself to observing that 'each of the applicant parties has a clear interest in the execution of the provisions relating to the Kiel Canal, since they all possess fleets and merchant vessels flying their respective flags.'[146]

Focusing on the possession of fleets and merchant vessels, the Court implicitly rejected other possible interpretations of the notion of interest. For example, it would have been certainly defensible had the Court required applicants to show that their economic interests were at stake, that their shipping depended on the free passage through the Kiel Canal, or that they were situated in the same geographic region as Germany. Instead, under the liberal test formulated by the Court, *every* seafaring State that was a party to the Treaty of Versailles would have been entitled to enforce the rules contained in articles 380 to 386 against Germany in an international forum.[147] As commentators did not fail to observe,[148] this was a remarkably broad interpretation of article 386. Even if the actual formulation of article 386 facilitated this approach, it is evident that in 1923, the PCIJ was far less hostile to the idea of a general right of State parties to institute judicial proceedings in response to treaty violations, than its successor was to be forty-three years later.

français, ont introduit la présente requête, y étaient autorisés.' Cf. Wolgast (1926), 28–29; Hutchinson (1988), 179 (his note 91).

146 PCIJ, Ser. A, No. 1 (1923), 20.

147 Given the objective character of the regime (which after all, had been 'permanently dedicated to the whole world'), it is tempting to speculate whether States not parties to the Treaty of Versailles would have been entitled to institute proceedings. The Court in *Wimbledon* did not have to address the issue. It is, however, discussed below, in the context of status treaties (section 2.2.2.b).

148 See e.g. Salvioli (1926), 11 (who found the Court's interpretation 'un peu excessive'); Wolgast (1926), 29 (arguing that the Court had relied on an interest of a non-legal nature); cf. also Voeffray (2004), 48–49; Gray (1987), 211. In view of some writers, the Court ought to have distinguished between the two cases of standing mentioned in article 386, namely violation complaints and requests for interpretation. Countries that had not sustained pecuniary losses, i.e. Italy, Japan, and the United Kingdom, in their view, would have been restricted to bringing requests for interpretation, see Salvioli (1926), 11–12; Wolgast (1926), 29–30. However, this view fails to take into account that under the express terms of article 386, applicants had to establish an 'interest' for both violations complaints and requests for interpretation. Also, not only did the Court treat all four applications alike, but it is clear from the proceedings that all four applicants submitted claims for an indemnisation of France, which suggests that they viewed their claims as violations complaints.

2.2.2 *The position in the absence of special treaty regulations*

Broad approaches to standing, even prior to the *Barcelona Traction case*, were, however, not limited to special treaty-based rules. In the absence of explicit clauses, a number of (customary or conventional) categories of obligations were said to be generally enforceable by all States. It must be conceded that these categories were often narrowly defined. What is more, the right of States to respond to breaches irrespective of individual injury was not always undisputed. Nevertheless, as the subsequent discussion shows, the general rules of standing were not monolithic, but capable of accommodating general interests of States. More particularly, four types of examples can be distinguished: interdependent obligations, status treaties, international judgments, and basic obligations of a humanitarian character. These will be addressed in turn.

2.2.2.a Interdependent obligations

The concept of interdependent obligations, which has been discussed already,[149] constitutes the first example in point. As has been stated, even under the restrictive structural analysis of multilateral obligations, interdependent obligations were the exception that confirmed the rule. Ever since the ILC's debates on the law of treaties, it seems to have been generally agreed that each State bound by a (customary or conventional) interdependent obligation is entitled to respond to any kind of breach of that obligation, irrespective of individually sustained injury.[150] Interdependent obligations therefore constitute the first (narrowly defined) category of obligations in whose observance all States have a legal interest.

2.2.2.b Status treaties

A similar trend can be discerned with regard to the rights of States to respond to breaches of so-called 'status treaties'.[151] The concept (also referred to as 'objective regimes') is an attempt to explain general (objective) effects of treaties, i.e. effects extending beyond the circle of State parties. Despite support in international jurisprudence, it has

[149] See above, section 2.1.1.

[150] See e.g. article 60, para. 2(c) VCLT; article 42(b)(ii) ASR.

[151] On the concept see Wyrozumska (1986), 251; Subedi (1994), 162; Mosler (1980), 221–245; Simma (1986b), 189; Ballreich (1954), 1; Ballreich (2000), 945 ; Delbrück (1999a), 29–35; Crawford (1979), 301–319; Roxburgh (1917); McNair (1957), 23–36; and, for a comprehensive discussion, Klein (1980).

remained controversial, as it is hard to reconcile with one of the key principles of treaty law: the maxim *pacta tertiis nec nocent nec prosunt*. This controversy has overshadowed the fact that the legal rules governing status treaties are exceptional in yet another respect, namely as regards their enforceability.[152] As will be shown, there is support for the view that where a treaty creates an objective status, all States are entitled to react against status breaches. Before addressing this departure from the general rules of standing, it is necessary briefly to summarise the debates about the concept as such.

Background

The concept of status regimes is based on the idea that in exceptional circumstances, States, by concluding a treaty, can lay down general rules defining the status of a particular piece of territory. Contrary to normal treaty law, these treaties are said to give rise to objective law, binding upon treaty members as well as third parties. Despite the fundamental character of the *pacta tertiis* rule, objective effects of treaties have indeed been recognised in exceptional situations. Treaties of cession, boundary treaties, or, more generally, treaties creating rights *in rem* (such as servitudes or other rights running with the land),[153] are generally held to be binding on – or at least opposable to – third States.[154] Status treaties are different from these dispositive or conveyance-type treaties in that the third-party effect is not incidental, but intentional: creating a generally binding (objective) regime is the very essence of the treaty.[155] In a now-classic dictum, Judge McNair described this in the following terms:

[152] For one of the rare discussions in literature see Klein (1980), 238–254.

[153] Whether the concept of servitudes forms part of international law is much discussed (contrast e.g. O'Connell (1970), Vol. I, 545–552 and Brownlie (2003) 366–368). There is, however, no denying that States, by agreement, have conveyed certain aspects of their territorial supremacy to other States, and that the easements or rights created by these agreements have, under certain conditions been held to 'run with the land'. Whether one describes them as servitudes thus seems largely a terminological question; see Dahm/Delbrück/Wolfrum (1989), 340.

[154] Verdross/Simma (1984), 477–478; Tomuschat (1988), 12–13; McNair (1961), 256; Klein (1980), 184–185; Bastid (1985), 152–153; but contrast Schwarzenberger (1957), 459.

[155] Waldock, Third Report, YbILC 1964, Vol. II, 32 (para. 15); Tomuschat (1988), 12–13. In contrast, treaties of cession or boundary treaties do not usually involve rights of third States. Exceptionally, such rights are recognised in special treaties; see e.g. article 1 of Protocol to the 1929 Treaty of Lima (94 LNTS 402) between Peru and Chile, pursuant to which both States agree not to cede parts of the formerly disputed territory without the other party's consent.

From time to time it happens that a group of great Powers, or a large number of States both great and small, assume a power to create by a multilateral treaty some new international regime or status, which soon acquires a degree of acceptance and durability extending beyond the limits of the actual contracting parties, and giving it an objective existence.[156]

The concept is said to have its roots in the nineteenth century, when the Great (European) Powers, acting within the Concert of Europe or the Holy Alliance, alleged a regulatory competence for matters of international peace and security.[157] As far as twentieth-century jurisprudence is concerned, the *Aaland*,[158] *Wimbledon*,[159] *South West Africa (Status)*[160] and *Reparations for Injuries cases*[161] are usually relied upon in support, since each of them recognises certain third-party effects of treaties. Based on this evidence, the ILC's Special Rapporteurs Fitzmaurice and Waldock suggested that the concept be codified in the future convention on the law of treaties.[162] Waldock's draft article 63, which defined the concept, however, failed to muster sufficient support within the ILC and was eventually withdrawn.[163] During the debates, members had stressed that the concept was open to abuse and difficult to define,[164] and that the exception to the *pacta tertiis* rule could not be convincingly explained.[165] Under the eventual provisions of the Vienna Convention,

[156] South West Africa (Status) case, Sep.Op. McNair, ICJ Reports 1950, 153.

[157] Delbrück (1999a), 20; and cf. Crawford (1979), 308.

[158] LNOJ, Special Supplement No. 3, Oct. 1920; and further below, section 2.2.2.b.

[159] PCIJ, Ser. A, No. 1 (1923); and further above, section 2.2.1.b.

[160] ICJ Reports 1950, 132–133, where the Court held that the South West African mandate remained in force after the demise of the League, even though the UN had not automatically succeeded into the legal position of its predecessor. To justify this finding, the Court stressed the objective character of the mandate.

[161] ICJ Reports 1949, 185, where the Court held that the UN's international legal personality was opposable to third States (such as Israel). In the view of the Court, 'fifty States, representing the vast majority of the members of the international community, had the power, in conformity with international law, to bring into being an entity possessing objective international legal personality'.

[162] Fitzmaurice, Fifth Report, YbILC 1960, Vol. II, 75–107 (commentaries to draft articles 14, 17, 18, 26); Waldock, Third Report, YbILC 1964, Vol. II, 5–65 (in particular commentary to draft article 63).

[163] YbILC 1964, Vol. II, 26.

[164] See e.g. YbILC 1964, Vol. I, 100 (para. 7) (de Luna); 101 (para. 22) (Jimenez de Arechaga); 103 (para. 45) (Tunkin). As is clear from draft article 63, para. 1, Waldock intended to restrict the concept to territorial or other geographically defined regimes, but had to accept that the *Reparations for Injuries case* did not fall into this category, see his commentary to draft article 63, para. 14, YbILC 1964, Vol. II, 31.

[165] As for the possible explanations or justifications of the concept, Waldock suggested a reverse rule on consent, pursuant to which failure to protest within a fixed period of time

third-party effects of treaties thus depend on the consent of that State,[166] or on the subsequent generation of a rule of custom.[167]

While the present state of the concept of status regimes therefore is open to doubt, it would be unjustified to exclude it from the present study altogether. For once, the ILC's decision not to adopt draft article 63 need not be interpreted as an outright rejection of the concept, which, since the conclusion of the Vienna Convention, has continually been invoked (e.g. in relation to the Antarctic Treaty, the 1992 Cambodian Settlement Agreement, or the Panama Canal).[168] What is more, the concept clearly enjoyed much support in the period prior to the Court's *Barcelona Traction* judgment, and ignoring it would convey an incomplete picture of the contemporary debate about standing. Remaining doubts notwithstanding, it therefore seems necessary to analyse how supporters of the concept of status treaties approached the question of responses against breaches.

Standing to react against breaches

When analysing the rights of States to respond to breaches of status treaties, it is necessary to distinguish between the rights of State parties and other, third States. Whether State parties have standing to respond is a matter of treaty interpretation.[169] In view of the allegedly objective

implied tacit consent to be bound (see draft article 63, para.2, YbILC 1964, Vol. II, 26–27). Others have accepted that States claiming to act in a general interest could exercise a semi-legislative function. This in turn has been based on concepts such as *negotiorum gestio*, trust, or representation; see e.g. Sep.Op. McNair, ICJ Reports 1950, 153; *Reparations for Injuries case*, ICJ Reports 1949, 185; Ballreich (1954), 19; and Delbrück (1999a), 29–35 (who proposes ways of generating 'public interest norms' in a legitimate process).

For an analysis of these approaches see Klein (1980), 191–216; Simma (1986b), 192–208.

166 Articles 35, 36 VCLT. Where treaties give rise to rights of third States, such consent may be presumed; see article 36, para. 2.

167 See article 38 VCLT (then draft article 34), which ILC members considered to be sufficient to cover the problem of status regimes (YbILC 1966, Vol. II, 230). In reality, article 38 merely states the obvious, namely that treaty rules may develop into rules of general international law. However, this can hardly be considered a case of third-party effects of a treaty, since third States are simply bound by the terms of the customary rule, see Aust (2001), 210–211; and Chinkin (1993), 34–35 (who describes the articles 34 to 38 VCLT as 'reductivist and formalist').

168 402 UNTS 71; 16 ILM (1977), 1022; 31 ILM (1992), 180, respectively. All of these treaties are discussed by Subedi (1994), 177–185. On the ILC's decision not to adopt draft article 63, and the continued relevance of the concept, see Sinclair (1984), 105–106; Reuter (1995), 114–116 (paras. 190–194), Aust (2001), 208–209.

169 See Klein (1980), 240–242, who argues for a right of all State parties to respond against breaches irrepective of individual injury. More generally, the same author has suggested that obligations arising under status regimes should be classified as

character of status treaties, the more interesting question is whether third States not party to the regime-creating treaty should have the same right. Unless the breach had specifically affected one of them, this would mean the recognition of a general interest of non-parties in seeing a treaty regime observed. International practice, while not conclusively settling the issue, indeed suggests that this should be the case. The United States' formal protest against violations of the Congo River regime[170] – to which the United States had not acceded – provides an early example, but admittedly stops short of any coercive interference requiring justification. Waldock's draft article 63 points in the same direction. Under that provision, third States, once integrated into the status regime and bound by its provisions, should assume considerable enforcement powers. Under para. 3(b), they notably were 'entitled to invoke the provisions of the régime and to exercise any general right which it may confer, subject to the terms and conditions of the treaty.'[171] The broad approach that informs this provision is in marked contrast to para. 4, under which only 'substantial[ly] interest[ed]' third States were entitled to participate in treaty amendments.[172]

As it failed to agree on the concept as such, the ILC hardly discussed these provisions. Nevertheless, it is interesting to note that draft article 63 as the most elaborate attempt to spell out the legal regime of status treaties recognised a right of non-State parties to respond against breaches. At least for Waldock, recognising the concept of status regimes therefore seemed to imply the recognition of a general right of response against breaches.

The Report of the Committee of Jurists in the *Aaland Islands* dispute confirms this approach.[173] Established by the League

interdependent obligations, which would lead to the same result; see Klein (1980), 234–237; and cf. above, section 2.2.2.a. on interdependent obligations.

170 See Roxburgh (1917), 49–50, Waldock, YbILC 1964, Vol. II, 29 (para. 9). Chapters I and IV of the 1885 Berlin General Act (165 CTS 485) had guaranteed the freedom of commerce and navigation on the Congo River.

171 YbILC 1964, Vol. II, 27. In contrast, Waldock's predecessor, Sir Gerald Fitzmaurice, had proposed to limit this right to States 'directly interested' in the matter: see his draft article 29, para. 2, YbILC 1960, Vol. II, 83. Waldock's approach is discussed by Klein (1980), 244–247.

172 See para. 24 of Waldock's commentary, YbILC 1964, Vol. II, 34.

173 'Report of the Committee of Jurists entrusted by the Council of the League of Nations with the task of giving an advisory opinion upon the legal aspects of the Aaland Islands Question', LNOJ, Special Supplement No. 3, October 1920. The League Council subsequently endorsed the findings of the Report in its Resolution of 24 June 1921.
On the dispute see Modeen (1992), 1; Suontausa (1950–51), 741–752; Klein (1980), 2–6; Ragazzi (1997), 28–37; Barros (1968); Castrèn (1960), 107–116. From the rich inter-War literature see in particular de Visscher (1921), 35; de Stael-Holstein (1922),

Council,[174] the Committee was asked to determine Finland's obligations relating to the demilitarisation of the Aaland islands, and thereby to help settle a Swedish-Finnish dispute that had arisen at the end of World War I.[175] Pursuant to article I of the 1856 Aaland Islands Convention,[176] concluded between Russia, France, and the United Kingdom and annexed to the Paris Peace Treaty of the same year,[177] Russia (as the then sovereign) had undertaken not to fortify the Aaland islands. In 1917, newly independent Finland – a third State in relation to both conventions – took possession of the archipelago. The Committee had to inquire whether Finland was obliged to observe the demilitarised status. It held that it was, as article I of the Aaland Island Convention created 'true objective law' that had been 'laid down in European interests'.[178] From this, it followed that not only Finland, but 'any State in possession of the Islands must conform to the obligations … arising out of the system of demilitarisation.'[179] While this pronouncement indeed provides powerful support for the concept of status treaties, it does not answer the question whether Sweden, which just as Finland was party to neither of the relevant conventions, had standing to raise the matter. As a preliminary issue, it may be pointed out that although the dispute had been referred to the Committee by the League Council, the proceedings were conducted in an adversarial way. Although

424–462; Steinmayr (1927); Söderhjelm (1928); Maury (1930); Vortisch (1933); Remsperger (1933).

[174] 'Resolution adopted at the seventh session of the Council of the League of Nations held in London from 9th to 12th July 1920', 5 LNOJ (July–August 1920), 249–250. The Commission consisted of three members, namely Professors Larnaude (France, President), Struycken (Netherlands) and Huber (Switzerland).

[175] This was the second of two questions put to the Committee. The first concerned Finland's obligations *vis-à-vis* the Swedish-speaking population and the scope of its domestic jurisdiction. The Committee's findings on this issue have had a considerable influence on the development of the modern law of self-determination; see Cassese (1995), 27–31.

[176] 15 NRG, 1st Ser., 788–790.

[177] 15 NRG, 1st Ser., 770–781. The treaty was concluded between Austria, France, the United Kingdom, Prussia, Russia, Sardinia, and the Ottoman Empire.

[178] See LNOJ, Special Supplement No. 3, Oct. 1920, 17 and 19 respectively. Among the arguments advanced in support of this finding were the following: (i) the strategic importance of the Aaland islands, (ii) the reference, in the preliminary proceedings to the 1856 treaty, to the 'interests of Europe'; (iii) the incorporation of the Aaland Convention into the framework of the Paris Peace Treaty; (iv) the wording of the preamble of the Aaland Convention; and (v) the interpretation given to it by the British Foreign Secretary, Lord Clarendon, in a speech before the House of Lords of which expressly mentions the 'national law of Europe'.

[179] LNOJ, Special Supplement No. 3, Oct. 1920, 19. This was much criticised in literature; see e.g. Steinmayr (1927), 32–33.

Sweden therefore was not an applicant in the technical sense, the Committee applied the standards governing contentious cases and required Sweden to establish a legal interest.[180]

In order to establish standing, Sweden sought to show that it had a special interest in the legal status of the Aaland islands. Its main contention was that the provisions on non-fortification were a servitude that had been introduced into the convention in its favour. Additionally, it claimed that its right to vindicate rights of the Aaland islanders on the international plane had been accepted in international practice. The Committee rejected the first of these contentions and held the second to be of ancillary relevance only.[181] When nevertheless admitting the claim, it did not rely on Sweden's allegedly special status, but held that '*every State interested* has the right to insist upon compliance with [the provisions of the 1856 Convention].'[182]

Although the term is not defined in the Report, the reference to 'interested States' signals a broad approach. Not only had the Committee referred to the interests of a number of different States; what is more, it had expressly observed that the Aaland status had been 'laid down the European interests'.[183] Against the background of this statement, and given the rejection of Sweden's attempts to establish a special legal position, it is difficult to see how the Committee should have taken a different view on claims brought by other European States. Quite to the contrary, its approach to questions of law enforcement competence suggests that it held the objective regime, created by the 1856 Convention, to be generally enforceable by all European States.[184] This is all the more remarkable since the Committee deliberately avoided relying on narrower grounds.

[180] LNOJ, Special Supplement No. 3, Oct. 1920, 18–19; and see de Visscher (1921), 40; Remsperger (1933), 18. It can also not be argued that Finland had accepted the Swedish right to bring the claim. While it agreed to an international resolution of the dispute, it maintained its objections, based on article 15, para. 8 of the Covenant, against the jurisdiction of the Commission.

[181] LNOJ, Special Supplement No. 3, Oct. 1920, 18–19. Contrast e.g. Steinmayr (1927), 21–23 (on the question of servitudes); and Maury (1930), 164 (on the relevance of international practice since 1856). Sweden's position as regards the 1856 Convention is discussed in detail by Vortisch (1933), 157–159, and Söderhjelm (1928), 100–110.

[182] LNOJ, Special Supplement No. 3, Oct. 1920, 19, point 2 of the *dispositif* (emphasis added).

[183] See LNOJ, Special Supplement No. 3, Oct. 1920, 17–18 and 19 (describing Sweden, Finland, and Germany as 'the Powers most directly interested on account of their geographical position', and Russia as 'an interested Party').

[184] Klein (1980), 245–247. This was criticised in literature as losing sight of the special situation of Sweden, see e.g. de Stael-Holstein (1922), 455.

The concept of status treaties therefore is another example of expansive tendencies in the field of standing. Although controversies about the concept as such have obscured the analysis of its enforcement regime, it has been shown that authorities supporting it were prepared to recognise a right of all States, including non-parties, to respond to breaches of the treaty-defined status.

2.2.2.c The duty to comply with judgments of the International Court of Justice

Broad approaches to standing were, however, not limited to complex legal concepts such as interdependent obligations and obligations arising under status regimes. A third example, discussed prior to the Court's *Barcelona Traction* judgment, was based on a relatively straightforward proposition. There was support for the view that all States should have a legal interest in seeing ICJ judgments observed, and should be entitled to enforce them by way of self-help. The crucial evidence derives from the proceedings in the *Monetary Gold case*, opposing Italy and the members of the Tripartite Commission established under the 1946 Paris Reparation Agreement and charged with restoring gold looted by Nazi Germany to its rightful owners.[185] Before the Commission, Italy and Albania each claimed title to Albanian gold reserves removed from Rome during World War II. The three States forming the Tripartite Commission – France, the United States, and the United Kingdom – decided to settle the question by way of arbitration, agreeing that should Albania's claim prevail, the gold would be transferred to the United Kingdom in partial fulfilment of the damages awarded in the *Corfu Channel case*.[186] At the time of the decision, none of the governments sought to justify this approach. Justification of course was readily available for the United Kingdom, which, as a party to the *Corfu Channel case*, would have been entitled to take coercive measures in order to enforce it.[187] Any such action by France and the United States, however, would have meant an infringement of Albania's rights.

[185] ICJ Reports 1954, 19.

[186] ICJ Reports 1949, 4. On the *Monetary Gold case* see Wühler (1997), 445. For the text of the Washington Agreement, which provided the basis for the *Monetary Gold arbitration*, see 91 UNTS 21; for the arbitral award see RIAA, Vol. XII, 13.

[187] See above, section 1.3.2, for comment.

It was only when Italy initiated ICJ proceedings against the arbitral award,[188] that the three governments justified their conduct. According to counsel for the United Kingdom,

> It must ... be a matter of importance to the family of nations ... that the judgments of the highest international tribunal ... should be respected and carried out. [...] [A]ll countries are, if not bound, at any rate entitled to take all such reasonable and legitimate steps as may be open to them to prevent such an occurrence, and either individually or by common action to do what they can to ensure that judgments ... are carried out.[189]

And further,

> On account of the fact that there was an outstanding judgment of the Court against Albania in favour of the United Kingdom which had never been satisfied, and in view of *the general interest ... which all countries can be regarded as having to further the implementation of the Court's judgments* – it would have been possible on these grounds for the three Governments to direct that the share attributable to Albania in the Gold Pool should be transferred to the United Kingdom.[190]

The assertion of law enforcement competence in the general interest could hardly have been formulated in clearer terms. Finding that it lacked jurisdiction, the Court did not address the issue. Its subsequent jurisprudence, stressing the *inter partes* character of proceedings, suggests that the defendants' claim may be problematic, as does article 94, para. 2 UNC, which distinguishes between States parties to the proceedings and third States.[191] As has been stated already, the ILC, in its work on State responsibility, has also argued that international judgments could be enforced by litigants only.[192] Nevertheless, it would be wrong to treat the above-quoted remarks as an isolated deviation from

[188] Jurisdiction was founded on a joint declaration accompanying the Washington Agreement, which allowed Italy to challenge the award before the ICJ; see 24 Department of State Bulletin (1951), 785. That Italy first initiated proceedings and then raised preliminary objections against the Court's jurisdiction (which resulted in the recognition, by the Court, of the absent third State rule) is one of the more remarkable facets of the case.

[189] ICJ Pleadings, *Monetary Gold case*, 126.

[190] *ibid.*, 131 (emphasis added).

[191] On article 94, para. 2 UNC see above, section 1.3.2.a, and further Sicilianos (1990), 104–105. As for the Court's subsequent jurisprudence, see notably the *Continental Shelf (Libya-Malta) case*, where the majority stressed that 'the principles and rules of international law found by the Court to be applicable [in a given case] ... cannot be relied on by the Parties against any other State'; ICJ Reports 1984, 26 (para. 42).

[192] Commentary to article 42 ASR, para. 7; and already draft article 40, paras. 2(b) and 2(c) of the ILC's 1996 text. See further above, section 1.3.2.a.

an otherwise accepted rule.[193] The above statement was not disputed at the time and also echoes frequent calls for compliance with ICJ decisions.[194] As for article 94, para. 2 UNC, the provision may be of lesser value than is sometimes maintained, as it does not address enforcement through self-help, but merely regulates which States are entitled to bring matters to the attention of the Security Council. In the light of this evidence, it seems at least arguable that States other than the States parties to the proceedings should have a right to enforce ICJ judgments.[195] While practice is undoubtedly scarce, and leaves many questions unaddressed,[196] the above-quoted remarks show that broader approaches to standing were discussed in relation to ICJ judgments.

2.2.2.d Basic humanitarian standards

The same applies to a fourth category of obligations: those protecting basic humanitarian standards. For centuries, it has been discussed whether States should be entitled to protect foreign citizens suffering under an inhumane regime. In terms of the academic debate, this category was by far the most disputed. To give but one example, Bluntschli, listing wrongful acts that should give rise to a general right to respond, argued that all States were entitled to respond against States practising slavery or brutally repressing the freedom of religion.[197] Conversely, when von Bulmerincq warned against intervention in the

[193] This, however, seems to be done by Alland (1994), 363; and Sicilianos (1990), 104–105. For critical comment see also Oliver (1955), 216.

[194] See e.g. GA Res. 43/49 (1988) (relating to the ICJ's *Nicaragua* judgment); and the institutional mechanisms referred to above, section 1.3.2.a. It should also be noted that international judgments have at times been enforced in courts of third countries, see *notably Anglo-Iranian Oil Co. v. Jaffrate (The Rose Mary)*, 20 ILR 316; and further Jenks (1964), 712–717; O'Connell (1990), 933–934.

[195] See also Elagab (1987), 58; Schachter (1960), 11–12; O'Connell (1990), 930–940; Akehurst (1970), 13–14; Jenks (1964), 705–706; Rosenne (1985b), 142. Rosenne's subsequent statement that 'in general, there is substance in the doctrinal view that a State can act as the agent of the international community and of international law, even when acting on its own account' is however altogether too sweeping.

[196] For example, it has been argued that States not parties to the proceedings should also be entitled to enforce judgments of international courts other than the ICJ; see Schachter (1960), 12; Akehurst (1970), 14. Another question is whether the right of response of other States should depend on a prior authorisation by the State party to the proceedings, or whether it exists independently (as the above-quoted statement seems to suggest).

[197] Bluntschli (1868), 265 (§ 472).

name of world justice, he was not primarily concerned with, say, a general right to enforce interdependent obligations (a category only to be devised in the next century), but mainly argued against coercive interference for humanitarian purposes.[198]

Actual practice in the field is manifold but inconclusive. It seems difficult to deny that States have, from time to time, responded against inhumane regimes even though they were not specially affected by the allegedly wrongful conduct. As regards countermeasures, the economic sanctions, by Ghana and Malaysia against South Africa in 1960, and by various European States against Greece in 1967, provide two illustrative examples. In the former case, Ghana and Malaysia sought to increase pressure on the South African apartheid regime by adopting economic sanctions. Following recommendations by the Second Conference of African Independent States, both countries banned all imports from South Africa, while Ghana also imposed an export boycott.[199] As will be discussed more fully below, such economic boycotts do not as such violate international law.[200] However, the situation is different under the rules of GATT, whose article XI prohibits quantitative trade restrictions such as quotas or embargoes.[201] All three countries being GATT members, the measures adopted by Malaysia and Ghana *prima facie* violated international law, and required justification. Since the GATT-specific exceptions did not apply, both countries had to justify their conduct as a countermeasure.[202] As the background to the measures suggests, Ghana and Malaysia claimed a right to take countermeasures because they considered that South Africa's policy of apartheid violated basic human rights of the majority of South Africans.

In the view of most European States, the same was true of the Greek military regime established in April 1967. As is well known, the military *coup* led to the so-called 'Greek case' before the European Human Rights Commission, in which Denmark, Norway, Sweden, and the Netherlands sought, and obtained, a pronouncement that the military regime was responsible for systematic violations of political freedoms and judicial guarantees, as well as for acts of torture and other

198 van Bulmerinq (1889), 84–85.

199 For a summary of the relevant measures see Rousseau (1960), 804–806.

200 See further below, Chapter 6.

201 On article XI GATT see e.g. Senti (2000), 244–254; and cf. GATT *Analytical Index* (1994), Vol. 1, 313–354, for a survey of the relevant case-law.

202 See also Dzida (1997), 252; Weschke (2001), 109–110.

ill-treatment.[203] In terms of standing, the case – just like the previous proceedings in *Pfunders* – did not raise serious questions, as (then) article 24 ECHR recognised the right of any State party, irrespective of individual injury, to institute inter-State proceedings.[204] In contrast, another, lesser-known, reaction, taken by member States of the European (Economic) Community, was not governed by any such special standing rule. When Greece continued to violate fundamental human rights obligations, these States partly suspended the Association Agreement concluded with Greece, and in particular decided to disregard their obligations, under Protocol 19 to that Agreement, to provide financial assistance to Greece.[205] Since neither the Association Agreement nor Protocol 19 had made this obligation conditional upon any human rights compliance, the relevant conduct *prima facie* violated international law and had to be justified as a countermeasure.[206]

Both instances provide early (pre-*Barcelona Traction*), little-known, examples of countermeasures taken to protect the general interest in seeing human rights obligations observed. Much more attention has focused on responses involving the use of military force, or so-called 'humanitarian interventions'.[207] Although the present study does not purport to address the legal regime governing law enforcement by means of force, this debate forms part of the background against which modern-day discussion of general legal interests has to be seen and may thus be briefly summarised.

[203] Applications No. 3321–3323/67 and 3344/67. For the Commission's admissibility decisions see 11 YbECHR (1968), 690 and 730; for its eventual Report see 12 YbECHR (1969: 'The Greek Case'), 1. For the Committee of Ministers' treatment of the issue cf. Resolution DH (70)1, 514; and, for a brief summary, Prebensen (1999), 447 and 449–450.

[204] See already above, footnote 11 and section 2.2.1.a.

[205] For the Association Agreement see OJ 1963, 294; for Protocol 19 *ibid.*, 340. Further on the dispute cf. Coufoudakis (1977–1978), 113; Krenzler (1971), 143–145.

[206] See also Dzida (1997), 252. On the E(E)C's subsequent practice to include human rights conditionality clauses into its international agreements see Brandtner/Rosas (1998), 473; Riedel/Will (1999), 723; and further below, section 6.2.1.a.

[207] See already above, Introduction, and for a discussion Gray (2000a), 26–42; Gray (2000b), 240; Chesterman (2001); Beyerlin (1995), 926; Lillich (1967–1968), 325; Lillich (1974), 229; Teson (1997); Brownlie (1974), 217; Brownlie (1963), 338–342; Akehurst (1984), 95; Stowell (1921); Charney (1999), 834; Verwey (1986), 57.

For definitions of the concept see e.g. Brownlie (1974), 217; Teson (1997), 1; Beyerlin (1995), 926; Chesterman (2001), 1. Others have used the term in a broader sense, encompassing non-military measures, or operations aimed at protecting nationals abroad.

As has already been stated in the Introduction, debates about law enforcement by means of military force have to take into account the changes brought about by article 2, para. 4 UNC, which for the first time introduced a comprehensive ban on the use of force.[208] In the pre-Charter era, in the absence of any comprehensive ban, the concept of humanitarian intervention, while not uncontroversial, indeed enjoyed considerable support. Admittedly, the conditions under which interventions should be justified (i.e. the types of breaches giving rise to it) were not clearly defined, and the concept was much abused by States seeking to lend credibility to nationalist policies.[209] Nevertheless, especially in nineteenth-century practice, it was much relied on by States.[210] The joint French–British–Russian intervention against Ottoman rule in Greece (1827),[211] the French occupation of Ottoman Syria in 1860–1861,[212] or the United States' intervention in Cuba following Spain's repression of the Cuban revolt in 1898[213] are prominent examples. Whether these interventions were prompted by purely humanitarian motives may be doubted. However, in all three cases, humanitarian concerns seemed genuine and certainly were a major factor influencing the decision to deploy military force. For example, it is widely accepted that atrocities committed during the Greek struggle for independence caused shock and disbelief in many European countries. In the Treaty of London 6 July 1827, France, the United Kingdom, and Russia proposed a transition to Greek self-rule, motivated 'no less by sentiments of humanity, than by interests for the tranquility of Europe'.[214]

Similarly, in 1898, in his message to Congress, President McKinley stressed America's special interests in the Spanish–Cuban crisis, but also stated that troops were deployed 'in the cause of humanity and to

[208] See Delbrück (1999b), 141–145; Brownlie (1963), 51–122 for historical surveys.

[209] The most blatant case was the proclamation on the German occupation of Bohemia and Moravia in March 1939. In the light of Germany's abuse of the concept, Thomas and Thomas (1956), 375, observed that humanitarian intervention 'was twisted and warped into a cloak for illegal intervention'. See further Chesterman (2001), 26–28.

[210] For comprehensive reviews of nineteenth-century practice see e.g. Fonteyne (1973), 203; Chesterman (2001), 24–35; and Stowell (1921).

[211] See Franck and Rodley (1973), 280–283; Abiew (1997), 48–49; Stowell (1921), 167–168.

[212] See Kloepfer (1985), 246; Pogany (1986), 182; Stowell (1921), 63–66.

[213] See Stowell (1921), 480–481; Chesterman (2001), 33–35.

[214] Treaty for the Pacification of Greece (77 CTS 307), second preambular paragraph. Rejection of the terms of the treaty led to the War of 1827. For the Porte's recognition of Greek independence see the Declaration of Accession to the 1827 Treaty (in Hertslet (1875), Vol. II, 812), and the Peace Treaty with Russia, 80 CTS 83.

put an end to the barbarities, bloodshed, starvation, and horrible miseries now existing [in Cuba]',[215] while it was 'no answer to say this is all in another country, belonging to another nation, and therefore none of our business.'[216]

Finally, when intervening to protect Christian Maronites in Greater Syria in 1860–1861, France and other European Powers formally declared that they would not use the intervention as a pretext for pursuing colonialist ambitions, and indeed left Syria once the mandate given to them had expired.[217]

These, and other, precedents were much discussed at the time, and have given rise to many conflicting interpretations. For present purposes, it is important to note that they are not merely of historic relevance, but continued to be invoked with a view to justifying the legality of humanitarian interventions in the Charter period. Clearly, the comprehensive ban on the use of force – especially in light of the Court's interpretation in the *Corfu Channel case*[218] – made arguments in favour of the concept much more difficult to sustain. Given the clear wording of article 2, para. 4, those arguing that States, even under the Charter, could use force to protect human rights therefore deliberately relied on pre-Charter law. Following their main argument, a customary rule authorising humanitarian intervention, dating from before 1945, continued to exist alongside article 2, para. 4 UNC.[219] Of course, the Court's subsequent jurisprudence, in the *Nicaragua case*, casts doubts on

[215] Special Message to Congress, reproduced in Moore (1898), Vol. VI, 211, 219–220.

[216] *Ibid.* For differing interpretations of the United States' conduct contrast e.g. Brownlie (1963), 340 (dismissing the case as a precedent) and Stowell (1921), 481 (declaring it 'one of the most important instances of humanitarian intervention').

[217] In response to massacres of Christian Maronites in Greater Syria, European Powers had forced upon the Ottoman Sultan the Convention and Protocols of Paris, authorising France to deploy troops and restore order in the region; see 122 CTS 488. For the declaration not to pursue colonialist ambitions see Second Protocol, 122 CTS 491 (para. 1); and further Chesterman (2001), 32–33.

[218] For the *Corfu Channel case* see ICJ Reports 1949, 35, where the Court stressed that even temporary infringements of another State's territorial integrity or political independence constituted a violation of article 2, para. 4. Apart from dismissing the United Kingdom's more liberal interpretation of the provision, the Court implicitly rejected claims that humanitarian interventions could be compatible with article 2, para. 4 UNC. On this view see e.g. Goodrich/Hambro (1946), 68–69; and, more recently, Teson (1997), 150–157; D'Amato (1987), 57–73; for the United Kingdom's argument see ICJ Pleadings, *Corfu Channel*, Vol. III, 296.

[219] See Lillich (1967), 325; Oppenheim/Lauterpacht, Vol. I (1955), 312–313 and 319–320; Fonteyne (1973), 203; and, more recently, Teson (1997), 177–179. Conversely, Brownlie (1963), 338–342, dismissing the concept of humanitarian intervention, did so on the basis

whether customary international law could have survived the adoption of article 2, para. 4.[220] But at the time of the *South West Africa* and *Barcelona Traction* judgments, this question was far from settled.

To sum up, it was a matter of controversy whether States, prior to the *Barcelona Traction case*, in the absence of individual injury, could enforce basic humanitarian standards. Of the various means of law enforcement, the concept of humanitarian intervention dominated debates. As has been briefly illustrated, it enjoyed considerable support in State practice, but, since 1945, had become difficult to bring in line with article 2, para. 4 UNC. Whether States could take non-forcible countermeasures in defence of general interests remained equally controversial, although the question was much less discussed and practice prior to 1970 remained rather limited. However, it has been shown that States at times did assert a right to take countermeasures in response to breaches that had not affected them in their individual capacity. Notwithstanding all these uncertainties, it seems fair to say that basic humanitarian standards constituted yet another category of obligations, in relation to which broad approaches to standing were discussed.

2.3 Concluding observations

The preceding analysis prompts a number of observations. First and foremost, it suggests that many cherished assumptions about the state of international law prior to 1970 are simplistic. One may readily subscribe to the view that international obligations traditionally were 'essentially relative';[221] this, however, only if the term 'essential' is understood as admitting of a number of exceptions. Undoubtedly, genuinely multilateral obligations did not square well with traditional conceptions of State responsibility – as witnessed by the Court's 1966 judgment in *South West Africa*. On a more general level, the structural approach to multilateral obligations, by emphasising the pattern along which obligations were to be performed, excluded individual enforcement action in response to breaches of absolute obligations.

of his more restrictive interpretation of nineteenth-century practice. It seems therefore fair to say that even after 1945, this practice continued to determine the debates.

220 See ICJ Reports 1986, 134–135 (para. 268), where the Court stressed the similarities between the customary and conventional prohibitions on the use of force and deliberately stated that 'the use of force could not be the appropriate method to monitor or ensure . . . respect for human rights.'

221 Cf. Verdross (1964), 126.

However, notwithstanding the dominance of a structural analysis of obligations, and the high profile of the *South West Africa case*, broad approaches to standing were accepted or discussed in a variety of different scenarios. The case of special treaty-based regulations recognising a general interest in the observance of a specific treaty (which is usually recognised as a possible exception to the general rules) presents few conceptual problems. What the previous analysis has tried to show is that such treaties, even prior to 1970, were much more common than is often admitted.

As regards ambiguous treaty clauses capable of broad or restrictive interpretations, jurisprudence was by no means uniform. In this regard, the 1966 *South West Africa case*, which indeed established a presumption against individual action in the general interest, needs to be contrasted with the *Wimbledon* judgment, in which the PCIJ adopted a very different approach. For all its notoriety, *South West Africa* (1966) therefore is not necessarily the one and only, or decisive, judicial pronouncement; it stands for one particular approach that was not always dominant.

Moreover, insofar as the *South West Africa* judgment, by implication, confirmed a narrow reading of the general rules of standing, the picture is also more diverse than is sometimes suggested. No doubt, in the absence of explicit treaty clauses, standing in the general interest remained exceptional. It is equally important to realise, however, that exceptions were accepted, or at least discussed, in different fields.

For once, it was generally accepted that all States should individually be entitled to respond to breaches of interdependent obligations. Narrowly defined as it was, the category of interdependent obligations shows that even outside specific treaty regulations, obligations could be generally enforceable by all States individually. The legal rules governing the enforcement of status obligations points in the same direction. Although the concept of status treaties remained controversial, the limited amount of evidence available suggests that all States should be entitled to respond against breaches. Finally, the same arguably applies to basic humanitarian concerns and the duty to comply with ICJ judgments. Admittedly, there is no conclusive support that third States not participating in proceedings should have been entitled to enforce ICJ judgments. However, such a right was asserted, and the general interest in seeing ICJ judgments complied clearly expressed. Finally, the same line of reasoning underlies the long-standing debate about interventions to safeguard basic humanitarian concerns. As has been shown, there was, prior to the Court's

Barcelona Traction judgment, at least some support in international practice for a right of States to take countermeasures in response to grave violations of human rights obligations. Whether States should even be entitled to use force in the name of humanity, was much debated, both before and after the adoption of article 2, para. 4 UNC. What is crucial to realise is that insofar as States invoked the concept of humanitarian intervention, they claimed for themselves, expressly or by implication, a right to exercise military force in defence of a general interest.

In the light of these developments, assertions that (by necessity and without exceptions) States, prior to the Court's *Barcelona Traction* judgment, could only respond to violations of international law that had affected their individual legal positions, are not only simplistic, but incorrect. Even before that judgment, it was hard to ignore the trend towards the recognition of general legal interest in the observance of specific categories of obligations. Paraphrasing a famous dictum by Judge Weeramantry, it seems fair to say that even prior to 1970, something not dissimilar to 'the *erga omnes* concept . . . [had] been at the door of [the] Court for many years.'[222]

[222] ICJ Reports 1995, 216.

PART II • LEGAL ISSUES RAISED BY THE *ERGA OMNES* CONCEPT

It is against the background set out in the preceding chapters that the concept of obligations *erga omnes* has to be seen. It emerged in a legal environment torn between traditional, restrictive concepts of individual injury on the one hand, and expansive approaches to standing on the other. As has already been stated in the Introduction, the instance of its emergence - two obscure, though soon-to-be-famous, paragraphs of a judgment otherwise concerned with the diplomatic protection of corporations - was a most unlikely one. The *Barcelona Traction* dictum however has been followed up by further references to the *erga omnes* concept, which to date has been mentioned in no less than eight other proceedings, namely in the orders or judgments in the *Namibia*, *Nuclear Tests*, *Nicaragua*, *East Timor*, *Genocide*, *Gabčíkovo*, *Armed Activities (Congo-Rwanda)*, and *Israeli Wall cases*. To these, a considerable number of separate and dissenting opinions has to be added.[1] Despite the frequent judicial endorsement, the 'masterpiece'[2] has escaped an easy classification. Three questions in particular - foreshadowed already in the *Barcelona Traction* dictum - have remained controversial.

The most fundamental of these is whether the *erga omnes* concept affects the rules of standing. In the *Barcelona Traction* dictum, the Court seemed to address this question when observing that obligations *erga omnes* are the 'concern of all States' and 'owed towards the international community as a whole'; that 'all States ... have a legal interest in their protection', and that they enjoy 'corresponding rights of protection'.[3] It did not, however, spell out the ways and means by which States could respond to violations of obligations *erga omnes*. Nor did the Court

[1] The relevant instances are discussed below.

[2] Cf. Weil (1992), 287: 'une des *pièces maîtresses* de l'arsenal conceptuel du droit international d'aujord'hui' (emphasis added).

[3] ICJ Reports 1970, 32–33 (paras. 33–34).

elaborate in any detail on how the new type of obligations should be identified. In passing, it referred to the 'nature' of obligations *erga omnes*; it distinguished them from obligations in the field of diplomatic protection and stated that it was '[i]n view of the importance of the rights involved [that] all States can be held to have a legal interest in their protection'.[4] However, this hardly amounts to a conclusive test. Finally, the Court's observation that some rights of protection concept had 'entered into the body of general international law' whereas others were 'conferred by international instruments of a universal or quasi-universal character'[5] seems to address the relation between enforcement rights attaching to the *erga omnes*, and treaty-based special rules of law enforcement. However, while hinting at the issue, the Court did not specify how these different rights of protection interrelate.

Even decades after the *Barcelona Traction* judgment, these different questions continue to puzzle commentators and courts. Subsequent chapters will attempt to answer them. More specifically, Chapter 4 assesses ways and means of identifying obligations *erga omnes*. Chapters 5 and 6 address the two means of law enforcement relevant to the present study; they discuss whether States can institute ICJ proceedings or take countermeasures in response to breaches of *erga omnes* breaches. Whereas these chapters focus on means of enforcing obligations *erga omnes*, Chapter 7 analyses the relation between possible *erga omnes* enforcement rights and other, treaty-based, enforcement systems. Taken together, Chapters 4 to 7 thereby address what are believed to be the most pressing questions raised by the *erga omnes* concept in the *Barcelona Traction* sense.

As has already been stated in the Introduction, the expression *erga omnes* has a considerably wider meaning and goes well beyond issues of standing or law enforcement. Before addressing specific aspects of the legal regime of obligations *erga omnes* in the *Barcelona Traction* sense, it is therefore necessary to distinguish the different meanings attributed to the notion. This will be done in Chapter 3, which identifies different types of *erga omnes* effects, and thereby seeks to delimit the scope of the subsequent inquiry in a more precise way.

[4] ICJ Reports 1970, 32 (para. 33). [5] ICJ Reports 1970, 33 (para. 34).

3 Distinguishing types of *erga omnes* effects

Before addressing the specific questions mentioned above, it is necessary further to delimit the field of analysis. Paradoxically, the need to do so is a consequence of the remarkable openness and success of the *erga omnes* concept. So far, it has been assumed that the concept affects the rules of standing and the invocation of responsibility. This approach indeed follows naturally from the wording and context of the above-quoted *Barcelona Traction* dictum. By mentioning 'legal interests' and 'rights of protection', the Court used terms that frequently appear in debates about standing and law enforcement. By distinguishing bilateral obligations in the field of diplomatic protection from obligations owed to the international community as a whole, it seemed to refer to these debates, and to the distinction between individual and general legal interests introduced above.[1] However, it is crucial to note that *erga omnes* effects have been referred to in a variety of different situations, often entirely unrelated to questions of standing or law enforcement. Not all of these statements have received the same degree of attention. In fact, those of the Court's references that are hard to bring in line with the *Barcelona Traction* dictum are often either ignored or treated *en passant*. This eclectic approach is of course convenient – not the least it allows commentators exclusively to focus on *erga omnes* effects in the field of standing and law enforcement. However, eclecticism comes at the price of comprehensiveness. Despite the considerable scholarly interest in the concept, the Court's jurisprudence on *erga omnes* effects is hardly ever analysed in an exhaustive way. What is more, commentators discussing *erga omnes* effects outside the field of law enforcement have often failed clearly to

[1] See above, sections 1.2 and 1.3.

distinguish them from *erga omnes* effects in the *Barcelona Traction* sense,[2] or have been accused of 'trivialising' the *erga omnes* concept.[3]

As will be shown in the following, it may indeed be helpful – or even necessary – to ignore some of the Court's express references to *erga omnes* effects. The reasons for so doing however have to be spelled out clearly. This is the purpose of the present chapter. In order to avoid trivialisation as well as (inadvertent) eclecticism, it categorises different types of *erga omnes* effects recognised by the Court and its members. By pointing to the different ways in which the term is used, it distinguishes *erga omnes* effects in the *Barcelona Traction* sense from 'other' *erga omnes* effects, which are often entirely unrelated to questions of standing, legal interests or law enforcement. This in turn has important consequences for the subsequent discussion of obligations *erga omnes* as a law enforcement concept. Having surveyed the field of possible *erga omnes* effects, and having drawn a distinction between different categories of them, it seems justified to focus, in subsequent chapters, on obligations *erga omnes* in the sense of the *Barcelona Traction case*, and to ignore the Court's other references.

Before introducing the different categories of *erga omnes* effects, it is necessary to make two preliminary remarks, both of which may help explain why the *erga omnes* concept has continued to present difficulties. The first point is that the term *erga omnes* is imprecise and does not have a clear and well-defined meaning. Secondly, and perhaps more importantly, debates about *erga omnes* effects by no means began with the *Barcelona Traction* dictum. Prior to 1970, however, the term had been used in a way that had little to do with questions of standing, or law enforcement. Apart from popularising it, the Court thus took an existing expression out of its original context. Before assessing the ICJ's jurisprudence relating to 'other' *erga omnes* effects, these two points need to be explored briefly.

2 See e.g. Ziemer (2000), 217–220; Feist (2001), 38–40 and 106–122; Sands (2003), 183; Juste Ruiz (1979), 225–233; Ragazzi (1997), 7–8; Delbrück (1999a), 20–25 (all failing to distinguish between *erga omnes* effects in the field of standing and *erga omnes* effects in the field of treaty law, a distinction reverted to in the subsequent discussion). A particular telling example of this confusion is the express reference, by the German *Bundesverfassungsgericht*, to the *Barcelona Traction* dictum, in a case concerning third-party ('*erga omnes*') effects of diplomatic treaties, see *GDR Ambassador case*, BVerfGE 96, 68 (para. 58).

3 Cf. Tomuschat's remarks on Rosenne's broad discussion of *erga omnes* effects: Tomuschat (1999), 83, and Rosenne (1998), 509, respectively.

3.1 Terminological imprecision

As for terminology, discussions about the *erga omnes* concept, and the confusion to which the term has given rise, exemplify the risks of using imprecise terms. Ideally, the name given to a legal concept has a certain explicatory value, and helps assess the specific legal consequences entailed by it. By speaking of a concept labelled 'obligations *erga omnes*', the International Court unfortunately failed to achieve this goal. Translated literally, '*erga omnes*' means 'against all', 'between all', or 'as opposed to all'. An obligation of international law that has *erga omnes* effects thus applies between all, or to all, others – presumably all other members of the international community, or, as the Court put it, to the international community as a whole. One problem with this use of terminology is that '*omnes*' has more than one meaning: it can either refer to all others collectively, or to each of the others individually.[4] This problem may be left to a side here, as it will be addressed more fully below when discussing the relation between individual States and the international community.[5] Still, in terms of clarity, the expression *erga omnes* leaves a lot to be desired.

A first – but unfounded – criticism is that the concept is described by a Latin term.[6] Of course, there is considerable debate as to whether the continued use of Latin expressions is a necessary feature of (international) legal discourse.[7] Whatever position one may take, it seems hard to deny that, in the case of obligations *erga omnes*, it is not the foreign language that causes problems, but the vagueness of the expressions used to describe the concept. Indeed, none of the translations given above would bring about much clarification.[8]

It would however have been helpful had the Court clarified what exactly it considered to be valid, or owed, *erga omnes*. As it stands, the

[4] Glare, *Oxford Latin Dictionnary*, 1051 ('omnis'). [5] Cf. below, section 5.2.3.

[6] See e.g. Crawford, Fourth Report, para. 49.

[7] See e.g. Reuter (1970), 445, who deplored the 'absence d'imagination [dans le vocabulaire du droit international] dont le recours au latin n'est pas le moindre signe!'

[8] The Court might have avoided some of the ensuing problems had it used the vernacular 'obligations owed to the international community as a whole' (see also para. 9 of the ILC's commentary on article 48 ASR, and further Crawford, Fourth Report, para. 49). By so doing, it would, however, have invited further discussion about the composition of that community, its status (or otherwise) as a subject of international law, or about the relation between rights of the community and rights of members exercised on behalf of it. While the vernacular might thus have conveyed more information, it would not have been uncontroversial either.

relevant passage can be interpreted in at least two ways. '*Erga omnes*' could notably be taken as a reference to the circle of States bound by the primary obligation in question. As a consequence, an obligation would be 'owed to all others' (or '*erga omnes*') if it applied between all States.[9] A brief glance at the passage as a whole however reveals that, in *Barcelona Traction*, the term *erga omnes* was not used in this sense. Had the Court merely wished to describe the circle of States between which the obligation applied, all obligations of general international law would qualify as obligations *erga omnes*, and the *Barcelona Traction* dictum would hardly deserve much attention.[10] Under this test, a coastal State's obligation not to hamper the innocent passage of foreign merchant ships would qualify as an obligation *erga omnes*, as would a receiving State's obligation to respect the inviolability of accredited diplomats – or indeed, the very obligation the Court sought to distinguish from obligations *erga omnes*, namely Spain's obligation to 'extend to [foreign investors, such as the Barcelona Traction Company] the protection of the law'.[11]

At least in *Barcelona Traction*, '*erga omnes*' seems to have been used in a different sense. As the reference to the 'legal interest' of all States, and to the 'corresponding rights of protection' suggests, the Court was not concerned with the scope of a *primary* obligation, but intended to describe specific features of the *secondary* rules governing the invocation of responsibility for violations of obligations called '*erga omnes*'. Not the obligation as such, but its performance in a specific case therefore is owed to all States (i.e. *erga omnes*). From a linguistic point of view, this is a defensible use of term, and Ago's remark that the expression 'obligations *erga omnes*' was a 'misnomer' seems exaggerated.[12] Nevertheless, it is equally clear that if the Court intended to make a statement about the secondary rules governing the enforcement of a special category of obligations, it did not express this intention in a very clear way. This is all the more unfortunate as it could have easily clarified matters – for example, as has been suggested, by speaking of 'obligation[s] the breach of which gives rise to responsibility *erga omnes*.'[13] As it stands, the passage enunciating the 'masterpiece'[14] of obligations *erga omnes* was drafted in a less than masterly way.

[9] Ago (1989), 237–238; Thierry (1990), 59 and 62; cf. also Seiderman (2001), 124.
[10] Even this is not undisputed: contrast e.g. the misleading observations by Ushakov, YbILC 1976, I, 71 (para. 36); Pellet (1996), 20; and Ago, YbILC 1976, Vol. I, 74 (para. 12).
[11] See ICJ Reports 1970, 32 (para. 33). [12] Ago (1989), 237.
[13] Thirlway (1989), 93; similarly Thierry (1990), 62–63. [14] Weil (1992), 287.

3.2 The traditional meaning of the term

However, not only did the Court use imprecise terminology, which seemed to invite misunderstandings; in addition it employed an expression that hitherto had been used in a different context. Today, it is often assumed that prior to the Court's decision in *Barcelona Traction*, the idea that certain obligations could have *erga omnes* effects had been unheard of. According to Seiderman, for example, '[t]he term *erga omnes* ... first gained prominence in international legal parlance through a pronouncement by the International Court of Justice in the Barcelona Traction case.'[15]

This assertion however does not withstand close scrutiny. Although the specific way in which the Court used the term was new, the phrase '*erga omnes*' was not. Rather, by 1970, there had been decades of discussion, in the literature, in practice and in the jurisprudence, about *erga omnes* effects under international law. The expression *erga omnes* thus was by no means a novelty when the Court used it in *Barcelona Traction*. *Erga omnes* effects in this traditional (i.e. pre-*Barcelona Traction*) meaning of the term, however, were very different from those that occupy the present study. They were discussed within the confines of the law of treaties, notably with reference to possible effects of specific treaties on third parties.[16] More specifically, four different types of such 'treaties producing effects *erga omnes*'[17] were distinguished.

Of these, the concept of objective regimes was the most controversial. Since it has been discussed already,[18] some remarks on terminology may suffice here. As has been stated above, treaties creating objective regimes were said to give rise to general, or objective, obligations binding on third States. When describing this alleged special effect, commentators often used the expression '*erga omnes*' as a synonym for 'general' or 'objective'. The ILC's commentary on draft article 34 provides the most prominent example. Summarising the debates about

[15] Seiderman (2001), 123.

[16] On the following see e.g. McNair (1957), 21; McNair (1961), 255–271; Rousseau (1944), 477–484; Guggenheim (1953), 97–103; for a brief reference to the earlier use of the term '*erga omnes*' see also Empell (2003), 132 (his note 135). That some treaties should entail *erga omnes* effects seemed to be widely accepted. For a contrary opinion see however Schwarzenberger (1957), 459, according to whom third-party effects of treaties depended not on alleged *erga omnes* validity or opposability, but on the application of concepts such as estoppel or acquiescence.

[17] Cf. the title of McNair's contribution to the *Festschrift Perassi* (1957).

[18] See above, section 2.2.2.b.

Waldock's proposed draft article 63, which had endorsed the concept, the Commission stated that it had 'considered whether treaties creating so-called "objective regimes", that is obligations and rights valid *erga omnes*, should be dealt with separately as a special case.'[19] As the record of the debates shows, ILC members had indeed debated the issue under the rubric of *erga omnes* effects and had had little qualms to claim that obligations under objective regimes were obligations *erga omnes*.[20]

The concept of obligations *erga omnes* (in this traditional sense), however, was not limited to controversial concepts such as objective regimes. Others used the term in a more general sense, denoting all legal positions imbued with objective validity or opposability. Treaties transferring territorial titles or creating other rights *in rem* - such as international servitudes, or rights of passage - were seen as a prime example.[21] Hence Switzerland, in the *Case Concerning the Free Zones of Upper Savoy and the District of Gex*, maintained that: 'les droits réels, en droit international, sont ceux qui se rapportent au territoire et qui, par essence, valent *erga omnes*',[22] whereas Huber, arbitrator, in the famous *Island of Palmas* award observed that the title to territory 'is valid *erga omnes*.'[23]

Thirdly, the same terminology was used in debates about the concept of international legal personality. The ICJ's observation that States, by

[19] YbILC 1966, Vol. II, 231 (para. 4) (emphasis added).

[20] See e.g. YbILC 1964, Vol. I, 83 (para. 29) (Lachs); 97 (para. 33) (Paredes); 99 (para. 3) (de Luna); 103 (para. 54) (Rosenne); 107–108 (paras. 27–28) (Lachs). Apparently based on the same understanding, the German *Bundesverfassungsgericht*, in the *GDR Ambassador case* (BVerfGE 96, 68, paras. 58–69), and Ress (2000), Doehring (1999), 68, discuss possible *erga omnes* effects of diplomatic immunity, while the Germany Society of International Law considered in detail the problems posed by treaties providing for the harmonisation of laws, which in its terminology entailed '*erga omnes* effects'; cf. Matscher/Siehr/Delbrück (1986).

[21] For brief references to these types of treaties see already above, section 2.2.2.b, and cf. further McNair (1961), 256; Guggenheim/Marek (1962), 540; Waldock, Third Report, YbILC 1964, Vol. II, 32 (para. 15); Westlake (1910), Vol. I, 294–295. Fitzmaurice cautioned against the recognition of automatic *erga omnes* effects, but proposed to recognise a general duty to recognise 'situations of law or of fact established by lawful and valid treaties *tending by their nature to have effects erga omnes*', see Fifth Report, YbILC 1960, Vol. II, 98 (draft article 18(c); emphasis added).

[22] PCIJ, Ser. C 17, I, Vol. III, 1654.

[23] RIAA, Vol. II, 840. See also Jennings' statement that '[i]f a title to sovereignty means anything at all it means a real title, a title *erga omnes*' (Jennings (1963), 5). Similar observations can be found in Oppenheim/Jennings/Watts (1992), 669; Verdross/Simma (1984), 639; and Shaw (1986), 16.

way of treaty, could 'bring into being an entity possessing objective international personality, and not merely personality recognized by them alone'[24] to many seemed to imply a modification of the third-party rule. The ICJ's advisory opinion in the *Reparations case* (as the *locus classicus*) thus prompted Rosenne to ask: 'What is that "objective international personality" if not personality *erga omnes*?'[25]

Finally, those concerned about the rigid formulation of article 59 ICJ Statute, pursuant to which ICJ judgments are binding between the parties only, argued in favour of recognising certain *erga omnes* effects of international judgments.[26] The Court itself, in its 1966 *South West Africa* judgment (of all cases), mentioned that exceptionally, a court decision could bring about a 'general judicial settlement' – and described this as an 'effect *erga omnes*'.[27]

The Court's dictum on obligations *erga omnes* in the *Barcelona Traction case* seems to have overshadowed these earlier, traditional, types of *erga omnes* effects.[28] This is unfortunate, since some of the Court's subsequent references to the *erga omnes* concept are informed by the traditional understanding, and can only be properly understood if seen in historical perspective.[29] For present purposes, it is crucial to note the differences between the traditional meaning of the term *erga omnes*, and its use, by the Court, in the *Barcelona Traction case*. These indeed are not difficult to identify. Traditionally, those claiming that treaty obligations qualified as obligations *erga omnes* intended to broaden the circle of States bound by the rule. Recognition of *erga omnes* effects thus modified the scope (*ratione personae*) of a primary rule of international law. Of course, this traditional *erga omnes* effect could eventually affect the

[24] ICJ Reports 1949, 185.

[25] Rosenne (1998), 513; and similarly McNair (1957), 30–33; Waldock, Third Report, YbILC 1964, Vol. II, 31 (para. 14).

[26] See e.g. Rosenne (1965), 629; similarly *id.* (1998), 519.

[27] See ICJ Reports 1966, 41 (para. 70). The reference is to the PCIJ's jurisdiction over the minorities treaties concluded after World War I; the *erga omnes* effect of PCIJ judgments was underlined by an express reference to article 13 of the Covenant.

[28] Few works assessing the relevance of the concept of obligations *erga omnes* in the field of law enforcement contain references to this traditional understanding. Some of the aspects are discussed in the works of Delbrück (1999a), 17, and Ragazzi (1997), who, however, do not specifically address the enforcement aspect of the *erga omnes* concept. There is also some reference to the traditional understanding in Rosenne (1998), 509. As noted above (see references in footnote 2) commentators acknowledging the traditional use of the term frequently fail to distinguish between the different *erga omnes* effects.

[29] See below, section 3.3.1.

secondary rules governing responses to breaches. As has been shown above, this process for example seemed to have taken place with respect to obligations under objective regimes, which – pursuant to Waldock's draft article 63, para. 3, and the Committee of Jurists' Report in the *Aaland* dispute – could be enforced by all States, irrespective of their participation in the regime-creating treaty.[30] Such modifications of the rules of standing however were by no means an automatic or necessary consequence. In the case of dispositive treaties, for example, is was widely agreed that even if the treaty's objective effects could be described as '*erga omnes* validity' (or similar), only treaty parties could react against breaches.[31] What is more, even in the case of objective regimes, discussions about *erga omnes* effects inevitably centred on the scope of the primary obligation, and the need to explain how the concept could be reconciled with the *pacta tertiis* rule. In contrast, possible effects on standing and the rules of law enforcement were largely ignored.[32]

When using the term '*erga omnes*' in this latter context, the Court in *Barcelona Traction* thus shifted the emphasis away from the traditional understanding of the *erga omnes* concept. It must be repeated that, given the openness of the term '*erga omnes*', the Court's use of terminology is defensible, and would have been unproblematic had the Court explained further what it was doing. However, by taking a well-established concept out of its traditional context and by failing to set out the reasons for doing so, the Court significantly increased the risk of terminological confusion.

3.3 'Other' *erga omnes* effects in the ICJ's jurisprudence

Developments since 1970 confirm the risks involved in employing a term as vague as *erga omnes*. Ever since the Court's *Barcelona Traction* judgment, claims that certain legal acts should have effects *erga omnes*

[30] See above, section 2.2.2.b.

[31] See e.g. Waldock, YbILC 1964, Vol. II, 32 (para. 15): 'These [dispositive] treaties differ from [status treaties] in that their purpose is to regulate the particular interests of the parties rather than to establish a general régime in the general interest. Other States, no doubt, may be affected – even to an important extent – by the conclusion of the treaty, but they are affected by the treaty only incidentally, not by the direct application of the treaty itself. Nor have the parties manifested any intention that other States should have or acquire any right or interest in the treaty, and other States cannot, in consequence, derive from the treaty any *legal* title for claiming a *locus standi* with regard to the maintenance or revision of the settlement established by the treaty.'

[32] For comment on the lack of academic discussion see already above, section 2.2.2.b.

have abounded in international jurisprudence, practice, and literature. This does not mean that the *erga omnes* concept was no longer relevant for questions of standing and law enforcement. To the contrary, many of the ICJ's references to *erga omnes* effects since 1970 attempt to clarify the meaning of the *Barcelona Traction* dictum, or have at least an indirect bearing on its interpretation. It is however equally relevant to note that - contrary to what is suggested by much of the literature - the *erga omnes* concept cannot be reduced to these matters. Instead, the Court and its members have identified *erga omnes* effects in situations that bore no relation to the problems posed by the *Barcelona Traction* dictum. The following section provides an overview of these other, often ignored, *erga omnes* effects. It does not purport to analyse them in any detail, or to assess whether the Court or its members were always correct in invoking the concept. Rather, it seeks to illustrate the heterogeneity of the concept by distinguishing obligations *erga omnes* in the *Barcelona Traction* sense from other types of *erga omnes* effects. Three of these other *erga omnes* effects can be identified.

3.3.1 *The traditional meaning*

Although the Court in *Barcelona Traction* took the term '*erga omnes*' out of its original (pre-*Barcelona Traction*) context, the traditional understanding has since then re-emerged in the Court's opinion on *Namibia*,[33] as well as in President Bedjaoui's declaration in the *Nuclear Weapons opinion*.[34]

In *Namibia*, the Court confirmed that the UN General Assembly had been entitled to revoke the South West African mandate, and that South Africa's continued presence in Namibia was in violation of SC Res. 276 (1970).[35] From this, it followed that all UN members were under a duty to refuse recognition of the South African exercise of administering power. More importantly, in the view of the Court, the resolutions of the two UN organs were also opposable to States not members of the

[33] ICJ Reports 1971, 16. [34] ICJ Reports 1996, 268.

[35] Even before SC Res. 276 (1970), South Africa's presence in Namibia had of course long been a matter of controversy, which, *inter alia*, had prompted the institution of contentious proceedings by Liberia and Ethiopia. On these proceedings see above, section 2.1.2. Following the Court's judgment of 18 July 1966, the UN General Assembly revoked the South African mandate in GA Res. 2145. Having repeatedly endorsed that GA Res. 2145, the UN Security Council, in SC Res. 276 (1970), stated that all acts taken by the South African administration after the revocation of the mandate were illegal. See further Klein (2000a), 497–499; Klein (1995a), 486–488; Bernhardt (1973), 13–37; and (for a comprehensive account) Dugard (1973) 376–542.

organisation.[36] Elaborating on this latter aspect, the Court stated that 'the termination of the Mandate and the declaration of the illegality of South Africa's presence in Namibia are opposable to all States in the sense of barring *erga omnes* the legality of a situation which is maintained in violation of international law'.[37]

This passage has at times been interpreted as an application of the Court's *Barcelona Traction* dictum, i.e. as affecting the secondary rules governing the invocation of responsibility. Two different readings have been advanced. First, some commentators have suggested that the Court intended to qualify South Africa's obligation to withdraw from Namibia as an obligation *erga omnes*.[38] This indeed would correspond to arguments made by Hungary during the proceedings before the Court.[39] It would also prompt the question whether all States had a legal interest in the observation of that obligation.[40] Secondly, the passage has also been interpreted to mean that the obligation of all States not to recognise the legality of South Africa's continued presence, was itself valid *erga omnes*.[41] As a consequence, all States arguably would have had a legal interest in ensuring that *other States* did not recognise South Africa's presence.

Both ways of reading the passage (and explaining it in ways similar to the *Barcelona Traction* dictum), however, neglect its precise context and ignore the information provided in some of the separate opinions. Rather than elaborating on South Africa's obligations or on obligations incumbent upon *all* States, the relevant paragraph is solely concerned with the effects of the relevant UN resolutions on States that are not themselves members of the organisation. While the legal effects of such resolutions on UN members are governed by the relevant UN Charter

[36] Cf. the judgment's operative paragraphs, ICJ Reports 1971, 58 (para. 133).

[37] ICJ Reports 1971, 56 (para. 126).

[38] See Thirlway (1989), 99; Antonopoulos (1996), 90. Cf. also Ragazzi (1997), 172 (his note 37) and the critical comment by Mann (1973b), 412–415.

[39] See ICJ Pleadings, *Namibia* opinion, Vol. I, 159–160, where Hungary submitted that 'Its [South Africa's] obligation to withdraw is an obligation *erga omnes*.' A similar position was taken by India, *ibid*., Vol. II, 119.

[40] Cf. the following statement by Thirlway (1989), 99: 'One possible view ... is that South Africa was under an obligation *erga omnes*, of the kind contemplated in the *Barcelona Traction* judgment, to withdraw from Namibia, such that any State could seek the enforcement of that obligation, without being required to show an individual interest in the matter.' For a similar statement see Thirlway (1990), 31; but contrast the subsequent change of view in Thirlway (1996), 4–5. Ragazzi (1997), 172 (his note 37), suggests that para. 118 of the Court's opinion supports this understanding.

[41] Ragazzi (1997), 167–168.

provisions, the Charter does not explain why resolutions should be binding on, or opposable to, non-members.[42] By holding that the resolutions of the General Assembly and Security Council 'barr[ed] *erga omnes* the legality' of South Africa's continued presence in Namibia, the Court clarified that non-members could not ignore their effects.[43] As a consequence, non-member States had to 'act in accordance' with the decisions of the competent UN organs.[44]

Thus interpreted, the Court's reference to *erga omnes* effects in *Namibia* bears all the hallmarks of the traditional use of the term.[45] By ascribing *erga omnes* validity to the resolutions of UN organs, the Court broadened the circle of States bound by them. Just as in the case of dispositive treaties or objective regimes, an obligation contained in a treaty or treaty-based resolution thus acquired general force in relation to third States. Not surprisingly, judges elaborating on the matter relied on analogies to the concepts of status regimes or absolute rights: Judge Ammoun, for example, stressed the mandate's 'objective institutional character', while Judge de Castro drew an analogy to the right of a proprietor to withdraw, with absolute effect, the mandate given to a person administering his property.[46] One year after launchng debates about *erga omnes* effects in the field of standing, the ICJ thus had reverted to the traditional meaning of the term.

The traditional understanding equally informs President Bedjaoui's brief reference to the '*erga omnes* opposability' of certain obligations, made in a declaration attached to the *Nuclear Weapons* opinion.[47] In his declaration, Bedjaoui commented on para. 2F of the *dispositif*, where the

[42] Article 2(6) of the UN Charter, which addresses the relationship between the Organisation and non-members, only applies to the 'Principles' of article 2. Article 25 expressly limits the binding effect of Security Council resolutions to UN members. On the two provisions see Graf Vitzthum (Article 2(6)) and Delbrück (Article 25) in: Simma (2002a).

[43] Klein (2000a), 499; Graf Vitzthum, in: Simma (2002a), Article 2(6), MN 15; Thirlway (1996), 5; Juste Ruiz (1979), 221–222. In his separate opinion, Judge de Castro indeed put the matter very clearly. Explaining the Court's reasoning, he stated: 'These [non-member] States have no obligation under the Charter. Nonetheless they should respect a declaration of forfeiture of the legal title to possess the territory pronounced by a legitimate authority, against a State which received the territory in order to administer it in the name of the international organization' (ICJ Reports 1971, 219).

[44] ICJ Reports 1971, 56 (para. 126). [45] See above, section 3.2.

[46] See ICJ Reports 1971, 73 (para. 4), and 219, respectively; and cf. Judge de Castro's dissent in the *Nuclear Tests cases*, ICJ Reports 1974, 387 (his note 1).

[47] ICJ Reports 1996, 273–274 (para. 23). The passage has been widely ignored. One of the few commentators addressing it considered it to be a 'slightly obscure reference to *erga omnes*' (Thirlway (1999), 432).

Court had unanimously held that States were under an obligation 'to pursue in good faith and to bring to an end negotiations leading to nuclear disarmament'. Whereas the judgment could be interpreted as a mere reiteration of the identical obligation contained in article VI of the Non-Proliferation Treaty,[48] Bedjaoui argued that it contained a '*general obligation*, opposable *erga omnes*'.[49]

As is clear from its terms and context, President Bedjaoui intended to clarify that the duty to pursue negotiations also applied to States not parties to that treaty – a question about which judges indeed had disagreed.[50] By qualifying this duty as 'opposable *erga omnes*', Bedjaoui thus broadened the circle of States bound by a treaty obligation.[51] Just as in the *Namibia case*, the term *erga omnes* therefore was used in its traditional meaning, denoting general effects of legal acts whose consequences would otherwise have been limited to specific States (such as State parties to the Non-Proliferation Treaty).

3.3.2 *The territorial restriction of obligations*

Whereas *Namibia* and President Bedjaoui's declaration in *Nuclear Weapons* recognised *erga omnes* effects that were already considered prior to 1970, the Court, in the 1996 *Genocide case*,[52] introduced a new facet of the *erga omnes* concept. In the circumstances of the case, it had to determine whether the dispute between Bosnia-Herzegovina on the one hand, and Yugoslavia on the other, was an 'international dispute' as required by article IX of the Genocide Convention. Yugoslavia disputed this, arguing, *inter alia*, that the conflict was of a domestic nature and had taken place on parts of the territory of Bosnia-Herzegovina, over which it had not exercised jurisdiction when the alleged genocidal acts had been committed.[53] In essence, its argument thus depended on the view that the obligations arising under the Genocide Convention only applied to member States in relation to

[48] Treaty on the Non-Proliferation of Nuclear Weapons, 729 UNTS 161. Article VI provides: 'Each of the Parties to the Treaty undertakes to pursue negotiations in good faith on effective measures relating to cessation of the nuclear arms race at an early date and to nuclear disarmament, and on a treaty on general and complete disarmament under strict and effective international control.'

[49] ICJ Reports 1996, 273–274 (para. 23) (italics in the original).

[50] Contrast, for example, the approaches of Judges Oda (ICJ Reports 1996, 373, para. 55) and Fleischauer (*ibid.*, 310, para. 7); and cf. Vice-President Schwebel's critical comments on para. 2F (*ibid.*, 329).

[51] See Thirlway (1999), 432, to whom the 'reference to *erga omnes* presumably means that the obligation rests on all states rather than that it is owed to all states.'

[52] ICJ Reports 1996, 595. [53] Cf. ICJ Reports 1996, 615 (para. 30).

territories under their jurisdiction. In response, the Court noted that States' obligations under the Genocide Convention were not territorially limited, and stressed the universal character of the condemnation of genocide and of the duty of 'co-operation required "in order to liberate mankind from such an odious scourge"'.[54] Because of this universality, the Court then found that the 'rights and obligations enshrined by the [Genocide] Convention are rights and obligations *erga omnes*'.[55] This in turn led it to hold that 'the obligation each State thus has to prevent and to punish the crime of genocide is not territorially limited by the Convention.'[56]

The reasoning underlying this passage is not entirely clear.[57] Pursuant to the Court, a right or obligation that applies *erga omnes* differs from other rights and obligations with respect to its territorial applicability. More specifically, the Court seems to suggest that where an obligation is valid *erga omnes*, States are precluded from arguing that acts had taken place outside their jurisdiction, and thus did not engage their responsibility.[58]

The implications of this statement have so far hardly been explored, and inferences drawn from it remain tentative.[59] What seems clear is that the type of *erga omnes* effect asserted by the Court is different both from *erga omnes* effects discussed in *Barcelona Traction* and those traditionally recognised. Unlike in *Barcelona Traction*, the *erga omnes* character of the obligation does not affect questions of standing or law enforcement - the applicants legal interest being undisputed.[60] Nor, however,

[54] ICJ Reports 1996, 616 (para. 31), citing ICJ Reports 1951, 23 and the Preamble to the Genocide Convention.

[55] ICJ Reports 1996, 616 (para. 31). [56] *Ibid.*

[57] For critical comment see e.g. Gray (1997), 692; Paulus (2001), 376; as well as Simma (1994a), 299 (whose work appeared after the judgment was rendered). According to Paulus, this effect ought to have been explained with reference to the peremptory character of the prohibition against genocide. Both Simma and Paulus have argued that the Court's statement conflated the two concepts of *jus cogens* and obligations *erga omnes*. For comment on the inter-relation between the two concepts see below, section 4.2.2.b.

[58] As Rosenne (1998), 512–513, has observed, unlike in *Barcelona Traction*, the fact that the obligation in question was an obligation *erga omnes* was essential for the Court's decision in the *Genocide case*; it constituted 'one of the central aspects of the *ratio decidendi* leading to the rejection of the relevant preliminary objection.'

[59] Although the statement has been referred to, there has been hardly any attempt to assess its effect on the rules of attribution or accountability. To give but two examples, neither the ILC (during its work on State responsibility) nor the Eur. Ct. HR (when assessing the territorial application of Convention rights in *Bankovic*) considered whether obligations *erga omnes* were subject to a special rule of accountability.

[60] But cf. below, section 5.2.3, for an analysis of Judge Oda's approach in this case.

can the relevant passage be explained as yet another reference to *erga omnes* effects in the traditional sense. Since it was bound by the 1948 Genocide Convention, Yugoslavia was obliged to prevent and punish genocidal conduct; references to traditional *erga omnes* effects would thus have been unnecessary. Rather than broadening the circle of States bound by the obligation, the new *erga omnes* effect recognised by the Court affected the content of the obligation in question. Being *erga omnes*, an obligation could not be territorially restricted, and thus imposed upon States a higher degree of accountability. For the sake of simplicity, one might say that whereas the *erga omnes* concept had traditionally affected the *breadth* of an obligation, the new type of *erga omnes* effect recognised in the *Genocide case* modified its *depth.*[61]

3.3.3 *The descriptive function*

Finally, the Court has also used the term in a purely descriptive way. Unlike in the cases discussed so far, its qualification that certain legal acts had *erga omnes* effects did not entail any immediate legal consequences. Observations made in the *Nuclear Tests cases*[62] and at the jurisdictional stage of the *Nicaragua case*[63] provide examples in point.

The two *Nuclear Tests cases*, in which Australia and New Zealand had invoked the *Barcelona Traction case* in order to establish standing, would have presented the Court with ample opportunity to elaborate on the implications of the concept in the field of law enforcement. While the issue is indeed discussed in many of the individual opinions attached to the decision,[64] the majority did not address it, holding that the legal dispute had become moot when France had unilaterally committed itself to stop atmospheric tests.[65] It nevertheless referred to certain *erga omnes* effects, albeit in different circumstances. Elaborating on the nature of the French unilateral commitment to stop atmospheric

[61] This may explain why some commentators would have preferred the Court to have relied on the *jus cogens* concept (see references in footnote 57). As will be shown below (section 4.2.2.b), it is generally accepted that this concept affects the content (or depth) of specific obligations. Similar observations were made during the ILC's debates about the relevance of concepts such as *jus cogens* and obligations *erga omnes* for debates about possible hierarchies in international law: cf. the summary contained in the ILC's Report on the work of its 56th session, UN Doc. A/59/10, paras. 352–358.

[62] ICJ Reports 1974, 253 and 457 respectively. [63] ICJ Reports 1984, 392.

[64] These are discussed below, section 5.2.5.a.

[65] ICJ Reports 1974, 269–270 (paras. 50–52) and ICJ Reports 1974, 474–475 (paras. 52–55). The statement was again referred to in the 1995 decision on New Zealand's Request for the Interpretation of the 1974 Judgement, ICJ Reports 1995, 306 (para. 64).

nuclear testing, it stated that 'the French government [had] conveyed to the world at large, including the Applicant, its intention to effectively terminate these [atmospheric] tests'.[66] This was so because the relevant oral statements by which the French President and government members committed their country were 'made publicly and *erga omnes*'.[67]

Compared to the statements discussed so far, this passage introduces yet another facet of the *erga omnes* concept. By qualifying the French statements as 'made ... *erga omnes*', the Court described to whom they were addressed and in relation to whom the newly created obligation had come into force. Of course, this use of terminology is related to the traditional understanding of the term, pursuant to which specific legal acts, if binding or opposable *erga omnes*, acquire general validity. However, there remains an important distinction. As has been shown, traditional references to *erga omnes* effects had served to broaden the circle of States bound by an otherwise specific obligation. In contrast, in the above-quoted statement, the Court was not concerned with the effects of legal acts on third States, but merely described in relation to whom a specific statement had been made. It did not intend to broaden the scope of an otherwise specific obligation, but simply used the expression *erga omnes* to identify the addressees of the relevant French statements.

This prompts the question whether the Court intended to recognise a legal interest on behalf of all States to hold France responsible for future breaches of that unilateral commitment. If this were so, the judgments in *Nuclear Tests* could be seen as a confirmation of the earlier decision in *Barcelona Traction*.[68] While the judgment does not expressly address the question, there is reason for caution. The applicants in their respective pleadings had stressed the importance of the alleged prohibition against atmospheric nuclear testing in order to establish its *erga omnes* validity. In contrast, the majority judgment was completely silent on – to borrow the language of the Barcelona Traction Case – the 'importance of the rights involved'.[69] Its main reason for accepting the *erga omnes* character of the promise was of a formal character. As the Court observed, the French promise was valid *erga omnes* because the relevant statements had been made in the public sphere, but not specifically

66 ICJ Reports 1974, 269 (para. 51); ICJ Reports 1974, 474 (para. 53).
67 ICJ Reports 1974, 269 (para. 50); ICJ Reports 1974, 474 (para. 52).
68 Cf. Weil (1983), 432. 69 ICJ Reports 1970, 32 (para. 33).

addressed to one specific country.[70] It seems unlikely that the Court, solely because of this formal reason, should have recognised an enforcement interest of all States.[71] In any event, it did not give the slightest hint that other States should have been entitled to challenge the French nuclear tests. The better view therefore is that the 'curious use of the expression "*erga omnes*"'[72] in the *Nuclear Tests* majority judgment did not entail *any* specific legal consequences. In fact, the decision would have been the same had the Court spoken of a 'unilateral undertaking made in relation to all States'. '*Erga omnes*' therefore seems to have been used in a merely descriptive way. By the same token, each and every obligation assumed in relation to all States – i.e. every obligation arising under general international law – could be qualified as having been undertaken *erga omnes*.[73]

The same, descriptive, use of the term recurs both in the Court's judgment and Judge Schwebel's dissent in the 1984 *Nicaragua (Jurisdiction) case*, more specifically in the respective passages addressing the effects of the United Sates' decision to withdraw its optional clause declaration. Under the terms of its previous optional clause declaration of 14 August 1946, such withdrawal should only take effect upon six months' notice.[74] Relying on considerations of reciprocity, the United States argued that at least in relation to Nicaragua, its withdrawal should take immediate effect, as that country's own declaration could be terminated without delay.[75] Taking up this argument, the Court, as well as Judge Schwebel, inquired whether 'the [immediate] termination . . . was effective *vis-à-vis* Nicaragua, if not effective *erga omnes*'.[76]

[70] ICJ Reports 1974, 269–270 (paras. 49–51), 474–475 (paras. 51–53). This was held notwithstanding the fact that some of the statements had been communicated to the Australian or New Zealand government, see *ibid.*, 269 (para. 50), 474 (para. 52). The nature of the French statements may be contrasted to e.g. the famous *Ihlen Declaration* which, in the words of the PCIJ, constituted a 'response to a request by the diplomatic representative of a [specific] foreign power', see *Eastern Greenland case*, PCIJ, Ser. A/B, No. 53, 53 (1933).

[71] Thirlway (1989), 11–12. Without formally distinguishing between different types of *erga omnes* effects, Gaja (1989), 153, also seems to take a cautious approach.

[72] Dominicé (1999), 359. [73] Cf. above, footnotes 9 and 10.

[74] See e.g. *Multilateral Treaties Deposited with the Secretary-General: Status as at 31 December 1982*, UN Doc. ST/LEG/SER.E/2 (1983). The relevant passage provided that 'this declaration shall remain in force for a period of five years and thereafter until the expiration of six months after notice may be given to terminate this declaration.'

[75] See ICJ Reports 1984, 415–421 (paras. 52–65). For comment cf. Briggs (1985), 373; D'Amato (1985), 385.

[76] ICJ Reports 1984, 416 (para. 55). For Judge Schwebel's very similar statement see *ibid.*, 627 (para. 116).

Again, just as in the *Nuclear Tests cases, erga omnes* was used here in a merely descriptive sense. Neither did it have any bearing on the secondary rules of law enforcement, nor did it modify the scope of the legal act in question. The reference to 'effects *erga omnes*' merely served to indicate between which legal actors the declaration could have taken effect. '*Erga omnes*' might have just as well been replaced by 'the world at large' (as in *Nuclear Tests*)[77] or simply 'all States'; it was used to describe the addresses of a legal act, but did not entail any specific legal consequences.

3.4 Concluding observations

To sum up, since *Barcelona Traction*, the Court and its members have recognised a variety of different *erga omnes* effects. '*Erga omnes*' has notably been used (i) to justify third party effects of treaties or UN resolutions, (ii) to preclude the territorial restriction of obligations, and (iii) in a descriptive way, as a substitute for 'all States'. Given this broad range of meanings, it is surprising that debates have largely remained focused on *erga omnes* effects in the *Barcelona Traction* sense. As the preceding discussion has shown, the narrow focus of the debate is unduly restrictive. Rather than purely concerned with questions of standing and law enforcement, the term '*erga omnes*' has become a legal *vademecum* prescribed to produce a wide array of legal effects. In terms of legal clarity and precision, this is not without its problems. It can only be repeated that the different uses of the expression '*erga omnes*' remain within the limits of a literal interpretation of the Latin term. However, by using an ambiguous term, taking it out of its original context, and subsequently employing it an inflationary way (without distinguishing its different aspects), the Court has rendered a clear analysis considerably more difficult.

The present study does not attempt to discuss the various other *erga omnes* effects in any detail. Clearly, each of them would require further analysis, as would the more general question whether it makes sense to speak of a single and unitary *erga omnes* concept rather than of a patchwork of loosely related *erga omnes* effects. For present purposes, the preceding discussion is important in mainly two respects. First, it serves a clarifying function. Although the distinction between different types of *erga omnes* effects is not usually drawn, it seems necessary for a better

[77] ICJ Reports 1974, 269 (para. 51); ICJ Reports 1974, 474 (para. 53).

understanding of the *erga omnes* concept, and may avoid confusion. Secondly, the distinction helps delimit the topic of the present inquiry more clearly. As has been shown, the Court's and judges' references to other *erga omnes* effects were made outside the context of standing and law enforcement. Despite the use of identical terminology, these references have no bearing on obligations *erga omnes* in the *Barcelona Traction* sense, and do not facilitate the analysis of obligations *erga omnes* as a law enforcement concept. Subsequent chapters discussing the obligations effects in the field of standing will therefore ignore the various pronouncements analysed in the preceding sections.

4 Identifying obligations *erga omnes*

Having distinguished different types of *erga omnes* effects, it is possible to discuss how the *erga omnes* concept affects the rules of law enforcement. The main questions arising in this regard have been summarised above.[1] The first of these, prompted by the Court's *Barcelona Traction* dictum, is which obligations qualify as obligations *erga omnes*. This is not an issue of law enforcement proper; however, it needs to be addressed, as the relevance of the *erga omnes* concept depends on it. Despite decades of discussions, the question has not been solved satisfactorily.[2] Michael Reisman expressed a widely-shared scepticism when professing that he 'was not certain as to how various norms entered into the magic *erga omnes* circle.'[3] Two factors are chiefly responsible for this problematic state of affairs.

First, the ICJ's jurisprudence is inconclusive. Having proclaimed the concept, the Court has subsequently taken a rather cautious approach, and has said very little on how to identify the new category of obligations.[4] To be sure, it has expressly recognised a number of narrowly defined examples of obligations *erga omnes*, namely the prohibitions against aggression, slavery, racial discrimination,[5] and genocide[6] whose

[1] See above, Introduction to Part II.

[2] See e.g. Weil (1992), 288; Schachter (1991), 211; Stein (1995), 115; Charney (1993), 158–159.

[3] Reisman (1993), 170.

[4] As Seiderman (2001), 123, observes, the Court's statements have focused on *erga omnes* effects rather than on the conditions under which an obligation acquires *erga omnes* status.

[5] *Barcelona Traction case*, ICJ Reports 1970, 33 (para. 34).

[6] *Barcelona Traction*, ICJ Reports 1970, 33 (para. 34); *Armed Activities case (Congo-Rwanda)*, available at www.icj-cij.org, para. 71.

erga omnes status is indeed widely accepted today.[7] More recently, the Court has gone beyond narrowly defined examples when observing that a concept as wide as the right of peoples to self-determination[8] or the rules of international humanitarian embodying 'elementary considerations of humanity'[9] applied *erga omnes*. In addition, individual judges have included the prohibition against the use of force (as opposed to the narrower category of aggression)[10] and, more generally, environmental obligations protecting the planetary welfare.[11] The 'beatification' of these obligations, however, has not been the result of a particularly transparent process: while qualifying some obligations as valid *erga omnes*, the Court has been cautious in saying why it has chosen these, and not other, examples. Although the language of the *Barcelona Traction* dictum suggests that such other examples indeed exist,[12] the Court's jurisprudence only hints at ways of indentifying them. Two statements are relevant in this regard.

For once, the Court has stressed that in order to be owed *erga omnes*, an obligation has to protect important values – hence it is '[i]n view of the importance of the rights involved, [that] all States can be held to have a legal interest of obligations ... *erga omnes*'.[13] Moreover, the Court has also drawn 'an essential distinction'[14] between obligations *erga omnes*, and obligations that were actually at stake in *Barcelona Traction*, i.e. reciprocal obligations in the field of diplomatic protection. As will be shown below, these two statements form the basis of the two dominant approaches to the question of identification. However, it is clear that they touch upon the question rather than exploring it in depth, and they fail to set out a conclusive test.

Secondly, State practice and the jurisprudence of other courts do not shed much light on the process of identifying obligations *erga omnes* either. While governments no longer call into question the relevance of

[7] See e.g. para. (9) of the ILC's commentary to Article 48 ASR; and the wealth of support cited by Ragazzi (1997), 74–131.

[8] *East Timor case*, ICJ Reports 1995, 102 (para. 29); *Israeli Wall case*, available at www.icj-cij.org, para. 88.

[9] *Israeli Wall case*, available at www.icj-cij.org, paras. 155 and 157 (quoting the *Corfu Channel* judgment, ICJ Reports 1949, 22).

[10] *Nicaragua case* (provisional measures), Diss.Op. Schwebel, ICJ Reports 1984, 198.

[11] *Gabčíkovo case*, Sep.Op. Weeramantry, ICJ Reports 1997, 117–118.

[12] This follows from the words 'for example' used at the beginning of the enumeration in para. 34. It is further underlined by the express reference to 'present-day international law', and by the phrase 'basic human rights including ...' (emphasis added).

[13] ICJ Reports 1970, 32 (para. 33).

[14] ICJ Reports 1970, 32 (para. 33).

the concept as such, there have been few general statements about its scope. Furthermore, courts other than the ICJ have only rarely mentioned the concept.[15] Occasional references can be found in the jurisprudence of the ICTY and some national courts, but the picture emerging from these statements is fragmentary and inconclusive.[16] In *Blaskić*, the ICTY has further complicated matters by introducing the category of treaty-based obligations *erga omnes* (so-called obligations *erga omnes partes* or obligations *erga omnes contractantes*).[17]

Given this absence of guidance, it is not surprising that commentators express widely diverging views on the scope of the concept. Leaving aside the problem of treaty-based obligations *erga omnes partes*, which has received considerable attention,[18] some commentators have expanded the concept to cover all obligations in the field of human rights,[19] or environmental law,[20] while other have largely focused on examples given by the ICJ.[21]

The present study does not intend to address these claims directly. While some remarks on examples of obligations *erga omnes* are inevitable, no attempt will be made to assess whether specific (groups of) obligations have acquired *erga omnes* status. This question has already received much attention in the literature. Also, trying to establish (or refute) the *erga omnes* status of specific examples, commentators have at times failed to analyse the characteristic features of the category. Rather than seeking to compile yet another list of obligations *erga omnes*, it therefore seems preferable to analyse the process by which these obligations can be identified.

This analysis is best divided into two steps. As a preliminary matter, it is first necessary to address the question of sources, and to comment on the relation between obligations *erga omnes* and obligations *erga omnes partes*. The bulk of this chapter then discusses how obligations *erga*

[15] See notably ICTY, *Furundzija case*, paras. 151–152; ICTY, *Kupreskic case* (evidence decision), 3; Brussels Court of First Instance, Order *In re Pinochet*, 119 ILR 356–357; German *Bundesverfassungsgericht*, 54 Neue Juristische Wochenschrift (2001), 1849.

[16] See, however, below, section 4.2.2 for a brief analysis of how national courts have analysed the relation between obligations *erga omnes* and norms of *jus cogens*.

[17] *Blaskić* case, 110 ILR 699–700 (para. 26).

[18] See below, section 4.1.

[19] See, amongst many others, *Institut de droit international* (1990), 341; Dinstein (1992), 16; Seiderman (2001), 129–135.

[20] See e.g. Birnie/Boyle (2002), 99–100; Brunnée (1989), 800–807; Xue (2003), 237–250; Kiss/Shelton (2000), 24–25; White/Abass (2003), 514; and, more cautiously, Okowa (2000), 212–217.

[21] See notably Ragazzi (1997).

omnes can be distinguished from other international obligations. While not presenting any neat and clear-cut test or even a checklist of criteria, the discussion - taking up Reisman's concern[22] - intends to shed some light on how obligations enter into the 'magic *erga omnes* circle'.

4.1 The question of sources

The first point to be addressed relates to the sources of law from which obligations *erga omnes* derive. The question has prompted considerable discussion, often with particular regard to notions such as *erga omnes partes* or *erga omnes contractantes*, used to describe treaty-based obligations in whose performance all contracting parties are said to have a legal interest.[23] The circle of obligations so labelled is broad, heterogenous and by no means universally agreed. In *Blaskić*, the ICTY expressly stated that article 29 of the ICTY Statute, imposing upon States a duty to cooperate with the Tribunal, was valid *erga omnes partes*.[24] As for academic debates, obligations *erga omnes partes* are notably said to arise under: human rights treaties, such as the ECHR or the CCPR;[25] the 1949 Geneva Conventions and 1977 Protocols, or international humanitarian law in its entirety;[26] international environmental law, notably under the Biodiversity Convention or the Ozone Protocol;[27] more specifically, marine environmental law (as evidenced by broad implementation clauses such as article 218 LOSC);[28] the WTO agreements (as evidenced

[22] See above, footnote 03.

[23] ICTY, *Blaskić case*, 110 ILR 699–700, para. 26; Arangio-Ruiz, Fourth Report, para. 92; Gaja (1989), 151–153; Kessler (2001), 42; Annacker (1994a), 29–30; (Annacker 1994b), 135–136; Paulus (2001), 382; Hutchinson (1988), 155–156. It should be noted that at times, commentators have asserted the existence of treaty-based obligations *erga omnes* (not: *erga omnes partes*) without clarifying that they would only be owed to the treaty parties. Hence Schindler (1995), 199–200, and Moir (2002), 244, state that obligations under the Geneva Conventions are obligations *erga omnes*, while Birnie/Boyle (2002), 99–100, argue that the *erga omnes* concept applies to obligations under environmental treaties. This use of terminology is imprecise, as it blurs the line between obligations *erga omnes* and obligations *erga omnes partes*, which - as will be shown in the following - needs to be maintained.

[24] *Blaskić case*, 110 ILR 699–700 (para. 26).

[25] See, amongst many others, ILC, commentary to article 48 ASR, para. 7; Karl (1994), 88, 108; Gaja (1989), 152–153; Günther (1999), 112–113 and 144–145.

[26] Provost (1994), 388; Schindler (1995), 199–200; Condorelli/Boisson de Chazournes (1984), 29–30; Zemanek (2000a), 5–6; Kessler (2001), 42; Abi-Saab (1984), 270.

[27] ILC, commentary to article 48 ASR, para. 7; Günther (1999), 129–142; Birnie/Boyle (2002), 99–100.

[28] Wolfrum (1990), 325–326; Ziemer (2000), 275; similarly Sachariew (1986), 82–83.

by the broad approach to questions of standing adopted by Panels and Appellate Body);[29] treaties imposing interdependent obligations.[30]

When attempting to assess the scope of the *erga omnes* concept, it is first necessary to determine whether such treaty-based obligations are possible candidates. For the sake of clarity, it should be noted at the outset that this does not require an assessment of whether international law recognises, or should recognise, a category of obligations *erga omnes partes*. It is of course possible to use this expression to describe a particular category of obligations. The questions is how the category so described relates to obligations *erga omnes* in the sense of the ICJ's *Barcelona Traction* jurisprudence; in particular, whether it is subject to the same legal regime.

This indeed is suggested rather frequently.[31] With respect to a particularly important field of obligations, the ILC's Special Rapporteur James Crawford, for example stated that: 'human rights obligations are either obligations *erga omnes* or obligations *erga omnes partes*, depending on their universality and significance'.[32] The subsequent section discusses whether the *erga omnes* concept is really as 'source-neutral' as this statement suggests. It does so in two steps: first, by assessing the the Court's relevant jurisprudence, and secondly, by advancing some more general considerations about the relation between obligations *erga omnes* and their alleged treaty-based counterpart. Although part of the question of sources, this discussion of course has a broader impact. Insofar as it clarifies the relation between obligations *erga omnes* and obligations *erga omnes partes*, it will be reverted to again in subsequent chapters, notably when discussing rights of protection available to States.

4.1.1 *The Court's jurisprudence*

In a first step, the ICJ's approach to the question of sources needs to be analysed. Courts and commentators differentiating between obligations

[29] Günther (1999), 142–144 and 242–247. Along similar lines, Tietje (1998), 163–173, and Matsushita/ Schoenbaum/Mavroidis (2003), 26–27, suggest that GATT law recognises an *actio popularis*, while Yenkong (2004), 768, argues that WTO obligations are 'a sort of "global common"' enforceable by all member States.

[30] Crawford, Third Report, para. 106(b) (his note 195). For the special case of disarmament treaties (the main category of treaties imposing interdependent obligations) see also the ILC's commentary to article 48 ASR, para. 7; Günther (1999), 122–124.

[31] Annacker (1994b), 135; Karl (1994), 88; similarly Kessler (2001), 42, with respect to international humanitarian law.

[32] Crawford, Third Report, his note 182.

erga omnes and obligations *erga omnes partes* usually assume that the former derive from general international law – hence the need to distinguish them from treaty-based obligations.[33] A quick glance at the ICJ's jurisprudence suggests that things are not quite as clear. Paragraph 34 of the *Barcelona Traction* judgment in particular seems to contradict the generally held held assumption. Discussing rights of protection attaching to obligations *erga omnes*, the Court took a more inclusive approach. In its view, such rights of protection could derive from general international law as well as 'international instruments of a universal or quasi-universal character.'[34] This in turn seems to imply that an obligation *erga omnes* could derive from (universal or quasi-universal) treaties.[35]

The reasons leading the Court to include this rather mysterious statement are not entirely clear. Taken at face-value it would stand in marked contrast to the overall thrust of the *Barcelona Traction* dictum, as well as the Court's subsequent jurisprudence, which quite clearly suggest that obligations *erga omnes* derive from general international law. Three aspects in particular are worth noting.

The first relates to terminology. Commentators interpreting para. 34 as an implicit recognition of obligations *erga omnes partes* do so with the proviso that these obligations would be owed not to the international community as a whole but to the particular community of treaty parties.[36] This, however, is not what the Court said: it did not mention communities of treaty parties, but quite clearly stated that *all States* (members of the international community) have a legal interest in seeing obligations *erga omnes* observed. This in turn suggests that these obligations indeed derive from general international law, since otherwise the Court would have recognised a legal interest of third States, not parties to the relevant treaty (allegedly imposing obligations *erga omnes*) in seeing its terms observed. As has been observed already, such legal interests of third States have only been recognised in very exceptional circumstances (notably under article 35 VCLT), and the more convincing interpretation is that all States have a legal interest in the observation of obligations *erga omnes* because they themselves are bound by it.

[33] In contrast, Crawford's Third Report on State responsibility contains the statement that 'there is no reason to exclude from the scope of obligations *erga omnes partes* obligations arising under general international law' (para. 106(b)). To the author's knowledge, this – indeed astonishing – statement has remained singular.

[34] ICJ Reports 1970, 33 (para. 34). [35] Gaja (1989), 152–153; Kessler (2001), 42.

[36] See e.g. Gaja (1989), 152–153; Kessler (2001), 40; Annacker (1994a), 29.

Secondly, this reading is also supported by the fact that *Barcelona Traction* was not decided on the basis of specific treaties, but on the basis of the general rules governing the treatment of aliens.[37] The 'essential distinction' between obligations in the field of diplomatic protection and obligations *erga omnes* was therefore drawn in the context of general international law.

Finally, the Court's subsequent jurisprudence on *erga omnes* effects in the field of standing points in the same direction. When explaining why a specific obligation should be valid *erga omnes*, the Court and its members have referred to features typical of general international law – such as their recognition in international jurisprudence or in UN practice.[38] To be sure, they have also mentioned that the obligations in question had been codified in treaty law; however, this served as further evidence of their acceptance as general international law.[39] Finally, in its *Israeli Wall case*, the Court carefully distinguished between the 1949 Geneva Conventions, and obligations *erga omnes* in the field of international humanitarian law.[40]

In the light of these considerations, the above-quoted passage is perhaps best interpreted as an indication that obligations *erga omnes* are often *also* protected by international treaties. On balance, the better arguments suggest that when recognising the category of obligations *erga omnes*, the Court indeed had in mind obligations arising under general international law.

4.1.2 *Further considerations*

Even so, the concept of obligations *erga omnes partes* could have of course emerged independently. Commentators endorsing it usually state that just as obligations *erga omnes* are owed to the international community, other obligations are owed to communities of treaty parties, and hence valid *erga omnes partes*.[41] The deliberate use of '*erga omnes* terminology' suggests that, but for the question of sources, these obligations would

[37] This is made particularly clear in the latter part of the judgment, where the Court briefly considered investment treaties protecting the economic interests of shareholders, but observed that neither of them was applicable; see ICJ Reports 1970, 46–47 (paras. 89–90).

[38] See e.g. *East Timor case*, ICJ Reports 1995, 102 (para. 29); Diss.Op. Weeramantry, *ibid.*, 194–196; Diss.Op. Skubiszewski, *ibid.*, 266 (paras. 136–138). Further criteria helping to identify obligations *erga omnes* are explored below, section 4.2.2.b.2.

[39] See e.g. *East Timor case*, Diss.Op. Weeramantry, ICJ Reports 1995, 194, 196 and 213-216.

[40] 43 ILM (2004), 1009 (paras. 157-160).

[41] See e.g. Kessler (2001), 40; Gaja (1989), 152; Annacker (1994a), 29.

be subject to the same legal rules. This in turn seems to imply that an analysis of obligations *erga omnes* would frequently have to refer to their treaty-based counterpart.

Attempts to conflate the two categories of obligations are, however, problematic. Of course, it has been stated already that concepts of general international law (such as obligations *erga omnes*) cannot be interpreted in isolation. Just as general international law can influence the interpretation of specific treaty provisions – as exemplified above with respect to the 1966 *South West Africa case* – treaties can help to identify rules of general international law.[42] This possibility however exists irrespective of whether a specific treaty obligation is labelled *erga omnes partes* or not.

What is more, a number of reasons suggests that the use of *erga omnes* terminology is misleading. In particular it seems to suggest that only treaties imposing obligations *erga omnes partes* could recognise a general legal interest of all parties. However, this would be rather simplistic. As has been shown above, the recognition of general legal interests, especially in the field of treaty law, clearly precedes the Court's *Barcelona Traction* judgment.[43] Well before 1970, all States, simply by virtue of their treaty participation and irrespective of any individually sustained injury, were entitled to respond to breaches of obligations contained in a considerable number of treaties, notably in the field of human rights or minority protection, but also under all treaties imposing interdependent obligations. The *erga omnes* concept, therefore, is not the earliest, let alone the only, mechanism allowing for the decentralised enforcement of general legal interests. By qualifying some, but not all,[44] generally enforceable treaty obligations as obligations *erga omnes partes*, commentators and courts risk presenting an undifferentiated picture of the international legal rules in the field of standing.

One might object that this remark is of purely terminological significance. However, there is another problem with treating obligations *erga omnes partes* as the conventional equivalent of obligations *erga omnes*.

[42] See above, section 1.3.3 and, for a discussion of the *South West Africa case*, section 2.2.1.

[43] See above, section 2.2.

[44] It is telling that, for example, the inter-War system for the protection of minorities, while in many respects similar to that under post-1945 human rights treaties, is hardly ever qualified as *erga omnes partes* (but cf. ILC, commentary to article 48 ASR, note 766, for a reference to the League's mandates system). If indeed, *erga omnes partes* status depended on the existence of specific rights of protection, available to all States, the TEC would also qualify (as Gaja (1989), 152–153, indeed seems to suggest).

Although the expression 'obligations *erga omnes partes*' is deliberately modelled on 'obligations *erga omnes*', there are crucial differences between the two concepts. The legal regime governing obligations *erga omnes partes* first and foremost depends on the express or implied terms of the treaty of which they form part. As a consequence, the rules governing the various obligations *erga omnes partes* referred to above are considerably more diverse than those governing obligations *erga omnes*. This may be briefly demonstrated with regard to two essential features of the concept: the conditions under which obligations qualify as obligations *erga omnes (partes)*, and the rights of reaction flowing from the respective status.

The first difference relates to the process of identifying the different categories of obligations. As regards obligations *erga omnes*, this question has yet to be addressed in detail. On the basis of the introductory remarks made above, it can be said that *erga omnes* status is likely to depend on the importance of specific obligations and/or their non-reciprocal structure, rendering them 'essentially different' from obligations in the field of diplomatic protection.[45] Of course, it is by no means excluded these factors should be relevant in the process of assessing whether all State parties have a legal interest in the performance of treaty obligations. However, other factors may equally be relevant, and the test is therefore far more flexible. Where – as in most cases of so-called 'obligations *erga omnes partes*' mentioned above – a treaty *expressly* recognises a general legal interest or confers specific rights of protection, one might even say that the question is of little relevance. States wishing to institute ICJ proceedings in response to alleged breaches of the Genocide Convention, or inter-State proceedings before the Human Rights Committee under article 41 CCPR, do not have to show that the relevant obligations are valid *erga omnes partes*.[46] Their right to react against treaty breaches exists because the respective treaties say so, not because of some special status of the obligation breached.[47]

In the absence of express provision, issues may be more complex but also, at least primarily, are one of treaty interpretation. Again, this interpretation may be influenced by factors other than the ones mentioned above, with respect to obligations *erga omnes* proper. WTO

[45] See above, Introduction.

[46] Cf. article 41 CCPR (providing for a system of optional inter-State complaints, irrespective of individual injury). On article IX of the 1948 Genocide Convention see already above, section 2.2.2.a.

[47] See Thirlway (1990), 100, for a similar argument.

dispute settlement organs, to take but one example, have accepted that trade rules protect conditions of trade, not actual trade flows.[48] This extensive treaty interpretation has prompted them to adopt a broad approach to questions of standing and to recognise a right of all State parties to bring violations complaints under article XXIII:1(a) GATT 1994[49] (which has led commentators to qualify WTO obligations as obligations *erga omnes partes*).[50] Similarly, when asserting the *erga omnes partes* character of article 29 of its Statute, the ICTY, in *Blaskić*, not only analysed the wording of that provision, but also relied on the text of Security Council Res. 827, which was held to express a general legal interest on behalf of all State parties in the functioning of the Tribunal.[51] In short, while obligations *erga omnes* and obligations *erga omnes partes* both protect a general legal interest, the conditions under which the respective status is acquired are not necessarily identical.

Secondly, similar considerations apply to the specific means by which States can enforce obligations *erga omnes* and obligations *erga omnes partes*. While in both cases, all States bound by the respective obligations have a legal interest in seeing them observed, their rights of protection may be very different. With respect to obligations *erga omnes*, it has already been stated that the existence of specific rights of protection is a matter of considerable controversy. Subsequent chapters will analyse in some detail whether States can avail themselves of the two means of enforcement addressed in the present study, namely ICJ claims and countermeasures. It is of course by no means excluded that State parties to treaties protecting general interests should be entitled to resort to the same forms of enforcement. However, just as with regard to the conditions of *erga omnes partes* status, the situation is considerably more diverse. This in particular because treaties protecting a general legal interest of all State parties often expressly recognise specific means of law enforcement. Depending on the character of the treaty, these may be

[48] See e.g. *Oilseeds case*, para. 150; *Japanese Leather*, paras. 47–55; *Tuna II* (unadopted Panel Report), 33 ILM (1994), 839, para. 5.6.

[49] See especially the Panel and Appellate Body Reports in the *Bananas III dispute*: WT/DS27/R (Panel), paras. 7.49–7.51, and WT/DS27/AB/R (Appellate Body), paras. 132–136; as well as the Panel Report in *Korea Dairy*, WT/DS98/R, para. 7.2. As for practice under GATT 1947 see the (unadopted) Panel Report in *Tuna II*, 33 ILM (1994), 839, paras. 3.84–3.87 and para. 5.6. For a discussion see Yenkong (2004), 766–768; Tietje (1998), 163–173; Waincymer (2002), 154–157. For a critical assessment of this jurisprudence cf. Pauwelyn (2003), 75–78 and 81–85.

[50] See above, footnote 29.

[51] See 110 ILR 699–700 (para. 26) (quoting operative paragraph 4 of SC Res. 827 (1993)).

very different. When limiting the analysis to the treaties mentioned above, one can distinguish committee-based procedures (under the CCPR or CAT) from proceedings before different international courts or court-like institutions (under the ECHR, the ICJ, or the WTO dispute settlement organs), while other provisions recognise the right of States to exercise jurisdiction in the general interest (e.g. under article 218 LOSC). These means of responding to treaty breaches are available to States simply as a matter of treaty law, and irrespective of whether the performance of specific obligations is owed to the community of treaty parties. Similarly, it is largely a question of treaty interpretation whether States not individually injured can rely on rights of protection not expressly recognised. With regard to human rights treaties or GATT, it has, for example, been hotly debated whether States should be entitled to resort to countermeasures in response to treaty breaches.[52] This question cannot be answered in the abstract; it depends on a thorough examination of each treaty regime, which cannot be substituted for by references to the *erga omnes* or *erga omnes partes* status of obligations.

What is more, whereas under the Court's jurisprudence, *all* States have a legal interest in seeing obligations *erga omnes* observed, treaties not infrequently delegate enforcement competence to specific actors. Again, the different regimes diverge widely. Article 218 LOSC extends the jurisdiction of port States, but says nothing about rights of other States not individually injured.[53] Having proclaimed that article 29 of its Statute was valid *erga omnes partes*, the ICTY, in *Blaskić*, suggested that States' legal interests notwithstanding, the duty of cooperation was primarily to be enforced by the UN Security Council.[54] Whether rights of protection also accrue to other actors not specifically designated again is a matter of treaty interpretation.

To sum up, whereas obligations *erga omnes* and obligations *erga omnes partes* are similar in that all States bound by the obligation have a legal interest in seeing it performed, the applicable legal rules may be very different. Since treaties often expressly regulate under which circumstances all States have a legal interest in seeing the treaty observed, and

[52] As regards human rights, the question is controversially discussed by e.g. Simma (1981), 635; Frowein (1983), 253–257; Graefrath (1987), 121–122 and 126–131; Sachariew (1988), 285–286; Sachariew (1986), 103–106. As for GATT, see e.g. Pauwelyn (2000), 335; Hahn (1996); von Unger (2004), 44–51. For further analysis see below, Chapter 7.

[53] On the provision see further König (1990); König (2002), 1; Smith (1988), 173–176.

[54] 110 ILR 699–700 (para. 26). For comment cf. Malanczuk (1998), 237–240; Stroh (2002), 298–299.

how this legal interest can be vindicated, the regime governing obligations *erga omnes partes* is considerably more flexible. Indeed, on the basis of the arguments summarised in the preceding paragraphs, it may be questioned whether anything approaching a coherent legal regime of obligations *erga omnes partes* has already emerged. At least at present, it seems that little would be lost if one continued to speak of treaties protecting general legal interests of all parties. Burdening the process of treaty interpretation with a notion as controversial as *erga omnes (partes)* often seems unnecessary, at least where treaties expressly list rights of protection available to States. In any event, obligations *erga omnes*, as well as the corresponding rights of protection flowing from that status, need to be assessed autonomously.

This does not mean that treaty law is irrelevant to the present study. As has been stated, treaty rules can support the existence of rules of general international law. What is more, as special rules, treaties can also derogate from general international law, and a subsequent chapter will therefore assess the relation between treaty and customary means of enforcement.[55] As a consequence, the subsequent discussion will frequently refer to treaty regimes. It will not, however, specifically address obligations *erga omnes partes*, but instead focus on those customary obligations that qualify as obligations *erga omnes*.

4.2 Distinguishing obligations *erga omnes* from other customary obligations

In order to define the scope of the concept, it is therefore necessary to analyse how obligations *erga omnes* are to be distinguished from other customary obligations. Given the scarcity of authoritative guidance, it is not surprising that this question has drawn widely divergent answers. As has already been stated, two approaches – both of which can be traced back to statements made by the Court – dominate much of the debate.[56]

[55] See below, Chapter 7.

[56] In addition to the two approaches discussed in the following, Ragazzi (1997) has sought to filter out common characteristics of obligations *erga omnes* expressly recognised by the Court. In his view (see pp. 132–134), the four examples recognised in *Barcelona Traction* are (i) prohibitions (as opposed to affirmative duties), (ii) obligations in the strict, Hohfeldian, sense (as opposed to liabilities, disabilities or no-claims), (iii) are narrowly defined, (iv) derive from peremptory norms of general international law (*jus cogens*), and (v) reflect fundamental moral values.

For a number of reasons, this 'inductive approach' will not be addressed separately. As Ragazzi concedes (cf. p. 134), the criteria given by him are not intended to be

. For the sake of convenience, the present study will address them in turn. Since they are not always properly distinguished, some preliminary remarks about their respective starting-points may be in order.

The first approach, based on the Court's reference to 'the importance of rights involved',[57] rests on a simple proposition. In order to be valid *erga omnes* – so the argument runs – an obligation has to be qualified in a material way: it has to protect important values. This *material approach* is indeed backed by the bulk of ICJ jurisprudence. Apart from general references to the importance of obligations, the Court and its members have for example recognised the *erga omnes* status of obligations deriving from 'essential principle[s] of contemporary international law',[58] or rules making up 'the basic tenets of modern international law'.[59] While frequently affirmed, the material approach of course is very difficult to apply in practice, as it relies on the inherently vague and indeterminate notion of 'importance'.

The second approach rests on a more complex proposition. It is based on the idea that there is 'an essential distinction'[60] between obligations *erga omnes* and obligations in the field of diplomatic protection. As the Court clarified, obligations in the latter field are owed to one State in particular and give rise to rights and duties between pairs of States. Pursuant to adherents of the second approach, obligations *erga omnes* (being essentially different) are 'non-reciprocal' or 'non-bilateralisable'. This of course is readily acceptable as far as the consequences triggered by breaches are concerned – by definition, responsibility for violations of obligations *erga omnes* exceeds the reciprocal legal relations between pairs of States, since all States have a legal interest in their observance. The vantage point of the second approach, however, is quite different. Rather than describing the consequences flowing from breaches, it addresses the pattern (or structure) along which obligations *erga omnes* have to be performed. In the view of commentators, the *erga omnes*

prescriptive, and not all obligations *erga omnes* would have to fulfil them. Furthermore, the value of Ragazzi's analysis is somewhat diminished, as it does not take into account the fifth example recognised by the Court, namely the right to self-determination. Even if one accepted that this could be understood as 'the prohibition against denial of self-determination' (in which case Ragazzi's first and second criteria would be met), this example would still be anything but narrowly defined; it would therefore not fulfil Ragazzi's third criterion. More generally, it may be doubted whether the first two criteria are of much help in distinguishing obligations *erga omnes* from other obligations of international law. Finally, criteria four and five seem to be aspects of what is labelled here as the 'importance requirement' and as such are addressed below, in section 4.2.2. For a critical analysis of Ragazzi's approach see Paulus (1999), 810.

57 ICJ Reports 1970, 32 (para. 33). 58 ICJ Reports 1995, 102 (para. 29).

59 ICJ Reports 1984, 198. 60 ICJ Reports 1970, 32 (para. 33).

status of an obligation is merely the consequence of its non-reciprocal structure of performance. Put differently, an obligation acquires *erga omnes* status precisely because it has to be performed in relation to all other States (or 'integrally'), and thereby transcends the reciprocal (or 'bilateral/bilateralisable') relations between pairs of States. In the words of Arangio-Ruiz, obligations *erga omnes* are thus 'legally indivisible',[61] whereas Annacker, in a much-quoted statement, has maintained that '[t]he distinguishing feature of an obligation *erga omnes* is its non-bilateralizable structure.'[62] This is clearly not the only way of reading the Court's statement about the 'essential difference'. However, it is a defensible one. Moreover, as the choice of terminology suggests, it builds on an existing analysis, namely the classification of obligations introduced by Fitzmaurice during his work as Special Rapporteur on the law of treaties, which had equally distinguished reciprocal and non-reciprocal obligations.[63] In order to underline this relation, the second approach will be referred to, in the following, as the *structural approach* to the *erga omnes* concept. Just as Fitzmaurice's analysis, it rests on a rational criterion – the structure of performance – and would considerably facilitate the identification of obligations *erga omnes*.[64]

Although not mutually exclusive, material and structural approaches thus proceed from very different starting-points. In the following, both will therefore be addressed in turn.

4.2.1 *The structural approach*

On the face of it, the structural approach seems difficult to reconcile with the Court's frequent affirmation that in order to be valid *erga omnes*, an obligation has to protect important values. While agreeing that obligations *erga omnes* would have to be non-reciprocal, structuralists have taken different views on how to accommodate these express statements. Adherents of what may be called the *strong version* of the structural approach seem to neglect the Court's comments; in their view, all non-bilateralisable obligations, irrespective of their importance, are valid *erga omnes*.[65] The point is made very clearly by

61 Fourth Report, para. 92.

62 Annacker (1994b), 136. See also Annacker (1994a), 53, 64–65; Seiderman (2001), 129; Sachariew (1986), 76 ('*nicht spaltbar*').

63 See above, section 2.2.1.

64 Cf. Paulus (2001), 382.

65 See e.g. Annacker (1994b), 135–136, 149; Seiderman (2001), 126–129; Bryde (1994), 167–169; Lefeber (1996), 113–114; Lopez Pegna (1998), 732–733. Feist (2001), 38–40 and 122–128, equates obligations *erga omnes* and absolute obligations.

Seiderman, who observes that 'the determination as to which norms give rise to obligations *erga omnes* is not an assessment as to which norms are most "important".'[66] In contrast, the *moderate version* of the structural approach, accepts that only important non-bilateralisable obligations qualify as obligations *erga omnes*.[67] As will be shown in the following, this differentiation has important consequences for the way the two versions of the structural approach are assessed. They will therefore be dealt with separately.

4.2.1.a The strong version

While allowing for a clear-cut identification, the strong version of the structural approach raises a number of problems. The most obvious point to make is that it simply ignores the one recurring theme in the ICJ's *erga omnes* jurisprudence, namely the Court's frequent references to the importance of the rights protected by obligations *erga omnes*. Even beyond that, however, the strong structural approach is unconvincing. As a proper application of Fitzmaurice's classification shows, it is based on a simplistic analysis of multilateral obligations.

If indeed, obligations *erga omnes* were solely characterised by their non-reciprocal (or non-bilateralisable/integral) structure, the concept would be considerably broader than its supporters acknowledge. Supporters have frequently stressed that on the basis of their analysis, obligations in the human rights or environmental field would qualify as *erga omnes*.[68] However, when following the strong structural approach to its conclusion, the concept could not be restricted to these fields, but would encompass two of the three categories of obligations identified

[66] Seiderman (2001), 129; similarly Arangio Ruiz, Fourth Report, para. 92; Voeffray (2004), 241–246. Bryde (1994), 169, recognises that this (structural) approach to obligations *erga omnes* moves away from the ICJ's *Barcelona Traction* dictum.

[67] Biermann (1996), 451; Künzli (2001), 65–66; Kessler (2001), 38–40, 42–47; Günther (1999), 99–101, 109–115; Simma (1993a), 132–133. See also Paulus (2001), 381–385, who argues that the two main criteria advanced by commentators (importance and specific structure of performance) are alternative rather than cumulative.

[68] Lefeber (1996), 113–114; Seiderman (2001), 126–129; (Annacker 1994b), 146–148; similarly the Commission's commentary to draft article 40 of the first reading text, YbILC 1985, Vol. II/2, 27 (stating that interests safeguarded by human rights obligations were 'not allocatable' to one State in particular, and hence could be vindicated by all States).

It should be stressed that the same view is shared by some adherents of the material approach. In their view, it is however based not on a structural analysis, but on the conviction that obligations under human rights or environmental law are sufficiently important to be valid *erga omnes*. See further below, section 4.2.2.

by Fitzmaurice: absolute and interdependent obligations. As has been shown above, the performance of neither of these obligations is owed to any particular State. If non-reciprocity was all that mattered, both absolute and interdependent obligations would be valid *erga omnes*.[69] With regard to both categories of obligations, this result is problematic.

As regards interdependent obligations, attributing *erga omnes* status would be quite unnecessary. As has been shown above, even prior to the *Barcelona Traction* judgment, interdependent obligations were subject to a special legal regime; all States had a legal interest in seeing them observed and were entitled to react against breaches.[70] Qualifying interdependent obligations as obligations *erga omnes* (a consequence of the strong structural approach) would thus not alter their regime of law enforcement.[71]

In contrast, with regard to absolute obligations, the strong structural approach would completely reverse Fitzmaurice's approach. As has been stated above, commentators had criticised that pursuant to Fitzmaurice's structural analysis, individual responses against breaches of absolute obligations were practically excluded.[72] By qualifying all absolute obligations as obligations *erga omnes*, structuralists would avoid this result; paraphrasing Marx' famous dictum on Hegel, they would thus 'invert' Fitzmaurice's analysis, which in their view most certainly was 'standing on its head'.[73]

As far as human rights or environmental obligations are concerned, it is of course open for debate whether the results of this *renversement*

[69] For the sake of clarity, it may be recalled that absolute obligations are to be performed not between States, but by each of them independently; they require States to adopt a parallel conduct within their own jurisdiction (see Fitzmaurice, Second Report, YbILC 1957, Vol. II, 54 (para. 125); Simma (1994a), 336). In contrast, interdependent obligations have to be performed between all parties, not independently by each of them. They are concluded on the basis of an implied understanding that the purpose of the obligation can only be attained if *each* party complies with it (Fitzmaurice, Second Report, YbILC 1957, Vol. II, 54 (para. 126); Simma (1994a), 336–337).
For comment on the viability of the distinction, and the confusing use of terminology, see above section 2.1.1.

[70] See above, Chapter 2; and cf. only article 60(2)(c) VCLT; article 42(b)(ii) ASR. For the respective commentaries see YbILC 1966, Vol. II, 255, para. 8; and commentary to article 42 ASR, para. 13.

[71] It must be conceded that this problem is avoided by authors who equate absolute obligations with obligations *erga omnes*, while maintaining interdependent obligations as a separate category; see notably Feist (2001), 38–40 and 122–128.

[72] See above, section 2.1.1.

[73] Cf. Marx' claim that with Hegel, dialectic materialism 'is standing on its head. It must be inverted, in order to discover the rational kernel within the mystical shell' (Marx (1867/1977), 103).

would be desirable. However, it has been shown above that, contrary to common perception, the concept of absolute obligations goes well beyond these two fields of law. If indeed, *erga omnes* status solely depended on the non-reciprocal structure, *all* absolute obligations (including the duties of States to harmonise national laws, to outlaw specific forms of behaviour, or to adopt other forms of conduct within their respective spheres of jurisdiction) would qualify.[74] One might object that absolute obligations are usually contained in treaties, and thus would not qualify as obligations *erga omnes*. But this is not necessarily the case, as the structural criterion upon which the distinction is based does not depend on an obligation's formal source.[75] In any event, there is little evidence that existing absolute obligations of general international law outside the human rights or environmental field are considered to be valid *erga omnes*. Solely relying on the structure of performance, the strong structural approach would be unable to distinguish between different types of absolute obligations.

To sum up, the strong structural approach leads to results that are either already accepted (in the case of interdependent obligations) or seem unduly broad (in the case of absolute obligations). While providing for a clear-cut definition of the concept, the strong structural approach therefore is not convincing.

4.2.1.b The moderate version

Given the problems of the strong structural approach, it is not surprising that adherents of the moderate version accept the need for a threshold limit, and restrict the *erga omnes* concept to obligations that are at the same time non-bilateralisable *and* important.[76] This accommodates the Court's affirmations of some form of importance requirement. At the same time, it forces supporters to determine how important non-bilateralisable obligations have to be in order to be valid *erga omnes*, and thus imports the main difficulty of the material approach.

This obstacle notwithstanding, the moderate structural approach is not supported by the Court's jurisprudence and is ultimately unconvincing. A quick glance at the list of examples expressly recognised by the

[74] For further examples and a discussion of the concept of absolute obligations see above, section 2.1.1.

[75] See above, section 2.1.1.

[76] Contrast the argument made by Paulus (2001), 382, in whose view both criteria are alternative, not cumulative. This is subject to the same criticism as the strong structural approach.

Court refutes the idea that in order to be valid *erga omnes*, an obligation had to be non-reciprocal (or non-bilateralisable/integral). Out of the five examples of obligations *erga omnes* expressly recognised by the Court, one is perfectly bilateralisable, while breaches of all others can at least give rise to (bilateral) responsibility between pairs of States.

The prohibition against aggression is the most obvious counter-example. As has already been stated, this prohibition is structurally not different from the rules preventing a State to violate reciprocal undertakings or indeed obligations owed to another State in the context of diplomatic protection.[77] Since aggression necessarily involves the use of force against another State,[78] every breach of the rule injures one (victim) State in its individual capacity. If acts of aggression nevertheless are held to affect the legal interests of other States, or the international community as a whole, the reason for this cannot be structural.[79]

However, aggression is not the only example of a bilateralisable obligation *erga omnes*; breaches of all other examples of obligations *erga omnes* can equally give rise to responsibility between pairs of States. The reason for this is that – as has been stated already – breaches of otherwise absolute or interdependent obligations can injure one State in its individual capacity if they specially affect it.[80] By the same token, a State that violates an important non-bilateralisable obligation (i.e. an obligation *erga omnes* in the sense of the moderate structural approach) in a way that specially affects one particular State incurs responsibility first and foremost in relation to that particular State.

The point can be illustrated by taking the example of a commonly accepted obligation *erga omnes*, such as the prohibition against genocide. If State A engages in genocidal conduct *vis-à-vis* the population of

[77] See above, sections 1.3 and 2.1.1. Cf. also de Hoogh (1996), 54–55, Paulus (2001), 382.

[78] See the definition of aggression adopted, in 1974, by the UN General Assembly, GA Res. 3314 (XXIX): all acts enumerated in article 3(a)–(g) expressly require that another State is targeted by the activity. Cf. further de Hoogh (1996), 54; Cassese (2001), 257.

[79] Annacker and Seiderman have argued that although aggression, by definition, affects one State in particular, it contains a non-bilateralisable component: In the words of Annacker: 'If non-compliance with an *erga omnes* obligation impairs the objective interests of all parties bound by the norm, and in addition the subjective interests of certain parties, then all States are affected directly, but in different interests' (Annacker (1994b), 149; similarly Seiderman (2001), 128).

This argument however fails to explain *why* all parties have an objective interest in seeing the obligation observed, and thereby 'reverse[s] cause and effect' (de Hoogh (1996), 54).

[80] For a discussion see sections 1.3.2 and 2.1.1. See also article 60, para. 2(b) VCLT; article 42(b)(i) ASR.

State B, responsibility – irrespective of any general legal interest of other States, or of the rights of the individual victims of the act – arises primarily between the perpetrator (A) and the State of nationality of the victims (B).[81] If the perpetrator State (A) is *also* responsible towards other States (C–Z), this cannot be explained as a consequence of an alleged non-reciprocal structure, but must be based on other arguments. Put differently, if responsibility arising from *erga omnes* breaches was necessarily non-bilateralisable, genocidal conduct *vis-à-vis* foreign nationals would not qualify.[82] In contrast, the Court has not distinguished between genocide committed against a State's own population and genocide committed against foreign nationals. Instead, it has recognised the *erga omnes* character of the prohibition against genocide irrespective of the nationality of the potential victims. Just as acts of aggression, *erga omnes* violations that specially affect individual States thus do not fit into the scheme of non-bilateralisable obligations.

It would seem to follow from this analysis that the moderate version of the structural approach cannot be reconciled with the Court's jurisprudence. Apart from ignoring the *erga omnes* character of the prohibition against aggression, it is based on a schematic application of Fitzmaurice's classification, and fails to explain that breaches of non-reciprocal obligations can specially affect individual States.

4.2.1.c Interim conclusion

To sum up, neither the strong nor the moderate version of the structural approach can be sustained. The reasons leading commentators to focus on the structure of obligations *erga omnes* are understandable. Quite apart from the misleading passage contained in para. 33 of the *Barcelona Traction* judgment, the *erga omnes* concept might have seemed an ideal vehicle to remedy the deficiencies of Fitzmaurice's approach, notably with regard to absolute obligations. However, as the above analysis shows, the concept of obligations *erga omnes* as recognised by the Court does not square with Fitzmaurice's distinction between three categories of obligations. Contrary to the basic premise of the structural approach, bilateralisable obligations may qualify as obligations *erga*

[81] Cf. the Bosnian and Croatian *Genocide cases* before the ICJ, which – although involving allegations of genocide – are traditional disputes between two States. See above, section 1.3.2, and the para. 12 of the ILC's commentary to article 42 ASR for further references.

[82] Curiously, violations of obligations *erga omnes* committed against foreign nationals are hardly ever discussed in literature. If at all, they are described as unusual cases; see Bryde (1994), 167–168; Seiderman (2001), 128.

omnes, while (contrary to the main argument put forward by adherents of its strong version) not all non-bilateralisable obligations have acquired that status. In short, the Court's jurisprudence suggests that obligations *erga omnes* defy clear-cut classifications, but have to be identified on the basis of a more flexible criterion.

4.2.2 *The material approach*

A more flexible test is put forward by adherents of what has been termed 'the material approach' to the *erga omnes* concept. As has been shown, the bulk of ICJ jurisprudence indeed suggests that obligations acquire *erga omnes* status because of their heightened importance. While enjoying much support, this importance test is very flexible indeed; in order to be applicable, it has to be given some practical meaning. The most obvious question arising is *how important* obligations have to be in order to be valid *erga omnes* - it is thus necessary to establish the required degree of importance. In addition, there is another, often neglected, problem. Even among those accepting the need for some importance test, there is considerable uncertainty as to which aspects of the legal relations arising from obligations *erga omnes* need to be important. This problem (which will be termed the 'point of reference' of the importance test) needs to be addressed before assessing the required degree of importance.

4.2.2.a The point of reference

Over the years, the importance test set out by the Court has been interpreted very differently by commentators. This is somewhat surprising, as the Court has taken a very straightforward approach. In the crucial statement, which has been quoted already, it observed that an obligation acquires *erga omnes* status '[i]n view of the importance of the rights involved'.[83] What is significant about this pronouncement is not so much the shift from the language of obligation to the language of right - after all, one might assume that where an obligation protects an important right, it could itself be characterised as an important obligation. However, it is crucial to realise that the importance is assessed by reference to the *quality* of a specific right. Simple as it may seem, this means that other considerations, often relied on by commentators, are irrelevant. Two aspects need to be addressed.

[83] ICJ Reports 1970, 32 (para. 33).

First, it is crucial to note that the Court distinguishes between different rights, not between different ways in which rights are infringed.[84] Of course, some of the examples of obligations *erga omnes* only protect against particular serious forms of misconduct.[85] However, the Court does not require that infringements of the rights in question should entail particularly serious consequences in a given case. Contrary to what is at times assumed by commentators,[86] an obligation thus acquires *erga omnes* status because it protects important rights, not because – or if – it is violated in a particularly serious way. As will be shown below, the intensity of breaches might be a relevant factor in assessing how States can respond to breaches of such obligations; equally it may of course be relevant when States decide whether or not they should make use of possible rights of protection. An obligation's *erga omnes* status as such, however, does not depend upon the effects of breaches.

Secondly, since the *erga omnes* status follows from the importance of the protected right, it does not depend on whether that right, in a concrete situation, actually requires protection. Contrary to arguments advanced in literature, the question of whether an obligation is owed *erga omnes* does not depend on functional criteria, such as the availability of other forms of protection, or the likelihood that States in a given situation will exercise rights of protection.[87] These considerations can be relevant in assessing how rights of protection derived from the *erga omnes* concept relate to other rights of protection (notably those derived from treaties).[88] The Court's express language however shows that *erga omnes* status has to be determined independently of such considerations of necessity or functionality.

[84] See also ICJ Reports 1995, 102 (para. 29), where the Court referred to the importance of the right of self-determination rather than the intensity of possible violations. Contrast however Judge Weeramantry's misleading reference to '*erga omnes* issues . . . of sufficient importance' in his separate opinion in *Gabčíkovo*, ICJ Reports 1997, 117–118.

[85] See notably the prohibition against aggression; aggression having been described as 'the most serious and dangerous form of the illegal use of force' (see the Preamble of GA Res. 3314 (XXIX); and further Frowein/Krisch, in: Simma (2002a), article 39, MN 13).

[86] Contrast e.g. Okowa (2000), 215–216 (arguing that the seriousness of breaches would be relevant in determining which environmental obligations are valid *erga omnes*). See also Oellers-Frahm (1992), 35, who misleadingly states that 'only gross violations on a widespread scale' clearly qualify as *erga omnes* breaches.

[87] Contrast notably Charney (1993), 159; Charney (1991), 154 and 161; and further Coffman (1996), 295–309.

[88] See below, Chapter 7.

4.2.2.b The required threshold of importance

No such clear answers can be given to the second, ultimately more important question. While affirming that only important obligations are valid *erga omnes*, the Court has failed to spell out *how important* they would have to be. As regards obligations in the human rights field, the Court's statement that obligations protecting 'basic human rights'[89] were valid *erga omnes* provides some guidance and suggests a cautious approach. While commentators have criticised the underlying distinction between basic and other human rights[90] it is difficult to ignore the fact that, at least in 1970, the Court was not prepared to admit the *erga omnes* character of all human rights.[91] Beyond that, however, it seems difficult to draw any firm conclusions from the Court's use of terminology.[92]

Unfortunately, other formulations used to describe the importance requirement (such as the references to 'essential principle[s]' or 'basic tenets' of international law giving rise to obligations *erga omnes*)[93] are also of limited help, since neither of the respective terms has a clear-cut meaning. Finally, while other vague, indeterminate notions of international law are often shaped through constant practice,[94] the *erga omnes* concept has not been regularly invoked in formalised proceedings.

Given these difficulties, it would be over-optimistic to expect that the required degree of importance could conclusively be established in the abstract. This does not mean, however, that identfying obligations *erga omnes* were a matter of pure speculation. Quite to the contrary, two very different approaches can help bring about at least some predictability.

89 ICJ Reports 1970, 33 (para. 34).

90 See e.g. Riedel in: Simma (2002a), Article 55(c), MN 12; Seiderman (2001), 131–133; Meron (1986), 10.

91 Oellers-Frahm (1992), 31; Ragazzi (1997), 140–141. It is frequently overlooked that by dismissing Belgium's claim, the Court implicitly held that the protection against denial of justice (whose violation had been alleged) was not a basic human right in the sense of para. 34.

92 For a more detailed discussion of the notion of 'basic human rights' see e.g. Ragazzi (1997), 139–141; Frowein (1983), 243–244; Meron (1986), 10–13; Seidermann (2001), 131–135.

93 ICJ Reports 1995, 102 (para. 29) and ICJ Reports 1984, 198 respectively. Cf. already above, Introduction to section 4.2.

94 Ill-defined or indefinable notions such as threat to peace or intervention (which, pursuant to Talleyrand, 'is largely the same as non-intervention', and, following Winfield (1922–1923), 130, at one time 'may [have been] anything from a speech of Lord Palmerston's in the House of Commons to the partition of Poland') come to mind. Both are concretised through application in practice.

First, the scope of the *erga omnes* concept can be determined in a comparative way, by assessing the relation between obligations *erga omnes* and peremptory norms of international law (*jus cogens*). As will be shown, rules of *jus cogens* are usually (though not exclusively)[95] considered to protect important values of the international community, and a comparison thus seems promising.[96] Secondly, it may be helpful to proceed pragmatically and simply single out other factors that are indicative of an obligation's importance. It is submitted that taken together, the two approaches (which are not mutually exclusive) give practical meaning to the Court's very general importance test.

Obligations erga omnes *and norms of* jus cogens

In the absence of a clear test for the identification of obligations *erga omnes*, commentators have often sought to define the scope of the concept by reference to the notion of peremptory norms (*jus cogens*) of general international law.[97] Article 53 VCLT, repeated *verbatim* in the 1986 Vienna Convention, stipulates that *jus cogens* rules are 'accepted and recognized by the international community of States as a whole as ... norm[s] from which no derogation is permitted and which can be modified only by ... subsequent norm[s] of general international law having the same effect.'[98] The relation between peremptory norms and obligations *erga omnes* is much discussed. That both concepts are somehow related is generally agreed and indeed supported by a considerable

[95] See below, footnote 109.

[96] Traditionally, obligations *erga omnes* have also been compared to obligations whose breach amounted to an international crime in the sense of draft article 19 of the ILC's first reading text on State responsibility; see e.g. Acosta Estevez (1995), 3; de Hoogh (1991), 183. With the demise of the notion of crimes, and its replacement by a category of 'serious breaches of obligations deriving from peremptory norms of general international law' (see article 40 ASR), it now seems possible to focus on the relation between obligations *erga omnes* and norms of *jus cogens*. Relevant comments on the concept of crimes will be integrated into this analysis; see especially text accompanying footnotes 149–151; and cf. *ibid.* for a short comment on the relation between crimes and serious breaches.

[97] The following section will focus on the relation between obligations *erga omnes* and peremptory norms of *general international law*. It does not purport to discuss the controversial question whether there can be treaty-based or regional norms of *jus cogens*. On this issue see notably American Commission on Human Rights, *Roach and Pinkerton v. United States*, 8 HRLJ (1997), 351 (holding that the execution of minors was prohibited by a norm of inter-American *jus cogens*), and further Byers (1999), 199–200; Kolb (1998), 98–103.

[98] For more recent discussion of the concept see in particular Kolb (2001); Kolb (1998), 69; Byers (1999), 183–203; Seiderman (2001), 35–121; Thierry (1990), 58–70; Weil (1992),

amount of circumstantial evidence. Although the ICJ has never expressly pronounced on the matter, its *erga omnes* jurisprudence seems to be inspired by debates about peremptory norms. The description of obligations *erga omnes* as obligations owed to the international community as a whole, but for the reference to States, takes up the language used to define the concept of *jus cogens*.[99] The *Barcelona Traction* judgment as the crucial judicial pronouncement was handed down a mere eight months after the adoption of article 53 VCLT, i.e. at a time when the concept of *jus cogens* dominated international legal debates.[100] Furthermore, in his separate opinion appended to the judgment, Judge Ammoun elaborated on the question of legal interests, distinguishing – just as the majority judgment – between individual interests of States, and general interests of the international community.[101] Unlike the majority, he did not use the concept of obligations *erga omnes*, but analysed community interests 'protected by norms of *jus cogens*.'[102] While the majority pronounced on *erga omnes* effects in the field of standing, Judge Ammoun thus treated the same issue under the rubric of peremptory norms.[103] Finally, the four examples of obligations *erga omnes* expressly referred to by the Court in *Barcelona Traction* had been named as prime examples of *jus cogens* norms during the Vienna Conference.[104]

In the light of these considerations, it seems beyond doubt that there is, at the very least, considerable overlap between obligations *erga omnes* and norms of *jus cogens*. In order to assess the scope of the *erga omnes* concept, it is necessary to analyse the relation in greater detail. Before proceeding with this analysis, it is also necessary briefly to introduce

262–282; Cassese (2001), 138–148; Frowein (1997a), 65; Paulus (2001), 330-363; Christenson (1988), 585; Hannikainen (1988); Macdonald 1987), 129–139; Kadelbach (1992). The controversial discussions preceding the adoption of article 53 VCLT are reflected in the works by Verdross (1966), 55; Schwarzenberger (1965), 455; Schwelb (1967b), 946; Virally (1966), 5; as well as the contributions to the *Lagonissi Conference* (1967).

99 de Hoogh (1991), 193; Seiderman (2001), 124; Günther (1999), 109; Kadelbach (1992), 117.

100 Ragazzi (1997), 189; de Hoogh (1991), 193; Tomuschat (2003), 196; Frowein (1987), 68. The Vienna Convention was adopted on 23 May 1969; the *Barcelona Traction* judgment was rendered on 5 February 1970. The adoption of ILC draft article 50 (which was to become article 53 VCLT), coinciding with the publication of the proceedings of the influential *Lagonissi Conference* (1967), gave rise to a wave of doctrinal debates about *jus cogens* in the second half of the 1960s.

101 ICJ Reports 1970, 325-327. 102 ICJ Reports 1970, 327; and cf. de Hoogh (1996), 55.

103 See further below, section 5.1.

104 de Hoogh (1991), 193; de Hoogh (1996), 55; Macdonald (1987), 138.

the concept of *jus cogens* and to spell out why a comparative approach can facilitate the identification of obligations *erga omnes.*

The merits of a comparative approach The merits of defining one concept by reference to another depend on whether that other concept is itself well defined. Debates in literature at times convey the impression that in order to define the scope of obligations *erga omnes*, one only had to clarify its relation to *jus cogens*. However, this is misleading; it neglects that at least conceptually, the latter concept is not much more clearly defined than the former. Taking up a comment by Krystyna Marek, one might wonder whether assessing obligations *erga omnes* by reference to *jus cogens* is more than a description of the unknown by reference to the unknown ('*ignotum per ignotum*').[105]

Indeed, the conceptual difficulties surrounding *jus cogens* can hardly be overstated. To some extent, they may have been caused by the problematic wording of article 53, which sets out a number of formal tests[106] but does not indicate in what respects the content of a peremptory norm differs from that of an ordinary norm of international law.[107] Not surprisingly, two very different approaches to the concept of *jus cogens* have emerged. Pursuant to a *substantive understanding*, a peremptory norm enjoys superior legal force because it protects basic values of the international community. In the words of the ILC, *jus cogens* norms

[105] Cf. Marek (1978–1979), 468, who commented on the ILC's attempt to rely on *jus cogens* to define international crimes in the following terms: 'One obscure notion ... is to serve as a basis for another obscure notion ..., an operation known as defining *ignotum per ignotum.*'

[106] For a discussion of the criteria referred to the text of article 53 – notably the requirement that peremptory norms have to be recognised and accepted by 'the international community of States as a *whole*' (emphasis added) – see Ago (1971), 323; Gaja (1981), 283; Alexidze (1981), 246–247, 258; Cassese (2001), 140–141. Cf. the much-quoted statement by Yasseen, Chairman of the Drafting Committee at the Vienna Conference: '[B]y inserting the words "as a whole" ..., the Drafting Committee had wished to stress that there was no question of requiring a rule to be accepted and recognized as peremptory by all States. It would be enough if a very large majority did so; that would mean that, if one State in isolation refused to accept the peremptory character of the rule, or if that State was supported by a very small number of States, the acceptance and recognition of the peremptory character of the rule would not be affected' (UN Doc. A/CONF.39/11, at 472 (para. 12)).

[107] See the criticism by Jiménez de Aréchaga (1978), 64; Weil (1992), 269–270; Tomuschat (1993a), 223; Nisot (1972), 694; Christenson (1988), 594; Simma (1994a), 286–287; Paulus (2001), 356; Cassese (2001), 140 (but contrast Fastenrath (1993), 323; Kolb (2001), 85–86; Pellet (1992), 38). On a similar note, Ragazzi (1997), 72, speaks of the 'test-oriented approach' informing article 53 (as opposed to the 'value-oriented approach' of the *Barcelona Traction* dictum).

are 'substantive rules of conduct that prohibit what has come to be seen as intolerable because of the threat it presents to the survival of States and their peoples and the most basic human values.'[108] In contrast, a *systemic approach* extends the concept to cover inherent rules, i.e. rules necessary for the functioning of a legal system, such as *pacta sunt servanda*, good faith, or the sovereign equality of States.[109]

For present purposes, it is not necessary to address this controversy, but merely to bear in mind its implications for the analysis of the *erga omnes* concept. Suffice it to say that if indeed, international law recognises the notion of systemic peremptoriness, the higher normativity allegedly attaching to the respective legal rules is based not on 'the importance of the rights involved',[110] but derives from their status as inherent rules. The rationale underlying systemic peremptory norms thus is different from that informing the *erga omnes* concept. As a consequence, systemic peremptory norms do not give rise to obligations *erga omnes*.[111]

Even when focusing on substantive *jus cogens* (which is based on a similar rationale as the *erga omnes* concept), uncertainties remain considerable. With the exception of articles 53 and 64 VCLT, there is little agreement on the legal consequences flowing from a norm's *jus cogens* status. To be sure, even articles 53 and 64 VCLT entail far-reaching effects. Under the express terms of the two provisions, whole treaties, irrespective of their actual implementation, are void if one of their provisions conflicts with an existing or emerging peremptory norm.[112] Neither provision however has to date had much practical significance.[113]

108 See ILC, commentary to article 40 ASR, para. 3. For similar 'substantive' definitions see Tomuschat (1993a), 223; Cassese (2001), 141; de Hoogh (1996), 45; Hannikainen (1988), 4–5; Simma (1994a), 288; Thierry (1990), 66–67; Macdonald (1987), 134. See also the succinct statement made by the Czechoslovakian delegation during the Vienna Conference, UN Doc. A/CONF.39/11, at 318.

109 See e.g. Abi-Saab (1999), 349; Abi-Saab (1987), 259; and further Kolb (2001), especially at 115–120 and 171–187. Cf. Wyler (2003), 115; Paulus (2001), 415 for a brief discussion. For critical comment on systemic *jus cogens* see Mosler (1968), 30–33; on systemic norms (*Rechtsvoraussetzungsnormen*) see also Verdross/Simma (1984), 59–60.

110 ICJ Reports 1970, 32 (para. 33).

111 Paulus (2001), 415; Abi-Saab (1999), 349.

112 As has been rightly observed, articles 53 and 64 VCLT thus are preventive in character; they prohibit the creation of legal exceptions; Gaja (1989), 158–159; Simma (1994), 285 and 300; Byers (1999), 201; Weil (1992), 268–269 ('*nullité draconienne*');.

113 For rare instances in which States relied on *jus cogens* in order to claim that specific treaties were invalid see e.g. the memorandum of the United States State Department regarding the 1978 Soviet-Afghan Treaty of Friendship, Goodneighborliness and Cooperation (allegedly justifying military intervention), reproduced in 74 AJIL (1980), 418; see further the arguments referred to in the two arbitrations of *Kuwait v. Aminoil*,

Difficulties multiply when analysing the legal effects of '*jus cogens* beyond the Vienna Convention'.[114] Initially a concept of treaty law, *jus cogens* has come to be applied to a variety of other fields of law. Relying on an extra-conventional[115] concept of peremptoriness, national, and international courts, as well as other international bodies, have discussed its effects on the rules governing jurisdiction,[116] immunities,[117] diplomatic protection,[118] reservations to treaties,[119] prosecution of human rights abuses,[120]

66 ILR 587–588, para. 90 (2); and *Maritime Boundary between Guinea-Bissau and Senegal*, 83 ILR 24–30. Cf. Gaja (1981), 288, for further references.

114 Cf. the title of the Giogio Gaja's Hague Lecture: Gaja (1981), 271.

115 There is considerable debate about the source of *jus cogens*, and in particular the *jus cogens* effects outside the Vienna Convention. In the view of some, the concept is best understood as a general principle of law in the sense of article 38, para. 1(c) of the ICJ Statute (Sur (1988), 128; Simma (1994a), 291–293; similarly the arbitral tribunal in *Guinea-Bissau v. Senegal*, 83 ILR 26, para. 44). Others have described it as 'an elite subset of the norms recognised as customary international law' (US Court of Appeals, 9th Cir., *Siderman de Blake v. Argentina*, 103 ILR 470–471; similarly Byers (1999), 187–195). For present purposes, it is important to recognise that the various *jus cogens* effects that have gained practical relevance in recent years do not derive from the Vienna Convention; hence the description as 'extra-conventional'. For a brief survey of the alleged extra-conventional effects see Karl (2003), 127–138.

116 There is considerable support for the proposition that all States are entitled to exercise universal jurisdiction over breaches of peremptory norms, see e.g. ICTY, *Furundzija case*, para. 156; House of Lords, *Pinochet III*, [2000] 1 A.C. 198 (per Lord Browne-Wilkinson); *ibid.*, 275 (per Lord Millett); Brussels Court of First Instance, Order *In re Pinochet*, 119 ILR 356–357; US Court of Appeals (District of Columbia), *Princz v. Germany*, Diss.Op. Judge Wald, 103 ILR 618; ICJ, *Arrest Warrant case*, Diss.Op. van den Wyngaert, para. 45.

117 See e.g. the ICTY's *Furundzija* judgment, para. 156, and Judge Wald dissent in *Princz* (103 ILR 618.); House of Lords, *Pinochet III*, [2000] 1 A.C. 278 (per Lord Millett) and 290 (per Lord Phillips); ICJ, *Arrest Warrant case*, Diss.Op. Al-Khasawneh, para. 7; Diss.Op. van den Wyngaert, para. 23 (all holding that international law precludes the plea of immunity in case of *jus cogens* breaches). Contrast however the majority judgment in the *Arrest Warrant case*, and decisions by the Eur. Ct. HR and the English courts in the *Al-Adsani case* (34 European Human Rights Reports (2002), 273; 103 ILR 420, and 107 ILR 536 respectively).

118 See e.g. Dugard, First Report on Diplomatic Protection, paras. 75–93, especially draft article 4 (1) (proclaiming a *duty* of States to exercise diplomatic protection in case of violations of *jus cogens* norms). Cf. also the *Abbasi case* before the (English) Court of Appeal, [2002] EWCA Civ. 159, paras. 28, 41.

119 See e.g. UN Human Rights Committee, General Comment No. 24 of 1994, UN Doc. CCPR/C/21/Rev.1/Add.6; similarly the opinions of Judges Padillo Nervo and Tanaka and Judge *ad hoc* Sørensen in the *North Sea Continental Shelf case*, ICJ Reports 1969, 97, 182, and 248 respectively.

120 In its *Furundzija* judgment, a trial chamber of the ICTY e.g. took the view that '[i]t would be senseless to argue, on the one hand, that on account of the *jus cogens* value of the prohibition against torture, treaties or customary rules providing for torture would be null and void *ab initio*, and then be unmindful of a State ... condoning torture or absolving its perpetrators through an amnesty law' (para. 155).

extradition,[121] and recognition of States,[122] as well as to various aspects of the law of State responsibility.[123]

Although nearly all of the alleged *jus cogens* effects have remained controversial, the considerable practice relating to *jus cogens* is highly relevant. In the course of proceedings involving *jus cogens*, national and international courts have frequently pronounced on whether specific legal rules are peremptory in nature. Although disagreeing on the implications flowing from *jus cogens* status, national and international jurisprudence provides a wealth of evidence as to the scope of the concept.[124] When adding to this the frequent statements by governments, made e.g. during the drafting of the Vienna Convention, one can ascertain with reasonable certainty whether a specific rule has acquired peremptory status.

Without entering into a detailed discussion, it may be helpful briefly to consider the examples of torture, war crimes and crimes against humanity, and the use of force (short of aggression). All three examples are often considered to give rise to obligations *erga omnes*, but authority supporting these claims is not abundant. For example, the Court yet has to confirm that the prohibitions against torture or the use of force (outside armed aggression) are valied *erga omnes*. War crimes and crimes

See also the position taken by the Spanish National Criminal Court (*Audencia Nacional*) in the *Pinochet case*, 119 ILR 344; and Decision No. 53 (1993) of the Hungarian Supreme Court (quoted by Cassese (2001), 141).

121 The Swiss Supreme Court (*Tribunal Fédéral*) as well as the *Institut de droit international*, for example, seem to take the view that conflicts with peremptory norms may constitute a reason to not to extradite individuals; see section IV of the *Institut's* 1983 resolution on 'New Problems of Extradition', 60-II Annuaire IDI (1983), 306. For the Supreme Court's position see e.g. decisions in *Bufano et al.*, Recueil Officiel, Vol. 108, I, 408–413 (para. 8a); Lynas, *ibid.*, Vol. 101, 541 (para. 7b); Sener, *ibid.*, Vol. 109, I, 72 (para. 6aa).

122 In its Opinion No. 10, the Arbitration Commission on Yugoslavia e.g. stated that while the recognition of States was a discretionary act, it was subject to compliance with '*les normes impératives du droit international général*' (96 RGDIP (1992), 594). See also article 41, para. 2 ASR proclaiming a general duty not to recognise situations brought about by serious breaches of obligations arising under peremptory norms.

123 See in particular the following provisions of the 2001 Articles on State Responsibility: (i) article 26: compliance with a peremptory norm as a circumstance precluding the wrongfulness of otherwise illegal conduct; (ii) articles 40, 41: a special regime of responsibility entailed by serious breaches of obligations arising under peremptory norms; (iii) article 50, para. 1(a): exclusion of countermeasures affecting obligations arising from peremptory norms. See further commentary to article 45, para. 4, and commentary to article 20, para. 7, for the question whether States can consent to, or waive the consequences of responsibility arising from, breaches of *jus cogens* norms.

124 Despite the remaining uncertainty, the evidence quoted in the preceding footnotes shows that, contrary to a famous observation, *jus cogens* is no longer 'the vehicle that hardly leaves the garage'; still less can it be said today that 'it does not have a lot of obvious relevance' (cf. Brownlie (1988b), 110).

against humanity might be covered by the Court's recent observation pursuant to which obligations of international humanitarian law apply *erga omnes*;[125] however, the Court's statement may be too sweeping to command general support. In contrast, a huge amount of evidence suggests that the relevant legal rules prohibiting torture,[126] the use of force,[127] and war crimes and crimes against humanity[128] are peremptory in nature. More generally, judging from concrete evidence provided by international practice, and despite all conceptual difficulties, it is thus considerably less cumbersome to establish a norm's peremptory character than its *erga omnes* status. This in turn means that pragmatically, using *jus cogens* to assess the scope of the *erga omnes* concept might be fruitful. It is on the basis of this assumption that the relationship between the two concepts will be assessed in the following.

125 *Israeli Wall case*, available at *www.icj-cij.org*, paras. 155–157.

126 Evidence supporting the peremptory character of the prohibition against torture is enormous; see in particular ICTY, *Furundzija case*, paras. 153–157; ICTY, *Delalić case*, para. 454; ICTY, *Kunarac case*, para. 466; and the decisions by the Eur. Ct. HR and the English courts in the *Al-Adsani case* (34 European Human Rights Reports (2002), 273; 103 ILR 420, and 107 ILR 536 respectively).

For further evidence see House of Lords, *Pinochet III* [2000] 1 A.C. 198 (per Lord Browne-Wilkinson), 247 (per Lord Hope), 278 (per Lord Millett), and 290 (per Lord Phillips); Ontario Superior Court of Justice, *Bouzari and Others v. Iran*, 124 ILR 427; US Court of Appeals (2nd Cir.), *Filartiga v. Peña-Irala*, 77 ILR 177–179; US Court of Appeals (9th Cir.), *Siderman de Blake v. Argentina*, 103 ILR 471; as well as *In re Fedinand E. Marcos Litigation (Trajano v. Marcos)*, 978 F.2d 500 (9th Cir. 1992); *Marcos Manto v. Thajane*, 508 U.S. 972 (1993) (cert. denied); *Cabiri v. Assasie-Gyimah*, 921F. Supp. 1189, 1196 (S.D.N.Y. 1996).

127 See the submissions of both parties in the *Nicaragua case*, ICJ Reports 1986, 100–101 (para. 190); and further the separate opinions of President Singh and Judge Sette-Camara, *ibid.*, 153 and 199. During the Vienna Conference, the same view was frequently expressed by governments, see UN Doc. A/CONF.39/11, at 294 (USSR), 296 (Kenya), 296–297 (Cuba), 297 (Lebanon), 300 (Sierra Leone), 301 (Ghana), 302 (Poland), 303 (Uruguay), 304 (United Kingdom), 306 (Cyprus), 307 (Belorussian SSR), 311 (Italy), 312 (Romania), 318 (Czechoslovakia), 318 (Germany), 320 (Ecuador), 322 (Ukrainian SSR), 323–324 (Switzerland), 326 (Malaysia). Cf. also the ILC's commentary on what was to become article 53 VCLT, YbILC 1966, Vol. II, 248 (para.3).

128 See ICTY, Trial Chamber II, *Prosecutor v. Kupreskic et al.*, Case IT-95-16 (Judgment of 14 January 2000), para. 520; Hungarian Supreme Court, Decision No. 53 of 13 December 1993, reproduced in *Az Alkotmànybirosg Hatà rosatai*, 1994, 2832, at 2836 (quoted by Cassese (2001), 141); House of Lords, *R v. Bow Street Metropolitan Stipendiary Magistrate*, ex parte *Pinochet Ugarte (No. 3)* [2000] 1 A.C. 242 (per Lord Hope); Brussels Court of First Instance, Order of 6 November 1998, *In re Pinochet*, 119 ILR, 355. In its commentary, the ILC had, more generally, mentioned acts criminal under international law, see YbILC 1966, Vol. II, 248 (para. 3). At the Vienna Conference, a number of governments took the view that international humanitarian law in its entirety was peremptory, see statements by, *inter alia*, Poland, Switzerland, and Italy at the Vienna Conference, UN. Doc. A/CONF.39/11, at 302, 311, and 324.

Implications for the *erga omnes* concept The relevance of *jus cogens*-related evidence for an analysis of obligations *erga omnes* depends on how exactly the two concepts relate. This question is controversial; views expressed range from mere overlap,[129] to partial identity (all peremptory norms imposing obligations *erga omnes*),[130] or complete identity.[131] At the present stage, all that needs to be decided is whether – as postulated by supporters of the identity and partial identity models – norms of (substantive) *jus cogens* necessarily give rise to obligations *erga omnes*.

When addressing this question, it is helpful to begin by analysing the dispute settlement provisions of the Vienna Convention. If, by necessity, all peremptory norms entail *erga omnes* effects, one should expect the Vienna Convention to recognise the general legal interest of all States in seeing peremptory norms observed.[132] Interestingly, this is not the case. While article 66 VCLT indeed establishes ICJ jurisdiction over disputes involving *jus cogens* norms, the provision adopts a very restrictive approach to the question of standing.[133] Of course, article 66(a) provides that '*any one of the parties to a dispute* concerning the application or the interpretation of articles 53 and 64 may, by a written application, submit it to the International Court of Justice for a decision ...'[134] This relatively open formulation however has to be read in line with the *chapeau* of article 66, which subjects article 66 VCLT to the

[129] See e.g. Frowein (1994), 364 and 405–406; Simma (1994a), 300–301; similarly para. 7 of the ILC's commentary to article 40 ASR.

[130] Paulus (2001), 413–415; Gaja (1981), 281; Gaja (1989), 158–159; Meron (1986), 11; Pellet (1999), 429; Künzli (2001), 74–75; Kadelbach (1992), 32–33; Günther (1999), 111–114; Biermann (1996), 451.The opposite view – pursuant to which all obligations *erga omnes* necessarily derive from peremptory norms – is rarely advanced; see, however, Kälin (1994), 12 (his note 16).

[131] Hannikainen (1988), 4–6, 269–292; Pieper (1997), 388–389; Reimann (1971), 97; Gomez Robledo (1981), 158; Ress (2000), 62; similarly Tomuschat (1999), 87 ('a number of rules which protect basic values by different procedural mechanisms').

[132] In contrast to the argument considered in the following, Byers (1999), 200–201, argues that *jus cogens* rules apply *erga omnes*, because 'illegal treaties and illegal rules of special customary law would never be struck down as inconsistent with *jus cogens* rules unless those rules also gave standing to other States.' This view fails to take account of the actual regulation adopted in articles 65, 66 VCLT.

[133] Since only States may be parties before the Court (see article 34 of the ICJ Statute), drafters of the 1986 Vienna Convention had to modify the Convention's dispute settlement clauses. Pursuant to article 66 [1986], international organisations are entitled to request advisory opinions by the ICJ. For comment see Menon (1992), 132–135.

[134] Emphasis added.

prior exhaustion of peaceful consensual dispute settlement under article 65 VCLT.[135] As the opening phrase of article 65, para. 1 clarifies, dispute settlement under article 65 can only be sought by States parties to the allegedly defective treaty.[136] As a consequence, the same applies to ICJ proceedings under article 66 VCLT.[137]

The reasons leading to the adoption of these provisions, which seem hard to bring into line with the community approach pervading the identification of *jus cogens* norms,[138] are difficult to re-establish. In fact, very few States during the Vienna Conference expressly endorsed the restrictive approach underlying article 66(a),[139] whereas a number of participants argued in favour of a general right of standing.[140] Nevertheless, the clear wording as well as a systematic reading of the provision mandates the conclusion that eight months before the *Barcelona Traction* judgment, the drafters of the Vienna Convention rejected the idea that all States have a legal interest in seeing peremptory norms observed. At least the Vienna Convention regime thus does not seem to imbue peremptory norms with *erga omnes* effect.

[135] The *chapeau* provides: 'If, under paragraph 3 of article 65 [providing for dispute settlement through means indicated by article 33 UNC] no solution has been reached within a period of 12 months following the date on which the objection was raised, the following procedure shall be followed . . . '

[136] The relevant part of article 65, para. 1 provides: 'A party which, under the provisions of the present Convention, invokes . . . a ground for impeaching the validity of a treaty, . . . must notify the other party of its claim.' When taking into account article 2 VCLT, it is clear that the term 'party' means a party to the allegedly defective treaty, not a party to the Vienna Convention.

[137] Weisburd (1995), 16–17; Ragazzi (1997), 205–206; de Hoogh (1996), 48; Jiménez de Aréchaga (1978), 68–69; Paulus (2001), 350; Gomez Robledo (1981), 157–158; Kadelbach (1992), 331; but contrast Weil (1992), 268; Byers (1999), 200–201. Contrary to a commonly held view (see e.g. Gomez Robledo (1981), 150–151; Rozakis (1976), 109–115), this does not necessarily mean that for treaties to be invalidated, States had to follow the procedure provided for in articles 65, 66 VCLT. As article 53, 64 VCLT do not mention any requirement of judicial involvement, the better view is that treaties conflicting with peremptory norms are automatically void (see Gaja (1981), 285–286; Paulus (2001), 350; de Hoogh (1996), 48). Standing to bring disputes under article 66 must also be distinguished from the separate question whether an ICJ judgment on matters of *jus cogens*, contrary to article 59 ICJ Statute, would effectively be binding *erga omnes* (as suggested by Rosenne (1998), 518). This is merely another instance in which the use of *erga omnes* terminology is misleading.

[138] Rozakis (1976), 119–120. [139] Stzucki (1974), 129.

[140] See notably the comments made by the representatives of Israel, Ethiopia, Pakistan, Canada, and Switzerland, reproduced in UN Doc./A/CONF.39/11, at 310, 314, 316, 323, and 324 respectively. For further references see de Hoogh (1996), 48 and 84 (his note 217).

Powerful as it may seem at first glance, this argument is not conclusive. It is not inconceivable that the restrictive treaty regulation adopted in 1969 should have been overcome through the recognition of subsequent non-written rules. As a consequence, the extra-conventional *jus cogens* concept could well go beyond the treaty regulation and entail *erga omnes* effects.[141] This all the more so since the argument based on articles 65 and 66 VCLT does not take into account a major distinguishing feature of *jus cogens* as recognised in the Vienna Convention. As has been mentioned above, articles 53 and 64 VCLT do not merely sanction breaches of *jus cogens* rules, but invalidate treaties irrespective of their actual implementation.[142] This '*nullité draconienne*'[143] clearly goes beyond possible *erga omnes* effects, which would only be triggered by actual breaches, and which would not affect the legal rule as such but merely enhance the prospects of its enforcement. Although this does not fully explain the restrictiveness informing articles 65 and 66 VCLT, it is at least understandable that drafters, concerned at preserving the stability of treaty relations, should have wanted to limit the availability of the draconian remedy, article 66, to a narrowly defined circle of States. Conversely, in the case of actual breaches, a general legal interest of all States (as flowing from *erga omnes* status) might be more readily acceptable. The main argument suggesting that substantive peremptory norms do not necessarily impose obligations *erga omnes* thus appears somewhat qualified.

When looking beyond the provisions of the Vienna Convention, two arguments strongly suggest that obligations arising under substantive peremptory norms are necessarily valid *erga omnes*.

The first of these arguments requires some further analysis of the rationale underlying substantive *jus cogens*. As has been stated, the substantive understanding is informed by the idea that certain fundamental norms are so important that no State may deviate from them by concluding treaties.[144] This, however, would seem to imply that third States, not themselves party to the treaty in question, have a legal interest in seeing the fundamental norm observed. Put differently, if substantive peremptory norms were not valid *erga omnes*, but only protected the legal interests of specific States, these States ought not

[141] See the argument made by Boellecker-Stern (1973), 88–89; de Hoogh (1996), 48; and Paulus (2001), 350; but contrast Kadelbach (1992), 33–34.

[142] See above, references in footnote 112. [143] Weil (1992), 268–269.

[144] See above, footnote 108.

to be prevented from disapplying the rule by concluding a treaty.[145] The substantive understanding of *jus cogens* norms thus seems to presuppose the existence of a general legal interest typical of *erga omnes* status.

Secondly, international practice and *opinio juris* confirm this analysis. States have only rarely felt the need to comment *in abstracto* on the relation between both concepts. Where they have done so, they have endorsed the view that all (substantive) peremptory norms impose obligations *erga omnes*. For example, governments' comments made during the ILC's work on State responsibility provide support for the view that all States have a legal interest in the protection of peremptory norms, and were injured by breaches.[146] During its second reading of the Articles on State Responsibility, the ILC – taking account of the views of governments – confirmed this position. The Commission's Report on the work of its 50th session noted the widely held view that 'all *jus cogens* norms were by definition *erga omnes*', whereas the Special Rapporteur observed that there was 'general agreement' about the 'narrower scope' of the *jus cogens* concept in comparison to that of obligations *erga omnes*.[147]

Occasional comments by national courts provide further support. Although the matter is not addressed in detail, decisions mentioning obligations *erga omnes* – such as the *Pinochet* order of the Brussels court of first instance, or the 2001 *Genocide case* decided by the German Federal Constitutional Court – seem to treat *erga omnes* effects as an automatic consequence of *jus cogens* status.[148]

Finally, the same view seems to have been implicitly endorsed by States commenting on the relation between obligations *erga omnes* and international crimes in the sense of draft article 19 [1996]. A proper assessment of this concept is outside the scope of the present inquiry,

[145] See Gaja (1989), 158, who pointedly asks: '[W]hy should [. . .] States not be able validly to conclude a treaty regulating matters that concern only them?' Cf. further Gaja (1981), 281; Annacker (1994a), 49; Paulus (2001), 414–415; Künzli (2001), 74; Brunnée (1989), 801.

[146] See e.g. Switzerland's comment on article 40, para. 3 of the 1996 first reading draft articles, reproduced in UN Doc. A/CN.4/488, 100; similarly the German government, *ibid.*, 137; and the Italian statement reproduced in: *Compilation of Statements on State Responsibility*, 69–70.

[147] YbILC 1998, Vol. II/2, 69 (para. 279) and 76 (para. 326). During the plenary debates, the same point was made e.g. by Pellet, Economides, Simma, Hafner, and Rodriguez Cedeño, see YbILC 1998, Vol. I, at 101 (para. 25), 104 (para. 49), 106 (para. 12), 117 (para. 10), and 140 (para. 33). Cf. also YbILC 1976, Vol. II/2, at 102 (para. 17).

[148] See especially the Belgian court's statement that norms of *jus cogens* were 'binding upon the domestic legal order with *erga omnes* effect', 119 ILR, 355. For the views of the German *Bundesverfassungsgericht* see 54 Neue Juristische Wochenschrift (2001), 1849.

and – given the ILC's decision to abandon it – may even no longer be required.[149] However, in the present context, governments' views on the scope of the concept and its relation to *jus cogens* and *erga omnes* are relevant. Notwithstanding the many areas of uncertainty, it was generally agreed that draft article 19 presupposed the violation of an obligation *erga omnes*.[150] This view of course has no direct bearing on the relation between *erga omnes* and *jus cogens*. However, it has to be seen in the light of the Commission's understanding that only breaches of (substantive) *jus cogens* norms could qualify as an international crime.[151] If both premises are accepted, the implications for the *erga omnes* concept are a matter of simple syllogical reasoning. If (i) the circle of peremptory norms and circle of rules whose breach might constitute a crime are identical, and if (ii) all State crimes are violations of obligations *erga omnes*, it follows (iii) that peremptory norms necessarily give rise to obligations *erga omnes*.

This interpretation received further support during the second reading of the Commission's work. Having decided to replace the notion of international crimes, the ILC initially considered to introduce a system of aggravated responsibility applicable to 'serious breaches of obligations owed to the international community as a whole', i.e. obligations *erga omnes*.[152] At its 2001 session, it eventually dropped the reference to *erga omnes* obligations from the relevant provisions (articles 40 and 41), and instead stipulated that the special regime was applicable to 'serious breaches of obligations *deriving from peremptory norms of general international law*'.[153] As debates in the Sixth Committee had shown, governments had argued for a restriction of the system of aggravated

[149] For extensive treatment of the concept see the contributions in Weiler/Cassese/Spinedi (1989); and Dupuy (2003).

[150] See Ago, YbILC 1976, Vol. I, 90 (para. 30); Spinedi (1989), 136–137; Hofmann (1985), 219–220; Gaja (1989), 157–158.

[151] Over the years, the ILC expressed slightly divergent views on the relation between rules of *jus cogens* and rules potentially giving rise to international crimes. A formulation contained in the commentary to former draft article 19 seemed to suggest that the circle of peremptory norms was wider than that envisaged in draft article 19 (see e.g. YbILC 1976, Vol. II/2, 119–120 (para. 62)). This was criticised by States, see e.g. the observation of the German government, reproduced in YbILC Vol. II/1, 75. The Commission later seemed to consider both circles of rules to be identical – 'crimes' being distinguished from *jus cogens* breaches on the basis of the intensity of the breach. On the issue see notably de Hoogh (1996), 56–64; Spinedi (1989), 135–136; Wyler (2002), 1155–1156.

[152] See draft article 41 of the interim text adopted in August 2000.

[153] Article 40 ASR (emphasis added). For comment on the relation between article 40 ASR and article 41 of the interim draft adopted in 2000, see Wyler (2002), 1147.

responsibility. That substituting *erga omnes* with *jus cogens* helped accommodate these concerns would seem to suggest that the latter category is narrower in scope.[154]

Interim conclusion The preceding discussion shows that the relation between norms of *jus cogens* and obligations *erga omnes* is a matter of considerable complexity. Both concepts pose great difficulties, and eschew an easy classification. As discussions about the systemic approach show, *jus cogens* is in many respects the more comprehensive concept. Since systemic *jus cogens* is based on a different rationale, the comparative analysis has to focus on the relation between obligations *erga omnes* and rules of substantive *jus cogens*.

In this regard, the better view is that obligations deriving from substantive peremptory norms are valid *erga omnes*. If legal interests of other, third States, were not at stake, it would be difficult to explain why treaties conflicting with substantive *jus cogens* should be invalid. International practice, while not abundant, points in the same direction. Extra-conventional *jus cogens* thus seems to have moved beyond the restrictive approach embodied in article 66 VCLT.

This in turn has important implications for the process of identifying obligations *erga omnes*. Since obligations deriving from norms of substantive *jus cogens* are automatically valid *erga omnes*, States invoking the *erga omnes* concept can rely on *jus cogens*-related evidence. As has been shown, this evidence is far more easily available. The comparative approach therefore considerably facilitates the identification of obligations *erga omnes*.

Beyond jus cogens: *obligation* erga omnes *not deriving from peremptory norms*

Erga omnes beyond *jus cogens* has so far remained rather uncharted territory. Of course, there is no shortage of claims that particular obligations, irrespective of their peremptory or dispositive character, should be valid *erga omnes*. However, it is not clear – nor indeed often discussed – how important an obligation would have to be in order to be already valid *erga omnes*, while not yet reaching peremptory status, or how this importance should be assessed. Given the scarcity of practice, and the vagueness of the importance requirement, the subsequent discussion can only advance tentative conclusions. It will address two separate

[154] See Crawford/Peel/Olleson (2001), 977–978; Crawford (2002a), 36–37.

questions. First, it needs to be assessed whether obligations *erga omnes* not deriving from peremptory norms exist at all. Secondly, some of the factors supporting an obligation's *erga omnes* status will be singled out.

Dispositive obligations *erga omnes*? As has been shown in the last section, rules of substantive *jus cogens* necessarily apply *erga omnes*. It is another question whether obligations *erga omnes* necessarily derive from peremptory norms. Should this be the case, the subsequent analyis would be unnecessary. The more convincing view however is that it is not, and that – as alleged by adherents of the partial identity model referred to above[155] – obligations *erga omnes*, at least in theory, can derive from dispositive rules of international law.

Unfortunately, the question is hardly addressed in international practice, and very little tangible evidence exists. The clearest position has been taken by the ILC. During the second reading of the draft articles on State responsibility, the dominant view was that obligations *erga omnes* could also derive from dispositive rules. In fact, in a passage that has been partly quoted already, the ILC Report not only observed that 'all *jus cogens* norms were by definition *erga omnes*', but further stated that 'not all *erga omnes* norms were necessarily imperative'.[156]

A comparison of the different consequences flowing from peremptory and *erga omnes* status supports this position. As has been stated already, article 53 VCLT is preventive in character; it precludes the mere conclusion of treaties conflicting with peremptory norms, and, in case of conflict, renders such treaties void.[157] In contrast, *erga omnes* status does not affect the validity of an obligation, but merely the prospects of responding against breaches. Where an *erga omnes* breach consists in the implementation of a treaty, that treaty could therefore well remain intact. The point was made very clearly by Giorgio Gaja:

> The existence of a peremptory norm implies two rules: one that imposes an obligation *erga omnes*, another which forbids the conclusion of a treaty directed towards infringing the obligation and thereby makes the treaty invalid. Reactions by [the] international society could well be confined to the actual violation of the obligation. Although the preventive measure concerning the validity of treaties no doubt contributes to the effectiveness of rules imposing obligations *erga omnes*,

[155] See above, footnote 129.

[156] See YbILC 1998, Vol. II/2, 69, para. 279; see further para. 280 and the reference to the 'narrower scope' of the *jus cogens* concept in para. 326.

[157] See above, footnote 112.

it cannot be said that the existence of this type of rule depends on the preventive measure [i.e. the possibility of invalidating treaties].[158]

Very little can be added to this statement, which indeed captures the essential difference between the two concepts. It would seem to follow that, at least in theory, breaches of obligations arising under dispositive rules can entail responsibility *erga omnes*.

Relevant factors The question remains which dispositive obligations are important enough to be valid *erga omnes*. This question is difficult to answer in the abstract, as there is simply no exhaustive canon of means by which the international community and its members can express which values they consider to be important. In principle, States seeking to establish that a particular obligation has acquired *erga omnes* status are thus not limited in their choice of arguments. Nevertheless, two approaches seem particularly relevant and may be briefly explored.

First, explicit statements by States or courts are the most obvious way of establishing that a specific obligation is important. Such direct evidence can take a variety of forms. The Court's *erga omnes* jurisprudence, however, provides some guidance as to which features should be relevant. The Court and its members have singled out specific factors which in their view underlined the importance of an obligation. When recognising the *erga omnes* status of a particular obligation, they have notably relied on the following factors: its recognition in the UN Charter,[159] in the practice of UN organs,[160] in other treaties, preferably universal treaties,[161] in general international law,[162] or in the jurisprudence of the ICJ.[163]

Clearly, these factors are a far cry from establishing a conclusive test. For once, they are interrelated – recognition in treaties e.g. can support

[158] Gaja (1989), 159; cf. also Gaja (1981), 281.

[159] *East Timor* judgment, ICJ Reports 1995, 102 (para. 29); Diss.Op. Skubiszewski, *ibid.*, 266 (para. 136); see also Diss.Op. Weeramantry, *ibid.*, 194–195 and 213–216.

[160] *East Timor case*, Diss.Op. Weeramantry, ICJ Reports 1995, 196 and 213–216; Diss.Op. Skubiszewski, *ibid.*, 266 (paras. 136–138); and further Delbrück (1999a), 31–32.

[161] *East Timor case*, Diss.Op. Weeramantry, ICJ Reports 1995, 194, 196, and 213–216; similarly Delbrück (1999a), 31–32.

[162] *East Timor case*, Diss.Op. Weeramantry, ICJ Reports 1995, 194 and 213–216. More generally, the same point was made in the *Hostages* judgment, ICJ 1980, 31 (para. 62), where the Court affirmed the gravity of the wrongful acts by arguing that they affected obligations that were not merely 'contractual . . . but also obligations under general international law'.

[163] *East Timor case*, ICJ Reports 1995, 102 (para. 29); Diss.Op. Weeramantry, *ibid.*, 197 and 213–216.

the customary character of an obligation.[164] Similarly, for an obligation to be valid *erga omnes*, it is not sufficient that one, or some, of the various factors are met. The UN Charter, for example, imposes many obligations, some of which are more important than others.[165] Equally, it is clear that recognition in general international law is a necessary, but by no means a sufficient condition for *erga omnes* status. These obstacles notwithstanding, the Court's jurisprudence has at least an indicative value. The various pronouncements convey an impression of how the Court and its members have interpreted the importance requirement. It seems likely that the same considerations should be relevant in future proceedings involving *erga omnes* claims. States seeking to establish that a specific obligation is owed *erga omnes* would thus be well advised to show that it meets the various factors referred to above.

Beyond that, a further argument is particularly relevant. Whether a specific obligation is considered important or not may depend not only on explicit affirmations, but also on indirect evidence, notably responses against breaches. While the Court has so far not specifically considered this point in relation to obligations *erga omnes*, it seems difficult to deny, as a general matter, that the importance of specific legal values may be judged by analysing reactions against wrongs.[166] As regards obligations *erga omnes*, commentators have at times doubted whether such indirect evidence should at all be relevant. It has been objected that the existence of rights of reaction is a consequence, not a condition, of *erga omnes* status.[167] However, this seems an unduly narrow approach. In fact, the status of other concepts is often inferred from responses against misconduct. When debating the concept of *jus cogens*, the drafters of the Vienna Convention, for example, analysed how the international community had responded to particular troublesome treaties or, more generally, to grave breaches of international law, and used this evidence to support the inclusion of articles 53 and 64 VCLT.[168]

[164] See *North Sea Continental Shelf case*, ICJ Reports 1969, 41 (para. 71).

[165] Contrast e.g. the obligation not to use force in the sense of article 2, para. 4 and the obligation to register treaties with the UN Secretary-General (article 102 para. 1 UNC).

[166] Cf. also Kessler (2001), 45–46; Thirlway (2003), 142; and further Taylor (1998), 98–102 (considering possible forms of responses).

[167] Ragazzi (1997), 202.

[168] See e.g. the frequent references to article 2(4) UNC as the cornerstone of the new (post-1945) international legal order, notably in para. 1 of the ILC's commentary on (then) draft article 50, YbILC 1966, Vol. II, 247. See further Rosenne, YbILC 1963, Vol. I., 74 (paras. 8 and 9) (referring to the Nuremburg tribunals, the Kellogg–Briand Pact and the Hague Conventions), Pal, *ibid.*, 65 (para. 65) (referring to the attempts, by the League of

Similarly, in the course of its work on responsibility, the ILC argued that a specific category of exceptionally serious wrongful acts (whether termed international crimes or otherwise) was justified precisely because responses against such acts allegedly differed from responses against ordinary breaches.[169] Reliance on indirect evidence is thus not peculiar to the *erga omnes* concept, and there is no reason to ignore it.

This has important implications for the subject of the present inquiry. It underlines that the identification of obligations *erga omnes* is more than a simple application of predetermined criteria. Instead, the scope of the concept can only be assessed on the basis of a dialectic process, in which rights of protection follow from an obligation's *erga omnes* status, while their actual exercise provides indirect evidence confirming that status. It follows that the identification of obligations *erga omnes* cannot be isolated from an analysis of responses against international wrongs.

Just as with regard to any other evaluation of international practice, the strength of the indirect evidence gained from such an analysis depends on a number of factors, notably the number of States involved, and the formality of the response.[170] Ideally, applicant States seeking to establish the *erga omnes* status of a particular obligation would thus be able to show that breaches of the obligation in question had previously prompted responses by a large number of States. As regards the forms of response, coercive measures or claims before international tribunals would provide particularly strong evidence.[171]

These considerations suggest that identifying obligations *erga omnes* deriving from dispositive rules of international law may be a rather

Nations, to maintain 'some sort of constitutional government'; Lachs, *ibid.*, 68 (paras. 7–10).

169 Hence the ILC's commentary to draft article 19 extensively discussed international practice and jurisprudence allegedly supporting the crimes/delicts distinction, see YbILC 1976, Vol. II/2, 95–122.

The commentary to article 41 ASR equally seeks to show that the prescribed specific consequences attaching to 'serious breaches of obligations arising under peremptory norms of general international law' (such as the duty of non-recognition) are accepted in international practice, see especially paras. 6–8, 10 and 12 of the commentary. Justifying the inclusion of a special regime, the Commission stated that it was necessary to reflect in the text the consequences flowing from the concept of 'serious breaches' of peremptory norms, see introductory commentary to articles 40 and 41 ASR, para. 7.

170 See already above, Introduction, for a differentiation between different means of law enforcement.

171 Hence Taylor (1998), 98–102, discusses New Zealand's arguments made in *Nuclear Tests* as a precedent upon which other States could rely, while Thirlway (2003), 142 refers to actual countermeasures as a form of international practice.

cumbersome process, and requires a detailed analysis of international practice. The Court's jurisprudence indicates which factors will be of particular relevance. In line with what has been said in the preceding paragraphs, it can be supplemented by indirect evidence, gained from analysing actual responses against international wrongs. It must be readily acknowledged that these two arguments provide only the starting-point for an analysis of obligations *erga omnes* beyond *jus cogens*. The contours of the importance test set out by the Court will only become clearly visible once the *erga omnes* concept is being invoked more frequently. The preceding discussion however indicates the lines along which discussions are likely to evolve. Although it leaves a lot to be desired conceptually, it is submitted that the pragmatic approach suggested facilitates the application of the *erga omnes* concept.

4.3 Concluding observations

The preceding discussion has deliberately refrained from assessing whether specific obligations are valid *erga omnes*. Instead, an attempt has been made to shed light on the process by which obligations *erga omnes* can be identified. The results of the inquiry can be summarised as follows:

First, obligations *erga omnes* are obligations of general international law; they should not be conflated with obligations *erga omnes partes*. Secondly, obligations *erga omnes* are distinguished from other obligations of general international law on the basis of their importance. When bearing in mind the antecedents addressed in Chapter 2, the *erga omnes* concept thus seems not dissimilar to the idea that all States can act to defend fundamental humanitarian values.[172] Thirdly, although the importance requirement is inherently vague, it is clearly established in the Court's jurisprudence. In contrast, unlike much of the literature, the Court has not taken up structural approaches to the concept pursuant to which obligations *erga omnes* are said to depend on a specific pattern of performance. Equally, *erga omnes* status does not depend on the intensity of breaches or functional criteria (such as the necessity of protecting specific obligations through rights of protection based on the *erga omnes* concept). Fourthly, when trying to define more clearly how important obligations have to be in order to be valid *erga omnes*, two very different approaches are helpful. On the basis of a

[172] Cf. above, section 2.2.2.d.

comparative approach, a core of obligations *erga omnes* can be identified with reasonable precision. It consists of obligations deriving from substantive peremptory norms of general international law, which *ipso facto* are valid *erga omnes*. When moving beyond *jus cogens*, the identification of obligations *erga omnes* becomes considerably more difficult. Pragmatically, it is possible to single out a number of factors that suggest that a specific obligation is important and thus likely to be valid *erga omnes* (such as specific forms of affirmations, or responses against previous breaches). While not amounting to a conclusive test, these factors should guide States seeking to establish that a particular obligation is valid *erga omnes*.

Whether these two approaches are sufficient to clarify how 'obligations enter into the magic *erga omnes* circle'[173] may be a matter of perspective. *Erga omnes* outside *jus cogens* is likely to remain uncharted territory until States begin to invoke the concept more frequently in formalised proceedings. Difficulties should however not be overstated. The preceding discussion shows that a core of obligations *erga omnes* can be identified with reasonable certainty, and at least indicates which other factors are relevant (and which irrelevant) when moving beyond that core. Although the scope of the concept cannot be determined in the abstract, identifying obligations *erga omnes* will usually not present unsurmountable problems. With this premise in mind, it seems fruitful to analyse, in subsequent chapters, the consequences that the 'magic' *erga omnes* status entails.

[173] Cf. the statement by Reisman (1993), 170.

5 Standing to institute ICJ proceedings

Identifying obligations *erga omnes* is only one of the problems to which the Court's jurisprudence gives rise. As important is the question how States can respond to *erga omnes* breaches – often described as 'the acid test of the *erga omnes* concept'.[1] Indeed, if violations of obligations *erga omnes* did not trigger any special rights of response, the concept, at least for the purposes of law enforcement, would be of rhetorical value only. For the reasons given in the Introduction, only two means of enforcement are addressed in the present study: ICJ proceedings and countermeasures. It is convenient to begin by discussing the former of these, as it has historically provided the starting-point for the debate about *erga omnes* effects in the field of standing.

Since 1970, it has been disputed whether all States should be entitled to bring ICJ proceedings in response to breaches of obligations *erga omnes*. The different points of view are defined relatively clearly. According to most commentators, the question hardly needs to be addressed; the Court is said to have conclusively settled it in *Barcelona Traction*, when recognising the legal interest of all States in seeing obligations *erga omnes* observed.[2] Byers, to take but one example, laconically states: 'Generality of standing ... is the essence of *erga omnes* rules.'[3] Following this interpretation (which will be referred to as the

[1] See e.g. Stein (1995), 115; similar observations have been made by Simma (1993a), 136 ('moment of truth'); Gaja (1989), 152 (his note 5).

[2] ICJ Reports 1970, 32 (para. 33).

[3] Byers (1999), 196. See also the ILC's commentary to former draft article 19, YbILC 1976, Vol. II/2, 99 (para. 10); Ago's Fifth Report, YbILC 1976, Vol. II/1, 29 (para. 89; but contrast *ibid.*, para. 90); Vadapalas (1993), 28 and 31–32; Seiderman (2001), 135–137; Antonopoulos (1996), 87–88; Graefrath (1985), 106; Dinstein (1992), 18; Hannikainen (1988), 271, 280; Oellers-Frahm (1992), 33; Kirgis (1990), 527–528; Empell (2003), 344.

broad approach), obligations *erga omnes* are another category of obligations allowing for a general right to respond against breaches. In terms of standing, their legal regime thus would follow the rules governing, for example, generally enforceable treaties (such as those mentioned in Chapter 2), or interdependent obligations.

This analysis is disputed by adherents of a *restrictive approach*, who question the broad interpretation of the Court's *Barcelona Traction* dictum and advance a variety of counter-arguments seeking to show that it has to be taken '*cum grano salis*' (as Judge de Castro famously put it).[4] Although frequently dimissed or ignored, these considerations need to be taken seriously. Three-and a-half-decades after *Barcelona Traction*, the Court has yet to admit a claim based on a violation of an obligation *erga omnes*. Just as States have only infrequently asserted their right to respond against breaches of generally enforceable treaties, they have hardly ever brought ICJ proceedings based on violations of obligations *erga omnes*. Where the *erga omnes* concept has been invoked before the Court, litigants have expressed widely diverging views about its implications.[5] All this suggests that the question of *erga omnes* proceedings needs to be approached, if not with a grain of salt, then at least with a measure of caution. Even if all States had standing to institute ICJ proceedings, they would be unlikely to make frequent use of this right. On the other hand, the relative absence of *erga omnes* claims may also reflect the continuing uncertainty about rights of protection triggered by *erga omnes* breaches; it shows that the question of standing before the ICJ is far from settled. The present chapter therefore deliberately addresses it in some detail. Before proceeding with the analysis, three preliminary remarks seem in order, which help spell out the points of contention more clearly.

First, before beginning to evaluate the competing arguments advanced by adherents of the different approaches, it may be helpful to note that there is general agreement about the area of controversy. The Court's reference to legal interests makes clear that, whatever its effects in the

[4] *Nuclear Tests cases*, Diss.Op. de Castro, ICJ Reports 1974, 387.

[5] The point may be illustrated with reference to Australia's changing views on the matter. When invoking the concept in *Nuclear Tests*, Australia argued that the alleged prohibition against nuclear testing, being owed *erga omnes*, could be invoked by all States (*Nuclear Tests cases*, Pleadings, Australian Memorial, ICJ Pleadings, Vol. I, 331–334, especially paras. 431 and 448). By the time it appeared as a defendant in *East Timor*, it took a more restrictive view, denying the right of all States to bring *erga omnes* proceedings (*East Timor case*, Pleadings, Australian Counter-Memorial, para. 262). For a more detailed analysis of both cases see below, sections 5.2.1 and 5.2.5; for comment on Australia's changing views on the matter see also Voeffray (2004), 85.

field of standing, the *erga omnes* concept does not affect the consensual character of the Court's jurisdiction. Even if all States should have standing to institute ICJ proceedings in *erga omnes* disputes, they could only avail themselves of that possibility where they have established jurisdiction. In the *East Timor case*, the Court clarified the matter by observing that 'the *erga omnes* character of a norm and the rule of consent to jurisdiction are two different things.'[6] In the circumstances of the case, this was controversial, as it provided the basis for the Court's application of the indispensable third party rule to *erga omnes* disputes.[7] But outside that specific context, the statement is unproblematic. It confirms that even where breaches of obligations *erga omnes* are at stake, the Court can only exercise jurisdiction where both parties to the proceedings have consented to it. Despite some uncertainty in the direct aftermath of the Court's decision, this is undisputed today.[8] Given the limited scope of the Court's jurisdiction, especially in disputes involving breaches of customary obligations (such as obligations *erga omnes*), this factor severely restricts the effectiveness of ICJ enforcement.[9]

Secondly, there is also agreement about the character of the rule of standing that could be affected by the *erga omnes* concept. As has been stated already, it is possible to distinguish treaty-based from general rules of standing.[10] Although the *Barcelona Traction* dictum is not free from ambiguity,[11] it seems clear that a possible rule recognising

[6] ICJ Reports 1995, 102 (para. 29); similarly para. 71 of the Court's interim order in the *Armed Activities (Congo Rwanda) case* (available at www.icj-cij.org).

[7] See further below, section 5.2.5.b.

[8] Seiderman (2001), 135–137; de Hoogh (1996), 356–360. For a discussion cf. Seidl-Hohenveldern (1975), 803. There has even been some discussion whether claims brought under *erga omnes* concept would fall within the scope of optional clause declarations made under article 36, para. 2 of the ICJ Statute; cf. Mann (1973a), 406–408. Since article 36, para. 2 expressly refers to 'all disputes', and since (as has been shown above, section 1.1) the existence of a dispute and the requirement of standing are two separate issues, this question can be answered in the affirmative. Unless States decide to exclude, by way of reservation, specific matters from the Court's jurisdiction, their optional clause declarations in principle cover all disputes brought in accordance with the Court's institutional law. Should all States have standing to institute ICJ proceedings in response to *erga omnes* breaches, article 36, para. 2 of the Court's Statute therefore would not exclude the possibility of *erga omnes* proceedings (see also Annacker (1994a), 102–104; Weschke (2001), 128; Bryde (1994), 180–181).

[9] See above, section 1.1. [10] See above, section 1.2.3.

[11] See especially the Court's reference to 'rights of protection [deriving from] general international law [or] conferred by international instruments of a universal or quasi-universal character'; ICJ Reports 1970, 33 (para. 34). For a discussion see above, section 4.1.

standing to institute *erga omnes* proceedings would belong to the latter category. Obligations *erga omnes* being customary in character, it is difficult to see how breaches should trigger treaty-based rights of protection. Instead, the crucial question prompted by *Barcelona Traction* is whether rights of protection (such as judicial enforcement or countermeasures) can be exercised *in the absence of specific treaty provisions.*[12]

Finally, as for terminology, this question is often addressed under the rubric of *actio popularis*, and has prompted considerable debate about the existence or otherwise of this concept.[13] The subsequent analysis will not address this controversy nor indeed use the term *actio popularis*. This, however, should not be taken to imply a particular position on the question; it is merely an attempt to avoid further terminological confusion (of which there is already no shortage). The notion of *actio popularis* would add to this, as it is used in two different ways. Many commentators restrict it to questions of standing; they speak of an *actio popularis* wherever all States, irrespective of individual injury, are entitled to institute legal proceedings in the general interest.[14] Others extend it to cover questions of jurisdiction as well; in their view, an *actio popularis* presupposes the availability of a judicial forum.[15] It has been stated already that the *erga omnes* concept does not affect questions of jurisdiction; it does not therefore imply the recognition of an *actio popularis* in this second, broader, sense.[16] Whether all States have standing to institute ICJ proceedings in response to *erga omnes* breaches is assessed in the following. This analysis however does not depend on a notion as controversial as *actio popularis*; its result is the same whether or not one chooses to employ the term.

In the light of these preliminary remarks, the issue to be addressed in the following can be refined: the question is whether, jurisdiction being

[12] Weil (1992), 284–285; Boellecker-Stern (1973), 88–90.

[13] See e.g. Silagi (1978), 10; M'Baye (1988), 316–318; Seidl-Hohenveldern (1975), 803; Ragazzi (1997), 210–214; Gray (1987), 211–215; Empell (2003), 356–363; Schwelb (1972), 46; for the most recent and comprehensive account see Voeffray (2004). As may be recalled, the ICJ, in *South West Africa*, had rejected the concept, see ICJ Reports 1966, 47 (para. 88). In their joint dissent in *Nuclear Tests*, Judges Onyeama, Dillard, Jimenez de Arechaga and Waldock left open the question, see ICJ Reports 1974, 369–370 (para. 118) and 521 (para. 52). For a discussion of the former case see above, section 2.1.2; on the joint dissent in *Nuclear Tests* see further below, section 5.2.5.a.

[14] See e.g. Hannikainen (1988), 271; Chinkin 1993, 217; M'Baye (1988), 316; Günther (1999), 152.

[15] Seidermann (2001), 136–137; Seidl-Hohenveldern (1975), 803.

[16] See above, text accompanying footnotes 6–9.

established, all States, even in the absence of any special treaty-based clause, have standing to institute contentious ICJ proceedings in response to breaches of obligations *erga omnes*. This is a matter of ICJ institutional law,[17] and not surprisingly, largely depends on an analysis of the relevant jurisprudence. The subsequent sections therefore assess how the Court and its members have approached the question of standing. More particularly, section 5.1 discusses the *Barcelona Traction* dictum upon which adherents of the broad approach place much emphasis, while section 5.2 evaluates the various counter-arguments advanced by adherents of the restrictive approach. Although it will only be fully resolved once the Court has admitted or dismissed a claim based on the *erga omnes* concept, it is submitted that on the basis of this analysis, the question of standing in *erga omnes* proceedings can be answered with sufficient clarity.

5.1 The *Barcelona Traction* dictum

Although the Court and its members, since 1970, have frequently pronounced on obligations *erga omnes* and their possible judicial vindication, the *Barcelona Traction* dictum remains the *locus classicus*. As has been stated already, supporters of the broad approach place considerable emphasis on this passage, more particularly the Court's recognition that 'all States can be held to have a legal interest in [the observance of] ... obligations *erga omnes*'.[18]

At first glance, the emphasis placed on this passage is somewhat surprising, as the statement is not unequivocal. While recognising the legal interest of all States, the Court did *not* state that this legal interest could be vindicated by way of ICJ proceedings (or indeed countermeasures). Whether this should be so, or whether standing to resort to specific means of enforcement should be subject to a more stringent test, depends on an analysis of the notion of legal interest, whose ambiguous nature has been explored already. As noted in Chapter 1, it is possible, in theory, to distinguish (i) legal interests required to invoke responsibility in a general sense, and (ii) legal interests required to resort to specific means of law enforcement (such as ICJ proceedings or countermeasures). The Court's statement thus need not necessarily be read as an endorsement of the broad approach.[19]

[17] Bryde (1994), 180; and already above, section 1.2.3.
[18] ICJ Reports 1970, 32 (para. 33).
[19] Similarly Paulus (2001), 371–372; Bryde (1994), 180–181.

On the other hand, in the light of the above considerations, much suggests that by recognising the legal interest of all States in seeing obligations *erga omnes* observed, the Court intended to confer upon them standing to institute judicial proceedings. As shown in Chapter 1, the distinction between legal interests to invoke responsibility and standing to institute ICJ proceedings has not usually been drawn in practice; the latter was considered to be a consequence of the former.[20] Closer analysis of the specific circumstances of the *Barcelona Traction* dictum confirms this interpretation. Three arguments can be distinguished.

First, the context suggests that paras. 33 and 34 concerns the question of standing before the Court. In the passage preceding the dictum on obligations *erga omnes*, the Court had clarified that instead of analysing the defendant's arguments in the order in which they had been raised, it would first assess whether Belgium had standing to bring a claim on behalf of a company incorporated under Canadian law. Having introduced the 'essential distinction' between obligations *erga omnes* and obligations arising in the framework of diplomatic protection, it stated that with regard to the latter type of obligations, only the State of nationality had standing to espouse claims. More specifically, as these obligations were 'not of the same category' as obligations *erga omnes*, '[a State wishing] to bring a claim in respect of the breach of such an obligation ... must ... establish its right to do so'.[21] The dictum on obligations *erga omnes* therefore is preceded and followed by comments on the rules of standing in ICJ proceedings. This suggests that the reference to 'legal interests' in para. 33 should also be read as a statement about this specific form of law enforcement.[22]

Secondly, the fact that paras. 33 and 34 are commonly seen as an attempt to reverse the effects of the 1966 *South West Africa* judgment[23] points in the same direction. As has been shown, in 1966 the judges disagreed on whether individual States, even in the absence of individual injury, could have standing before the Court.[24] If indeed the Court intended to move away from the 1966 judgment, it needed to make a statement about the rules governing standing in ICJ proceedings.[25]

20 See above, section 1.2.3. Cf. also Paulus (2001), 371; Günther (1999), 152.

21 ICJ Reports 1970, 33 (para. 35) (referring to ICJ Reports 1949, 181–182).

22 de Hoogh (1996), 50–51; Paulus (2001), 371; Gaja (1989), 154; see also Dupuy (1979), 548.

23 See above, Introduction, footnote 58; section 2.1.2.

24 See above, section 2.1.2.

25 This is conceded by Thirlway (1989), 94, who otherwise adopts a very restrictive approach to the *erga omnes* concept (92–102). See also Mann (1973b), 406–408.

Finally, Judge Ammoun's separate opinion further supports the broad approach. As the only member of the Court elaborating on the matter,[26] Judge Ammoun expressly recognised the right of States to institute ICJ proceedings in defence of general interests of the international community.[27] In his separate opinion, he considered in detail the legal and political issues underlying the protection of foreign investments. Just as the majority judgment had done in paras. 33 and 34, Judge Ammoun drew a distinction between different categories of international legal actions, namely (i) individual actions by States on the basis of their subjective rights, or of rights of a company, and (ii) actions brought in defence of general interests.[28] Although the Belgian claim did not fall into the second category, Judge Ammoun – just as the majority – considered the legal rules applicable to it. Unlike the majority, however, he did not merely speak of general legal interests, but expressly endorsed the right of States to institute ICJ proceedings in response to breaches affecting 'the principles of an international or humane nature, translated into imperative legal norms (*jus cogens*)'.[29]

It must be conceded that Judge Ammoun did not specifically explore the relevance of the *erga omnes* concept, but instead relied on the notion of peremptory norms (*jus cogens*). However, there is little to suggest that by choosing to take a more explicit stance on the issue, he intended to place himself in disagreement with the majority. Instead, the parallelism between his, and the Court's, reasoning, and the close relationship between obligations *erga omnes* and norms of *jus cogens*, suggest that his statement should be interpreted as a clarification of the majority's rather brief remarks.[30]

On the basis of these arguments, it seems fair to say that by recognising the legal interest of all States in the observance of obligations *erga omnes*, the Court, in *Barcelona Traction*, indeed seemed to accept that all

[26] In his dissent, Judge *ad hoc* Riphagen seemed to caution against the categorical nature of the 'essential distinction' between *erga omnes* and other obligations. He did not, however, elaborate on the implications of the *erga omnes* concept, nor indeed reject it altogether (ICJ Reports 1970, 338–340).

[27] ICJ Reports 1970, 325–327. For comment see Paulus (2001), 372.

[28] ICJ Reports 1970, 325 and 327.

[29] ICJ Reports 1970, 325. See also *ibid.*, 326, where Judge Ammoun invoked the 1962 *South West Africa case* judgment, as well as a number of international conventions providing for a general right to respond to violations, in support.

[30] This reading is further supported by the fact that Judge Ammoun expressly criticised the 1966 *South West Africa* judgment, which the majority intended to disavow. The relation between *jus cogens* and *erga omnnes* is discussed above, section 4.2.2.b.

States would have standing to respond to *erga omnes* breaches by instituting ICJ proceedings.

5.2 Possible counter-arguments

Many adherents of the restrictive approach accept that, if read on its own, the Court's recognition of a legal interest in the observance of obligations *erga omnes* supports the broad approach. However, they argue that it should not be taken at face value. In order to justify this claim, they have advanced a variety of very different considerations. Some have sought to play down the importance of the Court's statement on legal interests by pointing to other passages of the *Barcelona Traction* judgment. Others have tried to deny its relevance, arguing that it was an isolated pronouncement and irrelevant to the case in which it was made. Still others assert that the Court's subsequent jurisprudence, or the general rules of standing (in whose context the *erga omnes* concept has to be seen), warrant a restrictive reading of the Court's *Barcelona Traction* dictum. The following sections break down these considerations into six different counter-arguments. By examining these arguments in turn, they also present a fuller analysis of the Court's jurisprudence on obligations *erga omnes* than the one given so far.

5.2.1 *Isolated pronouncements?*

Pursuant to a first counter-argument, the Court's pronouncements on obligations *erga omnes* lack consistency and therefore are of limited relevance. The gist of this counter-argument was clearly expressed by Sir Ian Sinclair to whom the passage was ... 'an isolated dictum, and more can be read into it than the Court meant to convey.'[31]

These and similar[32] statements are informed by a measure of pragmatism. Not every judicial pronouncement is of the same authoritative value; isolated statements might be mere aberrations. On the basis of the preceding discussion of *erga omnes* effects outside the field of law

[31] Sinclair (1989), 225.

[32] For example, in his Fifth Report, Roberto Ago had cautioned that 'the position taken in the judgment on the *Barcelona Traction* case is perhaps still too isolated to permit the conclusion that a definite new trend in international judicial decisions has emerged', YbILC 1976, vol. II/1, 29 (para. 90); see also YbILC 1976, Vol. II/2, 99 (para. 11). It is important to note that the argument continues to be made to date; for more recent scepticism see e.g. Rosenstock (1994), 325; Jørgensen (2000), 221, 223; Chinkin 1993, 214–215; Gray (1987), 214; Rubin (1993), 172; and Schulte (1999), 535.

enforcement, it should also be added that not every use of the term *erga omnes* can be taken as a confirmation of the *Barcelona Traction* dictum.[33]

However, a brief look at the Court's jurisprudence shows that since the *Barcelona Traction* judgment, 'the notion of obligations *erga omnes*' – to quote Judge Weeramantry – 'has developed apace',[34] and is more than an aberration. Since some of the relevant passages have been mentioned already, and all of them will be explored more fully below, brief references may be sufficient here.[35]

The 1995 *East Timor case* between Portugal and Australia provided the Court with an opportunity to discuss the effects of the *erga omnes* concept on the rules governing the enforcement of obligations.[36] In its application, Portugal had claimed a right to vindicate the right of self-determination of the East Timorese people, relying – for the purposes of standing – on its status as the former administering power as well as on the *erga omnes* status of the right in question.[37] The Court affirmed the *erga omnes* status of the right of self-determination, but dismissed the Portuguese claim for procedural reasons, as any decision on the matter would have implied a judgment about a conduct of an absent third State (Indonesia's conduct *vis-à-vis* East Timor).[38] Although the *erga omnes* claim therefore was not admitted, the proceedings affirm the relevance of the *erga omnes* concept in the field of law enforcement. More recently, in the *Israeli Wall case*, the Court observed that since the wall constructed by Israel violated obligations *erga omnes*, all States were 'to see to it that any impediment [. . .] to the exercise by the Palestinian people of its right to self-determination is brought to an end', without however exploring which forms their enforcement action could take.[39]

Many more references to the *erga omnes* concept can be found in separate and dissenting opinions appended by judges. While these of course do not have the same value as pronouncements by the Court itself, they are 'an integral part of the collective work of the Court'[40] and

[33] See above, section 3.3. Contrast Ragazzi (1997), 12 (his note 49).

[34] *East Timor case*, Diss.Op. Weeramantry, ICJ Reports 1995, 215 (footnote omitted).

[35] For further analysis see above, Chapter 4, and below, section 5.2.5.

[36] ICJ Reports 1995, 90. [37] See e.g. paras. 8.01–8.17 of the Portuguese *réplique*.

[38] ICJ Reports 1995, 102 (para. 29).

[39] *Israeli Wall case*, available at www.icj-cij.org, para. 159.

[40] Shahabuddeeen (1996), 196. The relevance of individual opinions is discussed *ibid.*, 177–208; see further Hambro (1956/57), 229; Jennings (1989), 343. Irrespective of their general importance, individual opinions are particularly relevant when assessing *erga omnes* effects in the field of standing, as there has so far been no unequivocal pronouncement by the Court itself.

often clarify issues left unresolved by the majority. For example, in the *East Timor case*, the separate and dissenting opinions provide much further information about *erga omnes* effects in the field of standing.[41] Similarly, no less than seven judges expressed views on the *erga omnes* concept in their opinions in the 1974 *Nuclear Tests cases*, in which the two applicants had claimed to protect both their individual interests as sovereign States, and general interests of the international community.[42] In addition, judges have at times discussed the *erga omnes* concept even where applicants had not actually invoked it as a basis of standing. Comments by Judges Schwebel, Weeramantry, and Oda in the *Nicaragua*, *Genocide*, and *Gabčíkovo cases* highlight different aspects of the concept, and at least by implication, facilitate its understanding.[43]

To sum up, although no *erga omnes* claim has so far been admitted, the Court and its members have repeatedly acknowledged the relevance of the concept for the rules governing standing. The *Barcelona Traction* dictum thus has prompted a considerable follow-up jurisprudence, and cannot be considered an isolated remark.

5.2.2 *An* obiter dictum *lacking legal relevance?*

According to a second counter-argument, the Court's recognition of *erga omnes* effects in the field of standing cannot be taken at face value, because

[41] See further below, section 5.2.5.b.

[42] Much has been written about the different litigation strategies pursued by the two applicants; see e.g. Elkind (1981), 117–122; or the dissenting opinion of Judge *ad hoc* Palmer in the 1995 *Nuclear Tests case*, ICJ Reports 1995, 414–416, paras. 99–100. While Australia initially formulated its claims in terms of the violation of sovereign rights, New Zealand, in its request for interim relief, opted for a more communitarian approach, seeking to protect the 'rights of all members of the international community, including New Zealand' (New Zealand's Request, ICJ Pleadings, Vol. II, 49, para. 2). For present purposes, it is important to note that in the course of the proceedings, both countries relied on the concept of obligations *erga omnes* as expounded in *Barcelona Traction*. Australia expressly argued that the prohibition against atmospheric nuclear tests was 'couched in terms of an *erga omnes* obligation and not in terms of an obligation owed in relation to particular States' (Australian memorial, ICJ Pleadings, Vol. I, 334, para. 448; see also *ibid.*, 331, para. 431). In the view of New Zealand, the rights of all members of the international community to remain free from atmospheric nuclear tests were 'held in common and the corresponding obligation imposed on France (and on any other nuclear power) is owed in equal measure to New Zealand and to every other member of the international community. It is an obligation *erga omnes*' (New Zealand's memorial, ICJ Pleadings, Vol. II, 204, para. 191). For a discussion of the individual injury aspect of the case see above, section 1.3.2; for comment on the majority judgment and its use of the term *erga omnes* see already above, section 3.3.3.

[43] See ICJ Reports 1984, 190; ICJ Reports 1996, 625; ICJ Reports 1997, 88.

it was irrelevant to the actual decision of the case. As has been mentioned already, the Court could have decided the *Barcelona Traction case* without mentioning the concept of obligations *erga omnes*. The well-known passage therefore did not form part of the *ratio decidendi*, but was an *obiter dictum*. In view of some, this seriously diminishes its legal relevance. Judge de Castro, in the passage quoted above, argued that the *Barcelona Traction* judgment had to be taken '*cum grano salis*' precisely because it was expressed in an '*obiter* reasoning'.[44] Similarly, to Stephen McCaffrey, the dictum was

> a gratuitous statement ... [that] can hardly be taken as authority for the proposition that there are certain internationally wrongful acts which are offences *erga omnes*. Granted the Court did say this, but it uttered this in what you might call a quintessential dictum in the context of a case whose facts and legal issues hardly required such a pronouncement.[45]

More than the other considerations advanced by supporters of the restrictive approach, this second argument is tailored to the specific features of paras. 33 and 34 of the *Barcelona Traction* judgment. Traditionally, this may have been one of the factors accounting for the popularity of the argument. As jurisprudence has moved beyond *Barcelona Traction*, the specific focus of the *obiter* argument however has turned into a weakness. In fact, it may most easily be rebutted by reference to the Court's, and judges', subsequent pronouncements, which depended on the application and interpretation of the *erga omnes* concept. The statement on *erga omnes* in the Court's *East Timor case*, for example, was of considerable relevance to the outcome of the decision. While the Court declined to exercise jurisdiction, it seemed to accept the concept as such, if only by subjecting it to the indispensable third party rule.[46] *East Timor* thus at least partly depended on the Court's specific (and controversial) interpretation of the *erga omnes* concept. The same applies to many of the dissenting and separate opinions discussed below. In *Nuclear Tests*, to take but one example, judges addressing the question of standing placed considerable emphasis on their respective readings of the *Barcelona Traction* dictum.[47] Jurisprudence since 1970 has thus required the Court

[44] See ICJ Reports 1974, 387.
[45] McCaffrey (1989), 243. See also Charney (1993), 159; and Mann (1973b), 418, who speaks of a dictum 'that was unnecessary to the decision and which convey[s] the impression of having been studiously planted into the text or artificially dragged into the arena.'
[46] See Paulus (2001), 372, for a more cautious assessment.
[47] See further below, section 5.2.5; and cf. further Shahabuddeen (1996), 160–161, for a discussion of *obiter* and *ratio* of individual opinions.

to move beyond the allegedly 'gratuitous' and 'quintessential' *obiter dictum* found in paras. 33 and 34 of the *Barcelona Traction case*.[48]

Even upon its own terms, however, the *obiter* argument is difficult to sustain. It is based on the proposition that international law recognises a neat distinction between *obiter dicta* and *ratio decidendi*. That this should be so is far from clear. What may be safely said is that the distinction does not apply in the way known to various common law systems, i.e. as a means of determining the extent to which courts are bound by earlier case-law.[49] That this traditional understanding has no place at the international level is evident: international law not being based on a system of binding precedents, no part of a judicial decision – whether *ratio* or *dictum* – binds other courts or later panels of the same court.[50]

There is, however, at least some support for what might be called an 'international law version' of the distinction between *ratio* and *obiter*. It is based on the fact that decisions of institutionalised international judicial bodies, while not binding in law, are hardly ever departed from, and thus constitute persuasive precedents.[51] Under which circumstances judicial pronouncements are likely to mature into authoritative statements of the law has proven difficult to explain. A number of factors are commonly held to be relevant; they include the fullness and cogency of the reasoning, the eminence of the judicial body rendering the decision, the margin by which that decision has been reached, the subsequent attitude of the international community, and the extent to which a judicial decision crystallises an existing rule of international law.[52] According to some commentators, the

48 See the statement by McCaffrey, quoted above, footnote 45.

49 On the common law approach, and in particular the relation between the distinction and the doctrine of *stare decisis* (or rather *stare rationibus decisis*) see e.g. Goodheart (1930), 161; Montrose (1957), 587; and, for a comprehensive account, Cross and Harris (1991).

50 Pursuant to article 38 (1)(d) of the Statute, the Court's judgments, just as other judicial decisions, are 'subsidiary means for the determination of rules of law.' This is further qualified by the prefatory statement that article 38(1)(d) applies '[s]ubject to the provisions of Article 59', which prescribes the *inter partes* validity of judgments. On the basis of these rules, Shahabuddeen (1996), 97, succinctly states: 'It is not in dispute that the doctrine [of binding precedents, or *stare decisis*] does not apply.' See further Fitzmaurice (1986), Vol. II, 584; Bos (1982), 46; Oppenheim/Jennings/Watts (1992), 41; Cassese (2001), 159; Verdross/Simma (1984), 395–396.

51 Shahabuddeen (1996), 107–109; Roeben (1989), 398–399. See also Judge Jessup's separate opinion in the *Barcelona Traction case*, where it is stated that 'the influence of the Court's decisions is wider than their binding force' (ICJ Reports 1970, 163, para. 9); similarly Judge *ad hoc* Guggenheim's dissent in *Nottebohm*, ICJ Reports 1955, 61.

52 See e.g. Schwarzenberger (1957), 31; Brownlie (2003), 19; and for a comprehensive discussion Shahabuddeen (1996), 67–96.

distinction between *ratio* and *obiter* is another relevant consideration. Consequently a judicial pronouncement is said to be of greater precedential value when it was necessary to decide the case at hand.[53] Amerasinghe, distinguishing *ratio* and *obiter*, for example states that '[m]ore authority naturally attaches to the former than to the latter.'[54] But there is nothing natural about this. On the contrary, neither conceptual arguments nor practical experience suggests that *obiter dicta* of international courts and tribunals should necessarily be of lesser relevance. As regards legal texts, article 38(1)(d) of the ICJ Statute – recognising the role of judicial decisions as a 'subsidiary means for the determination of rules of law' – does not contain any hint that the *ratio* of a judgment should *per se* be of greater precedential value than considerations made *obiter*. What is more, if the authority of ICJ judgments derives from the fact that they crystallise rules of international law, there is no reason why only the *ratio decidendi* should be able to fulfil this crystallising function. Judge Anzilotti's dissent in the *Factory of Chorzów (Interpretation) case* captures the gist of this argument. In Anzilotti's words:

> The grounds of a judgment are simply logical arguments, the aim of which is to lead up to the formulation of what the law is in the case in question. And for this purpose there is no need to distinguish between essential and non-essential grounds, a more or less arbitrary distinction which rests on no solid basis and which can only be regarded as an inaccurate way of expressing the different degree of importance which the various grounds of a judgment may possess for the interpretation of its operative part.[55]

The practice of the Court also provides no conclusive support for the international law version of the distinction between *ratio* and *obiter*. The Court's recent jurisprudence indeed suggests that *obiter dicta* can even form part of a judgment's *dispositif*.[56] Admittedly, individual judges have occasionally qualified specific passages of judgments as *obiter dicta*,

[53] Shahabuddeen (1996), 157–160; Beckett (1932), 144; Bos (1982), 48–50; Condorelli (1987), 308.

[54] Amerasinghe (1967), 33. Admittedly, he goes on to say that *obiter dicta* 'are also valuable expressions of opinion.'

[55] PCIJ, Ser. A., No. 13, 24. For a similar comment see Lauterpacht (1958), 61.

[56] See the *Oil Platforms case*, available at www.icj-cij.org, para. 125(1), where the Court dismissed possible defences of the respondent's conduct even though it had held that this conduct did not violate the applicable Treaty of Amity. The majority's decision to address the question of defences was of course highly controversial: contrast e.g. paras. 2–10 of Judge Buergenthal's separate opinion and paras. 3–16 of Judge Simma's separate opinion (both available *ibid.*).

apparently so to lessen their authority.[57] However, a closer look reveals that they have rarely ever succeeded in so doing, as may be illustrated by reference to comments by Judges Schwebel and Gros, which (apart from the above-quoted remark by Judge de Castro) constitute the most prominent examples in question. Dissenting in *Nicaragua*, Judge Schwebel took the view that the Court need not have pronounced on the United States' right of counter-intervention, and that the relevant passage could 'be treated as *obiter dictum*'.[58] Notwithstanding this criticism, the Court's conclusion that Nicaragua's alleged violations of international law could not justify the United States' forcible intervention is widely regarded today as the most powerful support for a restrictive analysis of customary international law governing forcible interventions.[59] Similarly, in his dissent in the *Barcelona Traction case*, Judge Gros took the view it was 'an *obiter dictum* void of judicial significance to assert at the present time the Canadian nationality of the Barcelona Traction company.'[60] However, experience since 1970 shows that the Court's elaboration on the nationality of corporations (including its express confirmation that Canada was the state of nationality) has been considered to be anything but 'void of judicial significance'; instead it is widely regarded as the crucial judicial pronouncement on the matter.[61] This does not mean that the two passages qualified as *obiter dicta* were beyond criticism.[62] Disagreement, however, relates to the *content* of the Court's pronouncements, whereas their *obiter* status added very little to the discussion. The mere fact that the distinction between *ratio* and *obiter dicta* is mentioned by judges thus need not be conclusive.

[57] See e.g. *Nicaragua case*, Diss.Op. Schwebel, ICJ Reports 1986, 349–350 (paras. 175, 177); *Barcelona Traction case*, Diss.Op. Gros, ICJ Reports 1970, 280 (para. 21); *Aegean Shelf case*, Sep.Op. Elias, ICJ Reports 1976, 28; *Certain Expenses case*, Sep.Op. Spender, ICJ Reports 1962, 193; and cf. Shahabuddeen (1996), 155–157, with further references. The Court itself has used the distinction at times (see e.g. ICJ Reports 1992, 599; ICJ Reports 1987, 65–66), but has not drawn any immediate consequences.

[58] ICJ Reports 1986, 349 (para. 175).

[59] According to Cassese (2001), 160, 'in *Nicaragua*, ... the Court set out in compelling terms ... (ii) the principles on the use of force, in particular under article 51 of the UN Charter; (iii) the principle of non-intervention'.

[60] ICJ Reports 1970, 280 (para. 21).

[61] See *ELSI case*, Sep.Op. Oda, ICJ Reports 1989, 83–87; Brownlie (2003), 466–471; Akehurst/Malanczuk (1997), 266–267.

[62] For recent criticism of the Court's approach to the nationality of corporations in *Barcelona Traction* see Henkin (1995), 89; Seidl-Hohenveldern (1996), 115. For further analysis of the *Nicaragua case* see below, section 6.1.3; and section 7.2.2.

When looking more generally at the development of international law by international courts, the position that *obiter dicta* should have lesser precedential value becomes even more difficult to maintain. While an exhaustive discussion is outside the scope of the present inquiry, it seems safe to say that many *obiter dicta* have shaped the development of rules of international law. As regards the remedies available under the law of State responsibility, this applies, for example, to the primacy of restitution over other forms of reparation, notably compensation.[63] A passage from the PCIJ's judgment in the *Chorzów Factory case*, in which the Court stated that compensation is due only 'if [restitution] is not possible', is widely regarded as the clearest judicial endorsement.[64] As has been pointed out, this statement was quite unnecessary, since Germany, as the applicant in the case, had never claimed restitution, but only demanded compensation.[65] Within the law of treaties, the modification of the *pacta tertiis* rule in cases of treaties creating rights of third States provides another example.[66] It is frequently noted that article 36 VCLT, accepting that rights of third States can be created without their consent, was heavily influenced by the PCIJ's judgment in the *Free Zones case*, in which the Court had stated that 'nothing [could] prevent the will of sovereign States from having this [third-party] effect'.[67] The passage immediately preceding this statement is cited less frequently, but equally relevant. With surprising frankness, the Court had observed that the just-quoted statement was entirely irrelevant to decide the case. Hence it observed that it 'need not consider the legal nature of the Gex [free] zone from the point of view of whether it constitutes a stipulation in favour of a third Party. *But were the matter also to be envisaged from*

[63] Article 36 (1) ASR provides: 'The State responsible for the internationally wrongful act is under an obligation to compensate for the damage caused thereby, *insofar as such damage is not made good by restitution*' (emphasis added). See also para. 3 of the commentary, which speaks of the 'primacy [of restitution] as a matter of legal principle'.

[64] PCIJ, Ser. A, No. 17 (1928), 47. Gray, who is otherwise very critical of the decision, states that the case 'includes the most famous affirmation of primacy', see Gray (1999), 416.

[65] Gray (1987), 96; Thomsen (2000), 230–231.

[66] Article 36 VCLT. The discussion preceding the adoption of the provision is recapitulated in the ILC's commentary on draft article 32 (which was to become article 36 VCLT), YbILC 1966, Vol. II, 228 (paras. 1–4); see further Sinclair (1984), 102–103; Reuter (1995), 103–104 (paras. 155–158).

[67] PCIJ, Ser. A/B, No. 46, at 147. See the ILC's commentary on draft article 32, YbILC 1966, Vol. II, 228 (para. 4); Fitzmaurice, Fifth Report, YbILC 1960, Vol. II, 102–104 (draft article 18).

this aspect, the following observations should be made'.[68] As the subsequent development of the law shows, this express proviso has not affected the authority of the Court's pronouncement on third-party effects of treaties.[69]

These examples are illustrative only.[70] They show that certain *obiter dicta* have played a crucial role in the development of international law. This in turn suggests that despite occasional references in separate and dissenting opinions, the distinction between *obiter* and *ratio* is not only conceptually problematic, but also inconsistently applied. This in turn does not mean that all aspects of a decision had the same precedential value; the above-mentioned factors (such as the cogency of the reasoning, the eminence of the court, etc.), will still be relevant. The discussion however suggests that it is difficult to draw any categorical distinctions between *ratio* and *obiter*. Whether a particular aspect of a judicial decision forms part of the former or the latter seems to be of secondary relevance. The fact that paras. 33 and 34 of the *Barcelona Traction* judgment were made by way of *obiter dictum* thus does not affect their significance.[71]

5.2.3 The international community as the exclusive beneficiary?

Unlike the arguments considered so far, the third counter-argument advanced by adherents of the restrictive approach accepts that the concept of obligations *erga omnes* has become part of international law. However, it is based on a vastly different analysis of the structure of these obligations. Since, according to the ICJ, obligations *erga omnes*

[68] PCIJ, Ser. A/B, No. 46, 147 (emphasis added). Cf. McNair (1961), 311–312.

[69] Lauterpacht (1958), 307, even argued that 'the fact that [the Court] expressed a view on a general and controversial issue, although it was not necessary to do so, adds weight to its pronouncement.'

[70] To the examples given in the text, one might want to add one of the most famous judicial pronouncements of all times, namely the PCIJ's recognition of the *Lotus presumption*, pursuant to which '[r]estrictions upon the independence of States cannot . . . be presumed' (PCIJ, Ser. A, No. 10 (1927), 18). For all the controversy generated by this sweeping statement, it is uncontroversial that the actual decision in *Lotus* did not depend on this abstract and general presumption; rather, the case was decided on the basis of the Court's analysis of international practice in the field of jurisdiction; see *ibid.*, 22–31, and cf. Lauterpacht (1958), 361; Beckett (1932), 144 (his note 1); Fisher Williams (1928), 364–365; Spiermann (1999), 137 for comment.

[71] This is conceded even commentators who otherwise support the international law version of the distinction between *ratio* and *obiter*, see notably Shahabuddeen (1996), 159. On a similar note, Schachter (1991), 344, states that: 'Although this comment [i.e. the *Barcelona Traction* dictum] . . . was pure *obiter dictum*, it has been widely influential.'

are owed to the international community as a whole, this community – so the argument runs – is the beneficiary of the obligations in question, and solely entitled to respond to breaches. In the words of Roberto Ago: 'It is not all States [acting individually], but rather the international community that is envisaged as the possible bearer of a right of reaction to this particular serious form of internationally wrongful act.'[72]

In his Declaration in the 1996 *Genocide case*, Judge Oda equally argued that the obligation *erga omnes* to prevent and punish genocide, as protected by the Genocide Convention, was 'borne in a general manner by the Contracting Parties in their relations with all other Contracting Parties to the Convention – or even with the international community as a whole – but ... *not* in relation to any specific and particular signatory Contracting Party.'[73]

Supporters of this third counter-argument (which may be referred to as the 'community argument') are divided on whether the UN and its organs should be entitled to act as the representative of the international community as a whole.[74] They do, however, agree that individual States are not entitled to respond.[75] Since article 34 of the ICJ Statute

[72] Ago (1989), 238.

[73] ICJ Reports 1996, 626 (para. 4) (emphasis in the original). As a consequence, Judge Oda rejected Bosnia's right to institute inter-State proceedings before the Court. Given that the case involved alleged acts of genocide committed against Bosnian citizens, and therefore did not present any specific problems of standing in the public interest, this interpretation is somewhat surprising and can only be explained on the basis of Judge Oda's interpretation of the 1948 Genocide Convention, which the Court did not share. For further discussion see below, section 5.2.5, and, insofar as the remarks concern the relation between obligations *erga omnes* and corresponding treaty obligations, also below, Chapter 7. For further support of the community argument see also the Australian counter-memorial in the *East Timor case*, para. 263; Sachariew (1988), 282–284.

[74] See e.g. Tomuschat, YbILC 1985, Vol. I, 127; McCaffrey, *ibid.*, 96–97; Boeglin Naumovic (1993), 365; and the summary of views given by Spinedi (1989), 137. For similar arguments advanced in the context of the debate about reactions against international crimes as envisaged in article 19 of the 1996 draft on State responsibility see Graefrath (1989), 164; Dupuy (1989), 182–183; Riphagen, Third Report, YbILC 1983, Vol. II/1, 11; *id.*, Preliminary Report, YbILC 1980, Vol. II/1, 121–122 (paras. 68–73).

[75] It is crucial to distinguish this approach from attempts to make *specific types of responses* (such as countermeasures or military enforcement action) subject to collective action. The community argument is based on the more fundamental assumption that, being the sole beneficiary of obligations *erga omnes*, the international community has the exclusive competence to respond to breaches. The point is very clearly put by Sachariew (1986), 101, who states that the violation of an obligation *erga omnes* ... 'betrifft die Rechte aller gleichzeitig und verlangt eine kollektive Reaktion' (simultaneously affects the rights of all and requires a collective response).

prescribes that only States may be parties before the Court, this in turn means that – following the community argument – the *erga omnes* concept would be irrelevant to disputes before the Court.[76]

At least at first glance, this interpretation indeed seems to be supported by the text of the *Barcelona Traction* dictum. If, on the one hand, obligations *erga omnes* are 'owed towards the international community as a whole',[77] while, on the other (as the Court had observed two decades earlier), 'only the party to whom an obligation is due can bring a claim in respect of a breach',[78] it would seem to follow that the international community should have a monopoly for the vindication of obligations *erga omnes*.

However, the reference to the international community as a whole is only one aspect of the *Barcelona Traction* dictum. If read in their entirety, paras. 33 and 34 provide at best lukewarm support for the community argument. It has been said already that the expression '*erga omnes*' is ambiguous, as an obligation that is owed 'towards all' members of the international community can be owed either towards each of them individually or to all of them together.[79] More importantly, however, the community argument neglects the Court's express references to States made in the course of paras. 33 and 34, namely its recognition that obligations *erga omnes* 'are the concern of all States', and that 'all States . . . have a legal interest in their protection'.[80] How the international community, or all States collectively, should have a legal interest remains unclear.[81]

The context in which the dictum appears further weakens the community argument. As has been stated already, paras. 33 and 34 form part of the Court's discussion of standing in ICJ proceedings.[82] Since article 34 of the ICJ Statute restricts standing *ratione personae* to States, it would be surprising if paras. 33 and 34 were concerned with legal entities other than States.[83] Furthermore, if the community argument were correct, the *Barcelona Traction* dictum could not be seen as an attempt to reverse the effects of the 1966 *South West Africa* judgment either, as that judgment concerned the standing of individual States.

[76] Cf. Greig (1994), 304; Kokott (1996), 49–50. [77] ICJ Reports 1970, 32 (para. 33).
[78] *Reparations for Injuries case*, ICJ Reports 1949, 181–182.
[79] See above, Introduction to Part II and cf. also Weil (1983), 432.
[80] ICJ Reports 1970, 32 (para. 33).
[81] See also Boellecker-Stern (1973), 85; de Hoogh (1996) 93; Gaja (1989), 152; Gaja (1981), 281; Paulus (2001), 371, 378; Karl (2003), 103.
[82] See above, section 5.1. [83] de Hoogh (1996), 93–94; Paulus (2001), 371.

Finally, the Court's subsequent jurisprudence would also seem to contradict the community argument. Judge Oda's above-quoted remark aside, judges have not questioned the possibility that individual States could rely on the *erga omnes* concept. Despite persisting differences as to its precise implications, neither of the judges participating in the *Nuclear Tests* and *East Timor cases* raised objections against the applicants' invocation of the concept.[84]

To sum up, the community argument is based on a one-sided textual interpretation of paras. 33 and 34 that is contradicted both by a contextual analysis of the dictum and the Court's subsequent jurisprudence. The mere fact that the Court described obligations *erga omnes* as 'obligations towards the international community as a whole' therefore does not mean that they cannot be vindicated by individual States.

5.2.4 *Contradictions within the judgment?*

Even when accepting that the text of paras. 33 and 34 favours a broad interpretation, adherents of the restrictive approach have warned against putting too much emphasis on the passage. Pursuant to a fourth counter-argument, a subsequent passage of the *Barcelona Traction* judgment qualifies the earlier dictum on obligations *erga omnes*, and deprives it of its legal value. The relevant statement is contained in para. 91 of the judgment; it runs as follows:

> With regard more particularly to human rights, to which reference has already been made in paragraph 34 of this Judgment, it should be noted that these also include protection against denial of justice. However, on the universal level, the instruments which embody human rights do not confer upon States the capacity to protect victims of infringements of such rights irrespective of their nationality. It is therefore still on the regional level that a solution to this problem has had to be sought; thus, within the Council of Europe, of which Spain is not a member, the problem of admissibility encountered by the claim in the present case has been resolved by the European Convention on Human Rights, which entitles each State which is a party to the Convention to lodge a complaint against any other contracting State for violation of the Convention, irrespective of the nationality of the victim.[85]

This passage, and its relation to paras. 33 and 34, has prompted much discussion.[86] Judge Gros considered the two statements to be

[84] For a more detailed analysis of the various pronouncements see below, section 5.2.5.

[85] ICJ Reports 1970, 47 (para. 91).

[86] See Boellecker-Stern 1973, 84–88; Kamminga (1992), 154–156; Simma (1981), 642–643; Simma (1994), 296–297; de Hoogh 1991, 197–199; Voeffray (2004), 76–78; Paulus (2001),

'inconsistent',[87] and commentators have long disagreed whether para. 91 was meant to restrict the earlier dictum on obligations *erga omnes*.[88] If international law at the universal level does not confer upon States the capacity to vindicate human rights of non-nationals, it is argued, how could paras. 33 and 34 be read to introduce a general right of standing in respect of obligations *erga omnes* including 'the basic rights of the human person'?[89]

Despite the considerable amount of discussion, the problem to which para. 91 gives rise is not always spelled out clearly. A preliminary (but often overlooked) point to make is that in its sweeping terms, the Court's assertion that universal human rights treaties, in 1970, did not recognise a right to protect rights of non-nationals is simply incorrect. Admittedly, the CCPR as a *general* universal human rights treaty entitling States to protect victims of infringements irrespective of their nationality had not entered into force at the time of the judgment.[90] However, the Court curiously seemed to neglect the various binding instruments embodying *specific* human rights (e.g. protection from genocide, slavery, etc.), whose jurisdictional clauses confer upon all member States a general right to respond to all treaty breaches.[91] As has been shown already,[92] a considerable number of treaties, in force by 1970, did in fact confer upon States 'the capacity to protect victims of infringements of such rights irrespective of their nationality'.

371–372; Annacker (1994a), 16–17; M'Baye (1988), 307–308; Thirlway (1989), 99–100; Crawford (2000), 26–27; Ragazzi (1997), 211–212; Frowein (1983), 245–246; Frowein 1994, 406; Seidl-Hohenveldern (1975), 804–805, 809–813; Meron (1986), 11–12.

87 *Nuclear Tests cases*, Sep.Op. Gros, ICJ Reports 1974, 290. In the same case, Judge Petrén said that the Court had created 'the impression of a self-contradiction' (p. 303). In the view of Marek (1978–1979), 480, the 'contradiction' was 'to say the least, somewhat embarassing'.

88 Contrast e.g. Ragazzi (1997), 211–212; Crawford (2000), 26–27; Thirlway (1989), 99–100; Linsi (1994), 61–62; and Judge de Castro's dissent in the *Nuclear Tests cases*, ICJ Reports 1974, 387, on the one hand, and de Hoogh (1996), 52–53; Paulus (2001), 371–372; Annacker (1994a), 17; Simma (1994a), 296–297; Simma (1981), 643; Tomuschat (1999), 84; Meron (1986), 11–12, on the other.

89 ICJ Reports 1970, 33 (para. 34).

90 See article 41 CCPR, and cf. de Hoogh (1996), 52; Frowein (1983), 245; Crawford (2000), 26–27. Pursuant to its article 49, the CCPR entered into force on 23 March 1976. The optional inter-State complaint procedure envisaged under Article 41 only entered into force on 28 March 1979 (see article 41, para. 2).

91 See also Seiderman (2001), 135–136; Empell (2003), 341–342; Quigley (1988), 130–132.

92 See above, Section 2.2.1.a.

Notwithstanding this criticism, the relation between the two passages must be addressed.[93] Read properly, para. 91 raises two questions, only one of which can be dealt with here. The first problem is whether para. 91 directly contradicts paras. 33 and 34, or excludes a specific interpretation of the earlier dictum. The answer to this question is much simpler than is usually assumed: para. 91 does not contradict paras. 33 and 34, as the two passages concern different subject matters. The Court's reference to 'the instruments which embody human rights' makes clear that para. 91 is solely concerned with treaty-based mechanisms for the enforcement of human rights; it presents a certain (incorrect) view of how *conventional* human rights provisions could be enforced in 1970. In contrast, the enforcement of obligations *erga omnes* (which derive, as has been shown, from customary international law) is not a matter of treaty law. The crucial question prompted by paras. 33 and 34 is whether by recognising the category of obligations *erga omnes*, the Court meant to confer upon States a right to vindicate these obligations *in the absence of express treaty provisions*.[94] Since para. 91 does not bear on this matter, it is difficult to see how it could contradict a specific interpretation of the *erga omnes* concept.

Secondly, para. 91 could also be read as an implicit derogation from paras. 33 and 34. Some commentators wonder whether by alluding to special treaty-based mechanisms of enforcement, the Court intended to state that these special mechanisms take precedence over enforcement measures not based on express treaty provisions.[95] Thus interpreted, para. 91 would prompt the question – already hinted at in para. 34 – whether treaty-based rights of protection can coexist with rights of protection based on the *erga omnes* concept. Whether this reading is

[93] The following discussion is based on the premise that para. 91 concerns the standing of States to vindicate human rights of foreign nationals. Interestingly, Judge Petrén, in his separate opinion in the *Nuclear Tests case*, seemed to advance a different interpretation. According to him, para. 91 merely intended to confirm the rather evident proposition that States wishing to vindicate human rights would have to establish a jurisdictional title (ICJ Reports 1974, 303; see also Kamminga (1992), 155–156). This interpretation (which of course would resolve all problems of contradiction) is, however, not convincing. While the term 'capacity to protect' (*qualité pour protéger*), which is used in para. 91, indeed can have a broader meaning than 'standing', the French text of the *Barcelona Traction* judgment suggests that both terms are used synonymously. Hence, after having discussed the problem of standing, the Court ultimately held that Belgium lacked the necessary *qualité* to file the claim (see e.g. paras. 101, 102). For a discussion of both terms see M'Baye (1988), 258–260; Günther (1999), 20–28.

[94] See Introduction to this chapter; and further Weil (1992), 285; de Hoogh (1996), 52–53.

[95] Thirlway (1989), 99–100; Kamminga (1992), 181; Boellecker-Stern (1973), 86–87.

convincing need not, and cannot, be decided here. It is part of the broader problem of competing (conventional and customary) enforcement mechanisms, and needs to be analysed in that broader context. Most importantly, it can only be addressed properly once it has been clarified which rights of protection are triggered by the *erga omnes* concept. In the light of these considerations, the suggested interpretation will be discussed when assessing the relation between *erga omnes* enforcement rights and treaties.[96]

To sum up, not all issues raised by para. 91 can be addressed here. Whether the Court's rather generalised (and incorrect) reference to human rights treaties was meant as an implicit derogation from paras. 33 and 34 will be assessed below. What can be said is that para. 91 does not directly contradict a broad interpretation of the *erga omnes* concept.

5.2.5 *Inconclusive jurisprudence since 1970?*

Recognition of the *erga omnes* concept in *Barcelona Traction* raised hopes that the Court's jurisprudence since 1970 has not fulfilled. Not only has the Court yet to admit a claim based on the *erga omnes* concept. What is more, in the view of many commentators, the Court, after the audacious step of introducing the concept, has shied away from further developing it. Aspects of the decisions in *Nicaragua* and *East Timor*, as well as a number of separate and dissenting opinions, have been interpreted as attempts to turn back the clock to before 1970. The essence of this fifth argument is expressed by Jørgensen, who concludes her review of ICJ jurisprudence by observing that:

> 'The theory of obligations *erga omnes* is that all States should have *locus standi* to protect certain rights which by their nature are vested in the entire international community. In practice, courts have been reluctant to allow third parties to enforce such rights. It is therefore unlikely for the time being that the notion of obligations *erga omnes* will assist in bringing cases involving international crimes [the subject of Jørgensen's inquiry] before the ICJ'.[97]

96 See below, section 7.2.2.a.

97 Jørgensen (2000), 222–223. It should be noted that Jørgensen criticises this cautious attitude, and goes on to observe that 'the possibility of increased judicial support for the rapidly developing hierarchy of international norms should not be ruled out for the future' (*ibid.*).

Put differently, there is support for the view that whatever the correct interpretation of the *Barcelona Traction* judgment, inconclusive jurisprudence since 1970 overshadows the dictum contained in paras. 33 and 34, and diminishes its legal relevance.[98] This fifth argument – which may be termed the 'inconclusiveness thesis' – proceeds from the correct assumption that discussions about obligations *erga omnes* need to move beyond the interpretation of a judgment rendered more than 30 years ago. It also points to the fact that jurisprudence since 1970 provides a wealth of information (not always taken into account) about the correct interpretation of the concept. Whether this body of jurisprudence supports the inconclusiveness thesis is another matter. It will be addressed in the following sections, which analyse the relevant aspects of the proceedings in the *Nuclear Tests*, *East Timor*, *Nicaragua*, *Genocide*, and *Gabčíkovo cases*.[99]

5.2.5.a The *Nuclear Tests cases*

It has been said already that the majority judgments in the *Nuclear Tests cases* did not pronounce on *erga omnes* effects in the field of standing, the Court having held that the dispute had become moot.[100] This is unfortunate, since both applicants had in fact invoked the *Barcelona Traction* dictum in order to establish standing, and the Court's response to these arguments might have clarified many issues.[101] Four of the separate and dissenting opinions attached to the judgment however discuss the issue, and present diverging interpretations of the *erga omnes* concept.

Judge de Castro's dissent, which has already been referred to, very clearly rejects the view that all States have standing in disputes involving obligations *erga omnes*. As the *Barcelona Traction* dictum had to be taken '*cum grano salis*', an applicant, in order to establish standing, had

[98] See further Tomuschat (1999), 83, in whose view 'the concept [of obligations *erga omnes*] was decisively diluted' after the 1970 judgment. Disappointment with the Court's subsequent jurisprudence is also expressed by Schulte (1999), 535–536; Zemanek (2000a), 11–12; Macdonald (1987), 137.

[99] Of course, this fifth argument is closely linked to the view that the Court's pronouncement on obligations *erga omnes* constitute isolated incidents (see above, section 5.2.1). However, the inconclusiveness thesis goes beyond that argument, in that it asserts that the Court's pronouncements are not only few and far between – a contention that has proven easy to reject – but that jurisprudence contradicts the above interpretation of the *Barcelona Traction* dictum.

[100] See above, sections 5.2.1 and 3.3.3.

[101] See Australian memorial, ICJ Pleadings, Vol. I, 331 and 334 (paras. 431 and 448) and New Zealand's memorial, *ibid.*, Vol. II, 204, para. 191; and cf. already above, section 5.2.1.

to show the existence of a 'right of its own' ('*un droit propre*').[102] Expressly denying the legal relevance of paras. 33 and 34 of the *Barcelona Traction* judgment, Judge de Castro was

> unable to believe that by virtue of this dictum the Court would regard as admissible, for example, a claim by State A against State B that B was not applying 'principles and rules concerning the basic rights of the human person' (*ICJ Reports 1970, p. 32, para. 34*) with regard to the subjects of State B or even State C.[103]

Judge *ad hoc* Barwick's view was diametrically opposed, but equally clear. Quoting paras. 33 and 34 of the *Barcelona Traction* judgment, Judge *ad hoc* Barwick held that each State had a right to see obligations *erga omnes* observed, and to vindicate this right before the Court. If the Court accepted the applicants' contention that the customary prohibition against nuclear testing was an obligation *erga omnes* - which was a question of the merits stage - it therefore, in his view, would have to accept that they had established standing.[104]

The relation between preliminary objections and the merits of a case was also touched upon in the joint dissenting opinion of Judges Onyema, Dillard, Jiménez de Aréchaga, and Waldock. Unlike Judge *ad hoc* Barwick, these judges took a more reserved approach. They felt unable to decide, at the preliminary objections stage, the hypothetical question whether the applicants would have standing if the Court accepted their argument based on the *Barcelona Traction case*. In their view, all depended on whether the alleged prohibition against nuclear testing could be vindicated by all States individually.[105] Nevertheless, they did concede that in the light of the Court's *Barcelona Traction* dictum, this question was 'capable of rational legal argument and a proper subject of litigation before this Court.'[106] This may be taken as a cautious endorsement of the applicants' position that *erga omnes* status implied a general right of all States to vindicate the obligation in question.[107]

The same can be said of Judge Petrén's separate opinion, which stressed the relevance of the *erga omnes* concept for the enforcement of international law. While rejecting the applicants' position that customary international law recognised a prohibition against nuclear

[102] ICJ Reports 1974, 387. [103] ICJ Reports 1974, 387. [104] ICJ Reports 1974, 437.
[105] ICJ Reports 1974, 369–370 (para. 118) and 521 (para. 52).
[106] ICJ Reports 1974, 369–370 (para. 118) and 521 (para. 52).
[107] For a similar interpretation see Günther (1999), 156–157.

testing, Judge Petrén discussed the evolution of an 'allied field', namely that of human rights law.[108] Summarising developments since 1945, he stressed that whereas traditionally international law had not imposed upon States obligations with regard to the treatment of their own nationals, the Court now no longer had to treat inter-State claims brought for the vindication of human rights of foreign nationals as 'inadmissible'. In his view, 'the Court [had] alluded to this in its Judgment in the case concerning the *Barcelona Traction, Light and Power Company, Limited (ICJ Reports 1970, p. 32).*'[109]

Admittedly, Judge Petrén's remarks were not expressly directed at the rules of standing, and could also be interpreted as a comment on the development of the primary rules of international law. In this case, it would, however, be difficult to explain why Judge Petrén should have referred to the *Barcelona Traction* dictum, and mentioned the admissibility of inter-State claims in the field of human rights.[110] Rather, he seemed to accept that the *Barcelona Traction* dictum had affected the conditions under which the Court would admit inter-State claims in the human rights field. Thus interpreted, his opinion supports a broad reading of paras. 33 and 34.

The separate and dissenting opinions in the *Nuclear Tests cases* thus show the degree of controversy provoked by the *erga omnes* concept. The preceding discussion however clarifies that the majority of judges expressing a view was prepared to take the *Barcelona Traction* dictum at face value and interpret it as a recognition of a general right of standing.

5.2.5.b The *East Timor case*

More than any other decision, the judgment in the *East Timor case*, has been interpreted as an attempt by the Court to reverse the effects of the *Barcelona Traction* judgment.[111] In the circumstances of the case, the ICJ had to decide whether Australia had violated the right of the East Timorese people to self-determination by entering into the Timor Gap Treaty with Indonesia. It has been observed already that while confirming the *erga omnes* status of the right of self-determination, the Court held that the indispensable third-party rule prevented it from

[108] ICJ Reports 1970, 303 and 305–306. [109] ICJ Reports 1970, 303.

[110] See also Günther (1999), 155–156.

[111] The most emphatic critique is John Dugard's '1966 And All That. The South West Africa Judgment Revisited in the East Timor Case' (Dugard [1996], 549). For further critical comment see Joergensen (2000), 221–223; Paulus (2001), 374–375; Chinkin (1996), 712; Lowe (1995), 484; Schulte (1999), 533; Coffman (1996), 285; Scobbie and Drew (1996), 185; Jouannet (1996), 673; Antonopoulos (1996); 75; Clark (1998), 631.

entertaining the case.[112] Although the question of standing thus was not conclusively settled, the proceedings reveal a considerable amount of information about the Court's interpretation of the *erga omnes* concept. Crucially, the *erga omnes* concept came into play at two different levels: as a basis of standing and as a potential bar against the strict application of the indispensable third party rule. Both of these aspects need to be addressed separately.

Obligations erga omnes *and the indispensable third-party rule*

Much of the proceedings in *East Timor* focused on the relation between obligations *erga omnes* and the indispensable third-party rule. In view of Portugal, the rule had to be modified where obligations *erga omnes* were at stake.[113] The Court dismissed this assertion, holding that

> whatever the nature of the obligation invoked, the Court could not rule on the lawfulness of the conduct of a State when its judgment would imply an evaluation of the lawfulness of the conduct of another State which is not a party to the case. Where this is so, the Court cannot act, even if the right in question is a right *erga omnes*.[114]

Much to the disappointment of commentators, it thereby subjected the *erga omnes* concept to 'the procedural rigours of traditional bilateralism'.[115] It is beyond the scope of this study to assess whether the Court's reliance on the indispensable third-party rule was altogether inevitable, or in line with its previous jurisprudence.[116] Given the

[112] See above, section 5.2.1.

[113] See e.g. paras. 5.42, 5.46 of the Portuguese memorial and para. 8.16. of the *réplique* (invoking the concept of 'international public service').

[114] ICJ Reports 1995, 102 (para. 29). The Court also rejected Portugal's argument that the *Monetary Gold* principle was inapplicable, since a series of international resolutions had determined the illegality of Indonesia's conduct; see *ibid.*, 103–104 (paras. 30–33).

[115] Simma (1994a), 298. See also Jouannet (1996), 694–695; Scobbie and Drew (1996), 197–207; Antonopoulos (1996), 86–96; Schulte (1999), 536–544.

[116] Two considerations can be distinguished. First, it is arguable that an ICJ decision would have only *confirmed* previous UN resolutions pronouncing on the illegality of Indoesia's conduct. That illegality could thus have been treated as given, which in turn might have warranted a modification of the indispensable third-party rule. Controversially, the Court dismissed this argument, arguing that previous UN resolutions did not impose upon Australia a duty not to recognise Indonesia's authority, see ICJ Reports 1995, 103 (paras. 30–31). Secondly, by strictly applying the *Monetary Gold* principle, the Court seemed to move away from its more lenient position in the *Nauru case*, in which it had admitted Nauru's claim against one of the three former administering powers, see ICJ Reports 1992, 261–262 (para. 55). For comment cf. Scobbie/Drew (1996), 195–208, and further Zimmermann (1995), 105.

largely critical reactions in the literature, it may, however, be worth noting that by subjecting the enforcement of obligations *erga omnes* to the *Monetary Gold* test, the Court did not prejudice the question of standing. What is more, disappointed with the decision, commentators at times seem to have overlooked that the circumstances of the *East Timor case* were rather exceptional; the implications of the decision are thus more limited than is suggested. When assessing the possibility of *erga omnes* proceedings before the Court, it has been assumed thoughout this study that claims would be brought against States principally responsible for the alleged breaches. Irrespective of whether one agrees with the Court's treatment of the indispensable third-party rule, it is clear that the *East Timor case* did not follow this normal pattern. Proceedings were instituted not against the State principally responsible for the violation of the obligation *erga omnes* (i.e. Indonesia), but against a State accused of having condoned *erga omnes* Indonesia's breaches by recognising their legal effects.[117] As regards possible violations of the East Timorese right of self-determination, Australia – even upon Portugal's reading – thus was at best an accomplice after the fact. By subjecting the *erga omnes* concept to the indispensable third party rule, the Court therefore did not restrict the enforcement of obligations *erga omnes* as such, but merely clarified that enforcement action could not be taken against States condoning another State's *erga omnes* breaches.[118] Despite the largely critical responses in the literature, this canalisation of *erga omnes* enforcement action however seems defensible. In terms of the practical results, it means that enforcement must be directed against principally responsible States – a result that, with respect to the other form of enforcement action

[117] It therefore is unconvincing merely to allege – as for example, Schulte (1999), 537, does – that since obligations *erga omnes* involve more than two States, *erga omnes* breaches would rarely be committed by one State alone.

[118] With respect to the *erga omnes* concept, the result would not have been much different had Portugal – as suggested by some commentators, such as e.g. Crawford (2001b), 35–36 – argued that Australia had breached its (self-standing) duty not to recognise the legal consequences of particularly serious wrongful acts. There is indeed support for the existence of such a self-standing duty of non-recognition (see notably the ICJ's advisory opinion in the *Israeli Wall case* (available at www.icj-cij.org, para. 159); and the references in the ILC's commentary to article 41 ASR, paras. 4–9). By invoking it, Portugal might have countered the Australian argument based on the indispensable third party rule. This change of strategy would however not have affected the reasoning set out in the text, as there is little indication that the self-standing duty of non-recognition should itself be valid *erga omnes*.

relevant to the present study (i.e. countermeasures) is generally accepted.[119]

To sum up the reasoning on this point, the Court's treatment of the indispensable third party rule, in *East Timor*, does not prejudice the question of standing. Furthermore, given the rather exceptional circumstances, the implications of the decision should not be overstated.

The issue of standing

Compared to the extensive debates about the indispensable third-party rule, *erga omnes* effects in the field of standing played a more limited role. In order to establish standing, Portugal had relied on its status as the former administering power as well as on the *erga omnes* status of the right in question.[120] Given its decision on jurisdiction, the Court did not have to address this question. Nevertheless, both the majority judgment and some of the opinions attached to it provide some further information, which on balance strengthen the broad interpretation of the *erga omnes* concept.

As for the judgment, the Court did not explicitly state whether Portugal could have established standing on the basis of the *erga omnes* character of the legal rule in question. It is worth noting however that, at the end of the passage quoted above, the Court held that '*even if* the right in question is a right *erga omnes*',[121] it could not decide the case. The use of the proviso 'even if' seems to suggest that, but for the absence of an indispensable third party, Portugal would have been entitled to respond to the alleged breach of an obligation *erga omnes*.[122] While not settling the matter conclusively, the passage can thus be interpreted as supporting the broad approach.

The opinions of Judges Weeramantry and Ranjeva point in the same direction.[123] Judge Weeramantry's endorsement in fact could have

119 See above, section 1.1; and further below, section 6.2.1 for a review of international practice.

120 See e.g. paras. 4.12.–4.56. and 8.09.–8.13. of the Portuguese *réplique*.

121 ICJ Reports 1995, 102 (para. 29) (emphasis added).

122 Similarly Empell (2003), 351; Günther (1999), 159.

123 ICJ Reports 1995, 139 and 129 respectively. On Judge Weeramantry's dissent see the discussion by Clark (1998), 631. In contrast, neither Judge Oda's declaration nor Judge *ad hoc* Skubiszewski's dissent provide much information about the question of standing in *erga omnes* disputes. In particular, Judge Oda's statement that Portugal '*lacks standing*' cannot be taken as support of the restrictive approach. In his view, the *East Timor case* solely concerned 'the title to the continental shelf [of East Timor], which Portugal claims to possess as a coastal State', but did not involve the right of peoples to

hardly been more emphatic. While accepting that Portugal had standing on the basis of its status as the former administering power,[124] he dealt at length with various aspects of the *erga omnes* concept. Having affirmed that all States have a legal interest in seeing obligations *erga omnes* observed, he stated that where such an obligation had been violated, the Court would 'grant . . . judicial relief'.[125] These statements show that in view of Judge Weeramantry, Portugal's right of standing did not depend on its special status as a former administering power. His remarks therefore support the broad approach.

Judge Ranjeva's separate opinion seems to be based on the same understanding. Discussing the majority's application of the indispensable third-party rule, Judge Ranjeva drew a distinction between disputes involving subjective rights and those concerning 'objective rights opposable *erga omnes*'.[126] In his view, the *Monetary Gold* principle did not limit the Court's competence to entertain disputes of the latter ('objective') type, which involved the legal interests of all States. Judge Ranjeva nevertheless supported the Court's decision because in his interpretation, Portugal had primarily brought the case in order to nullify the legal effects of the Timor Gap treaty – which he considered to involve a question of subjective rights.[127] While this interpretation may be problematic, the express reference to legal interests of third States suggests that had he considered the case to concern 'objective rights opposable *erga omnes*', Judge Ranjeva would not have dismissed it for lack of standing.[128]

While specific circumstances enabled the Court to avoid a definitive answer, the *East Timor* judgment and the opinions of Judges Weeramantry and Ranjeva thus support, rather than contradict, the broad interpretation of the *Barcelona Traction* dictum. Notwithstanding the Court's controversial analysis of the relation between obligations *erga omnes* and the indispensable third-party rule, the *East Timor case* therefore provides no argument for the restrictive approach.

self-determination (see ICJ Reports 1995, 118 and 108 respectively). Conversely, Judge *ad hoc* Skubiszewski's finding that Portugal had standing to bring the case was based on his interpretation of the legal interest of an administering power; see *ibid.*, 255–257 (paras. 100–104).

[124] ICJ Reports 1995, 178–192. [125] ICJ Reports 1995, 215.

[126] ICJ Reports 1995, 131. [127] ICJ Reports 1995, 132.

[128] See Günther (1999), 160. It is worth mentioning that Judge Ranjeva frequently stressed the *erga omnes* status of the rights and obligations involved, but remained completely silent on Portugal's role as administering power. This provides further support for the view that he would have accepted the broad theory had the case (in his view) primarily been about *erga omnes* issues.

5.2.5.c The *Genocide case*

In addition to these cases, the proceedings in the *Nicaragua*, *Genocide*, and *Gabčíkovo cases* provide further evidence as to the judges' interpretation of the *erga omnes* concept. Judge Oda's declaration attached to the 1996 *Genocide* judgment, which has been mentioned already, provides clear support for the restrictive analysis of the *Barcelona Traction* dictum. As has been shown, the case provided the Court with an opportunity to explore the effects of the *erga omnes* concept on the territorial applicability of obligations.[129] In his declaration, Judge Oda discussed the enforcement system of the Genocide Convention, and the possible impact of the *erga omnes* concept, from a more general angle. In his interpretation, the Convention did not protect States' rights, but solely rights of individuals.[130] No State, not even the victims' State of nationality, therefore could invoke the responsibility of the responsible State. Nor did the *erga omnes* status of the obligation to prevent and punish genocide affect this result, as obligations *erga omnes* were 'borne in a general manner ... by [States] in their relations with ... the international community as a whole'.[131]

Although these remarks are directed at one specific obligation *erga omnes*, they are based on a restrictive analysis of the category of obligations *erga omnes* as such.[132] On the basis of this analysis, which takes up the problematic community argument discussed earlier, Judge Oda denied the right of individual States to bring ICJ proceedings in response to breaches of obligations *erga omnes*.

5.2.5.d The *Nicaragua case*

The same is often said to follow implicitly from the Court's decision in the *Nicaragua case*.[133] The United States' withdrawal from the proceedings of course prevented the Court from exploring many aspects of the *erga omnes* concept, which might otherwise have arisen at the merits stage. Even though, the Court discussed whether the United States' conduct in Nicaragua could be justified as response to alleged prior

[129] See above, section 3.3.2.

[130] ICJ Reports 1996, 626 (para. 4), and 628 (para. 6).

[131] ICJ Reports 1996, 626 (para. 4). See above, section 5.2.3 for a critical assessment of this community approach.

[132] Apart from the remark just quoted, see also Judge Oda's comment that the Genocide Convention had been adopted 'in parallel with the emergence of the concept of the protection of human rights and humanity'; ICJ Reports 1996, 626–627 (para. 4).

[133] See e.g. Pieper (1997), 387; Sachariew (1988), 286.

violations by Nicaragua of human rights of its nationals. In a passage relied on as evidence of a restrictive understanding of the *erga omnes* concept, the Court noted that 'where human rights are protected by international conventions, [their] protection takes the form of such arrangements for monitoring or ensuring respect for human rights as are provided for in the conventions themselves.'[134] Although the United States, which would have had to rely on means of ensuring respect not provided for the applicable convention(s), 'might form its own appraisal of the situation' in Nicaragua, 'the use of force could not be an appropriate method to monitor or ensure such respect.'[135]

As will be shown below,[136] this passage is based on a controversial understanding of the relation between conventional and customary means of protecting human rights, and in that respect is not without implications for the regime governing the enforcement of obligations *erga omnes*. To interpret it as restricting the right of States to vindicate obligations *erga omnes* before the ICJ, however, seems problematic. Just as para. 91 of the *Barcelona Traction* judgment,[137] it does not concern the existence (or otherwise) of enforcement rights based on the *erga omnes* concept, but the consequential question whether conventional enforcement mechanisms exclude rights of protection not expressly provided for in the relevant treaties.[138] To this, it may be added that the above-quoted passage is concerned with the protection of human rights rather than with the *erga omnes* concept (which had not been invoked by the defendant),[139] and that the Court was faced not with claims for judicial relief, but with unilateral measures amounting to forcible

[134] ICJ Reports 1986, 134 (para. 267).

[135] ICJ Reports 1986, 134 (para. 268). The United States' invocation of the right of self-defence in response to previous interventions, by Nicaragua, against El Salvador, Honduras, and Costa Rica, was dismissed in even clearer terms by the Court. As noted on p. 127 (para. 249): 'The acts of which Nicaragua is accused ... could only have justified proportionate counter-measures on the part of the State which had been the victim of the act, namely Salvador, Honduras or Costa Rica. They could not justify counter-measures taken by a third State, and particularly could not justify interventions involving the use of force.'

[136] See below, section 7.2.2.a. [137] On which above, section 5.2.4.

[138] Cf. Frowein (1987), 76–77; *id.* (1994), 398–401; Thirlway (1989), 100–101.

[139] Annacker (1994a), 24–25.

and non-forcible intervention – hence the express reference to the use of force as an inappropriate form of redress.[140]

While therefore the *Nicaragua* judgment does not directly affect the question of standing in *erga omnes* disputes before the Court, Judge Schwebel's dissent to the 1984 order on provisional measures is relevant.[141] In order fully to appreciate his comments, it is necessary to distinguish between their immediate subject matter and possible implications. On the face of it, his dissent did not concern the question of standing to institute ICJ proceedings, but the entitlement of a defendant to invoke rights of third States as a justification.[142] In view of Judge Schwebel, the Court had not paid sufficient regard to rights of third States (such as El Salvador or Honduras), which allegedly had been violated by Nicaragua. The United States had been entitled to invoke these alleged violations as a defence, as they concerned 'rights … *erga omnes*', namely the fundamental rights of States to live in peace and security.[143] Relying explicitly on the *Barcelona Traction* judgment, Judge Schwebel concluded that '[t]he United States has, in the specific term of *Barcelona Traction*, 'a legal interest' in the performance by Nicaragua of its fundamental international obligations',[144] and consequently could invoke before the Court Nicaragua's responsibility incurred through conduct *vis-à-vis* third States.

In many respects, these comments remain obscure. In particular, it is not quite clear how they should have influenced the Court's decision whether or not to grant interim relief. Nor indeed did Judge Schwebel clarify what forms of reactions against Nicaragua's conduct would have been justified. The passage is nevertheless relevant – if not so much for what it explcitly states, then for what it implies. According to Judge Schwebel, the legal interest of all States in seeing obligations *erga omnes* observed was sufficient to justify otherwise illegal conduct and to invoke before the Court the responsibility of other States *as a*

[140] This express reference has given rise to very different interpretations. While Günther (1999), 157–158, argues that the Court implicitly accepted that the use of other (non-forcible) might well be appropriate, Frowein (1989), 227 and Paulus (2001), 374 (note 200) take the opposite view. See further Charney (1989), 57; Hutchinson (1988), 193–194, and below, section 6.1.

[141] ICJ Reports 1984, 196–198.

[142] In addition, they were made in the context of Judge Schwebel's discussion of whether the Court ought to have taken into account the interests of third States when exercising its competence to issue provisional measures pursuant to article 41 of the Statute.

[143] ICJ Reports 1984, 196. [144] ICJ Reports 1984, 198.

justification. If however defendant States are entitled to invoke the responsibility of applicants, arising from *erga omnes* breaches, *as a justification*, it seems difficult to deny applicants the right to invoke the responsibility of defendants arising from the same type of breaches – all that distinguishes the two cases are the respective roles of the litigant States. While made in a formally different context, Judge Schwebel's remarks therefore seem to imply a broad approach to the *erga omnes* concept.[145]

5.2.5.e The *Gabčíkovo case*

Judge Weeramantry's separate opinion in *Gabčíkovo* provides further support for the broad approach.[146] Just as with regard to Judge Schwebel's dissent in *Nicaragua*, his remarks were made in a formally different context, but are based on a specific interpretation of the *erga omnes* concept. On the face of it, Judge Weeramantry was concerned with an issue that the majority judgment had left open, namely the question of estoppel.[147] In the circumstances of the case, Hungary had claimed a right to suspend, and terminate, a bilateral treaty envisaging the construction of a joint Hungaro-Czechoslovakian system of locks, arguing that its implementation would have entailed devastating environmental consequences.[148] However, it did so only after the 1989 change of government, whereas beforehand it had agreed to carry out the project. In Judge Weeramantry's view, Hungary would have, under normal circumstances, been estopped from relying on the legal effects of its suspension. Yet he questioned whether the rules on inter-State litigation, such as estoppel, could be applied in cases involving 'the greater interests of humanity and planetary welfare.'[149] In his view,

> [t]he Court, in the discharge of its traditional duty of deciding *between the parties*, makes the decision which is in accordance with justice and fairness *between the parties*. The procedure it follows is largely adversarial. Yet this scarcely does

[145] One might object that the majority of the Court did not share Judge Schwebel's approach; in its view, the United States could not simply claim to act in defence of other States' rights without having sought their prior approval (see especially ICJ Reports 1984, 184–186). However, the majority's statement concerned the actual justification of the United States' conduct. Insofar as Judge Schwebel had asserted a right of defendants States to invoke before the Court the applicant States' responsibility, the majority did not reject it. For a brief comment cf. Chinkin (1993), 214–215.

[146] ICJ Reports 1997, 115–119.

[147] On estoppel see Müller/Cottier (1995), 116; Sinclair (1996), 104.

[148] Cf. ICJ Reports 1997, 24–27 (paras. 21–23).

[149] ICJ Reports 1997, 118.

justice to rights and obligations of an *erga omnes* character – least of all in cases involving environmental damage of a far-reaching and irreversible nature. [. . .] There has been conduct on the part of Hungary which, in ordinary *inter partes* litigation, would prevent it from taking up wholly contradictory positions. But can momentous environmental issues be decided on the basis of such *inter partes* conduct? In cases where the *erga omnes* issues are of sufficient importance, I would think not.[150]

In view of Judge Weeramantry, the *erga omnes* concept thus modified the rules governing estoppel. By implication, this interpretation would seem to affect the rules governing standing.[151] The reason for this is that although they concern different aspects of international law, the rules on estoppel and standing, in one aspect, function along parallel lines. As a ground entailing the loss of a right to invoke responsibility, estoppel presupposes that initially, the said right has come into existence. Just as standing, estoppel – or, for that matter, other grounds entailing the loss of the right to invoke responsibility, such as acquiescence or waiver[152] – therefore presupposes injury.[153] By holding that Hungary's conduct, which otherwise would have amounted to estoppel, did not entail the loss of the right to suspend the treaty, Judge Weeramantry, by implication, accepted that other States had a legal interest in the subject-matter of the dispute, i.e. in 'the greater interests of humanity and planetary welfare'.[154] What is more, this legal interest was not of an inferior or secondary character, as States possessing it were in a position to prevent Hungary from disposing of the right to suspend the treaty.

Given its brevity, this statement touches upon, rather than fully explores, the various issues. Just as with respect to Judge Schwebel's

150 ICJ Reports 1997, 117–118 (emphasis in the original).

151 See also Lefeber (1998), 4–7.

152 Lefeber (1998), 6–7; Tams (Manuel), para. 14. Pursuant to Lefeber (1998), 6–7 the *erga omnes* concept has consequences on other circumstances precluding wrongfulness. The ICTY seems to have gone a similar way when commenting on the relation between the *erga omnes* concepts and the *tu quoque* principle; see *Prosecutor v. Kupreskic case* (evidence); Schabas (2000), 342. In contrast, articles 20 to 26 ASR do not develop the idea, but rather rely on the concept of peremptory norms as a bar to all circumstances precluding wrongfulness, see especially commentary to article 26 ASR para. 6; commentary to article 20, para. 7.

153 See the ILC's commentary to article 45 ASR, para. 1; and further Tams (Manuel), paras. 11–17.

154 The ILC seems to agree, see commentary to article 45 ASR, para. 4. The problem that Judge Weeramantry seems to neglect is that Hungary as the other party to the bilateral treaty, and furthermore as the State bearing the bulk of the devastating environmental consequences, would have been 'specially affected', and therefore in a position different to that of other States. The point is explored in Tams (Manuel), para. 17.

dissent in *Nicaragua*, Judge Weeramantry's approach however seems to imply a particular understanding of the *erga omnes* concept. If a State, because of its legal interest in a specific subject matter, is entitled to influence the disposability of a right, it seems at least highly likely that it should equally be entitled to vindicate its legal interest in other ways, for example by instituting proceedings before the ICJ.[155] While not conclusively settling the matter, Judge Weeramantry's separate opinion therefore provides further support for the broad interpretation of the *erga omnes* concept.

5.2.5.f Summary

The preceding survey has shown that even when focusing on *erga omnes* effects in the field of standing, jurisprudence since 1970 has provided the Court and its members with an opportunity to explore many facets of the *erga omnes* concept. Although the picture emerging from the analysis is far from homogeneous, jurisprudence since 1970, on balance, confirms a broad interpretation of the *Barcelona Traction* dictum. Judge de Castro's dissent in *Nuclear Tests* and Judge Oda's declaration in *Genocide* are the only two pronouncements that support a restrictive analysis of that passage. In contrast, the view that all States have standing to vindicate obligations *erga omnes* before the Court has been expressly endorsed by Judge *ad hoc* Barwick's dissent in *Nuclear Tests* and Judge Weeramantry's dissent in *East Timor*. It is further – if less clearly – supported by the majority judgment and Judge Ranjeva's separate opinion in that latter case, and the joint dissent of four judges as well as Judge Petrén's separate opinion in *Nuclear Tests*. Finally, Judge Schwebel's dissent in the 1984 *Nicaragua case* and Judge Weeramantry's separate opinion in *Gabčíkovo*, by implication, point in the same direction. To sum up, there is, within the spectre of heterogeneous views expressed since 1970, a marked tendency to take the *Barcelona Traction* dictum at face value, and to accept that all States have standing in disputes involving breaches of obligations *erga omnes*. Lastly, it should be noted that this interpretation is not affected by the Court's treatment of the indispensable third party rule in *East Timor*. The case was directed against a State that did not bear principal responsibility for the alleged *erga omnes* breach, and on that basis can be distinguished from *erga omnes* claims envisaged here.

[155] See Lefeber (1998), 4–7, for a similar analysis.

5.2.6 *A restrictive, contextual interpretation?*

Ultimately, adherents of the restrictive approach have advanced a sixth counter-argument, which goes beyond the Court's jurisprudence on obligations *erga omnes*. Some commentators stress the need to interpret the *erga omnes* dictum within its broader context, namely against the background of the general regime of standing. In their view, international law remains hostile to the idea that States – in the absence of specific treaty provisions to the contrary – could vindicate general interests. Two arguments in particular are invoked to support this claim. Thirlway, for once, argues that the *erga omnes* concept should be interpreted in the light of the Court's 1966 *South West Africa* judgment, which indeed encapsulates a restrictive approach.[156] Similarly, van Dijk relies on what he considers to be a cautious approach to questions of dispute settlement in international agreements:

> The very resistance of many States to the broad formulation of jurisdictional clauses in multilateral conventions ... do[es] not permit for the *lex lata* any other conclusion but that the right to bring an action in the public interest does not ensue from general international law; such a right must have been agreed upon – expressly or impliedly – between the States concerned in a treaty or on an *ad hoc* basis.[157]

According to adherents of the sixth counter-argument, the *erga omnes* concept stands out in a legal environment premised on the notion of individual legal interests. This in turn affects its interpretation: the contextual reading is said to warrant a restrictive interpretation of the concept.[158]

The preceding discussion already indicates that the contextual reading is unconvincing. Since rebutting it helps situate the *erga omnes* concept in the broader context of general international law, it may nevertheless be convenient to summarise the main concerns. Two points in particular are worth stressing.

The first point relates to the methodological approach adopted by adherents of the sixth counter-argument. As has been remarked above, it is of course possible to interpret special rules (whether special treaties or special concepts of general international law, such as the *erga omnes*

[156] Thirlway (1989), 92–102. On the *South West Africa case* see already above, section 2.1.2.

[157] van Dijk (1980), 474.

[158] See especially van Dijk (1980), 474. For a similarly cautious assessment cf. Mann (1973a), especially 406–408.

concept) in the light of the general rule surrounding them.[159] One classic example of this 'contextualisation' has been addressed already – the Court's approach in the 1966 *South West Africa case*, in which a broad jurisdictional clause was interpreted in the light of general international law, and thus read restrictively.[160]

On the other hand, it has equally been shown that this contextual reading has its limits; in particular, that it is unhelpful where the special rule in question deliberately deviates from the general rule. In *South West Africa*, the Court controversially held that article 7(2) of the mandate agreement was not clear enough to disapply the general rule. Irrespective of whether that was a correct interpretation, much suggests that with respect to obligations *erga omnes*, the situation is different. The above discussion shows that, when introducing and subsequently confirming the concept, the Court was fully aware of its special character – hence the 'essential distinction' between obligations *erga omnes* and traditional rules of diplomatic protection, or the proviso that 'even if' an obligation was valid *erga omnes*, the Court's jurisdiction would remain consensual.[161] The continued reliance on *South West Africa* seems particularly difficult to justify when bearing in mind that *Barcelona Traction* deliberately moved away from that judgment.[162] Finally, supporters of the sixth counter-argument seem to assume that the *erga omnes* concept had an existence of its own, separate and independent from the rest of international law. Conceptually, this is problematic. It neglects that the concept itself is part of the rules of international law; it influences these general rules just as much as it is influenced by them. A contextual interpretation therefore is no one-way street.[163]

Secondly, and more importantly, the sixth counter-argument rests on a questionable assumption. It presupposes that international law remains premised on the notion of individual legal interests. It has been noted already that this assumption indeed is often restated, and that *South West Africa* is almost inevitably cited in support.[164] The preceding discussion, however, has shown that matters are more complex than is usually assumed. As discussed in Chapter 2, expansive approaches

[159] See already above, section 1.2.3. [160] For an analysis cf. above, section 2.1.2.

[161] ICJ Reports 1970, 32 (para. 33); ICJ Reports 1995, 102 (para. 29) (emphasis added). For further affirmations of the concept's special character see above, section 5.2.5.

[162] Cf. already above, Introduction, footnote 58; and section 2.1.2, for references.

[163] See already above, section 1.2.3, for a brief comment.

[164] See e.g. above, Introduction to Chapter 2.

to standing do not begin with the *erga omnes* concept. Especially in the field of treaty law, the recognition of general legal interests preceded the Court's *Barcelona Traction* judgment, as evidenced by developments in fields such as human rights or minorities law, status treaties, or interdependent obligations.[165] Contrary to the argument advanced by van Dijk, special treaty-based jurisdictional clauses bring out this development with particular clarity.[166] Insofar as the *South West Africa* judgment is relied on, the preceding discussion suggests that the judgment has to be seen in the context of earlier decisions (such as the *Wimbledon* or *Memel Statute cases*), in which an equally eminent court adopted a far less restrictive approach.[167] Even at the time of the *Barcelona Traction* judgment, the trend towards the recognition of general legal interest in the observance of specific categories of obligations was difficult to ignore.

What is more, developments since 1970 further undermine the assumption upon which the sixth counter-argument rests. It is of course not possible to analyse in detail the manifold tendencies evidencing the trend 'From Bilateralism to Community Interest'.[168] However, it seems difficult to deny that, if anything, the foundations of the sixth counter-argument have been further shaken. As regards treaty law, States have continued to conclude treaties protecting general interests of communities of States in fields such as human rights, environmental protection, or economic integration. Post-*Barcelona Traction* treaties recognising the right of States to institute inter-State proceedings irrespective of individual injury notably include the 1981 African Charter on Human and Peoples' Rights (the 'Banjul Charter'), the 1984 Convention Against Torture, the 1979 Convention on the Elimination of All Forms of Discrimination Against Women, or the Vienna Convention and Montreal Protocol for the Protection of the Ozone Layer.[169] Not all of these recognise a right to seize the ICJ, and many of the respective procedures – just as the many of those existing at the

[165] See above, section 2.2, for a discussion. [166] See above, section 2.2.1. [167] *Ibid.*

[168] Cf. the title of Bruno Simma's Hague lectures: Simma (1994a), 217.

[169] See article 47 Banjul Charter, article 22 and 30 CAT, article 29 CEDAW, and article 11 of the Vienna Convention for the Protection of the Ozone Layer respectively. For the Non-Compliance Procedure established pursuant to article 8 of the Montreal Protocol to the Vienna Convention see 32 ILM (1993), 874 (Decision IV/5), Annex IV, para. 1. For a comprehensive account of generally enforceable treaty rules see Voeffray (2004), 107–218. The relation between these conventional enforcement rules and the *erga omnes* concept is analysed below, in Chapter 7.

time of the *Barcelona Traction* judgment – have hardly ever been used by States.[170] However, at least as regards treaties protecting general interests, 'the broad formulation of jurisdictional clauses' (to quote again van Dijk)[171] seems to have become the rule rather than the exception.

As regards general international law, the *erga omnes* concept itself has gained prominence, as evidenced by the Court's subsequent jurisprudence. According to at least one judge, even by 1984, the restrictive approach informing the *South West Africa* judgment had been 'effectively displaced' by the Court's jurisprudence on obligations *erga omnes*.[172] In the field of State responsibility, the ILC's work (widely commented on and accepted by States) expressly recognises that responsibility can no longer be reduced to bilateral relations between pairs of States,[173] and makes express provision, in article 48 ASR, for the invocation of responsibility in the general interest. To simply assert that international law remains premised on the notion of individual legal interests therefore seems simplistic. This in turn affects the process of interpretation. As there is simply no uniform, restrictive general rule of standing, the contextual interpretation loses much of its force.

Neither methodologically, nor as regards its basic assumption, the sixth counter-argument therefore is convincing. While the *erga omnes* concept cannot be assessed in clinical isolation, a contextual interpretation does not entail a restrictive interpretation.

5.3 Concluding observations

To sum up the preceding discussion, none of the arguments advanced by adherents of the restrictive approach ultimately warrants a restrictive reinterpretation of paras. 33 and 34 of the *Barcelona Traction* judgment. As has been shown, the passage is neither an isolated pronouncement, nor does the fact that it was made *obiter* deprive it of legal relevance. Moreover, neither the reference to the international community as a whole, nor the Court's problematic analysis of human

[170] There have to date been no inter-State proceedings under CAT or CEDAW. For inter-State proceedings under the Banjul Charter see notably *Communication 227/99 (Democratic Republic of Congo v. Burundi, Rwanda and Uganda)*. Practice under the Montreal Protocol's Non-Compliance Procedure is discussed by Victor (1996), 28–31; Yoshida (1999), 95.

[171] van Dijk (1980), 474.

[172] *Cf. Nicaragua case* (provisional measures), Diss.Op. Schwebel, ICJ Reports 1984, 197.

[173] See commentary to article 1 ASR, para. 4.

rights treaty law put forward in para. 91 of the *Barcelona Traction* judgment precludes individual States from seeking judicial relief against violations of obligations *erga omnes*. Finally, neither the Court's jurisprudence since 1970 nor the allegedly cautious approach dominating the general rules of standing on balance support a restrictive reading.

It has been stated at the outset that in the absence of a clear ICJ decision on the matter, any interpretation of the law is bound to remain provisional. By the same token, the preceding analysis cannot claim to produce a definitive answer, and stands to be corrected by subsequent Court decisions. However, it is worth noting that while the Court has yet to settle the matter conclusively, its jurisprudence on obligations *erga omnes* provides considerable support for a broad interpretation of the *Barcelona Traction* dictum pursuant to which all States have standing in ICJ disputes involving obligations *erga omnes*. In terms of para. 34 of the *Barcelona Traction* judgment, ICJ proceedings thus constitute a 'right of protection' flowing from the *erga omnes* concept. Where jurisdiction is established, all States can institute proceedings against States principally responsible for violations of obligations *erga omnes*.

6 Standing to take countermeasures

Although made in the context of ICJ proceedings, the *Barcelona Traction* dictum is claimed to have affected other forms of responses. In particular, it has prompted discussion about whether individual States, irrepective of individual injury, should be entitled to take countermeasures in respect of breaches of obligations *erga omnes*. As has been shown above, the traditional regime of countermeasures had been in a state of tension: while standing was largely restricted to individually injured States, exceptions were recognised or discussed in a number of areas (such as, for example, obligations under interdependent treaties, status treaties, or deriving from ICJ judgments).[1] In contrast, despite some evidence in State practice,[2] there had been only limited support for the view that all States should be entitled to respond, by way of countermeasure, against breaches of particularly important obligations. The present chapter assesses whether the *erga omnes* concept has affected these legal rules, more particularly: whether all States are entitled to take countermeasures in response to breaches of those particularly important obligations that qualify as obligations *erga omnes*.

It is evident that such a development would be of fundamental importance. Unlike the right to institute *erga omnes* proceedings before the ICJ, the right to take countermeasures would not be subject to jurisdictional constraints; it could be exercised by all States, and, more importantly, *against* all States (and not only against States having consented to the Court's jurisdiction). What is more, given the relative flexibility of the regime of countermeasures, States would be given scope to suspend the performance of a wide range of obligations owed

[1] For a discussion of these instances see above, section 2.2.

[2] See above, section 2.2.2.d for references to State practice prior to 1970.

to States responsible for *erga omnes* breaches, restricted only by the procedural conditions governing resort to countermeasures, the rules excluding specific forms of countermeasures, or the requirement of proportionality, but, for example, not subject to any form of prior, independent, assessment of the responsible State's conduct.[3] It is therefore not surprising that the matter is much discussed. It nevertheless has remained controversial, and three problems complicate much of the academic debate.

First, the complexity of the matter is not always appreciated. Supporters of a right to take countermeasures (referred to here, for the sake of simplicity, as 'supporters') sometimes seem to assume that their position is a natural consequence of the Court's jurisprudence on obligations *erga omnes*.[4] As will be shown, this view is oversimplified and cannot be sustained.

Secondly, legal analysis is often obscured by what might be labelled the problem of *politicisation*. At least some critics of a right to take countermeasures ('critics') replace legal arguments by considerations of legal policy. In their view, a system authorising individual States to take countermeasures in the general interest would be open to abuse. In graphic terms, prophets of gloom have predicted 'mob violence' and 'vigilantism', and warned that 'under the banner of law, chaos and violence would come to reign'.[5] Predictably, supporters have responded by invoking considerations of effectiveness. 'Were States not even allowed to adopt countermeasures', argues Gaja (neglecting the concept's influence on ICJ litigation) 'one would probably have to conclude that law rather protects the infringements of [community] interests.'[6]

While these comments contain elements of truth, they cannot substitute for a more profound analysis. By stressing the risks of abuse on the one hand, and of an ineffective legal regime on the other, commentators outline basic policy considerations that influence the

[3] As has been stated in Chapter 1, the present inquiry focuses on the rules of standing and does not purport to analyse how the *erga omnes* concept would affect the other conditions governing countermeasures. It is therefore assumed that, if indeed all States could resort to countermeasures in response to *erga omnes* breaches, this right would be subject to the conditions that apply to ordinary countermeasures within the bilateral inter-State relations.

[4] See below, footnote 16, for references.

[5] See Marek (1978–1979), 481; McCaffrey (1989), 244; and Weil (1983), 432–433 respectively. For similar observations see de Hoogh (1991), 210–211; Dupuy (1983), 546; Alland (1994), 370–371.

[6] Gaja (1989), 156. Cf. also Dzida (1997), 267; Tomuschat (1993a), 366–367.

development of the law. However, their general, even stereotyped, observations are of little value in answering the most important question – to assess *how* present-day international law strikes the balance between effective protection and risk of abuse.

Finally, apart from simplification and politicisation, debates about countermeasures and obligations *erga omnes* suffer from a third problem: that of vagueness. Unfortunately, vagueness is the key feature of the most important attempt to codify the existing law, namely the ILC's Articles on State Responsibility. Caught between the different policy considerations set out above, the Commission ultimately decided not to decide. Articles 49 to 53 ASR, spelling out the legal regime of countermeasures, restrict standing to injured States in the sense of article 42 ASR, i.e. States individually affected and States parties to interdependent obligations.[7] This, however, does not mean that countermeasures by other States are excluded. Instead, article 54 ASR seeks to safeguard their position by stipulating that the Articles do 'not prejudice the right of any State, entitled under article 48, paragraph 1 [addressing *inter alia* obligations *erga omnes*] to invoke the responsibility of another State, to take lawful measures against that State.' Whether or not countermeasures aimed at protecting obligations *erga omnes* would qualify as 'lawful measures' was deliberately left open.[8] In fairness, it must be conceded that the ILC adopted the Janus-faced article 54 ASR under pressure from governments and in order to secure the acceptance of the text as a whole.[9] However, in so doing it clearly failed to introduce the legal clarity and predictability for which codification efforts are generally undertaken.

The present chapter seeks to answer the question left open by article 54 ASR, while at the same time avoiding the problems of simplification and politicisation. Although dealing with a different means of law enforcement, in many respects this chapter builds on the results of the previous analysis. For example, it has been shown in Chapter 5, that the Court's *erga omnes* jurisprudence has to be taken seriously; it cannot simply be dismissed with reference to alleged contradictions or

[7] On article 42 ASR see above, section 1.3.

[8] See paras. 6 and 7 of the ILC's commentary on article 54 ASR; and further the Statement of the Chairman of the ILC's Drafting Committee for 2001, available at http://www.un.org/law/ilc/sessions/53/english/dc_resp1.pdf, 63; Tams (2002a), 789–790; Dupuy (2002b), 389–390. For a more cautious reading of article 54 see von Schorlemmer (2003), 282–283. The ILC's approach is discussed below, section 6.2.2.

[9] See further below, section 6.2.2.

the *obiter* status of particular pronouncements. Moreover, it can be taken for granted that by recognising the concept of obligations *erga omnes*, the Court meant to confer upon *individual* States specific rights of protection rather than exclusively empowering international organisations or the international community as a whole.[10] Of course, it is not inconceivable that a requirement of institutional or collective action should have emerged as a separate condition governing the legality of countermeasures in the general interest. However, such a requirement is not inherent in the *erga omnes* concept; consequently, it cannot be presumed that countermeasures could only be taken by institutions, or collectively.[11] Finally, when distinguishing institutional from non-institutional responses, this chapter builds on the notion of decentralised law enforcement explored above.[12] The term 'decentralised' therefore is interpreted broadly; it encompasses measures taken by a plurality of States, as well as conduct coordinated within the framework of international organisations, but directed against non-member States.

As to its structure, the present chapter is divided in two sections. Section 6.1 discusses whether the Court's jurisprudence provides specific guidance on the question of standing to take countermeasures. Given the non-institutional, private character of most countermeasures, it comes as no surprise that – compared to standing in ICJ proceedings addressed in Chapter 5 – this jurisprudence has had a more limited influence on the rules of standing. As a consequence, section 6.2 analyses international practice in the field of countermeasures and assesses how States have approached the question of standing.

6.1 The Court's jurisprudence

The Court's jurisprudence provides the starting-point of the analysis. However, for two reasons, it can be analysed in rather summary form. For once, the Court's pronouncements on obligations *erga omnes* have already been discussed in some detail in Chapter 5, and there is no need to repeat the analysis.[13] More importantly, most of the statements discussed above are only of limited relevance for the question of countermeasures. Of course, judges advocating a restrictive interpretation of

[10] See above, Chapter 5, especially section 5.2.3.

[11] Whether a requirement of collective action has emerged as a separate condition governing resort to countermeasures is discussed below, section 6.2.1.d (pp. 240–241).

[12] See above, Introduction. [13] See above, Chapter 5, especially section 5.2.5.

the *Barcelona Traction* dictum would probably be even less inclined to recognise a right of States to take countermeasures in defence of obligations *erga omnes*. However, as has been shown, such sceptical statements were few and far between. Most of the (more numerous) statements suggesting a broad interpretation are also of limited relevance. In particular, it cannot simply be assumed that judges accepting a right to institute ICJ proceedings in response to *erga omnes* breaches would automatically recognise other rights of protection (such as a right to respond by way of countermeasure). Quite the contrary, the majority of statements specifically focus on enforcement by means of ICJ proceedings. To take only two examples, the *East Timor* majority judgment or the various dissents in the *Nuclear Tests cases* do not provide much guidance as to how obligations *erga omnes* could be enforced outside the Court, nor enforcement by way of countermeasure.[14] Similarly, Judge Weeramantry's repeated endorsement of the *erga omnes* concept has to be seen in the light of his very critical remarks about the legality of countermeasures, made in his dissent in the *Nuclear Weapons* opinion.[15] To argue that as a strong supporter of the *erga omnes* concept, Judge Weeramantry would necessarily recognise a general right to take countermeasures would thus be unconvincing.

From the range of judicial pronouncements mentioned in Chapter 5, only the *Barcelona Traction* dictum therefore merits a more detailed analysis. In addition, the 1986 *Nicaragua* judgment, although not expressly discussing obligations *erga omnes*, also implies a certain position. Finally, it is necessary briefly to comment on the *Namibia* and *Hostages cases*, which are frequently relied on by commentators.

6.1.1 *The* Barcelona Traction case

It has been stated already that the Court's *Barcelona Traction* judgment, while not specifically mentioning countermeasures, is much discussed in this context also. Many supporters of a right to take countermeasures assume that *Barcelona Traction* not only supports their position but even settles the question conclusively. Since all States have a legal interest in seeing obligations *erga omnes* observed – so the argument runs – they should automatically be entitled to adopt countermeasures in response to breaches. Annacker, for example, simply lists countermeasures

[14] See above, section 5.2.5.a and 5.2.5.c.

[15] ICJ Reports 1996, 542–544. See above, section 5.2.5.b and 5.2.5.e for an analysis of Judge Weeramantry's approach.

among the permissible forms of individual responses, while Erasmus and Klein state that a general right to take countermeasures is a 'logical consequence' of the Court's *Barcelona Traction* dictum.[16] In contrast, some critics deny the relevance of the dictum altogether, simply ignoring it in their discussion of standing to take countermeasures.[17]

On the basis of the discussion in Chapter 1, it can be said that the notion of legal interest is more complex than these two positions suggest. Clinging to the immediate context in which the *Barcelona Traction* dictum was made, critics fail to recognise the *general nature* of that concept, which governs standing to take countermeasures as well as standing to institute ICJ proceedings. Furthermore, they overlook that when recognising the legal interest of all States to see obligations *erga omnes* observed, the ICJ did not refer to a specific means of law enforcement (such as, for example, ICJ proceedings), but used very general language.[18] The Court's recognition of a legal interest of all States therefore is relevant for the discussion of countermeasures.

On the other hand, contrary to the assumptions of many supporters, the Court's pronouncement is not conclusive. While recognising, in a general way, the legal interest of all States, the Court did not elaborate on specific means by which this general interest could be vindicated. At least some elaboration would have been necessary. As mentioned above,[19] States possessing a legal interest do not necessarily have standing to respond to breaches by way of countermeasure, especially where an obligation protects general rather than individual interests. As regards the more immediate context of the dictum, it should be borne in mind that paras. 33 and 34 were preceded and followed by comments about standing in judicial proceedings. As has already been shown, this factor (as well as Judge Ammoun's separate opinion and the relation between *Barcelona Traction* and *South West Africa*) strongly suggests that the Court meant to recognise a general right to institute ICJ proceedings.[20] In contrast, the circumstances of the *Barcelona Traction* dictum do not support the claim that the Court necessarily intended to confer

16 See Annacker (1994a), 86–88; Erasmus (1992), 133–134; Klein (1998a), 51 and 69 respectively. The same view has e.g. been put forward by Elagab (1987), 59; and Delbrück (1995), 152–153.

17 See notably Zoller (1984), 103–118, who fails to appreciate the dictum's potential impact on the rules of standing.

18 Hence the need to discuss, in Chapter 5, whether this general legal interest could be vindicated in contentious proceedings before the Court.

19 See above, section 1.2.3; and cf. also Bryde (1994), 178.

20 See above, section 5.1.

upon States a right to respond by way of countermeasure, an issue remote from that actually faced by the Court.

The *Barcelona Traction* dictum therefore only marks the beginning of the analysis. Given its broad terms, the statement paves the way for a discussion of countermeasures in the general interest. Whether such a right actually exists, however, needs to be assessed separately; it is by no means an automatic consequence of the *erga omnes* concept.

6.1.2 *The* Namibia *and* Hostages cases

Although not directly bearing on the matter, passages of the Court's decisions in the *Namibia* and *Hostages cases* are sometimes said to support a right of all States to respond to *erga omnes* breaches by way of countermeasures. Since the decisions have not been addressed in Chapter 5, these claims may be briefly assessed.

As for *Namibia*, emphasis is at times placed on the Court's finding that the South West Africa mandate had been terminated with *erga omnes* effect, and that non-members of the organisation had to 'act in accordance' with the relevant resolutions.[21] In the literature, this has been interpreted as a recognition that non-member States could adopt countermeasures against South Africa.[22] On the basis of the above discussion of different types of *erga omnes* effects,[23] this interpretation can be dismissed relatively quickly. As has been shown, the term '*erga omnes*' was used in the *Namibia opinion* in its traditional sense, denoting objective effects of legal acts, which, but for their *erga omnes* validity, would have applied to treaty parties only. By proclaiming their *erga omnes* effect, the Court thus sought to apply the relevant resolutions to third (non-member) States. There is little indication that it intended to confer upon these States any rights, and to read *Namibia* as an encouragement to adopt countermeasures against South Africa seems far-fetched.

Similarly, the Court's judgment in the *Hostages case* provides less evidence than is often assumed.[24] True, the Court, in that judgment, drew 'the attention of the entire international community ... to the irreparable harm that may be caused by events of the kind now before the Court' and stressed that Iran's conduct threatened to 'undermine the edifice of law carefully constructed by mankind over a period of

[21] ICJ Reports 1971, 56 (para. 126). [22] See e.g. Sicilianos (1990), 152.

[23] See above, Chapter 3.

[24] Commentators stressing the relevance of the judgment include Annacker (1994a), 21–22; Frowein (1983), 244–245; Hailbronner (1992), 4 (referring to collective contermeasures); similarly Stein (1992), 47.

centuries.'[25] While thereby hinting at a general interest in the observation of basic rules of diplomatic law, the Court refrained from discussing by which means States could seek to protect the 'edifice of law' endangered by Iran's conduct, nor less explored the question of countermeasures.[26] *Namibia* and *Hostages* are thus of little help in assessing the rules of standing to take countermeasures.

6.1.3 *The* Nicaragua case

In contrast, the 1986 *Nicaragua* judgment is highly relevant. The crucial (and often neglected)[27] statement is to be found in one of the less prominent parts of the judgment.[28] In addition to its claims based on the use of force and intervention, Nicaragua had accused the United States of having violated a bilateral FCN treaty concluded in 1956.[29] According to the Court, the United States had *prima facie* violated this treaty by mining and attacking Nicaraguan ports in 1983–1984, and by adopting a general trade embargo in May 1985.[30] When assessing possible justifications, the Court largely focused on the national security exception contained in article XXI of the 1956 treaty, and concluded that its conditions were not met.[31] Irrespective of whether one agrees with this interpretation,[32] the Court's discussion of possible justifications is remarkable for its omissions. Having found article XXI to be inapplicable, the Court did not analyse whether the United States'

[25] ICJ Reports 1980, 43 (para. 92).
[26] See also Sicilianos (1990), 152; Gaja (1989), 153–154.
[27] But cf. Frowein (1989), 227–228; Frowein (1994), 371–376; Sicilianos (1990), 152–154.
[28] Commentators addressing the *Nicaragua case* often focus on another passage of the judgment, namely the Court's controversial observation that the protection of conventional human rights 'takes the form of such arrangements ... as are provided for in the conventions themselves' (ICJ Reports 1986, 134, para. 267). As has been shown in section 5.2.5.d, this passage does not concern the existence of rights of protection deriving from the *erga omnes* concept, but the relation between such rights and treaty-based enforcement mechanisms; as such, it will be analysed below as part of the discussion of obligations *erga omnes* and treaties (see below, Chapter 7).
[29] See ICJ Reports 1986, 135–142 (paras. 270–282).
[30] ICJ Reports 1986, 138–140 (paras. 275–279). For the trade embargo see President Reagan's Executive Order and Message to the Congress, reproduced in 24 ILM (1985), 809; for the diplomatic note addressed to Nicaragua see *ibid.*, 811.
[31] ICJ Reports 1986, 140–142 (paras. 280–282).
[32] Judge Jennings, for one, strongly disagreed: see his dissent, ICJ Reports 1986, 540–542. For further criticism see Frowein (1994), 374–376. For further analysis of the scope of national security exceptions, and their relation to the rules of self-defence see the judgment in the recent *Oil Platforms case* (paras. 30–78); for a comparative assessment of different treaty clauses Akande/Williams (2003), 365.

treaty violations could be justified as a countermeasure.[33] Insofar as the United States conduct involved the use of force (such as in the case of the attacks on ports), this is readily acceptable, forcible countermeasures being excluded under modern international law. The situation is different with respect to the United States' non-forcible conduct, notably the adoption of a trade embargo. In this regard, the Court's failure to discuss the rules of countermeasures is remarkable. Not only had the United States, albeit in a general way, justified its conduct with reference to Nicaragua's previous conduct, which, in its view, violated both human rights law and the prohibition against the use of force.[34] What is more, the Court itself had partly accepted this argument when finding that the transborder incursions conducted, and sponsored, by Nicaragua between 1982 and 1984 qualified as an illegal use of force.[35] Put differently, although Nicaragua had previously used force and the United States had cited Nicaraguan conduct as a justification for its trade embargo, the Court did not consider the question of countermeasures. Had it done so, it would have had to address the problem of standing. Given the nature of Nicaragua's previous wrongful conduct, it seems likely that the *erga omnes* concept would have played a major part in the discussion.[36]

The question is what to make of the ICJ's failure to address the matter. Seeking to diminish its relevance, supporters of a right to take countermeasures might stress that the *erga omnes* concept was never invoked in the *Nicaragua case*, and that the Court's discussion thus was of little relevance to its interpretation. To an extent this is a valid argument, and the passage just discussed certainly cannot be construed as a definitive rejection of countermeasures in the general interest. On the other hand, in order to pronounce on Nicaragua's claims against a defendant that no longer took part in the proceedings, the Court was required to

[33] See already ICJ Reports 1986, 105 (para. 199) for the Court's view that in the absence of an express request, the United States could not invoke a right to exercise collective self-defence on behalf of other Latin American States.

[34] Cf. ICJ Reports 1986, 130–135 (paras. 257–269) for the Court's discussion of the human rights argument. When justifying the trade embargo of 1 May 1985, the United States had specifically referred to Nicaragua's 'support for armed insurrection, terrorism and subversion in neighboring countries'; see the diplomatic note addressed to Nicaragua, reproduced in 24 ILM (1985), 813.

[35] ICJ Reports 1986, 86–87 (paras. 161–164).

[36] Contrast Sicilianos (1990), 153, who argues that Nicaragua's wrongful acts were of a minor character and did not qualify as violations of obligations *erga omnes*. This explanation is unconvincing, as it neglects the Court's findings on the use of force.

assess all possible justifications, whether pleaded or not. By not addressing the concept of countermeasures, it therefore seemed to suggest that that specific justification was not available. To sum up, *Nicaragua* does not settle matters conclusively, but it provides support for critics denying that the right to take countermeasures in defence of general interests.

6.1.4 *Interim conclusions*

The ICJ's jurisprudence on the question of countermeasures and obligations *erga omnes* does not provide conclusive guidance. What is more, the limited evidence seems to point in different directions. Whereas supporters of a right to take countermeasures can rely on the general language of the *Barcelona Traction* dictum, critics find comfort in the Court's cautious approach in *Nicaragua*. Unlike in the case of ICJ proceedings, the Court's influence on the rules governing standing to take countermeasures thus remains limited. Of course, it is largely due to the Court's jurisprudence that the *erga omnes* concept has emerged. In order to assess its relevance for rules governing countermeasures, it is however necessary to look beyond ICJ jurisprudence. This will be done in the following section.

6.2 International practice

Given the ICJ's failure to answer the question conclusively, much depends on how States themselves have approached the question of standing to take countermeasures. The remainder of this chapter will therefore analyse international practice, i.e. actions, statements, and other forms of conduct that might help assess whether the *erga omnes* concept has actually influenced the rules governing countermeasures. For that to be the case, there would have to be, in the words of the Court, a 'settled practice' of countermeasures in response to *erga omnes* breaches, which was 'evidence of a rule of law'.[37] In order to assess this question in a meaningful way, it is necessary to evaluate a rather large amount of evidence. For the sake of convenience, this material is presented in two parts. Section 6.2.1 analyses how States, in specific instances of State practice, have responded against breaches of obligations *erga omnes*; section 6.2.2 assesses how they have approached

[37] Cf. *North Sea Continental Shelf case*, ICJ Reports 1969, 44 (para. 77); *Nicaragua case*, ICJ Reports 1986, 108–109 (para. 207).

the same problem when commenting on the ILC's work on State Responsibility.

6.2.1 Specific instances of state practice

The actual conduct of States provides the most tangible form of evidence. This section therefore analyses specific instances in which States, not individually injured, have taken countermeasures in response to wrongful acts of another State. Although the concept of countermeasures has been introduced already,[38] it may be convenient, at the outset of the analysis, to recapitulate a number of basic points.

The first remark concerns the often intricate distinction between countermeasures and retorsions. In order to qualify as a countermeasure, a particular response (or 'sanction'[39]) must affect treaty or customary rights of the target State. It will therefore have to be shown that when responding against wrongful acts, States have actually violated legal obligations. The distinction is based on a legal assessment and does not take into account the actual effects on the target State; in particular, it does not mean that countermeasures were automatically a more effective means of inducing compliance. Moreover, it may be worth repeating that the line between countermeasures and retorsions is not static. Whether a particular form of conduct is still unfriendly but lawful, or already involves a violation of international law, often depends on the terms of a treaty and thus cannot be determined in the abstract. Equally, rules of general international law are open to change, and conduct that has been considered unlawful may subsequently become accepted (or *vice versa*).

Secondly, countermeasures have to be distinguished from other responses affecting rights of the target State. For present purposes, the crucial distinction is between countermeasures on the one hand, and sanctions authorised by the specific terms of a treaty on the other. Since the latter are treaty-specific, they are only of limited relevance for the question of standing under the general rules of countermeasures. In contrast, as has been stated above,[40] the line between countermeasures on the one hand, and other generally available justifications (such as self-defence or grounds for the suspension or termination of treaties) may at times be difficult to draw and often largely depends on

[38] See above, section 1.1.
[39] See above, Introduction, footnote 29, for comment on the use of the term.
[40] See above, section 1.1.

statements made by the responding State. Bearing in mind the Court's warning not to 'ascribe to States legal views which they do not themselves advance',[41] the subsequent discussion of countermeasures - in the absence of clear statements to the contrary - covers responses that might have equally been justified under other concepts. In order to illustrate the close relation between the various justifications, some responses justified under different concepts are equally included.

Finally, in order to free the subsequent analysis from unnecessary discussion, it may be helpful to state at the outset how three very common responses are treated. In line with the generally held view, the subsequent discussion will assume that diplomatic boycotts or other acts affecting the diplomatic relations between States are not prohibited under general international law.[42] Although the matter is more controversial, measures of economic coercion (such as embargoes, quotas, or boycotts) will also be treated as intrinsically lawful, unless they are specifically prohibited by treaty.[43] In contrast, another measure frequently resorted to, the freezing of foreign assets, constitutes a coercive interference with another State's property, and requires justification.[44]

As to its structure, the present section is divided in four parts. The first three of these introduce the relevant examples of State practice; further distinguishing (i) instances in which States, in the absence of individual injury, have actually adopted countermeasures; (ii) instances in which they have asserted a right to take countermeasures, but ultimately decided not to exercise it, and (iii) instances in which they have violated rights of another State, but relied on justifications other than the concept of countermeasures (which might have equally been available). Finally, the fourth and last part assesses the available evidence.

6.2.1.a Actual violations

In a considerable number of instances since 1970, States not individually injured have responded against previous wrongful acts by taking countermeasures in response against the responsible State. In chronological order, the following instances can be cited as examples.

[41] Cf. *Nicaragua case*, ICJ Reports 1986, 108–109 (para. 207).

[42] See also Crawford, Third Report, para. 388; Kausch (1992), 485.

[43] See also Dicke (1995), 13; Kausch/Langefeldt (1995), 58; and, for a comprehensive discussion, Elagab (1987), 190–213; and Ress (2000), 12–42.

[44] See e.g. Elagab (1987), 214; Crawford, Third Report, para. 391.

Western countries – Uganda (1971–1978)

Western States' responses against Idi Amin's regime constitute the first example in point.[45] Having seized power in 1971, the former army officer established a dictatorship that systematically disregarded basic human rights of Ugandans, expelled ethnic minorities, and eventually led to an estimated loss of 300,000 lives. After initial hesitation, the United States as well as other western countries began to exercise pressure on the regime. The United States' measures culminated in the adoption of the Uganda Embargo Act in October 1978.[46] Section 5(c), (d) of the Act prohibited exports of goods and technology to Uganda. As was pointed out during the drafting, this embargo *prima facie* violated the United States' obligations owed to Uganda under GATT, more specifically the prohibitions against export restrictions and non-discrimination set out in articles XI and XIII.[47] As to possible justifications, the United States itself admitted that none of the GATT-specific exceptions (such as articles XIX–XXI GATT) applied. In contrast, provisions of the Act expressly pointed to the atrocities committed within Uganda. According to section 5(b), 'the United States should take steps to dissociate itself from any foreign government which engages in the international crime of genocide.'[48] The breaking off of trade relations thus served to stigmatise criminal conduct of a foreign government.

The member States of the European (Economic) Community took a more guarded approach. Faced with increasing demands for sanctions, the European Commission initially argued that the human rights abuses committed within Uganda did not affect obligations (notably in the field of development assistance) owed to Uganda under the then applicable Lomé I Convention. It is interesting to note that despite this

[45] The subsequent discussion focuses on measures adopted by western States. As a forcible measure, the Tanzanian military intervention that eventually put an end to Idi Amin's dictatorship, is outside the scope of the present study. For an assessment see e.g. Franck (2002), 143–145; Chesterman (2001), 77–79.

[46] 22 USC s. 2151 (1978).

[47] See the statements of the US administration before the House of Representatives: United States–Uganda Relations, Hearings Before the Subcommittee on Africa, International Organizations and International Economic Policy and Trade (established by the House Committee on International Relations), 95th Cong., 2nd Session (1978), at 61 and 64 (statements by W. C. Harrop and R. H. Meyer). For further references cf. Fredman (1979), 1156–1165; Talkington (1979), 210.

[48] 22 USC s. 2151 (1978). Cf. also the statement by Representative Pease (in *House Hearings*, last footnote, at 67) who observed that 'in the case of Uganda, not unlike that of South Africa, there are higher principles involved than blind adherence to free trade dogma.'

assessment, development assistance was suspended between 1977 and 1979.[49] This suspension had to be seen in the light of the 'Uganda Guidelines', in which the EC Council of Ministers had condemned the systematic disregard of human rights.[50] As Uganda's right to development assistance under the Lomé I Convention was not conditional upon the observance of human rights, this measure could not be justified under the specific terms of the treaty, and had to be justified as a countermeasure.[51]

European countries - Liberia (1980)

In 1980, following a military coup in Liberia, European countries adopted a very similar response. The new government under Samuel Doe repressed opposition groups, *inter alia*, executing thirteen dissidents after show trials. After having condemned this repression, the European Commission declared that because of Liberia's disregard for human rights, development assistance owed under the Lomé I Convention would be suspended.[52] As has been observed above with respect to the case of Uganda, this measure violated Liberia's right to development assistance under the Lomé I Convention, and could not be justified under the terms of that treaty.[53]

G77 and socialist countries - colonial regimes (1970s–1990s)

Compared to the instances examined so far, the third example in point involves problems of a considerably more complex character. Rather than one specific incident, it concerns the general problem posed by foreign States' involvement in struggles for national liberation and self-determination. For present purposes, the crucial question is whether States have been prepared to violate their international obligations in order to support such struggles. When leaving to a side forms of support that in itself would *prima facie* amount to a use of force (which are

[49] While not formally suspending its obligations, European countries refused to implement the relevant provisions of the Lomé I Convention. For details and further references see Oestreich (1990), 45–48, 304–307; Arts (1995), 268; Hoffmeister (1998), 11–12.

[50] EC Bull. 1977, No. 6, para. 2.2.59.

[51] Oestreich (1990), 442–443; Weschke (2001), 114–116. It is interesting to note that the difficulties experienced in the case of Uganda were one of the crucial factors leading to the gradual inclusion of human rights clauses into the EC's development agreements; see Hoffmeister (1998), 11–14.

[52] Statement by Commissioner Cheysson, 8 July 1980, in: Europe, Vol. 28, No. 2495 (new series), at 11. For further references see Oestreich (1990), 320–322.

[53] Cf. above, footnote 51; and further Oestreich (1990), 447–449.

outside the scope of the present study) the available evidence clearly suggests that they have. In fact, in official statements, a clear majority of States has asserted, or accepted, the legality of such support. Statements made by G77 States bring out the point with particular clarity. At their 1983 meeting in New York, the G77 foreign ministers for example called for 'more vigorous and concrete steps ... in order to end ... colonialism, ... *apartheid*, racism, all forms of racial discrimination and all forms of foreign aggression'.[54] At their previous meeting, they had already expressly affirmed 'the legitimacy ... of economic sanctions and other measures in the struggle against *apartheid*, racism, all forms of racial discrimination and colonialism ... [and] emphasized the right of developing countries, individually and collectively, to adopt such sanctions and other measures.'[55]

As regards permissible forms of assistance, non-aligned and socialist countries supported a right to provide diplomatic, political, and military support, while most western States tended to dispute the legitimacy of military assistance.[56] For present purposes, these differences are not crucial. Even the more restrictive position maintained by most western States ran counter to the traditional rules of non-intervention, under which any support of liberation movements would have qualified as an intervention in the internal affairs of the State concerned.[57] States asserting a right to provide such support thus were required to justify their conduct.

It remains to be seen whether the relevant conduct is relevant to an analysis of the *erga omnes* concept. Although the question of self-determination struggles has often been treated as a separate question, subject to distinct legal rules,[58] the more convincing view is that it is. While G77 States might have been particularly concerned with struggles for national liberation, their respective pronouncements are not limited to violations of the right of self-determination. Quite to the contrary, the above-quoted statements expressly assert a right to respond against 'all

[54] Declaration Adopted During at the Seventh Annual Meeting of G77 Foreign Ministers (1983), reproduced in Sauvant/Müller (1995), 430.

[55] Declaration Adopted During at the Sixth Annual Meeting of G77 Foreign Ministers (1982), reproduced in Sauvant/Müller (1995), 420.

[56] For clear summaries see Gray (2000a), 48–50; Cassese (1995), 152–155.

[57] Cf. Verdross/Simma (1984), 306–308 and 243–246.

[58] See e.g. Quaye (1991), 287–308; similarly the Court's ambiguous remarks in the *Nicaragua case*, ICJ Reports 1986, 108 (para. 206). Others have treated military assistance as an aspect of the legal regime of collective self-defence; see e.g. Dugard (1967), 157.

forms of racial discrimination and foreign aggression',[59] i.e. two other obligations *erga omnes* expressly recognised by the Court. Although stressing one particular aspect (just as western States, in the examples given so far, tended to stress the importance of political human rights), declarations by G77 States thus took up legal interests protected by the *erga omnes* concept. It would seem to follow that the above-quoted statements are relevant for the legal regime governing obligations *erga omnes*.[60]

As regards the actual implementation of the views summarised above, it is not possible here to assess in any detail the manifold instances in which foreign States have provided support for national liberation movements. The general pattern underlying their conduct may instead briefly be illustrated with reference to the reactions of African States against South Africa's continued administration in Namibia.[61] Since its beginning in 1966, African States were closely involved in the armed struggle led by the South West African People's Party (SWAPO) against the South African administration. The so-called 'Front Line States' allowed SWAPO to operate from their territory, helped train SWAPO fighters and provided logistic and military support. Although the actual implementation varied, African States adopted a variety of trade and other sanctions so to weaken the South African administration.[62] Without going into a detailed assessment, it seems safe to observe that States not only asserted a right to support liberation struggles, but took concrete steps to support them.

Western countries – Poland (1981)

On 13 December 1981, the Polish government under General Jaruzelski imposed martial law; subsequently, it banned the independent trade union *Solidarnosć* and interned approximately 12,500 dissidents. Western countries immediately expressed their concern. As for more concrete measures, the United States adopted a number of trade sanctions, which did not violate legal obligations owed to Poland.[63] Beyond that, it

[59] See above, footnote 55.

[60] Similarly Cassese (1995), 152; Sicilianos (1990), 167–169.

[61] For a more detailed treatment, and comment on South Africa's assertion of a right to exercise self-defence against Front Line States, see Kwakwa (1987), 421; Botha (1985–1986), 138; Dugard (1967), 157; Gray (2000a), 99–103.

[62] For South Africa's accusations in this regard see e.g. UNYB 1980, 263; UNYB 1981, 217 and 238; UNYB 1985, 189. For the UN's endorsement of Front Line States' involvement see SC Res. 428 and 445.

[63] Cf. Weschke (2001), 118–122. For a survey of the various measures see Moyer/Mabry (1983), 64–67 and 74–75.

suspended, with immediate effect, a bilateral aviation agreement providing for landing rights of Poland's national airline LOT.[64] In the ensuing discussions, LOT representatives referred to article XV, pursuant to which the agreement could only be denounced upon twelve months' notice.[65] The US authorities made it clear that they did not rely on article XV, but asserted a general right to suspend treaties with immediate effect in cases of 'exceedingly serious world events'.[66] Admitting that the suspension was 'of the most extraordinary nature', the relevant statement claimed that 'there resides in the [US] President ample authority to suspend application of an [aviation agreement] ... whether or not such suspension is provided for under the specific terms of the Agreement.'[67] European States initially disagreed on the appropriate course of conduct; the French foreign minister at one point even characterised the events as a domestic issue.[68] Eventually, however, a number of western European countries followed the US lead and temporarily suspended LOT landing rights on their territory.[69] At least in the case of Switzerland and the United Kingdom, this measure violated Poland's rights under applicable aviation agreements, and could not be justified under the terms of the relevant agreements.[70]

United States–Soviet Union (1981)

Events in Poland also had an impact on the United States treaty relations with the Soviet Union, which had amassed troops along the Polish border and, according to President Reagan, deserved 'a major share of the blame for development in Poland.'[71] Based on this assessment, the US authorities suspended import licences for Soviet products and deferred decisions pending treaty negotiations.[72] While most of the various measures remained mere retorsions, the United States violated its obligations under a bilateral aviation agreement by suspending, with immediate

[64] 23 UST 4269.

[65] Cf. the references in Nash (1982), 381. The agreement contained a suspension clause (article IV), which, however, only covered the non-observance of safety regulations, and thus did not apply. Cf. further Malamut (1983), 191–192.

[66] Statement of the US Civil Aeronautics Board of 28 December 1981, reproduced in Nash (1982), 381.

[67] Nash (1982), 381. [68] Cf. the statement reproduced in Moyer/Mabry (1983), 79.

[69] Cf. Rousseau (1982), 607.

[70] Cf. e.g. *Amtliche Sammlung* (Switzerland) 1977, 1659, for the text of the agreement.

[71] Statement of 28 December 1981, reproduced in Nash (1982), 380.

[72] For a survey see Nash (1982), 382; Moyer/Mabry (1983), 67–73.

effect, landing rights of Aeroflot.[73] Just as the US–Polish treaty referred to above, this agreement did not permit parties to suspend obligations with immediate effect, and thus could not justify the US conduct.[74]

Western countries – Argentina (1982)

Argentina's invasion of the Falklands/Malvinas islands in April 1982 was condemned as a 'breach of the peace' by the UN Security Council, which stopped short of adopting coercive measures.[75] In contrast, a number of western countries imposed sanctions.[76] Leaving aside a variety of unfriendly acts (such as arms embargoes), two types of measures are of particular relevance: general import embargoes adopted by the European Community, Canada and Australia;[77] and the suspensions, by Germany and New Zealand, of their respective bilateral aviation agreements.[78] It seems undisputed that these measures *prima facie* violated obligations owed to Argentina under GATT and the respective aviation treaties. In contrast, the question of justifications has remained controversial. The general import embargo in particular gave rise to considerable discussion among GATT member States.[79] Some Latin American States condemned the measure; however, they seemed to do so largely because they accepted Argentina's territorial claim to the islands.[80] For their part, EC members, Australia and Canada conceded that the import embargo affected Argentina's rights under GATT; it was, however, justified 'on the basis of their [GATT member States'] inherent right of which article XXI of the General Agreement is a reflection.'[81] Despite the reference to the national security exception contained in

[73] See 6 ILM (1967), 82 for the text of the agreement and 7 ILM (1968), 571 for a subsequent modification.

[74] Cf. article XVII of the agreement (providing for denunciation upon twelve months' notice).

[75] SC Res. 502 (1982) (calling for an immediate withdrawal of Argentinean troops).

[76] For a survey of the various measures see Rousseau (1982), 744–749; Lindemann (1984a), 557–558; Charpentier (1982), 1025–1026.

[77] For the measures adopted by the European Community see Regulations 877/82, OJ 1982, L 102/1 and 1176/82, OJ 1982, L 136/1; as regards the parallel measures adopted by the European Coal and Steel Community see Regulations 82/221/ECSC, OJ 1982, L 102/3, and 82/320/ECSC, OJ 1982, L 136/2. For the Australian and Canadian sanctions see the statements reproduced in Mestral (1983), 337, and 10 Australian YIL (1987), 573 respectively.

[78] Cf. Lindemann (1984a), 557–558; Keesing's 1982, 31533.

[79] See GATT Doc. C/M/157; and cf. Kuyper (1982), 151–154; Hahn (1996), 328–334.

[80] Cf. Sicilianos (1990), 163 (his note 341) for references.

[81] Joint Communiqué (EC, Canada, Australia, 'Trade Restrictions Affecting Argentina Applied for Non Economic Reasons', GATT Doc. L/5319/ Rev.1 (para. 1b).

article XXI, the circumstances suggest that the western countries did not seek to invoke a treaty-specific justification. As the EC representative made clear during the debates, 'inherent rights constituted a *general exception* to the GATT'.[82] This suggests that in the view of EC members, Canada and Australia, the import embargo could be justified under general international law, which had been codified in article XXI GATT. In any event, the general import ban also violated Argentina's rights under two sectoral agreements (on trade in textiles and trade in mutton and lamb), for which the security exceptions of GATT did not apply.[83] The more convincing view therefore is that the embargo measures are relevant for an analysis of general international law.

The question remains which of the different generally available justifications applied. It has at times been suggested that the various sanctions could be justified as measures of collective self-defence in the sense of article 51 UNC;[84] accordingly, the conduct would provide only limited support for the existence of a right to respond to *erga omnes* breaches by way of countermeasure. Argentina's conduct having been qualified as a 'breach of the peace' and 'an invasion',[85] the United Kingdom was indeed entitled to exercise self-defence and, for that purpose, could seek forcible and non-forcible assistance by other States. Although the conditions governing collective self-defence therefore were met, there is little evidence that the responding States exclusively relied on that concept. As the statements made before the GATT council suggest, they were asserting the legality of their conduct in a general way, without mentioning article 51 UNC.[86] Similarly, when justifying the suspension of the bilateral aviation agreement, the German government did not claim to act in collective self-defence, but argued that Argentina's illegal use of force gave rise to an extra-conventional right to suspend the treaty.[87] To evaluate the relevant conduct merely in terms of article 51 UNC is thus unconvincing; it is equally relevant for the rules of countermeasures.

[82] GATT Doc C/M/157, at 10 (emphasis added). Cf. further Weschke (2001), 105; but contrast Sicilianos (1990), 163 (his note 342).

[83] For the text of the agreements see OJ 1979, L 298/2 and OJ 1980, L 275/14. Cf. further Kuyper (1982), 154–156; and Sicilianos (1990), 163–164.

[84] Kuyper (1982), 154–156; Weschke (2001), 105. A study by the Austrian foreign ministry seems to point in the same direction, cf. Fischer/Hafner (1982), 389–392.

[85] SC Res. 502 (1982).

[86] See e.g. the statements quoted above, footnotes 81 and 82. Contrast the statement by the Austrian foreign ministry referred to in footnote 84.

[87] Cf. Lindemann (1984a), 557–558.

Western countries – Soviet Union (1983)

On 1 September 1983, Soviet aircraft shot down a Korean Air Lines jumbo jet that had entered Soviet airspace; this caused the death of 269 passengers and crew. While the UN Security Council was paralysed by veto threats, a majority of Security Council members condemned the conduct as a violation of basic principles of international law.[88] Acting outside the UN framework, a number of western countries temporarily suspended landing rights of Aeroflot planes on their territory.[89] In the cases of Germany, Switzerland, Austria, Japan, and Canada, these measures violated existing aviation agreements and could not be justified under the specific terms of the treaties.[90] Japan and Canada nevertheless did not need to rely on a right to take countermeasures in the general interest. As both States made clear, they had been individually injured by the Soviet action, which had caused the deaths of their nationals.[91] Such special justification being unavailable, other States had to assert a right to respond irrespective of any individual injury. The Swiss government did so with particular clarity, justifying its treaty suspension with reference to the previous 'violation of basic principles of public international law'.[92]

Western countries – South Africa (1985–1986)

Following the declaration, in July 1985, by the South African government, of a state of emergency, international concern about the government's apartheid policy increased, and the hitherto cautious attitude of western countries began to change. Within the UN Security Council, they nevertheless rejected proposals for binding economic sanctions

88 See the statements in UN Doc. S/PV.2470-PV.2476. For the text of a draft resolution submitted to the Security Council see UN Doc. S/15966/Rev. 1.

89 See Rousseau (1984), 446. In contrast, the French government refrained from any such measure, arguing that the French-Soviet aviation agreement did not recognise a right of suspension; see Rousseau (1984), 446; Lakehal (1984–1985), 175–176.

90 For the relevant agreements see BGBl. 1972, II, 1575 (Germany); Amtliche Sammlung 1968, 1068 (Switzerland); 12 Japanese Annuals of International Law (1968), 268 (Japan); 835 UNTS 54 (Canada). That the legality of the measures in question depended on general international law also seems to be accepted in a statement by the ICAO council, which observed that 'such use of armed force constitutes a violation of international law and invokes generally recognized consequences'; 23 ILM (1984), 37 (emphasis added).

91 Cf. the statements reproduced in Oda/Owada (1988), 140; and 22 ILM (1984), 1199–1200.

92 See the statement quoted in *Neue Zürcher Zeitung* of 15 September 1983, 31 ('Verletzung elementarer Grundsätze des Völkerrechts'). On the Swiss conduct see further Linsi (1994), 232–235; for the German response Raub/Malanczuk (1985), 735.

pursuant to article 41 UNC. Instead, the Council (deciding not to act under Chapter VII UNC) merely recommended that member States adopt sectoral economic boycotts, including export bans on technology and import bans on industrial products.[93] In terms of the law, this meant that the resolution could not in itself justify conduct that would otherwise be unlawful.[94] When EC member States adopted and implemented the recommended measures, their conduct was thus not mandated by UN law, but had to be justified with reference to general international law.[95]

More importantly, the United States Congress adopted sanctions that went beyond the measures recommended in SC Res. 569 (1985). Section 306 of the 1986 Comprehensive Anti-Apartheid Act[96] e.g. suspended a bilateral aviation agreement concluded in 1947.[97] Contrary to article IX of that agreement – to which representatives of South African Airways referred in a protest note – this suspension was effective immediately,[98] and was meant to encourage the South African government 'to adopt measures leading towards the establishment of a non-racial democracy.'[99] For present purposes, it is important to note that despite the UN's involvement, these measures qualify as decentralised enforcement action directed against South Africa's apartheid policy.

93 SC Res. 569 (1985). An arms embargo had already been imposed by SC Res. 418 (1977). In contrast to the argument developed in the following, Rosenstock (1994), 330, has argued that the sanctions adopted by western States were intrinsically lawful and thus did not require to be justified. In view of the specific treaties referred to in the text, this assertion cannot be sustained.

94 Cf. Frowein/Krisch, in: Simma (2002a), article 39, MN 31, and article 41, MN 33. The point is controversial, and others have argued that even Security Council recommendations should justify conduct that would otherwise be unlawful: see e.g. Stein (1987), 60; Cassese (1986), 244. This view would seem to neglect the distinction between measures intending to produce legal effects (such as resolutions or authorisations) and recommendations deliberately qualified as non-binding.

95 For the measures see EC Bull. 1985, No. 9, para. 2.5.1; EC Bull. 1986, No. 9, para. 2.4.2.

96 26 ILM (1987), 79.

97 66 UNTS 233.

98 See the Implementation Order of the US Department of Transportation (Order 86-11-29), 26 ILM (1987), 104. Cf. *ibid*., 105, for the complaints by South African Airways.

99 *Ibid*., 105. According to Rousseau (1986), 949, Australia equally suspended Aeroflot landing rights, and thereby violated an existing aviation agreement. In contrast, Canada's similar measures remained mere retorsions, as Canada had not assumed any treaty obligations in relation to South Africa (cf. the statement of Secretary of State, Joe Clark, 24 ILM (1985), 1470–1471).

Various countries – Iraq (1990)

Iraq's invasion of Kuwait, on 2 August 1990, provides further evidence of the often intricate interplay between institutional and decentralised responses against wrongful acts. As is well known, the invasion prompted a series of Security Council resolutions. Actual sanctions were first authorised in SC Res. 661 of 6 August 1990.[100] By that time, a great number of countries – including Japan, Australia, the United States, the member States of the European Community, and Czechoslovakia – had already imposed economic sanctions on Iraq, with immediate effect, notably by freezing Iraqi assets.[101] As is clear from the sequence of events, and is indeed acknowledged in some of the statements,[102] this conduct initially could not be justified as an enforcement measure under Chapter VII UNC. Instead, measures taken prior to SC Res. 661 constituted decentralised enforcement measures, as did measures taken by non-member States such as Switzerland.[103] Finally, it may be pointed out that, although Iraq's conduct amounted to an armed attack in the sense of article 51 UNC, States did not specifically justify their conduct as acts of collective self-defence. Just as in the case of the Falklands/Malvinas crisis, there is thus no reason to exclude it from the present analysis.

[100] For the earlier condemnation of Iraq's conduct see SC Res. 660 of 2 August 1990.

[101] See the statement by the Japanese Chief Cabinet Secretary (5 August 1990), annexed to UN Doc. S/21449; statement of the Australian Attorney-General and Acting Foreign Minister (6 August 1990), annexed to UN Doc. S/21520; US President Bush's Executive Order No. 12722 (2 August 1990), reproduced in 84 AJIL (1990), 903–905; statement of the Government of the Czech and Slovak Federal Republic on the Iraqi aggression (3 August 1990), reproduced in Bethlehem (1991), 101; and the statement by the EC member States of 4 August 1990, reproduced *ibid.*, 111–112. As for (European) national implementation measures taken before the relevant Security Council resolution see e.g. Decree No. 90-681 of the French Minister if the Economy, Finance and Budget (2 August 1990); Decree-Law No. 220 of the Italian President (6 August 1990); Regulation of the Luxemburg Grand Duchy (6 August 1990); Sanctions Decree 1990/No. G 90/1463 of the Dutch Ministers for Foreign Affairs and Finance (6 August 1990); Order No. 19202 of the Spanish Minster of the Economy and Finance (all reproduced in Bethlehem (1991), 120–121, 178–179, 218, 232–233, 294 respectively).

[102] See e.g. Japan's commitment (in the statement referred to in the last footnote) that UN measures would be implemented 'when a resolution on sanctions is approved by the Security Council'.

[103] See Swiss *note verbale* to the UN Secretary-General (22 August 1990), UN Doc. S/21585; and cf. Ordinance Instituting Economic Measures Against the Republic of Iraq and the State of Kuwait (7 August 1990). Both documents are reproduced in Bethlehem (1991), 307–308. Cf. further Linsi (1994) for a comprehensive assessment of the change of Swiss foreign policy marked by the Iraqi sanctions.

European and Commonwealth countries – Nigeria (1995)

On 10 November 1995, the Nigerian dissident Ken Saro-Wiwa and eight associates were executed after having been sentenced to death by a Nigerian special court. The Nigerian military government was widely perceived to be responsible for this incident, as well as for the systematic violation of basic human rights taking place since the annulment of the democratic elections in 1993. The UN General Assembly 'condemn[ed] the arbitrary execution ... and express[ed] deep concern about other violations of human rights and fundamental freedoms in Nigeria.'[104] European and Commonwealth States, while shying away from imposing an oil embargo, adopted a variety of sanctions, ranging from sports boycotts to travel restrictions.[105] For present purposes, two specific measures are of particular relevance. First, when discussing possible responses, EC member States were prepared to freeze Nigerian bank accounts in Europe,[106] which would have meant a violation of their obligations under general international law. When realising that this measure would not have produced any meaningful effect (most assets having already been transferred to Swiss bank accounts), they eventually refrained from adopting it. This decision was based on functional, rather than legal, considerations; the fact that the measure was discussed suggests that a violation of international law would have been considered justified.[107]

Secondly, Commonwealth member States suspended Nigeria from the organisation, and threatened to expel it if it did not restore democracy.[108] Unlike the (planned) freezing of assets, this measure is more difficult to evaluate in legal terms. The first question that needs to be addressed is whether the suspension affected rights of Nigeria, and thus required to be justified. The more convincing view is that it did. Despite its informal structure, the Commonwealth constitutes an international organisation, whose membership brings with it obligations (notably to make financial contributions) as well as rights (such as the right to participate in the decision-making process of the organisation, or the right to receive technical and development assistance).[109] Of course, by

[104] GA Res. 50/199 (1995).

[105] For a survey and further background information see Tomaševski (2000), 288–293; Torelli (1996), 234–236.

[106] Cf. Dzida (1997), 263–264, for references.

[107] Weschke (2001), 124–125; and further Dzida (1997), 263–264.

[108] Cf. 66 BYIL (1995), 626.

[109] On the legal character of the Commonwealth, and its character as an international organisation see Dale (1982), 451; Duxbury (1997), 346–349; Bowett/Sands/Klein (2001),

suspending Nigeria, the members of the Commonwealth mainly decided to send a political message. However, the suspension also meant that Nigeria was precluded from exercising its membership rights. As it was not taken by organs of the institution, but by the Commonwealth Heads of Governments, the decision would seem to be attributable to the States supporting the action.

As regards possible justifications, the situation is more straightforward. Quite clearly, the suspension could not be justified with reference to specific institutional rules of the organisations. While the 1971 Singapore Declaration of Commonwealth Principles and the 1991 Harare Commonwealth Declaration lay down basic principles of the organisation, neither document addresses the question of suspension of membership.[110] In order to justify the violation of Nigeria's membership rights, Commonwealth members thus had to rely on justification deriving from general international law. Among commentators, the general view seems to be that suspensions from membership, in the absence of an express provision, are to be characterised as a countermeasure.[111]

African States – Burundi (1996)

The assassinations of Presidents Ndadaye and Ntaryamira, in 1993–1994, derailed the process of Burundi's democratisation. Between 1994 and 1996, the country was gripped by inter-ethnic terror and counter-terror opposing Hutu rebels and the Tutsi-led military, leading to a humanitarian catastrophe deplored, for example, by the United Nations and First Arusha Summit of East African States.[112] On 25 July 1996, Burundi's former military ruler, Pierre Buyoya, seized power in a military coup, dissolved parliament, and banned political opposition parties. East African States involved in the Arusha process immediately

145–146. Interestingly, unlike in the case of most other international organisations, these rights are mostly not based on written treaty provisions, but customary in character. This is but a consequence of the Commonwealth's peculiar non-institutionalised character, and does not affect the legal nature of the rights in question.

[110] Both declarations are available at http://www.thecommonwealth.org/whoweare/declarations. On their relevance see Schiavone (1997), 67.

[111] See e.g. Bowett/Sands/Klein (2001), 545–546. Contrast Simma (1970), 66–67, who invokes article 60, para. 2(a) VCLT.

[112] See, *inter alia*, SC Res. 1012 (1995); GA Res. 50/159 (1995); UN Doc. S/PRST/1995/10; UN Doc. S/PRST/1995/13; and, for the Joint Communiqué of the First Arusha Summit, UN Doc. S/1996/557. For a brief overview see Tomaševski (2000), 238–247.

condemned the coup and demanded the restoration of democratic institutions. Beyond that, they agreed to 'exert maximum pressure on the [new] regime in Bujumbara', and to this effect, adopted a trade embargo, cut air links with Burundi and imposed a travel ban on the new leaders.[113] Burundi protested against these measures, which it considered to be 'in every respect contrary to the Charter of the United Nations, the Charter of the Organization of African Unity, and to international law as a whole.'[114] It must be admitted that the relative lack of documentation renders a proper evaluation of these sanctions difficult. On the basis of statements by both Burundi and the responding States, it can, however, be said that the trade embargo, initially covering arms and supplies, evolved into a general boycott, from which exemptions for fertilisers and seeds were granted once the Buyoya regime had restored parliament.[115] In terms of the law, these measures *prima facie* would have violated Burundi's rights under the WTO agreements, especially articles XI and XIII GATT. This in turn means that Kenya, Rwanda, Uganda, and Tanzania, which by July 1996 had become WTO members, were in breach of their international obligations.[116] Furthermore, Rwanda and Zaire/DRC arguably were in breach of the Treaty establishing the Economic Community of the Countries of the Great Lakes (CEPGL),[117] which obliges member States to facilitate economic integration and which, although defunct, had never been formally suspended or denounced.[118] In any event, the language of the resolutions, especially the commitment to exercise 'maximum pressure' or 'the necessary pressure',[119] seems to suggest that in view of the participating States, sanctions involving breaches of international law were considered to be justified.

[113] See Joint Communiqué of the Second Arusha Summit, para. 11; UN Doc. A/51/264–S/1996/620; and cf. also the brief summary in Angelet (2003), 226–227.
[114] UN Doc. A/51/409–S/1996/788; and already UN Doc. S/1996/690.
[115] Cf. the summary in UNYB 1996, 84.
[116] For the relevant information on membership see http://www.wto.org/english/thewto_e/whatis_e/tif_e/org6_e.htm.
[117] Cf. http://www.cepgl.com for the text of the agreement.
[118] Cf. Schiavone (1997), 94–95, for a brief survey of the CEPGL. The *Oil Platforms* and *Nicaragua cases* (involving treaties of amity and friendship between countries whose relations at the time of the proceedings were characterised by neither) show that even where the original circumstances leading to the conclusion of treaties have changed, one should not lightly presume that the legal obligations arising thereunder had ceased to apply.
[119] Cf. the Joint Communiqués adopted at the Second and Third Arusha Summits, UN Doc. A/51/264–S/1996/620 (para. 11) and UN Doc. A/51/513–S/1996/857 (para. 9) respectively.

European countries – Yugoslavia (1998)

Throughout the year 1998, European States discussed how to respond to the mounting crisis in Kosovo. On 7 May and 29 June 1998, the Council of Ministers, having deplored the repression of ethnic Albanians within Kosovo, decided to freeze Yugoslavian assets and to impose upon Yugoslavia an immediate flight ban.[120] These measures went beyond the international sanctions regime imposed by the UN Security Council.[121] For all participating States, the decision to freeze assets constituted a violation of international obligations. In addition, at least in the case of France and the United Kingdom, the flight ban was in violation of existing bilateral aviation agreements, none of which allowed for the immediate suspension of landing rights.[122] While France implemented it without further discussion, the decision-making process within the British government reveals the tension between treaty adherence on the one side, and effective sanctions on the other. Questioning the legality of an immediate suspension, the Foreign and Commonwealth Office proposed to denounce the treaty in accordance with the procedure prescribed in article 17, which would have triggered a 12 months' grace period.[123] Under pressure by other European countries, the British government eventually suspended the agreement with immediate effect.[124] The Foreign Secretary's statement to Parliament shows that this decision caused considerable uneasiness: 'President Milosevic's ... worsening record on human rights means that, *on moral and political grounds*, he has forfeited the right of his Government to insist on the 12 months' notice which would normally apply.'[125]

[120] See Common Position 98/326/CFSP, OJ 198, L 143/1, and Common Position 98/426/CFSP, OJ 1998, L 190/3. For the implementation see Regulation 1091/98, OJ 1998, L 248/1.

[121] By SC Res. 1160 of 31 March 1998, the Security Council had imposed an arms embargo. Further sanctions were imposed in SC Res. 1199 of 23 September 1998, i.e. after the relevant actions by European States.

[122] For the texts of the agreements see RTAF 1967, No. 69; UKTS 1960, No. 10 respectively. The subsequent discussion is based on the assumption that the respective treaties, originally concluded with the Federal Socialist Republic of Yugoslavia, continued to apply in relation to the Federal Republic of Yugoslavia. This view was implicitly taken by the British government; cf. the statement in 70 BYIL (1999), 555. Contrast, however, Wibaux (1998), 279–280.

[123] See Wibaux (1998), 263 and 267 (summarising the debates among European States).

[124] See the statements by Foreign Secretary Cook (denying that other European States had exercised pressure), reproduced in 69 BYIL, 580–581 and 70 BYIL (1999), 555–556, and further Wibaux (1998), 267.

[125] 69 BYIL (1998), 580–581 (emphasis added). Cf. also the subsequent statement reproduced in 70 BYIL (1999), 555–556.

Various countries – Zimbabwe (2002–2003)

Finally, the on-going international pressure mounted by western and Commonwealth States against the government of Zimbabwe in the years 2002–2003 provides the most recent evidence in point.[126] As in the instances examined above, the various sanctions are a mix of retorsions and measures requiring justification. The case of Zimbabwe, however, differs from the previous cases in that it involves a treaty that recognises the essential relevance of human rights and good governance. Under article 96 of the framework treaty governing relations between European States and Zimbabwe, the Cotonou Agreement (which replaces the earlier Lomé Conventions),[127] the Community and its member States are specifically entitled to adopt 'appropriate measures' – including, as a last resort, the suspension of the agreement – if another party 'has failed to fulfil an obligation stemming from respect for human rights, democratic principles, and the rule of law'.[128] Unlike in the cases of Uganda and Liberia examined above, the decision to suspend, from February 2002, financial aid and development assistance owed to Zimbabwe, therefore could be based on the specific terms of article 96 of the Cotonou Agreement, and did not have to be justified as a countermeasure.[129]

In contrast, no such specific justification applies to a second type of sanction imposed on Zimbabwe. Deploring the violation of civil and political rights and the intimidation of opposition groups, the EC Council of Ministers decided to adopt a variety of economic sanctions, including the freezing of assets of members of the Zimbabwean government.[130] Since this measure violated Zimbabwean rights under general

126 For an analysis of the measures adopted by the European Community see Pillitu (2003), 55.

127 OJ 2000, L 317/3; and for the regime of transitional application Decision 1/2000 of the ACP-EC Council of Ministers, OJ 2000, L 195/46. On the evolution of human rights clauses in the external relations of the European Community see Brandtner/Rosas (1998), 473; Riedel/Will (1999), 723.

128 See Cotonou Agreement, article 96, para. 2(a); as for the scope of 'appropriate measures' see article 96, para. 2(c)(i). In addition, article 9 prescribes that respect for human rights is an 'essential element' of the EC–ACP cooperation.

129 Cf. EC Bull. 2002, No. 1/2, 147 (para. 1.6.155–156); and further Pillitu (2003), 63–72. For the Community's response against Uganda and Liberia see above, sections 6.2.1.a.1 and 6.2.1.a.2.

130 Common Position 2002/145/CFSP, OJ 2002, L 50/1 (article 3 and 4); for the implementation see Regulation EC 310/2002, OJ 2002, L 50/4. The measures initially applied for twelve months, but were renewed in early 2003, cf. Common Position 2003/115/CFSP, OJ 2003, L 46/30; Regulation 313/2003, OJ 2003, L 46/6.

international law rather than the Cotonou Agreement, it did not fall within the scope of article 96, nor could it be justified under any other specific treaty. The same reasoning applies to the identical measures adopted by the United States in March 2003.[131] Finally, the decision to suspend Zimbabwe from the Commonwealth[132] finds no basis in any specific treaty document either. Following the argument developed above, with respect to Nigeria,[133] this measure violates actual membership rights, and thus requires to be legally justified. All three responses therefore qualify as countermeasures.

6.2.1.b Statements implying a right to take countermeasures

In addition to these examples, States have at times asserted a right to resort to countermeasures in response to another State's previous wrongful conduct; their actual responses, however, have remained mere retorsions. While not of the same evidentiary value, the respective statements show that a violation of international law would have been considered justified, and are thus relevant. The planned freezing, by EC member States, of Nigerian assets has been considered already.[134] In addition, the following instances may serve to illustrate the point.

G7 declarations on aircraft hijacking (1978/1981)

Determined to strengthen international cooperation against aircraft hijacking, the governments of the G7 States, at their 1978 meeting, adopted the so-called 'Bonn Declaration on Air-Hijacking'.[135] Under its terms – reaffirmed at the Ottawa and Tokyo summits[136] – the G7 States agreed to take joint action against countries harbouring hijackers. Where another country refused to extradite hijackers, or to return the hijacked aircraft, G7 States would 'take immediate action to cease all

[131] 'Blocking Property of Persons Undermining Democratic Processes or Institutions in Zimbabwe', Executive Order of 7 March 2003, available at: http://www.ustreas.gov/offices/eotffc/ofac/sanctions/t11zimb.pdf.

[132] See the statement by the Commonwealth Chairpersons' Committee, 19 March 2002, available at: http://www.thecommonwealth.org/whoweare/declarations. The measure, initially valid for one year, was confirmed at the Commonwealth General Meeing on 7 December 2003, prompting Zimbabwe to withdraw from the organisation. See 'Statement on Zimbabwe' of 7 December 2003, available at http://www.chogm2003.info, and cf. 'Zimbabwe Has Last Word Over Expulsion', *The Times*, 8 December 2003, available at http://www.timesonline.co.uk.

[133] Cf. above, pp. 220–221 (discussing Nigeria's suspension from the Commonwealth).

[134] See above, section 6.2.1.a (pp. 220–221). The Nigerian case was included in the above list because Nigeria's suspension from the Commonwealth amounted to an actual violation.

[135] 17 ILM (1978), 1285. [136] 20 ILM (1981), 956; 25 ILM (1986), 1005.

flights to that country ... [and] halt all incoming flights from that country or from any country by the airlines of the country concerned.'[137] Debates at the summit show that the declaration was intended to cover the immediate suspension of aviation agreements.[138] As is clear from the preceding discussion, this conduct would almost inevitably entail the breach of such agreements, few of which recognise a right of immediate suspension. Nor could it have been justified under the terms of the 1970 Hague Convention for the Suppression of Unlawful Seizure of Aircraft, which does not envisage the suspension of air links.[139] Although never invoked to justify the suspension of treaties,[140] the Bonn Declaration thus implicitly recognised a right of G7 States to take countermeasures irrespective of individual injury.[141]

Western countries - Iran (1979–1980)

The collective measures adopted by western States against Iran in the wake of the Hostages crisis provide another example.[142] Following the condemnation of the Iranian conduct[143] by the ICJ and the UN Security Council, European and other western States adopted a variety of trade sanctions and, *inter alia*, decided to suspend all contracts concluded with Iran after the seizure of the US embassy. Since the United States' attempts to adopt a Security Council resolution ordering sanctions proved unsuccessful, these measures constituted decentralised enforcement action.[144] At least arguably, they remained intrinsically lawful, and did not require to be justified.[145] Statements by the European

[137] 17 ILM (1978), 1285 (paras. 2 and 3).

[138] Frowein (1994), 418; Oppermann (1981), 512.

[139] Bussutil (1982), 479–481; and cf. 10 ILM (1971), 133. As Bussutil observes, the Bonn Declaration did not distinguish between States parties to the 1970 Convention and third States.

[140] When, in 1981, Afghanistan refused to extradite hijackers responsible for the seizure of a Pakistan International Airlines aircraft, G7 States decided to act according to the principles set out in the declaration. States that actually had entered into aviation agreements with Afghanistan decided to follow the denunciation procedure prescribed in the treaty; cf. Chamberlain (1983), 628; Weschke (2001), 99–100.

[141] Frowein (1994), 418; Weschke (2001), 99–100.

[142] For further analysis see Schröder (1980), 121–124; Sicilianos (1990), 159–160; Frowein (1994), 417.

[143] See SC Res. 457 (1979) and 461 (1979); as well as the ICJ's interim order, ICJ Reports 1979, 7.

[144] For the United States' draft resolution see UN Doc. S/13735 (1980).

[145] Unlike in many other examples examined so far, GATT law (which would have been violated) did not apply, as Iran was not a party to the agreement. For an analysis of the various measures see Lindemeyer (1981), 10; Enderlein (1980), 453.

Parliament and the Council of Ministers however suggest that the possibility of countermeasures was implied. Hence the Parliament expressly encouraged States to adopt 'all measures necessary' to bring about the liberation of the hostages, while the Council of Ministers took the view that, despite the UN's paralysis, general international law permitted the imposition of coercive measures.[146]

6.2.1.c Actual non-compliance justified differently

Finally, States not individually injured have at times invoked other justifications (notably the doctrine *clausula rebus sic stantibus*) in order to justify non-compliance with treaty obligations. Admittedly, their conduct is thus not directly relevant to the law of countermeasures. The examples to be given in the following, however, illustrate what has been stated already – that the difference between countermeasures and other generally available justifications is very fine indeed. In fact, in instances examined, commentators have suggested that the conduct *should* have been justified as a countermeasure. Both factors justify a brief treatment of two illustrative cases.

Netherlands–Surinam (1982)

A Dutch-Surinamese dispute of 1982 constitutes the first relevant instance. Under agreements concluded in 1975, Surinam was entitled to economic subsidies and financial assistance for the maintenance of its military.[147] In 1980, a new military government seized power in Surinam and, in December 1982, cracked down on dissidents, imprisoning and torturing opposition members, journalists, and unionists, and executing at least fifteen persons. The Dutch government responded by formally suspending the 1975 treaties, sharply protesting against the human rights violations, which it considered to be 'contrary to the most fundamental concepts of constitutional government'.[148] Since Surinam's right under the treaties did not depend on the observation of human rights, the Dutch government could not rely on any

[146] See the statements reproduced in EC Bull. 1980–4, points 1.2.6–1.2.9. For the various national implementation measures see *ibid.*, point 1.5.4.; for the measures adopted by other (non-European) western countries cf. Rousseau (1980), 888.

[147] See Tractatenblad 1975, Nos. 135 and 140 respectively. The financial assistance owed under the latter treaty was later formalised in the Surinamese Armed Forces Transitional Financial Provisions Scheme (Stb. 1977 No. 710).

[148] Statements quoted in Siekmann (1984), 321. On the dispute see further Lindemann (1984b), 64.

treaty-specific justification. Neither did it claim a right to resort to countermeasures. Instead, it argued that Surinam's disregard for human rights constituted a fundamental change of circumstances, which was said to justify the suspension.[149]

European countries–Yugoslavia (1991)

The suspension and subsequent denunciation, by EC member States, of the 1983 Co-operation Agreement with Yugoslavia, provides a second example. In the autumn of 1991, the disintegrating parts of Yugoslavia had agreed on a negotiated Peace Agreement. When fighting again broke out, the European Community suspended, and later denounced, the 1983 Co-operation Agreement.[150] This led to the general repeal of trade preferences on imports, and thus went beyond the weapons embargo ordered by the Security Council in SC Res. 713 (1991). Both suspension and denunciation were incompatible with the terms of the agreement, which did not provide for immediate suspension but only for denunciation upon six months' notice.[151] Justifying their response, EC member States stressed their concern at the renewed fighting. Following the pattern of the Dutch statement cited above, the relevant decisions suggest reliance of the *clausula rebus sic stantibus*. In its 1998 decision in the *Racke case*,[152] the ECJ accepted this line of reasoning, without questioning whether EC member States would have been entitled to invoke the Yugoslav conflict as a relevant fundamental circumstance.[153]

6.2.1.d An assessment

The list of cases discussed in the preceding sections is certainly not exhaustive. In many other instances, often involving bilateral treaties, it has not been possible to establish with sufficient certainty whether the responding States' conduct actually violated international law. Mexico's decision to cut economic ties with Spain in 1976 (following

149 Cf. Siekmann (1984), 321. In literature, it has been argued that the measure should have been justified as a countermeasure, see e.g. Lindemann (1984b), 81–91; Frowein (1994), 420–421.

150 The agreement can be found in OJ 1983, L 41/1. See OJ 1991, L 315/1 for the suspension and OJ 1991, L 325/23 for the denunciation.

151 See article 60, para. 2 of the agreement and cf. Chinkin (1997b), 196–197.

152 *Racke case* [1998] ECR I-3655, paras. 52–59.

153 For criticism of this approach see e.g. Crawford, Third Report, para. 396 (especially his note 36), and further Klabbers (1999), 179.

the execution of Basque separatists)[154] or France's and Belgium's refusal, in 1979 and 1990 respectively, to implement treaties providing for military and economic aid to the Central African Republic and Zaire (following the killing of demonstrators in Bangui and Kinshasa)[155] are typical examples.[156] More generally, the lack of proper documentation, both as regards the measures adopted and the possibly affected treaties, renders an exhaustive coverage almost impossible. Finally, lack of documentation also makes an assessment of more recent, or on-going, sanctions very difficult. These factors notwithstanding, the preceding survey reveals a considerable amount of evidence in point. Before beginning to evaluate it, some key features may briefly be summarised.

It has been shown that in at least thirteen cases, States not individually injured have taken countermeasures in response to previous wrongful acts of another State. In various other cases, they have either asserted a right to do so, or have violated international law but justified their conduct under doctrines of general treaty law. In most instances, a considerable number of (mostly western) States adopted countermeasures, acting either in concert or independently. With one possible exception,[157] all responses were directed against States principally responsible for the alleged wrongful act, whereas States condoning the conduct in question have not been targeted.

With respect to the types of responses, countermeasures were usually taken alongside retorsions. In some cases, they went hand in hand with institutional sanctions, or where taken following an independent condemnation of a previous wrongful act. Their actual effects were often rather trivial, notably in the frequent cases involving temporary suspensions of landing rights. In fact, practice suggests that commentators hoping for a truly effective system of protection of obligations *erga*

[154] Cf. Rousseau (1976), 590–598 for a summary of the dispute.

[155] See Rousseau (1980), 363–364; and Dzida (1997), 263, respectively. Lattanzi (1983), 322, qualifies the former, Dzida (1997), 263 the latter case as a countermeasure.

[156] Another response, often qualified as countermeasures, but for which it has been impossible to establish beyond doubt that a violation has occurred, is the reaction by western States against the Soviet Union following the 1979 invasion in Afghanistan. For a survey of the measures see Weschke (2001), 101–102; for a different analysis cf. Sicilianos (1990), 157–159; Kessler (2001), 84–85.

[157] It may be argued that western States' responses against the Soviet Union, in connection with the imposition of martial law in Poland, did not target the principally responsible State. On the other hand, it seems undeniable that the Soviet Union was heavily involved in the decision-making process preceding the adoption of repressive measures, and also amassed troops along Poland's eastern border, thereby exercising considerable influence on the situation.

omnes might have been over-optimistic. Conversely, the repeated warnings against abuse are perhaps even more exaggerated; practice examined in the previous sections does not suggest that the recognition of a right to take countermeasures would necessarily lead to 'mob violence' or a 'reign of chaos'.[158]

As regards the types of breaches prompting countermeasures, States have not responded against isolated or minor violations, but only if the previous breach had assumed considerable proportions. Although an exact threshold is difficult to establish, it seems fair to say that countermeasures were taken in response to large-scale or systematic breaches.

Finally, with respect to the legal rules concerned, two broad, and often overlapping, categories can be identified. In most cases, States have responded against breaches of obligations protecting human rights of individuals or groups. Most other responses have been directed against forcible conduct of another State (whether amounting to an illegal use of force in the sense of article 2, para. 4 UNC or not), giving rise to breaches of humanitarian law or causing serious humanitarian concerns.

The question remains how this body of international practice affects the rules governing countermeasures and obligations *erga omnes*. This question will now be assessed. For the sake of convenience, it seems preferable to begin by giving a brief preliminary assessment. This will be refined in subsequent sections, which evaluate the main arguments advanced by commentators.

A preliminary evaluation

At first glance, international practice seems to warrant two rather straightforward conclusions. A first, brief observation concerns the States targeted by responses. In the light of the controversies caused by the Court's *East Timor* judgment,[159] it is worth noting that responses have been directed against States that (in the terminology used above) were principally responsible for the wrongful conduct. Practice with regard to obligations *erga omnes* thus confirms the general rule pursuant to which countermeasures cannot affect rights of third States.[160]

[158] Cf. Marek (1978–1979), 481; and Weil (1983), 432–433.

[159] See above, section 5.2.5.b.

[160] See above section 1.1. Insofar as States condoning conduct of other States might be in breach of their self-standing duty not to recognise consequences of grave wrongful acts, this breach would usually not give rise to responsibility *erga omnes*. See further

More important are the findings concerning States entitled to take countermeasures. Here, practice equally seems straightforward. On the face of it, it clearly contradicts the widely held view that countermeasures could only be taken by individually injured States. In a surprisingly large number of cases (most of which involved conduct of a considerable number of States, and often violations of different obligations), States have rejected this restrictive approach by resorting to countermeasures, although they could not claim to have been individually injured. Given the problems of documentation, it seems likely that the actual number of such cases is considerably higher. That said, even the documented evidence has forced critics to concede that countermeasures in the general interest account for a large portion of the overall practice regarding countermeasures.[161] To these instances, one has to add statements in which States not individually injured have asserted a right to take countermeasures in response to serious wrongful acts. Finally, even where States have relied on other concepts (such as the *clausula rebus sic stantibus*), their conduct cannot be ignored altogether. It shows that States are willing to interpret other generally available justifications in the light of community interests and thus further undermines the traditionally restrictive approach governing responses to international wrongs. In the light of these considerations, it seems over-cautious to qualify practice – as the ILC and its Special Rapporteur have done – as 'sparse' or 'embryonic'.[162] Quite to the contrary, at least in the case of systematic or large-scale breaches of international law, there seems to exist a settled practice of countermeasures by States not individually injured.

Counter-arguments examined

Predictably, given the sensitivity of the topic, this preliminary evaluation is not generally shared. Those disagreeing with it have raised a

above, section 5.2.5.b; and cf. Delbrück (1992d), 91–97, for attempts to justify countermeasures taken against States other than the principally responsible State.

161 See Alland (1994), 364–365, who concedes that 'un part non négligeable de la pratique étatique des contre-mésures au cours de la dernière décennie est le fait d'Etats qui n'étaient pas directement lésés par le fait internationalement illicite auquel ils répondaient.'

162 See para. 6 of the ILC's commentary on article 54 ASR; and para. 8 of the introductory commentary to Part Three, Chapter II. See also Crawford, Fourth Report, para. 71; but contrast Crawford, Third Report, para. 395 (speaking of 'a considerable number of cases'). For criticism of the ILC's assessment see Sicilianos (2002), 1142–1143.

number of interrelated points, which in their view warrant a more cautious assessment. On the basis of their comments, five counter-arguments will be examined in the subsequent sections. By engaging with them, the analysis will move beyond the preliminary assessment given so far.

The relevance of the *erga omnes* concept The first question is whether the practice discussed above has actually been influenced by, and is relevant for, the *erga omnes* concept. The point needs to be addressed because States have hardly ever expressly cited the *erga omnes* concept in order to justify their conduct.[163] Given the (albeit scarce) existence of pre-1970 precedents, one might wonder whether international practice regarding countermeasures has evolved independently, and whether the *erga omnes* concept has really made much of a difference. Three considerations suggest that it has, and that it is correct to assess international practice in the light of the newly emerged concept.

For once, some pre-1970 cases notwithstanding, there has been, since *Barcelona Traction*, a considerable increase in the number of cases in which States not individually injured have been prepared to adopt countermeasures in response to previous breaches of international law. Furthermore, States' responses, while not expressly referring to the notion of obligations *erga omnes*, often express the *ratio* upon which that concept is based, namely the idea that because of their importance, certain obligations are the concern of all States. Justifying the measures adopted by its country during the *Teheran Hostages* crisis, the Japanese foreign ministry, for example, stated that the dispute 'was not simply a bilateral issue but a problem for the international community as a whole.'[164] In similar terms, many statements justifying or announcing the measures discussed above stress the fundamental character of the obligations violated.[165] In short, while (understandably) refraining from using Latin legal terminology, States have taken up the gist of the Court's *Barcelona Traction* dictum.

Finally, and most importantly, there is a large overlap between the circle of obligations whose breach has prompted responses and that of obligations commonly considered to be valid *erga omnes*. Admittedly, the difficulty precisely to define the scope of the *erga omnes* concept

[163] Okowa (1999), 408. [164] Cf. the statement reproduced in Oda/Owada (1986), 93–94.
[165] See e.g. the statements cited in footnotes 48, 92, and 104.

complicates this assessment. As has been shown in Chapter 4, only a core of obligations *erga omnes* can be identified with precision, while the status of others has to be assessed on the basis of international practice (including, of course, State practice relating to countermeasures).[166] However, it is interesting to note that in the clear majority of cases, States have taken countermeasures in situations that often amongst other violations, involved breaches of recognised 'core' obligations *erga omnes*. Hence responses were directed against the illegal use of force,[167] policies of apartheid and racial discrimination,[168] acts of genocide,[169] conflicts about self-determination claims,[170] or the practice of torture (often combined with other human rights violations).[171] In all these instances, the *erga omnes* character of the obligation was beyond doubt.

What is more, in cases not involving 'core' obligations *erga omnes*, States have usually adopted countermeasures in response to wrongful acts affecting obligations that count among the candidates most likely to have acquired *erga omnes* status. By way of example, suffice it to mention other human rights, such as the right to life, fair trial guarantees, freedom of expression, or the freedom from arbitrary detention.[172] In fact, the Teheran Hostages crisis, which, despite its humanitarian implications, mainly involved breaches of diplomatic and consular law, seems to be the only instance of State practice that concerns obligations *not* commonly considered to be valid *erga omnes*.

In short, although not expressly mentioning the *erga omnes* concept, States have, in nearly all instances, responded against breaches of obligations that are either recognised obligations *erga omnes* or count among the most likely candidates. In line with what has been said above, about the dialectic process of determining obligations *erga omnes*,[173] this practice has implications for the identification of obligations *erga omnes*. Practice summarised in the preceding chapter notably supports the view that the various human rights obligations mentioned

[166] See above, section 4.2.2.
[167] E.g. the cases of Iraq–Kuwait and Argentina–Falklands/Malvinas.
[168] E.g. the different instances involving South Africa. [169] As in the case of Uganda.
[170] E.g. the cases of Yugoslavia 1998 and 1991, or the frequent instances involving support for anti-colonial struggles.
[171] E.g. the cases of Burundi, Liberia, Uganda, or Surinam.
[172] E.g. the cases of Poland/Soviet Union (1981), Nigeria, or Zimbabwe.
[173] Cf. above, section 4.2.2.b.

above are not only candidates, but actually have acquired *erga omnes* status.[174] In any event, the almost complete congruence between obligations prompting responses and obligations considered to be valid *erga omnes* suggests that international practice is affected by the *erga omnes* concept.

The selectivity of practice To many commentators, the alleged irregularity, or sparsity, of practice is a second cause of concern. The ILC's Special Rapporteur on the law of State responsibility, James Crawford, for example observed that 'in the majority of cases involving breaches of ... obligations [owed to the international community], no reaction at all has been taken, apart from verbal condemnations.'[175] Indeed, even some supporters note 'the absence of much state practice',[176] while others mention the lack of responses in specific instances (such as during Pol Pot's Cambodian reign of terror).[177] Selectivity, in turn is said to weaken the case for the recognition of countermeasures in the general interest.[178]

Whether one agrees with this counter-argument largely depends on a factual assessment. The general proposition underlying it is hard to dispute. Evidently, the more widespread the practice of countermeasures against breaches of obligations *erga omnes*, the less difficult it is to agree on the existence of the respective legal right. Also, it is obvious that countermeasures have not been taken in all relevant instances, nor even in all instances involving egregious international wrongs; in this regard, practice can clearly be characterised as selective.

The real question that needs to be addressed, however, is a different one: it needs to be determined whether practice, as some commentators argue, is *too selective*, i.e. whether the relevant examples of State practice can be qualified as isolated incidents rather than a settled practice. The above survey strongly suggests that this is not the case. In fact, when recapitulating the relevant examples, it may come as a surprise that in

[174] Conversely, in may be noted in passing that practice provides little support for the view that obligations in the field of international environmental law should be valid *erga omnes*.

[175] Crawford, Third Report, para. 396. See also Empell (2003), 85 and 424–425; Dzida (1997), 264–266.

[176] Kamminga (1992), 161; similarly Frowein (1994), 422.

[177] See e.g. Hannum (1989), 82, especially at 137–138, for a strong condemnation of the international failure to respond against the Pol Pot regime. On the relevance of the Cambodian precedent cf. also Koskenniemi (2001), 341–342.

[178] Cf. Kamminga (1992), 161–163.

many of the high-profile disputes of the last thirty years – including the humanitarian tragedy in Uganda, the Teheran Hostages crisis, the Falklands/Malvinas conflict, the decade-long fight against Apartheid, the Iraqi invasion of Kuwait, the Yugoslav and Kosovo conflicts, or more recently the struggle for democracy and human rights in Zimbabwe – States not individually injured have been prepared to take countermeasures against *erga omnes* breaches. Although practice is not uniform, it may thus be not as selective as frequent comments suggest.

Finally, it is worth pointing out that if international practice amounts to a settled practice (which, it is submitted, the survey suggests), then this finding cannot be disputed by singling out individual instances in which States have not been prepared to respond. Of course, where States remain passive when faced with egregious breaches of obligations *erga omnes* (as in the case of Cambodia), they will risk losing political or moral credibility. When assessing the existence of a legal right to respond, their conduct in a specific instance, however, is of limited relevance only. As with respect to countermeasures generally, the conduct remains an option, or *faculté*, of which States will avail themselves when they see fit, having regard to a variety of legal and other considerations.[179] Just as within bilateral relations (in which resort to countermeasures is the exception rather than the norm), their decision not to do so in a specific case therefore does not as such affect the continued existence of the right.

The dominance of western practice Following a third counter-argument, practice is dominated by a small group of western States, and thus lacks the required degree of generality.[180] Just as with regard to the charge of selectivity, this counter-argument largely depends on a factual assessment. As regards the law, it is accepted that the conduct of groups of States, even if consistent, cannot alter rules of international law against the expressed will of the majority of States.[181] As regards the

[179] Stein (1995), 122–123; Sicilianos (1990), 174. See already above, Introduction, footnote 43, for brief references to works assessing the questions of a duty to intervene.

[180] Cf. only Crawford, Third Report, para. 396; Sachariew (1988), 283–284; Empell (2003), 85, 424–425; similarly Poland in its comments on the ILC's work on State responsibility, UN Doc. A/CN.4/515, Add. 2, 18–19.

[181] Cf. the Court's judgment in the *North Sea Continental Shelf case*, ICJ Reports 1969, 43–44 (paras. 75–76); and further Bernhardt (1992), 900; Akehurst/Malanczuk (1997), 41–42; Dahm/Delbrück/Wolfrum (1989), 58–59. For a discussion of the required degree of generality see Mendelson (1998), 211–227.

available evidence, the situation is more controversial. At the outset, it may be pointed out that the group of western States is not as small and homogenuous as some commentators seem to suggest. The (allegedly) exclusively western practice analysed above involves countries of four continents and comprises States as diverse as New Zealand, Japan, and (neutral) Switzerland.

More importantly, the survey also shows that the attitude of non-western countries is far more ambiguous than is often assumed. Two points seem particularly relevant.

First, although in the clear majority of cases, only western States have taken countermeasures, there is some practice by non-western States. By supporting the armed struggle against apartheid, African States violated their obligations *vis-à-vis* South Africa. More generally, (then) Socialist countries, as well as the members of the G77 (representing about two-thirds of the the countries of the world) have consistently claimed a right to support anti-colonial and anti-apartheid movements. With respect to self-determination and apartheid/racial discrimination, international practice thus is decidedly non-western.[182] As regards breaches of other obligations *erga omnes*, there also is some non-western practice. Commonwealth countries (mostly non-western), in 1995 and 2001, supported the suspensions of Nigeria and Zimbabwe. (Then) Czechoslovakia was among the first States to adopt concrete measures against the Iraqi invasion of Kuwait. Finally, East African countries saw fit to impose sanctions on Burundi in 1996. In the light of this evidence, reports about the exclusively western character of international practice seem, if not greatly exaggerated, then at least unbalanced.

A second point is of equal relevance. While not themselves resorting to countermeasures, non-western States usually seemed to accept western States' conduct. In fact, one of the most astonishing aspects of international practice is the lack of protests against countermeasures by States not individually injured. Of course, States are not obliged to protest against conduct they consider unlawful, and their silence need not necessarily be qualified as tacit acceptance, especially where the responses affected bilateral treaties, of which others States might not

[182] Cf. also Sicilianos (1990), 167–169; Sicilianos (2002), 1143. It may be recalled that Ghana and Malaysia were among the first countries to adopt economic sanctions against South Africa, thereby violating their obligations under GATT (cf. above, section 2.2.2.d).

have been aware.[183] However, it is crucial to note that even where responses violated general international law or widely ratified treaties and where they were widely discussed, States other than the target State almost never voiced concern or critcism. Three examples may serve to illustrate the point. During the Kosovo crisis (during which, *inter alia*, 132 member States of the G77 subsequently were to condemn NATO's military campaign),[184] the G77 States did not support Yugoslavia's protests, made in public discussions before the Security Council,[185] against the European flight embargo. Similarly, the clear majority of members of the UN Security Council and international aviation organisations supported the international sanctions against the Soviet Union following the 1983 shooting down of a Korean aircraft.[186] Finally, no State seemed unduly perturbed by the freezing of Iraqi assets in early August 1990, when that conduct had not yet been mandated by the United Nations. In fact, on the basis of the available evidence, it seems that only the countermeasures against Argentina (adopted during the Falklands crisis) gave rise to serious discussions. As has been shown above, States denouncing them did not dispute a general right to respond against acts of aggression. Supporting Argentina's territorial claim to the Falklands/Malvinas islands, they simply took the view that the conditions governing responses were not met.[187]

Even when accepting that silence makes for ambiguous evidence, it seems therefore difficult to escape the conclusion that non-western States have frequently tolerated countermeasures adopted by western countries. This in turn suggests that even if practice were exclusively western (which it is not), it would not necessarily be opposed by the non-western majority of States. Taken together, both considerations undermine the third counter-argument.

A lack of *opinio juris* A fourth counter-argument focuses not on the features of international practice discussed above, but on the attitude of States responding to breaches. Its adherents take the view that

[183] As to the role of silence, or absence of protests, see Mendelson (1998), 207–209. The *Anglo-Norwegian Fisheries case* highlights the relevance of lack of protests with particular clarity, see ICJ Reports 1951, 136–139. For a comprehensive account of jurisprudence see Breutz (1997), 141–160.

[184] See Ministerial Declaration, 24 September 1999, available at http://www.g77.org/Docs/Decl1999.htm (para. 69).

[185] Cf. UN Doc. S/1999/216. [186] See above, references in footnote 88.

[187] See above, text accompanying footnote 80.

practice is dominated by political, rather than legal, considerations. In legal terms, it might be argued that although States, in the absence of individual injury, have disregarded international law frequently, they have not claimed a right to do so. Practice, while arguably settled enough, would not be 'accepted as law', i.e. would not be accompanied by the required *opinio juris*.[188]

In order to evaluate this fourth counter-argument, it is necessary briefly to address the two different components of general international law. Both practice and *opinio juris* have so far deliberately been addressed together. This approach is based on the assumption that in the absence of specific indications to the contrary, the conduct of States will be based on an accompanying legal conviction; *opinio juris* thus can usually be inferred from State practice.[189] The fourth counter-argument raises the question whether international practice in the field of countermeasures bears out this assumption. Two factors might be said to contradict it.

First, doubts would quite clearly be justified if the responding States had conceded that their conduct was not justified in legal terms. The United Kingdom's conduct during the Kosovo crisis indeed seems to point in this direction. As has been stated above, the British Foreign Secretary, justifying the flight ban imposed during the Kosovo crisis, stated that '*on moral and political grounds*', Yugoslavia had forfeited its rights under the British–Yugoslavian aviation treaty, while conspicuously omitting any reference to international law.[190] On the other hand, the survey also shows that this form of conduct is exceptional. No similar disclaimer was made regarding Yugoslavia's rights under customary international law, which the United Kingdom was prepared to disregard when supporting the European freezing order. Nor is there evidence suggesting that – to take but two examples – the United

[188] Cf. e.g. the remarks by the ILC's Special Rapporteur, summarised in the ILC Report 2000, UN Doc. A/55/10, para. 356. For the quotation cf. *North Sea Continental Shelf case*, ICJ Reports 1969, 44 (para. 77); for a succinct discussion of the role of *opinio juris* Bernhardt (1992), 899–900.

[189] See Judge Tanaka's dissent in the *North Sea Continental Shelf case*, ICJ Reports 1969, 176; Lauterpacht (1958), 380; Dahm/Delbrück/Wolfrum (1989), 60; Akehurst/Malanczuk (1997), 44; similarly Kirgis (1987), 149. Brownlie (2003), 8–9, notes that in the majority of cases, the ICJ has followed this approach. For further judicial support see e.g. *Gulf of Maine case*, ICJ Reports 1984, 293–294 and 299 (paras. 91–93, 111); *Anglo-Norwegian Fisheries case*, ICJ Reports 1951, 128; *Barcelona Traction case*, ICJ Reports 1970, 42 (para. 70).

[190] Cf. above, footnote 125.

Kingdom's decisions to freeze Iraqi or Zimbabwean assets gave rise to similar qualms. Finally, other States, during the Kosovo crisis as well as in the other instances discussed above, have not qualified their position either. All this suggests that the United Kingdom's above-quoted statement cannot be generalised.

Secondly, it might also be argued that practice was dominated by political motives - hence, for example, the frequent countermeasures, by western States, against the Soviet Union during the 1980s.[191] In response, it must be clarified that politically motivated conduct does not necessarily lack *opinio juris*. On the contrary, as has been stated above, a State's decision to adopt countermeasures will inevitably involve non-legal considerations. For practice to be legally irrelevant, it would have to be shown that it is not only politically motivated, but that the political motives have replaced the legal assessment.[192] This, however, does not seem to have been the case. In the cases addressed above, western States publicly condemned previous breaches of international law - often specifically referring to, for example, the freedom of expression and association (as during the Polish crisis of 1981–1982) or the prohibition against the use of force (after the shooting down of the Korean aircraft in 1983) - and claimed to act in defence of international law. While their decision to resort to countermeasures (as opposed to other forms of response) might have been influenced by political considerations, their assessment of the underlying dispute thus was legally relevant.

To sum up, neither aspect of the fourth counter-argument is ultimately convincing. Only in one single case has a State publicly relied on political and moral, rather than legal, considerations. In other cases, politically motivated decisions to take countermeasures were based on a legal assessment of the situation. On balance, States responding against countermeasures considered their conduct to be accepted by law; practice thus does not lack the required *opinio juris*.

[191] Cf. e.g. the views of ILC members summarised in the ILC Report 2000, UN Doc. A/55/10, para. 367.

[192] The Court's language has at times been misleading, notably its pronouncement in the *Asylum case*, where it distinguished legally relevant conduct from conduct influenced by 'considerations of political expediency' (ICJ Reports 1951, 277). Despite this use of language, the Court, when interpreting customary international law, has not shied away from taking account of politically motivated statements. More generally, Brownlie (2003), 6, and Ferrari Bravo (1985), 271–273, list 'policy statements' among the most relevant manifestations of State practice.

The requirement of collective action Finally, it is necessary at least briefly to address a fifth argument often advanced in the literature. Pursuant to many commentators, in order to limit the risks of abuse, the right to take countermeasures should be restricted to conduct of groups of States.[193] It is not always very clear whether this plea for collective action is advanced *de lege ferenda*, or intended to form a separate condition limiting the exercise of the right. In the former case, one might readily agree that conduct by groups of States would be less likely to be qualified as 'mob violence' or 'vigilantism',[194] and therefore preferable. However, the real question is not whether international law *should* incorporate a requirement of collective conduct, but whether practice suggests that it actually *does*. This cannot simply be presumed: as has been stressed, obligations *erga omnes* do not necessarily require enforcement by groups of States or even the international community as a whole.[195] More importantly, the above survey suggests that a requirement of collective action has not been accepted in international practice. While most countermeasures have been taken by groups of States, there is no general pattern suggesting that only collective conduct was considered justified. Not only are there instances in which one country alone responded by way of countermeasure.[196] Moreover, different countries often acted independently of each other rather than on the basis of a collective decision-making process. If, nevertheless, countermeasures were usually taken by groups of States, this may reflect the growing internationalisation of foreign policies, or be due to a shared perception of wrongful conduct. There is, however, little evidence to suggest that States should have accepted a legal requirement of collective action. Popular as it is in academic writings, the fifth argument thus is not sustained by international practice.

193 See e.g. Oellers-Frahm (1992), 34–35; Rosenstock (1994), 333; Sachariew (1988), 280 and 284; Graefrath (1989), 166; similarly Frowein (1983), 258–259. A similar position had been taken by Special Rapporteur Riphagen, see his draft articles 6 and 9, YbILC 1984, Vol. II/1, 3; and already *id.*, YbILC 1980, Vol. II/1, 121–122 (paras. 68–73); YbILC 1982, Vol. II/1, 45 (paras. 140–141); YbILC 1983, Vol. II/1, 12–13 (paras. 65–67). Cf. also para. 12 of the ILC's commentary to draft article 30 of the first reading text, YbILC 1979, Vol. II/2, 118–119.

194 Cf. Marek (1978–1979), 481; McCaffrey (1989), 244.

195 See above, section 5.2.3, and Introduction to this chapter.

196 See e.g. the Dutch-Surinamese dispute of 1982 or the United States' reaction against the Soviet Union in the wake of the Polish crisis of 1981–1982.

Interim conclusion To sum up, none of the five counter-arguments therefore is ultimately convincing. It must be conceded that each of them points to inconsistencies and uncertainties in the practice of States. Taken together, they might want a more cautious assessment of international practice than the one given above, by way of preliminary conclusions.[197] Even though, the main features of that assessment remain unaffected. In a remarkable number of cases, States not individually injured have taken countermeasures against systematic or large-scale breaches of international law. Obligations whose breach has prompted these responses either belong to the agreed core of the obligations *erga omnes* or count among the most likely candidates. State practice therefore confirms and refines the results of the above approach to identifying obligations *erga omnes.* Contrary to the arguments made by commentators, practice is neither exclusively dominated by western States nor too selective nor less supportive of a requirement of collective action. Finally, States resorting to countermeasures have hardly ever denied the legal relevance of their conduct. In short, practice provides strong support for the view that even in the absence of individual injury, States are entitled to respond to serious breaches of obligations *erga omnes.* It is in the light of this assessment that governments' comments on the ILC's work will be analysed in the following.

6.2.2 *Governments' comments on the ILC's work on State responsibility*

The comments by government on the ILC's work on State responsibility provide a considerable amount of further evidence and help clarify some issues left unaddressed in the preceding section. Very often, these comments have had a decisive influence on the eventual content of the ILC's text. As has been stressed already, pressure by governments was one of the reasons eventually leading the ILC to adopt article 54 ASR, which deliberately leaves open the question of countermeasures in response to *erga omnes* violations.[198] What has so far not been said is that for the ILC, this decision marked a clear departure from the position taken only one year earlier. Unlike the eventual provision, article 54 of the provisional set of draft articles adopted, after much discussion, in 2000 ('article 54 [2000]') had expressly recognised a right of all States to take countermeasures in response to serious breaches of obligations *erga omnes*. The relevant statements, which prompted the ILC to alter its

[197] See above, pp. 230–231. [198] See above, Introduction (to this chapter).

text in the last minute,[199] will be assessed in the following. They are, however, only part of the overall picture. In fact, already during the first reading of the ILCs work, governments had commented on the question of countermeasures in the general interest. Although most of these comments did not directly address obligations *erga omnes*, but were made in the context of debates about international crimes in the sense of former draft article 19, they are relevant to the present study: as shown above, under the ILC's approach, an international crime presupposed a serious breach of an obligations *erga omnes*.[200] Before focusing on the drafting history of article 54 ASR, the relevant first reading comments will therefore briefly be evaluated.

6.2.2.a Comments made during the first reading

Ever since the ILC's recognition of the concept in 1976, it was discussed whether international crimes in the sense of former draft article 19 should entail a right of all States to resort to countermeasures.[201] Since the ILC had not yet begun to spell out the legal regime applicable to international crimes, governments were initially unable to comment on any specific draft provisions. Furthermore, debates were overshadowed by the more fundamental disagreement about draft article 19 as such, which often prevented a meaningful debate about means of responding against breaches.[202] As a result of both factors, most governments were content to affirm that breaches in the sense of draft article 19 involved responsibility *vis-à-vis* all other States.[203] Whether this meant that all

199 Koskenniemi (2001), 341, speaks of 'a last-ditch compromise'.

200 See above, section 4.2.2.b (text accompanying footnotes 149–151).

201 The relevant debates are recapitulated by Spinedi (1989), 64–77.

202 This does not mean that both questions were inextricably linked. Indeed, some governments opposed to the concept of crimes seemed to accept that States not individually injured could exercise right of protection; see UN Doc. A/C.6/37/SR.46, para. 29 (Portugal); UN Doc. A/C.6/37/SR.48, para. 9 (Australia); UN Doc. A/C.6/37/SR.52, para. 22 (United States). Conversely, at least two governments supporting the concept denied that crimes would trigger any rights of protection of individual States; see the comments by Sweden and Madagascar, UN Doc. A/C.6/37/SR.41, para. 12; UN Doc. A/C.6/37/SR.46, para. 117.

203 For early support of this thesis see e.g. the observations by Egypt, UN Doc. A/C.6./31/SR.30, para. 76–78; the Netherlands, UN Doc. A/C.6/31/SR.22, para. 5; or Somalia, UN Doc. A/C.6/31/SR.31, para. 15. Cf. further Spinedi (1989), 72–73 (her footnote 232) and Sicilianos (1990), 169–170 (his notes 379 and 381). As Spinedi (1989), 73, has pointed out, this position was accepted even by States that initially had remained opposed to the notion of crimes, such as France or Greece (cf. UN Doc. A/C.6/37/SR.38, para. 13; and UN Doc. A/C.6/SR.40, paras. 45 and 47).

States could take countermeasures in order to implement responsibility was another question, usually left open.

Some governments, however, did address it. While not unanimous, their statements, on balance, support the view that in the case of a crime, all States – irrespective of individual injury and any previous collective decision – could take countermeasures. Japan was one of the few governments unequivocally rejecting the idea.[204] On the other hand, Indonesia, Sri Lanka, the Netherlands, and the (then) two German States expressly supported a general right to take countermeasures in response to crimes;[205] more cautiously phrased statements by other States at least point in the same direction.[206] To Indonesia, the situation seemed particularly clear; hence its succinct statement that in the case of a crime 'an injured State [defined as a State individually injured] can take reprisals, and the other States can do the same.'[207] Finally, the United States' position deserves to be mentioned, as it shows that not all countries rejecting the concept of crimes were necessarily opposed to countermeasures in the general interest. Strongly condemning all attempts to criminalise international responsibility, the US government, during the General Assembly's 39th session, invited the ILC to clarify under which circumstances States not individually injured could respond to international wrongs by means of unilateral countermeasure.[208] This in turn seems to imply that such circumstances could exist.

The ILC's first reading text, eventually adopted in 1996, went along with these proposals. Although omitting any reference to obligations *erga omnes*, draft article 40 [1996] put forward a very broad notion of injury, and, in para. 3, expressly provided that ' "injured State" means, if the internationally wrongful act constitutes an international crime, all other States.'[209] More importantly, article 47 recognised, without

[204] UN Doc. A/C.6/31/SR.21, para. 8 (stressing the risk of abuse).

[205] See UN Doc. A/C.6./31/SR.30, para. 33 (Indonesia); UN Doc. A/C.6./31/SR.31, para. 15 (Sri Lanka) (specifically citing the right of self-determination of peoples); UN Doc. A/C.6./31/SR.22, para. 5 (Netherlands); YbILC 1981, Vol. II/1, 75 and UN Doc. A/C.6./35/SR.45, para. 11 (Federal Republic of Germany); and UN Doc. A/C.6./41/SR.36, para. 45 (German Democratic Republic).

[206] See e.g. UN Doc. A/C.6/39/SR.42, para. 3 (Soviet Union); UN Doc. A/C.6/40/SR.24, para. 37 (Jamaica); UN Doc. A/C.6/40/SR.24, para. 89 (Paraguay). For further references see Sicilianos (1990), 171 (his note 389).

[207] UN Doc. A/C.6./31/SR.30, para. 33 (Indonesia).

[208] UN Doc. A/C.6/SR.42, para. 10.

[209] Unfortunately, the commentary to that provision is of little explanatory value, merely asserting that 'it is clear from the very wording of article 19 of part 1 of the draft articles that, in the first instance, all States other than the author State are to be considered "injured States"'; YbILC 1985, Vol. II/2, 27 (para. 26).

further restriction, the right of all injured States to respond to international wrongful acts by way of countermeasure.[210]

Although the first reading text was the subject of extensive scrutiny,[211] very few States opposed the substance of this regulation. Those that criticised it did so largely because they were generally hostile to the notion of crimes,[212] or because they objected to the unitary concept of injury that article 40 [1996] enshrined.[213] Only three countries specifically warned against recognising a right of all States to adopt countermeasures in response to international crimes.[214] In contrast, a considerable number of other States, either directly or in a general way, endorsed the rules on countermeasures. Ireland – which rejected the concept of crimes – even warned that the regime of countermeasures should not 'unduly restrict a State's ability to take effective countermeasures in respect of certain wrongful acts involving obligations *erga omnes*, for example human rights.'[215] To sum up, governments' first reading comments do not settle matters, but refine the results of the previous analysis. As appears from both their express comments, and from the relative absence of protests against articles 40, para. 3, and 47 of the 1996 text, the majority of governments seemed prepared to recognise a right of all States to take countermeasures in response to those serious breaches of obligations *erga omnes* that amounted to an international crime. Governments' comments therefore confirm the above discussion in that (i) States, in the absence of individual injury, can take countermeasures in the general interest, but (ii) can do so only in the case of serious breaches of particularly important obligations.

210 As noted by Crawford, it is therefore incorrect to state that the first reading text left open the question of countermeasures in the general interest (Third Report, para. 390; but contrast Dzida (1997), 267). For further discussion of articles 40 and 47 [1996] see e.g. Bederman (1998), 291; von Trautmannsdorff (1998), 211; Kawasaki (2000), 17; Crawford (2000), 27.

211 The concept of crimes in particular attracted extensive comments; see UN Doc. A/CN.4/488, 50–66, 105–106, 133–141; and UN Doc. A/CN.4/488, Add. 1, 5–6; UN Doc. A/CN.4/488/Add. 2, 3–6; UN Doc. A/CN.4/492, 8–9. Cf. further the analysis in Crawford's First Report, UN Doc. A/CN.4/490, Add. 1, 6–9.

212 See e.g. UN Doc. A/CN.4./488, 100 (Switzerland); *ibid.*, 101–102 (United States).

213 See e.g. UN Doc. A/CN.4/488, 100 (Germany); *ibid*, 96 (Austria).

214 See UN Doc. A.CN.4/492, 11–12 (Japan); UN Doc. A.CN.4/488, 141 (France); *ibid.*, 138 (Czech Republic).

215 UN Doc. A.CN.4/488, 126.

6.2.2.b Comments made during the second reading

Governments' comments made during the second reading are much more frequent. They have to be seen in the light of the ILC's attempts to overcome the impasse reached over draft article 19. As part of these attempts, the Commission, during its 52nd session (2000), decided to replace the category of crimes with that of 'serious breaches of obligations owed to the international community as a whole', i.e. breaches of obligations *erga omnes* that involve 'a gross or systematic failure ... to fulfil the obligation, risking substantial harm to the fundamental interests protected thereby.'[216] Apart from triggering specific aggravated consequences (listed in draft article 42 [2000]),[217] this category of serious *erga omnes* breaches would have had implications on the regime of countermeasures. Under article 50 [2000], States could, in principle, take countermeasures only if they were individually injured or in response to an interdependent obligation. In two exceptional situations, however, other States could do so as well. First, they could assist an injured State and take countermeasures at its request (article 54, para. 1 [2000]). Secondly, and more importantly, irrespective of any such request, all States could take countermeasures in the case of serious *erga omnes* breaches (article 54, para. 2 [2000]). Especially the latter provision had been very controversial, but eventually met with a 'significant level of approval'.[218]

216 See article 41, para. 2 [2000].

217 These notably included the duty to pay 'damages reflecting the gravity of the breach' (commonly understood to mean exemplary, non-compensatory damages). Under article 42, para. 2 [2000], all other States were obliged not to recognise the situation created by the serious breach, not to render aid or assistance that might help to maintain the situation so created, and to cooperate to bring the breach to an end. During the Commission's 2001 session, the first of these special consequences (the duty to pay exemplary damages) was deleted. For a discussion of the various special consequences attaching to serious breaches, both under the provisional draft adopted in 2000 and the eventual text adopted in 2001, see Sicilianos (2002), 1127; Wyler (2002), 1161; Tams (2002b), 1181; and Gattini (2002), 1201.

218 See ILC Report 2000, UN Doc. A/55/10, paras. 364–373, for a summary of the debates and *ibid.*, para. 385 for the Special Rapporteur's concluding remarks on the subject (referring to draft articles 50A and 50B, on which draft article 54 [2000] was based). While the plenary debates clearly expose the different views, the crucial decision in favour of draft article 54 [2000] was taken by the Commission's Drafting Committee whose debates are not published. The Drafting Committee's considerations were summarised by its Chairman, Giorgio Gaja, in his statement to the plenary, available at http://www.un.org/law/ilc/sessions/52/d_cstate.pdf, at 49–51.

Unlike the relevant provisions of the 1996 draft, article 54 [2000], and especially its second paragraph, prompted a flood of observations by governments, which led the ILC to drop the provision in favour of article 54 ASR in its eventual (enigmatic) form. At least at first glance, this sequence of events seems to suggest that governments had roundly rejected the earlier proposal providing for a right to take countermeasures in response to serious *erga omnes* breaches. Although the explanatory commentary qualifies article 54 ASR as a saving clause, which does not prejudice the future development of the law,[219] the Commission itself supported this interpretation by stressing the 'strong opposition' that article 54 [2000] had provoked among governments.[220] Its Special Rapporteur went considerably further when observing that 'the thrust of Government comments is that article 54 [2000], and especially paragraph 2, has no basis in international law.'[221] This indeed seems to suggest that governments demanded a very cautious approach to the question of countermeasures. However, before jumping to premature conclusions, it is necessary to analyse the actual comments by governments'. Compared to the Special Rapporteur's clear-cut assessment, these present a surprisingly nuanced spectre of views. Quite clearly, a number of governments were unconvinced by article 54 [2000], criticising it as 'destabilizing',[222] arguing against the permissibility of individual (as opposed to collective) responses,[223] or calling for further refinement.[224] In the view of Japan, the most outspoken critic, article 54, para. 2 went 'far beyond the progressive development of international law [and] should be called "innovative" or "revolutionary" development.'[225]

On the other hand, an even larger number of governments did not share that view but, expressly or by implication, accepted that in the

[219] See commentary to article 54 ASR, paras. 6–7; similarly introductory commentary to Part Three, Chapter Two, para. 8.

[220] Cf. the Commission's summary of governments' comments, UN Doc. A/CN.4/513, para. 175, and, more generally, paras. 176, 177 and 181.

[221] Crawford, Fourth Report, UN Doc. A/CN.4/517, para. 72.

[222] See UN Doc. A/C.6/55, SR.15, para. 25 (Israel); and similarly *ibid.*, para. 63 (Botswana); UN Doc. A/CN.4/515, 89 (United Kingdom); *ibid.*, para. 69 (China).

[223] See UN Doc. A/CN.4/515, Add. 1, 9–12 (Mexico); UN Doc. A/C.6/SR.15, para. 17 (Iran); UN Doc. A/C.6/SR.18, para. 59 (Cuba); UN Doc. A/C.6/SR.17, para. 85; similarly UN Doc. A/CN.4/515, Add. 2, 18–19 (Poland) (but contrast the Polish statement cited below, footnote 231).

[224] UN Doc. A/C.6/SR.18, para. 5 (Algeria); UN Doc. A/C.6/SR.18, para. 17 (Jordan); UN Doc. A/CN.4/515, 89 (Korea).

[225] UN Doc. A/CN.4/515, 89.

case of serious breaches of obligations *erga omnes*, all States could resort to countermeasures. As for express support, France fully accepted article 54, para. 2 [2000] and even proposed to strengthen the position of responding States under article 54, para. 1 [2000].[226] New Zealand considered article 54 [2000] to be 'a logical extension' of the recognition of a general legal interests of all States in the observance of obligations *erga omnes*,[227] whereas Austria,[228] Italy,[229] and Costa Rica[230] suggested minor modifications while otherwise accepting the basic idea that all States could respond to serious *erga omnes* breaches by way of countermeasure.[231] A number of other States - including Spain, Bahrain, Australia, Chile, Slovenia, and South Africa (speaking on behalf of the 14 SADC members) – endorsed the rules on countermeasures adopted in 2000 (including article 54 [2000]) in a general way.[232] Finally, the Netherlands, Argentina and Brazil recognised the innovative nature of that provision, but seemed prepared to accept it.[233]

Given these comments, the Special Rapporteur's summary of comments quoted above seems rather difficult to sustain. While article 54 [2000] undoubtedly proved controversial, it was by no means generally rejected. Given the need for a quick finalisation of its work on State responsibility, the ILC understandably decided to modify its position. Contrary to what might have been suggested by the sequence of events, or by the above-quoted remarks, this decision however had not been demanded by a majority of States.

For present purposes, this (re-)evaluation is of crucial relevance. The drafting history of article 54 ASR suggests that a provision expressly recognising a right of all States to respond to *erga omnes* breaches by way of countermeasure does not, at present, enjoy the universal support of

[226] UN Doc. A/CN.4/515, 88. [227] UN Doc. A/C.6/SR.16 59.

[228] UN Doc. A/CN.4/515, 88–89 and UN Doc. A/C.6/SR.17, para. 76 (stressing the need for previous request(s) by the State(s) taking countermeasures).

[229] UN Doc. A/C.6/SR.16, 73 (seeking clarification about the relation between paras. 1 and 2 of article 54 [2000]).

[230] UN Doc. A/C.6/SR.17, 99–100 (wondering whether the requirement of prior negotiation should apply in case of serious breaches of obligations *erga omnes*).

[231] In addition, Poland, in apparent contradiction with its statement quoted above (footnote 223) also seemed to accept that all States could take countermeasures to secure the cessation (as opposed to reparation) of serious *erga omnes* breaches.

[232] See UN Doc. A/C.6/SR.16, 63; UN Doc. A/C.6/SR.19, 163; UN Doc. A/C.6/SR.16, 80; UN Doc. A/C.6/SR.17, 97; UN Doc. A/C.6/SR.18, 124; UN Doc. A/C.6/SR.14, 2 respectively.

[233] See UN Doc. A/CN.4/515, 87; UN Doc. A/CN.4/515/Add. 3, 9; A/C.6/SR.18, 143 respectively.

States. On the other hand, it is equally relevant to note that to the majority of States, such a provision would have been acceptable.

6.2.2.c Interim conclusions

Governments' comments on the ILC's work provide a wealth of evidence, but no conclusive guidance. One aspect they do confirm is that if at all, a general right to take countermeasures would be restricted to serious breaches of obligations *erga omnes*. During the first reading, this followed from the very definition of crimes in the sense of draft article 19, which presupposed a serious breach of an obligation *erga omnes*. During the second reading, the requirement was expressly included in draft article 41 [2000] and thus would have applied to countermeasures under draft article 54 [2000]. Clearly, it is difficult to say in the abstract under which circumstances a breach qualifies as (sufficiently) serious. The mere reference to seriousness does not allow for a clear-cut differentiation between breaches triggering a right to take countermeasures, and breaches remaining below the required threshold; accordingly, it has been criticised as imprecise.[234] However, on balance, the restriction to serious breaches, as well as the ILC's definition of serious breaches as a 'systematic or gross failure ... to fulfil [an] obligation',[235] did not raise major concerns. Experience during the ILC's work on State responsibility thus confirms the results gained from an analysis of State practice, namely that States cannot take countermeasures in response to minor or isolated breaches of obligations *erga omnes*.[236] Since they have, in practice, only responded to large-scale and systematic breaches, the lower limit of the threshold thus remains to be assessed in future. Notwithstanding this uncertainty, the restriction to serious *erga omnes* breaches, while conceptually unsatisfactory, seemed broadly acceptable to States.

In contrast, it has remained a matter of considerable controversy *whether* States can take countermeasures in response to such serious *erga omnes* breaches. It is interesting to observe that governments' views, as expressed in observations on the ILC's work, often markedly differed from their actual conduct in specific disputes. Given the preponderance

234 See Crawford, Fourth Report, para. 48, for references.

235 See article 40, para. 2 ASR; similarly draft article 41, para. 2 [2000]. For further attempts to clarify the meaning of that phrase see paras. 7-8 of the ILC's commentary to article 40 ASR; Wyler (2002), 1157-1159; Salmon (2001), 311.

236 See commentary to article 40 ASR, para. 7. For an analysis of State practice see above, section 6.2.1.

(though not exclusivity) of western practice, it comes as a surprise that at least some western States (such as Japan or the United Kingdom) were strongly opposed to draft articles 40, para. 3, and 47 [1996] of the first reading text or draft article 54 [2000]. On the other hand, reactions among non-western States were considerably more favourable than comments about the 'western' character of practice might have suggested.

As regards the actual division of views, a majority of governments commenting on the ILC's work seemed prepared to recognise a right of all States to respond to serious breaches of obligations *erga omnes*. As regards first reading comments, this view was shared by a rather clear majority; however, the number of governments expressing a view on the matter remained limited. During the second reading, some States strongly objected to, and eventually prevented the adoption of, draft article 54 [2000]. Nevertheless, the discussion has shown that a majority of governments would have been prepared to accept that provision.

6.3 Concluding observations

Whether States are, under present-day international law, entitled to resort to countermeasures against breaches of obligations *erga omnes* is a problem of considerable complexity. The preceding analysis shows that the problem has not only generated a wealth of discussion in the literature, but is also the object of much international practice. Debates preceding the adoption of article 54 ASR show both the practical relevance of the topic and the difficulty of securing universal agreement. Insofar as the Commission's eventual decision has prevented a further polarisation of views and paved the way for the conclusion of an important codification effort, the adoption of article 54 ASR in its eventual form may present an acceptable compromise. The question remains whether on the basis of present-day international law, the Commission could have said more than article 54 ASR says. It is submitted that it could.

Although of course not free from ambiguity, the evidence discussed in the preceding sections would seem to suggest that individual States are entitled to take countermeasures in response to systematic or large-scale breaches of obligations *erga omnes*. Admittedly, the ICJ's jurisprudence does little to sustain this view; as has been shown in section 6.1, it is inconclusive, and neither supports nor excludes it. As regards governments' comments on the ILC's work on State responsibility, the picture is ambiguous, but more favourable. On the one hand, the recent debates about article 54 [2000] show that the position does not command universal support, and that a number of governments are not prepared to recognise a right to take countermeasures in express form. It has also been shown that, both during the first and second reading of the Commission's work, a majority of governments expressed support for the substance of article 54 [2000]. Although some of the 'official' summaries of views quoted above may convey a rather different impression, governments' comments, on balance, support rather than undermine the existence of a right to take countermeasures. Finally, this view is strongly supported by actual conduct of States in specific disputes involving serious breaches of obligations *erga omnes*. As has been shown, States not individually injured have asserted and exercised a right to take countermeasures in a variety of instances. Contrary to views held by commentators, practice is neither exclusively western, nor lacks the required *opinio juris*, nor indeed is too selective. In the light of this evidence, it seems justified to conclude that present-day international law recognises a right of all States, irrespective of individual injury, to take countermeasures in response to large-scale or systematic breaches of obligations *erga omnes*.

This conclusion of course has important consequences on the legal regime governing obligations *erga omnes*. On the one hand, it increases the likelihood that States responsible for *erga omnes* breaches, even in the absence of centralised reactions, will be forced to comply with their international obligations. On the other hand, States that invoke the *erga omnes* concept in bad faith can claim to act 'under the banner of law'.[237] Just as within the bilateral inter-State relations, agreement on conditions governing resort to countermeasures minimises this problem, but does not exclude it. In the case of obligations *erga omnes*, the restriction to systematic and large-scale breaches provides some further protection; comments on the ILC's work suggest that States view it as a workable criterion.

Nothwithstanding these restrictions, it cannot be denied that an international system recognising a right to take countermeasures in the general interest is more open to abuse. The preceding discussion has attempted to show that the recognition of this right is not an automatic consequence of the *erga omnes* concept, but instead follows from an analysis of international practice and governments' comments.

[237] Weil (1983), 433.

Judging from their own conduct, States thus seem prepared to accept the increased risk of abuse in exchange for the increased possibility of responding against particularly serious wrongful conduct. The preceding survey also shows that countermeasures in the general interest are taken cautiously, and the hopes and fears with which the topic is approached in the literature are exaggerated. Political considerations rather than legal conditions thus seem to provide the most effective guarantee against abuse.

7 *Erga omnes* enforcement rights and competing enforcement mechanisms

The preceding chapters have shown that States can respond to breaches of obligations *erga omnes* by instituting ICJ proceedings and, if the breach is of a serious character, by resorting to countermeasures. As discussed in Chapter 4, these *erga omnes* enforcement rights are triggered by breaches of customary international law, on which the preceding analysis has consequently focused. The present chapter moves beyond customary international law and assesses whether the enforcement of obligations *erga omnes* could be affected by treaties. This could notably be the case if treaties protect the same interests as the *erga omnes* concept but confer upon States rights of protection that are substantially different from those deriving from the *erga omnes* concept. Where this is so, the State responsible for the wrongful conduct apparently incurs responsibility for the treaty breach *and* the breach of customary international law. State parties to the treaty in question may thus hold two sets of enforcement rights: as members of the international community, they have enforcement rights based on the *erga omnes* concept; as treaty parties, they have enforcement rights based on the treaty. The present section analyses the relation between these distinct sets of enforcement rights. More particularly, it inquires whether treaty-based enforcement systems *complement* or *exclude* the right of States to institute ICJ proceedings or take countermeasures in response to (serious) *erga omnes* breaches. Since the rules governing responses against *erga omnes* breaches are not peremptory in character, nothing would stop States from opting for a different regime.

Whether they actually have done so has been much discussed. Although there is no shortage of extreme views,[1] both basic positions

[1] For a discussion see in particular below, section 7.2.1.

on the issue – exclusivity and complementarity – seem at least plausible. The argument in favour of treaty exclusivity can be formulated as a simple question: why should States agree on complex treaty procedures if these could always be circumvented by recourse to extra-conventional means of enforcement? On the other hand, the crucial argument supporting complementarity seems equally plausible. If one accepts that treaties aim at strengthening the law (by clarifying its content, developing it, establishing systems of compliance control, etc.), why should they take away existing means of enforcement and replace them by treaty-based enforcement regimes, which – as will be shown – are often poorly developed?

Refined versions of these arguments have been advanced ever since treaties began to establish enforcement regimes. As regards the specific conflict relevant here, academic debate has largely centred on the relation between treaties and the customary right to take countermeasures, a question dominated by concepts such as *lex specialis* and self-contained regimes. This focus, however, is problematic in a number of respects. As regards rights of response, the focus on countermeasures is unduly restrictive. There is no reason why treaties could not affect other enforcement rights. It is therefore necessary to look beyond countermeasures and to analyse conflicts between treaty-based enforcement systems and the right of State to institute *erga omnes* proceedings before the ICJ.

As regards methodology, it is submitted that the importance of notions such as *lex specialis* and self-contained regimes is often overstated. Both tend to obscure the fact that what is called for is first and foremost a thorough interpretation of the two conflicting enforcement rules. *Lex specialis derogat legi generali* – the idea that the more special norm prevails over the more general – is one factor influencing this interpretation, just as is *lex posterior derogat legi priori*. However, as will be shown below, other considerations may equally be relevant. More importantly, neither *lex specialis* nor *lex posterior* constitute categorical rules. Whether States, by agreeing on special (later) rules, intend to derogate from general (earlier) rules, needs to be assessed on a case-by-case basis, having regard to the two conflicting enforcement systems. As counsel in the *Southern Bluefin Tuna case* observed, there is 'no special magic' about *lex specialis* (or *lex posterior*); they are but interpretative tools embodying 'common-sense approach[es]' to the interpretation of competing legal rules.[2]

[2] Statement by Sir Elihu Lauterpacht, *Southern Bluefin Tuna case* (arbitral award), Oral Hearings of 10 May 2000, available at http://www.worldbank.org/icsid/bluefintuna/0510icsi.pdf, at 48.

More problematic is the notion of self-contained regimes. In fact, it may be doubted whether the term is of much help in addressing conflicts between different enforcement mechanisms. Following a literal interpretation, in order to be self-contained, a regime would have to be 'independent of external means'.[3] Commentators criticising the notion have correctly observed that if that test were taken seriously, no treaty would qualify:[4] even comprehensive treaty regimes depend on external rules, not contained in the treaty, in order to address problems of interpretation, attribution, or consequences of breach.[5] In contrast, courts and commentators qualifying treaties as 'self-contained regimes' usually do not assert independence in a comprehensive sense. All that is claimed is that a particular treaty is exclusive in one particular respect – for example by excluding extra-conventional means of responding against treaty breaches.[6] Whether this is a particularly apposite use of the term 'self-contained regime' need not be discussed here. Suffice it to say that self-contained regimes in this second, more modest, sense are hardly different from *leges speciales* derogating from extra-conventional rules of enforcement. It follows that the matter again is one of interpreting two competing rules.

In the light of these considerations, the present chapter will refrain from discussing whether a particular treaty is a *lex specialis* or a *lex posterior*, and will not enter into the misleading terrain of self-contained regimes. Instead, it will assess whether by agreeing on specific treaty enforcement regimes, States have 'contracted out'[7] of *erga omnes*

[3] See *Shorter Oxford Dictionary* (1973), Vol. II, 1933 ('self-contained').

[4] Simma (1985), 111; Marschik (1997), 170–181; Pauwelyn (2003), 35–40; Sicilianos (1990), 34; Zemanek (1987), 41; Arangio-Ruiz, Fourth Report, para. 113.

[5] To take but one example, the jurisprudence of Panels and Appellate Body clearly disproves the (still popular) claims that WTO law was self-contained in this comprehensive sense. While WTO members might have contracted out of certain enforcement rights (such as the right to take unilateral countermeasures), or agreed on different (more future-looking) consequences of international wrongs, Panels and Appellate Body have applied extra-conventional rules with respect to areas as diverse as treaty interpretation, burden of proof, or *compétence de la compétence*; see respectively *US – Hot-Rolled Steel*, *WT/DS184/AB/R*, para. 60; *US – Shirts and Blouses*, WT/DS33/AB/R, 19; *US – Anti-Dumping Act of 1916*, WT/DS136/AB/R, note 30. For a comprehensive discussion with many further referencess cf. Pauwelyn (2003), 207–212.

[6] See ICJ Reports, 40 (para. 86); and the following discussion about the alleged 'self-contained nature' of diplomatic law. It is crucial to note that the Court merely stated that the Diplomatic Convention exhaustively listed the means by which a receiving State could react against abuses of diplomatic privileges; see Marschik (1997), 106–107. For criticism of that more modest claim see Zemanek (1987), 40; Simma (1985), 118–123; Baarnholm (1994), 39.

[7] Pauwelyn (2003), 212.

enforcement rights. By way of caveat, it should be stated at the outset that it focuses on the legal rules applicable *prior to the taking of enforcement measures*. It will thus be inquired whether treaty mechanisms preclude States from exercising their *erga omnes* enforcement rights altogether. In contrast, no attempt is made to assess whether States that have opted to pursue treaty-based dispute settlement procedures remain free to fall back on extra-conventional means of law enforcement.[8] This question (frequently addressed with respect to countermeasures *sub judice*) depends on the circumstances of the concrete case, notably the good or bad faith of the State against which treaty-based dispute settlement is commenced;[9] it is thus difficult to assess in the abstract. This limited focus means that although *erga omnes* enforcement rights should be excluded, a fall-back might be permitted if the target State is acting in bad faith.

Even when focusing on the situation prior to the taking of enforcement measures, the relation between *erga omnes* and treaty enforcement rights depends less on abstract principle than on a detailed examination of specific conflicts. When addressing it, it is necessary to interpret the relevant legal rules conferring enforcement rights, and to assess whether States, when agreeing on treaty enforcement mechanisms, sought to exclude ICJ proceedings, countermeasures, or both. This interpretation may of course be guided by international practice and jurisprudence. As regards the latter, it has already been stated that a number of ICJ pronouncements are said to address the relation between treaties and *erga omnes* enforcement rights.[10] Furthermore, other decisions, addressing conflicts between other competing enforcement mechanisms may also be helpful. First and foremost, however, it requires a comparison between enforcement rights conferred by treaty and those deriving from the *erga omnes* concept. Section 7.1 of the present chapter therefore identifies the main areas of divergence, and singles out three specific types of conflicts. Section 7.2 analyses these specific conflicts, and thereby clarifies whether the enforcement of obligations *erga omnes* is affected by treaties.

[8] On this question see article 52, para. 3b ASR and paras. 7–9 of the ILC's commentary; Dzida (1997), 162–170; Zoller (1984), 122–124.

[9] See e.g. article 52, para. 4 ASR.

[10] See above, sections 5.2.4 and 5.2.5.d.

7.1 Identifying areas of conflict

Competition between different enforcement mechanisms is only problematic if the two regimes are in conflict.[11] Conflicts exist if a specific subject matter is governed by two or more legal rules (overlap), and if these legal rules provide for different rights of enforcement (difference). Applied to the present context, this means that *erga omnes* enforcement rights can only be affected by treaty-based enforcement regimes if and where (i) interests safeguarded by obligations *erga omnes* are also protected by treaty, and (ii) the breach of this other obligation triggers rights of response that differ from *erga omnes* enforcement rights. In order to identify areas of conflict, both aspects need to be addressed.

7.1.1 Overlapping legal rules

As regards the first question, the situation is relatively straightforward. Although obligations *erga omnes* derive from customary international law, they are not independent from treaties. One aspect of this interrelation has been discussed already. It has been shown that affirmation in treaties may indicate that an obligation is considered to be important, and thus indirectly help establish its *erga omnes* status.[12] For the purposes of the present section, a related aspect is relevant: it must be assessed whether obligations that have acquired *erga omnes* status are actually protected by treaties. Uncertainties about the precise scope of the *erga omnes* concept of course complicate this assessment. Difficulties however need not be overstated. Given the proliferation of treaties codifying questions of general interest, the overlap of different legal rules has become, as the Arbitral Tribunal in the *Southern Bluefin Tuna case* noted, a 'commonplace of international law and State practice'.[13] This is particularly so with respect to the basic values protected by the *erga omnes* concept. It is therefore almost inevitable that an obligation *erga omnes* will also be protected by one or more treaties.

The point may be illustrated by reference to the five examples of obligations *erga omnes* expressly recognised in the Court's jurisprudence, all of which are protected by major universal agreements. Acts of aggression not only violate an obligation *erga omnes*, but also article 2,

[11] Cf. also commentary to article 55 ASR, para. 4. Courts and tribunals have often found that two overlapping provisions were not incompatible, and that there was no need to consider the question of derogation; cf. only the *Neumeister case*, ECHR, Ser. A, No. 17 (1974), 12–14 (paras. 28–31).

[12] See section 4.2.2.b. [13] *Southern Bluefin Tuna case* (arbitral award), para. 52.

para. 4 UNC (191 State parties); acts of genocide affect article I of the Genocide Convention (134 State parties); disregard for self-determination runs counter to common article 1 CCPR and CESCR (149 and 147 parties); practices of slavery violate articles II and III of the 1926 Slavery Convention (95 parties), article 1 of the 1956 Supplementary Slavery Convention (119 parties), and article 8 CCPR (149 parties); by practising racial discrimination, a State violates its obligations under articles 2 and 3 CERD (169 parties), and possibly the Apartheid Convention (101 parties). In addition, the latter four examples would also be covered by the general obligation, derived from articles 1(3), 55(c), and 56 UNC, to respect human rights.[14] To these universal treaties, one would have to add the various regional human rights conventions (such as the ECHR, ACHR, or the Banjul Charter), which are affected by *erga omnes* breaches in the field of human rights. Beyond that, it is by no means excluded that values protected by obligations *erga omnes* should have been enshrined in lesser-known treaties, such as ILO conventions,[15] defence pacts,[16] or even bilateral FCN treaties.[17]

This brief survey (which could be undertaken with respect to nearly all other candidates of obligations *erga omnes*)[18] suggests that customary obligations *erga omnes* almost inevitably have a conventional counterpart. Without going into a detailed examination, it also seems safe to say the various treaties not only cover the same area of law, but impose upon States obligations that are either identical in scope or further-reaching than the respective customary obligations *erga omnes*.[19] Given the number, and wide acceptance, of the above-mentioned treaties, it is

[14] On this general obligation see Riedel in: Simma (2002a), Article 55(c), MN 24–60; Wolfrum in: Simma (2002a), Article 1, MN 32.

[15] See e.g. ILO Conventions No. 29 and No. 105 (prohibiting forced labour).

[16] See e.g. article 1 NATO Treaty or article 22 of the OAS Charter (both prohibiting the use of force).

[17] See e.g. the FCN treaties between the United States and Iran or the United States and Nicaragua, which were at issue in the *Nicaragua* and *Oil Platforms cases*, and which in view of the applicants excluded the use of force. For the Court's cautious treatment of these claims see e.g. *Oil Platforms case* (Preliminary Objections), ICJ Reports 1996, 803.

[18] For example, torture is protected by CAT, article 7 CCPR, the American and European Anti-Torture Conventions and the three regional human rights conventions (cf. article 3 ECHR, article 5, para. 2 ACHR, article 5 Banjul Charter). Obligations in the field of international humanitarian law would be covered by the comprehensive rules set out in the four Geneva Conventions and Additional Protocols. Given the sheer number of agreements covering questions of environmental law, possible obligations *erga omnes* in that field would also be likely to be covered by treaties.

[19] For example, CERD not only prohibits policies of racial discrimination, but also imposes upon States a positive obligation to take measures aimed at combating racial

thus highly likely that a State violating an obligation *erga omnes* will at the same time be in breach of one, or more, treaty obligations.

7.1.2 *Different enforcement rights*

The overlap between obligations *erga omnes* and treaty law would be relatively unproblematic if it only concerned the substance of legal obligations. However, this is not the case. Instead, nearly all treaties regulating matters that are protected by obligations *erga omnes* contain at least some provisions on enforcement. The multiplication of substantive legal rules thus is paralleled by a proliferation of enforcement mechanisms. It is not the purpose of this study to describe these mechanisms in detail, each of which could, in principle, contract out of *erga omnes* enforcement rights. Instead, differences will be illustrated by focusing on a handful of exemplary treaties. In the light of the above considerations, it seems convenient to restrict the discussion to the major universal treaties that safeguard expressly recognised examples of obligations *erga omnes* (i.e. the UN Charter, the Genocide and Slavery Conventions, CERD, and the CCPR) and the three regional human rights conventions (ECHR, ACHR, Banjul Charter).[20] In order to identify conflicts, it is necessary to first assess how these treaties approach the question of enforcement, and then evaluate to what extent the respective enforcement regimes differ from enforcement rights deriving from the *erga omnes* concept. It is submitted that this analysis identifies the main types of problems and that conflicts with other treaties (not covered) can by solved by way of analogy.

prejudices (article 7). In contrast, the Court has so far only affirmed the *erga omnes* status of the prohibition on racial discrimination.

20 In addition to the treaties mentioned in the text, *erga omnes* breaches in the field of self-determination and racial discrimination are likely to affect obligations under article 1 CESCR and the Apartheid Convention respectively. The latter, however, does not contain any enforcement procedure; there is thus no conflict of enforcement rights. As regards the CESCR, the Committee on Social, Economic and Cultural Rights, established by ECOSOC resolution 1985/17 of 28 May 1985, is competent to receive State reports. However, contrary to the enforcement regime of the CCPR, there is at present no mechanism for inter-State or individual complaints. Since breaches of article 1 CESCR would equally affect article 1 CCPR, it seems justified to focus on this, more developed, enforcement regime. On the Committee on Social, Economic and Cultural Rights see Simma (1991), 75; on the proposals for the establishment of an individual complaints procedure see the comprehensive discussion by Engels (2000).

7.1.2.a Treaty-based systems of enforcement: a survey

Although limited in scope, the present analysis discusses treaties that embody very different approaches to the question of enforcement. Three broad categories can be distinguished.

First, the three regional human rights conventions, CERD, and CCPR establish monitoring bodies competent to safeguard compliance with the respective treaties. Despite considerable differences, all treaties rely on three types of procedures. Under reporting systems,[21] States periodically inform treaty-monitoring bodies about their compliance record; in response treaty bodies can criticise non-compliant States, but have no formal power of decision.[22] In addition, all five treaties establish individual complaint procedures,[23] by which individuals can protest against infringements of their treaty rights. The different procedures vary considerably. Most importantly, while mandatory under the three regional human rights conventions,[24] CERD and CCPR establish optional systems, which only apply in relation to States that have accepted the treaty-monitoring body's competence to receive individual complaints.[25] Furthermore, while individual complaints under the ECHR system (and exceptionally under the ACHR)[26] lead to binding court decisions, the other treaties envisage proceedings before commissions or committees, at the end of which the respective bodies publish formally non-binding reports or

[21] Cf. article 40 CCPR, article 9 CERD, article 52 ECHR, article 42 ACHR, article 62 Banjul Charter. For a survey see Tomuschat (2003), 136–158.

[22] Practice is not uniform. Especially the Human Rights Committee - based on an unduly restrictive interpretation of article 40, para. 4 CCPR, advocated by East European members - traditionally refrained from criticising States failing to comply with their obligations under the CCPR; cf. the controversy between Graefrath (1990), 305–306 on the one hand, and Opsahl (1992), 409–410; Opsahl (1989), 273 on the other. The importance of reporting procedures seems to decrease where systems function effectively (notably under the ECHR), cf. Frowein/Peukert, Article 57, MN 2. For a comparative survey of reporting systems see the different contributions in Klein (1998b).

[23] Terminology varies considerably. For the sake of simpliciy, the different treaty proceedings (labelled communications, petitions, or similar) are referred to here as a 'complaints'.

[24] Cf. article 34 ECHR, article 44 ACHR, article 55 Banjul Charter. Prior to the entry into force of the Eleventh Additional Protocol (in 1998), the ECHR was also based on an optional system (cf. ex-article 25).

[25] Cf. article 14 CERD and the First Optional Protocol to the CCPR.

[26] Individual complaints can reach the American Court of Human Rights if the State concerned has recognised the Court's competence under article 62 ACHR. As of December 2004, 21 States had made the relevant declaration.

views.[27] Finally, all systems provide for inter-State complaint procedures, by which all State parties, irrespective of individual injury, can respond against breaches, and which result in either binding judgments (under the ECHR and exceptionally the ACHR) or reports/views.[28] Optional under CCPR and ACHR, this inter-State complaint procedure is compulsory under CERD, ECHR, and the Banjul Charter. Pursuant to article 22 CERD, States parties to CERD can furthermore institute ICJ proceedings where the treaty-specific means of dispute settlement have failed.[29]

Secondly, the two Slavery Conventions and the Genocide Conventions adopt a much less complex approach to the question of enforcement. Unlike the more recent human rights conventions, they do not establish reporting systems or individual complaints procedures. Instead, as has been stated above,[30] they are early examples of treaties recognising a general right, of all State parties, to institute ICJ proceedings in response to treaty breaches, which can be exercised irrespective of any individual injury.

Thirdly, the UN Charter as a comprehensive framework agreement addresses questions of enforcement only in a rudimentary way. The relevant provisions largely deal with institutional enforcement. Most confer upon Charter organs the power to address specific situations and to make non-binding recommendations.[31] In contrast, Chapter VII UNC

[27] Karl (1994), 109–110; Graefrath (1990), 314; Sands/Mackenzie/Shany (1999), 171, 182, 228–229, 244. This is clearly expressed in the text of the agreements, see e.g. article 13 CERD ('recommendations'), article 50, para. 3 ACHR ('proposals and recommendations'). According to the American Court's judgment in *Loayaza Tamayo*, 19 HRLJ (1998), 203 (para. 80), ACHR parties are obliged to make every effort to apply recommendations contained in final decisions of the American Commission (so-called 'article 51 reports').

It should be noted that the 1998 Optional Protocol to the Banjul Charter, which entered into force in January 2004 has brought about a major reform of the African system of human rights protection. Notably, it will establish an African Court of Human Rights whose judgments are binding and final (cf. article 28, para. 2 of the Protocol). Similar to the ACHR system, individuals do not have access to the Court. However, their complaints can be submitted to it by the Commission or by the State of nationality (see article 5 of the Optional Protocol). For a discussion see Naldi/Magliveras (1998), 431.

[28] Cf. article 33 ECHR, article 45 ACHR, article 47 Banjul Charter, article 11 CERD, article 41 CCPR.

[29] On article 22 CERD cf. already above, section 2.2.1.a. [30] Cf. above, section 2.2.1.a.

[31] See e.g. article 36 UNC (recognising the Security Council's right to recommend measures aimed at the pacific settlement of disputes) or articles 10–14 and 62 UNC (recognising the competence of the General Assembly and ECOSOC to pass non-binding resolutions).

regulates under which circumstances the Security Council can take coercive enforcement action against member States. It is important to note that this specific form of Chapter VII enforcement does not presuppose a prior breach of the law.[32] However, there is no doubt that the Security Council *can* take Chapter VII enforcement action in situations which involve *erga omnes* breaches (such as in the case of aggression or massive human rights violations).[33] By comparison, the Charter is almost silent on enforcement rights of other actors. Article 51 UNC, affirming the inherent right of self-defence against armed attacks and implicitly recognising a right to take non-forcible measures, is the only provision indirectly bearing on decentralised responses by States. As for direct recourse, ECOSOC subsidiary organs have established different procedures for addressing human rights complaints by individuals or other non-State actors. In particular, under ECOSOC resolutions 1235 (1967) and 1503 (1970), the UN Human Rights Commission and its subsidiary organs investigate and examine situations revealing a 'consistent pattern of gross and reliably attested violations of human rights' and can set up country-specific working groups.[34]

7.1.2.b Specific types of conflict

Evidently, the brief survey only presents a very rough sketch of how the different treaties approach the question of enforcement. However, no more than a rough sketch is necessary to clarify the fact that treaties hardly ever confer upon State parties enforcement rights that are identical to those deriving from the *erga omnes* concept. The potential for derogation is thus immense. Three specific types of conflicts between treaty and *erga omnes* enforcement rights can be identified.

Contracting out of decentralised enforcement altogether: First, whereas *erga omnes* breaches trigger enforcement rights of States, many of the treaties provide for enforcement by non-State actors. Under a majority of treaties, individuals can lodge complaints against violations of their conventional human rights. In addition, the various reporting systems allow for institutional responses against treaty breaches, while the UN Charter confers upon UN organs the power to respond against breaches.

[32] Cf. Introduction, footnote 23.

[33] For two pertinent examples see e.g. SC Res. 661 (1990) (authorising enforcement measures following the Iraqi invasion against Kuwait), and SC Res. 253 (1968) (condemning the violation, by the Rhodesian regime, of the right of self-determination and international human rights).

[34] See Riedel in: Simma (2002a), Article 68, MN 84–111; Karl (1994), 104–106.

As a first step, it might thus be asked whether by recognising rights of non-State actors, States intended to give up their decentralised enforcement rights altogether.

Contracting out of specific erga omnes *enforcement rights*: Secondly, insofar as decentralised enforcement is concerned, treaties regularly confer upon States rights of response that are very different from those triggered by *erga omnes* breaches. This is particularly evident with respect to the right to take countermeasures, which only article 51 UNC (implicitly) recognises. In all other cases, it has to be analysed whether States intended to contract out of the right to take coutermeasures. The situation is similar with respect to ICJ proceedings. Under five treaties (ECHR, ACHR, Banjul Charter, CERD, CCPR), inter-State disputes are dealt with by treaty-monitoring bodies, while the ICJ has either a subsidiary role (in the case of CERD) or no role at all.

Special factors restricting treaty enforcement: Finally, even where treaties recognise the right to take countermeasures or to institute ICJ proceedings, conflicts cannot be excluded. Article 51 UNC subjects self-defence (including non-forcible responses) to very strict conditions, which might equally apply to countermeasures based on the *erga omnes* concept. Moreover, the right of States to institute ICJ proceedings in response to breaches of the Genocide Convention and the 1926 Slavery Convention may be excluded, if the respondent has registered a reservation against the relevant compromissary clauses.[35]

To sum up, conflicts between *erga omnes* enforcement rights and treaty enforcement systems are the rule rather than the exception. Obligations *erga omnes* are almost inevitably protected by treaties addressing questions of enforcement. The relevant treaties rarely confer upon States the right to take countermeasures or to institute ICJ proceedings. Even where they do, special factors may limit the exercise of the right. Given this factual assessment, it is of vital importance to analyse whether the relevant conflicting treaties contract out of *erga omnes* enforcement rights. This analysis will be undertaken in the next section.

[35] In contrast, article 9 of the 1956 Supplementary Slavery Convention prohibits reservations.

7.2 Addressing conflicts

The preceding survey shows the extent of the problem, and also its complexity. Each of the different conflicts identified at the end of the last section raises specific issues. It is unlikely that the relation between ICJ enforcement and Chapter VII UNC should be governed by the same rules as, for example, the effect of reservations, registered against compromissary clauses, on parallel claims based on customary law. The present section therefore separately inquires whether by entering into any of the relevant treaties, States have (i) contracted out of decentralised enforcement of obligations *erga omnes* altogether, (ii) contracted out of specific *erga omnes* enforcement rights, or (iii) accepted that the exercise of these rights would be subject to further conditions. As will be shown, these three conflicts are governed by very different principles. Each of them, however, needs to be approached in the same way. In line with what has been said above, the fundamental task is to ascertain the intention of States parties to the respective treaty. This will be done according to the normal rules of interpretation, as codified in articles 31–33 VCLT and reflected in international practice and jurisprudence.

7.2.1 Contracting out of decentralised enforcement by States

In a first step, it needs to be analysed whether any of the relevant treaty regimes contracts out of State enforcement measures altogether. As shown above, many treaties indeed envisage enforcement by individuals or institutions. The question is whether their enforcement competence affects the right of States to adopt decentralised responses against breaches.

7.2.1.a Direct recourse by individuals

Treaties providing for direct recourse by individuals pose relatively few problems. It is certainly not inconceivable that treaties should solely, or at least primarily, rely on direct recourse. Article 27 of the ICSID Convention, which precludes States from exercising diplomatic protection in disputes that could be, or are being, submitted to ICSID arbitration, is a well-known example.[36] However, when focusing on treaties

[36] Schreuer (2001), Article 27, MN 6 and 10–21; Shany (2003), 198–199. Article 27, para. 2 preserves the right of States to make use of diplomatic channels in order to facilitate the settlement of the dispute. *E contrario*, both countermeasures and ICJ claims are excluded. As regards the ICJ, see also article 64 of the ICSID Convention (establishing

relevant to the present study, it is difficult to think of any comparable provisions. On the contrary, a quick glance at the text of the agreements suggests that even for treaty breaches (let alone breaches of parallel customary provisions) direct recourse complements rather than excludes enforcement by States. The various individual complaints procedures established under the CCPR, CERD, ECHR, ACHR, and the Banjul Charter exist alongside inter-State procedures, and there is no indication that one form of enforcement is intended to enjoy priority over the other.[37] While the relevant treaties might restrict the permissible forms of decentralised enforcement (a question yet to be addressed), they do not *per se* exclude responses by States.

7.2.1.b Institutional enforcement

As regards institutional enforcement, it is necessary to distinguish State reporting systems under the various human rights agreements from coercive forms of institutional responses available under the UN Charter. As regards the former, it may already be doubted whether the practice of treaty bodies to criticise non-compliance qualifies as an enforcement measure. While possibly influential, the critical comments are not usually directed against concrete breaches, but respond to periodic reports.[38] In any event, reporting systems exist alongside inter-State and individual complaints procedures. Just as individual complaint systems, they therefore plainly do not exclude measures of decentralised enforcement.

More problems arise with respect to institutional responses under the UN Charter, in particular with regard to Security Council enforcement measures under Chapter VII UNC.[39] It seems undisputed that individual States retain their right to respond against breaches if the Council has not considered the matter. In contrast, where the Council is seized of

the Court's jurisdiction). As the *travaux* clarify, this provision cannot be used to undermine the jurisdiction of ICSID tribunals, see Schreuer (2001), Article 27, MN 21.

37 With respect to CERD, Partsch (1971), 14, graphically speaks of the 'three pillars' (State reports, individual complaints, inter-State complaints) upon which the enforcement mechanism rests; similarly Lerner (1970), 84.

38 Karl (1994), 101–104; Simma (1981), 640.

39 In contrast, the various non-binding responses (e.g. by the General Assembly or under Chapter VI UNC) clearly do not intend to restrict the scope of decentralised enforcement. In fact, article 36, para. 3 UNC encourages dispute settlement before the ICJ. In the *South West Africa case*, the Court clarified that it could entertain disputes addressed by the General Assembly, see ICJ Reports 1962, 345.

the matter, it is controversial whether individual UN members can still respond against breaches.

As regards ICJ proceedings during Security Council involvement, the question presents itself as a conflict between two different UN organs. Unlike the relation between Security Council and General Assembly,[40] this conflict is not expressly regulated; however, it has been addressed in the subsequent practice of both organs. Commentators and defendants before the Court have argued that article 24, para. 1 UNC – recognising the Security Council's primary responsibility for the maintenance of international peace and security – excluded ICJ proceedings over disputes addressed by the Security Council.[41] Others have invoked the concept of litispendence, i.e. the rule against parallel proceedings concerning the same subject matter between the same parties.[42] Neither argument is convincing.

Under article 24, para. 1, the Council has 'primary' but not exclusive, responsibility; as the Court has noted, this suggests that other organs have a (secondary) role to play.[43] As for litispendence, there are obvious difficulties with applying this concept, which was developed to regulate conflicts between different judicial bodies, to conflicts between political and judicial UN organs. Whether ICJ proceedings about obligations *erga omnes* (based on the interpretation and application of the law) concern the same subject matter as Security Council action under Chapter VII (guided by political considerations) may be doubted.[44] More importantly, subsequent Charter practice shows that neither the Court nor the Security Council have accepted the litispendence argument. Instead, the Court has entertained a number of cases that concerned disputes addressed by the Council. In the *Hostages case*, for example, it ordered provisional measures at a time the Security

[40] See article 11, para. 2, and article 12, para. 1 UNC (which, however, have to be read in the light of GA Res. 377 (V) – Uniting for Peace). Cf. similarly article 298, para. 1c LOSC, under which States are specifically entitled to exclude from the Part XV LOSC matters dealt with by the Security Council.

[41] Elsen (1986), 68–69; similarly Judge Alvarez' dissent in the *Anglo-Iranian Oil Co. case*, ICJ Reports 1952, 134.

[42] See e.g. Klein (1983), 474; Ciobanu (1976), 209; de Visscher (1966), 174–176; Fraas (1998), 116–123, and already above, Chapter 1 (references in footnote 21).

[43] *Certain Expenses*, ICJ Reports 1962, 163; *Nicaragua case* (jurisdiction and admissibility), ICJ Reports 1984, 434–435; and cf. Delbrück in: Simma (2002a), Article 24, MN 4–9 for a discussion.

[44] Delbrück in: Simma (2002a), Article 24, MN 9; Mosler/Oellers-Frahm in: Simma (2002a), Article 92, MN 88; Klein (1983), 474–478.

Council had already qualified the 'grave situation' in Teheran as 'a serious threat to international peace and security'.[45] In its judgment on the merits (which was reaffirmed on this point in the *Nicaragua case*)[46] the Court noted that the Security Council, in SC Res. 461 (1979), had expressly referred to the interim order, and that 'it does not seem to have occurred to any member of the Council that there was or could be anything irregular in the simultaneous exercise of their respective functions by the Court and the Security Council.'[47]

Perhaps more importantly, litispendence played no role in the *East Timor* or *Genocide cases*, although the Security Council in the latter had long qualified the Yugoslav conflict as a breach of the peace and taken enforcement action under Chapter VII.[48] And in *Lockerbie*, Libya's request for provisional measures was not dismissed because the Security Council had acted in the matter, but because, in view of the Court, Libya's obligations under SC Res. 748 (1992) prevailed over treaty rights whose breach it had alleged.[49]

No doubt each of these cases was instituted by individually injured States rather than on the basis of the *erga omnes* concept. However, it is difficult to see that this should affect the underlying legal issue. Charter practice thus suggests that even where the Security Council has taken enforcement action under Chapter VII UNC, States retain the right to institute ICJ proceedings in response to *erga omnes* breaches.[50] While Chapter VII enforcement measures, by virtue of article 25 UNC, may influence proceedings,[51] the mere fact that the Security Council is involved does not exclude the institution of ICJ proceedings.

As regards the countermeasures taken against serious *erga omnes* breaches, the matter is equally controversial. As discussed above,

[45] ICJ Reports 1979, 7; for the quotation see SC Res. 457 (1979).

[46] ICJ Reports 1984, 433–434 (para. 93). [47] ICJ Reports 1980, 21 (para. 40).

[48] See e.g. SC Res. 713 (1991).

[49] ICJ Reports 1992, 3 and 114 respectively. The point was clarified by a considerable number of judges, cf. Judge Ni's Declaration, *ibid.* 20–23 and 132–135; the Joint Declaration of Judges Evensen, Tarassov, Guillaume and Aguilar Mawdsley, *ibid.*, 24–25 and 136–137; Sep.Op. Lachs, *ibid.*, 26–27 and 189–139; Sep. Op. Shahabuddeen, *ibid.*, 28–29 and 140–141. The matter was left open in the 1998 judgment on preliminary objections, where the Court observed that SC Res. 748 (1992) had been adopted after the filing of the application and therefore could not affect its jurisdiction, see ICJ Reports 1998, 23–24 (paras. 37–38) and 128–129 (paras. 36–37).

[50] It is another question whether the Security Council, as part of its enforcement competence under articles 41, 42, could order States to discontinue or suspend proceedings. For brief comment on this aspect cf. Klein (1983), 479–481.

[51] For an example see the interim orders in the *Lockerbie case*, ICJ Reports 1992, 3 and 114.

there is considerable academic support for the view that countermeasures in response to *erga omnes* breaches should, as a general matter, only be permitted if exercised collectively - a view that has been rejected.[52] As a variation on this theme, some commentators have argued that individual States should only be entitled to resort to countermeasures if the Security Council has not taken action.[53] Article 51 UNC, according to which the right of self-defence ceases once the Security Council has taken 'measures necessary to maintain international peace and security', indeed seems to support this view. Two considerations, however, suggest that, on balance, it cannot be sustained.

The first relates to article 51 UNC. The strict limits on the use of individual self-defence are inspired by the drafters' intention to minimise the use of armed force and form part of of the comprehensive ban on the use of military force.[54] Since there is no comparable rule against the taking of non-forcible countermeasures, a reasoning by way of analogy seems problematic.[55]

More importantly, practice shows that States have not accepted the precedence of Security Council action. Instead, in a number of instances, they have taken individual countermeasures in response to *erga omnes* breaches, although the matter had been addressed by the Security Council. Since the relevant instances have been discussed above, brief references will suffice. The United States' 1986 Comprehensive Anti-Apartheid Act - adopted at a time when South Africa was already subjected to institutional enforcement measures - provides the first example in point.[56] The countermeasures, taken by European States against Yugoslavia during the mounting Kosovo crisis, are equally relevant. When European States decided to freeze Yugoslavian assets and imposed a flight ban, the Security Council had long been seized of the matter and had taken enforcement action under Chapter VII UNC.[57] Both examples suggest that Security Council

[52] Cf. above, section 6.2.1.d (pp. 240–241).

[53] See e.g. Simma (1993a), 136–137 (for the case of *effective measures*); similarly Schreuer (1993), 149. Cf. Empell (2003), 406–409 for a discussion.

[54] Cassese (2001), 310; Empell (2003), 406. Which measures would be sufficient to exclude the right of self-defence is controversial, cf. Dinstein (2001), 187–189; Halberstam (1996–1997), 229.

[55] Contrast Empell (2003), 408.

[56] See above, section 6.2.1.a (pp. 217–218). As noted there, some of the sanctions against South Africa had been recommended by the Security Council, others had been imposed under Chapter VII UNC.

[57] See above, section 6.2.1.a (pp. 223–224); and cf. notably SC Res. 1160 (1998).

enforcement action does not affect the right of individual States to take countermeasures against *erga omnes* breaches.[58] Clearly, such parallel responses, by the Security Council and individual member States, raise a number of complex consequential issues, notably questions of proportionality or coordination. However, decentralised enforcement is not *per se* excluded.

7.2.1.c Summary

To sum up, there is little evidence that States, by conferring enforcement rights upon non-State actors intended to contract out of decentralised enforcement altogether. In the absence of specific provisions to the contrary, State and non-State enforcement measures thus complement each other.

7.2.2 Contracting out of specific forms of decentralised enforcement

Even if decentralised enforcement as such remains possible, treaties might contract out of specific means of enforcement, such as countermeasures or ICJ proceedings. Of the different conflicts, this is clearly the most controversial, even though academic debate has largely centered on the question of countermeasures. In the light of the above considerations,[59] the relation between treaty enforcement and *erga omnes* proceedings before the ICJ needs to be studied as well. The two forms of responses will be studied separately, as treaties might well contract out of one extra-conventional enforcement right but leave the other unaffected. Whether this is so can only be determined by interpreting the two relevant conflicting rules. Their interpretation however takes place on the basis of a considerable body of jurisprudence, which has (or is claimed to have) established certain general guidelines of interpretation. Before addressing specific conflicts, these guidelines may be set out.

7.2.2.a General considerations

Although courts have so far hardly had to address conflicts between treaty regimes and enforcement rights deriving from the *erga omnes* concept, they have frequently addressed conflicts between other competing enforcement mechanisms. Their jurisprudence provides certain general guidelines for the analysis of specific conflicts. The present section

[58] See also Zoller (1984), 119; Tomuschat (1993b), 157–158.
[59] See above, Introduction (to this chapter).

attempts to filter out these guidelines, which will subsequently be applied to specific conflicts relevant here. At the outset, it is necessary to engage with a rather radical approach to the question: the *exclusivity thesis*, pursuant to which *all* treaty-based enforcement systems are exclusive.

The exclusivity thesis

By stressing the need for a case-by-case approach, and warning against a schematic application of the *lex specialis* principle and similar maxims, the preceding analysis has already taken a stance against clear-cut solutions to the problem of competing enforcement mechanisms. Nevertheless, it cannot be denied that one clear-cut approach – the exclusivity thesis – commands considerable support among commentators. At least for the field of human rights law, it is argued that wherever a treaty provides its own system of enforcement, that system should exclude extra-conventional means of enforcement (including those deriving from the *erga omnes* concept). This radical position would render the subsequent analysis superfluous and thus needs to be addressed at the outset.

Alleged support in international jurisprudence Traditionally advanced mainly (though not exclusively)[60] by writers from socialist countries,[61] the exclusivity thesis is said to find support in a passage from the Court's *Nicaragua case* and para. 91 of the *Barcelona Traction* judgment. Given the eminence of Court, and their potential implications, these statements need to addressed in some detail.

The *Nicaragua case* is of particular relevance. In a passage that has already been mentioned,[62] the Court discussed whether the United States' conduct could be justified as response to Nicaragua's alleged human rights violations.[63] The Court stated that it could not, holding that 'the use of force could not be an appropriate method to monitor or ensure . . . respect [for human rights].'[64]

60 See e.g. Karlshoven (1978), 143; Grabenwarter (2003), 152; Ermacora (1968), 396–397 (but contrast Ermacora (1980), 357–358).

61 See e.g. *Völkerrechts-Lehrbuch der Akademie der Wissenschaften* (1973), Vol. I, 329; Mohr (1983), 52–53; Graefrath (1973), 688; Graefrath (1987), 126–128; Sachariew (1986), 98–106; and the detailed discussion by Mohr (1981). Cf. Szawlowski (1979), 778, with further references.

62 See above, section 5.2.5.d. 63 See ICJ Reports 1986, 132–135 (paras. 262–269).

64 ICJ Reports 1986, 134 (para. 268). In even clearer terms, the Court rejected the United States argument based on collected self-defence. As noted on p. 127 (para. 249): 'The acts of which Nicaragua is accused . . . could only have justified proportionate countermeasures on the part of the State which had been the victim of the act, namely

Crucially, this conclusion (concerning an enforcement measure outside the scope of the present study) was based on very broad reasoning. Not content to clarify why, in the circumstances of the case, the use of force should be excluded, the Court observed in para. 267: '[W]here human rights are protected by international conventions, that protection takes the form of such arrangements for monitoring or ensuring respect for human rights as are provided for in the conventions themselves.'[65] On the face of it, this statement clearly seems to support the exclusivity thesis. By mentioning human rights generally (without indicating any particular source), but then focusing on treaty-specific means of enforcement, the Court seemed to suggest that where treaties applied, States could only respond to human rights violations (whether customary or conventional) by treaty-specific means.[66]

The second relevant pronouncement, para. 91 of the *Barcelona Traction* judgment, is said to support this view. As has been stated above, this passage and its relation to the earlier statement, in paras. 33 and 34, on obligations *erga omnes* has prompted much discussion.[67] It has been shown already that it does not *directly* contradict the *Barcelona Traction* dictum. For present purposes, the second interpretation mentioned above is relevant. Pursuant to some commentators, the Court's (incorrect) observation that 'on the universal level, the instruments which embody human rights do not confer upon States the capacity to protect victims of infringements of such rights irrespective of their nationality',[68] has a double meaning. Apart from putting forward a restrictive interpretation of the state of human rights treaty law, the Court is said to have implicitly qualified its earlier statement on obligations *erga omnes*. Kamminga, for example, wonders whether the Court had meant that 'states parties [to human rights agreements] are not entitled to resort to any remedies under general international law to respond to

Salvador, Honduras or Costa Rica. They could not justify counter-measures taken by a third State, and particularly could not justify interventions involving the use of force.'

65 ICJ Reports 1986, 134 (para. 267).

66 Cf. Thirlway (1989), 99–100; Teson (1987), 176; Teson (1997), 282–283; Annacker (1994a), 25; Kiwanuka (1988), 476–477; Empell (2003), 393–398; Frowein (1993), 123–124. Thirlway (1989), 99; and Teson (1987), 176, consider a second interpretation of the statement. In their view, the Court could have also wanted to deny that there existed *any* customary human rights. This reading however is not supported by the text of para. 267, in particular the Court's statement that in the absence of treaty commitments, Nicaragua 'could not with impunity violate human rights'. It also neglects the fact that the crucial sentence (cited in the text) is introduced by the proviso '*where* human rights are protected by international conventions'.

67 See above, section 5.2.4. 68 ICJ Reports 1970, 47 (para. 91).

breaches of these instruments',[69] while according to Thirlway, para. 91 marks 'an apparent withdrawal on human rights'.[70]

It is readily apparent that this interpretation of the two ICJ pronouncements would render the *erga omnes* concept almost meaningless. Given the number, and wide acceptance, of human rights treaties, in practice every breach of an obligation *erga omnes* protecting human rights at the same time violates treaty obligations. If all these treaties were exclusive, one could hardly disagree with Zemanek that 'the whole idea of *erga omnes* obligations ... would be but a *chimera*.'[71]

Its rejection The question is whether the above interpretation of the two passages should be accepted. Two considerations suggest that it should not. For one, *Nicaragua* and *Barcelona Traction* are difficult to reconcile with the bulk of international practice and jurisprudence, which on balance contradict the exclusivity thesis. Perhaps more importantly, closer analysis refutes the above interpretation of the two passages. As international practice and other cases will be addressed more fully below, it is proposed to focus on this second consideration. To that extent, both passages relied on by adherents of the exclusivity thesis will be dealt with separately.

In the case of para. 91 of the *Barcelona Traction* judgment, this can be done summarily, as the passage has been discussed already and the argument based on it is very difficult to sustain. To begin with a literal interpretation, the text of the passage clearly does not support the exclusivity thesis. As has been shown, enforcement rights based on the *erga omnes* concept are extra-conventional.[72] In contrast, the above-quoted sentence, which contains the essence of para. 91, refers to treaty law. Irrespective of whether one agrees with the Court's interpretation of universal human rights treaties,[73] there is simply no indication in para. 91 that these treaties should exclude claims based on extra-conventional mechanisms.[74] Claims that the passage should *implicitly* exclude extra-conventional enforcement rights are equally unconvincing. It appears at the end of the Court's discussion of issues of standing,

[69] Kamminga (1992), 181. It should be noted that in Kamminga's view, this is not the most convincing explanation, see *id.*, 154–156 and cf. above, Chapter 5 (footnote 92), for comment on his approach. Whether para. 91 supports the exclusivity thesis is further discussed by Weschke (2001), 47–51; Simma (1994a), 296.

[70] Thirlway (1989), 100. [71] Zemanek (2000a), 17; similarly Teson (1987), 176.

[72] See above, section 4.1; and Introduction to Chapter 5.

[73] Cf. above, section 5.2.4 for critical comment. [74] Empell (2003), 334–335 and 338.

at a stage at which the Court had already dismissed Belgium's claim based on the customary rules of diplomatic protection, and had clarified that the prohibition against denial of justice did not qualify as an obligation *erga omnes*. By including para. 91, the Court merely affirmed that treaties (which might have warranted a different reading) did not apply. To read it as an implicit derogation from paras. 33 and 34 neglects this context. Finally, it may be added that had the Court intended to exclude extra-conventional enforcement rights based on the *erga omnes* concept, one would have expected it to say so expressly. However, not only does para. 91 fail to mention the expression *erga omnes*; it also concerns a circle of obligation that is both broader and narrower than that of obligations *erga omnes* (human rights *tout court* as opposed to basic human rights and obligations *erga omnes* outside the human rights field).[75] Read properly, para. 91 does not support the view that treaty-based enforcement rights should, as a general matter, exclude extra-conventional means enforcement.[76]

By comparison, para. 267 of the *Nicaragua* judgment gives rise to many more problems. By stating that '[human rights] protection takes the form ... provided for in the conventions',[77] the Court clearly accepted some form of exclusivity. The question remains for which circle of human rights obligations the exclusionary rule should apply. The more natural reading indeed is that the Court wished to exclude extra-conventional means of enforcement for *all* human rights protected in international conventions, i.e. customary human rights codified in the convention and those conventional human rights that have not entered into customary international law and are only protected by treaty. Following this broad interpretation, para. 267 would indeed support the exclusivity thesis. Paragraph, 267 however, can be read in a much more restrictive way.[78] It is possible that when proclaiming the exclusivity of treaty-based means of enforcement, the Court did not refer to *all* human rights, but merely to conventional human rights. Following this restrictive interpretation, para. 267 (just as para. 91 of the *Barcelona Traction* judgment) would not affect the enforcement of (customary) *erga omnes* obligations.

[75] See also de Hoogh (1996), 52–53; Paulus (2001), 371–372; Annacker (1994a), 17; Simma (1994a), 296–297; *id.* (1981), 643.

[76] See also Meron (1986), 11–12; Tomuschat (1999), 84; Henkin (1977), his footnote 22.

[77] ICJ Reports 1986, 134 (para. 267). [78] Cf. Empell (2003), 395–396.

One might object that this restrictive interpretation would contain a rather trivial statement, which the Court would be unlikely to make. However, in the circumstances of the case, it was not as trivial as one might think. To clarify the point, it is necessary to consider which types of human rights breaches the United States had alleged. As appears from a Congress Report of July 1985 (referred to in para. 267 of the judgment), the United States mainly accused Nicaragua of violating the 'freedom of press, assembly and organization' and specifically cited reports by the Inter-American Commission of Human Rights to support its allegations.[79] Although the Report did not refer to any specific source of law, Congress thereby alleged breaches of human rights, which, as of 1985, at least arguably had not entered into the body of customary human rights law. As appears from para. 267 of the judgment, the Court certainly seemed to take this view - hence it considered Nicaragua's human rights compliance with reference to the ACHR only. Crucially, this agreement, while ratified by Nicaragua, did not apply in relation to the United States.[80] Even if one does not agree with the Court's rather restrictive view of customary human rights law, it is surely relevant for the interpretation of para. 267. The above considerations suggest that, in the view of the Court, the United States had accused Nicaragua of breaching human rights that had not acquired customary status but were only protected by conventions to which the United States was not a party. Seen in this perspective, it might not have been a triviality for the Court to affirm that treaty obligations were to be enforced through treaty mechanisms.

Three considerations suggest that this restrictive interpretation of para. 267 is not only plausible but convincing. Since it runs counter to the natural reading of the crucial sentence (which indeed supports the exclusivity thesis), these considerations need to be developed in some detail.[81] A close analysis of the Court's use of language provides the first argument. As observed above, the Court stated that 'where human rights are protected by international conventions, *that* protection takes the form ... provided for in the conventions themselves.'[82] The

[79] ICJ Reports 1986, 90–92 (paras. 179–180).

[80] The United States signed the Convention on 1 June 1977, but had not ratified it at the time of the judgment (nor indeed since then).

[81] Given the potential implications of the statement, and the eminence of the Court, it is surprising that para. 267 is often ignored or glossed over. For a detailed treatment see Empell (2003), 391–398.

[82] ICJ Reports 1986, 134 (para. 267) (emphasis added).

use of the word 'that' is significant. Had the Court wanted to suggest that even customary human rights could only be protected by means provided for in applicable treaties, it might have used a more neutral expression (such as 'their', or 'the') instead. By using the demonstrative pronoun 'that', it seemed to refer back to the specific form of human rights protection mentioned in the first part of the sentence, namely protection through human rights conventions.

When moving beyond the wording of the crucial sentence, two other arguments suggest that the broad interpretation favoured by adherents of the exclusivity thesis is highly unlikely. For once, the exclusivity argument is contradicted by a contextual reading of para. 267. In the passage immediately following the crucial sentence, the Court gave a specific reason why, in the particular case, Nicaragua's alleged human rights breaches could not justify the United States' conduct. In its view, the United States' assertion of a right to respond was misplaced, because - as witnessed by two Country Reports of the American Commission for Human Rights - 'the mechanisms provided for [in the conventions] have functioned.'[83] Of course, one need not agree with this assessment - as Teson notes, it would be surprising if country reports were enough to make a human rights system function.[84] However, the Court seems to accept that had the mechanism not functioned, the United States' could have availed itself of rights of protection not provided in the Convention. It follows that not *all*, but only *functioning*, treaty regimes exclude extra-conventional means of enforcement. In the light of this later passage, the broad interpretation favoured by adherents of the exclusivity thesis seems more difficult to uphold.

Furthermore, it stands in marked contrast to the most celebrated (and controversial) aspect of the *Nicaragua* judgment, namely the Court's discussion of the United States' multilateral treaty reservation, and its effects in the field of customary international law.[85] When discussing this aspect, the Court had frequently stressed the separate existence of treaty and customary rules, even if both rules were identical in scope; this in turn led it to hold that the United States' reservation did not exclude Nicaragua's arguments based on customary law.[86] Admittedly, these considerations were part of the analysis of the applicable law and

[83] ICJ Reports 1986, 134 (para. 267). [84] Teson (1987), 176.

[85] On the Court's reasoning cf. further below, section 7.2.3.b.

[86] See ICJ Reports 1986, 92-97 (paras. 172-182); and cf. already ICJ Reports 1984, 424 (para. 73). Contrast the dissents of Judges Jennings and Oda, ICJ Reports 1986, 216-219 and 529-537; and cf. the discussion by Crawford (1997), 373-374; Briggs (1987), 80-83.

did not necessarily imply a view on the availability of different enforcement mechanisms. However, the Court drew support for its approach from the fact that treaty and custom were often subject to different enforcement mechanisms. In its view, a State might conclude a treaty not only to codify rules of customary international law, but also

> because the treaty establishes ... desirable institutions or mechanisms to ensure implementation of the rule. Thus, if that [treaty] rule parallels a rule of customary international law, two rules of the same content are subject to separate treatment as regards the organs competent to verify their implementation, depending on whether they are customary rules or treaty rules.[87]

At least when discussing the effect of reservations, the Court therefore seemed to assume the separate existence of enforcement mechanisms, which would complement, rather than exclude, each other. It is difficult to see how that statement could have been made if treaties (at least in the field of human rights) *per se* excluded enforcement rights deriving from general international law.[88]

Finally, the broad interpretation of para. 267 seems unlikely to have been intended by the Court because it would produce results that go far beyond the mere recognition of the exclusivity thesis. It has been stated already that even this thesis is radical enough. However, its effects would pale in comparison to the (not always considered) consequences flowing from a broad interpretation of para. 267. As has been stated, *Nicaragua* did not concern the (possibly exclusive) effect of treaty regimes *on State parties*, as the relevant treaty (the ACHR) was not binding on the United States.[89] If indeed, the Court had held that customary human rights could only be enforced by treaty means, the above-quoted sentence would have a far more radical effect than acknowledged so far. It would imply that a treaty-based enforcement system such as the ACHR could exclude the legality of enforcement measures *taken by third States*.[90] As a consequence, States concluding a treaty could establish an enforcement regime binding (and exclusive) not only *inter partes*, but even in relation to third States. How such a 'super-exclusivity' could possibly be reconciled with basic concepts of treaty law is not clear. That the Court should have endorsed it seems unlikely.

None of these considerations puts into question the conclusion reached by the Court. As a non-party, the United States could not simply

[87] ICJ Reports 1986, 95–96 (para. 178).
[88] Cf. however Marschik (1997), 96–98, who defends the Court's distinction.
[89] Empell (2003), 396–397. [90] Similarly Teson (1987), 176; Teson (1997), 285.

invoke (and auto-interpret) the ACHR mechanisms, nor indeed enforce conventional human rights standards by forcible means. However, the discussions suggests that the broad interpretation of para. 267 of the *Nicaragua* judgment (which would have provided crucial support for the exclusivity thesis) cannot be sustained. It would imply recognition of a super-exclusivity of treaty regimes and is contradicted by a contextual reading of para. 267. On balance, the more convincing view is that when proclaiming that human rights had to be enforced through conventional means, the Court referred to human rights that had not acquired customary status and are *only* protected in treaty form. Following this restrictive reading, para. 267 of the *Nicaragua* judgment does not support the exclusivity thesis. Since para. 91 of the *Barcelona Traction* judgment is of even more limited help, it can be concluded that – contrary to a widely held view – that thesis has not been endorsed by the ICJ.

Guidelines for the analysis of specific conflicts

It has been stated already that even if the *Nicaragua case* and para. 91 of the *Barcelona Traction* judgment supported the exclusivity thesis (which they do not), they would be contradicted by the bulk of international practice and jurisprudence. When assessing conflicts between competing enforcement mechanisms, courts and tribunals have not accepted radical solutions along the lines of the exclusivity thesis. Instead, they have taken into account a number of broad and flexible principles. These principles cannot replace the interpretation of conflicting enforcement systems, and do not address all problems. However, they provide guidelines for the interpretation, and suggest how conflicts can be approached. Four points seem worth stressing.

Explicit conflict rules The first, and most obvious, point to make is that the matter may have been specifically regulated by a conflict clause. Conflict clauses can, in principle, be found in either of the two competing enforcement mechanisms; they can speak in favour of exclusivity or indicate non-exclusivity. Examples relevant to the present study will be addressed below. To illustrate the point, it may be helpful briefly to mention two typical examples without immediate relevance to the present study. As appears from article 282 LOSC, dispute settlement under Part XV LOSC is not only non-exclusive, but even residual: under the provision, special dispute settlement procedures that can be instituted unilaterally and that entail a binding decision disapply

Part XV LOSC.[91] In contrast, article 292 TEC indicates that disputes about questions covered by European Community law are exclusively to be dealt with by the ECJ; this has been interpreted to exclude not only other dispute settlement fora but also countermeasures between EC member States.[92] In the presence of such explicit conflict clauses, the problem of competing enforcement mechanisms can often be solved by way of simple treaty application.

Effectivity In the absence of conflict clauses, it must be assessed whether treaties implicitly exclude recourse to extra-conventional means of enforcement. Whether they do is of course a matter of interpretation. However, this interpretation is guided by one very general guideline: international jurisprudence suggests that enforcement regimes are more likely to be exclusive if they are effective. This presumption in favour of effectivity of course is not absolute. States remain free to agree on ineffective mechanisms and to replace more effective enforcement rights. This, however, would have to be indicated and has not usually been presumed.[93]

The relevance of the effectivity criterion has been expressly confirmed in the comments of States on the ILC's work on State responsibility,[94] and is also underlined by a variety of judicial pronouncements, only a handful of which need to be mentioned. The relevant passage of the *Nicaragua* judgment has been referred to already.[95] The *Hostages* and *Air Services cases* support the same position. In the former, the Court held that the Diplomatic Convention conferred upon receiving States 'entirely efficacious' means of responding against treaty breaches; as a consequence, extra-conventional enforcement measures were excluded.[96] Similarly, the Arbitral Tribunal in the *Air Services case* accepted that there was no general rule excluding countermeasures pending third-party dispute settlement proceedings, but conceded

[91] Shany (2003), 201–202. For an application see the Arbitral Tribunal's suspension order in the *Mox Plant case*, available at http://www.pca-cpa.org/ENGLISH/RPC.

[92] *Commission v. Luxemburg and Belgium*, Cases 90 and 91/63[1964] ECR631.

[93] Pursuant to the highly controversial arbitral award, this was e.g. the case in the *Southern Bluefin Tuna case*, see paras. 53–59 for the Tribunal's interpretation based on article 281 LOSC. For critical comment see Oxman (2002), 277; Shany (2003), 203.

[94] See e.g. UN Doc. A/C.6/47/SR.26, 6 (France); and cf. already *Institut de droit international* (1934), 708.

[95] See above, section 7.2.1 and cf. ICJ Reports 1986, 134 (para. 267), where the Court observed: '[T]he mechanisms provided for [in the conventions] have functioned.'

[96] ICJ Reports 1980, 40–41 (paras. 87 and 86 respectively).

that the situation would be different where 'the proceedings form part of an institutional framework ensuring some degree of enforcement of obligations'.[97] These statements suggest that in the absence of explicit conflict clauses, much depends on whether the allegedly exclusive mechanism is effective.

Formal indications of effectivity While jurisprudence thus provides ample evidence supporting the effectivity criterion, its application is problematic. This in particular because – unlike in the case of countermeasures *sub judice*[98] – effectivity must be assessed irrespective of a concrete dispute. Instead, it depends on a value judgement about the character of dispute settlement as envisaged in the treaty. When called upon to perform that value judgement, courts and tribunals have frequently recurred on four different factors. These do not form a checklist that could be easily applied. However, they are at least formal indications of a treaty system's (in)effectivity, and may thus be helpful.

First, as a general matter, it will be a sign of effectivity if a treaty system is capable of assessing treaty breaches objectively, and provides non-discretionary third-party procedures for settling them. Secondly, as regards the available remedies, the PCIJ's jurisprudence suggests that special treaty systems will only be considered effective if they provide for comprehensive remedies.[99] Thirdly, tribunals, e.g. in the *Air Services case*, have stressed the importance of instantly available protection against breaches.[100] Finally, it may be worth clarifying that effectivity requires not only the existence, but the actual functioning, of treaty enforcement systems – hence the above-mentioned reference to procedures that 'form part of an institutional framework ensuring some degree of enforcement of obligations.'[101]

The character of the breach Finally, whether a treaty restricts extra-conventional enforcement rights might also depend on the character

[97] 54 ILR 340 (para. 94), and more generally *ibid.*, paras. 89–95.
[98] On which above, Introduction (to this chapter).
[99] Cf. e.g. *Chorzow Factory (Jurisdiction) case*, PCIJ, Ser. A, No. 9 (1927), 30 (mixed arbitral tribunals not exclusive, as parties could not obtain full compensation). For a discussion see Shany (2003), 231–232.
[100] Cf. *Air Services case*, 54 ILR 340–341 (para. 96) (where the Tribunal addressed the question of interim protection). See also ILC, commentary to article 52 ASR, para. 8.
[101] *Air Services case*, 54 ILR 340 (para. 94). The relevance of institutional mechanisms was also underlined by the ICTY in the *Furundzija* judgment, 38 ILM (1999), para. 152.

of the violation against which the response is directed. This is evident insofar as certain responses are only available in the case of qualified breaches of the law (such as, in the present case, the right to take countermeasures in response to serious *erga omnes* breaches). Beyond that, it is possible that a specific treaty should exclude recourse to general mechanisms in the case of normal breaches, but allow for a fall-back in response to serious breaches. The award in the *Southern Bluefin Tuna case* provides a clear example in point. While controversially holding that dispute settlement under Part XV LOSC had been excluded by a special implementation convention, the Tribunal conceded that 'there might be instances in which the conduct of a State Party to UNCLOS and to a fisheries treaty implementing it would be so egregious, and risk consequences of such gravity, that a Tribunal might find that the obligations of UNCLOS provide a basis for jurisdiction'.[102] The required value judgement about the effectivity of a special enforcement system may thus be influenced not only by the characteristic features of the possibly exclusive treaty, but also by the nature of the violation against which the response is directed.

Summary

It is clear that the preceding considerations do not establish an easy-to-apply rule governing conflicts between competing treaty mechanisms. Given the wide range of conflicts, no hard and fast conflict rule exists. Attempts to solve *all* conflicts in favour of treaty exclusivity are misguided and find no support in international jurisprudence. Instead, the problem is best approached in two steps. First, one of the competing enforcement rules may explicitly regulate the conflict. Secondly, in the absence of conflict clauses or any other clear guidance, jurisprudence suggests that systems are more likely to be exclusive if they function effectively, and indicates a number of factors relevant in this regard. On the basis of these general considerations, the conflicts between treaties and *erga omnes* enforcement rights will be analysed in the following.

7.2.2.b Contracting out of ICJ proceedings

As has been stated above, most of the relevant treaties (ECHR, ACHR, Banjul Charter, CERD, CCPR) provide for some form of inter-State dispute settlement. Disputes however are dealt with by treaty-monitoring

[102] *Southern Bluefin Tuna case* (arbitral award), para. 64 (referring to the good faith obligation contained in article 300 LOSC).

bodies, while the ICJ has either a subsidiary role (in the case of CERD) or no role at all.[103] All five treaties therefore could exclude or restrict the possibility of *erga omnes* proceedings before the ICJ. This in particular because the various treaty procedures were designed to accommodate special concerns of treaty parties, often involving a deliberate decision against too much ICJ influence. The *travaux préparatoires* to the CCPR, to take but one example, reveal a gradual shift away from a judicial system of supervision, under which the ICJ would have had an important role to play, towards a system of merely optional inter-State complaints to a special treaty committee.[104] Given this background, it is certainly not inconceivable that parallel proceedings before ICJ might be excluded. Most conflicts can nevertheless be solved relatively easily, as the relevant treaties address it. There is thus no need to enter into discussions about the effectivity of treaty-based enforcement; instead, the matter is largely one of treaty interpretation, which mostly leads to very clear results. Three different forms of conflict regulation can be distinguished.

Non-exclusivity clauses

The situation under CCPR and CERD is straightforward, as both treaties contain explicit non-exclusivity clauses. In near-identical terms, article 44 CCPR and article 16 CERD provide that the respective enforcement systems 'shall not prevent the States Parties . . . from having recourse to other procedures for settling a dispute in accordance with general or special international agreements in force between them.'[105]

As is clear from the drafting history, the reference to 'general or special international agreements' was inserted to preserve the possibility of inter-State judicial proceedings before other fora. The different non-judicial procedures therefore were intended to complement, rather than exclude, other means of enforcement.[106] As to the types of 'other procedures for settling a dispute', drafters were mainly concerned to preserve the availability of regional human rights mechanisms. There is however little doubt that the reference to 'other procedures' also covers ICJ proceedings brought under article 36 of the ICJ Statute[107] and would

103 See above, section 7.1.2.a.

104 See Pechota (1981), 47–49; Robertson (1981), 334–336.

105 Article 44 CCPR was in fact modelled on article 16 CERD, which was based on article 12, para. 3 of the 1962 UNESCO Protocol. For guidance on the drafting history see Bossuyt (1987), 723–726.

106 Robertson (1981), 356; Kamminga (1992), 180; Simma (1981), 647; Linsi (1994), 70.

107 Nowak (1993), article 44, MN 8; Kamminga (1992), 179–180; Lerner (1970), 97–98.

consequently also cover proceedings aimed at vindicating obligations *erga omnes*. In the case of CERD, article 22 – recognising the right of all State parties to institute ICJ proceedings once treaty-specific mechanisms have failed – further supports this interpretation. Far from excluding recourse to the ICJ, CERD recognises its role as one (if only secondary) forum of dispute settlement.

Practice equally confirms the non-exclusive character of the enforcement mechanisms. States protesting against breaches of CCPR or CERD have frequently side-stepped the treaty procedures and instead relied on extra-conventional means of enforcement.[108] One particularly telling example may illustrate the point. As stated above, Portugal, in the *East Timor case*, claimed that by concluding the Timor Gap Treaty, Australia had violated the right of self-determination of the people of East Timor. When the Timor Gap Treaty was concluded in 1991, both Australia and Portugal were bound by the provisions of the CCPR and thus, under article 1, had to respect the right of self-determination.[109] Although the matter was therefore governed by a human rights treaty, there was little doubt that Portugal could institute ICJ proceedings under the optional clause. In fact, it is telling that neither the defendant nor the Court even mentioned the question of exclusivity.[110] Neither CERD nor CCPR thus affect the right of States to institute ICJ proceedings in response to *erga omnes* breaches.[111]

[108] For express confirmation see also the German government's statements in the Bundestag, cited in Simma (1985), 134.

[109] See http://www.unhchr.ch/html/menu3/b/a_ccpr.htm. Since Australia had not made any declaration under article 41 CCPR, enforcement would have been virtually impossible.

[110] In contrast, the Chilean government, in 1979, did raise the matter. In its view, the CCPR procedures excluded the establishment, by the UN Human Rights Commission, of *ad hoc* working groups investigating human rights abuses. Within the United Nations, this claim was roundly rejected. The Commission's Special Rapporteur expressly clarified that Chile could not 'plead that the procedures established under the International Covenant on Civil and Political Rights should be applied to the situation . . . at the exclusion of other procedures which the United Nations may consider appropriate' (UN Doc. A/34/503, para. 12 (1979)). While concerning a different type of conflict (namely the relation between CCPR and Human Rights Commission procedures), the two situations are comparable. The UN's handling of the matter further supports the view that treaties such as CCPR or CERD complement rather than exclude other means of human rights protection. On the dispute cf. Meron (1986), 215–216.

[111] In line with the interpretation advocated in the text, the UN Human Rights Committee recently observed in its General Comment No. 31: '[T]he mere fact that a formal interstate mechanism for complaints to the Human Rights Committee exists in

Implied non-exclusivity

The situation is similarly clear with respect to ACHR and the Banjul Charter. Although neither treaty contains an express clause along the lines of article 44 CCPR or article 16 CERD, both implicitly recognise the non-exclusivity of the respective enforcement mechanisms. In the case of the ACHR, this follows from article 46, para. 1c, under which proceedings are only admissible if 'the subject of the petition or communication is not pending in another international proceeding for settlement.'[112] As the *chapeau* and the express reference to 'petition[s] or communication[s]' clarify, this requirement applies to inter-State as well as individual complaints.[113] Similarly, under article 48 of the Banjul Charter, an inter-State communication can only be forwarded to the Commission if 'within three months ... the issue is not settled to the satisfaction of the two States involved through bilateral negotiation *or by any other peaceful procedure*'.[114]

Both provisions imply that States can avail themselves of such 'other peaceful procedure[s]' for the settlement of the dispute.[115] While drafters first and foremost had in mind the relation between the respective regional and universal human rights treaty regimes,[116] the formulation of the respective provision is broad enough to cover ICJ proceedings based on the optional clause. In line with this interpretation, African States parties to the Banjul Charter, have not challenged the admissibility of human rights claims before the ICJ.[117] On the contrary, the only

respect of States Parties that have made the declaration under article 41 does not mean that this procedure is the only method by which States Parties can assert their interest in the performance of other States Parties. On the contrary, the article 41 procedure should be seen as supplementary to, not diminishing of, States Parties' interest in each others' discharge of their obligations.' (See UN Doc. CCPR/C/74/CRP.4/Rev.6 of 21 April 2004, available at http://www.unhchr.ch/tbs/doc.nsf).

112 See also article 39, para. 1 of the Regulations of the Inter-American Commission on Human Rights, which by virtue of article 49, para. 2, applies to inter-State communictions. Similarly, article 47 (d) ACHR provides that communications are inadmissible if they are 'substantially the same as one previously studied by the Commission *or by another international organization*' (emphasis added).

113 Contrast the more limited scope of article 35, para. 2b ECHR, which applies only to individual complaints.

114 Emphasis added. See also article 93, para. 2c of the African Commission's Rules of Procedure.

115 Weschke (2001), 54; (Carrie 1994), 179.

116 Cf. the remarks on article 42 [47] in *Minutes of the 4th Session of Committee II*, Doc. 47, Corr. 2 (1970), reproduced in: Buergenthal/Norris (1982), Part Two, Chapter I, 193.

117 For recent examples see e.g. *Armed Activities (Congo-Rwanda)* (alleged breaches of CAT, CEDAW, CERD, and the Genocide Convention); *Ahmadou Sadio Diallo* (unlawful imprisonment, violation of property rights).

inter-State complaint admitted under the Banjul Charter was accompanied by parallel ICJ proceedings, brought under the optional clause.[118] Neither ACHR nor the Banjul Charter thus affect the right of States to institute ICJ proceedings in response to *erga omnes* breaches.

Flexible exclusivity clauses

Finally, the ECHR, just like the other four treaties, addresses the question of competing enforcement mechanisms. The relevant provision, article 55 (ex-article 62), however is considerably more ambiguous; it provides:

The High Contracting Parties agree that, except by special agreement, they will not avail themselves of treaties, conventions or declarations in force between them for the purpose of submitting, by way of petition, a dispute arising out of the interpretation or application of this Convention to a means of settlement other than those provided for in this Convention.

This provision may be qualified as a flexible exclusivity clause[119] – exclusive in that it gives priority to the ECHR, flexible in that it recognises the right of State parties to enter into 'special agreements' with a view to conferring jurisdiction on another judicial body. While the provision has hardly ever been invoked in ECHR[120] or other judicial proceedings,[121] States and commentators have much discussed how the

[118] *Communication 227/99 (Democratic Republic of Congo v. Burundi, Rwanda and Uganda)*; cf. Viljoen (2002), 98.

[119] Cf. Shany (2003), 188.

[120] Turkey invoked the provision in the *Cyprus/Turkey case*, arguing that Cyprus and Turkey had agreed to address the subject matter of the application – the issue of missing persons – exclusively within the framework of the UN Committee on Missing Persons. In its admissibility decision, the European Commission of Human Rights had little difficulty in dismissing this application, as Turkey was not involved in the work of the UN Commission, the Commission did not provide for a petition system (to which article 55 solely refers), and Cyprus clearly denied that the existence of a special agreement; cf. 39 YbECHR (1996), 160–162.

For present purposes, the decision is of little relevance, as it assesses whether States can use the exception recognised in article 55 (ex-article 62) in order to *avoid* dispute settlement before the Convention organs. In contrast, in the present scenario, article 55 ECHR would be invoked to exclude the availability of *other fora*.

[121] See, however, below, footnote 132, for brief comment on the *Certain Properties case*. In addition, it deserves to be mentioned that Austria and Italy sought to establish the ICJ's jurisdiction over the dispute relating to South Tyrol. As the 1957 European Convention for the Settlement of Disputes would have been inapplicable *ratione temporis*, both States, in 1971, concluded a bilateral treaty specifically disapplying the non-retroactivity rule found in article 27(a). While this shows that States parties to the ECHR have been prepared to avoid recourse to the Strasbourg Court, it is of little

balance between exclusivity and flexibility should be struck. In this regard, two questions arise.

First, before entering the discussion between exclusivity and flexibility, it is necessary to define to which type of disputes article 55 ECHR applies. On the basis of a formal reading, one could argue that the provision only intends to preclude disputes about Convention rights, but does not affect the right of States to bring other inter-State proceedings based on the violation of parallel human rights protected in customary international law or other treaties. The express reference to 'dispute[s] arising out of the interpretation or application of *this Convention*'[122] seems to support this formal reading.[123] However, it is hard to reconcile with the State parties' aim of avoiding – but for cases of special agreements – the possibility of jurisdictional conflicts between different courts. More importantly, it is clearly contradicted by the subsequent practice of States. When seeking to clarify the relation between different inter-State enforcement procedures (such as article 41 CCPR and article 33 ECHR), States have consistently referred to article 55 ECHR, and thereby implicitly accepted that it has a bearing on that matter.[124] Both arguments suggest that the restrictive interpretation (which would have avoided conflicts) is unconvincing, and that article 55 ECHR equally applies to disputes about parallel provisions, including customary human rights that have acquired *erga omnes* status.

Consequently, it must be analysed whether parallel ICJ proceedings about obligations *erga omnes* should be excluded. Since these will almost inevitably be brought under the optional clause,[125] it must be assessed whether the recognition, by two ECHR member States, of the ICJ's jurisdiction under article 36, para. 2 ICJ Statute would amount to a 'special agreement' (*compromis spécial*) in the sense of article 55 ECHR.[126] Three considerations suggest that this is not the case. Article 55 ECHR only recognises one narrowly formulated exception to the

help to the present study, as the 1971 agreement (referring to one specific dispute) plainly qualifies as a 'special agreement'. For a discussion see Zeller (1989), 85–89; and cf. already above, Introduction to Chapter 2, for a brief reference to the *Pfunders case*.

122 Emphasis added.

123 Cf. Eissen (1972–1973), 188–189; Meron (1984), 235.

124 See notably Committee of Ministers, Resolution (70) 17 (assessing the relationship between CCPR and ECHR mechanisms) reproduced in 18 YbECHR (1970), 265.

125 See above, section 1.1.

126 The following discussion is based on the assumption that article 55 ECHR contemplates 'special agreement[s]' concluded by the States parties to the respective dispute. In contrast, Frowein and Peukert have argued that in order to fulfil the requirements of the provision, a special agreement would have to be entered into by *all*

exclusivity rule; the negative phrasing ('will not – except') also implies that the term 'special agreement' ought to be read restrictively.[127] In contrast, optional clause declarations are the most general form of recognising the Court's jurisdiction. Furthermore, a systematic reading confirms the need for a restrictive interpretation. The reference, in article 55 ECHR, to 'special agreement[s]' is in marked contrast to other conflict clauses, such as article 44 CCPR and article 16 CERD both of which refer to '*general or special* international agreements'.[128] Finally, the *travaux préparatoires* show that drafters were anxious to avoid the possibility of contentious ICJ proceedings based on the optional clause.[129] All three factors support a robust interpretation of article 55 ECHR, pursuant to which States parties to the ECHR cannot institute ICJ proceedings concerning obligations *erga omnes* in the field of human rights, if these could equally form the subject of an inter-State complaint to the Strasbourg Court.

It must be conceded though that the subsequent practice is more ambiguous. While not addressing the present conflict, States have expressed differing views on the relation between article 33 ECHR and inter-State proceedings under article 41 CCPR. Signs of ambiguity notably appear in a resolution, adopted by the Committee of Ministers in 1970. Having noted 'differences of opinion ... as regards the exact scope of the obligation resulting from Article 62 [as it then was]', the Committee of Ministers stated that States

> should *normally* utilise only the procedure established by the European Convention in respect of complaints against another Contracting Party to the European Convention relating to an alleged violation of a right which in substance is covered by the European Convention (or its protocols) and by the UN Covenant on Civil and Political Rights, it being understood that the UN procedure may be invoked in relation to rights not guaranteed in the European Convention (or its protocols) or in relation to States which are not Parties to the European Convention.[130]

Although stressing the priority of ECHR proceedings, the resolution qualifies the robust interpretation by adding the word 'normally'.

State parties; cf. Frowein/Peukert (1996), commentary on Article 62 (sole MN). This view however finds no support in the *travaux* and would deprive the provision of its meaning; see Vierdag (1994), 138–139.

[127] Cf. European Commission on Human Rights, *Cyprus/Turkey case* (admissibility), 39 YbECHR (1996), 162.

[128] Emphasis added. [129] See Velu/Ergec (1990), 749–751, for references.

[130] Resolution (70) 17, reproduced in 18 YbECHR (1970), 265 (emphasis added).

However, there is no attempt to clarify when a situation would cease to be normal. In the light of these considerations, the more convincing view seems to be that article 55 ECHR excludes *erga omnes* proceedings before the ICJ.[131] While the matter certainly is not beyond doubt, it is generally understood that the provision applies to parallel disputes about obligations *erga omnes* in the field of human rights. Moreover, despite the ambiguous attitude of States, the better arguments suggest that acceptance of the ICJ's jurisdiction under the optional clause would not amount to a 'special agreement', and thus not fall within the recognised exception.[132]

Interim conclusion

In conclusion, the relevant treaties address conflicts between treaty-enforcement rights and contentious ICJ proceedings. Under the CCPR, CERD, ACHR, and Banjul Charter, the relevant provisions, expressly or by implication, recognise the right of States to use other, extraconventional means of dispute settlement, including ICJ proceedings. In contrast, the much more ambiguous article 55 ECHR on balance points towards exclusivity. State parties to the European Convention on Human Rights therefore have contracted out of the right to bring contentious ICJ proceedings about matters falling within the jurisdiction of the Strasbourg Court.

7.2.2.c Contracting out of countermeasures

This leaves the much-discussed question whether treaties affect the right of States to take countermeasures in response to serious *erga omnes* breaches. Unlike the problem of ICJ proceedings, this question cannot be answered by interpreting conflict clauses. Explicit conflict clauses contained in treaties do not usually cover the question.[133] Nor can the conflict be solved by analysing the general regime of countermeasures. As discussed above, whether treaty rules prescribing specific

[131] For similarly robust interpretations of article 55 ECHR see Kamminga (1992), 180; Simma (1981), 639; Kooijmans (1990), 93; Grabenwarter (2003), 147.

[132] It is worth noting that in its judgment of the *Certain Properties case* (available at www.icj-cij.org), the ICJ did not pronounce on article 55 ECHR. While this may be astonishing (given that the case involved a dispute about human rights between two ECHR members), it may be explained with reference to the previous proceedings, on the same subject-matter, before the Strasbourg Court.

[133] See below, p. 288, for brief comment on article 44 CCPR.

forms of third-party dispute settlement exclude countermeasures is a matter of interpreting the specific treaty.[134] As the ILC's debates show, there is, at present, no *general* rule covering all conflicts between countermeasures and conventional dispute settlement mechanisms either.[135] Attempts by various ILC Special Rapporteurs, to subject countermeasures to the prior exhaustion of *all* dispute settlement procedures (culminating in Arangio-Ruiz' famous draft article 12(1)(a) submitted in 1992),[136] proved much too radical to be acceptable.[137] The Commission's eventual text leaves open the question, instead merely regulating the relation between countermeasures and prior negotiations.[138] It thereby implicitly suggests that at the present stage of international law, no general conflict rule exists. This result is in line with international jurisprudence[139] and the plea for a case-by-case approach advocated here, and also does justice to the diversity of treaty mechanisms and the variety of conflicts thus arising.

Conflicts thus are to be addressed by interpreting the relevant treaty regimes, having regard to the various factors singled out above.[140] In order to avoid having to deal with each treaty separately, the subsequent sections place them in different groups, according to the rights of protection available to parties responding against breaches. In this regard, a basic distinction can be drawn between situations in which States could institute inter-State proceedings under the relevant treaty, and situations in which no such possibility exists. It seems convenient to begin by addressing the latter scenario.

[134] See above, section 1.1.

[135] The point has been, and is, much discussed; see e.g. Dzida (1997), 134–150; Bennouna (1994), 62; Schachter (1994), 471; Tomuschat (1994), 79; Bowett (1972b), 1.

[136] Arangio Ruiz, Fourth Report, 40. Under the provision, States would only have been entitled to take countermeasures once they had exhausted 'all the amicable settlement procedures available under general international law, the United Nations Charter or any other dispute settlement instrument.' For a similar proposal (though formulated more ambiguously) see already Riphagen, Sixth Report, YbILC 1984, Vol. II/1 (draft article 10, para. 1). Both provisions made room for interim measures of protection which could be taken prior to, or during, dispute settlement procedures.

[137] For criticism among States see e.g. UN Doc. A/C.6./47/SR.25, para. 50 (CSSR); *ibid.*, para. 90 (Marocco); *ibid.*, SR.26, para. 11 (France); *ibid.*, para. 47 (Austria); *ibid.*, SR.27, para. 37 (United States); *ibid.*, para. 15 (Uruguay). See Dzida (1997), 142–143, for references to discussions among ILC members. As the same author notes, there has not been a single case in which States had exhausted *all* dispute settlement procedures provided for in article 33 UNC before resorting to countermeasures (135–136).

[138] Cf. article 48, para. 1 [1996] and article 52, para. 1b ASR.

[139] See *Air Services case*, 54 ILR 340 (paras. 94–95).

[140] See above, section 7.2.2.a (pp. 276–279).

No inter-State procedures available

Few problems arise if treaties provide for merely optional inter-State procedures (such as CCPR and ACHR), and if the State allegedly responsible for the breach has not accepted the treaty-monitoring body's competence to entertain inter-State complaints. If the respective treaties contracted out of countermeasures, States would not have any expressly recognised enforcement rights at their disposal. Still, at least with respect to the CCPR, representatives of socialist States have occasionally argued in favour of treaty exclusivity.[141] Article 44 CCPR, which in the case of ICJ proceedings had proved the decisive counter-argument, does not directly contradict this view. While expressly recognising the right of States to pursue 'other dispute settlement procedures' (which might include dispute settlement by way of countermeasure), it only refers to procedures based on 'general or special international agreements' and thus does not cover the customary concept of countermeasures.[142]

When considering the various other criteria mentioned above, the view that the compulsory CCPR (or ACHR) enforcement mechanism excluded countermeasures however cannot be sustained. As a general matter, a treaty system solely relying on reporting systems and (optional)[143] individual complaint procedures is hardly equipped with tools for an effective protection. Since reports are submitted periodically and individual complaints (if possible) require the exhaustion of local remedies,[144] there is no possibility of responding against on-going breaches. Even where treaty-monitoring bodies have robustly interpreted their right to comment on State reports, they have no competence to order any remedies, nor is there any mechanism ensuring that reports are actually implemented.[145]

Finally, practice clearly shows that by entering into the relevant treaties, States did not intend to contract out of countermeasures. As has been analysed above, States have frequently taken countermeasures in response to serious *erga omnes* breaches in the field of human rights. In the clear majority of cases, States targeted by these countermeasures (such as Poland in 1981, Surinam in 1982, or Burundi in 1996, to name

141 See the references in Meron (1989), 229 (his note 304).

142 Cf. Simma (1981), 647, for a broader interpretation.

143 Contrast the Optional Protocol to the CCPR (optional individual complaints) and article 44 ACHR (compulsory).

144 See article 1 OP CCPR; article 46, para. 1a ACHR.

145 Simma (1981), 640; Opsahl (1992), 419.

but a few)[146] were parties to the CCPR, but had not accepted the Human Rights Committee's competence to receive inter-State complaints. Had the CCPR regime been exclusive, none of these countermeasures could have been taken. As has been shown above, not only were they taken, but they also provoked surprisingly few protests.[147] In the light of these considerations, there is little doubt that at least where inter-State procedures are not available, the CCPR or ACHR enforcement mechanisms do not affect the right of States to take countermeasures in response to serious *erga omnes* breaches.

Inter-State procedures available

Where inter-State procedures are available (either because they are compulsory or because the target State has made the required declaration), conflicts between countermeasures and treaty enforcement systems pose more problems. In principle, States seeking to respond against breaches could institute proceedings before an impartial and independent institution, which (to quote the *Furundzija* judgment), 'makes it possible for compliance ... to be ensured in a neutral and impartial manner.'[148]

Whether the more neutral and impartial means of ensuring compliance are not merely an option, but actually restrict the right to take countermeasures, depends on a case-by-case application of the various criteria listed above. For the sake of convenience, a basic distinction may be drawn between judicial and non-judicial proceedings.

Non-judicial procedures Under CCPR, CERD, and the Banjul Charter, as well as regularly under the ACHR,[149] inter-State complaints are addressed by treaty commissions or committees, and result in formally non-binding reports or views. In terms of the criteria mentioned above, this factor of course raises considerable doubts as to the effectivity of the enforcement systems. Neither of the relevant institutions is in a position to make binding decisions, and to impose upon States legal obligations. In the last resort, compliance with eventual reports or views thus remains a voluntary act, and States failing to comply do not incur responsibility.[150] On the other hand, the mere fact that proceedings are formally non-binding does not settle matters. Even formally

[146] See above, section 6.2.1.a. [147] See above, section 6.2.1.d (pp. 236–237).
[148] *Furundzija* judgment, 38 ILM (1999), para. 152. [149] Cf. above, footnote 26.
[150] See above, references in footnote 27.

non-binding systems can of course secure a high degree of compliance; as noted above, the effectivity of an enforcement system does not solely depend on whether it imposes upon States binding obligations.[151] It is therefore necessary to look beyond the question of bindingness.

In line with the above considerations, it may be helpful to look at the question of compliance first. Given the almost complete lack of practice, it is impossible to draw up proper records of compliance. With due caution, one might point to the fact that States parties to CCPR, CERD, and the ACHR (although not necessarily under the Banjul Charter) have usually accepted the outcome of *individual* complaint procedures.[152] Whether the same would hold true for inter-State procedures remains to be tested, but experience under the Banjul Charter (as the only of the four inter-State procedure having been used) warrants a note of caution.[153] This is underscored by the almost complete absence of mechanisms capable of ensuring compliance with committee or commission views. Under the Banjul Charter, the Assembly of Heads of States may take action, but has very limited powers.[154] No supervisory organs exist under CERD, CCPR, and the ACHR.[155]

Secondly, a brief look at the nature of inter-State proceedings confirms these doubts. As appears from the relevant provisions, all of the four treaties leave considerable room for discretion.[156] Under the Banjul Charter, CERD, and CCPR, complaints are to be preceded by negotiations between the parties. Even after the matter has been transferred to the respective treaty bodies, the focus remains on the friendly settlement of disputes rather than a formalised assessment of treaty compliance. Under article 52 of the Banjul Charter, the African Commission is to use 'all appropriate means to reach an amicable solution'[157] before beginning to prepare a report. Perhaps most importantly, eventual reports are, as a general matter, not published but only submitted to the Assembly of Heads of States.[158] In proceedings under the ACHR, CCPR, and CERD, the treaty bodies are also encouraged to establish

[151] See above, section 7.2.a.2.

[152] See e.g. Tomuschat (1995), 624–625; Cohen Jonathan (1995), 920.

[153] The only complaint submitted so far, communication 227/99, has so far not led to any result.

[154] See e.g. article 58, para. 2 Banjul Charter.

[155] It should be noted that treaty bodies have at times appointed Special Rapporteurs entitled to monitor compliance, see Schmidt (1992), 650.

[156] Karl (1994), 109–110. For brief descriptions of the respective procedures see Sands/Mackenzie/Shany (1999), 176–177, 183–184, 226–229, 241–244.

[157] Article 52 Banjul Charter. [158] *Ibid.*

conditions conducive to an amicable resolution of the dispute.[159] Under CCPR and CERD, disputes are transferred to an *ad hoc* conciliation commission upon whose composition the parties to the dispute retain considerable influence.[160] In the light of these considerations, one may doubt whether inter-State proceedings would 'make[s] it possible for compliance ... to be ensured in a neutral and impartial manner.'[161] On the contrary, much suggests that the four treaty enforcement systems are not sufficiently effective to warrant a restriction of the right to take countermeasure.

Finally, this interpretation is also borne out by international practice. In at least some of the cases examined above, States parties to the respective agreements were prepared to take countermeasures without pursuing non-binding inter-State procedures. Western States' countermeasures against Zimbabwe provide an example in point. Although Zimbabwe recognises the possibility of inter-State complaints to the Human Rights Committee,[162] none of the CCPR State parties apparently felt the need to pursue this possibility before resorting to countermeasures. Neither did African States exhaust the possibility of inter-State recourse under the Banjul Charter before imposing economic sanctions on Burundi in 1996.[163] Finally, although Yugoslavia, during the Kosovo crisis, arguably was in breach of its obligations under CERD, none of the States taking countermeasures (and subsequently using military force) considered the possibility of inter-State proceedings pursuant to articles 11–13 CERD.[164] All this suggests that treaties providing for non-judicial inter-State proceedings do not exclude the right of States to take countermeasures in response to serious *erga omnes* breaches.

Judicial procedures Unlike the other relevant agreements, the Slavery and Genocide Conventions as well as the ECHR open the possibility of a proper judicial challenge, resulting in a binding judgment by an international court. The three respective agreements are

[159] See article 48, para. 1f ACHR; article 41, para. 1b, 1g, and 1h CCPR; article 11, para. 2 CERD.

[160] See article 42, para. 1b CCPR; article 12, para. 1a CERD. Pursuant to article 42, para. 1a, even conciliation under the CCPR is subject to the prior consent of the parties; cf. Karl (1994), 109–110.

[161] *Furundzija* judgment, 38 ILM (1999), para. 152.

[162] See http://www.unhchr.ch/html/menu3/b/a_ccpr.htm. On the dispute see above, section 6.2.1.a (pp. 224–225).

[163] See above, section 6.2.1.a (pp. 221–223). [164] See above, section 6.2.1.a (pp. 223–224).

therefore much more likely to be considered effective (and thus to contract out of countermeasures) than the treaty mechanisms analysed so far. Proceedings before both relevant institutions (ICJ and the Strasbourg Court) also would fulfil most of the other formal indications of effectivity listed above. The ICJ has jurisdiction to award a variety of remedies, ranging from declaratory judgments to orders of compensation or restitution.[165] It is in a position to respond instantly if applicants request provisional measures. Furthermore, as recently clarified in the *LaGrand case*, interim orders of protection impose upon States binding legal obligations.[166] Finally, article 94, para. 2 UNC, recognising the Security Council's competence to enforce ICJ judgments, establishes an institutional framework capable of ensuring compliance.[167]

The situation is similar with respect to proceedings before the Strasbourg Court. Rule 39 of the ECHR Rules of Procedure enables the Court to grant interim measures of protection, whose binding nature has recently been affirmed in the *Mamatkulov case*.[168] Under article 46, para. 2 ECHR, the Committee of Ministers of the Council of Europe is competent to supervise the execution of judgments, which it can do by means of resolutions. As regards available remedies, article 41 ECHR only mentions the Court's power to order 'just satisfaction'. In practice, however, this restrictive formula has been interpreted broadly, covering *inter alia* the award of extensive damages.[169] This brief survey suggests that proceedings under the Genocide and Slavery Conventions and the ECHR would meet most or all of the various criteria mentioned above.

On the other hand, it has been stated already that the criteria are formal indications of effectivity, and that they are therefore mere starting-points for the analysis. It is therefore necessary to look beyond the

[165] Collier/Lowe (1999), 250–252; Brownlie (1996), 557. For a comprehensive discussion see Gray (1987), who questions the power of international tribunals to order restitution (11–17, 95–96).

[166] *LaGrand case*, ICJ Reports 2001, paras. 102–103. [167] See above, section 1.1.

[168] *Mamatkulov and Abdurasulovic v. Turkey*, paras. 106–107. The judgment is particularly important becauses it reverses the Eur.Ct. HR's earlier position taken in *Cruz Varas v. Sweden*, ECHR, Ser. A, No. 201 (1991). For comment see Tams (2003), 681.

[169] See e.g. *Stran Greek Refineries and Stratis Andreadis case* (Merits and Just Satisfaction), ECHR, Ser. A, No. 301B (1994) (involving a particularly substantial award of damages); *Papamichalopolous and Others v. Greece* (Just Satisfaction), ECHR, Ser. A, No. 330B (1995), para. 34 (clarifying that 'just satisfaction' under the Convention comprises all forms of reparation recognised under general international law). Cf. Gray (1987), 153–160, for criticism of the Court's practice in calculating compensation.

text of the relevant agreements and to assess the actual experience with judicial enforcement of the relevant agreements. Given the differences between proceedings before the two courts, this analysis needs to distinguish between treaties providing for recourse to the ICJ, and the European system establishing the jurisdiction of the Strasbourg Court.

Proceedings before the ICJ: When looking beyond the formal indications listed above, a number of factors suggest that the exclusivity of ICJ proceedings should not simply be presumed. Again, questions of compliance may be looked at first. Past experience suggests that States (at least prior to the *LaGrand case*) have frequently disregarded the interim orders, but generally complied with the Court's final judgments.[170] The good compliance record with respect to final judgments may reflect the fact that in a great number of cases, the Court's jurisdiction was founded on a *compromis*. Conversely, the most notorious instances of non-compliance involve highly politicised cases brought by way of unilateral application.[171] Since potential *erga omnes* claims would presumably fall into that latter category, compliance should not be taken for granted. This in particular because the compliance mechanism provided for in article 94, para. UNC has proven to be of rather limited practical relevance: it has been been invoked only once, and never been applied in practice.[172]

As noted above, the nature of breaches triggering the respective enforcement rights may be another factor influencing the analysis. This factor equally suggests that despite meeting the various formal indications mentioned above, proceedings before the ICJ need not necessarily exclude countermeasures. As shown in Chapter 6, countermeasures can only be taken against serious breaches of obligations *erga omnes*. In contrast, inter-State proceedings under the respective compromissary clauses can be commenced against all treaty breaches; there is no limitation to particularly important obligations (such as those having acquired *erga omnes* status) or qualified violations (such as large-scale or systematic breaches). In theory, inter-State proceedings under the Genocide and Slavery Conventions would therefore be possible against, for example, States failing to free slaves taking refuge on board ships,[173]

[170] See Collier/Lowe (1999), 178 and 175.

[171] See e.g. the *Corfu Channel* and *Nicaragua cases*, ICJ Reports 1949, 4, and 1986, 14. For the eventual settlement of the former case see the Memorandum of Understanding of 8 May 1992, 63 BYIL (1992), 781.

[172] Collier/Lowe (1999), 178.

[173] Cf. article 4 of the 1956 Supplementary Slavery Convention.

or States asserting a right to try individual perpetrators of genocide in violation of established principles of jurisdiction.[174] In line with the above considerations, one might argue that whereas treaties would normally be exclusive, countermeasures should remain available when directed against large-scale or systematic breaches of particularly important obligations.

This interpretation does indeed seem to be borne out by the subsequent practice of States and judicial bodies under the respective agreements. Particularly in the case of genocide, the international community has stressed the need for effective responses against what has been termed 'the crime of crimes',[175] whereas arguments in favour of treaty exclusivity would probably be disqualified as formalistic.[176] It must be conceded that practice in the field of countermeasures (as examined above) is of little help, as States parties to the Genocide Convention have not taken countermeasures in response to breaches by other States parties.[177] However, they have at times asserted a right to respond by forcible means, even though recourse to the ICJ would have been available.[178] In order to justify the military campaign against Yugoslavia during the Kosovo crisis, a number of western governments

[174] As in the *Pakistani Prisoners of War case* (following Pakistan's controversial interpretation of article VI Genocide Convention), ICJ Pleadings, 3. For the Court's brief treatment of the case see ICJ Reports 1973, 328 (provisional measures), and 347 (removal from the list); and further Schabas (2000), 425–427.

[175] ICTR, *Kambanda case*, para. 16.

[176] This is particularly clear in discussion about the legality of forcible measures to prevent genocide; see notably Secretary-General Kofi Annan's address to the UN General Assembly, 20 September 1999: 'To those for whom the greatest threat to the future of the international order is the use of force . . ., one might ask . . . if, in those dark days and hours leading up to the [Rwandan] genocide, a coalition of States had been prepared to act in defence of the Tutsi population, but did not receive prompt Council authorization, should such a coalition have stood aside and allowed the horror to unfold?' (UN Doc. A/54/PV.4, at 2). For similar considerations see Nolte (1999), 953-954; Tomuschat (1999), 224–226.

[177] The only relevant instance examined above, western States' countermeasures against the Idi Amin regime, were taken at a time when Uganda had not yet become a party to the Genocide Convention; see http://www.unhchr.ch/html/menu3/b/treaty1gen.htm.

[178] It must be conceded that two of the most pertinent instances of forcible intervention in response to genocidal conduct cannot be relied on. As regards the forcible overthrow of the Idi Amin regime by Tanzanian forces, it has already been stated that Uganda was not bound by the terms of the Genocide Convention. Similarly, Vietnam's intervention in Cambodia is of little help: although Cambodia was in breach of its obligations under the Genocide Convention, Vietnam could not invoke responsibility for the treaty breach, as it only became a party in 1981 (see http://www.unhchr.ch/html/menu3/b/treaty1gen.htm).

qualified the Yugoslavian repression as 'genocidal'.[179] There is no need here to assess the validity of that accusation (which seems to have been abandoned rather quickly), nor indeed the legality of the use of force. What is important to note is that western States could have instituted ICJ proceedings, pursuant to article IX, against Yugoslavia in order to verify their assertion.[180] The fact that they did not do so, but instead relied on self-help suggests that in their view, judicial recourse did not exclude extra-conventional means of responding against alleged acts of genocide. Conversely, none of the States condemning NATO's intervention seemed to argue that article IX of the Genocide Convention excluded private means of redress.

The Indian intervention in East Pakistan in December 1971 seems to point in the same direction. Again it need not be assessed whether India had a right to intervene, nor indeed whether Pakistani forces indeed committed acts of genocide.[181] For present purposes, it is important to note that Indian representatives in the Security Council had referred to breaches of the Genocide Convention (ratified by both countries)[182] eight months before fighting broke out.[183] If India had considered that article IX of the Convention precluded private means of self-help, it would have had ample opportunity to institute ICJ proceedings. As regards responses by other States, India's conduct gave rise to heated

[179] See e.g. German Defence Minister Scharping's statement of 27 March 1999, in: Scharping (1999), 84. Similar statements were made by (then) British Foreign Secretary Robin Cook (cf. The Times, 31 October 1999: 'Cook accused of misleading public on Kosovo massacres', available at http://www.timesonline.co.uk) or (then) British Defence Secretary George Robertson (cf. CNN, 29 March 1999: 'NATO, British leaders allege "genocide" in Kosovo', available at: http://www.cnn.com/WORLD/europe/9903/29/refugees.01/). For an assessment of these claims see Mennecke (2004).

[180] At the time of the Kosovo crisis, Yugoslavia considered itself bound by the 1948 Convention and thus could have been a party to cases brought under article IX. Matters only changed in March 2001, when Yugoslavia, following the 2000 change of government, newly applied for UN membership and entered a reservation against article IX of the Genocide Convention. Also, according to the Court's view adopted in 1999, Yugoslavia, notwithstanding problems of State succession, had access to the Court under articles 35, 36 of its Statute – hence it could act as applicant in the *Kosovo cases* and seek an interim order. For the Court's subsequent change of position on articles 35, 36 see the eventual judgments in the *Kosovo cases* (preliminary objection), available at www.icj-cij.org. For well-founded criticism of the Court's change of view see the Joint Declaration appended to that judgment (*ibid.*).

[181] Cf. Franck (2002), 139–143; Gray (2000a), 26–27 and 39; Franck/Rodney (1973), 275.

[182] See http://www.unhchr.ch/html/menu3/b/treaty1gen.htm. On *Pakistan's* subsequent attempts to apply the Convention see above, footnote 174.

[183] See the statement reproduced in UNYB 1971, 140; and Franck (2002), 139–140 for further references.

debates.[184] Even States criticising it however did not seem to suggest that the Genocide Convention excluded self-help.

Practice in the field of slavery is considerably more difficult to assess. The above survey suggests that States have not responded against breaches of the Slavery Conventions by taking countermeasures or forcible action. However, two instances of State practice, both concerning Liberia, suggest that judicial enforcement by the ICJ was not intended to exclude other forms of enforcement action. The first instance has been briefly dealt with already. In 1961, Portugal filed inter-State procedures against Liberia pursuant to article 26 of the ILO Constitution, alleging breaches of ILO Convention No. 29, the so-called 'Forced Labour Convention'.[185] At the relevant time, both countries were parties to the 1926 Slavery Convention, which not only outlaws slavery, but safeguards, in article 5, the right to remain free from forced or compulsory labour. When filing its complaint under article 26 of the ILO Constitution, Portugal thus implicitly accepted that the 1926 Slavery Convention would not exclude the parallel ILO mechanisms. This of course does not necessarily mean that countermeasures should equally remain possible. However, it indicates that efforts to outlaw slavery and related forms (such as forced labour) should as a general rule be complementary.

Secondly, earlier attempts to exercise pressure on Liberia support this conclusion. During the early 1930s, Liberia's practice of slavery had been heavily criticised by the United Kingdom and the United States, whose allegations had been largely confirmed by a commission of inquiry, set up by the League of Nations.[186] When Liberia failed to accept the recommendations of that commission, the British government moved to exclude Liberia from the League.[187] At that time, both States were parties to the 1926 Convention. Again, the incident, while not amounting to an exercise of countermeasures against States breaching the Slavery Convention, suggests that judicial supervision by an international court – the PCIJ – was not meant to exclude other forms of sanctions.

To sum up this review, there is thus at least some evidence suggesting that even when recognising a right of all parties to enforce treaties before the ICJ, States did not intend to contract out of other forms of

[184] Cf. Franck (2002), 140–142 for references.
[185] 46 ILO Bull. (1963), No. 2, Suppl. II; and cf. above, section 2.2.1.a.
[186] von Gretschaninow (1935), 174–178. [187] LNOJ 1934, 511.

law enforcement. Finally, it deserves to be mentioned that in a general way, the Court seemed to accept this position in the *Hostages case*. Following the seizure of the embassy, the United States took a variety of measures against Iran, including legal proceedings (before the ICJ), institutional action (before the Security Council), and decentralised sanctions (retorsions and countermeasures), to which the abortive attempt to liberate the hostages ('Operation Rice Bowl') added a further element.[188] For present purposes, it is crucial to note that while Operation Rice Bowl was only undertaken after Iran's failure to respect the ICJ's interim order had become manifest, the other responses were pursued before and during ICJ preoceedings. This already suggests that in view of the United States, countermeasures were an alternative option that could be taken even prior to the institution of legal proceedings. More importantly, the Court, by implication, seemed to endorse this view. While observing that Operation Rice Bowl might 'undermine respect for the judicial process of international relations',[189] it failed to condemn the other measures taken by the United States. It thus seemed to accept that the United States could adopt non-forcible countermeasures in parallel with judicial proceedings.[190]

These different arguments suggest that although ICJ proceedings under the Slavery or Genocide Conventions fulfil most of the formal indications mentioned above, States agreeing on them did not intend to contract out of the customary right to take countermeasures in response to breaches of parallel customary obligations. States parties to the respective conventions thus retain their right to take countermeasures in response to treaty breaches which at the same time qualify as serious violations of obligations *erga omnes*.

Proceedings before the Strasbourg Court: Proceedings before the Strasbourg Court in principle raise the same issue. Just with regard to the Slavery or Genocide Conventions, it is conceivable that in the case of serious breaches, States should be entitled to take countermeasures without having to exhaust the available means of dispute settlement. The fact that the Convention recognises the right of States to bring inter-State proceedings in response to even minor breaches (such as, for example, the practice of States to censor prisoners' letters

[188] For a discussion see Stein (1982), 499. [189] ICJ Reports 1980, 43 (para. 93).

[190] Cf. Diss.Op. Morozov, ICJ Reports 1980, 52. See also Marschik (1997), 106–107; Elagab (1987), 172; Stein (1982), 517.

containing derogatory remarks about prison authorities),[191] but does not contain any special procedures for dealing with large-scale breaches might support this conclusion. However, in a number of ways, experience with the ECHR is different from that under the Slavery or Genocide Conventions. One factor worth noting is that judgments of the Strasbourg Court have been complied with in all cases. Unlike in the case of the ICJ, this good compliance record also covers interim orders[192] and politically sensitive cases.[193] It may be added that unlike in other systems, State parties have actually invoked the mechanism for inter-State proceedings. While commentators have criticised the failure to make more frequent use of inter-State applications, notably during the Chechen conflict,[194] it seems fair to say that the European system comes closest to developing a culture of inter-State enforcement of human rights standards. Both factors suggest that judicial proceedings under the ECHR are better developed than the equivalent procedures under the Slavery and Genocide Conventions, and thus more likely to exclude the right of countermeasures.

On balance, practice would seem to support this assessment. When complaining about other ECHR parties' compliance with human rights, States have usually made use of the Convention procedures and not relied on coercive means of self-help. More importantly, in the one instance involving countermeasures between ECHR members, the acting States first sought to secure compliance by judicial means. As noted above, European States in 1967 partly suspended financial assistance owed to Greece under Protocol 19 to the Greek Association Agreement.[195] The decision to take this countermeasure, however, was preceded by frequent calls on Greece to comply with its obligations under the ECHR.[196] What is more, it was taken after four ECHR member States had initiated inter-State proceedings before the Strasbourg organs, which produced no immediate results. Unlike, for example, the United States in the *Hostages case*, State parties to the ECHR thus seemed to accept that before resorting to self-help, they ought to seek

[191] Cf. article 8 ECHR as interpreted in *Pfeifer and Plankl v. Austria*, ECHR Ser. A, No. 227 (1992).

[192] Cf. *Cruz Varas case*, ECHR, Ser. A, No. 201 (1991), para. 100.

[193] Cf. Schlette (1995), 915.

[194] See Recommendations 1456 and 1478 (2000), adopted by the Parlamentary Assembly of the Council of Europe. For comment cf. Voeffray (2004), 151–152, and more generally Kamminga (1994), 153.

[195] See above, section 2.2.2.d.

[196] Coufoudakis (1977–1978), 114.

judicial relief. It may be added that at the relevant time, recourse to the ECHR was considerably less likely to produce any immediate results, as the Strasbourg organs had not yet made use of their power to issue interim measures of protection.

To sum up, there is considerable support for the view that by entering into, and subsequently strengthening, the enforcement mechanism of the ECHR, States have implicitly accepted restrictions on their right to take countermeasures. The preceding considerations suggest that where serious violations of obligations *erga omnes* at the same time violate parallel ECHR provisions, State parties could not immediately resort to countermeasures, but would first have to seek judicial relief before the Strasbourg Court. As noted above, a right to take countermeasures might eventually revive once the defendant State fails to cooperate in the judicial proceedings.[197] However, in principle, ECHR members have contracted out of their right to take countermeasures.

Interim conclusion

The controversial issue of the relation between countermeasures and treaty-based dispute settlement procedures thus defies a clear-cut answer. Unlike the relation between treaty enforcement and ICJ proceedings, the matter is not covered by explicit conflict clauses. Nor does the general regime of countermeasures solve it. Instead, much depends on whether treaty systems ensure the effective protection of treaty rights. When assessing the effectivity of the relevant treaty enforcement systems, it is necessary to distinguish between (i) treaties providing for no inter-State procedure, (ii) treaties providing for non-judicial inter-State procedures, and (iii) treaties providing for judicial inter-State procedures. The former two categories of treaties clearly do not exclude a right to take countermeasures. The situation is more difficult where treaties (such as the Genocide or Slavery Conventions or the ECHR) provide for judicial enforcement. Practice and jurisprudence, as well as general considerations about the compliance with ICJ decisions, suggest that neither the Slavery nor the Genocide Conventions exclude countermeasures. In contrast, States parties to the ECHR have accepted that countermeasures can only be taken once recourse to the Strasbourg Court has proved unsuccessful.

[197] See above, Introduction (to this chapter).

7.2.3 *Special factors restricting treaty enforcement*

Finally, even where treaties recognise the same enforcement rights that derive from the *erga omnes* concept, conflicts cannot be excluded. As stated above, treaties not infrequently subject enforcement measures to special constraints not applicable to *erga omnes* enforcement. Two specific problems need to be addressed in this regard: (i) special conditions restricting the exercise of self-defence (incuding non-forcible measures) under article 51 UNC, and (ii) the effects of reservations, registered against treaty-based compromissary clauses, on parallel *erga omnes* proceedings.

7.2.3.a Article 51 UNC

While implicitly recognising the right of States to respond against wrongful acts by way of non-forcible countermeasure, article 51 UNC subjects such responses to two conditions not applicable to countermeasures taken against serious *erga omnes* breaches. First, States other than the direct victim of the armed attack can only exercise collective self-defence following a prior request by that direct victim;[198] secondly, responses are only permitted against breaches that qualify as 'armed attacks'.[199] The question is whether any of these special conditions should equally apply to responses based on the *erga omnes* concept.

Although conceptually, the first issue is of considerable relevance, it can only be addressed in a cursory way here. It depends on whether enforcement rights based on the *erga omnes* concept presuppose a prior authorisation of direct victims (if any), i.e. whether they are autonomous or derivative in character. As stated in the Introduction, this issue cannot be covered exhaustively in the present study. However, it may be briefly noted that in situations involving armed attacks, the conceptual difficulties have hardly given rise to practical problems. Practice suggests that States not individually injured have only responded against *erga omnes* breaches with the approval of the direct victim State. For example, responses against Argentina or Iran during the Falklands/Malvinas and Teheran Hostages crises were coordinated with the United Kingdom and the United States, while the international community's reaction against Iraq in 1990 was preceded by

198 This does not necessarily follow from the text of article 51 UNC, but from the ICJ's judgment in the *Nicaragua case*, ICJ Reports 1986, 105 (para. 199).
199 For an interpretation see Gray (2000a), 96–105; Dinstein (2001), 165–169.

prior Kuwaiti requests for help.[200] At least in cases involving the illegal use of force, other States thus seem to accept the primary role of the victim State's assessment. The idea informing article 51 UNC thus seems acceptable.[201] For the sake of clarity, it should be pointed out that this does not prejudice the broader conceptual issue whether responses based on the *erga omnes* concept could only ever be taken in the interest of direct beneficiaries of the obligations in question.[202]

The second question – the requirement that responses be taken only against armed attacks – can equally be dealt with briefly. Unlike the first question, it does not raise major difficulties. Even though acts of self-defence are only permitted in response to armed attacks, there is little indication that the same restriction should apply to non-forcible countermeasures taken in response to serious *erga omnes* breaches. It has already been stated that the armed attack requirement is based on a specific reasoning: the idea that exceptions to the prohibition against the use of force should be construed narrowly.[203] Since this consideration does not apply in the case of non-forcible countermeasures taken against *erga omnes* breaches, there is little reason to subject these responses to the same restriction. This reading is confirmed by the *Nicaragua* judgment, in which the Court even seemed to admit that States might use proportionate, small-scale force to counter another State's use of force not amounting to an armed attack.[204] This interpretation is of course difficult to reconcile with the text of articles 2, para. 4 and 51 UNC;[205] however, few problems arise if States limit themselves to non-forcible responses.

[200] Hence operative para. 9 of SC Res. 661 (1990), recognises the right of States to provide 'assistance' to the legitimate Kuwaiti government.

[201] See also para. 5 of the ILC's commentary to article 54 ASR; and Schorlemmer (2003), 284–287.

[202] For brief comment see above, Introduction. Judge Vereshchetin's separate opinion in the *East Timor case* (in which he alleged that Portugal had failed to show that its claim was supported by the people of East Timor) provides the clearest support for a *derivative reading*; see ICJ Reports 1995, 136–138; similarly article 48, para. 2b ASR and para. 12 of the commentary. In contrast, a number of States' comments on the ILC's work on State responsibility (see notably France, UN Doc. A/CN.4/515, 88) as well as Judge Weeramantry's separate opinion in *Gabčíkovo* by implication suggest an *autonomous reading*: as noted above (section 5.2.5.e), Judge Weeramantry argued that although Hungary (as a specially affected State) would have been estopped from raising the question of treaty breaches, other States had a legal interest sufficient to disapply the rules of estoppel. This argument could not have been made if the legal interest of other States had been derivative. For further discussion see Tams (Manuel), para. 14.

[203] See above, section 7.2.1.b. [204] ICJ Reports 1986, 110 (210); Hargrove (1987), 138.

[205] See Dinstein (2001), 174–175.

To sum up, State practice suggests that the first special condition restricting collective self-defence – the requirement of a prior authorisation by the direct victim – should equally govern responses based on the *erga omnes* concept. In contrast, such countermeasures can be taken even where the second special condition – the requirement of an armed attack – is not met.

7.2.3.b The effects of reservations

A similar conflict arises where treaties (such as the Genocide and the Slavery Conventions) recognise the right of States to institute ICJ proceedings in response to breaches, but where States have registered reservations against the respective compromissary clauses. In this case, States parties to the Convention could seek to circumvent the jurisdictional problem by instituting proceedings on the basis of the *erga omnes* concept. Especially with respect to the Genocide Convention, the question is highly relevant, as a great number of States have excluded the Court's compulsory jurisdiction under article IX.[206] It therefore has to be determined whether such reservations would equally bar ICJ proceedings based on the *erga omnes* concept.[207] The answer to this question may depend on the wording of the respective reservation. However, the ICJ's jurisprudence on the matter provides considerable guidance. Two questions have to be distinguished.

First, it is necessary to assess the legal effects of the respective reservation. Neither the 1926 Slavery Convention nor the Genocide Convention explicitly exclude reservations.[208] Given the importance of the respective treaty enforcement machineries, one might wonder whether they are incompatible with the treaties' object and purpose,

[206] Cf. the information available at http://www.unhchr.ch/html/menu3/b/treaty1gen.htm. Prior to 1989, similar reservations had been made by most socialist countries, but have since been gradually withdrawn. Cf. further Cassese (1990), 174–175; Akhavan (1991), 287.

[207] This is of course not the only conceivable conflict. In addition, treaties may subject recourse to ICJ to special conditions that do not apply to *erga omnes* proceedings. The range of such special conditions is, in principle, unlimited. Treaty clauses could e.g. restrict standing to specially affected parties, in which case it would have to be decided whether the more restrictive approach should exclude *erga omnes* proceedings. Similarly, in the *Armed Activities (Congo Rwanda) case*, Rwanda invoked article 29 CEDAW, under which parties were required to pursue negotiations before submitting disputes to the ICJ; cf. paras. 78–79 of the interim order. Since the two relevant treaties (the Genocide and the Slavery Convention) do not seem to contain any such special conditions, the discussion in the text is limited to questions of reservations.

[208] Contrast article 9 of the 1956 Supplementary Slavery Convention.

and thus invalid.[209] The background to the ICJ's 1951 *Genocide* opinion, in which the Court recognised the 'object and purpose' test, reinforces these doubts: proceedings were initiated following controversies about reservations, submitted by a number of socialist countries, against article IX of the Genocide Convention. In its more recent jurisprudence, the Court has largely ignored these arguments. Refraining from any 'object and purpose' test, it has had few qualms to uphold the effects of reservations registered against article IX of the Genocide Convention and article 22 CERD, where these had not been objected by the applicant State.[210] By the same token, it seems inevitable that States could exclude the application of article 8 of the 1926 Slavery Convention. Notwithstanding the importance of judicial supervision, reservations registered against compromissary clauses would thus be valid unless they had been objected to.

The question remains whether such valid reservations would equally exclude the Court's jurisdiction over parallel *erga omnes* claims. This, of course, first and foremost depends on an analysis of the wording of the respective reservation. On the basis of the Court's previous (controversial) jurisprudence, a preclusionary effect would however be rather unlikely. A very similar question had arisen in the *Nicaragua case*, where the Court held that the defendant's multilateral treaty reservation did not exclude the applicant's claim brought under the optional clause.[211] This decision was partly informed by the Court's conviction that even identical rules of custom and treaty would retain their separate existence.[212] More importantly, it was based on a restrictive interpretation of the defendant's reservation, which, in the view of critics, effectively undermined its effects.[213] In the light of this jurisprudence, it seems unlikely that States, by registering reservations against treaty-based compromissary clauses, could exclude the Court's jurisdiction over parallel *erga omnes* claims.

209 Cf. article 19(c) VCLT, which represents customary international law and would thus apply to the two relevant conventions.

210 See *Armed Activities (Congo Rwanda) case*, paras. 67 and 71–72 (available at http://www.icj-cij.org); *Kosovo case (Yugoslavia/United States)*, ICJ Reports 1999, 761, paras. 21–25; *Kosovo case (Yugoslavia/Spain)*, ICJ Reports 1999, 916, paras. 29–33.

211 See ICJ Reports 1986, 92–97 (paras. 172–182).

212 ICJ Reports 1986, 94–96 (paras. 177–179); and already above, text accompanying footnotes 85–88.

213 ICJ Reports 1986, 96–97 (paras. 180–182). For criticism of the decision see e.g. the dissents of Judges Jennings and Oda, ICJ Reports 1986, 216–219 and 529–537; and further Crawford (1997), 373–374.

To sum up, the legal effects of reservations registered against compromissary clauses is largely determined by the Court's controversial jurisprudence. Contrary to what might be suggested by article 19(c) VCLT, the Court would be likely to uphold the validity of such reservations. Contrary to the probable intention of the declaring State, the reservation would only exclude the Court's jurisdiction over treaty claims, while leaving the possibility of parallel *erga omnes* claims unaffected.

7.3 Concluding observations

The preceding discussion shows that *erga omnes* enforcement rights almost inevitably conflict with enforcement rights derived from treaties. When discussing the relation between these competing enforcement rules, three different conflicts need to be distinguished.

(i) Treaties conferring enforcement rights upon non-State actors do not exclude the exercise of *erga omnes* enforcement rights. In the case of enforcement by individuals, this follows from the text of the treaties itself. With respect to institutional enforcement action under Chapter VII UNC, an analysis of UN practice shows that even where the Security Council is seized of a matter, UN members retain the right to institute ICJ proceedings or to take countermeasures.

(ii) As regards conflicts betweeen specific rights of decentralised enforcement conferred by treaty, and decentralised enforcement on the basis of the *erga omnes* concept, the situation is more complex. Most of the relevant treaties (CCPR, CERD, ACHR, the Banjul Charter, etc.) do not exclude the exercise of *erga omnes* enforcement rights. The right of parties to circumvent the treaty-specific procedures and instead institute ICJ proceedings is usually recognised in the treaty itself. In the case of countermeasures, most treaty procedures are not exclusive, as they alone would not guarantee the effective protection of treaty rights. With respect to both *erga omnes* enforcement rights, the ECHR is the exception that proves the rule. Article 55 ECHR suggests that member States could not institute ICJ proceedings in response to breaches of human rights obligations protected by the ECHR. Given the effectivity of the ECHR mechanism of protection, and the general reluctance to make use of extra-conventional means of enforcement, it also seems that member States could only take countermeasures *inter se* once inter-State proceedings have proved unsuccessful.

(iii) Finally, where treaties recognise enforcement rights identical to those flowing from the *erga omnes* concept, specific conditions restricting their exercise could equally apply to *erga omnes* enforcement. With respect to article 51 UNC, the more convincing view is that in cases of *erga omnes* breaches involving the use of force, other States could only respond in the interest of the individually injured State. In contrast, article 51 UNC does not preclude the possibility of responses against forcible conduct that does not qualify as an armed attack. Lastly, on the basis of the Court's jurisprudence, it would seem that reservations registered against treaty-based compromissary clauses do not affect the right of States to institute parallel proceedings directed against *erga omnes* breaches.

When looking beyond the relevant conflicts discussed in the preceding chapter, two general points seem worth noting. First, the preceding chapter clarifies that radical solutions - such as the exclusivity thesis pursuant to which all treaties are exclusive, or attempts by ILC Special Rapporteurs to introduce a general rule, making countermeasures dependent on the prior exhaustion of dispute settlement mechanisms - are of little help. Instead, conflicts between treaty-specific mechanisms and *erga omnes* enforcement rights need to be addressed on a case-by-case basis, having regard to the two competing rules. Secondly, the case-by-case analysis of specific conflicts, undertaken in the preceding chapter, shows that in the vast majority of cases, treaty-based mechanisms do not exclude *erga omnes* enforcement rights. On balance, practice and jurisprudence therefore have largely been guided by the above-mentioned argument in favour of complementarity and have not accepted that treaty mechanisms take away existing means of enforcement.

This in turn is of crucial relevance for the enforcement of obligations *erga omnes*. If States, by agreeing on treaty-specific enforcement systems, had intended to exclude extra-conventional means of enforcement, they would have reduced the *erga omnes* concept to little more than a paper tiger (or a *chimera*, for that matter).[214] Conversely, that they have not done so is further evidence of the concept's relevance as a means of protecting general interest of the international community.

[214] Cf. the above-quoted remark by Zemanek (2000a), 17.

Conclusion

1.

The present study began by noting two dominant features of the on-going debate about obligations *erga omnes*: (i) the strong views provoked by the concept, and (ii) the lack of agreement about basic issues. Having addressed some of these basic issues, one can hardly avoid the conclusion that the former are the main source of the latter. Throughout the present study, strong feelings about the obligations *erga omnes* concept have resurfaced in the form of assertion or legal argument. If the concept is still 'very mysterious indeed',[1] this is largely due to hopes and fears that commentators project onto it, and that often stand – to borrow a comment on an equally mysterious area of international law (namely recognition) – 'like a bank of fog on a still day, between the observer and the contours of the ground which calls for investigation'.[2] Three different fog banks (or myths) have been encountered throughout the preceding chapters, and need to be briefly commented on: the idealist myth, the realist myth, and the myth of uniqueness.

The Idealist Myth: Clearly discernable in many debates about obligations *erga omnes* is the voice of idealism – the conviction that the *erga omnes* concept marks a paradigm shift towards a better international law, a value-oriented constitutional order. Based on an idealist reading, *erga omnes* effects are often simply taken for granted, or deduced from the perceived nature of the concept: all States *naturally* have standing to institute ICJ proceedings; all States *naturally* can take countermeasures in response to breaches; finally (a structural variation of the idealist theme) all obligations in the field of human rights or environmental law

[1] Brownlie (1988a), 71. [2] Brownlie (1983b), 627.

are *naturally* valid *erga omnes*. While some of these results are defensible (and have indeed been defended in the preceding chapters), the approach by which they are arrived at is problematic. 'The nature of the concept' is a rather lofty notion, especially if deduced from no more than the Court's cursory remarks in *Barcelona Traction*. If not supported by concrete evidence, this dictum would – if one may be permitted to quote *South West Africa* in this regard – hardly be 'capable of carrying the load [idealists] seek to place on it'.[3] The preceding discussion has shown that few things flow 'naturally' or inevitably from the *erga omnes* concept. The legal regime governing it cannot simply be deduced. More generally, it may be doubted whether the constitutionalisation of the international community is likely to be a matter of deduction.

The Sceptical Myth: Perhaps more problematic is the sceptical myth – the conviction that obligations *erga omnes* are 'an empty gesture' and 'purely theoretical category'[4] inspired by nothing more than 'the wishful thinking of some publicists who have no money to spend, no troops to send, no children likely to die in a military action.'[5]

Sceptical approaches appear in different shapes and sizes, ranging from assertion (e.g. Rubin, McCaffrey)[6] to thorough yet unduly restrictive analysis (e.g. Thirlway)[7]. They are informed by profound mistrust against natures of concepts and idealist deduction. Consequently, *Barcelona Traction* is 'taken *cum grano salis*',[8] or disqualified as 'an isolated dictum',[9] and much is made of the lack of actual *erga omnes* cases admitted by the ICJ. While this approach may be defensible at some level, the results are problematic. In particular, sceptical readings do not reflect the broad acceptance of obligations *erga omnes* by both States and the Court. The Court has frequently affirmed the 'isolated dictum'. With few exceptions, judges have taken it at face value rather than with a grain of salt. While States have not regularly filed *erga omnes* claims, they have frequently taken countermeasures in response to serious *erga omnes* breaches and have affirmed the concept in their comments on the ILC's work on State responsibility. Despite all remaining uncertainty, this evidence shows that States recognise the importance as well as the practical relevance of the concept. The *Barcelona Traction* gesture may thus not have been so empty.

[3] ICJ Reports 1966, 39 and 42 (paras. 65 and 72 respectively).
[4] Thirlway (1989), 100 and 102 respectively. [5] Rubin (1993), 172.
[6] Rubin (1993), 172; McCaffrey (1989), 243. [7] Thirlway (1989), 94–102.
[8] *Nuclear Tests cases*, Diss.Op. de Castro, ICJ Reports 1974, 387. [9] Sinclair (1989), 225.

The Myth of Uniqueness: Underlying both idealist and realist approaches is the third, and perhaps most influential, of all *erga omnes* myths – the conviction that the concept is revolutionary and unique. This third myth is the reason both for realists' undue concerns and idealists' excessive expectations. According to the former, the concept, being revolutionary, has to be contextualised and re-read restrictively. Following the latter, the fact that it entitles States to vindicate general interests makes it unique – to the point where treaties conferring similar powers are labelled *erga omnes partes* (as if only something called *erga omnes* could protect general interests).

It would be rather surprising for a thesis focusing on obligations *erga omnes* to conclude that there was nothing special about the concept. The preceding chapters have tried to show that it is indeed special, and that it has a marked impact on the legal rules governing responses against international wrongs. However, it is not as unusual or extraordinary as many supporters or critics claim. By the time of the *Barcelona Traction* judgment, there had been decades of discussion about the right of individual States to respond against wrongful acts not affecting their individual interests. The possibility of decentralised enforcement in the general interest was admitted in restrictive codification attempts (such as article 60 VCLT with respect to interdependent obligations). It was discussed with respect to obligations arising under ICJ judgments or status treaties, or basic humanitarian standards. States themselves moved beyond individual interest requirements by including broadly formulated jurisdictional clauses in treaties – treaties, which at that time did not have to be called *erga omnes partes* to be generally enforceable. The *Aaland Islands*, *Wimbledon* or *Memel Statute cases*[10] show the willingness of courts and tribunals to entertain such claims at a time when the term '*erga omnes*' (in its traditional meaning) was still exclusively used to describe, or assert, objective effects of legal transactions.

Needless to say, none of this deprives the ICJ's *erga omnes* jurisprudence of its relevance. Apart from signalling that it had understood the message of the *South West Africa case*, the Court, in *Barcelona Traction* and since, has moved beyond treaty law and has laid the basis for a more systematic approach to the protection of fundamental general interests of the international community. However, when so doing, it was able to draw on a variety of antecedents. Just as many other

[10] LNOJ, Special Supplement No. 3, Oct. 1920; PCIJ, Ser. A, No. 1 (1923); PCIJ, Ser. A/B, No. 47 (1932), 243, respectively.

'*pièce[s] maitresse[s]*',[11] the concept of obligations *erga omnes* thus builds on solid preparatory work.

The present study does not offer any grand theory to replace the different *erga omnes* myths. On the contrary, it suggests that the concept, after three-and-a-half-decades of often heated debates, deserves the level of sober acceptance accorded to other basic concepts of international law: it is part of the existing legal language, but not an avenue to some alternative form or level of discourse. The *pragmatic approach* thus advocated may not match the inspirational force of the idealist myth, or the appealing simplicity of its sceptical opposite. For two reasons, it seems nevertheless appropriate. For once, practical experience with obligations *erga omnes* suggests that idealist hopes are as exaggerated as the fears of realists. A dose of pragmatism – an approach relating to the facts, as opposed to theoretical concepts[12] – may thus be in order. More importantly, it may be worth noting that – contrary to scepticists' assertions – the *erga omnes* concept *can* today be analysed in a pragmatic way: the preceding chapters show that the concept is now a part of the *reality* of international law, established in the jurisprudence of courts and the practice of States. Tangible evidence is thus much more common than is often assumed; an approach relating to facts, as opposed to theoretical concepts, is therefore possible.

2.

When analysing obligations *erga omnes*, the present study has sought to focus as much as possible on this tangible evidence. Having focused on *erga omnes* effects in one specific field (the decentralised enforcement of the law), it cannot claim to have solved the *erga omnes* mystery altogether. However, it hopefully has succeeded in clearing some of the fog banks that stand between observers and the contours of the ground calling for investigation. In concluding, the main features of the *erga omnes* picture emerging from this investigation can be summarised in ten propositions.

1. The concept of obligations *erga omnes*, as enunciated in paras. 33 and 34 of the *Barcelona Traction* judgment, first and foremost affects the question of law enforcement. *Erga omnes* effects in the field of law enforcement need to be distinguished from other *erga omnes* effects,

[11] Cf. Weil (1992), 287.

[12] Cf. *Oxford Pocket Dictionnary* (2002), entry 'pragmatic': '*pragmatikos*' (greek) = 'relating to facts'.

discussed both prior to and after the *Barcelona Traction* judgment, and affecting questions as diverse as third-party effects of legal acts or the territorial application of obligations.

2. Obligations *erga omnes* derive from general international law. Despite considerable academic (and some jurisprudential) support, attempts to introduce a treaty-based counterpart, so-called 'obligations *erga omnes partes*', are of limited usefulness. Whether and by which means States can respond against treaty breaches largely depends on an interpretation of the relevant treaty. While concepts of general international law can influence this process, it need not usually be burdened with a notion as controversial as *erga omnes* (*partes*).
3. Obligations *erga omnes* differ from other obligations of general international law in that they protect values of heightened importance. In contrast, structural approaches to the concept (pursuant to which *erga omnes* status depends on the structure of performance of a particular obligation) cannot be sustained.
4. Although a threshold requirement of importance is inherently vague and conceptually unsatisfactory, the identification of obligations *erga omnes* will usually not present unsurmountable problems. Obligations arising under (substantive) *jus cogens* rules are, by necessity, valid *erga omnes*; as a consequence, the considerable State practice and jurisprudence relating to peremptory norms can be used as evidence. Outside that core of obligations *erga omnes*, the ICJ's jurisprudence and international practice indicate a number of factors by reference to which the importance of a particular obligation can be assessed. These notably include its recognition in widely ratified treaties, the practice of UN organs, or the character of other States' responses against breaches.
5. As regards legal consequences applicable to breaches, the *erga omnes* concept considerably enhances the prospects of enforcement. Contrary to a widely held view, responses against *erga omnes* breaches need not necessarily be taken by the international community as a whole, acting collectively or through international institutions.
6. With respect to the judicial enforcement of obligations, all States have standing to institute ICJ proceedings in response to *erga omnes* breaches. While not unequivocal, the *Barcelona Traction* dictum on balance strongly supports this view. The broad interpretation of the dictum is not contradicted by para. 91 of the *Barcelona Traction* judgment, and the fact that it was *obiter* does not affect its legal relevance. Jurisprudence since 1970 suggests that the Court would

admit *erga omnes* claims brought in defence of general interests of the international community. On the other hand, proceedings could only be brought against States that have accepted the Court's jurisdiction to entertain claims based on breaches of customary international law.

7. With respect to private means of law enforcement, all States are entitled to take countermeasures in response to serious breaches of obligations *erga omnes*. In a great number of instances, States have asserted a right to respond against systematic and large-scale *erga omnes* breaches even though these did not affect their individual interests. Contrary to popular arguments, practice is neither insufficient, nor exclusively western in provenance, nor does it lack the required *opinio juris*. Although jurisprudence is inconclusive, practice therefore supports a broad approach to the question of standing.
8. Government comments on the ILC's work on State responsibility on balance support, rather than contradict, this view. It must be conceded that there is at present no universal support for a provision expressly enshrining a right to take countermeasures in response to serious *erga omnes* breaches. A majority of States, both during the first and second reading of the ILC's work, however endorsed the substance of such a regulation. Article 54 ASR (which leaves open the question) therefore is unduly restrictive and unfortunate.
9. Both *erga omnes* enforcement rights can only be exercised against the State principally responsible for the violation. In the case of countermeasures, it is generally accepted that measures adopted against third States (not themselves responsible for the wrongful act) are not justified; State practice regarding *erga omnes* breaches confirms this view. As regards judicial proceedings, the Court's *East Timor* judgment in practice leads to the same result. Despite academic criticism, the idea underlying this decision is defensible.
10. States can restrict their *erga omnes* enforcement rights by agreeing on special treaty provisions. Whether a particular treaty mechanism excludes recourse to countermeasures or ICJ proceedings can only be assessed on a case-by-case basis. Closer analysis reveals that most treaties complement *erga omnes* enforcement rights. In contrast, the European Convention on Human Rights excludes proceedings before the ICJ and also restricts the availability of countermeasures; these can only be taken once inter-State proceedings have proved unsuccessful.

Epilogue

Nearly five years have passed since the manuscript of this book was finalised for the hardback edition. Since then, the notion of obligations *erga omnes* has continued to occupy international lawyers. The International Court of Justice and its members have shown a renewed willingness to consider and apply the concept to specific aspects of disputes before them. There is still no clear-cut *erga omnes* case, but the notion seems to have become almost a common phrase in ICJ proceedings on issues such as genocide or armed activities but also those concerning domestic proceedings for alleged acts of torture.[1] "[D]octrinal fascination with the [*erga omnes*] concept"[2] has, if anything, increased. Specialised *erga omnes* literature continues to flourish. Two studies stand out among the host of new publications.[3] The *Institut de droit international* addressed the topic on the basis of reports by Professor

[1] References to the more recent ICJ decisions are given below.

[2] B. Simma, Universality of International Law from the Perspective of a Practitioner, European Journal of International Law 20 (2009), 265, at 272.

[3] In addition to the references in footnotes 4 and 5 see notably the monographs by S. Villalpando, *L'émergence de la communauté internationale dans la responsabilité des Etats* (Paris 2005); P. Picone, *Comunità internazionale e obblighi "erga omnes"* (Naples 2006); and the relevant sections in Theodor Meron's Hague lectures (*The Humanization of International Law*; Leiden et al. 2006).

Cf. further C. Dominicé, A la recherche des droits *erga omnes*, in *Droit du pouvoir – pouvoir du droit. Mélanges offerts à Jean Salmon* (Brussels 2007), 357; B. Simma, Human Rights and State Responsibility, in Reinisch/Kriebaum (eds.), *The Law of International Relations*. Liber Amicorum *Hanspeter Neuhold* (Utrecht 2007), 359; I. de la Rasilla del Moral, *Nihil Novum Sub Sole* Since the South West Africa Cases? On *Ius Standi*, the ICJ and Community Interests, International Community Law Review 10 (2008), 171; M. Dawidowicz, Public Law Enforcement without Public Law Safeguards? Analysis of State Practice on Third-Party Countermeasures and Their Relationship to the UN Security Council, British Yearbook of International Law 77 (2006), 333; M. Benzing, Community Interests in the Procedure of International Courts and Tribunals, Law and Practice of International Courts and

Giorgio Gaja and, at its 71st session in Cracow, adopted an important resolution on "Rights and obligations *erga omnes*".[4] While the *Institut* mainly focused on the enforcement side of the concept, the contributions to *The Fundamental Rules of the International Legal Order*, edited by Tomuschat and Thouvenin,[5] address a broad range of actual and alleged *erga omnes* and *jus cogens* effects.

The subsequent sections do not purport to engage with the more recent literature comprehensively. Instead, they offer a number of 'variations on the *erga omnes* theme' forty years after *Barcelona Traction*. These 'variations' pursue a number of inter-related aims. In the light of recent developments, they re-visit arguments made five years ago and assumptions on which the book is based; and they seek to provide a number of broader perspectives on the current role of the *erga omnes* concept.

* * *

Different Categories of *Erga Omnes* Effects

One assumption that merits further consideration concerns the function(s) served by the *erga omnes* concept. In this respect, the book deliberately adopts a narrow approach. As the Introduction and in fact in the title clarify, the focus is on the *enforcement* of obligations *erga omnes*. The underlying assumption is obvious: the *erga omnes* concept – whatever its precise consequences – is presumed to affect the enforcement of international law, or more generally the law of State responsibility. This assumption was uncontroversial five years ago and is unlikely to cause much concern today.

It is an entirely different question whether the *erga omnes* concept can be restricted to this enforcement function. As noted in chapter 3, this is

Tribunals 5 (2006), 369;.M. M. Toufayan, A Return to Communitarianism? Reacting to "Serious Breaches of Obligations Arising under Peremptory Norms of General International Law" under the Law of State Responsibility and United Nations Law, Canadian Yearbook of International Law 42 (2004), 197; A. Vermeer Künzli, A Matter of Interest: Diplomatic Protection and State Responsibility *Erga Omnes*, International and Comparative Law Quarterly 56 (2006), 553. Needless to say that the list is not exhaustive.

4 See Professor Giorgio Gaja's First and Second Reports on 'Obligations and Rights *Erga Omnes* in International Law', reproduced (together with comments by members of the Institute's fifth commission) in Annuaire de l'Institut de droit international vol. 71-I (2005), 119–212; as well as the plenary debates held at the Institute's Cracow session and final resolution on the topic in Annuaire de l'Institut de droit international vol. 71-II (2006), 83–137 and 286–289.

5 C. Tomuschat/J.-M. Thouvenin (eds.), *The Fundamental Rules of the International Legal Order. Jus Cogens and Obligations Erga Omnes* (Leiden *et al.* 2006).

usually done. Chapter 3 criticises this approach as eclectic and draws attention to 'other' *erga omnes* effects. It argues that by the time of *Barcelona Traction*, the expression '*erga omnes*' had been used for decades (if typically in a different way), and that since 1970 the Court as well as writers have continued to refer to different categories of alleged *erga omnes* effects, often entirely unrelated to questions of law enforcement. Recent developments suggest that this is an on-going trend, which has yet to be properly evaluated. The matter therefore deserves more attention than it usually receives.

Erga Omnes Effects Outside the Field of Law Enforcement

Recent developments bring out very clearly that the expression '*erga omnes*' is used in a variety of legal settings and in order to justify many different legal consequences, often unrelated to questions of law enforcement. Three examples, all taken from the Court's recent jurisprudence, may serve to illustrate the point.

i. Judge Kreća's dissent appended to the 2007 *Bosnian Genocide* judgment[6] underlines the continuing importance of the traditional (i.e. pre-*Barcelona Traction*) understanding of the term.[7] It primarily[8] uses the expression *erga omnes* to denote the "objective legal situation"[9] brought about by General Assembly Resolution 55/12 (admitting the FRY to the United Nations), which is said to have created "a status with *erga omnes* effects".[10] Just as in the pre-*Barcelona Traction* era, the term *erga omnes* therefore is employed to explain, or simply to describe, absolute effects of status decisions.
ii. The Court's reliance on *erga omnes* effects in the final part of its *Wall* opinion is more difficult to classify.[11] In a controversial passage, the majority of the Court suggested that *because* Israel had violated

[6] Application of the Convention on the Prevention and Punishment of the Crime of Genocide (Bosnia and Herzegovina *v.* Serbia and Montenegro) ["*Genocide case*"], Judgment of 27 February 2007, available at www.icj-cij.org.

[7] Cf. pp. 103–110 of the book for references to the 'traditional meaning of the term *erga omnes*'.

[8] In addition to the references in the text see also para. 117 of the dissent, where the *erga omnes* character of obligations arising under the Genocide Convention is affirmed, apparently to underline their importance.

[9] *Genocide case*, Diss. Op. Kreća, para. 57.

[10] *Ibid.* For similar statements see also paras. 51 and 58.

[11] *Legal Consequences of the Construction of a Wall in the Occupied Palestinian Territory* ["*Wall* opinion", ICJ Reports 2004, 136, at paras. 154–160.

certain obligations *erga omnes*, other States were under a duty not to recognise the situation resulting from the construction of the wall.[12] The majority's approach seems to be based on the idea that the *erga omnes* character affects the *substantive scope* of an obligation, namely by imposing upon third States certain ancillary duties. This might be seen as a return to the curious reference to *erga omnes* effects in the 1996 judgment in the *(Bosnian) Genocide case*, in which the Court had invoked the *erga omnes* concept to justify another change in the substantive scope of an obligation – namely to deny the territorial restriction of an obligation.[13] Not surprisingly, the new (just as the old) statement has been criticised.[14]

iii. The majority's allegation of certain substantive *erga omnes* effects in the *Wall* opinion pales in comparison to Judge Cançado Trindade's ambitious approach to the concept set out in the recent *Belgium Senegal* order.[15] Dissenting at the interim stage of proceedings, Judge Cançado Trindade touched upon rather than explored many of the issues.[16] Even though, it is immediately clear that in his view, the *erga omnes* concept, "heralding the advent of the international legal order of our times, committed to the prevalence of superior common values",[17] requires a broad-ranging re-interpretation of traditional international law. This re-interpretation would notably affect "the prerequisites for the indication of provisional measures"[18] (warranting interim protection under more lenient conditions) and the consensual character of international

12 See *ibid.*, para. 159: "Given the character and the importance of the rights and obligations involved, the Court is of the view that al1 States are under an obligation not to recognize the illegal situation resulting from the construction of the wall in the Occupied Palestinian Territory, including in and around East Jerusalem." The context suggests that by mentioning the "character and importance of the rights and obligations involved" the Court intended to refer to their *erga omnes* status (which had been affirmed in paras. 155–157). The separate opinions of Judges Higgins and Kooijmans (discussed below, in section 2b of the epilogue) are equally based on this reading.

13 ICJ Reports 1996, 595, at para. 31. For comment see pp. 110–112 of the book.

14 See further below, text accompanying notes 22 and 23.

15 *Questions relating to the Obligation to Prosecute or Extradite* (Belgium v. Senegal) ["*Belgium Senegal case*"], Order of 28 May 2009, available at www.icj-cij.org.

16 Many of the points are elaborated in A.A. Cançado Trindade, *International Law for Humankind: Towards a New* Jus Gentium, Recueil des Cours, vols. 316 & 317, 2005, especially at pp. 347–364 of vol. 316.

17 *Belgium Senegal case* (*supra* note 15), Diss. Op. Cançado Trindade, at para. 71.

18 Ibid., para. 69.

law more generally.[19] Perhaps most importantly, Judge Cançado Trindade insisted on the "vertical dimension" of obligations *erga omnes*, which equally bound "natural persons *(simples particuliers)*, in their inter-individual relations",[20] i.e. acquired that particular quality referred to, in European human rights law, as *Drittwirkung*.[21]

These brief references illustrate how liberally the expression *erga omnes* continues to be used. They do not put into question the link between *erga omnes* status and issues of law enforcement, but suggest that the concept is increasingly relied on to justify a broad range of diverse other effects.

How to Deal With Them

These other *erga omnes* effects - at least those referred to in the *Wall* opinion and Judge Cançado Trindade's dissent - have yet to be fully appreciated. Just as five years ago, the most common "strategy" is to simply ignore them, and to focus (intuitively, as it were) on the enforcement side of the *erga omnes* concept. Chapter 3 of the book avoids this eclecticism and instead adopts a pragmatic approach: it acknowledges other *erga omnes* effects, distinguishes them and *on that basis*, restricts the analysis to the enforcement of obligations *erga omnes*. More recently, a third strategy has emerged alongside that of eclecticism and pragmatism, which might be termed as one of 'resistance': in their separate opinions in the *Wall* opinion, Judges Kooijmans and Higgins strongly criticised the majority's allegation of substantive *erga omnes* effects, and defended a narrow approach to the *erga omnes* concept. Judge Kooijman

19 Cf. ibid., para. 71: "The consolidation of *erga omnes* obligations of protection, ensuing from the imperative norms of international law, in my understanding overcomes the pattern erected in the past upon the autonomy of the will of the State, which can no longer be invoked or pursued in view of the existence of norms of *jus cogens*. These latter transcend the law of treaties, and encompass nowadays the domain of State responsibility. Those obligations, in their turn, clearly transcend the individual consent of States, heralding the advent of the international legal order of our times, committed to the prevalence of superior common values, in the ongoing construction of the international law for humankind."

20 Ibid., para. 72. For similar statements see already Judge Cancado Trindade's concurring opinion appended to the Inter-American Court's advisory opinion on the *The Juridical Condition and Rights of Undocumented Migrants* (Advisory Opinion of 17 September 2003), Inter-American Court of Human Rights, Ser. A, No. 18 (2003), at paras. 74–85.

21 See e.g. P. van Dijk / G.J.H. van Hoof, Theory and Practice of the European Convention on Human Rights (3rd edn., Leiden et al. 1998), at 22–26. Since "*Drittwirkung* " is frequently described as producing "horizontal effect", the term "vertical dimension" may be misleading.

expressed "considerable difficulty in understanding why a violation of an obligation *erga omnes* by one State should necessarily lead to an obligation for third States".[22] Judge Higgins went further, setting out her understanding of the *Barcelona Traction* dictum in a more general manner. In her view:

"The Court's celebrated dictum in *Barcelona Traction, Light and Power Company, Limited, Second Phase (Judgment, 1. C.J. Reports 1970*, p. 32, para. 33) is frequently invoked for more than it can bear. Regrettably, this is now done also in this Opinion, at paragraph 155. That dictum was directed to a very specific issue of jurisdictional *locus standi*. As the International Law Commission has correctly put it in the Commentaries to the draft Articles on the Responsibility of States for Internationally Wrongful Acts (A/56/10 at p. 278), there are certain rights in which, by reason of their importance "all states have a legal interest in their protection". It has nothing to do with imposing substantive obligations on third parties to a case."[23]

This criticism may indicate an increasing awareness that if the *erga omnes* concept in the *Barcelona Traction* is to be operationalised, its field of application needs to be delimited more clearly. According to Judges Higgins and Kooijmans, the way to do so is to limit it to the sphere of law enforcement[24] and to resist its extension into other areas of international law.

Neither strategy of responding to the challenge posed by other *erga omnes* effects is however fully satisfactory. The *eclectic approach* dominating much of the debate is clearly the most problematic. Simply ignoring the host of statements on other *erga omnes* effects outside the field of law enforcement, its adherents fail to appreciate the complexity of the concept. As noted in chapter 3, this complexity should not (or in any event: should *no longer*) be ignored. Other *erga omnes* effects appear in legal writing

22 *Wall* opinion, *supra* note 11, Sep. Op. Kooijmans, para. 40.

23 *Wall* opinion, *supra* note 11, Sep. Op. Higgins, para. 37. For a similar statement see already R. Higgins, *Problems and Process. International Law and How We Use It* (Oxford 1994), 57. Cf. also Sep. Op. Higgins, para. 38: "The obligation upon United Nations Members not to recognize South Africa's illegal presence in Namibia, and not to lend support or assistance, relied in no way whatever on '*erga omnes*'."

24 According to Judge Higgins, the concept, as employed in *Barcelona Traction*, has an even narrower scope, as the Court in 1970 merely addressed "a very specific issue of jurisdictional *locus standi*" (*Wall* opinion, *supra* note 11, Sep. Op. Higgins, at para. 37 [emphasis added]). This however is an unduly restrictive interpretation: as argued in chapters 1 and 6 of the book, the *Barcelona Traction* dictum, while made in the context of judicial proceedings, is better seen as a pronouncement on questions of standing generally, and thus equally affects questions of standing to take countermeasures.

as well as the ICJ's jurisprudence, and they appear with some regularity. Some of them may indeed far-fetched, but they merit critical and systematic analysis. To ignore them simply is no longer a viable option.

Resistance is a much better approach. The separate opinions of Judges Kooijmans and Higgins rightly engage with alleged other *erga omnes* effects. They are based on the correct assumption that expansive readings of the *erga omnes* concept will further complicate its analysis and undermine its coherence. On the other hand, they may be based on static an approach to a concept that seems very much capable of evolution. In fact, it bears reminding that the *Barcelona Traction* dictum itself took an ambiguous term out of its original context and postulated a new *erga omnes* effect, at that time in the new field of law enforcement. Experience since the 1920s (when the term appeared in international and arbitral practice), but certainly since 1970, suggests that there is no 'one true meaning' of the term *erga omnes*, and the recognition of new or other *erga omnes* effects should not be excluded.

Pragmatically, these problems can be avoided or mitigated by restricting the analysis on *erga omnes* effects in one particular field (such as the enforcement of international law), and to expressly acknowledge – as chapter 3 does – that this approach is based on a narrow approach. It is submitted that this approach remains defensible, as *erga omnes* effects in the field of law enforcement can be distinguished from other (alleged) effects. They may have, as has recently noted, been "overworked"[25] in the literature, but academic debate as well as the Court's jurisprudence and the work of the ILC have established a widely-agreed conceptual framework that debates about substantive *erga omnes* effects still lack.

Pragmatism however comes at a price. It cannot purport to offer a comprehensive account of the *erga omnes* concept. In the long run, it is no substitute for a systematic and critical assessment of *erga omnes* effects outside the field of law enforcement. Recent developments – and Judge Cancado Trindade's dissent in particular – reinforce the need for such a systematic and critical assessment. As explored further below,[26] this analysis will have to the mere assertion of other *erga omnes* effects, whose existence (especially if they involve a fundamental re-interpretation of existing concepts) should not be lightly assumed. In contrast, it requires a detailed examination of international practice and jurisprudence, which may or may not have accepted the link

[25] *Belgium Senegal case, supra* note 15, Diss. Op. Cançado Trindade, at para. 72.

[26] See below, section 3s of the epilogue.

between *erga omnes* status and non-recognition or have recognised the alleged "vertical dimension" of the concept.

Forty years after *Barcelona Traction*, these questions should be taken seriously. Just as writers, from the 1980s onwards rightly began to focus their attention on "*Jus Cogens* Beyond the Vienna Convention",[27] it may now be time to address "obligations *erga omnes* beyond *Barcelona Traction*". Focused on the enforcement of obligations *erga omnes*, the book does not provide such an analysis. Yet it may be hoped that the distinctions drawn in chapter 3 could be of some value to those applying themselves to the task.

The Question of Sources

The argument made in the book is based on a second assumption: it considers obligations *erga omnes* to be obligations under general international law and on that basis distinguishes them from treaty-based obligations protecting interests of communities of treaty members (typically referred to as obligations *erga omnes partes* or *erga omnes contractantes*). This distinction is not absolute, but chapter 4 is deliberately critical of all attempts to conflate obligations *erga omnes* and obligations *erga omnes partes* and questions the value of the latter notion.[28]

Since the initial publication of this book, there have been many further instances of (deliberate or accidental) conflation. If anything, the notion of obligations *erga omnes partes* has become more popular. The *erga omnes* label appears to be so attractive that it cannot be reserved for rules of general international law, and there is continued debate about the *erga omnes partes* nature of obligations arising under WTO law, global or regional human rights treaties, the 1949 Geneva Conventions, and even the ICAO Convention.[29] In a number of ICJ proceedings, judges have explored the common foundations of obligations *erga omnes* and

[27] Cf. Giorgio Gaja, *Jus Cogens* Beyond the Vienna Convention, Recueil des Cours 172 (1981 III), 271.

[28] See especially pp. 124 et seq. as well as p. 310 (proposition 2).

[29] See e.g. T. Gazzini, The Legal Nature of WTO Obligations and the Consequences of Their Violation, European Journal of International Law 17 (2006), 723; E. de Wet, The International Constitutional Order, International and Comparative Law Quarterly 55 (2006), 51; M. Craven, For the 'Common Good': Rights and Interests in the Law of State Responsibility, in Fitzmaurice/Sarooshi (eds.), *Issues of State Responsibility Before International Judicial Institutions* (2004), 105, at 111–112; J. Huang, Aviation Safety, ICAO and Obligations *Erga Omnes*, Chinese Journal of International Law 8 (2009), 63; S. Förster, *Internationale Haftungsregeln für schädliche Folgewirkungen gentechnisch veränderter*

obligations *erga omnes partes*.[30] In its work, the *Institut de droit international*, having initially restricted its work to obligations arising under general international law,[31] subsequently decided to include obligations *erga omnes partes* as well, as these "may share some of the characteristics of obligations *erga omnes* under general international law."[32]

These recent developments suggest that the distinction drawn in chapter 4, between obligations *erga omnes* and obligations *erga omnes partes* may have been over-stated. International practice and jurisprudence typically adopt a more flexible approach than the one advocated in the book - an approach focusing on the common features, rather than the distinction between, the two notions of *erga omnes* and *erga omnes partes*. In retrospect, it may have indeed been preferable to place greater emphasis on these common features. In particular, chapter 4 should have probably acknowledged more prominently that treaties just as custom can protect important community values, and that this importance may be translated into a general right of all members of the community to react against breaches. It may have also been preferable to draw a clearer distinction between the source of the obligation protecting community interests and the source of the enforcement right asserted by a State seeking to respond against a breach.

On the other hand, even under a more flexible approach to the question of sources, crucial differences between the respective enforcement regimes remain. The point is made in chapter 4, but in the light of recent developments, it deserves to be re-iterated that the enforcement of treaty-based community obligations primarily depends on an interpretation of the respective treaty. In two respects, these treaty regimes can affect the *erga omnes (partes)* enforcement regime.

i. Many treaties recognise a general right of all State parties to respond against treaty breaches.[33] If that is the case, as e.g. under many human rights treaties, there is no need to invoke the *erga omnes*

Organismen, at 179–188. References to earlier discussions can be found on pp. 120–121 of the book.

30 See especially Judge Cançado Trindade's dissent in the *Belgium Senegal case*, and cf. also Judge Simma's separate opinion in *Congo Uganda*. Both are addressed more fully below, section 3b.

31 See Professor Gaja's First Report (*supra* note 4), at 122–124.

32 Giorgio Gaja, Second Report (*supra* note 4), at 191. Cf. further Article 1(b) of the *Institut's* resolution (*supra* note 4); as well as Meron (*supra* note 3), 280.

33 See pp. 71-76 of the book for examples. For a comprehensive account cf. F. Voeffray, L'actio popularis - *ou la défense de l'intérêt collectif devant les juridictions internationales* (Geneva 2004).

(partes) status of an obligation to establish standing. The admissibility of inter-State cases before the European Court of Human Rights e.g. does not depend on arguments about the *erga omnes* status of ECHR obligations; Article 33 of the Convention settles the matter. By the same token, with respect to genocide, Giorgio Gaja rightly notes that under Article IX of the Genocide Convention, "[n]o special interest needs to be shown by a State in order to bring a claim before the [International] Court [of Justice]."[34] For the purposes of ICJ proceedings,

> Article IX simply makes it unnecessary to rely on *erga omnes* enforcement rights; the real question is one of interpreting a compromissory clause.

ii. Problems arise if treaties adopt differentiated approaches.[35] Differentiated approaches come in different forms. Some treaties entrust the role of enforcement agents to specific States – such as coast States under Article 218 LOSC. More frequently, treaties designate specific means of enforcement – typically by providing for judicial proceedings (e.g. under Article IX of the Genocide Convention or Article 33 ECHR) or quasi-legal complaints procedures (under many global human rights treaties). In both cases, it must be inquired whether the differentiated enforcement regime set out in the treaty is meant to displace or modify enforcement rights derived from the *erga omnes (partes)* concept – notably the right to resort to countermeasures.

The question, then, may be less one of the source of the obligation qualifying as *erga omnes (partes)* than of the inter-relation between different sets of enforcement rights. This inter-relationship is governed by regular conflict rules, notably by the *lex specialis* principle. Its application means that a State seeking to defend general legal interests of the international community or a treaty community will only need to rely on the *erga omnes (partes)* concept if its enforcement competence does not already follow from the terms or interpretation of a given treaty. Where treaty rules provide for some form of enforcement, it cannot be excluded that the treaty enforcement regime should displace *erga omnes (partes)* enforcement rights. Chapter 7 of the book however suggests that this will rarely be the case, as treaties, even though they are *leges*

34 First Report on Rights and Obligations *Erga Omnes* (*supra* note 4), at 123.

35 For further detail see pp. 125–128 of the book.

speciales, typically do not intend to derogate from the general enforcement mechanisms. In this respect, it is submitted that the guidelines governing the inter-relation between treaties and *erga omnes* enforcement rights identified in chapter 7 would also apply to the inter-relation between treaty mechanisms and *erga omnes partes* enforcement rights. If the *erga omnes* concept is to be operationalised (and especially if this is done on the basis of a more flexible approach to the question of sources), academic debate will have to deal with the very practical issues raised there more fully than it has to date.

Reactions Against *Erga Omnes* Breaches

While the book explores general concepts such as standing and adopts a particular approach to the *erga omnes* concept, the bulk of the analysis focuses on two distinct means of responding against *erga omnes* breaches, namely ICJ proceedings and countermeasures. More specifically, chapters 5 and 6 argue that all States have standing to institute ICJ proceedings in response to *erga omnes* breaches and are entitled to resort to countermeasures in response to *erga omnes* breaches of a serious nature. Developments since 2005 seem to provide further support for these arguments, both with respect to ICJ proceedings (b) and countermeasures (c). Before reviewing the more recent evidence, some brief comments on the method of establishing *erga omnes* effects may be in order (a).

Inductive versus Deductive Approaches

The discussion in Chapters 5 and 6 of the book presupposes that the legality of responses to *erga omnes* breaches cannot simply be assumed, but has to be established in international practice and jurisprudence. In retrospect, it may have been better to address the underlying methodological argument in a separate section. Even though, readers will sense the author's scepticism vis-à-vis deductions from the allegedly obvious nature of the *erga omnes* concept.

Since 2005, different methodological approaches to value-loaden normative concepts have received considerable attention. Much of the debate has focused on *jus cogens* (especially the "virtually unlimited [range of] special effects"[36] said to derive from peremptory status), but the methodological arguments can be applied to debates about

[36] C. Focarelli, Promotional *Jus Cogens*: A Critical Analysis of *Jus Cogens'* Legal Effects, Nordic Journal of International Law 77 (2008), 429, at 439.

obligations *erga omnes* as well. Two trends can be discerned in the literature: First, since 2005, deductive approaches have been carried to new levels of sophistication.[37] Second, in response, sceptics have drawn attention to the problems of simply deducing consequences from concepts.[38] It is submitted that these exchanges have led to a more informed debate about how to approach concepts such as obligations *erga omnes* or *jus cogens* and have brought out the risks of deductive approaches very clearly. Of particular relevance seems the distinction, drawn by Focarelli, between "purely deductive", "semi-deductive" and "fully inductive" ways of establishing special effects flowing from a given concept.[39] Adopting that terminology, the analysis in chapters 5 and 6 could be said to follow a "fully inductive" approach. This methodological choice affects the analysis in many respects. It means that elegant forms of syllogistic reasoning are typically not available; instead, there is no avoiding the cumbersome process of interpreting and evaluating international practice and jurisprudence. Yet on balance, an inductive approach is preferable for a range of reasons: it can help avoid dogmatism; it mirrors the reality of international law, which typically does not accept logical deductions, but applies concepts such as *jus cogens* and *erga omnes* in a pragmatic way; and by relying as much as possible on tangible evidence, it may offer results that are more likely to be accepted and applied in international practice. This does not mean that concepts such as *jus cogens* or obligations *erga omnes* were devoid of significance. They channel debates and shape international practice. They are not "independent from empirical verification",[40] but – as shown in the book – in fact very often *can* be verified empirically. Recent debates suggest that, whether one agrees with the results reached in the book or not, methodologically, the inductive approach employed is the correct one.

While inductive approaches seem to be gaining ground, they are often applied inconsistently. As regards the enforcement side of the *erga omnes* concept, it seems increasingly agreed that there is no

[37] As far as *jus cogens* is concerned, Alexander Orakhelashvili's *tour de force* presents the most ambitious attempt (*Peremptory Norms in Public International Law*, Oxford 2006). With respect to obligations *erga omnes* see notably Judge Cançado Trindade's above-mentioned dissent in the *Belgium Senegal case* (*supra* note 15).

[38] See especially C. Tomuschat, Reconceptualizing the Debate on *Jus Cogens* and Obligations *Erga Omnes* – Concluding Observations, in Tomuschat/Thouvenin (*supra* note 5), 425; Focarelli (*supra* note 36), 429.

[39] Focarelli, *supra* note 36, at 444–449.

[40] Focarelli, *supra* note 36, at 452.

"mechanical link"[41] between *erga omnes* breaches and responses by way countermeasure – hence most contemporary discussions of what used to be called "third-party reprisals" draw on international practice.[42] Yet matters are different with respect to ICJ proceedings. Here deductive approaches continue to hold sway: standing is frequently assumed, or the *Barcelona Traction* dictum played down, but there continue to be few detailed discussions of how the dictum has been interpreted in international practice or in the Court's subsequent jurisprudence.[43] This may be due to the absence of clear-cut public interest proceedings vindicating legal interests of the international community (an issue to be addressed below), or the conceptual difficulty of fitting ICJ proceedings and pronouncements by ICJ judges into neat categories of 'international practice'. However, it needs to be stressed that a "fully inductive" approach would have to go beyond a brief Court dictum and instead evaluate other pieces of evidence. Chapter 5 of the book suggests that there is indeed much more evidence than is usually assumed. The subsequent section evaluates developments since 2005.

Standing to Institute ICJ Proceedings

As will be shown, there is indeed some new evidence, but it is still not conclusive. Forty years after the *Barcelona Traction case*, the Court has yet to admit a single claim based on the *erga omnes* concept. Under the strict approach to sources adopted in the book, it may in fact not often have an opportunity to do so: the bulk of ICJ case-law on alleged wrongful conduct concerns *treaty breaches*; jurisdictional strictures mean that breaches of customary law can only come before the Court in optional clause cases or cases brought under dispute settlement conventions.[44] The more

[41] Tomuschat (*supra* note 38), at 436.

[42] See e.g. Dawidowicz (*supra* note 3); C. Hillgruber, The Right of Third States to Take Countermeasures, in Tomuschat/Thouvenin (*supra* note 5), 265. Tomuschat makes the point with particular clarity when observing that "the admissibility of countermeasures needs to be assessed in each and every single case" (*supra* note 38, at 434).

[43] In this respect, it is telling that the collection of essays edited by Tomuschat and Thouvenin (*supra* note 5), while evaluating a broad range of *erga omnes* and *jus cogens* effects, addresses standing to institute ICJ proceedings only in passing, namely in contributions addressing the Court's jurisdiction to handle public interest proceedings by Ruffert and Thouvenin (at pp. 295 and 311 respectively).

[44] The point is much neglected and requires further study. For brief comment see Meron (*supra* note 3), 280–281; and further C. Tams, The Continued Relevance of Compromissory Clauses as a Source of ICJ Jurisdiction, in Giegerich (ed.), *A Wiser Century? Judicial Dispute Settlement, Disarmament and the Laws of War 100 Years after the Second Hague Peace Conference* (Berlin 2009), 461.

flexible approach to sources dominant in international practice alleviates this problem to some extent. It can interpret proceedings instituted in defence of the general legal interests *of treaty parties* as evidence in point. Pursuant to that understanding, the pending *Belgium Senegal case*[45] might eventually turn out to be the first instance of successful 'public interest litigation' before the Court. At the present stage of proceedings, it is of course too early to tell how the Court and the parties will approach the problem of standing. Yet it seems clear that Belgium will have to do more than to simply assert its legal interest in the proper administration of justice by Senegal. Judging from exchanges during the interim stage of proceedings,[46] the alleged *erga omnes (partes)* nature of some of the obligations involved could help settle this point. If that were so, Belgium (the State suffering from the Court's narrow approach to diplomatic protection in *Barcelona Traction*) might eventually be the first successful applicant invoking *erga omnes (partes)* obligations in ICJ proceedings.

In the meantime, even in the absence of conclusive evidence, practice and jurisprudence provide indications of how the Court would handle *erga omnes* cases. Largely drawing on the Court's jurisprudence between 1970 and 2005, chapter 5 suggests there is "considerable support for a broad interpretation of the *Barcelona Traction* dictum pursuant to which all States have standing in ICJ disputes involving obligations *erga omnes*."[47] Evidence since 2005 would seem to support that view.

i. Just as before 2005, the individual opinions of judges entail important insights. Two of them stand out. Judge Simma's separate opinion in the 2005 *Congo Uganda case*[48] contains a clear endorsement of the broad interpretation of the *Barcelona Traction* dictum. In the last part of his opinion, Judge Simma elaborated on the potential scope of Uganda's counterclaims.[49] In the circumstances of the case, Uganda had accused the Democratic Republic of the Congo of having violated rights of Ugandan nationals under human rights law and humanitarian law. The counter-claim thus presented itself as an instance of diplomatic protection and did not raise serious issues of standing. Since the DRC's conduct had however also affected rights of individuals without Ugandan nationality, Judge Simma clarified

[45] *Supra* note 15.

[46] Cf. the uncorrected verbatim record of the public sittings of 6 April 2009 (3 p.m.) and 7 April 2009 (4.30 p.m.): CR 2009/9, at pp. 58–59 and CR 2009/10, at pp. 14–15.

[47] At p. 197. [48] ICJ Reports 2005, 201.

[49] Ibid., Sep. Op. Simma, at paras. 32–41.

that had it chosen to broaden its counterclaims, "Uganda ... would undoubtedly have had standing to bring such claims [relating to rights of non-nationals]".[50] This reasoning was primarily based on treaty law, as the treaties in question – such as the Geneva Conventions and the Covenant on Civil and Political Rights – gave rise to obligations "owed to a group of States including Uganda, and [were] established for the protection of a collective interest of the States parties".[51] With respect to the Geneva Conventions, that result was indicated by the express terms of common Article 1, pursuant to which all States, irrespective of individual injury, were required to "ensure respect" with international humanitarian law. The Covenant contained no such express clause, but Judge Simma considered the obligations deriving from it to be "instances *par excellence* of obligations that are owed to a group of States ..., and ... established for the protection of a collective interest of the States parties to the Covenant".[52]

In addition to affirming Uganda's standing to raise treaty breaches (even where no express clause so provided), Judge Simma also clarified that "the core of the obligations deriving from the rules of international humanitarian and human rights law are valid *erga omnes*", which implied a general legal interest of all States in their protection.[53] His approach to standing therefore did not depend on the source of the obligation, but flowed from "the community interest underlying international humanitarian and human rights law".[54] Although formally concerned with standing to invoke treaty breaches by way of counter-claim, the reasoning underlying the separate opinion supports a broad approach to standing more generally. In fact, it is difficult to see how the standing of States to raise violations of international law *by way of counter-claim* should be governed by rules different from those governing the standing to raise violations by way of regular ICJ proceedings. By recognising Uganda's right to raise broadly-formulated counter-claims, Judge Simma thus implicitly affirmed the broad interpretation of the *Barcelona Traction* dictum advocated in chapter 5.

[50] Ibid., para. 32.

[51] Ibid., para. 35. The formulation draws on Article 48 of the International Law Commission's 2001 Articles on State Responsibility.

[52] *Congo Uganda case, supra* note 48, Sep. Op. Simma, at para. 35.

[53] *Ibid.*, paras. 39–40. [54] Ibid., para. 38.

ii. In his dissent appended to the recent interim order in the *Belgium Senegal case*, Judge Cançado Trindade went much further. As noted above, he largely focused on *erga omnes* effects outside the field of law enforcement.[55] For present purposes, it is important to note that in his ambitious design of *erga omnes* effects, the concept's enforcement side continued to feature. In the circumstances of the case, the issue arose with respect to breaches of the Convention Against Torture. Specifically addressing issues of decentralised enforcement, Judge Cançado Trindade expressly recognised that "*all States parties* have the corresponding right, on the basis of the Convention, to see to it that these obligations are duly complied with. They are entitled by the Convention to exercise such right *erga omnes partes*."[56] Just as Judge Simma, he did not however restrict his analysis to one particular source. That the "right to the realization of justice"[57] were generally enforceable by all States did not depend on its acceptance in a particular treaty such as the Convention Against Torture, but on its character as a collective guarantee of fundamental community values. Hence the dissent assimilates obligations *erga omnes* and obligations *erga omnes partes*, without suggesting that their respective enforcement structure were any different.[58] Whatever one makes of the broader claims about other *erga omnes* effects, it thus is clear that at least by implication, Judge Cançado Trindade was prepared to recognise a general right of all States to institute ICJ proceedings in response to *erga omnes* breaches.

iii. In addition to these individual opinions, the approach adopted by the *Institut de droit international* deserves to be mentioned. Just as Judges Simma and Cançado Trindade, the *Institut* accepted the broad interpretation of the *Barcelona Traction* dictum. Article 3 of its resolution on rights and obligations *erga omnes* expressly

[55] See *supra* section 1a of the epilogue.

[56] *Belgium Senegal case*, *supra* note 15, Diss. Op. **Cançado** Trindade, at paras. 68–69.

[57] Ibid., at para. 60.

[58] Cf. *ibid.*, para. 70: "If customary international law were to be brought into the picture, one would be before a right corresponding to obligations *erga omnes*, disclosing a wider horizon, not circumscribed to the States parties to the United Nations Convention against Torture." See also at para. 73: "There could hardly be better examples of a mechanism for the application of the obligations *erga omnes* of protection (at least in the relations of the States parties *inter se*) than the methods of supervision provided for the human rights treaties themselves, such as the 1984 United Nations Convention against Torture, for the exercise of the *collective guarantee* of the protected rights."

recognises the right of all States to institute ICJ proceedings in response to *erga omnes* breaches:

> "In the event of there being a jurisdictional link between a State alleged to have committed a breach of an obligation *erga omnes* and a State to which the obligation is owed, the latter State has standing to bring a claim to the International Court of Justice or other judicial institution in relation to a dispute concerning compliance with that obligation."[59]

That provision prompted very little debate. Most of the *Institut*'s members considered it to be in line with the *Barcelona Traction* dictum. Moreover, the ILC's "translation" of that dictum into Article 48, para. 1(b) of the Articles on State Responsibility seemed to have settled matters. Karl Zemanek's comment brings out this approach very clearly. In his view, "if a State other than the [directly] injured State is entitled to invoke responsibility under certain circumstances, it would be absurd to deny it the right to submit an eventually ensuing legal dispute to a procedure for peaceful settlement if the necessary jurisdictional link exists."[60]

As was observed in chapter 5, that certainly is not the only possible view, and one could plausibly draw a distinction between (i) the legal interest to invoke responsibility, and (ii) the legal interest to do so by means of court proceedings. However, from its deliberations, it is clear that the *Institut* felt comfortable to adopt a more straightforward approach. This suggests that restrictive readings of the *Barcelona Traction* dictum are on the defensive.

Developments since 2005 therefore support the argument set out in chapter 5. It seems more likely than ever that, jurisdiction being established, the Court would recognise the standing of States to institute *erga omnes* proceedings in defence of general legal interests of the international community.

Standing to Take Countermeasures

While the subject remains controversial, there also seems to have been some development in the perception of 'third party countermeasures'. Chapter 6 of the book contains a rather detailed examination of the issue aimed at clarifying whether States can resort to non-forcible

[59] Annuaire de l'Institut de droit international, vol. 71-II (2006), at 289.

[60] Zemanek, Written comment on Professor Gaja's first report, reproduced in Annuaire de l'Institut de droit international, vol. 71-I (2005), at 168.

countermeasures in response to *erga omnes* breaches. Largely drawing on State practice, it goes beyond the approach adopted in the ILC's Articles on State Responsibility[61] and argues that "individual States are entitled to take countermeasures in response to systematic or large-scale breaches of obligations *erga omnes*."[62] Developments during the last five years would seem to support this view. Two points are particularly relevant:

i. The most important point to make is that States have continued to resort to countermeasures in response to wrongful conduct that did not specially affect them. For example, Western States continue to impose sanctions on Zimbabwe and its leaders; these include the suspension of economic aid as well as asset freezes and travel bans.[63] As noted in Chapter 6, the suspension, by the European Community, of economic aid can be justified under Article 96 of the Cotonou Agreement and therefore need not be explained as a countermeasure.[64] No treaty-based justification however is available for the travel ban and assets freeze imposed by the European Community, or for sanctions imposed by the United States.[65] As regards new instances of State practice, Western States have e.g. taken or contemplated coercive measures in response to human rights violations in Belarus. Referring to wide-spread and systematic breaches of civil and political rights, the United States, by Presidential executive order of 19 June 2006, froze President Lukashenko's assets.[66] Protesting against "violations of international electoral standards ... and international human rights law", EC member States, already in 2004, had imposed a travel ban on members of the Belarus government.[67] This ban was extended in April 2006; in addition,

[61] See Article 54 of the ILC's text. For comment on the ILC's approach cf. pp. 241–249 of the book.

[62] At p. 249 pf the book.

[63] For the EC's measures see e.g. Official Journal 2005, L48/28 (of 19 February 2005); Official Journal 2005, L 200/98 (of 30 July 2005); Official Journal 2006, L26/28 (of 31 January 2006). The most relevant measure adopted by the United States is President Bush's executive order 13391 of 23 November 2005, available at http://www.treas.gov/offices/enforcement/ofac/legal/eo/13391.pdf.

[64] Cf. p. 224 of the book.

[65] For a fuller treatment see Dawidowicz (*supra* note 3), at 394–396.

[66] See http://www.treas.gov/offices/enforcement/ofac/programs/belarus/belarus.pdf.

[67] See Official Journal 2004, L 301/67 (of 28 September 2004). For further evidence see e.g. statements by the European Parliament (in EU Bulletin No. 3/2005 of 10 March 2005, at 1.2.4, and EU Bulletin 1-2/2006 of 16 February 2006, at 1.32.26).

both the European Parliament and the Council of Ministers asserted a right to freeze assets of government members.[68] The U.S. *Syria Accountability and Lebanese Sovereignty Restoration Act*[69] of late 2003, designed to stop Syria's interference in Lebanon's domestic affairs as well as its alleged sponsoring of terrorist organisations, provides a final example in point. Its section 5 authorises the U.S. President to, *inter alia*, freeze Syrian assets or suspend civil aviation with Syria. From 2004 onwards, these powers have at least partly been used.[70]

As previously, poor documentation complicates the proper evaluation of international practice. The three examples mentioned in the last paragraph are unlikely to be the only instances of recent third-party countermeasures. They do however confirm two points made in chapter 6. First, while often ignored, practice is (and continues to be) surprisingly wide-spread. In fact, it is probably easier today to find evidence of third-party countermeasures than of countermeasures adopted in the classic bilateral context. And second, it would be wrong to expect too much of third-party countermeasures. Just as in earlier instances, the actual effects of countermeasures have usually been rather trivial. Both factors suggest that the recognition of an exceptional right of all States to take countermeasures in the general interest may have less dramatic consequences than critics fear and supporters hope.

ii. The argument made in chapter 6 of course is complicated by the cautious approach adopted in Article 54 of the ILC's text on State Responsibility. That provision stands, and it is highly unlikely that States should expressly endorse a general right to respond to *erga omnes* breaches should they ever decide to turn the ILC's text into a binding Convention on State Responsibility.[71] However it is noteworthy that in its resolution on rights and obligations *erga omnes*, the *Institut de droit international* was much less cautious. Drawing on its earlier resolution adopted at the 1989 session at Santiago de

[68] Cf. Dawidowicz (*supra* note 3), at 397–298, for further details.

[69] HR 1828 of 12 April 2003, enacted as Public Law 108–75 of 12 December 2003.

[70] See President Bush's executive order of 11 May 2004, available at http://www.treas.gov/offices/enforcement/ofac/sanctions/t11syria.pdf.; and further Dawidowicz (*supra* note 3), at 396–397.

[71] According to Tomuschat, Article 54 of the ILC's text, notwithstanding its indeterminacy, has now "in itself [become] a *rocher de bronze* which nobody can remove easily" (*supra* note 38, at 434).

Compostela,[72] it recognised a right of States to vindicate obligations *erga omnes* by coercive means. The point is expressly addressed in Article 5(c), which provides as follows:

> "Should a widely acknowledged grave breach of an *erga omnes* obligation occur, all the States to which the obligation is owed: [...] are entitled to take non-forcible counter-measures under conditions analogous to those applying to a State specially affected by the breach."[73]

In his reports, Giorgio Gaja had referred to instances of State practice, which he – in apparent contradistinction to the ILC[74] – considered to be "far from scarce".[75] The *Institut*'s debates suggest that while the risk of abuse remained an important concern, the idea that *erga omnes* breaches, at least in clear-cut cases, could trigger a right of all States to resort to countermeasures commanded broad support.

To sum up, evidence since 2005 provides growing support for the position advocated in chapter 6 – i.e. of a general right to take countermeasures in defence of the public interest embodied in obligations *erga omnes*, at least in the case of systematic or large-scale breaches.

Obligations *Erga Omnes* – Forty Years After *Barcelona Traction*

The preceding discussion indicates an emerging consensus (or at least some further agreement) on the permissibility of reactions against *erga omnes* breaches. While the topic continues to prompt discussion, few today would describe the Court's *Barcelona Traction* dictum as "an empty gesture".[76] Whatever one makes of other *erga omnes* effects (yet to be critically examined), the concept does have important effects on the enforcement of international law. If "[v]iewed realistically, the world of obligations *erga omnes* [can still be said to belong to] the world of the

[72] Institut de droit international, 'La protection des droits de l'homme et le principe de non-intervention dans les affaires des Etats', Annuaire de l'Institut de droit international vol. 63-II (1990), 338.

[73] Annuaire de l'Institut de droit international, vol. 71-II (2006), at 289.

[74] Cf. para. 6 of the ILC's commentary on Article 54 of its text, as well as para. 8 of the introductory commentary to Part Three, Chapter II (both reproduced in Report of the International Law Commission on the Work of its Fifty-Third Session, UN Doc. A/56/10, 43)

[75] Giorgio Gaja, Second Report (*supra* note 4), at 200.

[76] Cf. Thirlway, The Law and Procedure of the International Court of Justice – Part One, British Yearbook of International Law 60 (1989), 1, at 100.

'ought' rather than of the 'is'",[77] this may to some extent reflect continuing uncertainty about the concept, but it is mainly due to States' unwillingness to make use of their *erga omnes* enforcement rights.

Four decades of often fierce debate about the concept may have contributed to the emerging consensus on the scope of *erga omnes* enforcement rights. Yet it is submitted that all too often, in arguments about legal detail have obscured the broader view on the *erga omnes* concept as an enforcement mechanism. Notwithstanding the wealth of literature, a number of essential features of the *erga omnes* concept are frequently not spelled out clearly. The subsequent paragraphs identify four such essential features. They suggest (i) that the *erga omnes* concept is *ambitious but straightforward*; (ii) that it is *autonomous* from other concepts; (iii) that it grants enforcement *rights, not duties*; and (iv) finally, that *erga omnes* enforcement rights *complement* other enforcement mechanisms. It is hoped that the following brief comments on each of these points may help situate the *erga omnes* concept alongside other enforcement mechanisms, and thereby contribute to its demystification.

(i) An ambitious but straightforward concept

Given the "very mysterious"[78] nature of the *erga omnes* concept, it is worth mentioning that its basic thrust - that all States should have standing to react against breaches of particularly important obligations - while certainly *ambitious*, is relatively *straightforward*. It is ambitious because it moves beyond a narrow view of international law that restricted inter-State legal relations to reciprocal exchanges of benefits and presumes the existence of general legal interests of the international community as a whole.[79] Yet it is straightforward in two other respects:

First, in order to justify the move away from bilateralism, it relies on an obvious criterion - namely "the importance of the rights

[77] As noted by Bruno Simma in 1993 (Does the UN Charter Provide an Adequate Legal Basis for Individual or Collective Responses to Violations of Obligations *Erga Omnes*?, in Delbrück [ed.], *The Future of International Law Enforcement. New Scenarios – New Law?*, at 125). Cf. also *id.*, The Universality (*supra* note 2), at 275.

[78] Cf. I. Brownlie, To What Extent Are the Traditional Categories of *Lex Lata* and *Lex Ferenda* Still Viable?, in Weiler/Cassese (eds.), *Change and Stability in International Law-Making* (Berlin *et al.* 1988), 66, at 71.

[79] As noted in chapter 2 of the book, that view probably never accurately reflected the reality of international law, but it was an important lens through which to approach inter-State legal relations.

involved".[80] *Erga omnes* enforcement rights therefore do not depend on 'structural approaches' or complex legal arguments about the 'indivisibility' of obligations.[81] They arise because a State violates fundamental values shared by the international community. This criterion may be difficult to apply, but conceptually, it is straightforward.

Second, the *erga omnes* concept is based on an egalitarian approach. Transcending bilateralism, it opts for the other extreme – it translates the general legal interest of the international community (or of communities of treaty parties) into enforcement rights of *each and every* State belonging to that community. It does not introduce distinctions based on criteria such as geographical proximity; the factual effects of breaches; the power and/or self-perception of States; or their own compliance with *erga omnes* obligations. These factors of course may decide whether States will make use of their enforcement rights. However, as a matter of law, they are irrelevant.

(ii) An autonomous concept

The *erga omnes* concept is part of broader developments, but retains its *autonomous* character. As noted in the Introduction to the book, the gradual recognition of obligations *erga omnes* is frequently viewed as an important step in the continuing constitutionalisation of public international law.[82] Within that context, the *erga omnes* concept is usually considered alongside substantive[83] *jus cogens* norms – the two triplets remaining after the sacrifice of the 'international crimes', as it were. Increasingly, however, both concepts are not only linked, but merged into a joint notion of "fundamental community values".[84] For conceptual and pragmatic reasons, these attempts should be resisted. While few would dispute the connections between the two

[80] *Barcelona Traction case*, ICJ Reports 1970, 3, at 32 (para. 33).

[81] The weaknesses of such structural approaches are addressed on pp. 128–136 of the book.

[82] See the sources cited on p. 3 of the book. In the recent literature, this point is notably explored by E. de Wet (*supra* note 29). To view obligations *erga omnes* as part of the constitutionalisation of modern international law is as such not problematic, as long as the concept is not tied to any constitutionalist approach: as clarified in chapter 2 of the book, the basic argument underlying obligations *erga omnes* emerged long before constitutionalist readings began to gain ground.

[83] Writers treating or assimilating the two concepts almost inevitably restrict themselves to norms of substantive *jus cogens* and ignore or sacrifice rules of systemic *jus cogens*. For comment on systemic and substantive approaches see pp. 141–142 of the book.

[84] See notably Tomuschat (*supra* note 37), *passim*. The point is also touched upon in James Crawford's foreword to the book (at p. xiii).

notions,[85] conceptually, *jus cogens* norms are norms of elevated hierarchical status, whereas obligations *erga omnes* can well operate on an ordinary hierarchical level. A norm's elevated hierarchical status may require the invalidation of conflicting norms; or it may protect a core of values from being affected through other legal acts – hence treaties conflicting with *jus cogens* norms are void, *jus cogens* may provide a red line that not even the Security Council can cross, and compliance with *jus cogens* norms may preclude the wrongfulness of otherwise illegal conduct. None of these arguments can be easily applied to the *erga omnes* concept. *Erga omnes* effects are not directed at legal validity/invalidity. They may (as 'other *erga omnes* effects') affect the scope of application of an obligation, but in essence, they concern responses against breaches. *Jus cogens* and obligations *erga omnes* may have entered the international legal discourse almost simultaneously, but follow different rationales.

Perhaps more importantly, attempts at conflation should be resisted for pragmatic reasons. They are likely to further complicate the analysis of controversial concepts. The preceding discussion has noted the risks inherent in an ever-broader approach to the *erga omnes* concept.[86] These risks are already felt very clearly with respect to *jus cogens* and its "virtually unlimited [range of] special effects"[87]. An over-arching concept of fundamental community values combining *jus cogens* and *erga omnes* features would probably become unmanageable. Fundamental values may lie at the heart of both *jus cogens* and obligations *erga omnes*, but anyone interest in operationalising the two concepts should defend their autonomous existence.

(iii) Enforcement rights, not duties

Insofar as it affects the enforcement of international law, the *erga omnes* concept serves an *enabling function*. At least for the time being, it entails enforcement rights, not duties. Recent years have witnessed new debates about the responsibility of States and other actors to prevent, or respond to, grave forms of wrongful conduct. In light of these debates, it must be stressed that the *erga omnes* concept at present does not impose upon States any obligation to respond against *erga omnes* breaches. This view has obvious drawbacks; as a matter of law, it allows the concept to remain part of "the world of the 'ought'".[88] Yet it seems

[85] For details see pp. 139–141 and pp. 146–151 of the book.
[86] See section 2 of the epilogue. [87] Focarelli, *supra* note 36, at 439.
[88] *Supra*, footnote 77.

the only realistic understanding of the concept. The discussion of remedies in particular suggests that States simply do not accept a duty to respond against *erga omnes* breaches; if anything they decide to make use of their enforcement rights in exceptional cases.

This does not mean that 'duties to react' were alien to international law. Some domestic legal systems, though probably not international law, impose upon States the duty to exercise diplomatic protection on behalf of nationals.[89] A duty to respond on behalf of foreigners might emerge from debates about the 'responsibility to protect'.[90] And finally, enforcement duties have been recognised for decades in international treaties, notably in common Article 1 of the 1949 Geneva Conventions.[91] For the time being, however, there is little indication that this particular facet of international humanitarian law should have acquired customary status and become part of the *erga omnes* concept. In fact, in the *Wall* opinion, the Court rather carefully distinguished between the treaty-based *duty* to react against breaches of the Conventions and the *right* to respond against Israel's breaches of obligations *erga omnes*.[92]

(iv) A complementary enforcement mechanism

Finally, *erga omnes* enforcement rights *complement* other law enforcement mechanisms, which remain available.[93] Conversely, other law enforcement mechanisms can affect the egalitarian nature[94] of the *erga omnes* concept. Although compliance with obligations *erga omnes* is "the concern of *all States*",[95] in some instances wrongful conduct

89 Cf. the discussion in the paras. 75–93 of the First Report on Diplomatic Protection, submitted by Professor John Dugard to the UN International Law Commission in 1999 (UN Doc. A/CN.4/506). The eventual Draft Articles on Diplomatic Protection (reproduced in UN Doc. A/61/10) do not recognise a duty to exercise diplomatic protection.

90 See the detailed discussion by Christoph Verlage, *Responsibility to protect : ein neuer Ansatz im Völkerrecht zur Verhinderung von Völkermord, Kriegsverbrechen und Verbrechen gegen die Menschlichkeit* (Tübingen 2009), at 185 *et seq.*; and further C. Stahn, Responsibility to Protect : Political Rhetoric or Emerging Legal Norm?, American Journal of International Law 101 (2007), 99.

91 Pursuant to Article 1, "[t]he High Contracting Parties undertake to respect and to ensure respect for the present Convention in all circumstances". As noted by Judge Simma in his separate opinion in the *Congo Uganda case* (*supra* note 48), States parties to the Geneva Conventions not only have the right, but "indeed the duty … to raise … violations of international humanitarian law" (at para. 34).

92 *Wall* opinion (*supra* note 11), at paras. 155–158.

93 The point has been addressed above (section 2 of the epilogue) with respect to treaties, but it can be generalised.

94 See supra, subsection 4(i).

95 *Barcelona Traction case*, ICJ Reports 1970, 3, at 32 (para. 33).

violating an obligation *erga omnes* at the same time specially affects individual States, such as the immediate victim of an aggression, the coastal State affected by an oil catastrophe, or the State of nationality of victims of human rights abuses. If this is the case, the specially affected State is, to use the terms of the ILC's Articles on State Responsibility, both an "injured State" and a State "other than an injured State entitled to invoke responsibility".[96] The latter status does not affect the former. Quite to the contrary, *erga omnes* enforcement rights in principle exist alongside rights of diplomatic protection[97] and - as noted above[98] - enforcement rights conferred by treaty.

In relation to these other enforcement mechanisms, *erga omnes* enforcement rights are residual. The point has been made with respect to treaties, but equally describes the relationship between *erga omnes* enforcement rights and those of specially affected States. The practical relevance of the *erga omnes* concept therefore depends on the construction of these other enforcement mechanisms - in particular, States can reduce it by concluding treaties providing for general enforcement rights, or by accepting broad definitions of special/individual injury.[99] What is more, being residual, *erga omnes* enforcement rights can be disapplied or modified by special enforcement mechanisms. In practice, this however hardly ever happens. The existing treaty enforcement mechanisms do not opt out of *erga omnes* enforcement rights altogether, and only rarely preclude the exercise of countermeasures in response to serious *erga omnes* breaches.[100] As regards traditional enforcement mechanisms, the International Law Commission's Draft Articles expressly acknowledge that rights of diplomatic protection

"are ... not intended to exclude or to trump the rights of States, including both the State of nationality *and States other than the State of nationality* of an injured

[96] Cf. Articles 42 and 48 of the ILC's text.

[97] The book addresses the point only in passing. For a detailed treatment see Vermeer Künzli (*supra* note 3); as well as S. Forlati, Protection diplomatique, droits de l'homme et réclamations 'directes' devant la Cour internationale de Justice: quelques réflexions en marge de l'arrêt *Congo/Ouganda*, Revue générale de droit international public 111 (2007), 89.

[98] Section 2 of the epilogue.

[99] One example in point is the recognition of a right to exercise diplomatic protection on behalf of stateless persons and refugees. Insofar as States espousing claims of stateless persons or refugees can do so by way of diplomatic protection, they do not need to rely on the *erga omnes* concept. For details see Article 8 of the International Law Commission's Draft Articles on Diplomatic Protection (reproduced with explanatory commentary in UN Doc. A/61/10, at 47-51).

[100] For details see chapter 7 of the book.

individual, to protect the individual under either customary international law or a multilateral or bilateral human rights treaty or other treaty."[101]

When looking at other instances of *erga omnes* breaches special affecting one particular State, there are good reasons to suggest that – following the ICJ's interpretation of collective self-defence – *erga omnes* responses against armed attacks should require the consent of the victim State.[102] That however is but a minor modification. On balance, the *erga omnes* enforcement regime, while residual, retains its important role. Its ambitious but straightforward recognition of a general law enforcement competence is not lightly disapplied.

* * *

It is unlikely that the members of the International Court of Justice, when including into the *Barcelona Traction* judgment two obscure paragraphs on obligations *erga omnes*, should have fully anticipated quite what an avalanche they were about to set off. The paragraphs of course did not appear by accident, but were an attempt to mitigate the effects of the "public relations disaster"[103] that had been the Court's (second) *South West Africa* judgment. In retrospect, one can only be amazed at the results of this 'PR exercise'. The Court's dictum was picked up and explored in practice and writing, and for the last four decades has provided a conceptual framework for modern discussions about law enforcement in the general interest.

To a large extent, the book is an attempt to move *erga omnes* debates beyond case studies of *Barcelona Traction* and instead to take full account of earlier approaches and of developments since 1970. However, as the *Barcelona Traction* judgment approaches its fortieth "anniversary", it may be fitting to conclude this epilogue by acknowledging the vision and wisdom of the judges that applied the *erga omnes* concept to the field of law enforcement. Their dictum not only sent a political signal, but since 1970 has proved capable of explaining, justifying and guiding international enforcement action in defence of community interests. As an exercise in dispute resolution, the Court's handling of the Belgian-Spanish dispute may have been a disappointment. However, the

[101] See para. (1) of the ILC's explanatory commentary to draft article 16 (emphasis added), reproduced in UN Doc. A/61/10, at 86.
[102] For details see pp. 300–302 of the book.
[103] Cf. James Crawford's remark in the foreword to the book (at p. xiii).

Barcelona Traction dictum found in paras. 33–34 provides an excellent example of the Court's ability to progressively develop international law. It is rightly celebrated as one of the Court's most important pronouncements.

Christian J. Tams
Glasgow
August 2009

Bibliography

Unless otherwise indicated [in square brackets], references in the footnotes are to the author's surname and year of publication, i.e. 'Abi-Saab (1999)'. Documents issued by the UN International Law Commission are listed separately.

Books and articles

Abiew, Francis K., *The Evolution of the Doctrine and Practice of Humanitarian Intervention* (1997)

Abi-Saab, Georges, *Les exceptions préliminaires dans la procédure de la Cour internationale* (1967)

'Les mécanismes de mise-en-oeuvre du droit humanitaire', 82 *RGDIP* (1978), 103

'The Specificities of Humanitarian Law', in: *Études et essais sur le droit international humanitaire et sur les principes de la Croix-Rouge en l'honneur de Jean Pictet* (Swinarski ed., 1984), 265

'Cours général de droit international public', 207 *RdC* (1987 VII), 9

'De la sanction en droit international. Essai de clarification', in: *Theory of International Law at the Threshold of the 21st Century. Essays in Honour of Krzystof Skubiszewski* (Makarczyk ed., 1994), 61

'Comment', in: *Increasing the Effectiveness of the International Court of Justice* (Peck and Lee eds., 1997), 67

'The Uses of Article 19', 10 *EJIL* (1999), 339

'The Concept of Sanction in International Law', in: *United Nations Sanctions and International Law* (Gowlland-Debbas ed., 2001), 29

Accioly, Hildebrando, 'Principes généraux de la responsabilité internationale d'après la doctrine et la jurisprudence', 96 *RdC* (1959 I), 349

Acosta Estevez, J. B., 'Normas de *jus cogens*, efecto *erga omnes*, crimes internacional y la teoria de los círculos concéntricos', 11 *Annuario de Derecho Internacional* (1995), 3

Ago, Roberto, 'Le délit international', 68 *RdC* (1939 II), 415

'Droit des traités à la lumière de la Convention de Vienne: Introduction', 134 *RdC* (1971 III), 297

'Obligations *Erga Omnes* and the International Community', in: *International Crimes of States* (Weiler, Cassese, Spinedi, eds., 1989), 237

Akademie der Wissenschaften der DDR (ed.), *Völkerrechts-Lehrbuch*, 2 Bde. (1973)

Akande, Dapo / Williams, Sope, 'International Adjudication and National Security Issues: What Role for the WTO?', 43 *Virginia JIL* (2003), 365

Akehurst, Michael, 'Reprisals by Third States', 44 *BYIL* (1970), 1

'Custom as a Source of International Law', 47 *BYIL* (1974–1975), 1

'Humanitarian Intervention', in: *Intervention in World Politics* (Bull ed., 1984), 95

Akehurst's International Law (7th ed., Malanczuk ed., 1997) [Akehurst/Malanczuk]

Alebeek, Rosanne van, 'The *Pinochet* Case: International Human Rights Law on Trial', 71 *BYIL* (2000), 29

Alexidze, L. A., 'Legal Nature of *Jus Cogens* in Contemporary International Law', 172 *RdC* (1981 II), 219

Alland, Dénis, 'International Responsibility and Sanctions: Self-Defence and Countermeasures in the ILC Codification of Rules Governing International Responsibility', in: *United Nations Codification on State Responsibility* (Simma and Spined eds., 1987), 143

Justice privée et ordre juridique international (1994)

'Countermeasures of General Interest', 13 *EJIL* (2002), 1221

Allott, Philip, *Eunomia* (reprinted version, Oxford 2001)

Amerasinghe, C. F., *State Responsibility for Injuries to Aliens* (1967)

Anand, R. P., *Studies in International Adjudication* (1968)

Angelet, Nicolas (ed.), 'Pratique du pouvoir exécutif et contrôle des chambres législatives en matiére de droit international (1995–1999)', 35 *RBDI* (2003), 5

Annacker, Claudia, *Die Durchsetzung von* erga omnes-*Verpflichtungen vor dem Internationalen Gerichtshof* (1994) [Annacker 1994a]

'The Legal Régime of Erga Omnes Obligations Under International Law', 46 *AJPIL* (1994), 131 [Annacker 1994b]

'Part Two of the International Law Commission's Draft Articles on State Responsibility', 37 *GYIL* (1994), 206 [Annacker 1994c]

Antonopulos, C., 'Effectiveness v. the Rule of Law Following the *East Timor Case*', 27 *NYIL* (1996), 75

Anzilotti, Dionisio, *Teoria generale della responsabilità dello Stato nel diritto internazionale* (1902)

Cours de droit international (French translation by G. Gidel, 1929)

Arangio-Ruiz, Gaetano, 'Human Rights and Non-Intervention in the Helsinki Final Act', 157 *RdC* (1977 IV), 195

Arts, Karin, 'European Community Development Cooperation, Human Rights, Democracy and Good Governance: at Odds or Ease with Each Other?', in: *Sustainable Development and Good Governance* (Ginther *et al.* eds., 1995), 259

Aust, Anthony, *Modern Treaty Law and Practice* (2001)

Badhawi El-Sheikh, I., 'The African Charter on Human and Peoples' Rights: Problems and Prospects', 7 *NQHR* (1989), 272

Ballreich, H., 'Völkerrechtliche Verträge zu Lasten Dritter' in: *Völkerrechtliche und staatsrechtliche Abhandlungen. Festschrift Bilfinger* (Schreibner and Mosler eds., 1954), 1

'Treaties, Effect on Third States', in: EPIL, Vol. IV (Bernhardt ed., 2000), 945

Barboza, Julio, 'State Crimes: a Decaffeinated Coffee', in: *The International Legal System in Quest of Equity and Universality - Liber Amicorum Georges Abi-Saab* (Boisson de Chazournes and Gowlland-Debbas eds., 2001), 357

Barnhoorn, L. A. N. M., 'Diplomatic Law and Unilateral Remedies', 25 *NYIL* (1994), 39

Barros, J., *The Aaland Islands Question: its Settlement by the League of Nations* (1968)

Bassiouni, M. Cherif, 'International Crimes: *Jus Cogens* and Obligation *Erga Omnes*', 59 *Law and Contemporary Problems* (Issue 4, 1996), 63

Bastid, Suzanne, *Les traités dans la vie internationale* (1985)

Bauer, Hartmut, *Geschichtliche Grundlagen der Lehre vom subjektiven öffentlichen Recht* (1986)

Beckett, W. E., 'Les question d'intérêt général au point de vue juridique dans la jurisprudence de la Cour permanente de Justice internationale', 39 *RdC* (1932 I), 135

Bederman, David J., 'Article 40(2)(E) & (F) of the ILC Draft Articles on State Responsibility: Standing of Injured States Under Customary International Law and Multilateral Treaties', 92 *Proc. ASIL* (1998), 291

'Counterintuiting Countermeasures', 96 *AJIL* (2002), 817

Benedek, Wolfgang, 'The African Charter and Commission on Human and Peoples' Rights: How to Make It More Effective', 11 *NQHR* (1993), 25

Bennouna, Mohamed, 'Le règlement des différends, peut-il limiter le "droit" de se faire justice à soi-même?', 5 *EJIL* (1994), 61

Berber, Friedrich, *Lehrbuch des Völkerrechts*, Bd. III (1964)

Bergbohm, Karl, *Verträge und Gesetze als Quellen des Völkerrechts* (1887)

Bernhardt, Rudolf, 'Homogenität, Kontinuität und Dissonanzen in der Rechtsprechung des Internationalen Gerichtshofes: Eine Fallstudie zum Südwestafrika/Namibia-Komplex', 33 *ZaöRV* (1973), 1

'Customary International Law', in: EPIL, Vol. I (Bernhardt ed., 1992), 898

Bethlehem, Daniel (ed.), *The Kuwait Crisis. Basic Documents* (1991)

Beyerlin, Ulrich, 'Die israelische Befreiungsaktion von Entebbe in völkerrechtlicher Sicht', 37 *ZaöRV* (1977), 213

'Humanitarian Intervention', in: EPIL, Vol. II (Bernhardt ed., 1995), 927

'State Community Interests and Institution-Building in International Environmental Law', 56 *ZaöRV* (1996), 602

Umweltvölkerrecht (2000)

Bianchi, Andrea, 'Immunity versus Human Rights: The Pinochet Case' 10 *EJIL* (1999), 237

Biermann, Frank, ' "Common Concern of Humankind": the Emergence of a New Concept in International Environmental Law', 34 *AVR* (1996), 426

Birnie, Patricia W. / Boyle, Alan E., *International Law and the Environment* (2nd. ed., 2002)

Black's Law Dictionary (7th ed., 1999), at 1413
Bleckmann, Albert, *Probleme der Anwendung multilateraler Verträge* (1974)
Bluntschli, Johann Caspar, *Das moderne Völkerrecht der civilisirten Staaten als Rechtsbuch dargestellt* (1868)
Boed, Roman, 'The Effect of a Domestic Amnesty on the Ability of Foreign States to Prosecute Alleged Perpetrators of Serious Human Rights Breaches', 33 *Cornell International Law Journal* (2000), 297
Boeglin Naumovic, N., 'Reflexions sur l'*actio popularis* en droit international, dans le cadre de la responsabilité internationale', in: *Responsibility of States. Thesaurus Acroasium* Vol. XX (1993), 359
Boellecker-Stern, Brigitte, *Le préjudice dans la théorie de la responsabilité internationale* (1973)
Bos, Marten, *Les conditions du procès en droit international* (1957)
'The Interpretation of International Judicial Decisions', 33 *Revista Española de Derecho Internacional* (1982), 11
Bossuyt, Marc J., *Guide to the* 'Travaux Préparatoires' *of the International Covenant on Civil and Political Rights* (1987)
Botha, C. J., 'Anticipatory Self-Defence and Armed Reprisals Re-examined', 11 *SAYIL* (1985–1986), 138
Bothe, Michael, 'International Obligations, Means to Secure Performance', in: EPIL, Vol. II (Bernhardt ed., 1995), 1278
'The Evaluation of Enforcement Mechanisms in International Environmental Law: An Overview', in: *Enforcing Environmental Standards: Economic Mechanisms as Viable Means?* (Wolfrum ed., 1996), 13
'Neue und alte Konzepte zur Durchsetzung des Humanitären Völkerrechts, in: *Brücken bauen und begehen. Festschrift für Knut Ipsen* (Epping *et al.* eds., 2000), 23
Bowett, Derek W., 'Reprisals Involving Recourse to Armed Force', 66 *AJIL* (1972), 1 [Bowett 1972a]
'Economic Coercion and Reprisals by States', 13 *Virginia JIL* (1972), 1 [Bowett 1972b]
'Treaties and State Responsibility', in: *Le droit international au service de la paix, de la justice et du développement. Mélanges Michel Virally* (1991), 137
'Crimes of State and the 1996 Report of the International Law Commission on State Responsibility', 9 *EJIL* (1998), 163
Bowett's Law of International Institutions (5th ed. by Sands and Klein, 2001) [Bowett/Sands/Klein]
Bradley, A. W., 'Judicial Protection of the Individual Against the Executive in Great Britain', in: *Gerichtsschutz gegen die Exekutive*, Bd. 1 (Mosler ed., 1969), 327
Brandtner, Barbara / Rosas, Alan, 'Human Rights and the External Relations of the European Community: an Analysis of Doctrine and Practice', 9 *EJIL* (1998), 468
Breutz, Iris, *Der Protest im Völkerrecht* (1997)
Brierly, J. L., *The Law of Nations. An Introduction to the International Law of Peace* (6th ed. by C. H. M. Waldock, 1963) [Brierly/Waldock]

Brierly, James L, 'The Lotus case', 44 *Law Quarterly Review* (1928), 154
Briggs, Herbert W., '*Nicaragua v. United States*: Jurisdiction and Admissibility', 79 *AJIL* (1985), 373
'The International Court of Justice Lives Up to Its Name', 81 *AJIL* (1987), 78
Brown Weiss, Edith, 'Invoking State Responsibility in the Twenty-first Century', 96 *AJIL* (2002), 798
Brownlie, Ian, *International Law and the Use of Force by States* (1963)
'Humanitarian Intervention', in: *Law and Civil War in the Modern World* (Moore ed., 1974), 217
System of the Law of Nations: State Responsibility: Part I (1983) [Brownlie 1983a]
'Recognition in Theory and Practice', in: *The Structure and Process of International Law* (MacDonald and Johnston eds., 1983), 627 [Brownlie 1983b]
'To What Extent Are the Traditional Categories of *Lex Lata* and *Lex Ferenda* Still Viable?', in: *Change and Stability in International Law-Making* (Weiler and Cassese eds., 1988), 66 [Brownlie 1988a]
'Comment', in: *Change and Stability in International Law-Making* (Weiler and Cassese eds., 1988), 108 [Brownlie 1988b]
'Remedies in the International Court of Justice', in: *Fifty Years of the International Court of Justice* (Lowe and Fitzmaurice eds., 1996), 557
The Rule of Law in International Affairs. International Law at the Fiftieth Anniversary of the United Nations (1998)
Principles of Public International Law (6th ed., 2003)
Brunnée, Jutta, '"Common Interest" – Echoes from an Empty Shell?', 49 *ZaöRV* (1989), 791
Bryde (1994), 'Verpflichtungen *Erga Omnes* aus Menschenrechten', 33 *BDGVR* (1994), 165
Buergenthal, Thomas / Norris, Robert E. (eds), *Human Rights: The Inter-American System* (4 vols., 1982)
Buergenthal, Thomas, 'Implementation in the Inter-American Human Rights System', in: *International Enforcement of Human Rights* (Bernhardt and Jolowicz eds., 1987)
Bulmerincq, August von, 'Die Staatsstreitigkeiten und ihre Entscheidung ohne Krieg', in: *Handbuch des Völkerrechts*, Bd. 4 (von Holtzendorff ed., 1889), 3
Bussutil, James J., 'The Bonn Declaration on International Terrorism: a Non-Binding International Agreement on Aircraft Hijacking', 31 *ICLQ* (1982), 474
Byers, Michael, 'Conceptualizing the Relationship Between *Jus Cogens* and *Erga Omnes* Rules', 66 *Nordic JIL* (1997), 1
Custom, Power, and the Power of Rules (1999)
Bynkershoek, Cornelius van, *De foro legatorum liber singularis* (3rd ed., 1744, English reprint 1946) [Bynkershoek 1744/1946]
Cahier, Philippe, 'Le problème des effets des traités à l'égard des Etats tiers', 143 *RdC* (1974 III), 589
Carnegie Endowment for International Peace (ed.), *The Concept of Jus Cogens in International Law. Conference Held at Lagonissi (Greece), 3 to 8 April 1966* (1967) [*Lagonissi Conference*]

Caron, David D., 'The ILC's Draft Articles on State Responsibility: The Paradoxical Relationship Between Form and Authority', 96 *AJIL* (2002), 857

Carrie, Heiko, *Das diplomatische Asyl im gegenwärtigen Völkerrecht* (1994)

'The Concept of "Legal Dispute" in the Jurisprudence of the International Court of Justice', 14 *Communicazione e Studi* (1975), 173

'Remarks on the Present Legal Regulation of Crimes of States', in: *International Law at the Time of Its Codification. Essays in Honour of Roberto Ago*, Vol. III (Giuffrè ed., 1987), 49

Human Rights in a Changing World (1990)

Self-Determination of Peoples. A Legal Reappraisal (1995)

International Law (2001)

Castrèn, E., 'Die Entmilitarisierung und Neutralisierung der Alandinseln', in: *Völkerrecht und rechtliches Weltbild. Festschrift für Alfred Verdross* (v.d. Heydte *et al.* eds., 1960), 107

Chamberlain, Kevin, 'Collective Suspension of Air Services With States Which Harbour Hijackers', 32 *ICLQ* (1983), 616

Charney, Jonathan I., 'Third State Remedies in International Law', 10 *MichJIL* (1989), 57

'Third-State Remedies for Environmental Damage to the World's Common Spaces', in: *International Responsibility for Environmental Harm* (Francioni and Scovazzi eds., 1991), 149

'Comment', in: *The Future of International Law Enforcement. New Scenarios – New Law?* (Delbrück ed., 1993), 158

'International Law-making – Article 38 of the ICJ Statute Reconsidered', in: *New Trends in International Law-Making – International "Legislation" in the Public Interest* (Delbrück ed., 1997), 171

'Anticipatory Humanitarian Intervention in Kosovo', 93 *AJIL* (1999), 834

Charpentier, Jean, 'Pratique française concernant le droit international', 25 *AFDI* (1979), 905

'Pratique française concernant le droit international', 28 *AFDI* (1982), 1017

Chesterman, Simon, *Just War or Just Peace? Humanitarian Intervention and International Law* (2001)

Chinkin, Christine, *Third Parties in International Law* (1993)

'The *East Timor Case* (Portugal v. Australia)'. 45 *ICLQ* (1996), 712

'Increasing the Use and Appeal of the Court: Presentation' in: *Increasing the Effectiveness of the International Court of Justice* (Peck and Lee eds., 1997), 43 [Chinkin 1997a]

'The Legality of the Imposition of Sanctions by the European Union in International Law', in: *Aspects of Statehood and Institutionalism in Contemporary Europe* (Evans ed., 1997), 183 [Chinkin 1997b]

Christenson, Gordon A., 'The World Court and *Jus Cogens*', 81 *AJIL* (1987), 93

'*Jus Cogens*: Guarding Interests Fundamental to International Society', 28 *Virginia JIL* (1988), 585

Churchill, Robin / Lowe, Vaughan, *The Law of the Sea* (3rd ed., 1999)

Ciobanu, Dan, 'Litispendence Between the International Court of Justice and the Political Organs of the United Nations', in: *The Future of the International Court of Justice*, Vol. I (Gross ed., 1976), 209

Clark, Roger S., 'Obligations of Third States in the Face of Illegality – Ruminations Inspired by the Weeramantry Dissent in the *Case Concerning East Timor*', in: *Legal Visions of the 21st Century. Essays Weeramantry* (Anghie and Sturgess eds., 1998), 631

Coffman, Peter D., 'Obligations *Erga Omnes* and the Absent Third State', 39 *GYIL* (1996), 285

Cohen Jonathan, Gérard, 'Human Rights Covenants', in: EPIL, Vol. II (Bernhardt ed., 1995), 915

Collier, John / Lowe, Vaughan, *The Settlement of Disputes in International Law* (1999)

Combacau, Jean, 'Sanctions', in EPIL, Vol. IV (Bernhardt ed., 2000), 311

Combacau, Jean / Sur, Serge, *Droit international public* (5th ed., 2001)

Condorelli, Luigi, 'L'autorité de la décision des juridictions internationales permanentes', in: *La juridiction internationale permanente. Colloque de Lyon* (Société française de droit international, 1987), 277

'Measures Available to Third States Reacting to Crimes of States', in: *International Crimes of States. A Critical Analysis of the ILC's Draft Article 19 of State Responsibility* (Weiler, Cassese, Spinedi eds., 1989), 264

Condorelli, Luigi / Boisson de Chazournes, Laurence, 'Quelques remarques à propos de l'obligation des États de "respecter et faire respecter" le droit international humanitaire "en toutes circonstances"', in: *Études et essais sur le droit international humanitaire et sur les principes de la Croix-Rouge en l'honneur de Jean Pictet* (Swinarski ed., 1984), 17

Corten, Olivier / Klein, Pierre, *Droit d'ingérence ou obligation de réaction* (2nd ed., 1996)

Cottereau, Gilles, 'Système juridique et notion de responsabilité', in: *La responsabilité dans le système international. Colloque du Mans* (Société française de droit international, 1991), 3

Coufoudakis, Van, 'The European Economic Community and the "Freezing" of the Greek Association, 1967–1974', 16 *Journal of Common Market Studies* (1977–1978), 114

Crawford, James R., *The Creation of States in International Law* (1979)

'The General Assembly, the International Court and Self-Determination', in: *Fifty Years of the International Court of Justice* (Lowe and Fitzmaurice eds., 1996), 585

'Military Activities Against Nicaragua Case (Nicaragua v. United States)', in: EPIL, Vol. III (Bernhardt ed., 1997), 371

'The Standing of States: A Critique of Art. 40 of the ILC's Draft Articles on State Responsibility', in: *Liber Amicorum in Honour of Lord Slynn of Hadley*, Vol. II (M. Adenas & D. Fairgrieve eds., 2000), 23

'The Relationship Between Sanctions and Countermeasures', in: *United Nations Sanctions and International Law* (Gowlland-Debbas ed., 2001), 57 [Crawford 2001a]

'The Right of Self-Determination in International Law: Its Development and Future', in: *Rights of Peoples* (Alston ed., 2001), 7 [Crawford 2001b]

'Introduction', in: *The International Law Commission's Articles on State Responsibility* (Crawford ed., 2002), 1 [Crawford 2002a]

'The ILC's Articles on State Responsibility of States for Internationally Wrongful Acts: A Retrospect', 96 *AJIL* (2002), 874 [Crawford 2002b]

'Responsibility to the International Community as a Whole', in: Crawford, *International Law as an Open System. Selected Essays* (2002), 341 [Crawford 2002c]

'Hague Lectures on Multilateralism' (forthcoming, Recueil des Cours, manuscript of Chapter 1 on file with the author) [Crawford, Hague Lectures]

Crawford, James R. / Bodeau, Pierre / Peel, Jacqueline, 'The ILC's Draft Articles on Responsibility of States for Internationally Wrongful Acts: Towards a Completion of the Second Reading', 94 *AJIL* (2000), 660

Crawford, James R. / Olleson, Simon, 'The Nature and Forms of International Responsibility', in: *International Law* (Evans ed., 2003), 445

Crawford, James R. / Peel, Jacqueline / Olleson, Simon, 'The ILC's Articles on Responsibility of States for Internationally Wrongful Acts: Completion of the Second Reading', 12 *EJIL* (2001), 963

Creifelds Rechtswörterbuch, 17. Auflage (2002)

Cross, R. / Harris, J. W., *Precedent in English Law* (4th ed., 1991)

Dahm, Georg, *Völkerrecht*, Bd. III (1961)

'Das Verbot der Gewaltanwendung nach Art. 2(4) der UNO-Charta und die Selbsthilfe gegenüber Völkerrechtsverletzungen, die keinen bewaffneten Angriff enthalten', 11 *JIR* (1962), 48

Dahm, Georg / Delbrück, Jost / Wolfrum, Rüdiger, *Völkerrecht*, Bd. I/1 (2nd ed., 1989)

Völkerrecht, Bd. I/3 (2nd ed., 2002)

Dale, William, 'Is the Commonwealth an International Organisation?', 31 *ICLQ* (1982), 451

D'Amato, Anthony, *International Law: Process and Prospect* (1987)

'Modifying U.S. Acceptance of the Compulsory Jurisdiction of the World Court', 79 *AJIL* (1985), 385

Danilenko, Gennadi, *Law-Making in the International Community* (1993)

Dashwood, Alan / White, Robin, 'Enforcement Action Under Articles 169 and 170 TEC', 14 *ELR* (1989), 388

David, Eric, 'Les sanctions économiques prises contre l'Argentine dans l'affaire des Malouines' 18 *RBDI* (1984–1985), 150

de Hoogh, André, *Obligations Erga Omnes and International Crimes* (1996)

Degan, V. D., 'Attempts to Codify Principles of Treaty Interpretation and the South-West Africa Cases', 8 *Indian JIL* (1966), 9

The Sources of International Law (1997)

Dehaussy, Jacques, 'Le problème de la classification des traités et le projet de convention établi par la Commission de droit international des Nations Unies', in: *Recueil d'études de droit international en hommage à Paul Guggenheim* (Geneva 1968), 305

Delbrück, Jost, 'A Fresh Look at Humanitarian Intervention under the Authority of the United Nations', 67 *Indiana Law Journal* (1992), 887 [Delbrück 1992a]

'Apartheid', in: EPIL, Vol. I (Bernhardt ed., 1992), 192 [Delbrück 1992b]

'Non-Judicial Procedures of Enforcement of Internationally Protected Human Rights with Special Emphasis on the Human Rights Practice of UNESCO', in: *Neuntes Deutsch-Polnisches Juristenkolloquium. Der internationale und nationale Schutz der Menschenrechte* (Delbrück ed., 1992), 31 [Delbrück 1992c]

'International Economic Sanctions and Third States', 30 *AVR* (1992), 86 [Delbrück 1992d]

'A More Effective International Law or a New "World Law"? Some Aspects of the Development of International Law in a Changing International System', 68 *Indiana Law Journal* (1993), 705

'The Impact of the Allocation of International Law Enforcement Authority on the International Legal Order', in: *Allocation of Law Enforcement Authority in the International System* (Delbrück ed., 1995), 135

' "Laws in the Public Interest" – Some Observations on the Foundations and Identification of *Erga Omnes* Norms in International Law', in: *Liber Amicorum Günther Jaenicke – Zum 85. Geburtstag* (Götz et al. eds., 1999), 17 [Delbrück 1999a]

'Effektivität des UN-Gewaltverbots', 74 *Friedens-Warte* (1999), 137 [Delbrück 1999b]

Diccionario de términos jurídicos – Spanish Law Dictionary (Peter Collin, 2000)

Dicke, Detlev Christian, *Die Intervention mit wirtschaftlichen Mitteln im Völkerrecht* (1978)

'Economic Coercion', in: EPIL, Vol. II (Bernhardt ed., 1995), 13

Dictionnaire économique et juridique Navarre (1992)

Dijk, Pieter van, *Judicial Review of Governmental Action and the Requirement of an Interest to Sue* (1980)

Dinstein, Yoram, 'The *erga omnes* Applicability of Human Rights', 30 *AVR* (1992), 16

War, Aggression and Self-Defence (3rd ed., 2001)

Doehring, Karl, 'Die Selbstdurchsetzung völkerrechtlicher Verpflichtungen', 47 *ZaöRV* (1987), 44

'The Unilateral Enforcement of International Law by Exercising Reprisals', in: *Essays in Honour of Wang Tieya* (MacDonald ed., 1993), 235

'Local Remedies, Exhaustion of', in: EPIL, Vol. II (Bernhardt ed., 1995), 240

Völkerrecht (1999)

Dominicé, Christian, 'Les répressailles en droit diplomatique', in: *Recht als Prozeß und Gefüge. Festschrift Hans Huber* (Bern 1981), 541

'The International Responsibility of States for Breach of Multilateral Obligations', 10 *EJIL* (1999), 353

Dugard, John, 'The South West Africa Cases, Second Phase, 1966', 83 *South African Law Journal* (1966), 429

'The Organization of African Unity and Colonialism: An Inquiry into the Plea of Self-defence as a Justification for the Use of Force in the Eradication of Colonialism', 16 *ICLQ* (1967), 157

Dugard, John (ed.), *The South West Africa/Namibia Dispute* (1973)
Dugard, John, '1966 and All That. The South West Africa Judgment Revisited in the East Timor Case', 8 *African Journal of International and Comparative Law* (1996), 549
Dupuy, Pierre-Marie, 'Action publique et crime international de l'Etat', 25 *AFDI* (1979), 539
'Observation sur la practique récente des "sanctions" de l'illicite', 87 *RGDIP* (1983), 505
'Le fait générateur de la responsabilité des Etats', 188 *RdC* (1984 V), 9
'Implications of the Institutionalization of International Crimes' in: *International Crimes of States. A Critical Analysis of the ILC's Draft Article 19 of State Responsibility* (Weiler, Cassese, Spinedi eds., 1989), 170
'The International Law of State Responsibility: Revolution or Evolution?' 11 *MichJIL* (1990), 105
'Responsabilité et légalité', in: *La responsabilité dans le système international. Colloque du Mans* (Société française de droit international, 1991), 263
'Quelques remarques sur l'évolution de la pratique des sanctions décidées par le Conseil de sécurité des Nations Unies dans la cadre du Chapitre VII de laCharte', in: *United Nations Sanctions and International Law* (Gowlland-Debbas ed., 2001), 47
'General Stocktaking of the Connections Between the Multilateral Dimension of Obligations and Codification of State Responsibility', 13 *EJIL* (2002), 1053 [Dupuy 2002a]
'L'unité de l'ordre juridique international. Cours général de droit international public', *RdC* 298 (2002), 9 [Dupuy 2002b]
Dupuy, Pierre-Marie (ed.), *Obligations multilatérales, droit impératif et responsabilité internationale* (2003)
Dutheil de la Rochère, Jacqueline, 'L'affaire de l'accident du Boeing 747 de Korean Airlines', 29 *AFDI* (1983), 749
Duxbury, Alison, 'Rejuvenating the Commonwealth - The Human Rights Remedy', 46 *ICLQ* (1997), 344
Dzida, Boris, *Zum Recht der Repressalie im heutigen Völkerrecht* (1997)
Eagleton, Clyde, *The Responsibility of States in International Law* (1928)
'International Organization and the Law of Responsibility', 76 *RdC* (1951 I) 323
Ebock, Kerstin, *Der Schutz grundlegender Menschenrechte durch kollektive Zwangsmaßnahmen der Staatengemeinschaft - Vom Interventionsverbot zur Pflicht zur humanitären Intervention?* (1999)
Eggers, Winfried, *Die Staatenbeschwerde* (1978)
Ehrmann, Markus, *Erfüllungskontrolle im Umweltvölkerrecht* (2000)
Eissen, M.-A., 'The European Convention on Human Rights and the United Nations Covenant on Civil and Political Rights: Problems of Coexistence, 22 *Buffalo Law Review* (1972–1973), 181
Elagab, Omer Y., *The Legality of Non-Forcible Countermeasures in International Law* (1987)
'The Place of Non-Forcible Countermeasures in Contemporary International Law', in: *The Reality of International Law. Essays in Honour of Ian Brownlie* (Talmon and Goodwin-Gill eds., 1999), 125

Elias, Tasmin E., *The Modern Law of Treaties* (1974)

Elkind, Jerome B., *Interim Protection. A Functional Analysis* (1989)

Elsen, T. J. H., *Litispendence Between the International Court of Justice and the Security Council* (1986)

Enderlein, Joachim, 'Die Sanktionen gegen den Iran auf dem Gebiet des Kapitalverkehrs', 26 *RIW* (1980), 453

Engels, Markus, *Verbesserter Menschenrechtsschutz durch Individualbeschwerdeverfahren? Zur Frage der Einführung eines Fakultativprotokolls für den Internationalen Pakt über wirtschaftliche, soziale und kulturelle Rechte* (2000)

Erasmus, Gerhard, 'Third States and Sanctions in Public International Law - the Position of South Africa', 30 *AVR* (1992), 128

Ermacora, Felix, 'Human Rights and Domestic Jurisdiction (Article 2, para. 7 of the Charter)', 124 *RdC* (1968 II), 371

'Die Probleme der Durchsetzung der UN-Konvention über zivile und politische Rechte', in: *Um Recht und Freiheit. Festschrift von der Heydte* (Kipp *et al.* eds., 1977), 141

'Über die völkerrechtliche Verantwortlichkeit für Menschenrechtsverletzungen', in: *Ius Humanitatis. Festschrift für Alfred Verdross zum 90. Geburtstag* (Miehsler *et al.* eds., 1980), 357

Falk, Richard, '*South West Africa Cases*: an Appraisal', 21 *International Organization* (1967), 1

Fassbender, Bardo, *UN Security Council Reform and the Right of Veto. A Constitutional Perspective* (1998)

'Der Schutz der Menschenrechte als zentraler Inhalt des völkerrechtlichen Gemeinwohls', 30 *Europäische Grundrechte-Zeitschrift* (2003), 1

Fastenrath, Ulrich, 'Relative Normativity in International Law', 4 *EJIL* (1993), 305

'Servitudes', in: EPIL, Vol. IV (Bernhardt ed., 2000), 387

Fawcett, James E. S., 'The Legal Character of International Agreements', 30 *BYIL* (1953), 1

The Law of Nations (1968)

Feinberg, Nathan, 'La jurisdiction et la jurisprudence de la Cour permanente de Justice internationale en matière de mandates et de minorités', 59 *RdC* (1937 I), 591

Feist, Christian, *Kündigung, Rücktritt und Suspendierung multilateraler Verträge* (2001)

Ferencz, Benjamin, *Enforcing International Law – a Way to World Peace*, 2 Vols., (1983)

Ferguson-Brown, Kevin W., 'The Legality of Economic Sanctions Against South Africa in Contemporary International Law', 14 *SAYIL* (1988–1989), 59

Ferrari Bravo, Luigi, 'Méthodes de recherche de la countume internationale dans la pratique des Etats', 192 *RdC* (1985 III), 233

Fiedler, Wilfried, 'Zur Verbindlichkeit einseitiger Versprechen im Völkerrecht', 19 *GYIL* (1976), 35

'Gegenmaßnahmen', in, *Gegenmaßnahmen (Counter Measures). Berichte der deutschen Gesellschaft für Völkerrecht*, Vol. 37 (Klein, Fiedler, Schnyder eds., 1998), 9

Fischer, Peter / Hafner, Gerhard, 'Aktuelle österreichische Praxis zum Völkerrecht', 33 *öZöR* (1982), 307

Fisher Williams, John, 'L'affaire du Lotus', 35 *RGDIP* (1928), 361

Fitzmaurice, Sir Gerald, *The Law and Procedure of the International Court of Justice* (2 vols., 1986)

Fleming, Brian, 'South West Africa Cases. Ethiopia v. South Africa; Liberia v. South Africa. Second Phase', 5 *CYIL* (1967), 241

Fonteyne, Jean-Pierre L., 'The Customary International Law Doctrine of Humanitarian Intervention: Its Current Validity Under the UN Charter', 4 *California Western International Law Journal* (1973), 203

Fraas, Michael, *Sicherheitsrat der Vereinten Nationen und Internationaler Gerichtshof: Die Rechtmäßigkeitsprüfung von Beschlüssen des Sicherheitsrates der Vereinten Nationen im Rahmen des VII. Kapitels der Charta durch den Internationalen Gerichtshof* (1998)

Franck, Thomas M., 'Fact-Finding in the I.C.J.', in: *Fact-Finding Before International Tribunals* (Lillich ed., 1992), 21

Recourse to Force: State Action Against Threats and Armed Attacks (2002)

Franck, Thomas M. / Rodney, Nigel S., 'After Bangladesh: The Law of Humanitarian Intervention by Military Force', 67 *AJIL* (1973), 275

Fredman, Steven J., 'U.S. Trade Sanctions Against Uganda: Legality under International Law', 11 *Law and Policy in International Business* (1979), 1149

Friedmann, Wolfgang G., 'The Jurisprudential Implications of the South West Africa Case', 6 *Columbia Journal of Transnational Law* (1967), 1

Frowein, Jochen Abr., 'The Interrelationship Between the Helsinki Final Act, the International Covenants on Human Rights, and the European Convention on Human Rights', in: *Human Rights, International Law and the Helsinki Accord* (Buergenthal ed., 1977), 71

'Die Verpflichtungen, *erga omnes* im Völkerrecht und ihre Durchsetzung', in: *Völkerrecht als Rechtsordnung – Internationale Gerichtsbarkeit – Menschenrechte. Festschrift Mosler* (Bernhardt *et al.* eds., 1983), 241

'Collective Enforcement of International Obligations', 47 *ZaöRV* (1987), 67

'Das Staatengemeinschaftsinteresse – Probleme bei der Formulierung und Durchsetzung' in: *Staat und Völkerrechtsordnung. Festschrift Doehring* (Ress and Hailbronner eds., 1989), 219

'Legal Consequences for International Law Enforcement in Case of Security Council Inaction', in: *The Future of International Law Enforcement. New Scenarios – New Law?* (Delbrück ed., 1993), 111

'Reactions by Not Directly Affected States to Breaches of Public International Law', 248 *RdC* (1994 IV), 345

'*Jus Cogens*', in: EPIL, Vol. III (Bernhardt ed., 1997), 65 [Frowein 1997a]

'Obligations *Erga Omnes*', in: EPIL, Vol. III (Bernhardt ed., 1997), 757 [Frowein 1997b]

Frowein, Jochen Abr. / Peukert, Wolfgang, *Europäische Menschenrechtskonvention. EMRK-Kommentar* (2nd ed., 1996)

Gading, Heike, *Der Schutz grundlegender Menschenrechte durch militärische Maßnahmen des Sicherheitsrates – das Ende staatlicher Souveränität?* (1996)
Gaja, Giorgio, '*Jus Cogens* Beyond the Vienna Convention', 172 *RdC* (1981 III), 271
'Obligations *Erga Omnes*, International Crimes and *Jus Cogens*: A Tentative Analysis of Three Related Concepts' in: *International Crimes of States. A Critical Analysis of the ILC's Draft Article 19 of State Responsibility* (Weiler, Cassese, Spinedi eds., 1989), 151
'Should All References to International Crimes Disappear from the ILC Draft Articles on State Responsibility?', 10 *EJIL* (1999), 365
'Is a State Specially Affected When Its Nationals' Human Rights Are Infringed?', in: *Man's Inhumanity to Man. Essays on International Law in Honour of Antonio Cassese* (Vorah *et al.* eds., 2003), 373
Gasser, Hans Peter, 'Ensuring Respect for the Geneva Conventions and Protocols: the Role of Third States and The United Nations', in: *Effecting Compliance* (Fox and Meyer eds., 1993), 15
GATT: *Analytical Index – Guide to GATT Law and Practice*, 2 Vols. (1994)
Gattini, Andrea, *Zufall und* Force Majeure *im System der Staatenverantwortlichkeit anhand der ILC-Kodifikationsarbeit* (1987)
'A Return Ticket to "*Communitarisme*", Please', 13 *EJIL* (2002), 1181
Gazzini, Tarcisio, 'Il contributo della Corte Internazionale di Giustizia al rispetto degli obblighi, *erga omnes* in material di diritti umani', 55 *La Comunità Internazionale* (2000), 19
Geck, Karl-Wilhelm, Diplomatic Protection, in: EPIL, Vol. I (Bernhardt ed., 1992), 1045
Gihl, Torsten, *International Legislation. An Essay on Changes in International Law and in International legal Situations* (1937)
Gilbert, Geoff, 'The Criminal Responsibility of States', 39 *ICLQ* (1990), 345
Ginther, Konrad, 'Die Verfassung der Völkerrechtsgemeinschaft im Lichte der Entscheidungen des Internationalen Gerichtshofes im sogenannten Südwestafrikastreit', in: *Internationale Festschrift für Alfred Verdross zum 80. Geburtstag* (Marcic *et al.* eds., 1971), 91
Glare, P. (ed.) *Oxford Latin Dictionnary* (1982)
Golsong, Heribert, 'Implementation of International Protection of Human Rights', 110 *RdC* (1963 III), 7
Gomaa, Mohammed, *Suspension or Termination of Treaties for Grounds of Breach* (1996)
Gomez Robledo, A., 'Le *jus cogens* international: sa génèse, sa nature, ses fonctions', 172 *RdC* (1981 III), 9
Goodheart, A. L., 'Determining the *ratio decidendi* of a Case', 40 *Yale LJ* (1930), 161
Goodrich, Leland M. / Hambro, Edvard, *Charter of the United Nations: Commentary and Documents* (1st ed., 1946; 3rd ed. – with Anne Patricia Simons – 1969)
Goodwin-Gill, Guy, 'Crime in International Law: Obligations *Erga Omnes* and the Duty to Prosecute', in: *The Reality of International Law. Essays in Honour of Ian Brownlie* (Talmon and Goodwin-Gill eds., 1999), 199
Gordon, Edward, 'Legal Disputes Under Article 36 (2) of the Statute', in: *The International Court of Justice at Crossroads* (Fisler Damrosch ed., 1987), 183

Gowlland-Debbas, Vera, 'Security Council Enforcement Actions and Issues of State Responsibility', 43 *ICLQ* (1994), 55

'Judicial Insights into the Fundamental Values and Interests of the International Community', in: *The International Court of Justice – Its Future Role After Fifty Years* (Muller ed., 1997), 327

Grabenwarter, Christoph, 'Probleme paralleler Rechtsverbürgungen durch Vertrag und Gewohnheitsrecht', in: *Menschenrechtsschutz durch Gewohnheitsrecht* (E. Klein ed., 2003), 147

Graefrath, Bernhard, 'Internationale Zusammenarbeit und Menschenrechte', 27 *Neue Justiz* (1973), 683

'Responsibility and Damages Caused: Relationship Between Responsibility and Damages', 185 *RdC* (1984 II), 9

'Völkerrechtliche Verantwortung für Verbrechen', in: *Probleme des Völkerrechts 1985* (Graefrath ed., 1985), 89

'Das Verantwortlichkeitsverhältnis im Völkerrecht und die Definition des "verletzten Staates"', in: *Probleme des Völkerrechts 1987* (Graefrath ed., 1987), 107

'International Crimes – A Specific Regime of International Responsibility of States and Its Legal Consequences', in: *International Crimes of States. A Critical Analysis of the ILC's Draft Article 19 of State Responsibility* (Weiler, Cassese, Spinedi eds., 1989), 161

'International Crimes and Collective Security', in: *International Law. Theory and Practice. Essays in Honour of Eric Suy* (Wellens ed., 1998), 237

Graefrath, B. / Oeser, E. / Steininger, P. A., *Völkerrechtliche Verantwortung der Staaten* (1977)

Grahl-Madsen, Atle, 'Decolonization: The Modern Version of a Just War', 22 *GYIL* (1979), 255

Gray, Christine D., *Judicial Remedies in International Law* (1987)

'Application of the Convention on the Prevention and Punishment of the Crime of Genocide, Bosnia and Herzegovina v. Yugoslavia (Serbia and Montenegro)', 43 *ICLQ* (1994), 704

'Bosnia and Herzegovina: Civil War or Interstate Conflict? Characterisation and Consequences', 67 *BYIL* (1996), 155

'Jurisdiction and Admissibility in the Genocide Case', 46 *ICLQ* (1997), 688

'The Choice Between Restitution and Compensation', 10 *EJIL* (1999), 413

International Law and the Use of Force (2000) [Gray 2000a]

'The Legality of NATO's Military Action in Kosovo: Is There a Right of Humanitarian Intervention?', in *International Law in the Post-Cold War World* (Wang Tieya and Sienho Yee eds., 2000), 240 [Gray 2000b]

'Types of Remedies in International Court of Justice cases: Lessons for the WTO', in *Improving WTO Dispute Settlement Procedures: Issues and Lessons from the Practice of Other International Courts and Tribunals* (Weiss ed., 2000), 401 [Gray 2000c]

'The Use of Force and the International Legal Order', in *International Law* (Evans ed., 2003), 589

Green, L. C., 'Protection of Minorities in the League of Nations and in the United Nations', in: *Human Rights, Federalism and Minorities* (Gottlieb ed., 1970), 180

Greig, Donald W., *International Law* (2nd ed., 1976)
'Reciprocity, Proportionality, and the Law of Treaties', 34 *Virginia JIL* (1994), 295
Gretschaninow, G. von, 'Der Versuch eines Ausschlußverfahrens gegen Liberia nach Art. 16 Abs. 4 der Völkerbundssatzung', 5 *ZaöRV* (1935), 174
Grotius, Hugo, *De iure belli ac pacis libri tres* (1646, English translation 1925) [Grotius 1646/1925]
Guggenheim, Paul, *Traité de droit international public* (tome I, 1953)
Guggenheim, Paul/Marekv, Krystina, 'Verträge, völkerrechtliche', in: *Wörterbuch des Völkerrechts*, Vol. III (Strupp and Schlochauer eds., 1962), 528
Guillaume, Gilbert, 'De l'exécution des décisions de la Cour internationale de Justice', 7 *Schweizerische Zeitschrift für internationales und europäisches Recht* (1997), 431
Günther, Carsten Alexander, *Die Klagebefugnis der Staaten in internationalen Streitbeilegungsverfahren* (1999)
Guttry, Andrea de, 'Some Recent Cases of Unilateral Countermeasures and the Problem of Their Lawfulness in International Law', 7 *Italian Yearbook of International Law* (1986–1987), 169
Hafner, Gerhard, 'Bemerkungen zur Funktion und Bestimmung der Betroffenheit im Völkerrecht anhand des Binnenstaates', 31 *GYIL* (1988), 187
'Rechtliche Grundlagen für die Sanktionen innerhalb der EU und die Rechtslage österreichs', in: *Aktuelle Probleme des Wehrrechts* (österreichisches Bundesministerium für Landesverteidigung ed., 1997), 488
'Should One Fear the Proliferation of Mechanisms for the Peaceful Settlement of Disputes?', in: *The Peaceful Settlement of Disputes between States: Universal and European Perspectives* (Caflisch ed., 1998), 25
'The Draft Articles on the Responsibility of States for Internationally Wrongful Acts', 5 *Austrian Review of International and European Law* (2000), 189
Hahn, Michael J., *Die einseitige Aussetzung von GATT-Verpflichtungen als Repressalie* (1996)
Hailbronner, Kay, 'Sanctions and Third Parties and the Concept of International Public Order', 30 *AVR* (1992), 2
Halberstam, M., 'The Right of Self-Defense Once the Security Council Has Taken Action', 17 *MichJIL* (1996–1997), 229
Hambro, Edvard, 'Dissenting and Individual Opinions in the International Court of Justice', 17 *ZaöRV* (1956/57), 229
Hannikainen, Lauri, *Peremptory Norms* (Jus Cogens) *in International Law. Historical Development, Criteria, Present Status* (1988)
Hannum, Hurst, 'International Law and Cambodian Genocide: The Sounds of Silence', 11 *HRQ* (1989), 82
Hanz, Martin, *Die völkerrechtliche Aktivlegitimation zum Schutze der Menschenrechte* (1985)
Hargrove, L., 'The *Nicaragua* Judgment and the Future of the Law of Force and Self-Defence', 81 *AJIL* (1987), 138
Heffter, August Wilhelm, *Das europäische Völkerrecht der Gegenwart* (8th ed. by Geffcken, 1882) [Heffter/Geffcken]

Henkin, Louis, '"Nationality" at the Turn of the Century', in: *Recht zwischen Umbruch und Bewahrung. Festschrift für R. Bernhardt* (Hofmann *et al.* eds., 1995), 89

'Human Rights and "Domestic Jurisdiction"', in: *Human Rights, International Law and the Helsinki Accord* (Buergenthal ed., 1977), 21

'Inter-State Responsibility for Compliance With Human Rights Obligations', in: *Man's Inhumanity to Man. Essays on International Law in Honour of Antonio Cassese* (Vorah *et al.* eds., 2003), 383

Higgins, Rosalyn, 'The International Court and South West Africa: the Implications of the Judgment', 42 *International Affairs* (1966), 573–599

'Aspects of the Case Concerning the Barcelona Traction, Light and Power Company, Ltd.', 11 *Virginia JIL* (1971), 327

Problems and Process. International Law and How We Use It (1994)

'Fundamentals of International Law', in: *Perspectives on International Law. Essays in Honour of Judge Manfred Lachs* (Jasentuliyana ed., 1995), 3

Hoffmeister, Frank, *Menschenrechts- und Demokratieklauseln in den vertraglichen Außenbeziehungen der Europäischen Gemeinschaft* (1998)

Hofmann, Rainer, 'Zur Unterscheidung Verbrechen und Delikt im Bereich der Staatenverantwortlichkeit', 45 *ZaöRV* (1985), 195

Hohfeld, W. N., *Fundamental Legal Concepts* (1923)

Hoogh, André de, 'The Relationship Between *Jus Cogens*, Obligations *Erga Omnes* and International Crimes: Peremptory Norms in Perspective', 42 *AJPIL* (1991), 183

Obligations Erga Omnes and International Crimes (1996)

'The Relationship Between *Jus Cogens*, Obligations *Erga Omnes* and International Crimes: Peremptory Norms in Perspective', 42 *AJPIL* (1991), 183

Hutchinson, D. N., 'Solidarity and Breaches of Multilateral Treaties', 59 *BYIL* (1988), 151

Institut de droit international, 'Le régime des répressailes en temps de paix' (résolution, session de Paris, 1934), 38 *Annuaire IDI* (1934), 708

Institut de droit international, 'New Problems of Extradition' (résolution, session de Cambridge, 1983) 60-II *Annuaire IDI* (1984), 304

Institut de droit international, 'La protection des droits de l'homme et le principe de non-intervention dans les affaires des Etats' (résolution, session de Santiogo de Compopstela, 1989), 63-II Annuaire IDI (1990), 338

International Law Association – Study Group on the Law of States Responsibility: First Report of the ILA's Study Group on the Law of States Responsibility, Submitted to the UN International Law Commission (2000) (Manuscript, on file with the author) [ILA Study Group 2000]

Jacobs and White: The European Convention on Human Rights (3rd ed., White and Ovey eds., 2002) [Jacobs/White/Ovey]

Jenks, C. Wilfred, *The Prospect of International Adjudication* (1964)

'The General Welfare as a Legal Interest', in: *Jus et Societas. Essays in Tribute to Wolfgang Friedmann* (Wilner ed., 1979), 151

Jennings, Robert Y., *The Acquisition of Territory in International Law* (1963)
'General Course on Principles of Public International Law', 121 *RdC* (1967 II), 323
'Gerald Gray Fitzmaurice', 55 *BYIL* (1984), 1
'The Judicial Enforcement of International Law', 47 *ZaöRV* (1987), 3
Jennings, Robert, 'The Collegiate Responsibility and Authority of the International Court of Justice', in: *International Law at a Time of Perplexity. Essays Rosenne* (Dinstein ed., 1989), 343
Jessup, Philip C., *A Modern Law of Nations* (1948)
Jhering, Rudolf von, *Der Geist des römischen Rechts* (3. Auflage, 1877)
Jiménez de Aréchaga, Eduardo, 'International Law in the Past Third of a Century', 159 *RdC* (1978 I), 1
Jiménez de Aréchaga, Eduardo / Tanzi, Attila, 'International State Responsibility', in: *International Law: Achievements and Prospects* (Bedjaoui ed., 1991), 347
Johnson, D. H. N., 'The South West Africa Cases (Second Phase)', 3 *International Relations* (1967), 157
Jørgensen, Nina H. B., 'State Responsibility and the 1948 Genocide Convention', in: *The Reality of International Law. Essays in Honour of Ian Brownlie* (Talmon and Goodwin-Gill eds., 1999), 273
Jørgensen, Nina H. B., *The Responsibility of States for International Crimes* (2000)
Jouannet, Emmanuelle, 'Le principe de l'*Or Monétaire* à propos de l'arrêt de la Cour Internationale de Justice du 30 Juin 1995 dans l'*Affaire du Timor Oriental (Portugal c. Australie)*', 100 *RGDIP* (1996), 673
Juste Ruiz, José, 'Las obligaciones, *erga omnes* en derecho internacional publico', in: *Estudios de Derecho Internacional. Homenaje al Profesor Miaja de la Muela* (Mostaza *et al.* eds, 1979), Vol. I, 219
Kadelbach, Stefan, *Zwingendes Völkerrecht* (1992)
Kälin, Walter, 'Menschenrechtsverträge als Gewährleistung einer objektiven Ordnung', 33 *BDGVR* (1994), 9
Kamminga, Menno T., *Inter-State Accountability for Violations of Human Rights* (1992)
'Is the European Convention Sufficiently Equipped to Cope with Gross and Systematic Violations?', 12 *NQHR* (1994), 153
Kappeler, D., 'La récente décision dans la Cour internationale de Justice dans les affaires du Sud-Ouest africain', 85 *Zeitschrift für Schweizerisches Recht* (1966), 335
Karl, Wolfram, 'Besonderheiten der internationalen Kontrollverfahren zum Schutz der Menschenrechte', 33 *BDGVR* (1994), 83
'Aktuelle Entwicklungstendenzen im internationalen Menschenrechtsschutz', in: *Paradigmenwechsel im Völkerrecht zur Jahrtausendwende* (Hummer ed., 2002), 275
'Menschenrechtliches ius cogens – Eine Analyse von "Barcelona Traction" und nachfolgender Entwicklungen', in: *Menschenrechtsschutz durch Gewohnheitsrecht* (E. Klein ed., 2003), 102
Karlshoven, Frits, 'International Concern with Human Rights: Can It Be Effective?', 21 *GYIL* (1978), 119

Kausch, Hans G., 'Boycott', in: EPIL, Vol. I (Bernhardt ed., 1992), 485
Kausch, Hans G. / Langenfeld, Christine, 'Embargo', in: EPIL, Vol. II (Bernhardt ed., 1995), 58
Kawasaki, Kyoji, 'The "Injured State" in the International Law of State Responsibility', 28 *Hitsobashi Journal of Law and Politics* (2000), 17
Kelsen, Hans, 'Unrecht und Unrechtsfolgen im Völkerrecht', 12 *ZöR* (1932), 481
'Collective Security and Collective Self-Defense under the Charter of the United Nations', 42 *AJIL* (1948), 783
Principles of International Law (2nd ed. by Tucker, 1955) [Kelsen/Tucker]
Kessler, Birgit, *Die Durchsetzung der Genfer Abkommen von 1949 in nicht-internationalen bewaffneten Konflikten auf Grundlage ihres gemeinsamen Art.* 1 (2001)
Khol, Andreas, *Zwischen Staat und Weltstaat. Die internationalen Sicherungsverfahren zum Schutz der Menschenrechte* (1969)
Kirgis, Frederic L., 'Custom on a Sliding Scale', 81 *AJIL* (1987), 146
'Standing to Challenge Human Endeavors that Could Change the Climate', 84 *AJIL* (1990), 525
Kiss, Alexandre / Shelton, Dinah, *International Environmental Law* (2nd ed., 2000)
Kiwanuka, Robert N., 'The International Human Rights Implications of the ICJ Decision in *Nicaragua v. United States*', 57 *Nordic JIL* (1988), 470
Klabbers, Jan, 'Case Note: A. Racke GmbH & Co. v. Hauptzollamt Mainz', 36 *CMLR* (1999), 179
Klein, Eckart, *Statusverträge im Völkerrecht. Rechtsfragen territorialer Sonderregime* (1980)
'Paralleles Tätigwerden von Sicherheitsrat und Internationalem Gerichtshof bei friedensbedrohenden Streitigkeiten', in: *Völkerrecht als Rechtsordnung – Internationale Gerichtsbarkeit – Menschenrechte. Festschrift Mosler* (Bernhardt *et al.* eds., 1983), 467
'Namibia' in: EPIL, Vol. II (Bernhardt ed., 1995), 485 [Klein 1995a]
'Genocide Case (Advisory Opinion)', in: EPIL, Vol. II (Bernhardt ed., 1995), 544 [Klein 1995b]
'Gegenmaßnahmen', in *Gegenmaßnahmen (Counter Measures). Berichte der deutschen Gesellschaft für Völkerrecht*, Vol. 37 (Klein, Fiedler, Schnyder eds., 1998), 39 [Klein 1998a]
Klein, Eckart (ed.), *The Monitoring System of Human Rights Obligations* (1998) [Klein 1998b]
Klein, Eckart, 'South West Africa/Namibia (Opinions and Judgments)', in: EPIL, Vol. IV (Bernhardt ed., 2000), 491 [Klein 2000a]
'Treaties, Effects of Territorial Changes', in: EPIL, Vol. IV (Bernhardt ed., 2000), 941 [Klein 2000b]
Klein, Pierre, 'Responsibility for Breaches of Obligations Deriving from Peremptory Norms of International Law and United Nations Law', 13 *EJIL* (2002), 1241
Kloepfer, Stephen, 'The Syrian Crisis, 1860–61: A Case Study in Classic Humanitarian Intervention', 23 *CYIL* (1985), 246
Kokott, Juliane, *Das interamerikanische System zum Schutz der Menschenrechte* (1986)

'Zum Spannungsverhältnis zwischen nationality rule und Menschenrechtsschutz bei der Ausübung diplomatischer Protektion', in: *Der diplomatische Schutz im Völker- und Europarecht. Aktuelle Probleme und Entwicklungstendenzen* (Ress and Stein eds., 1996), 45

Kolb, Robert, 'The Formal Source of *Ius Cogens* in Public International Law', 53 ZöR (1998), 69

Théorie du Jus Cogens *International* (2001)

König, Doris, *Durchsetzung internationaler Bestands- und Umweltschutzvorschriften auf Hoher See im Interesse der Staatengemeinschaft* (1990)

'The Enforcement of the International Law of the Sea by Coastal and Port States', 62 *ZaöRV* (2002), 1

König, Ludger, Die Klagebefugnis Privater im englischen Verwaltungsprozess (Diss. Münster, 1979)

Kooijmans, Pieter H., 'Inter-State Dispute Settlement in the Field of Human Rights', 3 *LJIL* (1990), Special Issue 1990: The United Nations Decade of International Law – Reflections on International Dispute Settlement, 87

'Comment', in: *Increasing the Effectiveness of the International Court of Justice* (Peck and Lee eds., 1997), 75

Koskenniemi, Marti, 'Solidarity Measures: State Responsibility as a New Legal Order?', 72 *BYIL* (2001), 337

Krenzler, Horst Günther, 'Die Beziehungen der EWG zu den Mittelmeerländern, 26 *Europa-Archiv* (1971), 139

Kreß, Claus, *Gewaltverbot und Selbstverteidigungsrecht nach der Satzung der Vereinten Nationen bei staatlicher Verwicklung in Gewaltakte Privater* (1995)

Krisch, Nico, 'The Establishment of an African Court on Human and Peoples' Rights', 58 *ZaöRV* (1998), 713

Künzli, Jörg, *Zwischen Rigidität und Flexibilität: der Verpflichtungsgrad internationaler Menschenrechte. Ein Beitrag zum Zusammenspiel von Menschenrechten, humanitärem Völkerrecht und dem Recht der Staatenverantwortlichkeit* (2001)

Kuyper, Pieter Jan, 'Community Sanctions Against Argentina: Lawfulness under Community and International Law', in: *Essays in European Law and Integration* (O'Keefe and Schermers eds., 1982), 141

Kwakwa, Edward, 'South Africa's 1985 Military Incursions into Neighbouring African States', 12 *Yale JIL* (1987), 421

Lachs, Manfred, 'Le développement et les fonctions des traités multilatéraux', 92 *RdC* (1957 II), 229

'Le juge international à visage découvert (les opinions et le vote)', in: *Estudios de Derecho Internacional. Homenaje al Profesor Miaja de la Muela*, Vol. II (Mostaza *et al.* eds, 1979), 939

'The Development and General Trends of International Law in Our Time. General Course on Public International Law', 169 *RdC* (1980 III), 9

'Jessup: Memorials and Reminiscences', 80 *AJIL* (1986), 896

Ladenburger, Felix, *Durchsetzungsmechanismen im Umweltvölkerrecht: 'Enforcement' gegenüber den Staaten* (1996)

Lagonissi Conference: Carnegie Endowment for International Peace (ed.), *The Concept of Jus Cogens in International Law. Conference Held at Lagonissi (Greece), 3 to 8 April 1966* (1967) [*Lagonissi Conference*]

Laitenberger, Birgit, 'Die Schutzmacht', 21 *GYIL* (1978), 180

Lakehal, Djamel-Eddine, 'Les sanctions à la déstruction du Boeing sud-coréen, le 1er Septembre 1983', 18 *RBDI* (1984–1985), 171

Lamers, Karl, 'Interpretation of Memel Territory Statute Case', in: *EPIL*, Vol. II (Bernhardt ed., 1995), 1431

Lattanzi, F., *Garanzie dei diritti dell' uomo nel dirito internazionale generale* (1983)

Lauterpacht, Hersch, *Private Law Sources and Analogies of International Law* (1927)

The Development of International Law by the International Court (1958)

Leckie, Scott, 'The Inter-State Complaints Procedure in International Human Rights Law: Hopeful Prospects or Wishful Thinking?', 10 *HRQ* (1988), 249

Lefeber, René, 'The Exercise of Jurisdiction in the Antarctic Region and the Changing Structure of International Law: The International Community and Common Interests', 21 *NYIL* (1990), 81

Transboundary Environmental Interference and the Origin of State Liability (1996)

'Editorial: Cum Grano Salis', 11 *Leiden JIL* (1998), 1

Lerner, Natan, *The U.N. Convention in the Elimination of all Forms of Racial Discrimination* (1970)

Lillich, Richard B., 'Forcible Self-Help by States to Protect Human Rights', 53 *Iowa Law Review* (1967), 325

'Humanitarian Intervention: A Reply to Ian Brownlie and a Plea for Constructive Alternatives', in: *Law and Civil War in the Modern World* (Moore ed., 1974), 229

Lindemann, Hans-Heinrich, 'Die völkerrechtliche Praxis der Bundesrepublik Deutschland im Jahr 1982', 44 *ZaöRV* (1984), 495 [Lindemann 1984a]

'Die Auswirkungen der Menschenrechtsverletzungen auf die Vertragsbeziehungen zwischen den Niederlanden und Surinam', 44 *ZaöRV* (1984), 64 [Lindemann 1984b]

Lindemeyer, Bernd, 'Das Handelsembargo als wirtschaftliches Zwangsmittel der staatlichen Außenpolitik', 27 *RIW* (1981), 10

Linsi, Christian, *Gegenmaßnahmen in der Form des Embargos zur Durchsetzung elementarer Völkerrechtsverpflichtungen in der schweizerischen Außenpolitik* (1994)

Lopez Pegna, Olivia, 'Counter-Claims and Obligations *Erga Omnes* Before the International Court of Justice', 9 *EJIL* (1998), 724

Lowe, Vaughan, 'The International Court in a Timorous Mood', 54 *CLJ* (1995), 484

Macdonald, R. St. John, 'Fundamental Norms in Contemporary International Law', 25 *CYIL* (1987), 115

Magid, Per, 'The Post-Adjudicative Phase', in: *Increasing the Effectiveness of the International Court of Justice* (Peck and Lee eds., 1997), 325

Malamut, Michael E., 'Aviation: Suspension of Landing Rights of Polish Airlines in the United States', 24 *Harvard ILJ* (1983), 190

Malanczuk, Peter, 'Countermeasures and Self-Defence as Circumstances Precluding Wrongfulness in the International Law Commission's Draft Articles on State Responsibility', 43 *ZaöRV* (1983), 705

'Zur Repressalie im Entwurf der International Law Commission zur Staatenverantwortlichkeit', 45 *ZaöRV* (1985), 293

'Countermeasures and Self-Defence as Circumstances Precluding Wrongfulness in the International Law Commission's Draft Articles on State Responsibility', in: *United Nations Codification on State Responsibility* (Simma and Spined eds., 1987), 197

'A Note on the Judgement of the Appeals Chamber of the International Criminal Tribunal for the Former Yugoslavia on the Issuance of *Subpoenae Duces Tecum* in the *Blaškic* Case', 1 *Yearbook of International Humanitarian Law* (1998), 229

Mandelstam, André, 'La protection des minorités', 1 *RdC* (1923), 363

Mann, F. A., 'The Protection of Shareholders' Interests in the Light of the Barcelona Traction Case', 67 *AJIL* (1973), 259 [Mann 1973a]

'The Doctrine of *Jus Cogens* in International Law', in: *Festschrift Scheuner* (Ehmke *et al.* eds., 1973), 399 [Mann 1973b]

'The Consequences of an International Wrong in International and National Law', 48 *BYIL* (1976–1977), 1

Marek, Krystina, 'Contribution à l'étude du *jus cogens* en droit international', in: *Mélanges Guggenheim* (Lalive and Freymond eds., 1968), 426

'Criminalizing State Responsibility', 14 *RBDI* (1978–1979), 460

Marschik, Axel, *Subsysteme in Völkerrecht. Ist die Europäische Union ein 'Self-Contained Regime'?* (1997)

'Too Much Order? The Impact of Special Secondary Norms on the Unity and Efficacy of the International Legal System', 9 *EJIL* (1998), 212

Martens, Georg Friedrich von, *Precis du droit des gens modern de l'Europe*, tome 2 (2nd ed., 1864)

Martin, Antoine, *L'estoppel en droit international public* (1979)

Marx, Karl, *Capital: A Critique of Political Economy* (1867, English translation 1977) [Marx 1867/1977]

Matscher, Franz / Siehr, Kurt / Delbrück, Jost (eds.), *Multilaterale Staatsverträge* erga omnes *und deren Inkorporation in nationale IPR-Kodofikationen–Vor- und Nachteile einer solchen Rezeption. Berichte der deutschen Gesellschaft für Völkerrecht*, Vol. 26 (1986)

Matscher, Franz, 'Standing Before International Courts and Tribunals', in: EPIL, Vol. IV (Bernhardt ed., 2000), 594

Matsushita, Mitsuo / Schoenbaum, Thomas J. / Mavroidis, Petros, *The World Trade Organization. Law, Practice, and Policy* (2003)

Maurer, Hartmut, *Allgemeines Verwaltungsrecht* (14. Auflage, 2002)

Maury, Pierre, *La Question des Iles d'Aland* (1930)

M'Baye, Keba, 'L'intérêt pour agir devant la Cour Internationale de Justice', 209 *RdC* (1988 II), 223

McCaffrey, Stephen, '*Lex Lata* or the Continuum of State Responsibility', in: *International Crimes of States. A Critical Analysis of the ILC's Draft Article 19 of State Responsibility* (Weiler, Cassese, Spinedi eds., 1989), 242

McNair, Arnold D., 'So-Called State Servitudes', 6 *BYIL* (1925), 111
'The Functions and Differing Legal Character of Treaties', 11 *BYIL* (1930), 100
'Treaties producing effects "erga omnes"', in: *Scritti di diritto internazionale in Onore di Tomaso Perassi*, Vol. II (Milan, Giuffrè, 1957), 21
The Law of Treaties (2nd ed., 1961)
McWhinney, Edward, *Judicial Settlement of International Disputes* (1991)
Judge Manfred Lachs and Judicial Law-Making, Opinions on the International Court of Justice, 1967–1993 (The Hague 1995)
Meadows, Frances, 'The First Site Visit by the International Court of Justice', 11 *LJIL* (1998), 609
Mendelson, Maurice H., 'The Formation of Customary International Law', 272 *RdC* (1998), 155
Meng, Werner, 'Die Kompetenz der EWG zur Verhängung von Wirtschaftssanktionen gegen Drittländer', 42 *ZaöRV* (1982), 780
Mennecke, Martin, 'Kosovo – A Question of Genocide', in: *Century of Genocide. Eyewitness Accounts and Critical Views* (Totten ed., 2nd ed., forthcoming 2004) [Mennecke 2004]
Mennecke, Martin / Tams, Christian J., 'The *LaGrand* Case (Germany v. United States)', 51 *ICLQ* (2002), 449
Menon, P. K., *The Law of Treaties Between States and International Organizations* (1992)
Meron, Theodor, *Human Rights Law-Making in the United Nations* (1984)
'On a Hierarchy of International Human Rights', 80 *AJIL* (1986), 1
Human Rights and Humanitarian Norms as Customary Law (1989)
War Crimes Law Comes of Age. Essays (1998)
Merrills, John G., *Judge Sir Gerald Fitzmaurice and the Discipline of International Law* (1998)
Modeen, Tore, 'Aaland Islands', in: EPIL, Vol. I (Bernhardt ed., 1992), 1
Mohr, Manfred, Fragen der Durchsetzung von Völkerrechtsnormen, dargestellt anhand der Antirassendiskriminierungskonvention von 1965 und der UN-Menschenrechtskonventionen von 1966 (thesis manuscript, East Berlin 1981)
'Völkerrechtliche Verfahrensfragen bei der Durchsetzung von Menschenrechten', in: *DDR-Komitee für Menschenrechte – Schriften und Informationen, Issue 2/1983* (1983), 52
'The ILC's Distinction Between "International Crimes" and "International Delicts" and Its Implications', in: *United Nations Codification of State Responsibility* (Simma and Spinedi eds., 1987), 115
Moir, Lindsay, *The Law of Internal Armed Conflict* (2002)
Montrose, J. L., 'The *ratio decidendi* of a Case', 20 *Modern Law Review* (1957), 587
Moore, John Bassett, *History and Digest of the International Arbitrations to Which the United States Has Been a Party* (6 vols., 1898)
Morrison, Fred L., 'The Role of Regional Organizations in the Enforcement of International Law', in: *Allocation of Law Enforcement Authority in the International System* (Delbrück ed., 1995), 39
Mosler, Hermann, '*Ius Cogens* im Völkerrecht', 25 *SchwJIR* (1968), 9

Mosler, Hermann (ed.), *Gerichtsschutz gegen die Exekutive* (3 vols., 1969–1971)
Mosler, Hermann, 'Völkerrecht als Rechtsordnung', 36 *ZaöRV* (1976), 30
The International Society as a Legal Community (1980)
Moyer, Homer E. Jr. / Mabry, Linda A., 'Export Controls as Instruments of Foreign Policy: The History, Legal Issues and Policy Lessons of Three Recent Cases', 15 *Law and Policy in International Business* (1979), 1
Müller, J. P. / Cottier, Th., 'Estoppel', in: EPIL, Vol. II (Bernhard ed., 1995), 116
Münch, Ingo von, *Das völkerrechtliche Delikt* (1963)
'Der diplomatische Schutz von Schiffen', in: *Recht über See. Festschrift Stödter* (Ipsen and Necker eds., 1979), 231
'The *Wimbledon*', in: EPIL, Vol. IV (Bernhardt ed., 2000), 1482
Musgrave, Thomas D., *Self-Determination and National Minorities* (1997)
Naldi, Gino J. / Magliveras Konstantin, 'Reinforcing the African System of Human Rights: The Protocol on the Establishment of a Regional Court on Human and Peoples' Rights', 16 *NQHR* (1998), 431
Nash, Martin, 'Contemporary Practice of the United States Relating to International Law', 75 *AJIL* (1981), 142
'Contemporary Practice of the United States Relating to International Law', 76 *AJIL* (1982), 374
Nettesheim, Martin, 'Die ökologische Intervention. Gewalt und Druck zum Schutz der Umwelt?', 34 *AVR* (1996), 168
Nielsen, Henrik Karl, 'The Supervisory Machinery of the International Labour Organisation', 64 *Nordic JIL* (1995), 129
Nisot, J., 'Le *jus cogens* et la Convention de Vienne sur les traités', 76 *RGDIP* (1972), 692
Nolte, Georg, 'Kosovo und Konstitutionalisierung: Zur humanitären Intervention der NATO-Staaten', 59 *ZaöRV* (1999), 941
'From Dionisio Anzilotti to Roberto Ago: The Classical International Law of State Responsibility and the Traditional Primacy of a Bilateral Conception of Inter-state Relations', 13 *EJIL* (2002), 1083
Nowak, Manfred, *CCPR. A Commentary* (1993)
Nussbaum, Arthur, 'The Arbitration Between the Lena Goldfields, Ltd., and the Soviet Government', 36 *Cornell Law Quarterly* (1950–1951), 31
O'Brien, John, *International Law* (2001)
O'Connell, Daniel P., *International Law* (2 vols., 2nd ed., 1970)
O'Connell, Mary Ellen, 'The Prospects of Enforcing Judgments of the International Court of Justice: A Study of Nicaragua's Judgment Against the United States', 30 *Virginia JIL* (1990), 891
'Enforcing the New International Law of the Environment', 35 *GYIL* (1992), 293
'Comment', in: *Allocation of Law Enforcement Authority in the International System* (Delbrück ed., 1995), 127
Oda, Shigeru / Owada, Hisashi, 'Annual Review of Japanese Practice in International Law XVI (1978–1980)', 29 *Japanese Annuals of International Law* (1986), 74
'Annual Review of Japanese Practice in International Law XVIII (1983–1984)', 31 *Japanese Annuals of International Law* (1988), 138

Oellers-Frahm, Karin, 'Zur Vollstreckung der Entscheidungen internationaler Gerichte im Völkerrecht', 36 *ZaöRV* (1976), 654

'Comment: The *erga omnes* Applicability of Human Rights', 30 *AVR* (1992), 28

'France–United States Air Transport Arbitration (1978)', in: *EPIL*, Vol. II (1995), 461

Oestreich, Gabriele, *Menschenrechte als Elemente der dritten AKP-EWG-Konvention von Lomé. Sanktionsinstrumente oder Zielvorgabe einer Entwicklungszusammenarbeit im Dienste des Menschen?* (1990)

Okowa, Phoebe N., 'Defences in the Jurisprudence of International Tribunals', in: *The Reality of International Law. Essays in Honour of Ian Brownlie* (Talmon and Goodwin-Gill eds., 1999), 389

State Responsibility for Transboundary Air Pollution in International Law (2000)

'Issues of Admissibility and the Law of International Responsibility', in: *International Law* (Evans ed., 2003), 473

Oliver, C. T., 'The Monetary Gold Decision in Perspective', 49 *AJIL* (1955), 216

Oppenheim's International Law, Vol. I: Peace, (8th ed., H. Lauterpacht ed., 1955) [Oppenheim/Lauterpacht]

Oppenheim's International Law, Vol. I: Peace (9th ed. by Jennings and Watts, 1992) [Oppenheim/Jennings/Watts]

Oppermann, Thomas, 'Der Beitrag des internationalen Rechts zur Bekämpfung des internationalen Terrorismus', in: *Staatsrecht – Völkerrecht – Europarecht. Festschrift für Hans-Jürgen Schlochauer* (von Münch ed., 1981), 495

'Intervention', in: EPIL, Vol. II (Bernhardt ed., 1995), 1436

Opsahl, Torkel, 'The General Comments of the Human Rights Committee', in: *Des Menschen Recht zwischen Freiheit und Verantwortung. Festschrift für Karl Josef Partsch zum 75. Geburtstag* (Jekewitz *et al.* eds., 1989), 273

'The Human Rights Committee', in: *The United Nations and Human Rights. A Critical Appraisal* (Alston ed., 1992), 369

Oxman, Bernhard H., 'The International Commons, the International Public Interest and New Modes of International Law-Making', in: *New Trends in International Law-Making – International "Legislation" in the Public Interest* (Delbrück ed., 1997), 21

'Complementary Agreements and Compulsory Jurisdiction', 96 *AJIL* (2002), 277

Palchetti, Paolo, 'Opening the International Court of Justice to Third Parties: Intervention and Beyond', 6 *Max Planck Yearbook of United Nations Law* (2002), 139

Partsch, Karl Josef, 'Vereinbarungstheorie', in: *Wörterbuch des Völkerrechts*, Vol. III (Strupp and Schlochauer eds., Berlin 1962), 489

Rassendiskriminierung. Die UN-Konvention und ihre Wirkungsweise (1971)

'The Committee on the Elimination of Racial Discrimination', in: *The United Nations and Human Rights. A Critical Appraisal* (Alston ed., 1992), 339

'Fact-Finding and Inquiry', in: EPIL, Vol. II (Bernhardt ed., 1995), 343

'Reprisals', in: EPIL, Vol. IV (Bernhardt ed., 2000), 200 [Partsch 2000a]

'Retorsions', in: EPIL, Vol. IV (Bernhardt ed., 2000), 232 [Partsch 2000b]

Paulus, Andreas, 'Book Review: The Concept of International Obligations *Erga Omnes* (Ragazzi) and Obligations *Erga Omnes* and International Crimes (de Hoogh)', 10 *EJIL* (1999), 810

'Reziprozität im Völkerrecht', in: *Korruption, Reziprozität und Recht* (Fikentscher and Jakob eds., 2000) 211

Die internationale Gemeinschaft im Völkerrecht (2001)

'The influence of the United States on the Concept of the "International Community"', in: *United States Hegemony and the Foundations of International Law* (Byers and Nolte eds., 2003), 57

Paulus, Andreas / Khan, Daniel-Erasmus, 'Gemeinsame Werte in der Völkerrechtsgemeinschaft?' in: *Frieden und Recht. 38. Assistententagung öffentliches Recht* (Erberich *et al.* eds., 1998), 217

Pauwelyn, Joost, 'Enforcement and Countermeasures in the WTO: Rules are Rules – Towards a More Collective Approach', 94 *AJIL* (2000), 335

Conflict of Norms in Public International Law. How WTO Law Relates to other Rules of International Law (2003)

Pechota, Vratislav, 'The Development of the Covenant on Civil and Political Rights', in: *The International Bill of Rights. The Covenant on Civil and Political Rights* (Henkin ed., 1981), 32

Pellet, Alain, 'The Normative Dilemma: Will and Consent in International Law-Making', 12 *Australian YIL* (1992), 22

'Remarques sur une révolution inachevée – le projet d'articles de la Commission du droit international sur la responsabilité des Etats', 42 *AFDI* (1996), 7

'Vive le crime! Remarques sur les degrés de l'illicite en droit international', in: *International Law on the Eve of the Twenty-first Century: Views from the International Law Commission* (UN International Law Commission ed., 1997), 287

'Can a State Commit a Crime? Definitely, Yes!', 10 *EJIL* (1999), 425

Perrin, Georges, 'La détermination de l'Etat lésé. Les régimes dissociables et les régimes indissociables', in: *Theory of International Law at the Threshold of the 21st Century. Essays in Honour of Krzystof Skubiszewski* (Makarczyk ed., 1994), 243

Phillimore, Robert, *Commentaries upon International Law* (3rd ed., 1879)

Picone, Paolo, 'Obblighi reciproci ed obblighi *erga omnes* degli Stati nel campo della protezione internazionale dell'ambiente maritimo dall'inquinamento', in: *Diritto internazionale e protezione dell'ambiente maritimo* (Starace ed., 1983), 15

Pictet, Jean (ed.), *Commentary on Geneva Convention I of 12 August 1949* (1952)

Pieper, Stefanie, *Neutralität von Staaten* (1997)

Pillitu, Paola Anna, 'Le sanzioni dell'Unione e della Communità europea nei confronti dello Zimbabwe e di esponenti del suo Governo par gravi violazioni dei diritti umani e dei principi democratici', 86 *Riv.D.I.* (2003), 55

Pogany, Istvan, 'Humanitarian Intervention in International Law: The French Intervention in Syria Re-Examined', 35 *ICLQ* (1986), 182

Politis, Nicolas, 'Le régime des représailles en temps de paix', 38 *Annuaire IDI* (1934), 1

Prebensen, Søren, 'Inter-State Complaints under Treaty Provisions – The Experience under the European Convention on Human Rights', 20 *HRLJ* (1999) 446

Provost, René, 'Reciprocity in Human Rights and Humanitarian Law', 65 *BYIL* (1994), 383

International Human Rights and Humanitarian Law (2002)

Quaye, Christopher O., *Liberation Struggles in International Law* (1991)

Quéneudec, Jean-Pierre, 'La notion d'État intéressé en doit international', 255 *RdC* (1995), 339

Quigley, John, 'The International Law Commission's Crime-Delict Distinction: A Toothless Tiger?', 66 *RDISDP* (1988), 117

Quoc Dinh, Nguyen / Daillier, Patrick / Pellet, Alain, *Droit international public* (7th ed., 2002)

Ragazzi, Maurizio, *The Concept of International Obligations* Erga Omnes (1997)

'International Obligations *Erga Omnes*: Their Moral Foundation and Criteria of Identification in the Light of Two Japanese Contributions', in: *The Reality of International Law. Essays in Honour of Ian Brownlie* (Talmon and Goodwin-Gill eds., 1999), 455

Raub, Gerlinde, 'Protecting Power', in: EPIL, Vol. III (Bernhardt ed., 1997), 1147

Raub, Gerlinde / Malanczuk, Peter, 'Völkerrechtliche Praxis der Bundesrepublik Deutschland im Jahr 1983', 45 *ZaöRV* (1985), 714

Réglade, M., 'De la nature juridique des traités internationaux et du sens de la distinction des traités-lois et des traités-contrats', 41 *Revue du droit publique et de la science politique* (1924), 505

Reimann, Heinrich Bernhard, *Ius Cogens im Völkerrecht* (1971)

Reisman, W. Michael, 'Revision of the South West Africa Cases: An Analysis of the Grounds of Nullity in the Decision of July 18th, 1966, and Methods of Revision', 7 *Virginia JIL* (1966–1967), 1

'Comment', in: *The Future of International Law Enforcement. New Scenarios – New Law?* (Delbrück ed., 1993), 168

Reisman, W. Michael / McDougal, Myres S., 'Humanitarian Intervention to Protect the Ibos', in: *Humanitarian Intervention and the United Nations* (Lillich ed., 1973), 167

Remsperger, Philip, *Die Rechtslage der Alandinseln* (1933)

Ress, Hans-Konrad, *Das Handelsembargo. Völker-, europa- und außenwirtschaftsrechtliche Rahmenbedingungen, Praxis und Entschädigung* (2000)

Reuter, Paul, 'Quelques réflexions sur le vocabulaire du droit international', in: *Mélanges offerts à M. le doyen Louis Trotabas* (Paris, LGDJ, 1970), 424.

Introduction au droit des traités (3rd ed., 1995)

Riedel, Eibe H., 'Damages', in: EPIL, Vol. I (Bernhardt ed., 1992), 929

'International Environmental Law – A Law to Serve the Public Interest?', in: *New Trends in International Law-Making – International 'Legislation' in the Public Interest* (Delbrück ed., 1997), 61

Riedel, Eibe H. / Will, Martin, 'Human Rights Clauses in External Agreements of the EC', in: *The European Union and Human Rights* (Alston *et al.* eds., 1999), 723

Riphagen, Willem, 'State Responsibility: New Theories of Obligation in Inter-State Relations', in: *The Structure and Process of International Law* (MacDonald and Johnston eds., 1983), 581

Robertson, A. H., 'The Implementation System: International Measures', in: *The International Bill of Rights. The Covenant on Civil and Political Rights* (Henkin ed., 1981), 332

Robinson, Jacob / Karbach, Oscar / Laserson, Max M. / Robinson, Nehemiah / Vichniak, Marc, *Were the Minorities Treaties a Failure?* (1943) [Robinson et al. (1943)]

Roeben, Volker, 'Le précédent dans la jurisprudence de la Cour internationale', 32 *GYIL* (1989), 382

Rolin, Henri, 'Observation', 52-II *Annuaire IDI* (1967), 358

Ronzitti, Natalino, *Rescuing Nationals Abroad Through Military Coercion and Intervention on Grounds of Humanity* (1985)

Rosas, Allan, 'Reactions to Non-compliance with the Chemical Weapons Convention', in: *The New Chemical Weapons Convention – Implementation and Prospects* (Bothe, Ronzitti and Rosas eds., 1998), 415

Rosenne, Shabtai, *The Law and Practice of the International Court* (2 vols., 1st ed., 1965)

'Bilateralism and Community Interest in the Codified Law of Treaties', in: *Transnational Law in a Changing Society. Essays in Honor of Philip C. Jessup* (Friedmann *et al.* eds., 1972), 202

Breach of Treaty (1985) [Rosenne 1985a]

The Law and Practice of the International Court (2nd ed., 1985) [Rosenne 1985b]

The Law and Practice of the International Court: 1920–1996 (4 vols., 1997)

'Some Reflections, *Erga Omnes*', in: *Legal Visions of the 21st Century. Essays in Honour of Judge Christopher Weeramantry* (Anghie and Sturgess eds., 1998), 509

'The Perplexity of Modern International Law. General Course of Public International Law', 291 *RdC* (2001), 9

Rosenstock, Robert, 'Crimes of States – an Essay' in: *Völkerrecht zwischen normativem Anspruch und politischer Realität. Festschrift Zemanek* (1994), 319

'An International Criminal Responsibility of States?', in: *International Law on the Eve of the Twenty-first Century: Views from the International Law Commission* (1997), 265

Rosting, Helmer, 'Protection of Minorities by the League of Nations', 17 *AJIL* (1923), 641

Rougier, Antoine, 'La théorie de l'intervention d'humanité', 17 *RGDIP* (1910), 469

Rousseau, Charles, *Principes généraux du doit international public* (tome I, 1944)

'Chronique des faits internationaux', 64 *RGDIP* (1960), 771

Droit international public, tome I (1973)

'Chronique des faits internationaux', 80 *RGDIP* (1976), 546

'Chronique des faits internationaux', 84 *RGDIP* (1980), 351 and 1068

'Chronique des faits internationaux', 85 *RGDIP* (1981), 842

'Chronique des faits internationaux', 86 *RGDIP* (1982), 543

Droit international public (tome V, 1983)

'Chronique des faits internationaux', 88 *RGDIP* (1984), 413

'Chronique des faits internationaux', 90 *RGDIP* (1986), 945

Roxburgh, Ronald F., *International Conventions and Third States* (1917)
Rozakis, Christos L., 'Treaties and Third States: a Study in the Reinforcement of Consensual Standards in International Law', 35 *ZaöRV* (1975), 1
The Concept of Jus Cogens *in the Law of Treaties* (1976)
Rubin, Alfred P., 'The International Legal Effects of Unilateral Declarations', 71 *AJIL* (1977), 1
'Comment', in: *The Future of International Law Enforcement. New Scenarios – New Law?* (Delbrück ed., 1993), 171
Ethics and Authority in International Law (1997)
'*Actio Popularis, Jus Cogens* and Offenses *Erga Omnes*' 35 *New England Law Review* (2001), 265
Rucz, Claude, 'Les mesures unilatérales de protection de droits de l'homme devant l'Institut de Droit International', 38 *AFDI* (1992), 579
Ruda, José Maria, 'Reservations to Treaties', 146 *RdC* (1975 III), 95
Ruffert, Mattias, 'Kommentar', in: *Menschenrechtsschutz durch Gewohnheitsrecht* (E. Klein ed., 2003), 292
Rumpf, Helmut, *Der internationale Schutz der Menschenrechte und das Interventionsverbot* (1981)
Sachariew, Kamen, *Die Rechtsstellung betroffener Staaten bei Verletzungen multilateraler Verträge* (thesis manuscript, East Berlin 1986)
'State Responsibility for Multilateral Treaty Violations: Identifying the Injured State and Its Legal Status', 35 *NILR* (1988), 273
'States' Entitlement to Take Action to Enforce International Humanitarian Law', 29 *International Review of the Red Cross* (1989), 177
Salmon, Jean, 'Les obligations quantitatives et l'illéicité', in: *The International Legal System in Quest of Equity and Universality – Liber Amicorum Georges Abi-Saab* (Boisson de Chazournes and Gowlland-Debbas eds., 2001), 311
Salvioli, Gabriele, 'La jurisprudence de la Cour permanente de Justice internationale', 12 *RdC* (1926 II), 5
'Problèmes de procédure dans la jurisprudence internationale', 91 *RdC* (1957 I), 553
Sands, Philippe, *Principles of International Environmental Law* (2nd ed., 2003)
Sands, Philippe / Mackenzie, Ruth / Shany, Yuval, *Manual on International Courts and Tribunals* (1999)
Sauvant, Karl P. / Müller, Joachim W. (eds.), *The Third World Without Superpowers (Second Series). The Collected Documents of the Group of 77*, Vol. XX (1995)
Scelle, Georges, *Précis du droit des gens*, Vol. II (1934)
Schabas, William A., *Genocide in International Law* (2000)
Schachter, Oscar, 'The Enforcement of International Judicial and Arbitral Decisions', 54 *AJIL* (1960), 1
'Philip Jessup's Life and Ideas', 80 *AJIL* (1986), 878
International Law in Theory and Practice (1991)
'Dispute Settlement and Countermeasures in the International Law Commission', 88 *AJIL* (1994), 471
Scharping, Rudolf, *Wir dürfen nicht wegsehen* (1999)

Scheuner, Ulrich, 'Conflict of Treaty Provisions with a Peremptory Norm of General International Law and Its Consequences. Comments on Arts. 50, 61 and 67 of the ILC's Draft Articles on the Law of Treaties', 27 *ZaöRV* (1967), 520

Schiavone, Giuseppe, *International Organizations: A Dictionary* (4th ed., 1997)

Schindler, Dietrich, 'Die *erga omnes*-Wirkung des humanitären Völkerrechts', in: *Recht zwischen Umbruch und Bewahrung. Festschrift Bernhardt* (Hofmann *et al.* eds., 1995), 199

Schlette, Volker, 'Das neue Rechtsschutzsystem der Europäischen Menschenrechtskommission: Zur Reform des Kontrollmechanismus durch das 11. Protokoll', 55 *ZaöRV* (1995), 905

Schlochauer, Hans-Jürgen, 'Die Entwicklung des völkerrechtlichen Deliktsrechts', 16 *AVR* (1974–1975), 239

Schmidt, Markus G., 'Individual Human Rights Complaints Procedures Based on United Nations Treaties and the Need for Reform', 41 *ICLQ* (1992), 645

Schoch, Friedrich / Schmidt-Aßmann, Eberhard / Pietzner, Rainer (eds.), *VwGO-Kommentar, Loseblatt-Sammlung* (Stand 2003)

Schorlemmer, Sabine von, 'Verfahrensrechtliche Aspekte bei Ansprüchen aus Verletzungen von Erga-omnes-Normen', in: *Menschenrechtsschutz durch Gewohnheitsrecht* (E. Klein ed., 2003), 238

Schreuer, Christoph, 'Comment', in: *The Future of International Law Enforcement. New Scenarios – New Law?* (Delbrück ed., 1993), 147

The ICSID-Convention. A Commentary (2001)

Schröder, Meinhard, 'Wirtschaftssanktionen der Europäischen Gemeinschaften gegenüber Drittstaaten', 23 *GYIL* (1980), 111

Schulte, Constanze, 'The Enforcement of Obligations *Erga Omnes* Before the International Court of Justice, Procedural Law and the *East Timor* Judgment', in: *Might and Right in International Relations. Thesaurus Acroasium*, Vol. XXVIII (1999), 533

Schwarzenberger, Georg, *International Law as Applied by International Courts and Tribunals*, Vol. I (1957)

'International *Jus Cogens?*', 45 *Texas Law Review* (1965), 455

International Law as Applied by International Courts and Tribunals, Vol. IV (1986)

Schweitzer, Michael, '*Jus Cogens* im Völkerrecht', 15 *AVR* (1971–1972), 197

Schwelb, Egon, 'Termination or Suspension of a Treaty as a Consequence of its Breach', 7 *Indian Journal of International Law* (1967), 309 [Schwelb 1967a]

'Some Aspects of *Jus Cogens* as Formulated by the ILC', 61 *AJIL* (1967), 946 [Schwelb 1967b]

'The *Actio Popularis* and International Law', 2 *Israel Yearbook of Human Rights* (1972), 46

Scobbie, Iain, 'The Invocation of Responsibility for Breach of Obligations Under Peremptory Norms of General International Law', 13 *EJIL* (2002), 1201

Scobbie, Iain / Drew, Catriona, 'Self-Determination Undetermined: The Case of East Timor', 9 *LJIL* (1996), 185

Seiderman, Ian D., *Hierarchy in International Law. The Human Rights Dimension* (2001)

Seidl-Hohenveldern, Ignaz, 'Der Barcelona-Traction-Fall', 22 *öZöR* (1971), 255
'*Actio Popularis* im Völkerrecht?', 14 *Communicazione e Studi* (1975), 803
'Der diplomatische Schtuz für juristische Personen und Aktionäre', in: *Der diplomatische Schutz im Völker- und Europarecht* (Ress and Stein eds., 1996), 115
Senti, Richard, *WTO: System und Funktionsweise der Welthandelsordnung* (2000)
Sette-Camara, José, 'Behind the World Bench', in: *International Law. Liber Amicorum Jiménez de Aréchaga* (Fundación de Cultura Montevideo ed., 1994), 1069
Shahabuddeen, Mohamed, *Precedent in the World Court* (1996)
Shaw, Malcolm N., *Title to Territory in Africa* (1986)
International Law (5th ed., 2003)
Shelton, Dinah, *Remedies in International Human Rights Law* (1999)
'Righting Wrongs: Reparations in the Articles on State Responsibility', 96 *AJIL* (2002), 833
Shihata, Ibrahim F. I., 'Implementation, Enforcement and Compliance with International Environmental Agreements – Practical Suggestions in Light of the World Bank's Experience' 9 *Georgetown International Environmental Law Review* (1996–1997), 37
Shorter Oxford Dictionary (1973)
Sicilianos, Linos-Alexandre, *Les réactions décentralisées à l'illicite. Des contre-mesures à la légitime défense* (1990)
'The Relationship Between Reprisals and Denunciation or Suspension of a Treaty', 4 *EJIL* (1993), 341
'The Classification of Obligations and the Multilateral Dimension of the Relations of International Responsibility', 13 *EJIL* (2002), 1127
Siekmann, R. C. R., 'Netherlands State Practice for the Parliamentary Year 1982–1983', 15 *NYIL* (1984), 267
Simma, Bruno, 'Reflections on Article 60 of the Vienna Convention on the Law of Treaties and its Background in General International Law', 20 *österreichische Zeitschrift für öffentliches Recht* (1970), 5
Das Reziprozitätselement im Zustandekommen völkerrechtlicher Verträge (1972)
'Termination and Suspension of Treaties: Two Recent Austrian Cases', 21 *GYIL* (1978), 74
'Zur bilateralen Durchsetzung vertraglich verankerter Menschenrechte: Aktivlegitimation und zulässige Mittel nach allgemeinem Völkerrecht', in: *Autorität und internationale Ordnung* (Schreuer ed., 1979), 129
'Fragen der zwischenstaatlichen Durchsetzung vertraglich vereinbarter Menschenrechte', in: *Staatsrecht – Völkerrecht – Europarecht. Festschrift für Hans-Jürgen Schlochauer* (von Münch ed., 1981), 635
'Consent: Strains in the Treaty System', in: *The Structure and Process of International Law* (MacDonald and Johnston eds., 1983), 485
'Self-Contained Regimes', 16 *NYIL* (1985), 111
'Grundfragen der Staatenverantwortlichkeit in der Arbeit der International Law Commission', 24 *AVR* (1986), 357 [Simma 1986a]
'The Antarctic Treaty as a Treaty Providing for an Objective Regime', 19 *Cornell International Law Journal* (1986), 189 [Simma 1986b]

'International Crimes: Injury and Countermeasures. Comments on Part 2 of the ILC's Work on State Responsibility', in: *International Crimes of States. A Critical Analysis of the ILC's Draft Article 19 of State Responsibility* (Weiler, Cassese, Spinedi eds., 1989), 283 [Simma 1989a]

'Bilateralism and Community Interest in the Law of State Responsibility', in: *International Law in a Time of Perplexity. Essays in Honour of Shabtai Rosenne* (Dinstein and Tabori eds., 1989), 821 [Simma 1989b]

'The Implementation of the International Covenant on Economic, Social and Cultural Rights', in: *Die Durchsetzung wirtschaftlicher und sozialer Rechte im Völkerrecht* (Matscher ed., 1991), 75

'Does the UN Charter Provide an Adequate Legal Basis for Individual or Collective Responses to Violations of Obligations *Erga Omnes*?', in: *The Future of International Law Enforcement. New Scenarios – New Law?* (Delbrück ed., 1993), 125 [Simma 1993a]

'International Human Rights and General International Law: A Comparative Analysis', in: *Collected Courses of the Academy of European Law*, Vol. IV, Book 2 (1993), 153 [Simma 1993b]

'From Bilateralism to Community Interest', 250 *RdC* (1994 VI), 217 [Simma 1994a]

'Countermeasures and Dispute Settlement: A Plea for a Differentiated Balance', 5 *EJIL* (1994), 102 [Simma 1994b]

'The Work of the International Law Commission at Its Forty-Ninth Session', 66 *Nordic JIL* (1997), 527

'Reservations to Human Rights Treaties – Some Recent Developments', in: *Liber Amicorum Professor Seidl-Hohenveldern* (Hafner *et al.* eds., 1998), 659 [Simma 1998a]

'The Work of the International Law Commission at Its Fiftieth Session', 67 *Nordic JIL* (1998), 431 [Simma 1998b]

'NATO, the UN, and the Use of Force: Legal Aspects', 10 *EJIL* (1999), 1 [Simma 1999a]

'The Work of the International Law Commission at Its Fifty-first Session', 68 *Nordic JIL* (1999), 293 [Simma 1999b]

'The Work of the International Law Commission at Its Fifty-second Session', 70 *Nordic JIL* (2001), 183

Simma, Bruno (ed.), *The Charter of the United Nations. A Commentary* (2nd ed., 2 vols., 2002) [Simma 2002a]

Simma, Bruno, 'The Work of the International Law Commission at Its Fifty-third Session', 71 *Nordic JIL* (2002), 123 [Simma 2002b]

Simma, Bruno / Alston, Philip, 'The Sources of Human Rights Law: Custom, *Ius Cogens*, and General Principles', 12 *Australian YbIL* (1992), 82

Simma, Bruno / Aschenbrenner, Jo / Schulte, Constanze, 'Human Rights Considerations in Development Cooperation Activities of the European Community', in: *The European Union and Human Rights* (Alston *et al.* eds., 1999), 571

Simma, Bruno / Spinedi, Marina (eds.), *United Nations Codification of State Responsibility* (1987)

Sinclair, Ian, *The Vienna Convention on the Law of Treaties* (2nd ed., 1984)

'State Responsibility and the Concept of Crimes of States', in: *International Crimes of States. A Critical Analysis of the ILC's Draft Article 19 of State Responsibility* (Weiler, Cassese, Spinedi eds., 1989), 223

'Estoppel and Acquiescence', in Fifty Years of the International Court of Justice (Lowe and Fitzmaurice eds., Cambridge 1996), 104

Skouris, Wassilios, *Verletztenklage und Interessentenklage im Verwaltungsprozess* (1979)

Smith, Brian D., *State Responsibility and the Marine Environment: the Rules of Decision* (1988)

Söderhjelm, J. O., *Démilitarisation et neutralisation des Iles d'Aland en 1856 et 1921* (1928)

Soerensen, Max, 'Principes de droit international public', 101 *RdC* (1960 III), 1

Spiermann, Ole, '*Lotus* and the Double Structure of International Legal Argument', in: *International Law, the International Court of Justice and Nuclear Weapons* (Sands and Boisson de Chazournes eds., 1999), 131

Spinedi, Marina, 'International Crimes of State: The Legislative History', in: *International Crimes of States. A Critical Analysis of the ILC's Draft Article 19 of State Responsibility* (Weiler, Cassese, Spinedi eds., 1989), 1

'From One Codification to Another: Bilateralism and Community Interest in the Genesis of the Codification of the Law of Treaties and the Law of State Responsibility', 13 *EJIL* (2002), 1099

Stael-Holstein, Baron L. de, 'La doctrine des servitudes internationales et son application en Scandinavie', 49 *Revue de Droit International et de Législation Comparé* (3e séries, 1922), 424

Starke's International Law (Shearer ed., 11th ed., 1994) [Starke/Shearer]

Stein, Eric, 'Collective Enforcement of International Obligations', 47 *ZaöRV* (1987), 56

Stein, Ted L., 'Contempt, Crisis and the Court: The World Court and the Hostage Rescue Attempt', 76 *AJIL* (1982), 499

Stein, Torsten, 'International Measures Against Terrorism and Sanctions by and Against Third States', 30 *AVR* (1992), 38

'Decentralized International Law Enforcement. The Changing Role of the State as Law-Enforcment Agent', in: *The Allocation of Law Enforcement in the International System* (Delbrück ed., 1995), 107

Steinmayr, Helmut, *Die völkerrechtliche Bedeutung der Alandsinseln in Geschichte und Gegenwart* (1927)

Stern, Brigitte, 'Conlusions: La responsabilité dans le système international', in: *La responsabilité dans le système international. Colloque du Mans* (Société française de droit international, 1991), 319

'Responsabilité internationale', in: *Répertoire Internationale. Encyclopédie Dalloz* (1998)

'Et si on utilisait la le concept de préjudice juridique? Retour sur une notion délaissée à l'occasion de la fin des travaux de la C.D.I. sur la responsabilité des États', 47 *AFDI* (2001), 3

Stowell, Ellory C., *Intervention in International Law* (1921)

Stroh, Dagmar P., *Die nationale Zusammenarbeit mit den internationalen Straftribunalen für das ehemalige Jugoslawien und für Ruanda* (2002)

Strupp, Karl, *Das völkerrechtliche Delikt. Handbuch des Völkerrechts*, Bd. III/4 (1920)

Stzucki, Jerzy, *Jus Cogens and the Vienna Convention on the Law of Treaties. A Critical Reappraisal* (1974)

Subedi, S. P., 'The Doctrine of Objective Regimes in International Law and the Competence of the United Nations to Impose Territorial or Peace Settlements on States', 37 *GYIL* (1994), 162

Suontausa, T., 'La situation juridique des iles d'Aland', 13 *ZaöRV* (1950–51), 741

Sur, Serge, 'Comment', in: *Change and Stability in International Law-Making* (Weiler and Cassese eds., 1988), 125

Swepston, Lee, 'Human Rights Complaint Procedures of the International Labor Organization', in: *Guide to International Human Rights Practice* (Hannum ed., 3rd ed., 1999), 85

Szasz, Paul C., 'Centralized and Decentralized Law Enforcement: The Security Council and the General Assembly Acting Under Chapters VII and VIII', in: *Allocation of Law Enforcement Authority in the International System* (Delbrück ed., 1995), 17

Szawslowski, R., 'The International Protectionof Human Rights – A Soviet and a Polish View', 28 *ICLQ* (1979), 778

Talkington, H. Alan, 'International Trade: Uganda Trade Embargo', 20 *Harvard ILJ* (1979), 206

Tams, Christian J., 'All's Well That Ends Well? Comments on the ILC's Articles on State Responsibility', 62 *ZaöRV* (2002), 759 [Tams 2002a]

'Do Serious Breaches Give Rise to Any Specific Obligations of the Responsible State?', 13 *EJIL* (2002), 1161 [Tams 2002b]

'Well-Protected Enemies of Mankind – Comment on the ECHR's Judgment in *Al-Adsani v. United Kingdom*', 61 *Cambridge Law Journal* (2002), 246 [Tams 2002c]

'Interim Orders by the European Court of Human Rights – Comments on *Mamatkulov and Abdurasulovic v. Turkey*', 63 *ZaöRV* (2003), 681

'Renonciation, acquièscement et préscription', in: *Manuel de la responsabilité internationale* (Crawford, *et al.*, eds., forthcoming) [Tams (Manuel)]

Tanzi, Attila, 'Is Damage a Distinct Condition for the Existence of an Internationally Wrongful Act?', in: *United Nations Codification of State Responsibility* (Simma and Spinedi eds., 1987), 1

Taylor, Prue, *An Ecological Approach to International Law* (1998)

Teson, Fernando R., 'Le Peuple, c'est moi! The World Court and Human Rights', 81 *AJIL* (1987), 173

Humanitarian Intervention: An Inquiry into Law and Morality (2nd ed., 1997)

Thierry, Hubert, 'L'évolution du droit international – Cours général de droit international public', 222 *RdC* (1990 III), 9

'Réflexions sur le "droit d'ingérence humanitaire" ', in: *The International Legal System in Quest of Equity and Universality – Liber Amicorum Georges Abi-Saab* (Boisson de Chazournes and Gowlland-Debbas eds., 2001), 219

Thirlway, Hugh W. A., 'The Law and Procedure of the International Court of Justice - Part One', 60 *BYIL* (1989), 1
'The Law and Procedure of the International Court of Justice - Part Two', 61 *BYIL* (1990), 1
'The Law and Procedure of the International Court of Justice - Part Eight', 67 *BYIL* (1996), 1
'The *Nuclear Weapons* Advisory Opinions: The Declarations and Separate and Dissenting Opinions', in: *International Law, the International Court of Justice and Nuclear Weapons* (Boisson de Chazournes and Sands eds., 1999), 390
'The Sources of International Law', in: *International Law* (Evans ed., 2003), 117
Thomas, Ann van Wynen / Thomas, A. J., *Non-Intervention. The Law and Its Import in the Americas* (1956)
Thomsen, Sabine, 'Restitution', in: EPIL, Vol. IV (Bernhardt ed., 2000), 229
Thornberry, Patrick, *International Law and the Rights of Minorities* (1991)
Tietje, Christian, *Normative Grundstrukturen der Behandlung nichttarifärer Handelshemmnisse in der WTO/GATT-Rechtsordnung: eine Untersuchung unter besonderer Berücksichtigung des Countertrade* (1998)
Tomaševski, Katarina, *Responding to Human Rights Violations 1946–1999* (2000)
Tomuschat, Christian, 'Repressalie und Retorsion. Zu einigen innerstaatlichen Aspekten ihrer Durchführung', 33 *ZaöRV* (1973), 179
'Völkerrechtlicher Vertrag und Drittstaaten', 28 *BDGVR* (1988), 9
'Some Reflections on the Consequences of a Breach of an Obligation Under International Law', in: *Im Dienst an der Gesellschaft. Festschrift für Dietrich Schindler* (Haller *et al.* eds., 1989), 147
'Obligations Arising for States With or Without Their Will', 241 *RdC* (1993 IV), 195 [Tomuschat 1993a]
'Comment', in: *The Future of International Law Enforcement. New Scenarios - New Law?* (Delbrück ed., 1993), 156 [Tomuschat 1993b]
'Are Counter-measures Subject to Prior Recourse to Dispute-Settlement Procedures?', 5 *EJIL* (1994), 77
'Die internationale Gemeinschaft', 33 *AVR* (1995), 1
'International Crimes of States - An Endangered Species?' in: *International Law. Theory and Practice. Essays in Honour of Eric Suy* (Wellens ed., 1998), 254
'International Law: Ensuring the Survival of Mankind on the Eve of a New Century', 281 *RdC* (1999), 9
Human Rights - Between Idealism and Realism (2003)
Torelli, Maurice (ed.), 'Chronique des faits internationaux', 100 *RGDIP* (1996), 197
Trautmannsdorf, Ferdinand, 'Die Verantwortlichkeit von Staaten für Verletzungen von völkerrechtlichen Verpflichtungen *erga omnes*', in: *Rechtsfragen an der Jahrtausendwende* (Kötz ed., 1998), 211
Triepel, Heinrich, *Völkerrecht und Landesrecht* (1899)
Unger, Moritz von, 'Die Zulässigkeit, "humaitärer" Wirtschaftssanktionen in und neben dem WTO-Recht', *Kritische Justiz* 2004, 37
Vadapalas, Vilenas, 'L'intérêt pour agir en responsabilité internationale', 20 *Polish Yearbook of International Law* (1993), 17

Vali, F. A., *Servitudes of International Law* (2nd ed., 1958)
Valticos, Nicolas, 'Les commissions d'enquête de l'Organisation internationale du travail', 91 *RGDIP* (1987), 847
van Alebeek, Rosanne, 'The *Pinochet* Case: International Human Rights Law on Trial', 71 *BYIL* (2000), 29
van Dijk, Pieter, *Judicial Review of Governmental Action and the Requirement of an Interest to Sue* (1980)
Vattel, Emer de, *Le droit des gens ou principes de la loi naturelle* (1758, English translation 1916) [Vattel 1758/1916]
Velu, Jacques / Ergec, Rusen, *La Convention européenne des droits de l'homme* (1990)
Verdross, Alfred, *Völkerrecht* (5th ed., 1964)
'*Jus Dispositivum* and *Jus Cogens* in International Law', 60 *AJIL* (1966), 55
Verdross, Alfred / Simma, Bruno, *Universelles Völkerrecht. Theorie und Praxis* (3rd ed., 1984)
Verwey, Wil D., 'Humanitarian Intervention', in: *The Current Legal Regulation of the Use of Force* (Cassese ed., 1986), 57
Victor, David G., *The Early Operation and Effectiveness of the Montreal Protocol's Non-Compliance Procedure* (International Institute for Applied Systems Analysis, May 1996)
Vierdag, Bert, 'Some Remarks About Special Features of Human Rights Treaties', 25 *NYIL* (1994), 119
Viljoen, Frans, 'Admissibility under the African Charter', in: *The African Charter on Human and Peoples' Rights* (Evans and Murray eds., 2002), 61
Virally, Michel, 'Réflexions sur le *jus cogens*', 12 *AFDI* (1966), 5
'Sur la classification des traités', 13 Communicazioni e Studi (1967), 16
Visscher, Charles de, *Aspects récents du droit procédural de la Cour Internationale de Justice* (1966)
Visscher, Fernand de, 'La Question des Iles d'Aland', 48 *Revue de Droit International et de Législation Comparé* (3e séries, 1921), 35
Voeffray, François, L'actio popularis – *ou la défense de l'intérêt collectif devant les juridictions internationales* (2004)
Vortisch, Friedrich, *Die Alandfrage. Ihre Entwicklung aus Natur und Geschichte Nordosteuropas, juristische Würdigung der um sie erwachsenen Völkerrechtsakte* (1933)
Waincymer, Jeff, *WTO Litigation: Procedural Aspects of Formal Dispute Settlement* (2002)
Wallace, Cynthia D., 'Barcelona Traction Case', in EPIL, Vol. I (Bernhardt ed., 1992), 356–360
Watts, Arthur, 'The Protection of Merchant Ships', 33 *BYIL* (1957), 52
'The Nationality of States: Some Relevant Concepts' in: *Fifty Years of the International Court of Justice* (Lowe and Fitzmaurice eds., 1996), 424
Weber, Hermann, 'League of Nations', in: *United Nations: Law, Policies and Practice*, Vol. II (Wolfrum ed., 1995), 848
Wehberg, Hans, 'Der Wimbledonprozeß vor dem Völkerbundsgerichtshof', Hansa 1923, 1255, 1277, 1301

Weil, Prosper, 'Towards Relative Normativity in International Law', 77 *AJIL* (1983), 413
'Le droit international en quête de son identité', 237 *RdC* (1992 VI), 9
Weisburd, A. Mark, 'The Emptiness of the Concept of *Jus Cogens* as Illustrated by the War in Bosnia-Herzegovina', 17 *MichJIL* (1995), 1
Wengler, Wilhelm, *Völkerrecht*, Bd. I (1964)
Werksman, Jacob, 'Compliance and Transition: Russia's Non-Compliance Tests the Ozone Regime', 56 ZaöRV (1996), 750
Weschke, Katrin, *Internationale Instrumente zur Durchsetzung der Menschenrechte* (2001)
Westlake, John, *International Law*, Vol. I (2nd ed., 1910)
White, Nigel D. / Abass, Ademola, 'Countermeasures and Sanctions', in: *International Law* (Evans ed., 2003), 505
Wibaux, Denys, 'A propos de quelques questions juridiques posées par l'interdiction des vols des compagnies yugoslaves', 44 *AFDI* (1998), 262
Wildhaber, Lucius, 'Treaties, Multilateral', in: EPIL, Vol. IV (Bernhardt ed., 2000), 949
Wilson, Heather A., *International Law and the Use of Force by National Liberation Movements* (1988)
Winfield, P. H., 'The History of Intervention in International Law', 3 *BYIL* (1922–1923), 130
Wolfke, Karol, '*Jus Cogens* in International Law', 6 *Polish Yearbook of International Law* (1974), 145
Wolfrum, Rüdiger, 'Purposes and Principles of International Environmental Law', 33 *GYIL* (1990), 308
United Nations–Law, Policies and Practice (2 vols., 1995)
'Means of Ensuring Compliance with and Enforcement of International Environmental Law', 272 *RdC* (1998), 9
Wolgast, E., *Der Wimbledonprozeß vor dem Völkergerichtshof* (1926)
Wühler, Norbert, 'Monetary Gold case', in: EPIL, Vol. III (Bernhardt ed., 1997), 445
Wyler, Eric, 'From "State Crime" to Responsibility for "Serious Breaches of Obligations Under Peremptory Norms of General International Law"', 13 *EJIL* (2002), 1147
'Du "crime d'Etat" à la "responsabilité pour violations graves d'obligations découlant des normes impératives de droit international général"', in: *Obligations multilatérales, droit impératif et responsabilité internationale* (Dupuy ed., 2003), 105
Wyrozumska, A., 'Treaties Establishing Territorial Regimes', 15 *Polish Yearbook of International Law* (1986), 251
Xue, Hanqin, *Transboundary Damage in International Law* (2003)
Yoshida, O., 'Soft Enforcement of Treaties: The Montreal Non-Compliance Procedure and the Functions of the Internal International Institutions', 10 *Colorado Journal of International Environmental Law and Policy* (1999), 95

Zeller, Karl, *Das Problem der völkerrechtlichen Verankerung des Südtirol-Pakets und die Zuständigkeit des Internationalen Gerichtshofs* (1989)

Zemanek, Karl, 'The Unilateral Enforcement of International Obligations', 47 *ZaöRV* (1987), 32

'General Course on Public International Law', 266 *RdC* (1997), 9

'Does International Law Need Reform or Just an Update?', in: *Development and Developing International and European Law. Essays Ginther* (Benedek *et al.* eds., 1999), 201

'New Trends in the Enforcement of Obligations *Erga Omnes*', 4 Max Planck Yearbook of United Nations Law (2000), 1 [Zemanek 2000a]

'Responsibility of States: General Principles', in: EPIL, Vol. IV (Bernhardt ed., 2000), 219 [Zemanek 2000b]

Zemanek, Karl / Salmon, Jean, *La responsabilité internationale* (1987)

Ziemer, Jonna, *Das gemeinsame Interesse an einer Regelung der Hochseefischerei. Dargestellt am Beispiel des Fish Stocks Agreement* (2000)

Zimmermann, Andreas, 'Die Zuständigkeit des Internationalen Gerichtshofes zur Entscheidung über Ansprüche gegen am Verfahren nicht beteiligte Staaten', 55 *ZaöRV* (1995), 105

Zoller, Elisabeth, *Peacetime Unilateral Remedies: An Analysis of Coutermeasures* (1984)

Enforcing International Law Through U.S. Legislation (1985)

Zygojannis, Philipp A., *Die Staatengemeinschaft und das Kosovo. Humanitäre Intervention und internationale Übergangsverwaltung unter Berücksichtigung einer Verpflichtung des Intervenienten zur Nachsorge* (2003)

Documents issued by the International Law Commission

1. *Texts on State responsibility*

- Draft Articles on State Responsibility Provisionally Adopted by the International Law Commission on First Reading (1996), reproduced in: Report of the International Law Commission on the Work of its Forty-Eighth Session, UN Doc. A/51/10, 125 ['First Reading Draft Articles']
- The International Law Commission's Draft Articles on Responsibility of States for Internationally Wrongful Acts (Second Reading, 2001), reproduced in: Report of the International Law Commission on the Work of its Fifty-Third Session, UN Doc. A/56/10, 43 ['Second Reading Draft Articles'; 'ASR']
- Provisional Set of Draft Articles Adopted On Second Reading (2000), UN Doc. A/CN.4/L.600, reproduced in: Report of the International Law Commission on the Work of its Fifty-Second Session, UN Doc. A/55/10, 124

2. *Reports on State responsibility by Special Rapporteurs Ago, Riphagen, Arangio-Ruiz, and Crawford*

a) Roberto Ago:

- First Report, YbILC 1969, Vol. II, 125
- Second Report, YbILC 1970, Vol. II, 177
- Third Report, YbILC 1971, Vol. II/1, 199
- Fourth Report, YbILC 1972, Vol. II/1, 71
- Fifth Report, YbILC 1976, Vol. II/1, 3
- Sixth Report, YbILC 1977, Vol. II/1, 3
- Seventh Report, YbILC 1978, Vol. II/1, 31
- Eighth Report, YbILC 1979, Vol. II/1, 3, and YbILC 1980, Vol. II/1, 13 (Add. 5–7)

b) Willem Riphagen:

- Preliminary Report, YbILC 1980, Vol. II/1, 107
- Second Report, YbILC 1981, Vol. II/1, 79
- Third Report, YbILC 1982, Vol. II/1, 22
- Fourth Report, YbILC 1983, Vol. II/1, 3
- Fifth Report, YbILC 1984, Vol. II/1, 1
- Sixth Report, YbILC 1985, Vol. II/1, 3
- Seventh Report, YbILC 1986, Vol. II/1, 1

c) Gaetano Arangio-Ruiz:

- Preliminary Report, YbILC 1988, Vol. II/1, 6
- Second Report, YbILC 1989, Vol. II/1, 6
- Third Report, YbILC 1991, Vol. II/1, 1
- Fourth Report, YbILC 1992, Vol. II/1, 1
- Fifth Report, YbILC 1993, Vol. II/1, 1
- Sixth Report, YbILC 1994, Vol. II/1, 3
- Seventh Report, UN Doc. A/CN.4/469 and Add. 1–2 (1995)
- Eighth Report, UN Doc. A/CN.4/476 and Add. 1 (1996)

d) James Crawford:

- First Report, UN Doc. A/CN.4/490 and Add. 1–7 (1998)
- Second Report, UN Doc. A/CN.4/498 and Add. 1–4 (1999)
- Third Report, UN Doc. A/CN.4/507 and Add. 1–4 (2000)
- Fourth Report, UN Doc. A/CN.4/517 and Add. 1 (2001)

3. *Reports on the law of treaties by Special Rapporteurs Fitzmaurice and Waldock*

a) Sir Gerald Fitzmaurice:

- Second Report, YbILC 1957, Vol. II, 16

- Third Report, YbILC 1958, Vol. II, 20
- Fourth Report, YbILC 1959, Vol. II, 37

b) Sir Humphrey Waldock

- Second Report, YbILC 1963, Vol. II, 36

4. *Other reports by Special Rapporteurs*

- Alain Pellet, Second Report on Reservation to Treaties, UN Doc. A/CN.4/ 477 and Add. 1 (1996)
- John Dugard, First Report on Diplomatic Protection, UN Doc. A/CN.4, 506 and Add. 1 (2000)
- P. S. Rao, Third Report on Prevention of Transboundary Damage from Hazardous Activities, UN Doc. A/CN.4/510 (2000)

5. *Other documents*

- State Responsibility: Comments and Observations Received from Governments, UN Doc. A/CN.4/488 and Add. 1–3 (1998)
- State Responsibility: Comments and Observations Received from Governments, UN Doc. A/CN.4/492 (1999)
- State Responsibility: Comments and Observations Received from Governments, UN Doc. A/CN.4/515 and Add. 1–3 (2001)
- Compilation of Statements Made Before the UN General Assembly's Sixth Committee During the Assembly's Fifty-Fifth Session (2000), available at the Lauterpacht Research Centre for International Law, Cambridge
- Statement of the Chairman of the Drafting Committee on State Responsibility (2000), Prof. Giorgio Gaja, 18 August 2000, available at http://www.un.org/law/ilc/archives/statfra.htm
- First Statement of the Chairman of the Drafting Committee on State Responsibility (2001), Mr. Peter Tomka, 29–31 May 2001, available at http://www.un.org/law/ilc/sessions/53/english/dc_resp1.pdf
- Second Statement of the Chairman of the Drafting Committee on State Responsibility (2001), made by Prof. Giorgio Gaja on behalf of Mr. Peter Tomka, 3 August 2001, available at http://www.un.org/law/ilc/sessions/ 53/english/dc_resp2.pdf

Index

Cambridge Studies in International and Comparative Law

Books in the series

Democracy, Minorities and International Law
Steven Wheatley

Vessel-Source Marine Pollution
The Law and Politics of International Regulation
Alan Tan

Enforcing Obligations Erga Omnes *in International Law*
Christian J. Tams

Non-Governmental Organisations in International Law
Anna-Karin Lindblom

Prosecuting International Crimes
Selectivity and the International Law Regime
Robert Cryer

Compensation for Personal Injury in English, German and Italian Law
A Comparative Outline
Basil Markesinis, Michael Coester, Guido Alpa and Augustus Ullstein

Dispute Settlement in the UN Covention on the Law of the Sea
Natalie Klein

The International Protection of Internally Displaced Persons
Catherine Phuong

Imperialism, Sovereignty and the Making of International Law
Antony Anghie

Necessity, Proportionality and the Use of Force by States
Judith Gardam

International Legal Argument in the Permanent Court of International Justice
The Rise of the International Judiciary
Ole Spiermann

Great Powers and Outlaw States
Unequal Sovereigns in the International Legal Order
Gerry Simpson

Local Remedies in International Law
C. F. Amerasinghe

Reading Humanitarian Intervention
Human Rights and the Use of Force in International Law
Anne Orford

Conflict of Norms in Public International Law
How WTO Law Relates to Other Rules of Law
Joost Pauwelyn

Transboundary Damage in International Law
Hanqin Xue

European Criminal Procedures
Edited by Mireille Delmas-Marty and John Spencer

The Accountability of Armed Opposition Groups in International Law
Liesbeth Zegveld

Sharing Transboundary Resources
International Law and Optimal Resource Use
Eyal Benvenisti

International Human Rights and Humanitarian Law
René Provost

Remedies Against International Organisations
Karel Wellens

Diversity and Self-Determination in International Law
Karen Knop

The Law of Internal Armed Conflict
Lindsay Moir

International Commercial Arbitration and African States
Practice, Participation and Institutional Development
Amazu A. Asouzu

The Enforceability of Promises in European Contract Law
James Gordley

International Law in Antiquity
David J. Bederman

Money Laundering
A New International Law Enforcement Model
Guy Stessens

Good Faith in European Contract Law
Reinhard Zimmerman and Simon Whittaker

On Civil Procedure
J. A. Jolowicz

Trusts
A Comparative Study
Maurizio Lupoi

The Right to Property in Commonwealth Constitutions
Tom Allen

International Organizations Before National Courts
August Reinisch

The Changing International Law of High Seas Fisheries
Francisco Orrego Vicuña

Trade and the Environment
A Comparative Study of EC and US Law
Damien Geradin

Unjust Enrichment
A Study of Private Law and Public Values
Hanoch Dagan

Religious Liberty and International Law in Europe
Malcolm D. Evans

Ethics and Authority in International Law
Alfred P. Rubin

Sovereignty Over Natural Resources
Balancing Rights and Duties
Nico Schrijver

The Polar Regions and the Development of International Law
Donald R. Rothwell

Fragmentation and the International Relations of Micro-States
Self-determination and Statehood
Jorri Duursma

Principles of the Institutional Law of International Organizations
C. F. Amerasinghe

For EU product safety concerns, contact us at Calle de José Abascal, 56–1°,
28003 Madrid, Spain or eugpsr@cambridge.org.

www.ingramcontent.com/pod-product-compliance
Lightning Source LLC
LaVergne TN
LVHW090301210926
848480LV00001B/88

* 9 7 8 0 5 2 1 1 2 8 8 9 6 *